RELATIVISM:
INTERPRETATION AND CONFRONTATION

RELATIVISM

INTERPRETATION AND CONFRONTATION

Edited with an Introduction by
MICHAEL KRAUSZ

University of Notre Dame Press
Notre Dame, Indiana

Library of Congress Cataloging-in-Publication Data

Relativism : interpretation and confrontation.

1. Ethical relativism.   2. Cultural relativism.
I. Krausz, Michael.
BJ37.R37   1989   149   88-40325
ISBN 0-268-01636-4

Manufactured in the United States of America

Contents

Introduction

Michael Krausz

This volume collects recent studies on relativism to exhibit its varieties and to rehearse its virtues and vices. Hardly a philosophical issue is untouched by the challenges of relativism, so any collection of essays on this topic will inevitably be wide-ranging and incomplete. Despite the size of this volume, then, no claim to comprehensiveness is made, nor has there been an attempt to represent the full range of pertinent idioms of philosophical discourse. These limitations reflect practicality, not principle.

The ways in which contributors take relativism vary considerably, as do their critical attitudes toward it. But we may broadly characterize relativism as holding, characteristically, that cognitive, moral, or aesthetic claims involving such values as truth, meaningfulness, rightness, reasonableness, appropriateness, aptness, or the like are relative to the contexts in which they appear. Often such contexts are formulated in terms of conceptual frameworks. And the range of such conceptual frameworks may extend from a highly localized person-specific or occasion-specific state to that of a community, culture, tradition, historical epoch, or the like. Relativism denies the viability of grounding the pertinent claims in ahistorical, acultural, or absolutist terms. Relativism is often motivated by the recognition of historical or cultural diversity, but that recognition cannot be equated with relativism. Cultural or historical diversity is logically compatible with either relativism or anti-relativism. So, while claims of such diversities often appear in accounts of why and how standards of evaluation sometimes do give out, relativism is not thereby necessitated. The counter "one ought to seek or develop further standards" remains open.

Of course, to be a relativist at very general levels is not to acceed to an extreme relativism, which holds that all claims involving truth and such are on a par. The extreme relativist might hold that each belief is as good as another because each belief should be judged according to the unique circumstances of its appearance. This is absurd, because (at least) the claim of uniqueness here carries with it an unwarranted implication of incomparability. Further, the claim that each belief is as good as another is itself a nonrelativistic claim. But other forms of relativism ought not be dismissed on these grounds. Even if one concedes relativism at general levels, extreme relativism is not necessitated.

Where standards of evaluation give out at the bounds of conceptual frameworks, relativists might expand the horizon of their inquiry. Where a disciplinary matrix gives out, they might place it within an ever-wider cultural matrix; where a cultural matrix gives out, they might place it within a cross-cultural matrix; where these give out, they might place them within a species-specific matrix or an historical matrix; and so on. Where these conceptual frameworks give out altogether, relativists (unlike, say, Hegelians) remain silent. And such silence may derive from the belief that here the search for pertinent standards makes no sense: standards are formulable only internal to conceptual frameworks; where they give out, so do standards. Here is where the controversy between relativists and the antirelativists is seen in its starkest form.

Besides characteristic "framework" relativisms, we should note "nonframework" ones, such as those which hold that of a given domain the range of ideally admissible interpretations is multiple. That is, more than one uniquely correct interpretation applies to it, on account of a multiplicity of its standards—which in turn may well be incongruent. This sort of relativism need not appeal to a framework for its formulation. What is common to both sorts of relativism is the absence of standards that would otherwise permit one to claim that such values as rightness, reasonableness, aptness, and appropriateness—serving as standards—might be uniquely applied to one of a number of contending interpretations.

The range of positions characterizable as relativistic is varied and heterogeneous, so careful discussion of its versions resists refutation en bloc. Indeed, under some characterizations of relativism some avowedly antirelativistic theorists turn out to be "closet relativists." This is due, in part, to the tendency to accept the term "relativist" as standing for its most extreme and least defensible formulations. What is important, of course, is a critical consideration of the views collectable under this name, not the credentials for the name's ownership.

Relativistic themes, then, prompt such questions as: How shall we construe "contexts" or "conceptual frameworks" in relation to which pertinent values are held to be relative? How shall we construe such conceptual frameworks as cultures, societies, traditions, points of view,

Weltanschauungen, forms of life, *noemata*, worlds, practices, linguistic frameworks, conceptual schemes, modes of discourse, systems of thought, disciplinary matrices, constellations of absolute presuppositions, perspectives, and the like? Is it appropriate to construe persons or selves as such frameworks? How shall we understand confrontation between pairs of conceptual frameworks? Can one translate between them? Is mutual understanding between them possible, whether or not they are mutually translatable? Are such frameworks systematically tight, such that incommensurability is necessitated? Or is it a mistake to characterize them with such a degree of systematicity? If there is partial incommensurability between conceptual frameworks, how should we characterize their confrontation?

With what opposing concept should relative values be contrasted? How shall we construe relative truth, for example, as contrasted with absolute truth? And how should we construe corresponding distinctions for such other values as meaningfulness, rightness, reasonableness, appropriateness, aptness, and so on? Can one coherently embrace a relativism as to some of these values and not others? And does this, in turn, depend upon the types of domains to which these values are meant to apply?

How shall we distinguish relativism from objectivism, universalism, or absolutism? Can one be a relativist and a universalist? Can the relativist concede to invariant universal features of all cultures or persons, such as one's ability to recognize individuals as persons in all cultures; the use of some form of indexical expressions in all cultures; the presence of some moral order in all cultures? Does universalism necessitate absolutism? What is the relation between those characteristic forms of relativism that are predicated on frameworks and those that are not? How should we construe the "conversation of human-kind," and what are its realistic prospects?

While not actually embracing relativism, Clifford Geertz unmasks a number of knee-jerking antirelativists with a rhetorical flourish. At the end of his provocative article he remarks:

> We see the lives of others through lenses of our own grinding and . . . they look back on ours through ones of their own. That this led some to think the sky was falling, solipsism was upon us, and intellect, judgment, even the sheer possibility of communication had all fled is not surprising.

For Geertz the decentering of any one perspective as the absolutely true one does not necessitate the disastrous consequences sometimes feared.

While some authors hold that such a decentering of perspective actually constitutes relativism, others hold that relativism is but one kind of response to such a decentering. Much of Richard Rorty's discussion, for example, is concerned to show that relativism is the epithet misapplied to pragmatism by realists, and that the issue of relativism should be placed within a larger discourse about how reflective human beings try to give sense to their lives. According to the way of objectivity one attaches oneself "to something which can be described without reference to any particular human beings." And according to the way of solidarity one "does not ask about the relation between the practices of the chosen community and some thing outside that community." For Rorty those who wish to ground solidarity in objectivity are realists; and those, like Rorty himself, who wish to reduce objectivity to solidarity are pragmatists.

Eddy Zemach is no "knee-jerking" antirelativist. The reader will find in his essay a kind of position that, if right, stops relativism (of certain sorts) in its tracks. Zemach argues for a metaphysical realism (i.e., the view that we can refer to entities in the world, that is, to an objective, verification-independent reality); a semantic realism (i.e., the view that terms are meaningful because there are meanings which they denote); and mentalism (i.e., the view that meanings are directly known mental entities). Zemach's treatment of the combination of these claims is perhaps as subtle as it is idiosyncratic in its antirelativism.

The question of the construal of "the world" has been an enduring one for Nelson Goodman, and we may read his spirited article "Just the Facts, Ma'am" as an elaboration of themes introduced in his book *Ways of Worldmaking*. Here Goodman emphasizes the conventionality of the distinction between facts and conventions. The world cannot be transparent in the way suggested by Zemach, for example. For, Goodman asks,

> How can the earth at the same time stand still, revolve around the sun, and move in countless other ways? How can divergent diagrams or versions be of the same fact, the same world? They must either be of no world or of different worlds. There must be many worlds if any.

Facts are conventional for Goodman, and so is the very distinction between fact and convention. But the line between fact and convention "is not capricious."

In a similar vein Catherine Elgin argues:

> Something that is right relative to one acceptable system may be wrong relative to another . . . so several answers to a given question, or several courses of action, may be right. But . . . not every answer or action is right . . . if many things are right, many more remain wrong.

For Elgin the acceptability of factual or evaluative sentences "derives from its place in a system of considered judgments in reflective equilibrium."

The idea of multiple objective worlds is also embraced by anthropologist Richard Shweder. Much as Goodman and Elgin would hold, Shweder observes that the denial that there is one uniform objective reality does not imply that there are no objective realities. As an anthropological method, then, Shweder invites us to adopt the stance of internal realism; and he urges us to view the world from the point of view of each of several prejudices in sequence, seeing as best we can with the received "dogmas" of the moment.

Clearly, the question of incommensurability between worlds, world-versions, conceptual schemes, or the like, looms large in discussions of relativism. David Wong, who accepts the notion that there is more than one form of life that is best, distinguishes between three kinds of incommensurability: (1) untranslatability between theories, (2) differences in basic premises about the nature of the world or in fundamental forms of reasoning, and (3) inability to judge one of several competing theories to be superior. Wong claims that authors who argue for incommensurability often derive (3) from (1) or (2). But, he suggests, arguments from (1) do not establish anything interesting about (3). And the furor over untranslatability has obscured the most interesting case of (3), which arises precisely from an understanding of what is believed in other cultures.

Different sorts of criticism of relativism are in currency, of course. As it presents itself as a claim of relative truth or relative evidence, relativism has been charged with a kind of self-referential inconsistency, or a self-excepting fallacy. Such a criticism has been tellingly pressed by Maurice Mandelbaum.[1] Another sort of criticism of relativism is found in the work of Donald Davidson, who addresses the question of the coherence of relativism. In his influential article "On the Very Idea of a Conceptual Scheme"[2] Davidson argues that the very idea of a conceptual scheme is incoherent. This view, if right, is devastating to those forms of relativism which are so formulated as to claim that values are relative to a conceptual scheme or its cognates. (We should note again that not all forms of relativism are of this sort.) Davidson argues, very roughly, that the coherence of the idea of a conceptual scheme requires the coherence of the idea of an alternative conceptual scheme. But this idea is incoherent too. If an alternative conceptual scheme is translatable into the first conceptual scheme, it is not "alternative," and if it is not thus translatable, nothing intelligent can be said about it to distinguish it from the first conceptual scheme. Since grounds for distinguishing a conceptual scheme from an alternative conceptual scheme do not obtain, the distinction collapses, and with it the coherence of the very idea of a conceptual scheme, and with that the coherence of most forms of relativism. In his contribution to the present volume Davidson extends his argument to suggest that, just as the distinction between conceptual scheme and alternative conceptual scheme cannot be made out, so the distinction between subjective and objective cannot be made out. Both distinctions collapse, and with them a range of philosophical claims that depend upon them. He says:

> Content and scheme . . . came as a pair; we can let them go together. Once we take this step, no *objects* will be left with respect to which the problem of representation can be raised. Beliefs are true or false, but they represent nothing. It is good to be rid of representations, and with them the correspondence theory of truth, for it is thinking there are representations that engenders thoughts of relativism.

Attacking the view that the subjective is the foundation of objective empirical knowledge, Davidson argues that empirical knowledge has no epistemological foundation, and needs none. In holding that empiricism is the view that the subjective is the foundation of objective empirical knowledge—that sensation plays an *epistemological* role in determining the contents of beliefs (this amounting to "the third dogma of empiricism)"—Davidson says:

> What is true is that certain beliefs directly caused by sensory experience are often veridical, and therefore often provide good reasons for further beliefs. But this does not set such beliefs apart in principle, nor award them epistemological priority.

Hilary Putnam presses for the possibility of a relativism by arguing, contra Davidson, that the assumption that an interpreter's own language needs to be singular is mistaken. That is, it is a mistake to assume that the radical interpreter need have only one language in which he can give the truth conditions for every sentence in every language he claims to be able to understand. Such an interpreter may have more than one "home" conceptual scheme, and translation practice may be governed by more than one set of constraints. So conceptual relativity does not disappear, on Putnam's view, when one inquires into the meanings of various conceptual alternatives.

Alternatively, Alasdair MacIntyre distinguishes between translatability and understanding, and claims that one can understand two cultures or appropriate "portions" thereof while not being able to translate between them. Indeed, MacIntyre holds, the bilingual needs to be able to do this in order to determine as he does what is not translatable from one culture to another. Just as untranslatability does not entail a limit on understanding, understanding does not entail translatability. Alasdair MacIntyre's argument undercuts Davidson's claim that the coherence of the idea of a conceptual scheme or an alternative conceptual scheme is a matter of translatability.

In turn, Gordon Bearn views Davidson's "conceptual schemes" arguments as charting the horizon of reason, and then formulates a relativism within that horizon. Bearn argues that epistemological relativism should be seen as a critique of the pretensions of reason, and that it need not reject the traditional realist conception of truth. When relativism is approached via the notion of "being a good reason" for a belief, it becomes clear that Davidson's transcendental argument against any form of relativism serves only to mark the horizon of what is recognizable at all as an epistemic practice: the horizon of reason. Within that horizon, Bearn claims, we may locate two distinctively relativistic observations: first, that there may be a diversity of incommensurable epistemic practices; and second, that the horizon of reason is itself without grounds.

Joseph Margolis' moderate or robust relativism is to be distinguished from Protagoreanism and incommensurabilism, and it is opposed to all familiar forms of skepticism, nihilism, anarchism, irrationalism, and the like. It is compatible with nonrelativistic theories of truth, as well as with theories that do not apply nonrelativistic truth-values to all domains of inquiry. This robust relativism defends the formal availability of truthlike values; judgments that would yield incompatible or contradictory judgments on a nonrelativistic or bipolar model of truth do not do so on this model. Further, Margolis holds that the nature or ontology of different sectors of the causal world is such that a relativistic theory is as reasonable as or more reasonable than a nonrelativistic theory.

The view that there is nothing to be said about truth or rationality apart from descriptions of procedures of justification is best represented by proponents of the so-called "strong program" in the sociology of knowledge. The strong program recommends that insofar as validity is reducible to credibility, equally credible beliefs be treated on a par. This view is discussed by Thomas McCarthy, and then by Russell Keat. In his account of learning McCarthy holds that the notion of truth, while essentially related to warranted assertability by the standards or warrants of this or that culture, cannot be reduced to any particular set of such standards or warrants. He holds that some differences between systems of belief are more than mere differences, because they can best be understood as the results of learning. The sociologist who weighs the claims to credibility of competing sociological data must be doing more than merely reflecting the contingent predilection of claims of warrant of his interpretive community.

Now, while both advocates and critics of the strong program (e.g., originally Barry Barnes and David Bloor, as well as Thomas McCarthy) generally agree that it entails cognitive relativism, Russell Keat holds that cognitive relativism does not justify the exclusion of conceptions of rationality from the theoretical vocabulary of such a science of sciences; nor would cognitive relativism rule out in principle the ascription of explanatory power to the conceptions of rationality accepted by members of a scientific community. Keat's contribution prompts the question, among others, whether the conventionally accepted assumption that relativism entails irrationalism is correct.

In the cross-cultural context this question arises in consideration of the idea of "development." Martha Nussbaum and Amartya Sen consider methodological and philosophical issues that are raised by an attempt to describe and assess the values of traditional Indian society. They distinguish two ways in which traditional values may be undermined: *object failure* obtains when the objects of valuation treasured by a particular traditional value system become more difficult to obtain and sustain as a result of material change; and *value rejection* obtains when there is a weakening of the holds those values have on the subjects. These authors argue that a method for the evaluation and criticism of tradition should be responsive to the need for criticism and also to concerns about external imposition. Criticism, they argue, must be *internal*, using resources taken from within human history and human experience. In addition, in the case of a particular culture, criticism should be *immersed* in, rather than detached from, the culture's way of life, its practices, even its emotions. And yet, third, it will have to be *genuinely critical*, subjecting traditional beliefs and practices to critical examination. Since cultures almost always contain a plurality of voices and much active debate, sufficient resources for criticism can frequently be found without moving outside the culture in question. This is all the more true since any culture is part of a larger community; and its communications with and responses to this larger world become a part of its own "internal" resources. But Nussbaum and Sen do not rule out the possibility that criticism might sometimes be entitled to appeal beyond the local culture to a broader area of human experience. These two strategies will frequently collapse in any case, since the criticism of culture A by culture B, once known, becomes a part of the internal reality of culture A.

Resisting a radical incommensurability between conceptual frameworks or their correlative worlds, Jitendra Mohanty argues that there is no opposition between diversity and unity. Rather than being a preexistent metaphysical entity, unity is being worked out in a gentle and tolerant, rather than a violent and imperious, way. Mohanty suggests that even for two world-noemata that are so far removed that any communication between them would seem impossible there can always be a series of intervening world-noemata that may link and overlap the initial pair. Thus, communication can be achieved. This presupposes that each noematic world is not a fully holistic system, for otherwise it would be impossible for one to share part of its contents with another.

Recognizing that real confrontation between cultures does take place (resulting in value rejection and value change), Bimal Matilal distinguishes between two faces of morality: (1) one that answers the needs of the "naked man"[3] and (2) another that answers local needs or local conventions in a given society. Regarding (1), Matilal considers the consequences (which he urges) of viewing the capabilities of the "naked man" as similar and equally valuable to all peoples. Here Matilal suggests that anthropologists and old liberal colonialists needlessly worry about misjudging the values of an "alien" culture, for if the "aliens" are judged as human, the way is open to judge their beliefs and values. Regarding (2), while a *rigid* version of moral relativism can be shown to be incoherent and misconceived, Matilal suggests that we can accept a *soft* version. Matilal considers two recent formulations (Bernard Williams' and Gilbert Harman's) and finds these unsatisfactory, for they face insuperable practical difficulties in that they depend upon the possibility of complete individuation of culture-groups. Matilal rejects possible answers to these difficulties, as well as further consequences of Harman's view.

Gilbert Harman holds that the issue between relativism and absolutism comes down to the dispute between naturalism and autonomous ethics. He uses the term "naturalism" for an approach to ethics dominated by a concern for the place of values in the natural world. And, in contrast, he calls any approach that is not so dominated or one that does not take the main question of ethics to be the naturalistic status of values and obligations an instance of "autonomous ethics." Harman holds that the most plausible versions of naturalism, which he endorses, involve moral relativism, which

denies that there are universal basic moral demands and says different
people are subject to different basic moral demands depending on the
social customs, practices, conventions, values and principles that they
accept.

Inevitably the question of relativism bears on the construal of
persons or selves, and thus on personal identity. Rom Harré holds that
while there is a common primary structure that every society recognizes
as human individuality in the form of persons, there are very wide
variations in secondary structures—or selves—which organize persons'
experienced thoughts, feelings, premonitions, and plans as their own.
He suggests that the constitution of the self involves being in possession
of a theory about one's self, a theory in terms of which a being orders,
partitions, and reflects on its own experience and becomes capable of
self-intervention and control. The organization of the self is as variable
as are the conventions through which the person is presented. It is
culture-specific.

In turn, Amélie Rorty holds that

[m]oral and political principles cannot be derived from "the" concept of
personhood because that concept is socially and politically constructed:
the defining characteristics of persons are set by. . . primary practices and
privileged actions.

Now, how does such a constructivist view bear on the question of
relativism? Amélie Rorty dissociates the issues, and she claims that the
relativism/antirelativism controversy is mistaken. The epistemological
difficulties on which relativists focus are compatible with there actually
being genuine intercultural communication—with which, in turn, constructivism is congenial. At issue is the holism of culture: the degree of
overlap between the institutions and practices that define different cultures. Of course, this view makes vulnerable only those forms of relativism which disallow the possibility of intercultural communication.

Mark Johnston argues for a method of theorizing about personal
identity which investigates what kind of thing we could be identifying
and reidentifying in the way in which we ordinarily identify and reidentify our selves and each other. In considering the possibility that the
kind so identified is not our substance-kind, but merely a kind which
corresponds to a phase through which we could live in circumstances
not yet realized, Johnston suggests that there is a certain relativity in the
application conditions of the concept of personal identity. He develops a
paradox for "simple-minded" relativism about personal identity and
shows that the resolution of that paradox lies in a higher-order consis-

tency, according to which what we can survive at any given time depends in part upon our socially enacted self-conception at that time.

If, in the course of these essays, the reader comes to see how engaging are the challenges of relativism, and how important are the multifarious responses to them, the aims of this volume will have been served. Besides the bibliographical references that appear at the end of individual essays, the reader who wishes to pursue further pertinent and recent materials will benefit from the bibliography which appears at the end of Harvey Siegel's useful book *Relativism Refuted* (Reidel, 1987).

For having helped to bring this volume to fruition, thanks are due to many people. First, thanks are due to John Ehmann of the University of Notre Dame Press for his consistent help and courtesies. Under Bryn Mawr College's Dana Internship Program Genevieve Bell was of considerable editorial assistance. Special thanks are due to Amélie Rorty, who, as something of an editor *sub rosa*, provided guidance and many helpful suggestions. It was she, in the first place, who proposed the present volume as something of a sequel to *Relativism: Cognitive and Moral*, coedited with Jack Meiland. Finally, thanks are due to the seventeen authors who prepared their essays for this volume, and to the five authors and their publishers for permission to have their essays reprinted.[4]

Notes

1. Maurice Mandelbaum, "Subjective, Objective, and Conceptual Relativism," reprinted in *Relativism: Cognitive and Moral*, ed. Jack W. Meiland and Michael Krausz (Notre Dame: University of Notre Dame Press, 1982).

2. Donald Davidson, "On the Very Idea of a Conceptual Scheme," ibid.

3. While this unfortunate phrase was originally offered by Stuart Hampshire and has been kept as such in pertinent discussions, its substitution by "naked person" would surely be seen as a welcome improvement by the authors. But then too the question whether "naked" and "man" *or* "person" can do the philosophical work for which it was introduced is itself open.-Ed.

4. The author gratefully acknowledges helpful suggestions of Frances Berenson, Joseph Margolis, Bimal Matilal, and James Winn.

Anti Anti-Relativism

CLIFFORD GEERTZ

I

A scholar can hardly be better employed than in destroying a fear. The one I want to go after is cultural relativism. Not the thing itself, which I think merely there, like Transylvania, but the dread of it, which I think unfounded. It is unfounded because the moral and intellectual consequences that are commonly supposed to flow from relativism— subjectivism, nihilism, incoherence, Machiavellianism, ethical idiocy, esthetic blindness, and so on—do not in fact do so and the promised rewards of escaping its clutches, mostly having to do with pasteurized knowledge, are illusory.

To be more specific, I want not to defend relativism, which is a drained term anyway, yesterday's battle cry, but to attack anti-relativism, which seems to me broadly on the rise and to represent a streamlined version of an antique mistake. Whatever cultural relativism may be or originally have been (and there is not one of its critics in a hundred who has got that right), it serves these days largely as a specter to scare us away from certain ways of thinking and toward others. And, as the ways of thinking away from which we are being driven seem to me to be more cogent than those toward which we are being propelled, and to lie at the heart of the anthropological heritage, I would like to do some- thing about this. Casting out demons is a praxis we should practice as well as study.

My through-the-looking-glass title is intended to suggest such an effort to counter a view rather than to defend the view it claims to be counter to. The analogy I had in mind in choosing it—a logical one, I trust it will be understood, not in any way a substantive one—is what,

Reprinted with permission of the American Anthropological Association from *American Anthropologist* 86: 2 (June 1984): 263-278. Not for further reproduction.

at the height of the cold war days (you remember them) was called "anti anti-communism." Those of us who strenuously opposed the obsession, as we saw it, with the Red Menace were thus denominated by those who, as they saw it, regarded the Menace as the primary fact of contemporary political life, with the insinuation—wildly incorrect in the vast majority of cases—that, by the law of the double negative, we had some secret affection for the Soviet Union.

Again, I mean to use this analogy in a formal sense; I don't think relativists are like communists, anti-relativists are like anti-communists, and that anyone (well . . . hardly anyone) is behaving like McCarthy. One could construct a similar parallelism using the abortion controversy. Those of us who are opposed to increased legal restrictions on abortion are not, I take it, pro-abortion, in the sense that we think abortion a wonderful thing and hold that the greater the abortion rate the greater the well-being of society; we are "anti anti-abortionists" for quite other reasons I need not rehearse. In this frame, the double negative simply doesn't work in the usual way; and therein lies its rhetorical attractions. It enables one to reject something without thereby committing oneself to what it rejects. And this is precisely what I want to do with anti-relativism.

So lumbering an approach to the matter, explaining and excusing itself as it goes, is necessary because, as the philosopher-anthropologist John Ladd (1982:161) has remarked, "all the common definitions of . . . relativism are framed by opponents of relativism . . . they are absolutist definitions." (Ladd, whose immediate focus is Edward Westermarck's famous book, is speaking of "ethical relativism" in particular, but the point is general: for "cognitive relativism" think of Israel Scheffler's [1967] attack on Thomas Kuhn, for "aesthetic relativism," Wayne Booth's [1983] on Stanley Fish.) And, as Ladd also says, the result of this is that relativism, or anything that at all looks like relativism under such hostile definitions, is identified with nihilism (Ladd 1982:158). To suggest that "hard rock" foundations for cognitive, esthetic, or moral judgments may not, in fact, be available, or anyway that those one is being offered are dubious, is to find oneself accused of disbelieving in the existence of the physical world, thinking pushpin as good as poetry, regarding Hitler as just a fellow with unstandard tastes, or even, as I myself have recently been—God save the mark—"[having] no politics at all" (Rabinow 1983:70). The notion that someone who does not hold your views holds the reciprocal of them, or simply hasn't got any, has, whatever its comforts for those afraid reality is going to go away unless we believe very hard in it, not conduced to much in the way of clarity in the anti-relativist discussion, but merely to far too many people spending far too much time describing at length what it is they do *not* maintain than seems in any way profitable.

All this is of relevance to anthropology because, of course, it is by way of the idea of relativism, grandly ill-defined, that it has most disturbed the general intellectual peace. From our earliest days, even when theory in anthropology—evolutionary, diffusionist, or *elementargedankenisch*—was anything but relativistic, the message that we have been thought to have for the wider world has been that, as they see things differently and do them otherwise in Alaska or the D'Entrecasteaux, our confidence in our own seeings and doings and our resolve to bring others around to sharing them are rather poorly based. This point, too, is commonly ill-understood. It has not been anthropological theory, such as it is, that has made our field seem to be a massive argument against absolutism in thought, morals, and esthetic judgment; it has been anthropological data: customs, crania, living floors, and lexicons. The notion that it was Boas, Benedict, and Melville Herskovits, with a European assist from Westermarck, who infected our field with the relativist virus, and Kroeber, Kluckhohn, and Redfield, with a similar assist from Lévi-Strauss, who have labored to rid us of it, is but another of the myths that bedevil this whole discussion. After all, Montaigne (1978:202-214) could draw relativistic, or relativistic-looking, conclusions from the fact, as he heard it, that the Caribs didn't wear breeches; he did not have to read *Patterns of Culture.* Even earlier on, Herodotus, contemplating "certain Indians of the race called Callatians," among whom men were said to eat their fathers, came, as one would think he might, to similar views (Herodotus 1859-61).

The relativist bent, or more accurately the relativist bent anthropology so often induces in those who have much traffic with its materials, is thus in some sense implicit in the field as such; in cultural anthropology perhaps particularly, but in much of archeology, anthropological linguistics, and physical anthropology as well. One cannot read too long about Nayar matriliny, Aztec sacrifice, the Hopi verb, or the convolutions of the hominid transition and not begin at least to consider the possibility that, to quote Montaigne again, "each man calls barbarism whatever is not his own practice . . . for we have no other criterion of reason than the example and idea of the opinions and customs of the country we live in" (1978:205, cited in Todorov 1983:113-144).[1] That notion, whatever its problems, and however more delicately expressed, is not likely to go entirely away unless anthropology does.

It is to this fact, progressively discovered to be one as our enterprise has advanced and our findings grown more circumstantial, that both relativists and anti-relativists have, according to their sensibilities, reacted. The realization that news from elsewhere about ghost marriage, ritual destruction of property, initiatory fellatio, royal immolation, and (Dare I say it? Will he strike again?) nonchalant adolescent sex naturally inclines the mind to an "other beasts other mores" view of things has led to arguments, outraged, desperate, and exultant by turns, designed to persuade us either to resist that inclination in the name of reason, or to embrace it on the same grounds. What looks like a debate about the broader implications of anthropological research is really a debate about how to live with them.

Once this fact is grasped, and "relativism" and "anti-relativism" are seen as general responses to the way in which what Kroeber once called the centrifugal impulse of anthropology—distant places, distant times, distant species . . . distant grammars—affects our sense of things, the whole discussion comes rather better into focus. The supposed conflict between Benedict's and Herskovits's call for tolerance and the untolerant passion with which they called for it turns out not to be the simple contradiction so many amateur logicians have held it to be, but the expression of a perception, caused by thinking a lot about Zunis and Dahomeys, that, the world being so full of a number of things, rushing to judgment is more than a mistake, it's a crime. Similarly, Kroeber's and Kluckhohn's pan-cultural verities—Kroeber's were mostly about messy creatural matters like delirium and menstruation, Kluckhohn's about messy social ones like lying and killing within the in-group—turn out not to be just the arbitrary, personal obsessions they so much look like, but the expression of a much vaster concern, caused by thinking a lot about *anthropōs* in general, that if something isn't anchored everywhere nothing can be anchored anywhere. Theory here—if that is what these earnest advices as to how we must look at things if we are to be accounted decent should be called—is rather more an exchange of warnings than an analytical debate. We are being offered a choice of worries.

What the relativists, so-called, want us to worry about is provincialism—the danger that our perceptions will be dulled, our intellects constricted, and our sympathies narrowed by the overlearned and overvalued acceptances of our own society. What the anti-relativists, selfdeclared, want us to worry about, and worry about and worry about, as though our very souls depended upon it, is a kind of spiritual entropy, a heat death of the mind, in which everything is as significant, thus as insignificant, as everything else: anything goes, to each his own, you pays your money and you takes your choice, I know what I like, not in the south, *tout comprendre, c'est tout pardonner.*

As I have already suggested, I myself find provincialism altogether the more real concern so far as what actually goes on in the world. (Though even there, the thing can be overdone: "You might as well fall flat on your face," one of Thurber's marvelous "morals" goes, "as lean too far over backward.") The image of vast numbers of anthropology readers running around in so cosmopolitan a frame of mind as to have no views as to what is and isn't true, or good, or beautiful, seems to me largely a fantasy. There may be some genuine nihilists out there, along Rodeo Drive or around Times Square, but I doubt very many have become such as a result of an excessive sensitivity to the claims of other cultures; and at least most of the people I meet, read, and read about, and indeed I myself, are all-too-committed to something or other, usually parochial. "'Tis the eye of childhood that fears a painted devil": anti-relativism has largely concocted the anxiety it lives from.

II

But surely I exaggerate? Surely anti-relativists, secure in the knowledge that rattling gourds cannot cause thunder and that eating people is wrong, cannot be so excitable? Listen, then, to William Gass (1981:53-54), novelist, philosopher, *précieux,* and pop-eyed observer of anthropologists' ways:

> Anthropologists or not, we all used to call them "natives"—those little, distant, jungle and island people—and we came to recognize the unscientific snobbery in that. Even our more respectable journals could show them naked without offense, because their pendulous or pointed breasts were as inhuman to us as the udder of a cow. Shortly we came to our senses and had them dress. We grew to distrust our own point of view, our local certainties, and embraced relativism, although it is one of the scabbier whores; and we went on to endorse a nice equality among cultures, each of which was carrying out its task of coalescing, conversing, and structuring some society. A large sense of superiority was one of the white man's burdens, and that weight, released, was replaced by an equally heavy sense of guilt.
>
> No more than we might expect a surgeon to say "Dead and good riddance" would an anthropologist exclaim, stepping from the culture just surveyed as one might shed a set of working clothes, "What a lousy way to live!" Because, even if the natives were impoverished, covered with dust and sores; even if they had been trodden on by stronger feet till they were flat as a path; even if they were rapidly dying off; still, the observer

could remark how frequently they smiled, or how infrequently their children fought, or how serene they were. We can envy the Zuni their peaceful ways and the Navaho their "happy heart."

It was amazing how mollified we were to find that there was some functional point to food taboos, infibulation, or clitoridectomy; and if we still felt morally squeamish about human sacrifice or headhunting, it is clear we were still squeezed into a narrow modern European point of view, and had no sympathy, and didn't—couldn't—understand. Yet when we encountered certain adolescents among indolent summery seaside tribes who were allowed to screw without taboo, we wondered whether this enabled them to avoid the stresses of our own youth, and we secretly hoped it hadn't.

Some anthropologists have untied the moral point of view, so sacred to Eliot and Arnold and Emerson, from every mooring (science and art also float away on the stream of Becoming), calling any belief in objective knowledge "fundamentalism," as if it were the same as benighted Biblical literalism; and arguing for the total mutability of man and the complete sociology of what under such circumstances could no longer be considered knowledge but only *doxa* or "opinion."

This overheated vision of "the anthropological point of view," rising out of the mists of caricatured arguments ill-grasped to start with (it is one of Gass's ideas that Mary Douglas is some sort of skeptic, and Benedict's satire, cannier than his, has escaped him altogether), leaves us with a fair lot to answer for. But even from within the profession, the charges, though less originally expressed, as befits a proper science, are hardly less grave. Relativism ("[T]he position that all assessments are assessments relative to some standard or other, and standards derive from cultures"). I.C. Jarvie (1983:45, 46) remarks,

> has these objectionable consequences: namely, that by limiting critical assessment of human works it disarms us, dehumanizes us, leaves us unable to enter into communicative interaction: that is to say, unable to criticize cross-culturally, cross-sub-culturally: ultimately, relativism leaves no room for criticism at all . . . [B]ehind relativism nihilism looms.

More in front, scarecrow and leper's bell, it sounds like, than behind: certainly none of us, clothed and in our right minds, will rush to embrace a view that so dehumanizes us as to render us incapable of communicating with anybody. The heights to which this beware of the scabby whore who will cut off your critical powers sort of thing can aspire is indicated, to give one last example, by Paul Johnson's (1983) ferocious new book on the history of the world since 1917, *Modern*

Times, which, opening with a chapter called "A Relativistic World" (Hugh Thomas's [1983] review of the book in the *TLS* was more aptly entitled, "The inferno of relativism"), accounts for the whole modern disaster—Lenin and Hitler, Amin, Bokassa, Sukarno, Mao, Nasser, and Hammarskjöld, Structuralism, the New Deal, the Holocaust, both world wars, 1968, inflation, Shinto militarism, OPEC, and the independence of India—as outcomes of something called "the relativist heresy." "A great trio of German imaginative scholars," Nietzsche, Marx, and (with a powerful assist—our contribution—from Frazer) Freud, destroyed the 19th century morally as Einstein, banishing absolute motion, destroyed it cognitively, and Joyce, banishing absolute narrative, destroyed it esthetically:

> Marx described a world in which the central dynamic was economic interest. To Freud the principal thrust was sexual . . . Nietzsche, the third of the trio, was also an atheist . . . [and he] saw [the death of God] as . . . an historical event, which would have dramatic consequences . . . Among the advanced races, the decline and ultimately the collapse of the religious impulse would leave a huge vacuum. The history of modern times is in great part the history of how that vacuum [has] been filled. Nietzsche rightly perceived that the most likely candidate would be what he called "The Will to Power" . . . In place of religious belief, there would be secular ideology. Those who had once filled the ranks of the totalitarian clergy would become totalitarian politicians . . . The end of the old order, with an unguided world adrift in a relativistic universe, was a summons to such gangster statesmen to emerge. They were not slow to make their appearance. [Johnson 1983:48]

After this there is perhaps nothing much else to say, except perhaps what George Stocking (1982:176) says, summarizing others—"cultural relativism, which had buttressed the attack against racialism, [can] be perceived as a sort of neo-racialism justifying the backward techno-economic status of once colonized peoples." Or what Lionel Tiger (Tiger and Sepher 1975:16) says, summarizing himself: "the feminist argument [for "the social non-necessity . . . of the laws instituted by patriarchy"] reflects the cultural relativism that has long characterized those social sciences which rejected locating human behavior in biological processes." Mindless tolerance, mindless intolerance; ideological promiscuity, ideological monomania; egalitarian hypocrisy, egalitarian simplisticism—all flow from the same infirmity. Like Welfare, The Media, The Bourgeoisie, or The Ruling Circles, Cultural Relativism causes everything bad.

Anthropologists, plying their trade and in any way reflective about it, could, for all their own sort of provincialism, hardly remain unaffected by the hum of philosophical disquiet rising everywhere around them. (I have not even mentioned the fierce debates brought on by the revival of political and moral theory, the appearance of deconstructionist literary criticism, the spread of nonfoundationalist moods in metaphysics and epistemology, and the rejection of whiggery and method-ism in the history of science.) The fear that our emphasis on difference, diversity, oddity, discontinuity, incommensurability, uniqueness, and so on—what Empson (1955, cited to opposite purposes in Kluckhohn 1962:292-293) called "the gigan-/-tic anthropological circus riotiously/[Holding] open all its booths"—might end leaving us with little more to say than that elsewhere things are otherwise and culture is as culture does has grown more and more intense. So intense, in fact, that it has led us off in some all-too-familiar directions in an attempt, ill-conceived, so I think, to still it.

One could ground this last proposition in a fair number of places in contemporary anthropological thought and research—from Harrisonian "Everything That Rises Must Converge" materialism to Popperian "Great Divide" evolutionism. ("We Have Science . . . or Literacy, or Intertheoretic Competition, or the Cartesian Conception of Knowledge . . . but They Have Not.")[2] But I want to concentrate here on two of central importance, or anyway popularity, right now: the attempt to reinstate a context-independent concept of "Human Nature" as a bulwark against relativism, and the attempt to reinstate, similarly, a similar one of that other old friend, "The Human Mind."

Again, it is necessary to be clear so as not to be accused, under the "if you don't believe in my God you must believe in my Devil" assumption I mentioned earlier, of arguing for absurd positions—radical, culture-is-all historicism, or primitive, the brain-is-a-blackboard empiricism—which no one of any seriousness holds, and quite possibly, a momentary enthusiasm here and there aside, ever has held. The issue is not whether human beings are biological organisms with intrinsic characteristics. Men can't fly and pigeons can't talk. Nor is it whether they show commonalities in mental functioning wherever we find them. Papuans envy, Aborigines dream. The issue is, what are we to make of these undisputed facts as we go about explicating rituals, analyzing ecosystems, interpreting fossil sequences, or comparing languages.

III

These two moves toward restoring culture-free conceptions of what we amount to as basic, sticker-price *homo* and essential, no additives *sapiens* take a number of quite disparate forms, not in much

agreement beyond their general tenor, naturalist in the one case, rationalist in the other. On the naturalist side there is, of course, sociobiology
and other hyper-adaptationist orientations. But there are also perspectives growing out of psychoanalysis, ecology, neurology, display-and-
imprint ethology, some kinds of developmental theory, and some kinds
of Marxism. On the rationalist side there is, of course, the new intellec-
tualism one associates with structuralism and other hyper-logicist orientations. But there are also perspectives growing out of generative linguistics, experimental psychology, artificial intelligence research, ploy and
counterploy microsociology, some kinds of developmental theory, and
some kinds of Marxism. Attempts to banish the specter of relativism
whether by sliding down The Great Chain of Being or edging up it—the
dog beneath the skin, a mind for all cultures—do not comprise a single
enterprise, massive and coordinate, but a loose and immiscible crowd of
them, each pressing its own cause and in its own direction. The sin may
be one, but the salvations are many.

It is for this reason, too, that an attack, such as mine, upon the
efforts to draw context-independent concepts of "Human Nature" or
"The Human Mind" from biological, psychological, linguistic, or for
that matter cultural (HRAF and all that) inquiries should not be mistaken for an attack upon those inquiries as research programs. Whether
or not sociobiology is, as I think, a degenerative research program
destined to expire in its own confusions, and neuroscience a progressive
one (to use Imre Lakatos's [1976] useful epithets) on the verge of extraordinary achievements, anthropologists will be well-advised to attend
to, with various shades of mixed, maybe, maybe not, verdicts for structuralism, generative grammar, ethology, AI, psychoanalysis, ecology, microsociology, Marxism, or developmental psychology in between, is
quite beside the point. It is not, or anyway not here, the validity of the
sciences, real or would-be, that is at issue. What concerns me, and
should concern us all, are the axes that, with an increasing determination bordering on the evangelical, are being busily ground with their
assistance.

As a way into all this on the naturalist side we can look for a
moment at a general discussion widely accepted—though, as it consists
largely of pronouncements, it is difficult to understand why—as a balanced and moderate statement of the position: Mary Midgeley's *Beast
and Man, The Roots of Human Nature* (1978). In the Pilgrim's Progress,
"once I was blind but now I see" tonalities that have become characteristic of such discourses in recent years, Midgeley writes:

> I first entered this jungle myself some time ago, by slipping out over the
> wall of the tiny arid garden cultivated at that time under the name of

British Moral Philosophy. I did so in an attempt to think about human nature and the problem of evil. The evils in the world, I thought are real. That they are so is neither a fancy imposed on us by our own culture, nor one created by our will and imposed on the world. Such suggestions are bad faith. What we abominate is not optional. Culture certainly varies the details, but then we can criticize our culture. What standard [note the singular] do we use for this? What is the underlying structure of human nature which culture is designed to complete and express? In this tangle of questions I found some clearings being worked by Freudian and Jungian psychologists, on principles that seemed to offer hope but were not quite clear to me. Other areas were being mapped by anthropologists, who seemed to have some interest in my problem, but who were inclined . . . to say that what human beings had in common was not in the end very important: that the key to all the mysteries [lay] in culture. This seemed to me shallow . . . I [finally] came upon another clearing, this time an expansion of the borders of traditional zoology, made by people [Lorenz, Tinbergen, Eibes-Eibesfeldt, Desmond Morris] studying the natures of other species. They had done much work on the question of what such a *nature* was—recent work in the tradition of Darwin, and indeed of Aristotle, bearing directly on problems in which Aristotle was already interested, but which have become peculiarly pressing today. [1978:xiv–xv; italics in original]

The assumptions with which this declaration of conscience is riddled—that fancies imposed on us by cultural judgments (that the poor are worthless? that Blacks are subhuman? that women are irrational?) are inadequately substantial to ground real evil; that culture is icing, biology, cake; that we have no choice as to what we shall hate (hippies? bosses? eggheads? . . . relativists?); that difference is shallow, likeness, deep; that Lorenz is a straightforward fellow and Freud a mysterious one—may perhaps be left to perish of their own weight. One garden has been but exchanged for another. The jungle remains several walls away.

More important is what sort of garden this "Darwin meets Aristotle" one is. What sort of abominations are going to become unoptional? What sort of facts unnatural?

Well, mutual admiration societies, sadism, ingratitude, monotony, and the shunning of cripples, among other things—at least when they are carried to excess:

Grasping this point ["that what is *natural* is never just a condition or activity . . . but a certain *level* of that condition or activity proportionate to the rest of one's life"] makes it possible to cure a difficulty about such concepts as *natural* which has made many people think them unusable. Besides their strong sense, which recommends something, they have a weak sense, which does not. In the weak sense, sadism is natural. This just means that it occurs; we should recognize it. . . . But in a strong and perfectly good sense, we may call sadistic behavior *unnatural*—meaning that a policy based on this natural impulse, and extended through some-body's life into organized activity, is, as [Bishop] Butler said, "contrary to the whole constitution of human nature." . . . That consenting adults should bite each other in bed is in all senses natural; that schoolteachers should bully children for their sexual gratification is not. There is some-thing wrong with this activity beyond the actual injury that it inflicts. . . . Examples of this wrong thing—of unnaturalness—can be found which do not involve other people as victims; for instance, extreme narcissism, suicide, obsessiveness, incest, and exclusive mutual admiration societies. "It is an unnatural life" we say, meaning that its center has been mis-placed. Further examples, which do involve victimizing others, are redir-ected aggression, the shunning of cripples, ingratitude, vindictiveness, parricide. All these things are *natural* in that there are well-known im-pulses toward them which are parts of human nature. . . . But redirected aggression and so on can properly be called *unnatural* when we think of nature in the fuller sense, not just as an assembly of parts, but as an organized whole. They are parts which will ruin the shape of that whole if they are allowed in any sense to take it over. [Midgeley 1978:79-80; italics in original][3]

Aside from the fact that it legitimates one of the more popular sophisms of intellectual debate nowadays, asserting the strong form of an argument and defending the weak one (sadism is natural as long as you don't bite too deep), this little game of concept juggling (natural may be unnatural when we think of nature "in the fuller sense") dis-plays the basic thesis of all such Human Nature arguments. Virtue (cognitive, esthetic, and moral alike) is to vice as fitness is to disorder, normality to abnormality, well-being to sickness. The task for man, as for his lungs or his thyroid, is to function properly. Shunning cripples can be dangerous to your health.

Or as Stephen Salkever (1983:210), a political scientist and follow-er of Midgeley's puts it:

Perhaps the best developed model or analogue for an adequate functional-ist social science is that provided by medicine. For the physician, physical features of an individual organism become intelligible in the light of a basic conception of the problems confronting this self-directed physical system and in the light of a general sense of healthy or well-functioning state of the organism relative to those problems. To understand a patient is to understand him or her as being more or less healthy relative to some stable and objective standard of physical well-being, the kind of standard the Greeks called *aretè*. This word is now ordinarily translated "virtue," but in the political philosophy of Plato and Aristotle it refers simply to the characteristic or definitive excellence of the subject of any functional analysis.

Again, one can look almost anywhere within anthropology these days and find an example of the revival of this "it all comes down to" (genes, species being, cerebral architecture, psycho-sexual constitution . . .) cast of mind. Shake almost any tree and a selfish altruist or a biogenetic structuralist is likely to fall out.

But it is better, I think, or at least less disingenuous, to have for an instance neither a sitting duck nor a self-destructing artifact. And so let me examine, very briefly, the views, most especially the recent views, of one of our most experienced ethnographers and influential theorists, as well as one of our most formidable polemicists: Melford Spiro. Purer cases, less shaded and less circumspect, and thus all the better to appall you with, could be found. But in Spiro we are at least not dealing with some marginal phenomenon—a Morris or an Ardrey—easily dismissed as an enthusiast or a popularizer, but with a major figure at, or very near, the center of the discipline.

Spiro's more important recent forays into "down deep" in the *Homo* anthropology—his rediscovery of the Freudian family romance, first in his own material on the kibbutz and then in Malinowski's on the Trobriands—are well-known and will be, I daresay, as convincing or unconvincing to their readers as psychoanalytic theory of a rather orthodox sort is in general. But my concern is, again, less with that than with the Here Comes Everyman anti-relativism he develops on the basis of it. And to get a sense for that, a recent article of his (Spiro 1978) summarizing his advance from past confusions to present clarities will serve quite well. Called "Culture and Human Nature," it catches a mood and a drift of attitude much more widely spread than its rather beleaguered, no longer avant-garde theoretical perspective.

Spiro's paper is, as I mentioned, again cast in the "when a child I spake as a child but now that I am grown I have put away childish things" genre so prominent in the anti-relativist literature generally. (Indeed, it might better have been titled, as another southern California-based anthropologist—apparently relativism seems a clear and present danger out that way—called the record of his deliverance, "Confessions of a Former Cultural Relativist."[4])

Spiro begins his apologia with the admission that when he came into anthropology in the early 1940s he was preadapted by a Marxist background and too many courses in British philosophy to a radically environmentalist view of man, one that assumed a *tabula rasa* view of mind, a social determinist view of behavior, and a cultural relativist view of, well . . . culture, and then traces his field trip history as a didactic, parable for our times, narrative of how he came not just to abandon these ideas but to replace them by their opposites. In Ifaluk, he discovered that a people who showed very little social aggression could yet be plagued by hostile feelings. In Israel, he discovered that children "raised in [the] totally communal and cooperative system" of the kibbutz and socialized to be mild, loving and noncompetitive, nevertheless resented attempts to get them to share goods and when obliged to do so grew resistant and hostile. And in Burma, he discovered that a belief in the impermanence of sentient existence, Buddhist nirvana and nonattachment, did not result in a diminished interest in the immediate materialities of daily life.

> In short, [my field studies] convinced me that many motivational dispositions are culturally invariant [and] many cognitive orientations [are so] as well. These invariant dispositions and orientations stem . . . from panhuman biological and cultural constants, and they comprise that universal human nature which, together with received anthropological opinion, I had formerly rejected as yet another ethnocentric bias. [Spiro 1978:349-350]

Whether or not a portrait of peoples from Micronesia to the Middle East as angry moralizers deviously pursuing hedonic interests will altogether still the suspicion that some ethnocentric bias yet clings to Spiro's view of universal human nature remains to be seen. What doesn't remain to be seen, because he is quite explicit about them, are the kinds of ideas, noxious products of a noxious relativism, such a recourse to medical functionalism is designed to cure us of:

> [The] concept of cultural relativism . . . was enlisted to do battle against racist notions in general, and the notion of primitive mentality, in particular. . . . [But] cultural relativism was also used, at least by some anthropologists, to perpetuate a kind of inverted racism. That is, it was used as a powerful tool of cultural criticism, with the consequent derogation of Western culture and of the mentality which it produced. Espousing the philosophy of primitivism . . . the image of primitive man was used . . . as a vehicle for the pursuit of personal utopian quests, and/or as a fulcrum to express personal discontent with Western man and Western society. The strategies adopted took various forms, of which the following are fairly representative. (1) Attempts to abolish private property, or inequality, or

aggression in Western societies have a reasonably realistic chance of success since such states of affairs may be found in many primitive societies. (2) Compared to at least some primitives, Western man is uniquely competitive, warlike, intolerant of deviance, sexist, and so on. (3) Paranoia is not necessarily an illness, because paranoid thinking is institutionalized in certain primitive societies; homosexuality is not deviant because homosexuals are the cultural cynosures of some primitive societies; monogamy is not viable because polygamy is the most frequent form of marriage in primitive societies. [Spiro 1978:336]

Aside from adding a few more items to the list, which promises to be infinite, of unoptional abominations, it is the introduction of the idea of "deviance," conceived as a departure from an inbuilt norm, like an arrhythmic heartbeat, not as a statistical oddity, like fraternal polyandry, that is the really critical move amid all this huffing and puffing about "inverted racism," "utopian quests," and "the philosophy of primitivism." For it is through that idea, The Lawgiver's Friend, that Midgeley's transition between the natural natural (aggression, inequality) and the unnatural natural (paranoia, homosexuality) gets made. Once that camel's nose has been pushed inside, the tent—indeed, the whole riotous circus crying all its booths—is in serious trouble.

Just how much trouble can perhaps be more clearly seen from Robert Edgerton's (1978) companion piece to Spiro's in the same volume, "The Study of Deviance, Marginal Man or Everyman?" After a useful, rather eclectic, review of the study of deviance in anthropology, psychology, and sociology, including again his own quite interesting work with American retardates and African intersexuals, Edgerton too comes, rather suddenly as a matter of fact—a cartoon light bulb going on—to the conclusion that what is needed to make such research genuinely productive is a context-independent conception of human nature—one in which "genetically encoded potentials for behavior that we all share" are seen to "underlie (our universal) propensity for deviance." Man's "instinct" for self-preservation, his flight/fight mechanism, and his intolerance of boredom are instanced; and, in an argument I, in my innocence, had thought gone from anthropology, along with euhemerism and primitive promiscuity, it is suggested that, if all goes well on the science side, we may, in time, be able to judge not just individuals but entire societies as deviant, inadequate, failed, unnatural:

> More important still is our inability to test any proposition about the relative adequacy of a society. Our relativistic tradition in anthropology has been slow to yield to the idea that there could be such a thing as a deviant society, one that is contrary to human nature. . . . Yet the idea of a

deviant society is central to the alienation tradition in sociology and other fields and it poses a challenge for anthropological theory. Because we know so little about human nature . . . we cannot say whether, much less how, any society has failed. . . . Nevertheless, a glance at any urban newspaper's stories of rising rates of homicide, suicide, rape and other violent crimes should suffice to suggest that the question is relevant not only for theory, but for questions of survival in the modern world. [Edgerton 1978:470]

With this the circle closes; the door slams. The fear of relativism, raised at every turn like some mesmeric obsession, has led to a position in which cultural diversity, across space and over time, amounts to a series of expressions, some salubrious, some not, of a settled, underlying reality, the essential nature of man, and anthropology amounts to an attempt to see through the haze of those expressions to the substance of that reality. A sweeping, schematic, and content-hungry concept, conformable to just about any shape that comes along, Wilsonian, Lorenzian, Freudian, Marxian, Benthamite, Aristotelian ("one of the central features of Human Nature," some anonymous genius is supposed to have remarked, "is a separate judiciary"), becomes the ground upon which the understanding of human conduct, homicide, suicide, rape . . . the derogation of Western culture, comes definitively to rest. Some gods from some machines cost, perhaps, rather more than they come to.

IV

About that other conjuration "The Human Mind," held up as a protective cross against the relativist Dracula, I can be somewhat more succinct: for the general pattern, if not the substantial detail, is very much the same. There is the same effort to promote a privileged language of "real" explanation ("nature's own vocabulary," as Richard Rorty [1983; cf. Rorty 1979], attacking the notion as scientistic fantasy, has put it); and the same wild dessensus as to just which language— Shannon's? Saussure's? Piaget's?—that in fact is. There is the same tendency to see diversity as surface and universality as depth. And there is the same desire to represent one's interpretations not as constructions brought to their objects—societies, cultures, languages—in an effort, somehow, somewhat to comprehend them, but as quiddities of such objects forced upon our thought.

There are, of course, differences as well. The return of Human Nature as a regulative idea has been mainly stimulated by advances in genetics and evolutionary theory, that of The Human Mind by ones in linguistics, computer science, and cognitive psychology. The inclination of the former is to see moral relativism as the source of all our ills, that of the latter is to pin the blame on conceptual relativism. And a partiality for the tropes and images of therapeutic discourse (health and illness, normal and abnormal, function and disfunction) on the one side is matched by a penchant for those of epistemological discourse (knowledge and opinion, fact and illusion, truth and falsity) on the other. But they hardly count, these differences, against the common impulse to final analysis, we have now arrived at Science, explanation. Wiring your theories into something called The Structure of Reason is as effective a way to insulate them from history and culture as building them into something called The Constitution of Man.

So far as anthropology as such is concerned, however, there is another difference, more or less growing out of these, which, while also (you should excuse the expression) more relative than radical, does act to drive the two sorts of discussions in somewhat divergent, even contrary, directions, namely, that where the Human Nature tack leads to bringing back one of our classical conceptions into the center of our attention—"social deviance"—the Human Mind tack leads to bringing back another—"primitive *(sauvage,* primary, preliterate) thought." The anti-relativist anxieties that gather in the one discourse around the enigmas of conduct, gather in the other around those of belief.

More exactly, they gather around "irrational" (or "mystical," "prelogical," "affective" or, particularly nowadays, "noncognitive") beliefs. Where it has been such unnerving practices as headhunting, slavery, caste, and footbinding which have sent anthropologists rallying to the grand old banner of Human Nature under the impression that only thus could taking a moral distance from them be justified, it has been such unlikely conceptions as witchcraft substance, animal tutelaries, godkings, and (to foreshadow an example I will be getting to in a moment) a dragon with a golden heart and a horn at the nape of its neck which have sent them rallying to that of The Human Mind under the impression that only thus could adopting an empirical skepticism with respect to them be defended. It is not so much how the other half behaves that is so disquieting, but—what is really rather worse—how it thinks.

There are, again, a fairly large number of such rationalist or neorationalist perspectives in anthropology of varying degrees of purity, cogency, coherence, and popularity, not wholly consonant one with another. Some invoke formal constancies, usually called cognitive universals; some, developmental constancies, usually called cognitive stages; some, operational constancies, usually called cognitive processes.

Some are structuralist, some are Jungian, some are Piagetian, some look to the latest news from MIT, Bell Labs, or Carnegie-Mellon. All are after something steadfast: Reality reached, Reason saved from drowning.

What they share, thus, is not merely an interest in our mental functioning. Like an interest in our biological makeup, that is uncontroversially A Good Thing, both in itself and for the analysis of culture; and if not all the supposed discoveries in what is coming to be called, in an aspiring sort of way, "cognitive science" turn out in the event genuinely to be such, some doubtless will, and will alter significantly not only how we think about how we think but how we think about what we think. What, beyond that, they share, from Lévi-Strauss to Rodney Needham, something of a distance, and what is not so uncontroversially beneficent, is a foundationalist view of Mind. That is, a view which sees it—like "The Means of Production" or "Social Structure" or "Exchange" or "Energy" or "Culture" or "Symbol" in other, bottom-line, the-buck-stops-here approaches to social theory (and of course like "Human Nature")—as the sovereign term of explanation, the light that shines in the relativist darkness.

That it is the fear of relativism, the anti-hero with a thousand faces, that provides a good part of the impetus to neo-rationalism, as it does to neo-naturalism, and serves as its major justification, can be conveniently seen from the excellent new collection of anti-relativist exhortations—plus one unbuttoned relativist piece marvelously designed to drive the others to the required level of outrage—edited by Martin Hollis and Steven Lukes (1982), *Rationality and Relativism*.[5] A product of the so-called "rationality debate" (see Wilson 1970; cf. Hanson 1981) that Evans-Pritchard's chicken stories, among other things, seem to have induced into British social science and a fair part of British philosophy ("Are there absolute truths that can be gradually approached over time through rational processes? Or are all modes and systems of thought equally valid if viewed from within their own internally consistent frames of reference?"[6]) the book more or less covers the Reason in Danger! waterfront. "The temptations of relativism are perennial and pervasive," the editors' introduction opens, like some Cromwellian call to the barricades: "[The] primrose path to relativism . . . is paved with plausible contentions" (Hollis and Lukes 1982:1).

The three anthropologists in the collection all respond with enthusiasm to this summons to save us from ourselves. Ernest Gellner (1982) argues that the fact that other people do not believe what we, The Children of Galileo, believe about how reality is put together is no argument against the fact that what we believe is not the correct, "One True Vision." And especially as others, even Himalayans, seem to him to be coming around, he thinks it almost certain that it is. Robin

Horton (1982) argues for a "cognitive common core," a culturally universal, only trivially variant, "primary theory" of the world as filled with middle-sized, enduring objects, interrelated in terms of a "push-pull" concept of causality, five spatial dichotomies (left/right, above/below, etc.), a temporal trichotomy (before/at the same time/after) and two categorical distinctions (human/nonhuman, self/other), the existence of which insures that "Relativism is bound to fail whilst Universalism may, some day, succeed" (Horton 1982:260).

But it is Dan Sperber (1982), surer of his rationalist ground (Jerry Fodor's computational view of mental representations) than either of these, and with a One True Vision of his own ("there is no such thing as a non-literal fact"), who develops the most vigorous attack. Relativism, though marvelously mischievous (it makes "ethnography. . . inexplicable, and psychology immensely difficult"), is not even an indefensible position, it really doesn't qualify as a position at all. Its ideas are semi-ideas, its beliefs semi-beliefs, its propositions semi-propositions. Like the gold-hearted dragon with the horn at the base of his neck that one of his elderly Dorze informants innocently, or perhaps not quite so innocently, invited him to track down and kill (wary of nonliteral facts, he declined), such "relativist slogans" as "peoples of different cultures live in different worlds" are not, in fact, factual beliefs. They are half-formed and indeterminate representations, mental stopgaps, that result when, less circumspect than computers, we try to process more information than our inherent conceptual capacities permit. Useful, sometimes, as place holders until we can get our cognitive powers up to speed, occasionally fun to toy with while we are waiting, even once in a while "sources of suggestion in [genuine] creative thinking," they are not, these academic dragons with plastic hearts and no horn at all, matters even their champions take as true, for they do not really understand, nor can they, what they mean. They are hand-wavings—more elaborate or less—of a, in the end, conformist, false-profound, misleading, "hermeneutico-psychedelic," self-serving sort:

> The best evidence against relativism is . . . the very activity of anthropologists, while the best evidence for relativism [is] in the writings of anthropologists. . . . In retracing their steps [in their works], anthropologists transform into unfathomable gaps the shallow and irregular cultural boundaries they had not found so difficult to cross [in the field], thereby protecting their own sense of identity, and providing their philosophical and lay audience with just what they want to hear. [Sperber 1982:180]

In short, whether in the form of hearty common sense (never mind about liver gazing and poison oracles, we have after all got things more or less right), wistful ecumenicalism (despite the variations in more developed explanatory schemes, juju or genetics, at base everyone has more or less the same conception of what the world is like), or aggressive scientism (there are things which are really ideas, such as "propositional attitudes" and "representational beliefs," and there are things that only look like ideas, such as "there's a dragon down the road" and "peoples of different cultures live in different worlds"), the resurrection of The Human Mind as the still point of the turning world defuses the threat of cultural relativism by disarming the force of cultural diversity. As with "Human Nature," the deconstruction of otherness is the price of truth. Perhaps, but it is not what either the history of anthropology, the materials it has assembled, or the ideals that have animated it would suggest; nor is it only relativists who tell their audiences what they would like to hear. There are some dragons—"tigers in red weather"—that deserve to be looked into.

V

Looking into dragons, not domesticating or abominating them, nor drowning them in vats of theory, is what anthropology has been all about. At least, that is what it has been all about, as I, no nihilist, no subjectivist, and possessed, as you can see, of some strong views as to what is real and what is not, what is commendable and what is not, what is reasonable and what is not, understand it. We have, with no little success, sought to keep the world off balance; pulling out rugs, upsetting tea tables, setting off firecrackers. It has been the office of others to reassure; ours to unsettle. Australopithicenes, Tricksters, Clicks, Megaliths—we hawk the anomalous, peddle the strange. Merchants of astonishment.

We have, no doubt, on occasion moved too far in this direction and transformed idiosyncrasies into puzzles, puzzles into mysteries, and mysteries into humbug. But such an affection for what doesn't fit and won't comport, reality out of place, has connected us to the leading theme of the cultural history of "Modern Times." For that history has indeed consisted of one field of thought after another having to discover how to live on without the certainties that launched it. Brute fact, natural law, necessary truth, transcendent beauty, immanent authority, unique revelation, even the in-here self facing the out-there world have all come under such heavy attack as to seem by now lost simplicities of a less strenuous past. But science, law, philosophy, art, political theory, religion, and the stubborn insistences of common sense have contrived nonetheless to continue. It has not proved necessary to revive the simplicities.

It is, so I think, precisely the determination not to cling to what once worked well enough and got us to where we are and now doesn't quite work well enough and gets us into recurrent stalemates that makes a science move. As long as there was nothing around much faster than a marathon runner, Aristotle's physics worked well enough, Stoic paradoxes notwithstanding. So long as technical instrumentation could get us but a short way down and a certain way out from our sense-delivered world, Newton's mechanics worked well enough, action-at-a-distance perplexities notwithstanding. It was not relativism—Sex, The Dialectic and The Death of God—that did in absolute motion, Euclidean space, and universal causation. It was wayward phenomena, wave packets and orbital leaps, before which they were helpless. Nor was it Relativism—Hermeneutico-Psychedelic Subjectivism—that did in (to the degree they *have* been done in) the Cartesian *cognito*, the Whig view of history, and "the moral point of view so sacred to Eliot and Arnold and Emerson." It was odd actualities—infant betrothals and nonillusionist paintings—that embarrassed their categories.

In this move away from old triumphs become complacencies, one-time breakthroughs transformed to roadblocks, anthropology has played, in our day, a vanguard role. We have been the first to insist on a number of things: that the world does not divide into the pious and the superstitious; that there are sculptures in jungles and paintings in deserts; that political order is possible without centralized power and principled justice without codified rules; that the norms of reason were not fixed in Greece, the evolution of morality not consummated in England. Most important, we were the first to insist that we see the lives of others through lenses of our own grinding and that they look back on ours through ones of their own. That this led some to think the sky was falling, solipsism was upon us, and intellect, judgment, even the sheer possibility of communication had all fled is not surprising. The repositioning of horizons and the decentering of perspectives has had that effect before. The Bellarmines you have always with you; and as someone has remarked of the Polynesians, it takes a certain kind of mind to sail out of the sight of land in an outrigger canoe.

But that is, at least at our best and to the degree that we have been able, what we have been doing. And it would be, I think, a large pity if, now that the distances we have established and the elsewheres we have located are beginning to bite, to change our sense of sense and our perception of perception we should turn back to old songs and older stories in the hope that somehow only the superficial need alter and that we shan't fall off the edge of the world. The objection to anti-relativism is not that it rejects an it's-all-how-you-look-at-it approach to knowledge or a when-in-Rome approach to morality, but that it imagines that they can only be defeated by placing morality beyond culture and knowledge beyond both. This, speaking of things which must needs be so, is no longer possible. If we wanted home truths, we should have stayed at home.

Notes

1. See Todorov 1983:113-144 for general discussion of Montaigne's relativism from a position similar to mine.

2. For materialism, Harris 1968; for "science" and "The Big Ditch," Gellner 1979; for "literacy," Goody 1977; for "inter-theoretic competition," Horton 1982; for "the Cartesian conception of knowledge," Lukes 1982; cf. Williams 1978. For Popper, from whom all these blessings flow, Popper 1963, 1977.

3. The "monotony" example occurs in a footnote ("Monotony is itself an abnormal extreme").

4. Baggish 1983. For another troubled discourse on "the relativism problem" from that part of the world ("I set out what I think a reasonable point of view to fill the partial void left by ethical relativism, which by the 1980s seems more often to be repudiated than upheld" [12]), see Hatch 1983.

5. There are also some more moderate, split-the-difference pieces by Ian Hacking, Charles Taylor, and Lukes, but only the first of these seems genuinely free of cooked-up alarms.

6. The parenthetical quotations are from the book jacket, which for once reflects the contents.

References

Baggish, H. 1983. "Confessions of a Former Cultural Relativist." In *Anthropology 83/84*. E. Angeloni, ed. Guilford, Conn.: Dushkin Publishing.

Booth, W. 1983. "A New Strategy for Establishing a Truly Democratic Criticism." *Daedalus* 112:193-214.

Edgerton, R. 1978. "The Study of Deviance, Marginal Man or Everyman." In *The Making of Psychological Anthropology,* ed. G. Spindler, pp. 444-471. Berkeley: University of California Press.

Empson, W. 1955. *Collected Poems.* New York: Harcourt, Brace and World.

Gass, W. 1981. "Culture, Self, and Style." *Syracuse Scholar* 2:54-68.

Gellner, E. 1979. *Spectacles and Predicaments.* Cambridge, England: Cambridge University Press.

———1982. "Relativism and Universals." In *Rationality and Relativism,* ed. M. Hollis and S. Lukes, pp. 181-200. Cambridge, Mass.: MIT Press.

Goody, J. 1977. *The Domestication of the Savage Mind.* Cambridge, England: Cambridge University Press.

Hanson, F. A. 1981. "Anthropologie und die Rationalitätsdebatte." In *Der Wissenschaftler und das Irrationale,* vol. 1, ed. H.P. Duerr, Frankfurt am Main: Syndikat.

Harris, M. 1968. *The Rise of Anthropological Theory.* New York: Crowell.

Hatch, E. 1983. *Culture and Morality: The Relativity of Values in Anthropology.* New York: Columbia University Press.

Herodotus. 1859-61. *History of Herodotus,* Bk. 3 Chap. 38. New York: Appleton.

Hollis, M., and S. Lukes. 1982. *Rationality and Relativism.* Cambridge, Mass.: MIT Press.

Horton, R. 1982. "Tradition and Modernity Revisited." In *Rationality and Relativism*, ed. M. Hollis and S. Lukes, pp. 201-260. Cambridge, Mass.: MIT Press.

Jarvie, I. C. 1983. "Rationalism and Relativism." *The British Journal of Sociology* 34:44-60.

Johnson, P. 1983. *Modern Times: The World from the Twenties to the Eighties.* New York: Harper & Row.

Kluckhohn, C. 1962. "Education, Values and Anthropological Relativity." In *Culture and Behavior,* ed. Clyde Kluckhohn. New York: Free Press.

Ladd, J. 1982. "The Poverty of Absolutism." In *Edward Westermarck: Essays on His Life and Works. Acta Philosophica Fennica* (Helsinki) 34:158-180.

Lakatos, I. 1976. *The Methodology of Scientific Research* . Cambridge, England: Cambridge University Press.

Lukes, S. 1982. "Relativism in Its Place." In *Rationality and Relativism,* ed. M. Hollis and S. Lukes, pp. 261-305. Cambridge, Mass.: MIT Press.

Midgeley, M. 1978. *Beast and Man: The Roots of Human Nature.* Ithaca, N.Y.: Cornell University Press.

Montaigne. 1978. *Les Essais de Michel de Montaigne,* ed. P. Villey, pp. 202-214. Paris: Universitaires de France.

Popper, K. 1963. *Conjectures and Refutations: The Growth of Scientific Knowledge.* London: Routledge and Kegan Paul

———1972. *Objective Knowledge: An Evolutionary Approach.* Oxford: Clarendon Press.

Rabinow, P. 1983. "Humanism as Nihilism: The Bracketing of Truth and Seriousness in American Cultural Anthropology." In *Social Science as Moral Inquiry,* ed. N. Haan, R. M. Bellah, P. Rabinow, and W. M. Sullivan, pp. 52-75. New York: Columbia University Press.

Rorty, R. 1979. *Philosophy and the Mirror of Nature.* Princeton: Princeton University Press.

———1983. "Method and Morality." In *Social Science as Moral Inquiry,* ed. N. Haan, R.M. Bellah, P. Rabinow, and W.M. Sullivan, pp. 155-176. New York: Columbia University Press.

Salkever, S. 1983. "Beyond Interpretation: Human Agency and the Slovenly Wilderness." In *Social Science as Moral Inquiry*, ed. N. Haan, R. M. Bellah, P. Rabinow, and W. M. Sullivan, pp. 195-217. New York: Columbia University Press.

Scheffler, I. 1967. *Science and Subjectivity.* Indianapolis, Ind.: Bobbs-Merrill.
Sperber, D. 1982. "Apparently Irrational Beliefs." In *Rationality and Relativism,* ed. M. Hollis and S. Lukes, pp. 149-180. Cambridge, Mass.": MIT Press.
Spiro, M. 1978. "Culture and Human Nature." In *The Making of Psychological Anthropology,* ed. G. Spindler, pp. 330-360. Berkeley: University of California Press.
Stocking, G. W., Jr. 1982. "Afterword: A View from the Center," *Ethnos* 47:172-186.
Thomas, H. 1983. "The Inferno of Relativism." *Times Literary Supplement,* July 8, p. 718.
Tiger, L., and J. Sepher. 1975. *Women in the Kibbutz.* New York: Harcourt Brace Jovanovich (Harvest).
Todorov, T. 1983. "Montaigne, Essays in Reading." In *Yale French Studies,* vol. 64, ed. Gérard Defaux, pp. 113-144. New Haven, Conn.: Yale University Press.
Williams, B. 1978. *Descartes: The Project of Pure Enquiry.* Harmondsworth, England: Penguin.
Wilson, B. 1970. *Rationality.* Oxford: Blackwell.

Solidarity or Objectivity?

Richard Rorty

There are two principal ways in which reflective human beings try, by placing their lives in a larger context, to give sense to those lives. The first is by telling the story of their contribution to a community. This community may be the actual historical one in which they live, or another actual one, distant in time or place, or a quite imaginary one, consisting perhaps of a dozen heroes and heroines selected from history or fiction or both. The second way is to describe themselves as standing in immediate relation to a nonhuman reality. This relation is immediate in the sense that it does not derive from a relation between such a reality and their tribe, or their nation, or their imagined band of comrades. I shall say that stories of the former kind exemplify the desire for solidarity, and that stories of the latter kind exemplify the desire for objectivity. Insofar as a person is seeking solidarity, he or she does not ask about the relation between the practices of the chosen community and something outside that community. Insofar as he seeks objectivity, he distances himself from the actual persons around him not by thinking of himself as a member of some other real or imaginary group, but rather by attaching himself to something which can be described without out reference to any particular human beings.

The tradition in Western culture which centers around the notion of the search for Truth, a tradition which runs from the Greek philosophers through the Enlightenment, is the clearest example of the attempt to find a sense in one's existence by turning away from solidarity to objectivity. The idea of Truth as something to be pursued for its own sake, not because it will be good for oneself, or for one's real or imaginary community, is the central theme of this tradition. It was perhaps the growing awareness by the Greeks of the sheer diversity of human communities which stimulated the emergence of this ideal. A fear of parochialism, of being confined within the horizons of the group into which one happens to be born, a need to see it with the eyes of a stranger, helps produce the skeptical and ironic tone characteristic of Euripides and Socrates. Herodotus' willingness to take the barbarians seriously enough to describe their customs in detail may have been a necessary prelude to Plato's claim that the way to transcend skepticism is to envisage a common goal of humanity—a goal set by human nature rather than by Greek culture. The combination of Socratic alienation and Platonic hope gives rise to the idea of the intellectual as someone who is in touch with the nature of things, not by way of the opinions of his community, but in a more immediate way.

Plato developed the idea of such an intellectual by means of distinctions between knowledge and opinion, and between appearance and reality. Such distinctions conspire to produce the idea that rational inquiry should make visible a realm to which nonintellectuals have little access, and of whose very existence they may be doubtful. In the Enlightenment, this notion became concrete in the adoption of the Newtonian physical scientist as a model of the intellectual. To most thinkers of the eighteenth century, it seemed clear that the access to Nature which physical science had provided should now be followed by the establishment of social, political, and economic institutions which were in accordance with Nature. Ever since, liberal social thought has centered around social reform as made possible by objective knowledge of what human beings are like—not knowledge of what Greeks or Frenchmen or Chinese are like, but of humanity as such. We are the heirs of this objectivist tradition, which centers round the assumption that we must step outside our community long enough to examine it in the light of something which transcends it, namely, that which it has in common with every other actual and possible human community. This tradition dreams of an ultimate community which will have transcended the distinction between the natural and the social, which will exhibit a solidarity which is not parochial because it is the expression of an ahistorical human nature. Much of the rhetoric of contemporary intellectual life takes for granted that the goal of scientific inquiry into man is to understand "underlying structures," or, "culturally invariant factors," or "biologically determined patterns."

Those who wish to ground solidarity in objectivity—call them "realists"—have to construe truth as correspondence to reality. So they must construct a metaphysics which has room for a special relation between beliefs and objects which will differentiate true from false beliefs. They also must argue that there are procedures of justification of belief which are natural and not merely local. So they must construct an epistemology which has room for a kind of justification which is not merely social but natural, springing from human nature itself, and made possible by a link between that part of nature and the rest of nature. On their view, the various procedures which are thought of as providing rational justification by one or another culture may or may not really *be* rational. For to be truly rational, procedures of justification *must* lead to the truth, to correspondence to reality, to the intrinsic nature of things.

By contrast, those who wish to reduce objectivity to solidarity— call them "pragmatists"—do not require either a metaphysics or an epistemology. They view truth as, in William James' phrase, what it is good for *us* to believe. So they do not need an account of a relation between beliefs and objects called 'correspondence,' nor an account of human cognitive abilities which ensures that our species is capable of entering into that relation. They see the gap between truth and justification not as something to be bridged by isolating a natural and transcultural sort of rationality which can be used to criticize certain cultures and praise others, but simply as the gap between the actual good and the possible better. From a pragmatist point of view, to say that what is rational for us now to believe may not be *true*, is simply to say that somebody may come up with a better idea. It is to say that there is always room for improved belief, since new evidence, or new hypotheses, or a whole new vocabulary, may come along.[1] For pragmatists, the desire for objectivity is not the desire to escape the limitations of one's community, but simply the desire for as much intersubjective agreement as possible, the desire to extend the reference of "us" as far as we can. Insofar as pragmatists make a distinction between knowledge and opinion, it is simply the distinction between topics on which such agreement is relatively easy to get and topics on which agreement is relatively hard to get.

"Relativism" is the traditional epithet applied to pragmatism by realists. Three different views are commonly referred to by this name. The first is the view that every belief is as good as every other. The second is the view that "true" is an equivocal term, having as many meanings as there are procedures of justification. The third is the view that there is nothing to be said about either truth or rationality apart from descriptions of the familiar procedures of justification which a given society—*ours*—uses in one or another area of inquiry. The pragmatist holds the ethnocentric third view. But he does not hold the self-refuting first view, nor the eccentric second view. He thinks that his views are better than the realists, but he does not think that his views correspond to the nature of things. He thinks that the very flexibility of the word "true"—the fact that it is merely an expression of commendation—insures its univocity. The term "true," on his account, means the same in all cultures, just as equally flexible terms like "here," "there," "good," "bad," "you," and "me" mean the same in all cultures. But the identity of meaning is, of course, compatible with diversity of reference, and with diversity of procedures for assigning the terms. So he feels free to use the term "true" as a general term of commendation in the same way as his realist opponent does—and in particular to use it to commend his own view.

However, it is not clear why "relativist" should be thought an appropriate term for the ethnocentric third view, the one which the pragmatist *does* hold. For the pragmatist is not holding a positive theory which says that something is relative to something else. He is, instead, making the purely *negative* point that we should drop the traditional distinction between knowledge and opinion, construed as the distinction between truth as correspondence to reality and truth as a commendatory term for well-justified beliefs. The reason that the realist calls this negative claim "relativistic" is that he cannot believe that anybody would seriously deny that truth has an intrinsic nature. So when the pragmatist says that there is nothing to be said about truth save that each of us will commend as true those beliefs which he or she finds good to believe, the realist is inclined to interpret this as one more positive theory about the nature of truth: a theory according to which truth is simply the contemporary opinion of a chosen individual or group. Such a theory would, of course, be self-refuting. But the pragmatist does not have a theory of truth, much less a relativistic one. As a partisan of solidarity, his account of the value of cooperative human inquiry has only an ethical base, not an epistemological or metaphysical one. Not having *any* epistemology, *a fortiori* he does not have a relativistic one.

The question of whether truth or rationality has an intrinsic nature, of whether we ought to have a positive theory about either topic, is just the question of whether our self-description ought to be constructed around a relation to human nature or around a relation to a particular collection of human beings, whether we should desire objectivity or solidarity. It is hard to see how one could choose between these alternatives by looking more deeply into the nature of knowledge, or of man, or of nature. Indeed, the proposal that this issue might be so settled begs the question in favour of the realist, for it presupposes that knowledge, man, and nature *have* real essences which are relevant to the problem at hand. For the pragmatist, by contrast, "knowledge" is, like "truth," simply a compliment paid to the beliefs which we think so well justified that, for the moment, further justification is not needed. An inquiry into the nature of knowledge can, on his view, only be a sociohistorical account of how various people have tried to reach agreement on what to believe.

This view which I am calling "pragmatism" is almost, but not quite, the same as what Hilary Putnam, in his recent *Reason, Truth and History*, calls "the internalist conception of philosophy."[2] Putnam defines such a conception as one which gives up the attempt at a God's eye view of things, the attempt at contact with the nonhuman which I have been calling "the desire for objectivity." Unfortunately, he accompanies his defense of the antirealist views I am recommending with a polemic against a lot of the other people who hold these views—e.g., Kuhn, Feyerabend, Foucault, and myself. We are criticized as "relativists." Putnam presents "internalism" as a happy *via media* between realism and relativism. He speaks of "the plethora of relativistic doctrines being marketed today"[3] and in particular of "the French philosophers" as holding "some fancy mixture of cultural relativism and 'structuralism'."[4] But when it comes to criticizing these doctrines all that Putnam finds to attack is the so-called "incommensurability thesis": vis., "terms used in another culture cannot be equated in meaning or reference with any terms or expressions *we* possess."[5] He sensibly agrees with Donald Davidson in remarking that this thesis is self-refuting. Criticism of this thesis, however, is destructive of, at most, some incautious passages in some early writings by Feyerabend. Once this thesis is brushed aside, it is hard to see how Putnam himself differs from most of those he criticizes.

Putnam accepts the Davidsonian point that, as he puts it, "the whole justification of an interpretative scheme . . . is that it renders the behavior of others at least minimally reasonable by *our* lights."[6] It would seem natural to go on from this to say that we cannot get outside the range of those lights, that we cannot stand on neutral ground illuminated only by the natural light of reason. But Putnam draws back from this conclusion. He does so because he construes the claim that we cannot do so as the claim that the range of our thought is restricted by what he calls "institutionalized norms," publicly available criteria for settling of arguments, including philosophical arguments. He rightly says that there are no such criteria, arguing that the suggestion that there are is as self-refuting as the "incommensurability thesis." He is, I think, entirely right in saying that the notion that philosophy is or should become such an application of explicit criteria contradicts the very idea of philosophy.[7] One can gloss Putnam's point by saying that "philosophy" is precisely what a culture becomes capable of when it ceases to define itself in terms of explicit rules, and becomes sufficiently leisured and civilized to rely on inarticulate knowhow, to substitute *phronesis* for codification, and conversation with foreigners for conquest of them.

But to say that we cannot refer every question to explicit criteria institutionalized by our society does not speak to the point which the people whom Putnam calls "relativists" are making. One reason these people are pragmatists is precisely that they share Putnam's distrust of the positivistic idea that rationality is a matter of applying criteria.

Such a distrust is common, for example, to Kuhn, Mary Hesse, Wittgenstein, Michael Polanyi and Michael Oakeshott. Only someone who did think of rationality in this way would dream of suggesting that "true" means something different in different societies. For only such a person could imagine that there was anything to pick out to which one might make "true" relative. Only if one shares the logical positivists' idea that we all carry around things called "rules of language" which regulate what we say when, will one suggest that there is no way to break out of one's culture.

In the most original and powerful section of his book, Putnam argues that the notion that "rationality . . . is defined by the local cultural norms" is merely the demonic counterpart of positivism. It is, as he says, "a scientistic theory inspired by anthropology as positivism was a scientistic theory inspired by the exact sciences." By "scientism" Putnam means the notion that rationality consists in the application of criteria.[8] Suppose we drop this notion, and accept Putnam's own Quinean picture of inquiry as the continual reweaving of a web of beliefs rather than as the application of criteria to cases. Then the notion of "local cultural norms" will lose its offensively parochial overtones. For now to say that we must work by our own lights, that we must be ethnocentric, is merely to say that beliefs suggested by another culture must be tested by trying to weave them together with beliefs we already have. It is a consequence of this holistic view of knowledge, a view *shared* by Putnam and those he criticizes as "relativists," that alternative cultures are not to be thought of on the model of alternative geometries. Alternative geometries are irreconcilable because they have axiomatic structures, and contradictory axioms. They are *designed* to be irreconcilable. Cultures are not so designed, and do not have axiomatic structures. To say that they have "institutionalized norms" is only to say, with Foucault, that knowledge is never separable from power—that one is likely to suffer if one does not hold certain beliefs at certain times and places. But such institutional backups for beliefs take the form of bureaucrats and policemen, not of "rules of language" and "criteria of rationality." To think otherwise is the Cartesian fallacy of seeing axioms where there are only shared habits, of viewing statements which summarize such practices as if they reported constraints enforcing such practices. Part of the force of Quine's and Davidson's attack on the distinction between the conceptual and the empirical is that the distinction between different cultures does not differ in kind from the distinction between different theories held by members of a single culture. The Tasmanian aborigines and the British colonists had trouble communicating, but this trouble was different only in extent from the difficulties in communication experienced by Gladstone and Disraeli. The trouble in all such cases is just the difficulty of explaining why other people disagree with us, of reweaving our beliefs so as to fit the fact of disagreement together with the other beliefs we hold. The same Quinean arguments which dispose of the positivists' distinction between analytic and synthetic truth dispose of the anthropologists' distinction between the intercultural and the intracultural.

On this holistic account of cultural norms, however, we do not need the notion of a universal transcultural rationality which Putnam invokes against those whom he calls "relativists." Just before the end of his book, Putnam says that once we drop the notion of a God's-eye point of view we realize that:

> we can only hope to produce a more rational *conception* of rationality or a better *conception* of morality if we operate from *within* our tradition (with its echoes of the Greek agora, of Newton, and so on, in the case of rationality, and with its echoes of scripture, of the philosophers, of the democratic revolutions, and so on . . . in the case of morality). We are invited to engage in a truly human dialogue.[9]

With this I entirely agree, and so, I take it, would Kuhn, Hesse, and most of the other so-called "relativists"—perhaps even Foucault. But Putnam then goes on to pose a further question:

> Does this dialogue have an ideal terminus? Is there a *true* conception of rationality, an ideal morality, even if all we ever have are our *conceptions* of these?

I do not see the point of this question. Putnam suggests that a negative answer—the view that "there is only the dialogue"—is just another form of self-refuting relativism. But, once again, I do not see how a claim that something does not exist can be construed as a claim that something is relative to something else. In the final sentence of his book, Putnam says that "The very fact that we speak of our different conceptions as different conceptions of *rationality* posits a *Grenzbegriff,* a limit-concept of ideal truth." But what is such a posit supposed to do, except to say that from God's point of view the human race is heading in the right direction? Surely Putnam's "internalism" should forbid him to say anything like that. To say that *we* think we're heading in the right direction is just to say, with Kuhn, that we can, by hindsight, tell the story of the past as a story of progress. To say that we still have a long way to go, that our present views should not be cast in bronze, is too platitudinous to require support by positing limit-concepts. So it is hard to see what difference is made by the difference between saying "there is only the dialogue" and saying "there is also that to which the dialogue converges."

I would suggest that Putnam here, at the end of the day, slides back into the scientism he rightly condemns in others. For the root of scientism, defined as the view that rationality is a matter of applying criteria, is the desire for objectivity, the hope that what Putnam calls "human flourishing" has a transhistorical nature. I think that Feyerabend is right in suggesting that until we discard the metaphor of inquiry, and human activity generally, as converging rather than proliferating, as becoming more unified rather than more diverse, we shall never be free of the motives which once led us to posit gods. Positing *Grenzbegriffe* seems merely a way of telling ourselves that a nonexistent God would, if he did exist, be pleased with us. If we could ever be moved solely by the desire for solidarity, setting aside the desire for objectivity altogether, then we should think of human progress as making it possible for human beings to do more interesting things and be more interesting people, not as heading towards a place which has somehow been prepared for humanity in advance. Our self-image would employ images of making rather than finding, the images used by the Romantics to praise poets rather than the images used by the Greeks to praise mathematicians. Feyerabend seems to me right in trying to develop such a self-image for us, but his project seems misdescribed, by himself as well as by his critics, as "relativism."[10]

Those who follow Feyerabend in this direction are often thought of as necessarily enemies of the Enlightenment, as joining in the chorus which claims that the traditional self-descriptions of the Western democracies are bankrupt, that they somehow have been shown to be "inadequate" or "self-deceptive." Part of the instinctive resistance to attempts by Marxists, Sartreans, Oakeshottians, Gadamerians and Foucauldians to reduce objectivity to solidarity is the fear that our traditional liberal habits and hopes will not survive the reduction. Such feelings are evident, for example, in Habermas' criticism of Gadamer's position as relativistic and potentially repressive, in the suspicion that

Heidegger's attacks on realism are somehow linked to his Nazism, in the hunch that Marxist attempts to interpret values as class interests are usually just apologies for Leninist takeovers, and in the suggestion that Oakeshott's skepticism about rationalism in politics is merely an apology for the status quo.

I think that putting the issue in such moral and political terms, rather than in epistemological or metaphilosophical terms, makes clearer what is at stake. For now the question is not about how to define words like "truth" or "rationality" or "knowledge" or "philosophy," but about what self-image our society should have of itself. The ritual invocation of the "need to avoid relativism" is most comprehensible as an expression of the need to preserve certain habits of contemporary European life. These are the habits nurtured by the Enlightenment, and justified by it in terms of an appeal of Reason, conceived as a transcultural human ability to correspond to reality, a faculty whose possession and use is demonstrated by obedience to explicit criteria. So the real question about relativism is whether these same habits of intellectual, social, and political life can be justified by a conception of rationality as criterionless muddling through, and by a pragmatist conception of truth.

I think that the answer to this question is that the pragmatist cannot justify these habits without circularity, but then neither can the realist. The pragmatists' justification of toleration, free inquiry, and the quest for undistorted communication can only take the form of a comparison between societies which exemplify these habits and those which do not, leading up to the suggestion that nobody who has experienced both would prefer the latter. It is exemplified by Winston Churchill's defense of democracy as the worst form of government imaginable, except for all the others which have been tried so far. Such justification is not by reference to a criterion, but by reference to various detailed practical advantages. It is circular only in that the terms of praise used to describe liberal societies will be drawn from the vocabulary of the liberal societies themselves. Such praise has to be in *some* vocabulary, after all, and the terms of praise current in primitive or theocratic or totalitarian societies will not produce the desired result. So the pragmatist admits that he has no ahistorical standpoint from which to endorse the habits of modern democracies he wishes to praise. These consequences are just what partisans of solidarity expect. But among partisans of objectivity they give rise, once again, to fears of the dilemma formed by ethnocentrism on the one hand and relativism on the other. Either we attach a special privilege to our own community, or we pretend an impossible tolerance for every other group.

I have been arguing that we pragmatists should grasp the ethnocentric horn of this dilemma. We should say that we must, in practice, privilege our own group, even though there can be no noncircular justification for doing so. We must insist that the fact that nothing is immune from criticism does not mean that we have a duty to justify everything. We Western liberal intellectuals should accept the fact that we have to start from where we are, and that this means that there are lots of views which we simply cannot take seriously. To use Neurath's familiar analogy, we can *understand* the revolutionary's suggestion that a sailable boat can't be made out of the planks which make up ours, and that we must simply abandon ship. But we cannot take his suggestion seriously. We cannot take it as a rule for action, so it is not a live option. For some people, to be sure, the option *is* live. These are the people who have always hoped to become a New Being, who have hoped to be converted rather than persuaded. But we—the liberal Rawlsian searchers for consensus, the heirs of Socrates, the people who wish to link their days dialectically each to each—cannot do so. Our community—the community of the liberal intellectuals of the secular modern West—wants to be able to give a *post factum* account of any change of view. We want to be able, so to speak, to justify ourselves to our earlier selves. This preference is not built into us by human nature. It is just the way *we* live now.[11]

This lonely provincialism, this admission that we are just the historical moment that we are, not the representatives of something ahistorical, is what makes traditional Kantian liberals like Rawls draw back from pragmatism.[12] "Relativism," by contrast, is merely a red herring. The realist is, once again, projecting his own habits of thought upon the pragmatist when he charges him with relativism. For the realist thinks that the whole point of philosophical thought is to detach oneself from any particular community and look down at it from a more universal standpoint. When he hears the pragmatist repudiating the desire for such a standpoint he cannot quite believe it. He thinks that everyone, deep down inside, *must* want such detachment. So he attributes to the pragmatist a perverse form of his own attempted detachment, and sees him as an ironic, sneering aesthete who refuses to take the choice between communities seriously, a mere "relativist." But the pragmatist, dominated by the desire for solidarity, can only be criticized for taking his own community *too* seriously. He can only be criticized for ethnocentrism, not for relativism. To be ethnocentric is to divide the human race into the people to whom one must justify one's beliefs and the others. The first group—one's *ethnos*—comprises those who share enough of one's beliefs to make fruitful conversation possible.

In this sense, everybody is ethnocentric when engaged in actual debate, no matter how much realist rhetoric about objectivity he produces in his study.[13]

What is disturbing about the pragmatist's picture is not that it is relativistic but that it takes away two sorts of metaphysical comfort to which our intellectual tradition has become accustomed. One is the thought that membership in our biological species carries with it certain "rights," a notion which does not seem to make sense unless the biological similarities entail the possession of something nonbiological, something which links our species to a nonhuman reality and thus gives the species moral dignity. This picture of rights as biologically transmitted is so basic to the political discourse of the Western democracies that we are troubled by any suggestion that "human nature" is not a useful moral concept. The second comfort is provided by the thought that our community cannot wholly die. The picture of a common human nature oriented towards correspondence to reality as it is in itself comforts us with the thought that even if our civilization is destroyed, even if all memory of our political or intellectual or artistic community is erased, the race is fated to recapture the virtues and the insights and the achievements which were the glory of that community. The notion of human nature as an inner structure which leads all members of the species to converge to the same point, to recognize the same theories, virtues, and works of art as worthy of honor, assures us that even if the Persians had won, the arts and sciences of the Greeks would sooner or later have appeared elsewhere. It assures us that even if the Orwellian bureaucrats of terror rule for a thousand years the achievements of the Western democracies will someday be duplicated by our remote descendants. It assures us that "man will prevail," that something reasonably like *our* world-view, *our* virtues, *our* art, will bob up again whenever human beings are left alone to cultivate their inner natures. The comfort of the realist picture is the comfort of saying not simply that there is a place prepared for our race in our advance, but also that we now know quite a bit about what that place looks like. The inevitable ethnocentrism to which we are all condemned is thus as much a part of the realist's comfortable view as of the pragmatists' uncomfortable one.

The pragmatist gives up the first sort of comfort because he thinks that to say that certain people have certain rights is merely to say that we should treat them in certain ways. It is not to give a *reason* for treating them in those ways. As to the second sort of comfort, he suspects that the hope that something resembling *us* will inherit the earth is impossible to eradicate, as impossible as eradicating the hope of surviving our individual deaths through some satisfying transfiguration.

But he does not want to turn this hope into a theory of the nature of man. He wants solidarity to be our *only* comfort, and to be seen not to require metaphysical support.

My suggestion that the desire for objectivity is in part a disguised form of the fear of the death of our community echoes Nietzsche's charge that the philosophical tradition which stems from Plato is an attempt to avoid facing up to contingency, to escape from time and chance. Nietzsche thought that realism was to be condemned not only by arguments from its theoretical incoherence, the sort of argument we find in Putnam and Davidson, but also on practical, pragmatic, grounds. Nietzsche thought that the test of human character was the ability to live with the thought that there was no convergence. He wanted us to be able to think of truth as:

> a mobile army of metaphors, metonyms, and anthromorphisms—in short a sum of human relations, which have been enhanced, transposed, and embellished poetically and rhetorically and which after long use seem firm, canonical, and obligatory to a people.[14]

Nietzsche hoped that eventually there might be human beings who could and did think of truth in this way, but who still liked themselves, who saw themselves as *good* people for whom solidarity was *enough*.[15]

I think that pragmatism's attack on the various structure-content distinctions which buttress the realist's notion of objectivity can best be seen as an attempt to let us think of truth in this Nietzschean way, as entirely a matter of solidarity. That is why I think we need to say, despite Putnam, that "there is only the dialogue," only *us,* and to throw out the last residues of the notion of "trans-cultural rationality." But this should not lead us to repudiate, as Nietzsche sometimes did, the elements in our movable host which embody the ideas of Socratic conversation, Christian fellowship, and Enlightenment science. Nietzsche ran together his diagnosis of philosophical realism as an expression of fear and resentment with his own resentful idiosyncratic idealizations of silence, solitude, and violence. Post-Nietzschean thinkers like Adorno and Heidegger and Foucault have run together Nietzsche's criticisms of the metaphysical tradition on the one hand with his criticisms of bourgeois civility, of Christian love, and of the nineteenth century's hope that science would make the world a better place to live, on the other. I do not think that there is any interesting connection between these two sets of criticisms. Pragmatism seems to me, as I have said, a philosophy of solidarity rather than of despair. From this point of view, Socrates' turn away from the gods, Christianity's turn from an Omnipotent Creator to the man who suffered on the Cross, and the Baconian turn from science as contemplation of eternal truth to science as instrument of social progress, can be seen as so many preparations for the act of social faith which is suggested by a Nietzschean view of truth.[16]

The best argument we partisans of solidarity have against the realistic partisans of objectivity is Nietzsche's argument that the traditional Western metaphysico-epistemological way of firming up our habits simply isn't working anymore. It isn't doing its job. It has become as transparent a device as the postulation of deities who turn out, by a happy coincidence, to have chosen *us* as their people. So the pragmatist suggestion that we substitute a "merely" ethical foundation for our sense of community—or, better, that we think of our sense of community as having no foundation except shared hope and the trust created by such sharing—is put forward on practical grounds. It is *not* put forward as a corollary of a metaphysical claim that the objects in the world contain no intrinsically action-guiding properties, nor of an epistemological claim that we lack a faculty of moral sense, nor of a semantical claim that truth is reducible to justification. It is a suggestion about how we might think of ourselves in order to avoid the kind of resentful belatedness—characteristic of the bad side of Nietzsche—which now characterizes much of high culture. This resentment arises from the realization, which I referred to at the beginning of this essay, that the Enlightenment's search for objectivity has often gone sour.

The rhetoric of scientific objectivity, pressed too hard and taken too seriously, has led us to people like B.F. Skinner on the one hand and people like Althusser on the other—two equally pointless fantasies, both produced by the attempt to be "scientific" about our moral and political lives. Reaction against scientism led to attacks on natural science as a sort of false god. But there is nothing wrong with science, there is only something wrong with the attempt to divinize it, the attempt characteristic of realistic philosophy. This reaction has also led to attacks on liberal social thought of the type common to Mill and Dewey and Rawls as a mere ideological superstructure, one which obscures the realities of our situation and represses attempts to change that situation. But there is nothing wrong with liberal democracy, nor with the philosophers who have tried to enlarge its scope. There is only something wrong with the attempt to see their efforts as failures to achieve something which they were not trying to achieve—a demonstration of the "objective" superiority of our way of life over all other alternatives. There is, in short, nothing wrong with the hopes of the Enlightenment, the hopes which created the Western democracies. The value of the ideals of the Enlightenment is, for us pragmatists, just the value of some of the institutions and practices which they have created. In this essay I have sought to

distinguish these institutions and practices from the philosophical justifications for them provided by partisans of objectivity, and to suggest an
alternative justification.

Notes

1. This attitude toward truth, in which the consensus of a community
rather than a relation to a nonhuman reality is taken as central, is associated not
only with the American pragmatic tradition but with the work of Popper and
Habermas. Habermas' criticisms of lingering positivist elements in Popper parallel those made by Deweyan holists of the early logical empiricists. It is important to see, however, that the pragmatist notion of truth common to James and
Dewey is not dependent upon either Peirce's notion of an "ideal end of inquiry"
nor on Habermas' notion of an "ideally free community." For criticism of these
notions, which in my view are insufficiently ethnocentric, see my "Pragmatism,
Davidson, and Truth," forthcoming in a festschrift for Davidson edited by
Ernest LePore (to be published by the University of Minnesota Press in 1985),
and "Habermas and Lyotard on Postmodernity" in *Praxis International,* 1984.

2. Hilary Putnam, *Reason, Truth, and History* (Cambridge: Cambridge
University Press, 1981), pp. 49-50.

3. Ibid., p. 119.

4. Ibid., p. x

5. Ibid., p. 114.

6. Ibid., p. 119. See Davidson's "On the very idea of a conceptual
scheme," in his *Inquiries into Truth and Interpretation* (Oxford: Oxford University Press, 1984) for a more complete and systematic presentation of this point.

7. Putnam, p. 113

8. Ibid., p. 126.

9. Ibid., p. 216.

10. See, e.g., Paul Feyerabend, *Science in a Free Society* (London: New
Left Books, 1978), p. 9, where Feyerabend identifies his own view with "relativism (in the old and simple sense of Protagoras)." This identification is accompanied by the claim that "'Objectively' there is not much to choose between anti-
semitism and humanitarianism." I think Feyerabend would have served himself
better by saying that the scare-quoted word "objectively" should simply be
dropped from use, together with the traditional philosophical distinctions between scheme and content (see the Davidson essay cited in note 6 above) which
buttress the subjective-objective distinction, than by saying that we may keep
the word and use it to say the sort of thing Protagoras said. What Feyerabend is
really against is the correspondence theory of truth, not the idea that some views
cohere better than others.

11. This quest for consensus is opposed to the sort of quest for authenticity which wishes to free itself from the opinion of our community. See, for
example, Vincent Descombes' account of Deleuze in *Modern French Philos-*

ophy (Cambridge: Cambridge University Press, 1980), p. 153: "Even if philosophy is essentially demystificatory, philosophers often fail to produce authentic critiques; they defend order, authority, institutions, 'decency,' everything in which the ordinary person believes." On the pragmatist or ethnocentric view I am suggesting, all that critique can or should do is play off elements in "what the ordinary person believes" against other elements. To attempt to do more than this is to fantasize rather than to converse. Fantasy may, to be sure, be an incentive to more fruitful conversation, but when it no longer fulfills this function it does not deserve the name of "critique."

12. In *A Theory of Justice* Rawls seemed to be trying to retain the authority of Kantian "practical reason" by imagining a social contract devised by choosers "behind a veil of ignorance"—using the "rational self-interest" of such choosers as a touchstone for the ahistorical validity of certain social institutions. Much of the criticism to which that book was subjected, e.g., by Michael Sandel in his *Liberalism and the Limits of Justice* (Cambridge, Cambridge University Press, 1982), has centered on the claim that one cannot escape history in this way. In the meantime, however, Rawls has put forward a meta-ethical view which drops the claim to ahistorical validity. (See his "Kantian constructivism in moral theory," *Journal of Philosophy,* 1977, and his "Theory of Justice: Metaphysical or Political?" forthcoming in *Philosophy and Public Affairs.*) Concurrently, T.M. Scanlon has urged that the essence of a "contractualist" account of moral motivation is better understood as the desire to justify one's action to others than in terms of "rational self-interest." See Scanlon, "Contractualism and Utilitarianism," in A. Sen and B. Williams, eds., *Utilitarianism and Beyond,* (Cambridge, Cambridge University Press, 1982). Scanlon's emendation of Rawls leads in the same direction as Rawls' later work, since Scanlon's use of the notion of "justification to others on grounds they could not reasonably reject" chimes with the "constructivist" view that what counts for social philosophy is what can be justified to a particular historical community, not to "humanity in general." On my view, the frequent remark that Rawls' rational choosers look remarkably like twentieth-century American liberals is perfectly just, but not a criticism of Rawls. It is merely a frank recognition of the ethnocentrism which is essential to serious, nonfantastical, thought. I defend this view in "Postmodernist Bourgeois Liberalism," *Journal of Philosophy,* 1983.

13. In an important paper called "The Truth in Relativism," included in his *Moral Luck* (Cambridge: Cambridge University Press, 1981), Bernard Williams makes a similar point in terms of a distinction between "genuine confrontation" and "notional confrontation." The latter is the sort of confrontation which occurs, asymmetrically, between us and primitive tribespeople. The belief-systems of such people do not present, as Williams puts it, "real options" for us, for we cannot imagine going over to their view without "self-deception or paranoia." These are the people whose beliefs on certain topics overlap so little with ours that their inability to agree with us raises no doubt in our minds about the correctness of our own beliefs. Williams' use of "real option" and "notional confrontation" seems to me very enlightening, but I think he turns these notions to purposes they will not serve. Williams wants to defend ethical relativism,

defined as the claim that when ethical confrontations are merely notional "questions of appraisal do not genuinely arise." He thinks they *do* arise in connection with notional confrontations between, e.g., Einsteinian and Amazonian cosmologies. (See Williams, p. 142.) This distinction between ethics and physics seems to me an awkward result to which Williams is driven by his unfortunate attempt to find *something* true in relativism, an attempt which is a corollary of his attempt to be "realistic" about physics. On my (Davidsonian) view, there is no point in distinguishing between true sentences which are "made true by reality" and true sentences which are "made true by us," because the whole idea of "truth-makers" needs to be dropped. So I would hold that there is *no* truth in relativism, but this much truth in ethnocentrism: we cannot justify our beliefs (in physics, ethics, or any other area) to everybody, but only to those whose beliefs overlap ours to some appropriate extent. (This is not a theoretical problem about "untranslatability," but simply a practical problem about the limitations of argument; it is not that we live in different worlds than the Nazis or the Amazonians, but that conversion from or to their point of view, though possible, will not be a matter of inference from previously shared premises.)

14. Nietzsche, "On Truth and Lie in an Extra-Moral Sense," in *The Viking Portable Nietzsche,* Walter Kaufmann, ed. and trans., pp. 46-47.

15. See Sabina Lovibond, *Realism and Imagination in Ethics* (Minneapolis: University of Minnesota Press, 1983), p. 158: "An adherent of Wittgenstein's view of language should equate that goal with the establishment of a language-game in which we could participate ingenuously, while retaining our awareness of it as a specific historical formation. A community in which such a language-game was played would be one . . . whose members understood their own form of life and yet were not embarrassed by it."

16. See Hans Blumenberg, *The Legitimation of Modernity* (Cambridge: MIT Press, 1982), for a story about the history of European thought which, unlike the stories told by Nietzsche and Heidegger, sees the Enlightenment as a definitive step forward. For Blumenberg, the attitude of "self-assertion," the kind of attitude which stems from a Baconian view of the nature and purpose of science, needs to be distinguished from "self-foundation," the Cartesian project of grounding such inquiry upon ahistorical criteria of rationality. Blumenberg remarks, pregnantly, that the "historicist" criticism of the optimism of the Enlightenment, criticism which began with the Romantics' turn back to the Middle Ages, undermines self-foundation but not self-assertion.

On Meaning and Reality

EDDY M. ZEMACH

This paper presents an antirelativistic theory of reality, language, and mind. It advocates metaphysical realism ("truth is correspondence to a theory-independent reality"), meaning realism ("to be meaningful is to have a meaning"), and psychologism ("meanings are mental entities"). The system itself is developed in sections 5-9, while sections 1-4 and 10 carry on a dialogue with its leading rivals; in order to be reasonably brief, a similar argument is used against most of them.

1: Sentences or Propositions?

The verifiability thesis is positivistic in origin, but it matured, and came to be used as a weapon against realism, only in the hands of Quine and Dummett. Its core claim is that the linguistic items that we learn to use, that are linked to behavior, that we actually reject or enjoin, and that face the tribunal of experience, are not the propositions expressed by our sentences, but those sentences themselves. The uttering of some sentences in certain circumstances can be observed, encouraged or discouraged, assented to or dissented from. On the other hand, what those sentences mean, whether they are about rabbits or Goedel numbers, cats or cherries, depends on our choice of an analytic hypothesis; but that choice is largely arbitrary and, at any rate, is immaterial for the empirical testing of the said sentences. Quine argues that all our terms are ontologically opaque, and Putnam extends the referential underdetermination of our terms to all possible worlds; verification needs no reference.

Quine's argument is well known: to interpret a language, we observe the behavioral reaction of assent and dissent of native speakers to the utterance of a given sentence in some given circumstances; that defines the stimulus meaning of that sentence. The assumption that the said sentence stands for mental entities called 'meanings' serves no purpose in the classification of the role that sentence plays in the large network of utterance circumstances, connections to propensities to utter other sentences, afferent stimuli, and efferent reactions of the organism. Given stimulus meaning, the traditional notion of meaning may be dispensed with. But, I wonder, can we have stimulus meaning without assuming the traditional notion of meaning as a mental entity? I have said earlier, echoing Quine, that assent and dissent are behavioral reactions; but surely that is not right. To assent is to express a belief that a given proposition is true; to dissent is to express a belief that it is false. If the grunts and groans produced by the native following the utterance of the stimulus sentence by the experimenter are all that there is to assent and dissent, how can we avoid the conclusion that water, for example, assents to mud or dissents from fire? There is, after all, a great regularity in the kind of noises produced by water in reacting to given stimuli. Indeed the overall type of behavior manifested by people is very different from that manifested by water, but it is certainly no less complex. Why, then, say that people's grunts are assents and dissents, while water sounds are not? If one answers that unlike water's, people's grunts express beliefs, then those beliefs must be somehow stored in the speaker's mind. In that case we have to assume the existence of a mental entity, that is, a mentally represented content that is assented to or dissented from by the believer.

Can one forego the mentally represented content and say that to assent is to treat a given utterance as appropriate under the circumstances? A Quinean may interpret Dummett's notion of warranted assertibility in that way, that is, as accepted utterability, and say that s assents to 'p' iff s treats 'p' as assertable. But utterability cannot replace truth, because one may treat 'p' as utterable even though one does not believe it is true, and vice versa. For example, it may be believed that although 'gavagai' is then true, one ought not say 'gavagai' when a rabbit is present, so as not to spoil the hunt; or it may be bad form for adults to utter obvious truths; and so on. On the other hand people may tell ghost stories without believing that there are any ghosts. In order not to be trivialized into questions of etiquette and tribal mores, the question of when is an assertion warranted must therefore be distinct from the question of utterability; assertibility must be restricted to genuine expressions of belief. But to make this distinction one must use the notion of belief as an attitude to some mentally represented contents, that is, the attitude of holding some of them to be realized in the world. The attitude in question cannot be a mere disposition to utter some sentences in some circumstances, or else assertability again collapses into mere utterability.

Moreover, sentences are not better off than fully interpreted predicates and propositions with respect to verification; they are *at least* as underdetermined by all the empirical data as any interpretation of them would be. For what would sanction their assertibility? No doubt, one can be in the habit of saying 'gavagai' whenever a rabbit goes by. Does that mean that uttering 'gavagai' is, according to that person, justified by rabbit-passing-by experiences? Only if we assume, first, that the person who manifests that behavior sees it as we see it; second, that his behavior is not a mere habit, that is, that it is intended; and third, that he believes that the said behavior is apt for the situation, that is, that it is *right*. (Even if the practice is prevalent in the society, it may still be considered wrong; norms are not a matter of statistics: a society may repeatedly violate a norm while still acknowledging its normative status.) But in order to answer the above questions one must interpret the manifested behavior by connecting it with some internal representations and attitudes. Thus, meaning is not parasitic upon independently established verification procedures for sentences; on the contrary, in order to verify any sentence (assuming for the moment that it makes sense to speak about the verification of sentences), that is, in order for the assertion of a given sentence to be epistemically right in certain circumstances, it must be linked to what the assertor internally represents, including the internal attitudes that are expressed by the speaker's symbols for assent and dissent. Further, since assent and dissent may reflect nonepistemic (e.g., moral or religious) acceptance or rejection, the said symbols must stand for the speaker's attitude of belief, that is, an attribution of truth or satisfaction. Once we have that, however, a full-fledged mentalistic semantics, in which terms are taken to stand for mental entities called 'meanings', is only one step away.

2: Sentences and Society

A more radical assertibility conditions semantics is attributed to Wittgenstein by Kripke. According to Kripke, Wittgenstein argues that no data about one's mental life or one's previous applications of a rule can justify a new application, since infinitely many rules, all of which are compatible with all those data, mandate different applications. "No course of action could be determined by a rule, because every course of action can be made to accord with the rule."[1] This is highly paradoxical, since we seem to know what we mean by our terms and do not hesitate in applying a rule (a concept) to a new case. I am sure that the correct answer to '68 + 57 = ?' is '125', that is, that I meant *addition* when I used the sign '+' in the past; I am sure that the answer to 'is this leaf green?'

is 'yes', that is, that it is the concept *green* (rather than, e.g., *grue,* in which case I should say 'no') that I meant when I used the term 'green'. But what can justify that belief if all data are compatible with the claim that I have always meant *quaddition* (a function whose value for 68 and 57 is 5) by '+', and *grue* (a function whose value for blue objects first examined after 5/5/85 is True) by 'green'?

Kripke's answer is that "Wittgenstein's skeptical solution to his problem depends on agreement, and on checkability—on one person's ability to test whether another uses a term as he does."[2] "The solution turns on the idea that each person who claims to be following a rule can be checked by others. Others in the community can check whether the putative rule follower is or is not giving responses that they endorse, that agree with their own."[3] Thus although the statement "by '+' I mean *addition*" has no truth conditions, I am justified in asserting it if my answers to problems involving '+' agree with the answers given by other members of my community.

That solution cannot work. Suppose that I ask Jones, "What color is this leaf?" and he says, "Green." By hypothesis, nothing in Jones' past use of this term determines what he means by it, nor is the interpretation constrained by any fact about Jones' mental representations. Instead, I must check whether Smith, too, says, "Green," and consider Jones' utterance justified if it agrees with Smith's. Now let us suppose that I am lucky: Smith, too, gives the answer "Green," and I therefore say, "they agree." But, by hypothesis, nothing in my past use of 'agree' or in my present mental contents constrains the interpretation of what I say, and hence gives no indication whatsoever on what I mean by the words 'they agree'. What, then, am I saying? Try to repeat the move: the meaning of my utterance cannot be determined by its truth conditions, because it has none; instead, it has assertibility conditions and is justified iff other members of my community say 'they agree' under the said circumstances. Let us suppose again that my luck has not run out, and everyone around me does say just that. Is that a reason to believe that Smith and Jones agree? Of course not. The only thing that happened is that people have uttered in unison the phoneme string 'they agree'. What this sound means one cannot say, since (by the Kripke/Wittgenstein argument) it is an instance of infinitely many *distinct* rules (concepts). But the suggested solution was not that Jones uses the concept *green* if, upon hearing him and Smith, I and my friends produce some noises. The suggested solution was that Jones has the concept *green* if his use of 'green' agrees with Smith's (and others') use of 'green'. To ascertain that, one has to determine whether the concept *agree* is satisfied by the pair [Jones' 'green', Smith's 'green']; and to do that, one has to know the *truth*-conditions of sentences of the form 'x and y agree', that is, know what 'agree' *means*. If this is impossible, it is impossible to say whether Jones and Smith agree. We can only say that members of the community went 'agree' when they heard Jones and Smith. There may be an inductive proof that whenever there is an agreement, the community makes that sound; but for an inductive proof to work, *agreement* must have some independent (e.g., mental) indicators other than the ones whose relation to agreement is to be established by the inductive proof, that is, the community's making the sound 'agree'. Otherwise, to agree will just *be* to say 'agree'.

Can agreement be given such a purely behavioral definition? Perhaps, like a computer, one "agrees to," "assents to," or "accepts" data iff, given those data, one goes on functioning well? In order for that definition to make any sense we must be able to distinguish the condition of malfunctioning, or being jammed, from the condition of one's working smoothly. To do that we need to know the purpose of the mechanism, but what can count as functioning and malfunctioning for human beings when there is no such obvious purpose for which they were constructed and which they ought to fulfill? Perhaps the interpreter should use his own interests to define a purpose; relative to that set of interests he can say when the society is "working smoothly" and when it is "jammed." But then the interpreter, at least, knows what these terms mean, that is, he knows the *truth* conditions for 'x is working smoothly' and for 'x is jammed'; he understands these predicates in the traditional sense, that is, knows what are their satisfaction conditions. The whole account is therefore question-begging. Further, such interpretation is entirely arbitrary; to attribute a meaning to an utterance because it causes the system to behave as the interpreter wants it to behave is like saying that the river means to say something by flowing south, just because I wish to go south. Surely, that a set of occurrences *a* suits me does not confer upon the members of *a* the status of meaningful sentences? It is a perfect caricature of interpreting when only what the interpreter means, and not what the interpretee means (since that is compatible with any interpretation whatsoever), counts! We can, then, interpret any system that has a bearing on our interests in any way we please; we can say that the stars praise our leader and rolling pennies recite stock market quotations.

Quine, Davidson, and Rorty may resign themselves to the parochial nature of interpretation. The very notion of meaning, they may say, is relative to the interpreter's values; there *is* no fact of the matter as to what *s* means by her term '*n*' apart from what I and my friends take her to mean; what '*n*' means *is* how we take it. But that is inconsistent;

in order to interpret any text according to the bearing it may have on my values and beliefs I have to know what are my beliefs and my values, and that is impossible without knowing what I mean by my words, what I desire, and what I have in mind. Yet according to the new relativists I cannot know what I mean on my own; meanings are not in the head, they say, since words do not carry their own meaning; and therefore in order to know what I mean I have to know whether my society agrees with my use of the terms I use. But as argued earlier, I cannot understand my society's verdict unless I already know what constitutes agreement, and hence what it is, for it to function "acceptingly." No matter what I do, my society would react in some way or other. Which reaction is the accepting one? People cannot tell me, since I would not understand their words until I know when they do, and when they do not, agree with the interpretation I give to their words. Should I interpret *that* reaction as agreement or as disagreement? Again, if the interpretation rests on my values and beliefs, I have to find out what they are, which depends on knowing what my words mean; but then I need the agreement of my society to give meaning to my words. This is a vicious circle: in order to interpret others you have to interpret yourself, but that is impossible without interpreting others. A global interpretation of my own and my society's actions all at once is out of the question, for what could possibly be the adequacy criteria for that interpretation? Such interpretation, with no constraints placed on it (because the content and message of all possible constraints would be subject to that very interpretation, depending upon how it may construe them), must be entirely arbitrary and hence utterly capricious.

The behavioristic medicine may be applied once more: you do not have to understand your own words or interpret those of your peers. Instead, simply react to the oncoming stimuli. Now that is a fine directive for a robot, but I am not one. I know that I think and that my words mean something that I have in mind. That knowledge is absolutely certain; it is certain that I cannot be wrong in thinking that I mean something, for in order to be wrong, I must mean something which is wrong, and thus mean something or other. I think that I think; *ergo*, I think.

3: Sentences in the Brain

According to the functionalist the role that a sequence of brain events plays in the brain's own career and its interaction with efferent and afferent stimuli can make it into a token of a syntactic type. The mind is a set of such syntactically identified brain events. According to most Fodorians (excluding Stich) some of these sentences are semantically interpreted; they represent external reality in virtue of their causal connections with external events.

But our above argument shows that interaction pattern is not meaning. One well-known version of this argument is due to John Searle; another, to Ned Block.[4] Here is yet another: take any object you think is *not* conscious of its surroundings and uses no language, say, a piece of rock. Identify those internal state-types of it that are caused by, and those that cause, all the interactions of that rock with its environment. Draw a flowchart which describes that rock's going from one such state to another, including intermediary states of the rock which serve to facilitate those transitions. The flowchart will be of the same order of complexity as that of the human brain. That is easy to ensure, since you can use any level of specificity (molecules, atoms, or elementary particles) in describing those interaction-types. Since those types are realized in the rock's internal structure, you may interpret them semantically as beliefs and desires about the environment; thus the rock thinks, represents its environment, and intentionally acts to change it. If that is rubbish, so is the functionalist account of meaning.

Eliminative materialists try to avoid this absurdity by foreswearing any interpretation of brain processes in psychological terms. According to them not only 'represents', 'believes', and 'desires' but all phenomenological terms (such as 'looks red', 'feels warm', etc.) are denotationless; they are the theoretical terms of an obsolete folkpsychology that ought to be discarded. But the said suggestion, I have argued,[5] eliminates the most important feature of science, the feature that distinguishes it from myth and fairy tales. Science is a theory that takes firsthand ascriptions of phenomenological properties to be *prima facie true if believed*. For the empirical scientist a mere belief that, for example, iron sinks in water, is not heedworthy, and does not serve as *prima facie* evidence that iron sinks in water, unless we seem to experience the said event, that is, believe that we have observed it. To describe our experience, however, we need a phenomenological vocabulary. Thus, if all sentences in which these terms occur are false, empirical science is impossible.

Some eliminative materialists (e.g., R. Rorty and P. Churchland[6]) answer that a phenomenological terminology is not necessary for direct observation reporting; a scientific terminology can replace it. "Brain states . . . are indeed know*able* by introspection. Just as one can learn to feel that the summer air is about 70°F or 21°C, so one can learn to feel that the mean KE of its molecules is about $6.2 \times 10\text{-}21$ joules" (Churchland, p. 21). Now it is true that people may be trained to report, "my C-fibers fire" and "the mean KE of air molecules here is n" instead of "I feel pain" and "I feel warm." But such statements fail to provide an essential piece of information provided by the above phenomenological statements: they omit the grounds of the report. If I merely have an *idée fixe* that the mean KE of the air is now n or that my C-fibers fire, the scientist need not pay any attention to what I say. Only if I felt it, that is, if I had a sensory experience to that effect, can my report be used as evidence. What the scientist gleans from my report is neither that I *say* that the mean KE is n (that is no evidence that the mean KE is n) nor that the mean KE is n (that would logically imply, rather than serve as inductive evidence for, the mean KE being n). Rather, what the scientist learns from my report, and uses as evidence that the mean KE is probably n, is that I *felt* that the mean KE is n.

To recapture this vital distinction, Rorty and Churchland may wish to retain the expression "I *feel* as if the mean KE of the air molecules is n" in their scientific Newspeak for reports of first-hand sense experience. But then phenomenological terms are reintroduced into the language; 'an n-KE-like feeling' is no less phenomenalistic an expression than 'a warm feeling'. The choice is therefore between a materialistic language that makes science impossible and a language of science that includes phenomenal terms and is therefore ontologically committed to mental entities.

4: Meaning and Possible Worlds

A term, I claim, has a meaning iff it has satisfaction conditions; an indicative sentence has a meaning iff it has truth conditions (I shall refer to both as "satisfaction conditions"). Thus, it seems that to understand a linguistic item is to know what satisfies it. But what counts as knowing those satisfaction conditions? That task may be construed as ridiculously easy or else as impossibly difficult. In one unwelcome sense all that it takes to know the satisfaction conditions of 'p' is to be able to use the disquotation principle. Surely "electrons are leptons" is true iff electrons are leptons; no other condition will quite do. But do I know the satisfaction conditions, and hence the meaning of, the sentence 'electrons are leptons' if all I can say about it is that it would be satisfied by the state of electrons being leptons? If so, anyone who knows how quotation works understands all sentences. But this is clearly wrong; one does not understand the quoted sentence if one does not understand the unquoted one; one may use the disquotation principle as above without having the faintest idea what are electrons or leptons, or while believing that electrons are cows and leptons are bovine animals. Mouthing words is not understanding. Perhaps, then, knowing the satisfaction conditions of 'p' is knowing all that is necessary and sufficient for it to be true. That condition, however, is far too stringent; I understand the sentence 'the cat is on the mat', but only an infinite mind may know all the facts that are necessary and sufficient for the cat to be on the mat. Further, if in order to understand the sentences stating those conditions one must also know *their* necessary and sufficient conditions, then only God knows anything at all.

An intermediate suggestion (made by Dummett[7]) is that one understands a sentence iff one can (in principle) recognize its proof. Understanding a term is then, I suppose, being able, in principle, to recognize whether a given item satisfies it. This suggestion may help us solve the problem, but I do not think that it can work unless we use possible worlds in the explication of "being able in principle." As it stands, Dummett's criterion compromises the crucial distinction between understanding a linguistic term and being able to ascertain whether it is satisfied in reality. Suppose that as a matter of fact Fermat's last theorem is never proved or disproved; does that imply that every mathematician who has worked on it was only contemplating a string of meaningless signs, never even understanding what is claimed by the theorem in question? That would be very odd indeed. As to incomplete proofs, Dummett insists on current evidence (let us assume that this demand makes sense, although I doubt it: *how* current should, or can, a piece of evidence be?). But there are past tense sentences (e.g., 'Homer was tall') for which there is no available evidence, yet we understand them perfectly well. No one has ever (even partially) proved a sentence saying of someone that she is a witch, yet it is preposterous to claim that a Salem witch hunter, who invariably misapplied 'witch', did not know what the word meant and understood no sentence of the form 'x is a witch'. Understanding cannot be a recognitional ability in the *real* world due to the existence of contingent factors that jeopardize recognition, but not understanding.

Possible worlds get us out of some difficulties. The proposition that-p divides all situations into those that are, and those that are not, p-situations. Now, since one can understand a given sentence better, worse, or not at all, let us use Dummett's suggestion in a possible world framework. Assume that a person can inspect whether a situation is or is not a p-situation not only in this but in all possible worlds. Then it seems that a person s understands the sentence 'p' better than $s*$ iff, given all worlds, s is less likely than $s*$ to err in telling p-situations from non-p ones. Allowed to inspect thoroughly a world where witches do exist, a Salem judge is more likely to identify them correctly than a person who does not understand the term 'witch' at all.

But something else is needed before we can proceed. To understand a term is to know what it means, but what is it that one knows when one knows what a term means? It is what enables one to say whether the term is satisfied by an inspected item. What can that be? It is certainly not a propensity triggered by p-situations (or a-things), to quack 'p' (or 'a') automatically upon encountering one of them. If understanding the meaning of 'p' were such a propensity to behave, consciousness would have been redundant for understanding; one would not need to be aware of what p-situations are like in order to understand the term 'p'. But that is surely false; the prisoner in Searle's Chinese room does not understand the messages he passes to the outside, and a Turing machine may play its game without attaching any meaning to the notes it manufactures. We, on the other hand, are conscious of the state of affairs that 'the cat is on the mat' alleges to obtain, and we can check whether an item satisfies 'cat' by comparing it with the satisfaction conditions of 'cat'. We can do all that because we are *aware* of the said satisfaction conditions, that is, we have them in mind.

Intuitionists, pragmatists, behaviorists, coherentists, and other antirealists try to challenge the correspondence theory of truth by attacking the truth-conditions theory of understanding. If to understand 'p' is to be aware of its satisfaction conditions, then 'p' is true iff those conditions obtain in reality. The antirealists, therefore, attempt to replace the traditional notion of understanding; instead of mentally representing satisfaction conditions, they say, understanding consists in some other fiat, for example, using an expression correctly in a given language-game, being able to identify a proof of it, processing it according to the right transformation rules, using it to one's advantage, and so on. What I want to say, however, is that none of these activities is understanding. There is a vast number of things I can do with a sentence you hand me. I can use it as a banner and wave it in the streets; I may press it to my heart or paste it on my door; I may put it into a mechanism that makes delicious lasagna out of it; I can stick it into a slot machine and hit a jackpot every time, and so on. But performing none of these wonderful tricks counts as understanding the sentence in question. To understand what is the state of affairs a sentence alleges to be the case (or, for a term, what item it denotes) is just that: to envisage the said situation (or thing), and to see it as such, that is, as that which satisfies the said expression. No other activity or response can replace it. It is true that he who understands the sentence 'p' (or the term 'a') possesses a strategy for identifying p-situations (or a-things), but not vice versa: to understand 'p' is not simply to possess a technique for identifying p-situations; a smoke detector, for example, reacts to smoke, but it is not conscious of the smoke it "detects," that is, it does not have a conscious mental representation of it. Understanding is one particular strategy of identifying what would satisfy an expression, and that strategy is: having that expression's satisfaction conditions mentally present to one, that is, having the item that would satisfy it in mind. Thus the meaning of 'cat', its satisfaction conditions, must somehow be "in my mind" for me to understand it.

But how can that be? What satisfies 'cat' is cats; surely there are no cats in my mind? On the other hand, if what is in my mind is some symbol or image that stands for cats, then Wittgenstein's argument shows that the said symbol (even with a rule intended to direct its application) may be applied, with complete impunity, to anything whatsoever. How, then, is a mentalistic theory of meaning possible? Strange as it may seem, I opt for the first alternative: there *are* cats in my mind. A real cat cannot exist in my mind, but possible cats take no real space or time. What I am going to suggest is, then, that my meaning of 'cat' is a possible cat that exists, so to speak, "in my mind." I shall claim that to know the meaning of a term 'n' is, quite literally, to have the entity that satisfies it, N, in mind. I shall also show how Wittgenstein's problem, about specifying the right way of relating that intramental entity to extramental ones, can be answered. In essence it was answered, I shall suggest, by Wittgenstein himself.

5: Objects and Entities

People project worlds. I shall alternatively use 'projected world' (using the metaphor of the cinema) and 'representation world' (using the metaphor of what we see "in" paintings) to refer to the possible worlds that we can envisage, sometimes at will. Representation worlds ('RW', for short), or course, do not exist; only the real world exists. But there are persons in the real world that are conscious of some things; for example, they can imagine things, or dream, or sense, or think. To speak of RW is thus nothing but a way of speaking about what those persons are. Just as possible worlds are nothing but reifications of some properties of real things, that is, their various possibilities, so peoples' RW are nothing but a reification of a certain property of persons, that is, their conscious life. To talk about RW is just a way of talking about what a person is, that is, about what one represents. RW are a modification of one's perfectly real property of being aware; for although what one represents, the mental entities that one projects, are (Moore and Searle to the contrary) *not* real, one's psychological experience of representing thus-and-so-ly is real enough. I shall therefore say that a person *s* understands an expression 'n' in *s*'s idiolect iff *s* assigns to 'n' an item in some RW that *s* projects ('*s*RW', for short) and sees it as such, that is, as satisfying the expression 'n'.

I distinguish between objects and entities; an object is a nonrepeatable item occurring at one index-triplet: a world *w*, a time *t*, and a place *p*; an entity recurs at several such triplets. Here are their definitions (for 'x = y' read, 'x is identical with y at z'):

$$z$$

$$A \text{ is an object iff } (x)\,[\,(\exists y)\,(A=x) \supset (y)\,(A=x)\,]$$
$$ y y$$

$$A \text{ is an entity iff } (\exists x)\,(\exists y)\,(z)\,[\,(x \neq y)\,\&\,(A=x)\,\&\,(A=y)\,].$$
$$ z x y$$

Socrates, who is found in various possible worlds and in many spatiotemporal locations, is an entity. Snow is also an entity: it recurs in various locations in many possible worlds. White is an entity, too, since you find *it* again and again at various times, places, and worlds; I hold that whatever you call 'white' *is* the entity White itself, at that location. Another entity is Cat; one can find it climbing a tree in the yard and, at the same time, sleeping on a mat a thousand miles away. In some locations it coincides with the entity White; in some it is black; in some locations, in other possible worlds (e.g., the one envisaged by Saki), Cat speaks English (i.e., its occurrence there is also an occurrence of the entity Speaker-of-English).[8]

RW are possible worlds that conscious beings envision. Objects in RW are therefore "in the mind" in the sense that they are our intentional objects: they are phenomenal, not noumenal (i.e., real) entities. A meaning, now, is such a mental entity: a meaning (I now define) is an entity that recurs at RW only. For example, there are many objects, in many possible worlds, to which *s* would be willing to apply the term 'cat'. Now the meaning of *s*'s term 'cat', M(*s*) 'cat', is the entity that recurs at all and only those objects in *s*RW that *s* would call 'cat'. The entity M(*s*) 'cat', that is, the meaning of the term 'cat' as used by *s*, is an entity that coincides with every object in any world in *s*RW to which *s* would apply 'cat'. (Where the person *s* is assumed, I shall write only "M'n'" instead of "M(*s*)'n'.") The terms 'cat', 'white', 'Socrates', and so on are meaningful to *s* because they have meanings: their meanings are the entities M'cat', M'white', and M'Socrates' that *s* represents, that is, that occur in *s*RW.

Entities that occur in RW may occur in the real world, too. Socrates, for example, is one such entity: he exists in *r*, the real world, as well as in many other possible worlds; some of them are RW, some are not. Thus the entity that I envisage, M'Socrates' (i.e., the meaning of my term 'Socrates'), *is* Socrates if it coincides with Socrates in all my RW. To say it otherwise, what I mean by the word 'Socrates' is an entity, M'Socrates', that recurs at some of my RW and coincides with Socrates wherever it, M'Socrates', is. In my RW, Socrates=M'Socrates'. Similarly, if I understand the word 'cat', then its meaning for me, M'cat', is the entity Cat as it is in my RW. Or take 'red': what that word means to me is the meaning M'red', which, not being blind, I do represent: I envision quite a few objects as being red. Thus, in my RW, Red itself is identical with that entity M'red'. For you to know what 'red' means is to be in the following position: every object *o* in your RW that you will call 'red' is identical at that *o* (i.e., at some index-triplet: objects, or locations, are index triplets) with M'red' and hence with Red itself.

Let me summarize: all terms (including both names and predicates) are names of entities. Those entities (e.g., Socrates, Snow, Red, Bigger Than, etc.) recur at various objects. An object is an occurrence of an entity at a world, a time, and a place. Entities overlap: thus, for example, to say that all dogs are animals is to say that Dog=Animal at Dog; to say that all animals are dogs is to say that Dog=Animal at Animal. Entities that occur in the real world are real entities. Some real entities, that is, those that occur in RW, are comprehensible, since in those worlds they overlap with meanings. Since meanings are what we are directly aware of, we can thereby be directly aware of the entities whose occurrences those meanings are. Since some of those entities exist in the real world, that is, are noumena, we can, in that rather circuitous way, be directly aware of some noumena. People who understand the term 'red' have the meaning M'red' in their minds and thus are directly aware of the entity Red. Those who understand the term 'Socrates' have in their minds the meaning M'Socrates' and are therefore directly aware of Socrates.

6: Belief and Other Representation Worlds

Among the many possible worlds that we imagine, dream up, or envisage, one is special to us: the perceptual everyday world that Wilfrid

Sellars has named "the manifest image." That world is so vividly projected that the majority of human beings take it to be the real world, the world as it really is. Even though many of us would deny that the world really is exactly as it appears to us to be, that is, that it is literally characterized by qualia such as smells or colors, we all feel so much at home in that familiar world of blue skies, warm air, and scented flowers that we tend to think of it as if it were real. That world exhibits how things look to us most of the time. I may have a sensory experience as of a white, fluffy cat, but if the real world has only pulsating energy fields in it, neither the energy field nor my experience of it is white and fluffy *in propria persona*, that is, in *r*. The white and fluffy object is therefore a phenomenal object, where phenomenal objects are a certain kind of intentional object, that is, a kind of meaning. That object is a segment of a possible world that does not exist, a sensible world which is my own way (being what I am) of representing what there really is. Let us call that world '*c*'.

Another interesting member of *s*RW is *s*'s belief world *b*; that world manifests what *s* takes *r* to be. I borrow the term 'belief-world' from Hintikka, who defines a belief world of *s* as a possible world *w* such that 'p' is true in *w* iff *s* believes that p.[9] Hintikka assumes that all possible worlds are ontologically complete, and therefore he needs an infinite set of belief-worlds to capture *s*'s beliefs: different worlds in this set differ in details *s* neither believes nor disbelieves to be the case, and they all share those features which according to *s* do characterize the real world. Thus, if P is the set of all worlds in which 'p' is true, then for Hintikka *s* believes that p iff every belief world of *s* is a member of P. I accept this definition, but since I like my model to be psychologically realistic, I cannot have an infinite set of worlds that include items undreamt of by *s* represent what *s* believes. Instead, I regard *s* as projecting exactly one belief world, *b*, which is an ontologically incomplete model of reality: the world according to *s*.

Some may argue that incomplete worlds are impossible; in every possible world *w* there is a definite number of cats, and each cat is fully determinate, down to the structure of each molecule in its body. But no one represents cats in such detail, nor need one have any belief about the number of cats in the world. Hence, one's belief world is not a possible world. I answer this objection by denying its premise: some objects are ontologically incomplete; an object *a* may be such that for some predicate 'F' neither '*Fa*' nor 'not F*a*' is true. In another essay[10] I argued that all ordinary objects are like that. Take the Empire State Building; since no one has decided, with respect to a huge number of items, whether they are parts of the building or are merely attached to it, there are infinitely many predicates (e.g., 'weighs more than n pounds' for a certain appropriately chosen number n) such that neither they nor their negations are true of the Empire State Building. Therefore, there are numerous ontologically complete *distinct* entities (e.g., one weighing more, the other weighing less, than n pounds) each of which qualifies with equal justification as the Empire State Building. If every entity is ontologically complete, it follows that there are infinitely many Empire State Buildings. Therefore, 'the Empire State Building' fails the uniqueness condition and denotes nothing; hence the Empire State Building does not exist. To avoid this outrageous conclusion we must admit that some objects are incomplete; the Empire State Building, for example, is one.

In RW all objects are ontologically incomplete: for example, any object x in b has *only* those features that s believes it has, and none other. Moreover, not only objects in RW but RW themselves are ontologically incomplete. Just as a person may be older than n seconds, younger than m seconds, but any sentence about that person being i seconds ($n<i<m$) old is truth-valueless, so an RW may have more than n cats, less than m cats, but any sentence about its having i cats ($n<i<m$) in it is truth-valueless. Hence, b can be such that any sentence 'p' is true in b iff s believes that p.

But what about impossible beliefs, for example, s's belief that 9 is a prime number or that water is not H_2O? How can they be true in a possible world? I shall return to the issue of the alleged "metaphysically impossible" beliefs in section 10. As to logically impossible beliefs my answer is that a possible world need not be governed by the classical logic calculus. Why can there not be possible worlds that realize other, nonclassical logics? If Finkelstein and Putnam are right, even the real world does not obey classical logic, since distributivity laws do not apply in quantum mechanics. The logics needed for belief worlds can be chosen from Anderson and Belnap's relevance logics, where each statement is indexed, and *modus ponens* is valid only for premises bearing the same relevance-index.[11] These logics can cash in Grices' contention that a person may have several belief "dossiers" that need not be integrated, and my own argument that Bp&Bq does not imply B(p&q).[12] If 'p' carries the belief-index (i) and 'not-p' is indexed (j), 'p&not-p' does not follow, and thus both 'p' and 'not-p' may be true in it, and yet the belief world b itself would be free of contradiction, since 'p&not-p' would not follow.

Armed with the notion of meaning explained above, we can now cope with difficulties that wrecked other realistic, nonrelativistic, Fregean theories of meaning. The meaning M'white' has instances (it exists at various locations) in s's world c, as well as in other (but perhaps not in all) of sRW. M'electron' exists in b, and in other worlds in sRW, but not in c. If s understands the word 'witch' but does not believe in witches, M'witch' exists neither in b nor in c, but it does exist in some other w in sRW. 'Socrates', too, has a meaning for s; that meaning is the entity M'Socrates' in some w in sRW. M'Socrates' in b can be described, and that description is, as Frege said, synonymous with s's token of 'Socrates'; it specifies what s believes Socrates really is. $M(s)$'Socrates' in other worlds in sRW is the realization of what, according to s, Socrates could have been. Again, just as Frege taught, the cognitive import of 'Socrates' for its user can be used to pick out what 'Socrates' denotes, for in sRW Socrates satisfies what 'Socrates' means to s. Similarly, Cat is the entity that satisfies in sRW what 'cat' means to s, and so on.

Frege's mistake was relatively modest; claiming that senses are entities, he incurred the just criticism of Russell, Wittgenstein, and Quine. Claiming that referents of meaningful terms satisfy those senses in the real world, he incurred the just criticism of Kripke, Putnam, and Kaplan: surely, Water, or Socrates, need not satisfy what John Doe believes about them? In the present model, however, these problems are removed. A meaning is a mental entity; to ask "What does 'n' mean to s?" is tantamount to asking, "What is the meaning of 'n' for s?" and that question is answerable by describing the meaning $M(s)$'n'. But having meanings in our ontology does not commit us to any Platonic entities, since mental entities do not exist: $M(s)$'n' is just N itself as it is in the set of possible worlds sRW. Furthermore, if 'Sx' is the conjunction of all the sentences about Socrates that s would assent to, s's term 'Socrates' is synonymous with '$(ix)\ (Sx,sRW)$', which is different from $(ix)\ (Sx,r)$. Thus Kripke's problem is also answered: even if Socrates does not satisfy *in reality* what s believes about him, he does satisfy it in sRW.

7: Sense: An Identity Function

The key argument of all relativists (including pragmatists, intuitionists, "internal" realists, idealists, and so on) is, perhaps, the argument from the opacity of reference: "How can the relation of reference between a mental item and a particular set of mind-independent, theory-independent entities," they ask the realist, "be ever specified?" As noted by Dummett and Putnam, the argument applies with full force even to phenomenalists such as Berkeley and Hume, who are realists about a small, privileged set of entities: opacity strikes any entity the realist attempts to refer to, be it psychological or physical. In his *Rea-*

son, Truth, and History Putnam discusses the two traditional attempts to answer that question, the similarity answer and the causal connection answer, and shows that each one of them presupposes reference and therefore cannot be used to define it. If the speaker defines 'E' as everything that resembles his current sensation, the definition, says Putnam, is empty, since everything is similar to everything else in some respect or other. If a certain respect R, or some sets of items that exemplify that kind of resemblance, is specified, then, asks Putnam, how did the speaker manage to refer to them? (p. 65) Putnam is surely right to claim that the answer "the speaker just directs his attention to those items" (given by Devitt and others) either begs the question or assumes a magical theory of reference. The same argument works against the causal theory of reference: "if I am able to specify what *is* the appropriate type of causal chain, I must already be able to refer to the kinds of things and properties that make up that kind of causal chain. But how did I get to be able to do that?"[13] (Putnam could have gone even further and asked not only how can the speaker refer to a particular kind of resemblance and to a particular kind of causal connection but also how can an intention to use resemblance, or causality, in order to define reference Q succeed in referring to the *real* relations of resemblance and causality. How does the intention "lasso" the right relation? What is to prevent one from interpreting the mental symbols 'resemblance' and 'causality' in some other, arbitrary way in reality?)

If that question is not answered properly, and without assuming any "magical" theory of reference, one is forever trapped (together with Quine, Davidson, Goodman, Rorty, and Derrida) in a parochial system of beliefs and practices, and the very stating of the metaphysical realistic position becomes meaningless. Let us start, then, from the beginning: How does one refer to one's own present experience? The obvious answer is that I am not separate from my experience; I am not a transcendental ego who directs a "mental gaze" upon a given experience and attaches a tag to it. I *am* that experience; to say that I experience it is to say that it is self-aware. Consciousness is the self-transparency of experience, and hence it is essentially an act of self-referring; reference is therefore nothing other than the basic datum of consciousness, that is, one's being present to oneself.

But how do we go from that minimal self-reference to refer to entities which are either nonpresent experiences or external, for example, physical, things? As indicated above, the solution will involve the idea that the object to which one refers in an immediate way, one's present meaning, is an occurrence of an entity that has other occurrences in my RW and in other possible worlds, including *r*. As many

relativists (especially Goodman and Putnam, who carry on Wittgenstein's examination) rightly remark, no trans-world-heirline, in fact not
even a trans-*index*-heirline, is given by its instance (or, for that matter,
by any number of instances); one can go from that instance to any other
object whatsoever. What can justify my saying that M(s)'Socrates' and
M(s)'woman' *are* Socrates and Woman in sWR? To provide that justification I shall use a revised version of the two traditional strategies of
reference discussed and discarded by Putnam. My answer, I believe, is
thoroughly Wittgensteinian, for it was Wittgenstein who *did* finally
show how an instance may indicate all the other instances of a rule of
which it is an instance.

The question of identity across possible worlds is the question,
how to compute the value of identity functions. Given an object, what
is the function that matches it with other objects, that are instances of
the same entity? We use two different functions for that purpose; the
way we identify occurrences of, for example, White is different from the
way in which we identify occurrences of, for example, Socrates. Essentialists like Kripke or Plantinga believe that the answer to the above
question ("An occurrence of which entity is a given object?") is determined by the essence of the given object. But that is much too easy; like
Quine, Hintikka, Goodman, and others, I think that essences are not *in
rem*; only within the framework of some discourse, inside a (Kuhnian)
paradigm, or when given a set of interests and research practices, we can
distinguish some properties as more central than others. Kripke's way
out is therefore blocked, because many kinds of trans-index function
may be used to explicate the concept of identity. Two such functions,
however, are of special interest to us and play a major role in organizing
our worlds: it is customary to call them 'Qualitative Identity' and 'Numerical Identity'.

These terms, however, are very misleading. In my nominalistic
theory (see note 8 above) White is a physical entity just like Socrates.
Indeed, in a given world the entity Socrates recurs at distinct nonsimultaneous spatiotemporal locations only, while White may also recur simultaneously at various spatial locations. But that is not a basic categorical difference. Not only Socrates but Sand, Woman, and The Lion,
too, may recur at various locations; all these entities are (like all entities)
repeatable: they recur at various objects (locations). The important
difference between Socrates and White is not that only Socrates is an
entity, while White is a universal; they are both full-fledged physical
entities. Rather, the difference is that we tend to compute which objects
they occur at in different ways.

One identity function, the "qualitative" one, picks up its values by similarity. Given my immediate acquaintance with the meaning M'white', I can reidentify it in many locations, having a rather good idea what white objects would be like in any possible world: they are all similar to M'white'. "But wait a minute," say Goodman and Putnam, "anything whatsoever is similar in some respect or other to that sample of white of which you are aware. Did not Wittgenstein show that one can go from that object to any other object, that is, that a sample gives you no rule for its future application?" It is my contention that Wittgenstein's point was exactly the opposite. Any object *can* be interpreted in any way you wish, and cats can be matched with cherries, but that kind of sorting looks to us, directly and immediately, awfully ugly and *wrong*. We do not see the cat as belonging together with cherries; we see it as belonging together with other cats. *That* is the point of Wittgenstein's famous duck-rabbit example, and of his entire discussion in *Philosophical Investigations* II, xi: every object we encounter is, in that respect, like the duck-rabbit; in principle (i.e., as a matter of logic) it is possible to see it in many ways and apply odd rules to it. A cat possesses a valid interpretation as a Putnamian cat* (to be matched with cherries); the sign '+' can be seen as standing for the Kripkean quaddition (whose value for 68 and 57 is 5), and so on. All that is legitimate. The point, however, is that we do not see things in that way. Given a fork, says Wittgenstein, I do not say that I see it *as* a fork; that would be pointless since I am not aware of any other way of seeing it as; I see it *only* as a fork; as I see it, it fits some things and not others. That is why Wittgenstein compares meaning in language to the meaning of a musical phrase; of course you can do anything at all with that motif, but given the way we see it, having heard the work up to this point, some developments would look absolutely wrong to us. The phrase in that work has a meaning: it "asks" to be dealt with in certain ways and not in others.

"But surely the relativists do not deny that, within a framework, a given item does have a sense of its own and cannot be arbitrarily classified! They only deny that it specifies that classification all by itself, outside our theories and interpretations!" Relativists who say that miss the entire point. The realist does not quarrel with the above contention; he uses it. What the relativist forgets is that whatever may have caused my seeing an item as manifesting an aesthetic preference for some objects and abhorrence of others, I need not be aware of that cause; I may just use the immediately given object in order to refer to those things that I am directly aware of its mandating as right for it. Thus, objects that are not immediately given, but are immediately seen by one as right for the item A which is given, that is, as fitting it, are referred to as "As" by whomever is aware of the given object A. It does not matter that the said classification is culture dependent. What does matter is that one can see an object *as* belonging together with some specific others; we know what is its *specific* use because we see it as an occurrence of some *specific* type: an A, a fork, a duck, or a rabbit. Reference is secured.

Here we have a theory-free way of specifying what one is talking about. One does not have to specify the respect in which the entity White (i.e., what he intends to refer to by means of the white sample he currently envisions) is similar to the sample that one is aware of now, nor does one need to refer to other sets of white things in order to define 'white' in extension. One does not even need the concept of similarity or any other concept. My seeing the sample *as* White is the object's determining for me, in the most immediate way, what other objects belong together with it. I can now define the entity that recurs with all these objects, calling it 'White'; I do not have to refer to any property or rule in order to compute which objects resemble my sample in the right way and thus are instances of the same entity (White) it is an instance of. I do not have to do that, because I *see* how to apply my sample, that is, what objects are genidentical with it. To see the stimulus object as such and such is precisely to be able to use it without referring to anything else (a property, an extension, a rule, or whatever). To see that sample as mandating another kind of application, as fitting other things, is to see it in a totally different way; it requires a radical, and immediately noticeable, change in my visual experience, a dramatic perceptual revelation ("*Aufleuchten des Aspekts*") that seldom happens.

White is, then, the entity which in any world occurs wherever there is an object that, according to s, is seen as similar to the given M'white'. An object o in w satisfies 'white' iff, had s represented w, she would have applied 'white' to o. I shall call that "qualitative" identity function the *sense function*. For every term 'n' of s there is a sense-function from M'n' to S'n', that is, from the meaning of 'n' (which exists in sRW only) to its *sense* (which exists in other possible worlds as well). M'n' and S'n' have in RW the same instances, that is, M'n' and S'n' overlap in M'n'. Usually if 'n' is a predicate, then N (the entity denoted by 'n') is none other than S'n'. Let us define S'n' (the sense of a token 'n' in s's idiolect) thus: $S'n' = o_i \ldots o_n$ (at each of $o_i \ldots o_n$) iff s sees M'n' as an instance of the entity they, too, are instances of.

8. Reference: Another Identity Function

Sense is not the only extension of meaning, and similarity is not the only trans-world-heir-line we use. With some terms (usually Q proper names) another, the so-called "numerical," identity function is employed. That function is used very liberally in counterfactual sentences, and I think that Kripke is right when he says that "generally, things aren't 'found out' about a counterfactual situation, they are stipulated."[14] Unlike Kripke, however, I think that the said stipulative nature of "numerical" identity allows us to genidentify an object o with any other object d (i.e., regard o and d as occurrences of the same entity). The ground for identification can be very slim (e.g., a location or a form; cf.: "Had *this* coat been made of leather") or very rich. There is no degree of similarity above which objects must be considered as occurrences of the same ("numerically identical") entity, and no degree of similarity below which they must be considered as occurrences of "numerically distinct" entities. That enormous freedom of stipulation is used, however, in counterfactual situations only; in real contexts the notion is much stricter.

The stricter notion of numerical identity is grounded in the concept of *the best explanation*. For any representation world w, say, s's dream, or s's world of sensory experience, there is an *external* explanation why that world is as it is, that relates items in it to items in the real world, r; it accounts for the provenance of items in w, for their *raison d'être*. That explanation is most likely to be an *interpretation*, that is, an assigning of objects in w to objects in r as occurrences of the same entity in both worlds. Think, for example, of interpreting the represented content in dreams, paintings, stories, and alien belief systems. Although explanations may be holistic, they often conclude with a piecemeal interpretation of items. An interpretation coordinates segments of worlds, regarding them as occurrences of the same entity. People interpret each other by matching items in their respective RWs and declare them to be the same; that is also the way we make an alien theory understandable to us. We use interpretations in the sciences ("genes are DNA molecules"; "temperature is mean kinetic energy"), in the arts ("this figure is Christ"; "the violin theme expresses despair"), in psychology ("gods are parent figures"; "the knife in your dream is a penis"), and elsewhere. Not every explanation is an interpretation, but without interpretation there could be no accumulation of knowledge, no communication, and no memory.

Again the relativist would insist that explanation is interest, and paradigm, relative. "Our methodological constraints," he says, "express our aesthetic taste and depend on anthropological and sociological factors; they reflect our preference for the elegant, the general, and the parsimonious. Within that theory we can specify a privileged causal connection obtaining between an item and what it denotes; but to claim that the said causal relation obtains between an experienced object and some *Ding an sich* is nonsense; used in that way the term 'causal connection' loses all meaning." Now the metaphysical realist can accept all that without batting an eyelid. What explanation is considered best is relative to the assumed aesthetic sensitivity; our methodological constraints, and, quite obviously, the concept of a cause, are indeed internal to our theory. Still, the following description of a noumenon referred to by an item in sRW is *not* relative to anything: "the item in r that would be assigned to the object o in sRW by the interpretation I, where I is the interpretation that s, according to his *own* methodological (i.e., aesthetic) criteria, would consider best." Thus, using s's own theory (and hence s's own aesthetic taste), we can specify a real object, a noumenon, whose existence and nature are completely independent of s's theory and its culture-bound constraints. I therefore agree that it is a mistake to suggest that our term 'Socrates' refers to the cause in r of the phenomenal Socrates, for we cannot say which item, if any, our term 'cause' denotes in r without presupposing reference. But we may characterize the referent of 'Socrates' as the item in r that we, had we been able to examine r, would have—using our concepts, our aesthetic sensitivity, and hence the theory which is best according to our criteria—regarded as the interpretandum of M'Socrates' (or as its cause).

The numerical identity function (call it "the *reference* function") specifies a transworld entity that may have instances in r for each meaning in sRW. To determine the referent R(s)'Socrates' of s's term 'Socrates', given the meaning M(s)'Socrates', we ask: "What entity in r would God, who knows all that there is to know about r, assign to M(s)'Socrates' (i.e., what, would he say, explains best the existence of M'Socrates') if He were to use s's own aesthetic taste, that is, abide by s's methodological constraints?" That algorithm gives the value of the reference function for the argument M(s)'n'. Even if we can never compute it, it has a solution: R(s)'n' is what the best explanation according to s would have designated as the interpretand of M(s)'n' in r had s inspected r.

Usually, given a name 'n', R'n' is simply N, but not always. Take, for example, Phlogiston: when we say that Phlogiston does not exist, we talk about S'phlogiston', the substance that is sufficiently similar to M'phlogiston'. If r is as our science says it is, then, for sure, S'phlogiston' does not exist in r. Yet Joseph Priestly did not talk about nothing when he used the word 'phlogiston'; the *referent* of his term, that is, R'phlogiston', does exist in reality. If the existence of oxygen in reality best explains the presence of phlogiston in b, R'phlogiston' in r is oxygen.

The procedure for computing the instances of R'n' in nonrepresentation possible worlds is similar, although much more trivial. Possible worlds are those worlds in which counterfactual properties of real objects are actualized. Thus, the fact that Socrates could have escaped from prison *externally* explains someone's having escaped from prison in some possible worlds *w*. The said escapee in *w* is an instance of R'Socrates' in *w* iff it is Socrates in *r* who best explains the existence, and the relevant features of, that escapee. To say it otherwise, Socrates in *w* is that entity whose escape from prison is best explained by Socrates' ability to escape in *r*. This "explanation," I admit, is trivial, unlike the genuine explanation that objects in *r* provide for objects in RW. But the very concept of possible worlds is tailor-made for one purpose only. It is, therefore, only fit and proper that the "explanation" that objects in *r* provide for objects in those worlds be that simplistic. That explanation, at any rate, makes it possible to assign instances in many possible worlds to R'Socrates': in any world *w*, R'Socrates' (i.e., Socrates) is identical with that object whose best interpretans is Socrates in *r* (where 'best' is interpreted as before).

Am I arguing, then, that names such as 'Socrates' have reference but no sense, and predicates such as 'white' have sense but no reference? Far from it. My definitions of S'n'and R'n' as distinct entities assigned to M'n' by two different identity functions is completely indifferent to the syntactical category of the term 'n'. There is absolutely no reason why we cannot specify the entities S'Socrates' and R'white' just as clearly as we specify S'white' and R'Socrates'. It is true, however, that the former two entities do not interest us very much. Usually we use the term 'Socrates' in order to talk about R'Socrates', and the term 'white' in order to talk about S'white'. But we may, if we wish, speak about R'white', the entity "numerically identical" to M'white'. The color of R'white' in *r*, for example, need not be white, since R'white' in *r* is an odd assortment of things that are white in RW, not in *r*. S'white' in *r*, on the other hand, is colored white. Similarly, S'Socrates' in *r* need not be, as we say, the real Socrates: if *s*'s views of Socrates are very mistaken, S'Socrates' in *r* may be Iris Murdoch. That is how *s* can be entirely wrong *about* Socrates: R'Socrates' need not be identical with S'Socrates' in *r*.

Questions about the manner of reference of indexicals and of definite descriptions were often used by the "new" semanticists to undermine the Fregean notion of reference via cognitive import. I shall say nothing about indexicals in this essay, since I have already given a detailed neo-Fregean account of the reference of indexicals somewhere else[15]; I argued that indexicals abbreviate definite descriptions that contain an item that is not referred to by a symbol but is itself displayed there. In another article[16] I offered a neo-Fregean view of definite descriptions, too, but I shall say a little more about them now, because the relation between definite descriptions and the other referential terms discussed above, that is, predicates, proper names, and sentences, seems to me now even closer than I had then realized. Each definite description, 'ixFx', has a meaning, and that meaning, M'ixFx', is an entity that in some contextually understood world w in RW (usually in b) is indeed the only F. Given that meaning, we wish to know what 'ixFx' denotes in other worlds, for example, r, and here too there are two available strategies. One identity function yields the entity R'ixFx', that is, that entity whose occurrences in any w are "numerically" identical with M'ixFx'. R'ixFx' need not be F in reality, but it (at r) is what accounts for the existence of M'ixFx'. In this way we get what Donnellan has called[17] "the referential use" of definite descriptions. We may, however, look for S'ixFx' too. That entity (denoted, according to Donnellan, when one makes an "attributive use" of a definite description) is the one that is sufficiently relevantly similar to M'ixFx' in some world w. The only difference between the sense of a definite description and the sense of a predicate or a proper name is that in the latter case the relevant similarity is unspecified; we rely on our aesthetic intuitions, scientific beliefs, contextually salient factors, or a rule like Putnam's division of linguistic labor in order to identify it. But in the case of definite descriptions we know exactly in what way every instance of S'ixFx' must be like M'ixfx': it, too, must be the only F in *its* world.

Usually a definite description behaves referentially; 'ixFx' would normally denote R'ix(Fx,b)', that is, R'ixFx'. To borrow Kripke's example[18], one may refer to a woman's lover by the expression 'her husband'. I explain that fact in the following way: the expression 'her husband' refers to M'her husband', whose existence in b is best explained by the existence of her lover in r; the latter is therefore the best interpretandum of M'her husband'. In other cases, however, 'ixFx' is understood to denote S'ixFx', and not R'ixFx': if all I know about her husband is that he (whoever he may be) is her husband, then my expression 'her husband' would probably be "attributive": relevant similarity is used as our identity function, and it takes us from M'her husband' to an appropriate counterpart in r, if there is any.

Let me sum up in one inaccurate, but serviceable, sentence: linguistic expressions may denote their senses or their referents; usually proper names and indexicals denote their referents, predicates and sentences denote their senses, and definite descriptions do both.

9: Truth

An indicative sentence, said Frege, is a name, and I think he was right. Unlike Frege, however, I think that sentences name situations, and a situation is an entity that may recur in several possible worlds, including r and RW. Since all entities exclusive to RW (i.e., meanings) are mental entities, a situation there is a mental entity, too; I shall call such entities 'propositions'. A proposition, then, is an occurrence of a situation in RW. In that way we get the traditional definition of a proposition as the meaning of a sentence: the meaning of the sentence 'p' is the proposition M'p', that is, the occurrence of the situation P in one's mind.

I cannot go into the many logical and ontological problems raised by the suggested analysis (but see the articles mentioned in note 8 above; I now think, however, that a situation is a complex substance, as defined there). Fortunately, what we need in the present context is only a quick review of its basic elements. An indicative sentence says of two items that they are identical at some item. Thus, if 'Socrates' refers to R'Socrates' (i.e., Socrates = R'Socrates') and 'mortal' denotes S'mortal' (i.e., Mortal = S'mortal'), what a speaker normally alleges by uttering the sentence 'Socrates is mortal' is that the following situation exists in r: R'Socrates' = S'mortal' *at* R'Socrates'. Let me say that again: the sentence that s utters, 'Socrates is mortal', denotes a proposition; if s speaks ordinary English (not using a code or a dialect), that proposition is a mentally represented situation in which Socrates is mortal. Since Socrates as he exists in s's mind is M'Socrates', and Mortal there is M'mortal', the proposition in question is an identity, obtaining at the domain Socrates-in-RW, between Socrates and Mortal. That situation, P, either does, or else does not, exist in r as well as in RW. It is important to notice that the situation P is S'p', and not R'p'. R'p', the situation that is numerically identical with the proposition of Socrates being mortal, is irrelevant to the truth or falsity of 'Socrates is mortal' as ordinarily understood (a moment's reflection may convince you that it need not include either Socrates or Mortal in it). The only situation that does matter here is S'p', that is, the identity, at R'Socrates' in r, of R'Socrates' and S'mortal'. We have therefore reached a traditional correspondence theory of truth; only this time, I hope, it is impervious to relativistic attacks. Our result is that s's sentence 'Socrates is mortal' is true iff Socrates (i.e., whoever s would have found to bear R to M'Socrates') is mortal (i.e., whatever s would have found to bear S to M'mortal'). A sentence 'p' of s is true, therefore, iff S'p' is in r; that is the case iff the interpretandum that would be assigned to the meaning of the sentence's subject by the best (according to s's aesthetic sensitivity) interpretation is, in reality, identical *at* that interpretandum, with the entity in reality that s would have found sufficiently (according to her aesthetic sensitivity) to resemble the meaning she associates with the sentence's predicate.

10: Contingent Identity

Finally, let me discuss the objection that mental states such as understanding or belief cannot have possible world models because their content may be impossible. No world has nonself-identical objects; yet s may believe that Dr. Jekyll is not Mr. Hyde, that the Evening Star is not the Morning Star, or that water is not H_2O. If these propositions violate metaphysical necessity, how can they occur in any world?

If s believes that Mr. Hyde is not Dr. Jekyll, 'Jekyll' and 'Hyde' have different meanings in s's idiolect. But if s's meaning M'Jekyll' is not identical with her meaning M'Hyde', then in s's belief-world b these are distinct entities. In RW, M'n'=R'n', and if 'n' is a name, then R'n'=N; therefore, in b Jekyll $\neq$ Hyde. We know, however, that in r Jekyll = Hyde. Are they, then, the same entity or not? The answer is that two entities need not have either all, or else none, of their occurrences in common; they may intersect. Identity is contingent: two entities may be the same in one location (object) and distinct in another. If contingent identity is feasible, a possible world model of belief can accommodate metaphysical impossibilities; the entities that s refers to by her terms 'Dr. Jekyll' and 'Mr. Hyde' are one and the same in r and distinct in b. In fact, s can refer to that single entity in r simply because she has in mind these two entities, M'Jekyll' and M'Hyde'. The pernicious problem of referential opacity is therefore solved in the simplest way, and the case is seen to be no more problematic than regular predication. To show that, let us use a simple example. How do we get the problem of epistemic opacity? Where 'B' is the belief operator, it was argued thus:

1. $B(a=a)$ & $-B(a=c)$
2. $a=c$
3. $B(a=a)$ & $-B(a=a)$

and we have a contradiction. But now rewrite that argument according to the present suggestion, using substance logic:

1. $a \underset{b}{=} a$ & $a \underset{b}{\neq} c$

2. $a = c$
   r

3. $a = a$ & $a \neq c$
   b   b

Now it is obvious why we cannot go from (1) and (2) to (3): if identity is contingent, the fact that a and c are identical in r does not imply that they are identical in b. The fallacy is now obvious, and similar to the following fallacious argument: since Socrates is mortal and Plato is mortal, that is, Socrates is identical with Mortal at Socrates, and Plato is identical with Mortal at Plato, Socrates and Plato are both identical with Mortal, and hence they are identical with each other. Obviously that does not follow, because although both Socrates and Plato are identical with Mortal, each is identical with it in a different domain.

But has not contingent identity been shown to be logically objectionable? I do not think so. The entire theory of predication above is based on the assumption that two entities, for example, This Shirt and White, may be identical at one location and not identical at others (e.g., when This Shirt is no longer White or where there is a White House). There is, however, an objection of D. Wiggins[19] that casts doubt on the notion of contingent identity; it runs as follows. Let 'Fx' abbreviate, 'x may not be b'. If identity is contingent, 'Fa' and '$a = b$' may both be true. By the indiscernability of identicals, however, if Fa, and $a = b$, then Fb. But it is not true that b may not be b. Hence, not Fa. Q.E.D. Let us reformulate this argument and adapt it for localized identity: Suppose that A $=$ B in I and A $\neq$ B in J. So A $=$ Nonidentical-with-B-in-J (for short, N) wherever it is, and, in particular, in I. Since A $=$ B in I, and A $=$ N in I, then (by the transitivity of localized identity) B $=$ N in I. But it is false, in I or anywhere else, that B is Nonidentical-with-B-in-J. Thus, contingent identity is untenable. That argument, however, although formally impeccable, is nothing but a confusion. Leibnizian logic cannot distinguish A $=$ NonA (in J), from A $=$ NonA-in-J (in I); both sound logically absurd. For substance logic, however, the distinction is crucial; the first statement is self-contradictory; the second is a trivial truism. A cat, for example, can never, nowhere, be a noncat; but it can now be identical with something, for example, some bunch of atoms, that at another time is not a cat. So, Cat is identical in I with Noncat-in-J. Every entity is somewhere identical with something that is not identical with it somewhere else: that is how entities are defined. The impression that this is a devastating objection is illusory, being due to the rhetorical mistake of reading a sentence as if it meant what a similar sentence would have meant in another logical system.

In this essay I tried to defend three philosophical tenets: metaphysical realism, that is, the view that we refer to entities in THE WORLD (an objective, verification-independent reality); semantic realism, that is, the view that terms are meaningful because there are meanings which they denote; and mentalism, that is, the view that meanings are directly known mental entities. These theses which, at first blush, seem to be quite alien to each other have turned out to be mutually dependent and almost merge into one, welded by substance logic, the logic of localized identity. We can have in mind entities that exist in an external, mind-independent reality because entities recur: they occur in representation worlds as well as in the real one.

Notes

1. L. Wittgenstein, *Philosophical Investigations,* 1, p. 201.

2. Saul A. Kripke, *Wittgenstein on Rules and Private Language* (Blackwell, 1982), p. 99.

3. Ibid., p. 101.

4. John Searle, "Minds, Brains, and Programs," *The Behavioral and Brain Sciences* 3(1980): 417-424, 450-457, and in *Minds, Brains, and Science* (Harvard, 1984), pp. 32-35. N. Block, "Troubles with Functionalism," in W. Savage, ed., *Perception and Cognition, Minnesota Studies in the Philosophy of Science,* vol. 9, (University of Minnesota Press, 1978). I have used a similar argument in E.M. Zemach, "Intention, Attention, and the Nature of Fiction," *Hebrew University Studies in Literature* 5(1977): 135-154.

5. Cf. E. M. Zemach, "The Possibility of a Materialistic Language," *Ratio* 25(1983): 169-170, and idem, "Truth and Beauty," *The Philosophical Forum,* 18:21-39 (1986).

6. Richard Rorty, "Mind-Body Identity, Privacy, and Categories," *The Review of Metaphysics* 19(1965): 24-54; idem, *Philosophy and the Mirror of Nature* (Princeton University Press, 1979; Paul Churchland, "The Direct Observation of Brain States," *The Journal of Philosophy* 82(1985): 3-28.

7. M. Dummett, "What Is a Theory of Meaning, II," in Evans and McDowell, *Truth and Meaning* (Oxford University Press, 1976).

8. For the logic and ontology of locally identical, recurring entities see E.M. Zemach, "Four Ontologies," *The Journal of Philosophy* 67(1970):231-247; "Substance Logic" (with E. Walther), *Boston Studies in the Philosophy of Science* 43(1974): 55-74; "On the Adequacy of Type Ontology," *Synthese* 31(1975): 509-516; "A Plea for a New Nominalism," *Canadian Journal of Philosophy* 12 1982: 527-537; "Numbers," *Synthese* 64(1985): 225-239.

9. J. Hintikka, *Knowledge and Belief* (Cornell University Press, 1962).

10. E.M. Zemach, "Schematic Objects and Relative Identity," *Nous* 16(1982): 295-305.

11. A. Anderson and N.D. Belnap, *Entailment: The Logic of Relevance and Necessity* (Princeton University Press, 1975).

12. E.M. Zemach, "Transparent Belief," *Australasian Journal of Philosophy* 60(1982): 55-65.

13. H. Putnam, *Reason, Truth, and History* (Cambridge University Press, 1981), p. 66.

14. S. Kripke, *Naming and Necessity* (Harvard University Press, 1980), p. 49.

15. E.M. Zemach, "*De Se* and Descartes: A New Semantics for Indexicals," *Nous* 19(1985): 181-204.

16. E.M. Zemach, "Singular Terms and Metaphysical Realism," *American Philosophical Quarterly* 23(1986): 299-306.

17. K. Donnellan, "Reference and Definite Descriptions," *Philosophical Review* 75(1966): 281-304; "Speaker Reference, Descriptions, and Anaphora," in *Contemporary Perspectives in the Philosophy of Language*, ed. P.A. French et al. (Minnesota, 1979) pp. 28-44.

18. S. Kripke, "Speaker's Reference and Semantic Reference," in *Contemporary Perspectives in the Philosophy of Language,* ed. P.A. French et al. (University of Minnesota Press, 1977), pp. 6-27.

19. David Wiggins, *Sameness and Substance* (Oxford University Press, 1980).

"Just the Facts, Ma'am!"

NELSON GOODMAN

The terms "convention" and "conventional" are flagrantly and intricately ambiguous. On the one hand, the conventional is the ordinary, the usual, the traditional, the orthodox as against the novel, the deviant, the unexpected, the heterodox. On the other hand, the conventional is the artificial, the invented, the optional as against the natural, the fundamental, the mandatory. Thus we may have unconventional conventions (unusual artifices) and conventional nonconventions (familiar facts). The two uses of "convention" are not only different but almost opposite—yet not quite so; for to say that something is usual carries some suggestion that there are less usual alternatives; and what is mandatory, without alternatives, is usual.

Philosophers have been primarily concerned with convention as fabricated form imposed on uninterpreted content. Sometimes they aim at clearing away artifice to discover pure fact, sometimes simply at distinguishing the contributions of convention and of content. But the conventional as the usual, the habitual, cannot be dismissed as merely a popular usage that occasions frequent confusion, for it plays a major role in some theoretical contexts. For instance, in a recent paper on literary theory the author writes: "In this essay, 'conventions' refers to *manifestations of shared practices.*"[1] But I shall begin by considering convention as contrasted with content, the conventional as the optional or artificial as contrasted with the mandatory or factual.

Consider the motion of the moon. The moon rotates in that its orientation to the sun changes in a certain regular way, but it is fixed on its axis in that its orientation to the earth never changes. Does it rotate or not, then? Well, Yes and No. If that seems self-contradictory, we like to say that the moon rotates relative to the sun but not relative to the earth. But this is a somewhat deceptive way of speaking; for to say that something "moves relative to" something else is not to impute any motion to it at all. To say that the moon rotates relative to the sun is entirely compatible with saying that the sun revolves about a fixed moon. And to say that the moon does not rotate relative to the earth is entirely compatible with the earth's revolving about a rotating moon, as well as with saying that both earth and moon remain at rest. So perhaps to avoid giving a false impression, one should say simply that different aspects of the moon face the sun at different times; and that the same aspect of the moon faces the earth at all times. No more about rotation, rest, revolution; no more indeed about motion. Motion disappears from the realm of fact. And that should have been expected from the start, when the question "Does the moon rotate or not?" is answered by "That depends upon what we take as frame of reference." It depends upon what we do; we *make* the moon rotate or stand still. Motion is optional, a matter of convention, of fabrication imposed upon what we find.

But, then, what *is* found? The size and shape of the moon vary, it seems, according to the speed and direction of its motion. Thus since motion is a matter of convention, so are size and shape, and these also must be subtracted from fact. And of course any description in terms of the sun, moon, earth, etc. is conventional in that there are alternative equally legitimate versions in terms of other concepts. Organization into these familiar units, like the organization of stars into constellations, is optional.[2] All fact threatens to evaporate into convention, all nature into artifice.

You are likely not to go along with this but to protest: "How can there be no fact, no content, but only alternative ways of describing nothing? Surely there must be something that is described, however many different ways there are of describing it. There must be some line between what there is and how we describe it."

Quite so. The two statements about the moon are alternatives in that they describe something in common: that they are about the same objects, that they agree with certain observations, measurements, and principles, that they are in some way descriptive of the same facts. Yet these objects, observations, measurements, principles are themselves conventional; these facts are creatures of their descriptions. Two versions are "of the same facts" to the extent that they share some terms, comprise some identical or kindred concepts, can be translated into one another. All convention depends upon fact, yet all fact is convention.

Is the distinction between convention and fact, then, indispensable but meaningless? Rather, I think the distinction is itself conventional. That, of course, is meaningless if the distinction between convention and fact is meaningless. And if all facts are conventions and all conventions are facts, how can the distinction be meaningful, especially for a hard-boiled extensionalist?

Consider for a moment the terms "immediate predecessor" and "immediate successor" as applied to the integers, or to the clockwise series of minute marks on a watch face. Every integer, or every mark, is both an immediate predecessor and an immediate successor, yet the distinction between "immediate predecessor" and "immediate successor" does not vanish. For they are not categorical terms sorting a realm into different classes, but relational terms. So also for the terms "rest" and "motion". They do not sort bodies into classes; all bodies are at rest and in motion. And so also for "conventional" and "factual." They do not sort statements or versions into classes but relate versions to each other.

In other words, two terms that apply to exactly the same things may have parallel compounds that apply to very different things. The pairs of terms just discussed are cases of what I have elsewhere explained as difference in meaning through difference in secondary extensions. Although all centaurs are unicorns and all unicorns are centaurs, simply because there are no centaurs and no unicorns, still "centaurs" and "unicorns" differ in meaning in that certain parallel compounds of them are not coextensive; for example, not all centaur pictures (or descriptions)—indeed very few—are also unicorn pictures or descriptions.[3] Likewise, while "immediate predecessor" and "immediate successor" are coextensive because both apply to all integers, still "immediate predecessor of the integer 5" and "immediate successor of the integer 5" name very different things. Again, while all bodies are both in motion and at rest, "moves relative to the earth" and "is at rest relative to the earth" do not apply to all the same things. And while "factual" and "conventional" are coextensive, applying to all versions, "factual relative to version V" and "conventional relative to version V" are not.

If we are asked under what circumstances an integer is immediate successor to another, we can readily reply that the immediate successor is that integer plus one. But if we are asked to explain under what circumstances one of two bodies moves relative to another, we may say, for the sun and the earth for example, "If the sun is fixed, the earth moves; if the sun moves, the earth is fixed." But the apparent conditionalization in the two clauses is specious. Compare such a sentence as "If the black horse wins, I'm rich; if the white horse wins, I'm broke," where each antecedent is true or false according to which horse wins. In contrast, since unrelativized statements of motion are incomplete, the antecedents "the sun is fixed" and "the sun moves" are vacuous. We cannot determine whether the earth moves or is fixed by finding out whether the sun is fixed or moves, for the sun and the earth and all other bodies are both fixed and moving. A slightly different, familiar formulation runs: "On the assumption that the sun is fixed, the earth moves; on the assumption that the sun moves, the earth is fixed." Plainly this is no better, for the "assumptions," like the antecedents before, are vacuous. All this may not dispel a dogged conviction that nevertheless, in some sense or other, if the sun is taken as fixed, the earth moves, while if the sun is taken as moving, the earth is fixed. Putting it this way may seem to be going from bad to worse. For what does "taken as" mean? We cannot take hold of the sun or the earth and keep it still or give it a push to get it moving. And how can taking one body as fixed or moving make another revolve or stop? But when "taken as" is read as "plotted as" (under a given system) and associated adjustments are made, we have something like "When the sun is plotted as a point, the earth is to be plotted as a surrounding closed curve; when the sun is plotted as a closed curve, the earth is to be plotted as a surrounded point." "Plotting" may be broadened here to include mathematical or verbal description. The faults of our former proposals vanish. Apparent talk of motion turns out to be talk of diagrams, descriptions, mathematical functions, versions.

Diagrams or other versions under a given system, differing only through what is taken as fixed, are alternatives, optional, conventional. Furthermore, a system of plotting whereby whatever is taken as fixed is shown as a point, and whatever is taken as moving is shown as a path, is itself conventional—one among alternative systems, each admitting various versions.

But what has become of "the facts"? What are all these versions versions of? You may feel like the inspector in the radio series who tires of talk and keeps insisting "Just the facts, ma'am!" But all that can be done to comply with a demand to say what the versions are versions *of* is to give another version. Each version tells what "the facts" are, but the several versions are at odds with each other. How can the earth at the same time stand still, revolve around the sun, and move in countless other ways? How can divergent diagrams or versions be of the same facts, the same world? They must be either of no world or of different worlds. There must be many worlds if any.

That may suggest to you that we have taken leave, if not of our wits, at least of everyday experience and ordinary discourse. Let's get back to solid ground. A friend of mine was stopped by an officer of the law for driving 56 miles an hour. She argued, "But officer, taking the car ahead of me as fixed, I was not moving at all." "Never mind that," replied the officer, "You were going 56 miles an hour along the road, and (as he stamped his foot) this is what is fixed." "Oh, come now, officer; surely you learned in school that this road as part of the earth is not fixed at all but is rotating rapidly eastward on its axis. Since I was driving westward, I was going slower than those cars parked over there." "O.K., lady, I'll give them all tickets for speeding right now—and you get a ticket for parking on the highway."

Where does this leave us? If everything is the way it is taken to be, and anything can be correctly taken in all sorts of opposing ways, are we condemned to chaos? No. For despite Bruno, and the speeder's sophistry, the officer was of course right in the first place. Although nothing is absolutely fixed or moving, and although whether it is fixed or how it moves depends upon how it is taken, that in turn depends upon context, circumstances, purpose. Where cars on the highway are concerned, the earth is taken as fixed, and the ticket for speeding is deserved. In other contexts the earth is rotating and revolving; we use an alternative version.

Almost always some *stance* or other is adopted. Merely noting that many alternative versions can be constructed does not provide us with any. We have to hold some things steady for a while as a working basis. Along with the recognition that there is no fixed distinction between fact and convention must go the recognition that nevertheless there is almost always *some* distinction or other between fact and convention—a transient distinction drawn by the stance adopted at the time. Adoption of a stance, as we have seen, turns a relational term into a categorical one: designation of an integer as origin divides the class of integers into origin, an immediate predecessor, an immediate successor, and all other integers; designation of certain bodies as fixed may sort other bodies into the fixed and the moving; designation of certain statements as mandatory may classify other statements as mandatory or optional. A shift in stance effects a re-sorting. The Copernican revolution constituted such a shift. It did not so much change cosmology to fit the facts as transform the facts by changing stance from earth to sun.

Although a stance may be taken anywhere, and shifted often and without notice, it is not arbitrary. Most of our stances and shifts of stance are habitual, instilled by practice. We commonly take the earth as fixed in describing the motion of a plane, but on an airplane we automatically take the plane as fixed in describing the motions of the cabin crew. Where a choice of stance is more deliberate, it may involve complex considerations of simplicity, convenience, suitability to context, efficacy for a purpose, and accessibility by those we must communicate with. Taking the tip of a fly's wing as fixed in describing the motion of bodies in the solar system would presumably fail on all these counts.

In sum, I have been arguing such obvious points as that there is no firm distinction between fact and convention, but that that distinction is very important; that the line between fact and convention shifts often and may be drawn anywhere but is not capricious; that when a convention (as option) becomes a convention (as the usual), it thus tends to become factual; and that rather than the facts determining how we take them, how we take them determines the facts—but that we had better be careful how we take them.

In a recent review of Italo Calvino's novel *Mr. Palomar* Michael Wood puts it more poignantly:

> A fact is what won't go away, what we cannot *not* know, as Henry James remarked of the real. Yet when we bring one closer, stare at it, test our loyalty to it, it begins to shimmer with complication. Without becoming less factual, it floats off into myth. Mr. Palomar looks at the sky, the lawn, the sea, a girl, giraffes, and much more. He wants only to observe, to learn a modest lesson from creatures and things. But he can't. There is too much to see in them, for a start. . . . And there is too much of himself and his culture in the world he watches anyway: the world is littered with signs of our needs, with mythologies.[4]

Readers wanting more particular applications of what I have been saying should have no trouble working some out. Getting the facts straight is easy enough so long as we bear in mind that the facts are paradoxical.

Notes

1. Steven Mailloux, "Rhetorical Hermeneutics," *Critical Inquiry* 11 (1985): 638, n. 5.

2. See further Nelson Goodman, *Of Mind and Other Matters* (Harvard University Press, 1984), pp. 40-42.

3. See Nelson Goodman, *Problems and Projects* (Hackett, 1972), pp. 221-238.

4. Michael Wood, "Theory with a Wife," *The London Review of Books* 7 (3 October 1985), p. 17.

The Relativity of Fact
and the Objectivity of Value

CATHERINE Z. ELGIN

Fact and value purport to be polar opposites: facts being absolute, material, objective, and impersonal; values relative, spiritual, subjective, and personal; facts being verifiable by the rigorous, austere methods of science; values being subject to no such assessment. The facts, they say, don't lie. So every factual disagreement has a determinate resolution. Whether barium is heavier than plutonium is a question of fact, and whatever the answer, there are no two ways about it. Values, if they don't precisely lie, are thought perhaps to distort. So evaluative disputes may be genuinely irresolvable. Whether, for example, a Van Gogh is better than a Vermeer might just be a matter of opinion. And on matters like these everyone is entitled to his own opinion. Such is the prevailing stereotype.

I believe that stereotype ought to be rejected, for it stifles our understanding of both fact and value. Far from being poles apart, the two are inextricably intertwined: the demarcation of facts rests squarely on considerations of value, and evaluations are infused with considerations of fact. So factual judgments are not objective unless value judgments are, and value judgments are not relative unless factual judgments are. I want to suggest that tenable judgments of both kinds are at once relative and objective.[1]

First, let's look at the facts. When we proclaim their independence from and indifference to human concerns, we forget that we are the ones who set and enforce the standards for what counts as a fact. We stipulate: "a thing cannot both be and not be"; or "no entity is without identity"; or "whatever is is physical." In effect we decree that whatever fails to satisfy our standards hasn't got what it takes to be a fact.

At the same time we arrange for our standards to be met. We construct systems of categories that settle the conditions on the individuation of entities and their classification into kinds. Thus, for example, we devise a biological taxonomy according to which a dachshund is the same kind of thing as a Doberman, but a horse is a different kind of thing from a zebra.

For all their clarity scientific examples may mislead. We are apt to think that constructing a biological taxonomy is simply a matter of introducing terminology for what is already the case. Then prior to our categorization dachshunds and Dobermans were already alike; horses and zebras, already different. The problem is that any two things are alike in some respects and different in others. So likeness alone is powerless to settle matters of categorization. In classing dachshunds and Dobermans together, horses and zebras apart, we distinguish important from unimportant similarities. That is, we make a value judgment.

The selection of significant likenesses and differences is not, in general, whimsical. It is grounded in an appreciation of why a particular classificatory scheme is wanted, and this, in turn, depends on what we already believe about the subject at hand. If our goal is to understand heredity, for example, it is reasonable to group together animals that interbreed. Then despite their obvious differences dachshunds and Dobermans belong together, and despite their blatant similarities horses and zebras belong apart.

More general considerations come into play as well. If our system is to serve the interests of science, the cognitive values and priorities of science must be upheld. Membership in its kinds should be determinate and epistemically accessible. There should be no ambiguity and no (irresolvable) uncertainty about an individual's membership in a kind. The classification should be conducive to the formulation and testing of elegant, simple, fruitful generalizations and should perhaps mesh with other scientific classifications of the same and adjacent domains. In constructing a system of categories suitable for science, then, we make factual judgments about what the values of science are and how they can be realized.

Science streamlines its categories in hopes of achieving exceptionless, predictive, quantitative laws. Narrative has quite different ends in view, being concerned with the particular, the exceptional, the unique. So schemes suited to narrative enterprises exhibit different features from those suited to science. Scientific vices—ambiguity, imprecision, immeasurability, and indeterminacy—are often narrative virtues.[2] The complex characterization of the emotional life that we find, for example, in the novels of Henry James requires a baroque conceptual scheme whose involuted categories intersect in intricate and subtle ways. And equally complex categories may be required to achieve the sort of understanding that biographers, historians, psychoanalysts, and serious gossips strive to achieve.

A category scheme provides the resources for stating various truths and falsehoods, for exhibiting particular patterns and discrepancies, for drawing specific distinctions, for demarcating conceptual boundaries. Purposes, values, and priorities are integral to the design. They constitute the basis for organizing the domain in one way rather than another. And the acceptability of any particular scheme depends on the truths it enables us to state, the methods it permits to employ, the projects it furthers, and the values it promotes. Together these constitute a system of thought. A failure of the components to mesh undermines the system, preventing it from doing what it ought to do.

We design category schemes with more or less specific purposes in mind and integrate into the scheme such values and priorities as we think will serve those purposes. But the values that our schemes realize are not always or only the ones we intend to produce. Some are simply mistakes; others, inadvertent holdovers from prior systems; yet others, unintended by-products of features we intentionally include. When pregnancy and aging are classified as medical conditions, they come to be considered and treated as diseases or disabilities—as deviations from a state of health. If Marx is right, the values of the ruling class are invisibly embedded in the social and economic categories of a society. And my students are convinced that a fundamental truth is revealed by the fact that witchcraft comes just after philosophy in the Library of Congress classification system.

As a first approximation, facts are what answer to true sentences. And different systems produce different truths. It is a truth of physics, not of botany, that copper is lighter than zinc. This alone does not lead to relativity, for such systems may complement one another or be indifferent to one another. Relativity emerges when systems clash—when what is true according to one system is false according to another. Evolutionary taxonomy so groups animals that crocodiles and lizards are close relatives; crocodiles and birds, distant ones. Cladistic classification shows crocodiles and birds to be close; crocodiles and lizards distant. Each system divulges some affinities among animals and obscures others. Neither invalidates the other. So whether it is a fact that crocodiles and lizards are closely related depends on a choice of system. According to one system any violation of the law is a crime; according to another only serious violations—felonies—are crimes. So whether spitting on the sidewalk is a crime depends on which system is in use.

According to one medical classification, health is the absence of disease; according to another, health is the absence of disease or disability. So whether a congenital defect renders a person unhealthy depends on which system is in effect. A single domain can be organized in a multitude of ways, while different schematizations may employ a single vocabulary. So under one schematization a given sentence—say, 'Spitting on the sidewalk is a crime'—comes out true; under another it comes out false. Truth then is relative to the system in effect.

Still, facts are objective. For once the system is in place, there is no room for negotiation. Events that are simultaneous relative to one frame of reference are successive relative to another. But it is determinate for each frame of reference whether given events are successive or simultaneous. Similarly, although some psychologistic systems consider neuroses to be mental illnesses and others do not, once a system is chosen there is a fact of the matter as to whether a compulsive handwasher is mentally ill.

Such objectivity might seem spurious if we can switch frameworks at will. What is true according to one framework is false according to another. So can't we simply choose our facts to fit our fantasy? There are at least two reasons why we can't. The first is that rightness requires more than truth.[3] We need to employ an appropriate framework—one that yields the right facts. For example, the fact that someone went to Choate neither qualifies nor disqualifies him for a federal judgeship. So a classification of candidates according to their secondary schools is inappropriate, even if it would enable us to choose the candidate we want. Correctness requires that the facts we appeal to be relevant. Psychoanalytic categories are powerless to settle the issue of criminal insanity because they mark the wrong distinctions. People who cannot be held criminally liable for their actions are supposed to be, in some important respect, different from the rest of us. And the categories in question reveal no difference. For they characterize everyone's behavior in terms of motives and desires the agent can neither acknowledge nor control. So the facts that psychoanalytic theory reveals do not suit the purposes of the criminal court: they do not discriminate the class of criminally insane. Rightness of categorization thus depends on suitability to a purpose. And an aspiring lepidopterist whose collection consists of larvae seems to have missed the point. Lepidopterists concentrate on mature forms—they collect butterflies, not caterpillars. Although biologists class butterflies and caterpillars together, butterfly collectors do not. Rightness here requires fit with past practice. The fellow fails as a lepidopterist because he employs radically nontraditional categories in selecting specimens for his collection.

Moreover, even though we construct the categories that fix the facts, we cannot construct whatever we want. If we take the notion of construction seriously, this will come as no surprise. Although we make all manner of inventions, we can't make a nonfattening Sacher Torte, a solar-powered subway, or a perpetual-motion machine. And although we design programs that endow computers with amazing abilities, we can't get a computer to translate a natural language or beat a grand master at chess.

Some of these incapacities are irremediable; others will eventually be overcome. My point in mentioning them is to emphasize that construction is something we do, and we can't do everything we want. Our capacities are limited, and our aspirations often interfere with one another. So there is no reason to think that we can convert any fantasy into fact by designing a suitable system. Plainly we cannot.

In constructing a political system, for example, we'd like to maximize both personal liberty and public safety. We'd like, that is, to arrange for as many actions as possible to fall under the predicate 'free to . . .' and as many harms as possible to fall under the predicate 'safe from . . . .' But we can't maximize both at once. The cost of security is a loss of liberty, and the cost of liberty, a risk of harm. With the freedom to carry a gun comes the danger of getting shot. So we have to trade the values of liberty and safety off against each other to arrive at a system that achieves an acceptable level of both.

In constructing a physicalistic system we'd like all the magnitudes of elementary particles to be at once determinate and epistemically accessible. But this is out of the question. For although we can measure either the position or the momentum of an electron, we can't measure both at once.

In building a system of thought we begin with a provisional scaffolding made of the (relevant) beliefs we already hold, the aims of the project we are embarked on, the liberties and constraints we consider the system subject to, and the values and priorities we seek to uphold. We suspend judgment on matters in dispute. The scaffolding is not expected to stand by itself. We anticipate having to augment and revise it significantly before we have an acceptable system. Our initial judgments are not comprehensive; they are apt to be jointly untenable; they may fail to serve the purposes to which they are being put or to realize the values we want to respect. So our scaffolding has to be supplemented and (in part) reconstructed before it will serve.

The considered judgments that tether today's theory are the fruits of yesterday's theorizing. They are not held true come what may but are accorded a degree of initial credibility because previous inquiry sanctioned them. They are not irrevisable, but they are our current best guesses about the matter at hand. So they possess a certain inertia. We need a good reason to give them up.[4]

System-building is dialectical. We mould specific judgments to accepted generalizations, and generalizations to specific judgments. We weigh considerations of value against antecedent judgments of fact. Having a (partial) biological taxonomy that enables us to form the generalization "like comes from like"--that is, progeny belong to the same biological kind as their parents—we have reason to extend the system so as to classify butterflies and caterpillars as the same kind of thing. Rather than invoke a more superficial similarity and violate an elegant generalization, we plump for the generalization and overlook obvious differences.

Justification is holistic. Support for a conclusion comes, not from a single line of argument, but from a host of considerations of varying degrees of strength and relevance. What justifies the categories we construct is the cognitive and practical utility of the truths they enable us to formulate, the elegance and informativeness of the accounts they engender, the value of the ends they promote. We engage in system-building when we find the resources at hand inadequate.[5] We have projects they do not serve, questions they do not answer, values they do not realize. Something new is required. But a measure of the adequacy of a novelty is its fit with what we think we already know. If the finding is at all surprising, the background of accepted beliefs is apt to require modification to make room for it, and the finding may require revision to be fitted into place. A process of delicate adjustments occurs, its goal being a system in wide reflective equilibrium.[6]

Considerations of cognitive value come into play in deciding what modifications to attempt. Since science places a premium on repeatable results, an observation that cannot be reproduced is given short shrift, while one that is readily repeated may be weighted so heavily that it can undermine a substantial body of theory. And a legal system that relies on juries consisting of ordinary citizens is unlikely to favor the introduction of distinctions so recondite as to be incomprehensible to the general public.

To go from a motley collection of convictions to a system of considered judgments in reflective equilibrium requires balancing competing claims against one another. And there are likely to be several ways to achieve an acceptable balance. One system might, for example, sacrifice scope to achieve precision; another trade precision for scope. Neither invalidates the other. Nor is there any reason to believe that a uniquely best system will emerge in the long run. To accommodate the impossibility of ascertaining both the position and the momentum of an electron, drastic revisions are required in our views about physics. But which ones? A number of alternatives have been suggested. We might maintain that each electron has a determinate position and a determinate momentum at every instant, but admit that only one of these magnitudes can be known. In that case science is committed to the existence of things that it cannot in principle discover. Or we might contend that the magnitudes are created in the process of measurement. Then an unmeasured particle has neither a position nor a momentum, and one that has a position lacks momentum (for the one measurement precludes the other). Physical magnitudes are then knowable because they are artifacts of our knowledge-gathering techniques. But from the behavior of particles in experimental situations nothing follows about their behavior elsewhere. Yet a third option is to affirm that a particle has a position and affirm that it has a momentum, but deny that it has both a position and a momentum. In that case, however, we must alter our logic in such a way that the conjunction of individually true sentences is not always true. That science countenances nothing unverifiable, that experiments yield information about what occurs in nature, that logic is independent of matters of fact—such antecedently reasonable theses are shown by the findings of quantum mechanics to be at odds with one another. Substantial alterations are thus required to accommodate our theory of scientific knowledge to the data it seeks to explain. Although there are several ways of describing and explaining quantum phenomena, none does everything we want. Different accommodations retain different scientific desiderata. And deciding which one to accept involves deciding which features of science we value most and which ones we are prepared, if reluctantly, to forego. "Unexamined electrons have no position" derives its status as fact from a judgment of value—the judgment that it is better to construe magnitudes as artifacts of measurement than to modify classical logic, or commit science to the truth of claims it is powerless to confirm, or to make any of the other available revisions needed to resolve the paradox.

Pluralism results. The same constellation of cognitive and practical objectives can sometimes be realized in different ways, and different constellations of cognitive and practical objectives are sometimes equally worthy of realization. A sentence that is right according to one acceptable system may be wrong according to another.

But it does not follow that every statement, method, or value is right according to some acceptable system. Among the considered judgments that guide our theorizing are convictions that certain things—for example, affirming a contradiction, ignoring the preponderance of legal or experimental evidence, or exterminating a race—are just wrong.

Such convictions must be respected unless we find powerful reasons to revise them. And there is no ground for thinking that such reasons are in the offing. So it is not the case that anything goes.

Nor does it follow that systems can be evaluated only by standards that they acknowledge. An account that satisfies the standards it sets for itself might rightly be faulted for being blind to problems it ought to solve, for staking out a domain in which there are only trivial problems, for setting too low standards for itself. An inquiry that succeeds by its own lights may yet be in the dark.

So far I have argued for the value ladenness of facts. I developed a scientific example in some detail, because science is considered a bastion of objectivity. If scientific facts can be shown to be relative and value laden, there is a strong *prima facie* case for saying that relativity and value ladenness do not undermine objectivity. Then, if the objectivity of normative claims is to be impugned, it must be on other grounds.

I want to turn to questions of value. Not surprisingly, I contend that value judgments are vindicated in the same way as factual judgments. Indeed, normative and descriptive claims belong to the same systems of thought and so stand or fall together. Still, some systems seem more heavily factual; others, more heavily evaluative. For now I will concentrate on the latter.

In constructing a normative category scheme, as in constructing any other scheme, we are guided by our interests, purposes, and the problem at hand. Together these factors organize the domain, so that certain considerations are brought to the fore. In restructuring zoning laws, for example, it is advisable to employ consequentialist categories. For we need the capacity to tell whether things would in fact improve if the building code were altered in one way or another. We need, then, the capacity to classify and to evaluate in terms of outcomes. If we are concerned with developing moral character, it may be advisable to use predicates that can be applied with reasonable accuracy in self-ascription. For the capacity for self-scrutiny is likely to be valuable in moral development.

For like cases to be treated alike the evaluations yielded by a moral or legal system must be coherent, consistent with one another, and grounded in the relevant facts. Fairness and equity are demanded of such a system; arbitrariness and caprice are anathemas to it. So logical and evidential constraints are binding on evaluation as well as on description.

The problems we face and the constraints on their solution often have their basis in the facts. Whether, for example, we ought to perform surgery to prolong the life of a severely defective newborn becomes a problem only when we acquire the medical resources to perform such surgery. Prior to the development of the medical techniques the question was moot. There was no reason to require a moral code to provide an answer. So a moral problem arises in response to changes in the facts.

Our previously acceptable moral code may never have needed, and so never have developed, the refinements required to handle the new case. Unanticipated facts can thus put pressure on a system by generating problems it cannot (but should) solve, thus yielding inconsistent evaluations or producing counterintuitive verdicts. Values that do not ordinarily clash may do so in special circumstances. Typically the physician can both prolong the lives of her patients and alleviate their pain. But not always. So a moral system that simply says she ought to do both is inadequate. It does not tell her how to proceed when the realization of one value interferes with the realization of the other. Our values then need to be reconsidered. In the reconception previously accepted conclusions are called into question, competing claims adjudicated, a new balance struck. Our goal again is a system of considered judgments in reflective equilibrium. Achieving that goal may involve drawing new evaluative and descriptive distinctions or erasing distinctions already drawn, reordering priorities or imposing new ones, reconceiving the relevant facts and values or recognizing new ones as relevant. We test the construction for accuracy by seeing whether it reflects (closely enough) the initially credible judgments we began with. And we test it for adequacy by seeing whether it realizes our objectives in theorizing. An exact fit is neither needed nor wanted. We realize that the views we began with are incomplete, and we suspect that they are flawed, while we recognize that our initial conception of our objectives is inchoate and perhaps inconsistent. So we treat our starting points as touchstones which guide but do not determine the shape of our construction.

Here, too, pluralism results, for the constraints on construction do not guarantee a unique result. Where competing considerations are about equal in weight, different tradeoffs might reasonably be made, different balances struck. If any system satisfies our standards, several are apt to do so.

In child rearing, for example, we regularly have to balance a concern for a child's welfare against the value of granting him autonomy. And responsible parents settle the matter differently, some allowing their children greater freedom, some less. A variety of combinations of permissions and prohibitions seem satisfactory, none being plainly preferable to the rest. It follows then that a single decision—say, to permit a child to play football—might be right or wrong depending on which acceptable system is in effect. Rightness is then relative to system.

But it does not follow that every act is right according to some acceptable system or other. It is irresponsible to permit a toddler to play with matches and overprotective to forbid a teenager to cross the street. From the fact that several solutions are right, it does not follow that none is wrong. Some proposed resolutions to the conflict between welfare and autonomy are plainly out of bounds.

Nor does it follow that to be right according to some acceptable system is to be right *simpliciter*. Rightness further requires that the system invoked be appropriate in the circumstances. Although my freshmen's papers would rightly be judged abysmal failures if evaluated according to the editorial standards of *The Journal of Philosophy*, those are clearly the wrong standards to use. To grade my students fairly, I must employ standards appropriate to undergraduate work. (Then only some of their papers are abysmal failures.)

Can we rest satisfied with the prospect of multiple correct evaluations? Disconcertingly, the answer varies. If the systems that produce the several evaluations do not clash, there is no difficulty. We easily recognize that an accurate shot by an opposing player is good from one point of view (excellence in playing the game) and bad from another (our partisan interest that the opposition collapse into incompetence). And there is no need to decide whether it is a good or bad shot all things considered.

In other cases multiplicity of correct evaluations may be rendered harmless by a principle of tolerance. We can then say that what is right according to any acceptable system is right. Thus one parent's decision on how best to balance paternalist and libertarian considerations in child rearing does not carry with it the commitment that all parents who decide otherwise are wrong. And one physician's decision on how to balance the value of alleviating pain against the value of prolonging life does not carry with it the commitment that all physicians who strike a different balance are wrong.

Tolerance is an option because the prescriptions for action apply to numerically distinct cases. So long as parents decide only for their own children, they can recognize that other parents might reasonably decide the same matters somewhat differently. Pluralism does not lead to paralysis here because the assignment of responsibility is such that conflicting right answers are not brought to bear on a single case.

Tolerance seems not to be an option, however, when systems dictate antithetical responses to a single case. For we must inevitably do one thing or another. The problem becomes acute in socially coordinated activity. If the several parties in a joint venture employ clashing systems, their contributions are likely to cancel each other out, diminishing the prospect of success. Although nothing favors the convention of driving on the right side of the road over that of driving on the left, leaving the choice to the individual driver would be an invitation to mayhem. We need then to employ a single system, even if the selection among acceptable alternatives is ultimately arbitrary.

In such cases, then, we invoke a metasystematic principle of intolerance. Even if there are several ways of equilibrating our other concerns, we mandate that an acceptable equilibrium has not been reached until a single system is selected. The justification for this mandate is the recognition that unanimity or widespread agreement is itself a desideratum that is sometimes worth considerable sacrifice to achieve.

To be sure, an intolerant system remains vulnerable to criticism, revision, and replacement by a better system. The argument for intolerance is simply that where divided allegiance leads to ineffectiveness, a single system must reign. Successors there can be, but no contemporaries.

In the cases I've spoken of so far, both tolerance and intolerance look like fairly easy options. We readily agree to be intolerant about rules of the road, not only because we appreciate the value of conformity in such matters but also because we recognize that nothing important has to be given up. It simply doesn't matter whether we drive on the left or on the right, so long as we all drive on the same side. And we readily tolerate a range of child-rearing practices, because so long as certain broad constraints are somehow satisfied, small differences don't much matter. The difference between a 10 PM curfew and a 10:30 one is unlikely to significantly affect a child's well-being. In such cases we can agree, or respectfully agree to disagree, precisely because no deeply held convictions are violated in the process.

Sometimes, however, conflicts run deep. Thus, the abortion problem arises because in an unwanted pregnancy, the value of personal autonomy clashes with the value of fetal life. Neither is trivial. So to achieve any resolution, a substantial good must be sacrificed. Each party to the dispute achieves equilibrium at a price the other is unwilling to pay: the one maintaining that even fetal life cannot compensate for the loss of liberty, the other maintaining that even liberty cannot compensate for the loss of fetal life. Nor can the parties civilly agree to disagree. For each is convinced that the position of the other is fundamentally immoral.

Both parties to the dispute can adduce powerful reasons to support their position. But neither has the resources to convince its opponents. Nor has anyone come up with a compromise that both sides can in good conscience accept.

The existence of such seemingly intractable problems might seem to support a subjective ethical relativism. Having found no objective way to resolve such dilemmas, we might conclude that all morality is relative to system, and the choice of a system is, in the end, subjective.

Without denying the difficulty that such problems pose I want to resist the slide into subjectivism. Our practice bears me out. Even in the face of widespread disagreement we don't treat such issues as subjective. If we did, we would probably be more charitable to those holding opposing views. How do we proceed?

Sometimes we deny that the problem remains unsolved. We contend that one of the positions, although still sincerely held, has actually been discredited. The holdouts, we maintain, overlook some morally relevant features of the situation or improperly weigh the relevant ones. This response may well be correct. Advocates of apartheid, however adamant, are simply wrong. And they remain wrong even if they are too ignorant, biased, or closed-minded to recognize it.

So the failure of an argument to convince its opponents may be due to defects in their understanding, not to weaknesses in the argument. This has its parallel in science. The inability of any argument to convince my accountant of the truth of the Heisenberg Uncertainty Principle does not discredit the objectivity of the principle; it discredits her claim to have mastered quantum mechanics.

Alternatively, we might concede that a question is unanswered without concluding that it is unanswerable. We then take it to be an outstanding problem for the relevant field of inquiry. All fields have such problems. And if our current inability to solve the problem of the origin of life does not impugn the objectivity of biology, our current inability to solve the problem of abortion should not impugn the objectivity of ethics. What such problems show is that more work remains to be done. This is no surprise.

The objectivity of ethics does not insure that we can answer every question. Neither does the objectivity of science. If a question is ill-conceived or just too difficult, or if our attempts are wrongheaded or unlucky, the answer may forever elude us. But that success is not guaranteed is just an epistemological fact of life.

Nor does objectivity insure that every properly conceived question has a determinate answer. So perhaps nothing determines whether the young man whom Sartre describes ought to join the Resistance or stay home and care for his aged mother.[7] If the relevant considerations are in fact equally balanced, either alternative is as good (or as bad) as the other. The choice he faces then is subjective. But this does not make ethics subjective. For to say that personal predilections are involved in deciding among equally worthy alternatives is quite different from saying that personal predilections are what make the alternatives worthy. Subjective considerations function as tiebreakers after the merit of the contenders has been certified by other means.

I have suggested that factual and evaluative sentences are justified in the same way. In both cases acceptability of an individual sentence derives from its place in a system of considered judgments in reflective equilibrium. Since equilibrium is achieved by adjudication, several systems are apt to be adequate. But since they are the products of different trade-offs, they are apt to disagree about the acceptability of individual sentences. So relativism follows from pluralism. Something that is right relative to one acceptable system may be wrong relative to another.

Still, the verdicts are objective. For the systems that validate them are themselves justified. The accuracy of such a system is attested by its ability to accommodate antecedent convictions and practices; its adequacy, by its ability to realize our objectives. Several applicable systems may possess these abilities, so several answers to a given question or several courses of action may be right. But not every system possesses them, so not every answer or action is right. The pluralism and relativism I favor thus do not lead to the conclusion that anything goes. If many things are right, many more remain wrong.[8]

Notes

1. Ruth Anna Putnam argues for a similar thesis in "Creating Facts and Values," *Philosophy* 60 (1985): 187-204.

2. Israel Scheffler, *Beyond the Letter* (London: Routledge and Kegan Paul, 1979), pp. 6-7.

3. Nelson Goodman, *Ways of Worldmaking* (Indianapolis: Hackett, 1978), pp. 109-140.

4. Nelson Goodman, "Sense and Certainty," in *Problems and Projects* (Indianapolis: Hackett, 1972), pp. 60-68.

5. But not only then. We may attempt to modify a working system out of curiosity—to see how it works and whether it can be made to work better.

6. Cf. Nelson Goodman, *Fact, Fiction, and Forecast* (Cambridge: Harvard University Press, 1984), pp. 65-68; John Rawls, *A Theory of Justice* (Cambridge: Harvard University Press, 1971); Catherine Z. Elgin, *With Reference to Reference* (Indianapolis: Hackett, 1983), pp. 183-193.

7. Jean Paul Sartre, *Existentialism and Humanism* (London: Methuen, 1968), pp. 35-37.

8. I am grateful to Israel Scheffler, Jonathan Adler, and William Lycan for comments on an earlier draft of this paper.

Post-Nietzschian Anthropology:
The Idea of Multiple Objective Worlds*

Richard A. Shweder

Kurt Vonnegut in his novel *Slaughterhouse Five* has some things to say about his education in relativism.

> I think of my education sometimes. I went to the University of Chicago for a while after the Second World War. I was a student in the department of anthropology. They taught me that nobody was ridiculous or bad or disgusting. Shortly before my father died he said to me—"You never wrote a story with a villain in it." I told him that was one of the things I learned in school after the war.

The aim of relativist teachings is to give permission to diversity and difference by justifying the permission it grants on the grounds of the coequality or noncomparability of divergent forms. I have tried to imagine myself listening in on a lecture promoting relativism as it might have been delivered forty years ago by one of Vonnegut's anthropological mentors.

As I imagine it, the mentor approaches his lecture anticipating that within the minds of his highly reflective modern audience resides unconsciously and comfortably a habit of mind called "ethnocentrism." "Ethnocentrism" is the belief that our ways, because they are ours, must be closer to truth, goodness, and beauty than are the ways of others. Forty years ago in academic circles "ethnocentrism" was thought to be a universal presumption of native thinking. Our mentor enters the lecture

*Parts of this essay were written while I was a John Simon Guggenheim Foundation Fellow and a Fellow at the Center for Advanced Study in the Behavioral Sciences. I am grateful for the financial support provided by the National Institute for Child Health and Human Development and by the Spencer Foundation. My thanks to Wayne C. Booth, G. David Greenstone, Haskell Levi, and Melford E. Spiro for their thoughtful commentary and to the members of the "Practical Reason" workshop at the University of Chicago for a stimulating discussion of the manuscript.

hall eager to raise to consciousness that presumption and to banish it through schooling.

So he begins his lecture with a challenging series of rhetorical questions: What is the proper language for human beings, English, Tamil, Chinese, or French? What is the proper diet for human beings, vegetarian or nonvegetarian? What is the proper mode of artistic expression, the surrealism of Dali, the cubism of Picasso, or the impressionism of Renoir?

It is a strong opening. A modern educated mind, even a relatively ethnocentric one, boggles at the presumptuousness of such questions; for, as our lecturer must have known, when we compare the diverse languages of the world or the diverse modes of artistic expression, we are not typically tempted to make overall judgments of which is better or which is worse. Rather we are tempted to respond that they are just different but in some sense equal, or perhaps that their differences are good for different things, and the different things they are good for are just different but in some sense equal. By stimulating in his audience a few relativistic intuitions the mentor has gotten his lecture off to a good start.

The lecture, as I imagine it, continues, at length, with a fascinating and detailed description of variations in human languages, musical forms, terminological classifications for kinsmen, preferences and aversions and taboos in food, and aesthetic standards and fashions for art, clothing, and hair style.

Finally the lecture concludes with the posit of a moral principle: there are no universally or uniformly valid (objective, binding, constraining, authoritative) requirements for what languages to speak or what foods to eat or what clothes to wear and so on. Others may speak Tamil or eat soured curds or wear kilts, etcetera, even if you don't!

Now I am confident that any thoughtful University of Chicago student in Vonnegut's era presented with that moral principle would have been up all night pondering the "etcetera"; and I suspect that for any thoughtful and liberal student engaged in "etcetera pondering" late at night it must have seemed but a short step to the idea that ethical injunctions, customary practices, and super-natural (i.e., meta-physical) beliefs are like the languages, foods, and aesthetic standards of human beings—different but equal. Others may have extramarital sex, circumcise their daughters at adolescence, or believe that "enthusiasm" is a heresy or that there is no random (or accidental) event, even if you do not!

It must have seemed an even shorter step to the conclusion that no one is "ridiculous or bad or disgusting," or wrong or deluded or confused, etcetera.

That conclusion, of course, is fallacious. Just because there is no single valid mode of artistic expression does not mean that any doodling with paint on canvas is a work of art or is entitled to our respect.

The fallacy can be stated in quite general terms: Just because there is no one uniform objective reality (constraint, foundation, Godhead, truth, standard) does not mean there are no objective realities (constraints, foundations, godheads, truths, standards) at all. The death of monotheism should not be confused with the death of god(s). Ontological atheism or subjectivism is not the only route into relativism. Polytheism or the idea of multiple objective worlds is the alternative.

Over the past several decades the practice of ridiculing with stock counterarguments certain fallacious interpretations and absurd exaggerations of the doctrine of relativism has become a customary recreational activity in a few scholarly disciplines (especially philosophy); and one of the favorite and easy targets is the burlesque claim that nothing is the same across cultures or that nothing can be ruled out as immoral or bad, etc. Perhaps the ridicule is deserved, and Vonnegut's teachers should have been more precise and thorough in tracing out the implications of their lectures.

Yet here I am forty years later, an anthropologist at The University of Chicago who thinks there may have been something important and valid (and perhaps even subtle) in their message. So by examining two major routes into relativism, ontological atheism (God is dead) and ontological polytheism (monotheism is dead), I am going to hazard to see if I can get that message right. (For a frontal assault on fallacies in relativistic thinking in anthropology see Spiro 1986; recent expositions, defenses, and critiques of relativism can be found in the volumes edited by Wilson 1970, Hollis and Lukes 1982, Shweder and LeVine 1984, Clifford and Marcus 1986, Fiske and Shweder 1986; also see Geertz 1984).

Seeking to get a message right, however, is not necessarily an innocent act; especially so when we live in a conflated world where for every truth there is some political (or personal) interest or end that may be served by drawing to it our attention or keeping it out of sight. The main aim of relativist doctrine in anthropology is to give permission to diversity and difference, by indicating why and when such permission ought to be granted. The truth in relativism is that there are times, not all times yet some times, when permission ought to be granted to diversity and difference. In drawing our attention to that truth by trying to be clearer about it, anthropology and other modern scholarly disciplines interested in relativism have in fact played a political role, which I shall discuss.

The Confrontation with Difference

For anthropologists the confrontation with diversity in belief, desire, and practice can be a radical one. Here is a short list of the things you can observe out there in the world of human beings if you look in the right places and with the right clearance: people hunting for witches, exorcising demons, propitiating dead ancestors, sacrificing animals to hungry gods, sanctifying temples, waiting for messiahs, scapegoating their sins, consulting the stars, decoding their dreams, flagellating themselves in public, prohibiting the eating of pork (or dog, or beef, or all swarming things except locusts, crickets, and grasshoppers), wandering on pilgrimage from one dilapidated shrine to the next, abstaining from sex on the day of the full moon, refusing to be in the same room with their wife's elder sister, matting their hair with cow dung, isolating women during menstruation, seeking salvation by meditating naked in a cave for several years, and so on and on.

Let us restrict our observations for the moment to one community in one part of the world. For some years I have been conducting research on moral development and moral reasoning in a Hindu temple town on the east coast of India among various Oriya Brahman subcastes and among various castes referred to as "scheduled" castes by the government of India ("scheduled" for affirmative action programs), referred to as "Harijans" ("children of God") by Mahatma Gandhi, and referred to as "chuuan" (unclean, polluted, untouchable) by the local Brahmans (see, e.g., Shweder, Mahapatra, and Miller 1987; Shweder and Much 1987; Shweder and Bourne 1984; Shweder 1985, 1986, 1987).

In all sorts of ways, although certainly not in all ways, Oriya Brahman belief, desire, and practice appear to be in contrast to our own. Eating beef is prohibited. Marriages are arranged. Dating and premarital sexual play are strictly forbidden. Widows may not remarry, and restrictions exist concerning the foods they are permitted to eat and the clothing they are permitted to wear. Menstruating women are not allowed to sleep in the same bed with their husband or enter the kitchen or engage in prayer or groom themselves or touch their children. Adult men prefer to eat their meals at home alone, and it is considered shameless for a husband and wife to eat together. Certain kinsmen, for example, a woman and her husband's elder brother and a man and his wife's elder sister, are not permitted in each other's presence. Children sleep in the same bed with a parent or grandparent (although not with a menstruating woman) until at least the age of six or seven years. Adult women are not allowed out of the house without permission. Untouchables are not allowed in the local temple, and no one can enter the temple for twelve days following a birth or death in the family. The corpse of an adult must be cremated, never buried, with the exception of a holy man, who must be buried, never cremated.

Each of those practices has associated with it a line of argumentation. For example, it is argued by Oriyas that so many people, including ancestral spirits, are affected in serious ways by the person you marry. How can the marriage decision possibly be left up to one young, vulnerable person driven by sex, passion, and infatuation?

Or it is argued that the human body is a temple with a spirit (what we call the self or the observing ego) dwelling in it, and it is a proper end in life to preserve the sanctity of the temple and keep it clean and pure. The body of a menstruating woman is impure. Hence she must stay at or be kept at a distance from all holy or sanctified ground, including all temples such as the body of her husband, the household prayer room and kitchen, and so on.

Each line of argumentation presupposes, makes use of, or culminates in several posits about what the world is like: people have souls, and they transmigrate in proportion to their sanctity; the body is a temple with a spirit dwelling in it; eating food is an oblation; you reap what you sow; nature is just, and received inequalities are a form of just desert; to be born a woman and to survive the death of your husband are indications of prior sin, which should be absolved before you die; ancestral spirits return to your wife's kitchen to be fed, and they will not accept food from your wife unless her caste status is appropriate, etc. Many residents in the temple town design, organize, and interpret their experiences guided by those conceptions of reality.

Confronted with such apparently different conceptions of reality and associated practices, anthropologists have reacted in one of three ways.

Some, let us call them the universalists, have tried to look beyond the differences and search for significant or deeper or more abstract points of similarity, while treating the diversity as merely apparent and the differences as trivial or unimportant or irrelevant.

Some, let us call them the developmentalists, have tried to see within the diversity a continuous or perhaps stagelike process of growth and adaptation, viewed as a battle between reason and superstition, education and ignorance, science and religion, enlightenment and dark-ness, secondary process thinking and primary process thinking, sophisti-cation and innocence, rationality and irrationality, modernity and tradi-tionalism.

Some, let us call them the relativists, have tried to give permission to the diversity by documenting the significance, relevance, and impor-tance (i.e., the genuineness) of the differences between apparently diver-gent forms, while arguing that not all differences should be ranked into higher and lower levels of development or adaptation.

In the eyes of their respective antagonists the relativists look "soft on superstition," the developmentalists appear "ethnocentric," and the universalists seem "colorless, vacuous, and banal"; the universalists (as the "late" Wittgenstein, an antagonist, might have put it) try to find the real artichoke by divesting it of its leaves.

Not being an antagonist interested in ridicule I prefer to demur to those epithets, especially since, in this case, it is not difficult to see something of value in all three types of responses. Each has its (partial) point within the terms of a well-known and powerful metaphysics of form (or conceptual architecture of likeness and difference), which I shall now tersely describe.

When it comes to thinking through the metaphysics of form, it is useful to start with the truism that no two things are identical, from which it follows inexorably that in some way any two things are differ-ent. The assertion of difference, however, raises the question "different in respect to what?" which presupposes a higher-order likeness. So it also follows that in some way any two things are alike. Any and all two things, it turns out upon reflection, are both different and alike.

Within that tidy conceptual structure for likeness and difference there are separate rooms, each with a view, for universalism, develop-mentalism, and relativism.

When the differences between things are trivial, unimportant, or irrelevant (that is, when what is true about the functioning of one thing is also true of the other things regardless of their differences), universal-ism is at a premium, and nonidentical things can, with profit, be treated as equivalent.

Yet sometimes the differences between things do matter, and noni-dentical things should not be treated as equivalent. The universals that unite the things are insufficient to explain their functioning; because of their differences the dynamics of their functioning is different, even though in other respects the things are alike.

When the differences between things matter in that way—because of their differences things function differently, even though in other ways they are alike—those differences are sometimes revelatory of progress or advance. This is especially true when the differences represent points or stages in the attainment of some adaptive equilibrium or some proper endstate. At such times developmentalism is at a premium.

Sometimes, however, the differences are significant, but neutral with respect to the issue of relative progress. This is especially true when they represent the existence of multiple equilibria or noncomparable endstates. At such times relativism is at a premium.

The merit of the relativistic stance, within the terms of that metaphysics of form, is that it gets us to recognize that there are cases of genuine and significant diversity that are not matters for developmental analysis, although not every case is such a case. And by that account it should be possible to construct a version of relativist doctrine relatively resistant to stock ridicule and misunderstanding.

In that version of the doctrine relativism becomes a type of explanation for diversity, in which it is argued that cases exist where differences are to be expected, because there is no authority worthy of universal respect defining *the* proper way to classify and understand reality or *the* proper ends of life or *the* proper way to design a society, etcetera. As we shall see later in this essay, different subtypes of relativist doctrine can be differentiated by examining the reasons and justifications adduced in support of that claim ("different but equal").

It is noteworthy that this version of relativist doctrine does not prohibit universals, although it does require the absence of any authority simultaneously worthy of universal respect and capable of specifying *the* proper way to understand and experience the world or *the* proper way to live. Relativism is perfectly compatible with the existence of authorities worthy of universal respect (for example, the logical principle of noncontradiction—"a thing cannot both be and not be"; or the moral principle of justice—"treat like cases alike and different cases differently") as long as those universal authorities are insufficient (they may be necessary) for drawing substantive conclusions about what to think or feel and how to live.

What a proper doctrine of relativism does claim is that to derive substantive conclusions of that sort (what to think or feel and how to live) one must *also* appeal presumptively to local authorities (scripture, communally held theories and assumptions about truth, beauty, and goodness) that are not entitled to universal respect. A proper doctrine of relativism, thus, must provide an account of the differences between the mandatory and the presumptive (discretionary) aspects of authority. And the doctrine must help us see why both aspects of authority, the mandatory and the presumptive, are necessary if we are to have practical guidance about how to think, feel, and live in the world.

For example, in some relativist accounts mandatory authority is equated with whatever can uniquely be induced from universally available experience or evidence or logically be deduced from undeniable first principles. Accordingly, according to that account there are major aspects of the authority of, say, the Old Testament or Darwin's origin story about the evolution of complex biological forms that are local or presumptive, for their first principles are not undeniable, and the evidence they powerfully interpret by means of their quite deniable assumptions can be powerfully reinterpreted from alternative conceptual starting points; or, at the very least, we must allow for that possibility.

In other words, the doctrine of relativism denies that it is the *sine qua non* of reason that its requirements converge or are uniform across space and time. According to the doctrine it is natural for human beings to be as different from each other as is allowed by their common rationality. Their common rationality is, after all, not all of their rationality but only that part that is common. Any total system of authority capable of giving guidance about what to believe or value or how to live will consist of interacting elements some of which are mandatory, common, or ecumenical and others of which are presumptive, variable, or denominational. In other words, and again, others may have two wives, or believe that all learning is reminiscence, or believe that human beings, "suspended between the angels and the beasts," descended from the angels, even if you don't believe so!

The story of relativism in anthropology, however, is not that simple. Complications arise because there are subtypes of relativist doctrine, each built on a somewhat different conception of the relevant state of mind (e.g., pretending that ___, fantasizing that ___, believing that ___) associated with the apparently alien ideas and practices of the "other." And each subtype of relativist doctrine is built, as well, on a somewhat different conception of the relationship between subjectivity and objectivity, interiority and exteriority, fantasy and reality, and imagining and witnessing in the interpretation of symbolic forms. Those complications are of main concern in the remainder of this essay.

Rationality, Realism, and the Interpretation of Symbolic Forms

Those complications arise because crosscutting the distinction among universalists, developmentalists, and relativists is an independent issue of interpretation and evaluation concerned with the question of the realism or rationality of "symbolic" forms. The issue concerns the proper way to attribute states of mind (e.g., pretending, believing, wishing) when interpreting and translating the "symbolic" forms of other peoples. For example, how are we to translate and interpret all those things people around the world say and do about witches, ghosts, and spirit possession? (See, e.g., Trevor-Roper 1967; Obeyesekere 1981; Malleus Maleficarum 1489; Shweder 1987.) What state of mind should we attribute to them (knowing? believing? pretending? imagining? wishing? hallucinating?), and why?

The answers given to that question divide the "God is dead" school for the interpretation of "symbolic" forms from schools of interpretive realism. That division roughly parallels the split between subjectivists and objectivists, emotivists and cognitivists, nonrationalists and rationalists. It is possible to be a relativist or universalist or developmentalist on either side of the divide, although in this essay I shall focus only on the two schools of relativism opposing each other across the emotivist versus cognitivist divide.

Before discussing the two sides of that divide, however, some terms and concepts need to be clarified concerning the interpretation of "symbolic" forms.

A "symbolic" form, just like many other "appearances" or "sensations" or "experiences" (e.g., a retinal image or a verbal utterance or a drawing on a pad) is a reality-posit. A reality-posit is a *representation* of a particular state of the world (e.g., "there is a unicorn in my garden") that functions as the content, the topic, the object, or the aim for any of the various states of the mind that we designate with such labels as fantasizing (that ___) or wishing (that ___) or believing (that ___) or perceiving (that ___) or remembering (that ___) or what have you. "Symbolic" forms are the reality-posits that fill in the "that" clause for a state of mind.

Just like many other "appearances-sensations-experiences," reality-posits are "symbolic" forms because they are about something else. Through their content reality-posits (e.g., "there is a unicorn in my garden") refer or point beyond themselves to another realm, that exteriorized framework that we call "reality" or the "world," connecting us to it by positing *of* it (as in fantasy or in memory or in belief) or positing *for* it (as in desire) a particular state of the realm.

A state of mind, on the other hand, is an interpretation or classification of the status (dream, fantasy, imagination, hallucination) of a reality-posit (e.g., "there is a unicorn in my garden") as a representational object or symbolic form. State of mind classifications are designed to interpret the nature of a reality-posit (e.g., seen "as if through a glass darkly"), the conditions of its occurrence (e.g., witnessed only while sleeping) or reproduction (e.g., brought to mind at will), its degree of availability as an experience to audiences of different kinds (e.g., witnessed only by me), and ultimately its source (e.g., it's only in the head).

States of mind (believing, fantasizing, wishing) can be postulated, but they cannot directly be viewed or known, which is why one of the most important things up for interpretation in the evaluation and classification of "symbolic" forms is the state of mind suggested by any particular reality-posit. How is this particular people's particular reality-posit (e.g., "people entering into compacts with the devil") to be translated? Is it indicative of a belief, a wish, a fantasy, a desire, and how can one tell? What is the difference, anyway, between, for example, perceiving that ___, believing that ___, imagining that ___, wishing that ___, etc., and how is it possible, if at all, to distinguish those reality-posits or "symbolic" forms that are realistic or rational or proportionate to "actual" states of the realm from those that are not?

The issue of the interpretation of the state of mind associated with any particular "symbolic" form or reality-posit is multileveled. First there is the problem of how to define the proper or ideal ratio of subjectivity to objectivity in reality-finding reality-posits, or in those rational or realistic reality-posits that are thought to be proportionate to or in graceful coincidence with actual states of the world.

Some claim that reality-posits that are rational or realistic or reality-finding are those in which subjectivity has been reduced to zero. That means that perfect rationality or realism (subjectivity set at zero) consists of a perspective-free ("unbiased") witnessing of the world. The idea is one of stepping completely out of your mind, personality, and position in the social order, so as to see the world the way it really is, as a thing in itself, uncontaminated and undistorted by projected traces of your intellectual point of view, wishes, desires, goals, emotions, and interests.

Others agree, but argue that since that is impossible, rationality and realism can never be achieved. As that argument goes, perspective-free perception is a God-like state of mind unattainable by human beings. Others argue that the least you can do is strive to be God-like, correcting for projections and distortions wherever possible. Still others argue that perhaps it is our prejudices that make it possible for us to see; perhaps our prejudices even make it possible for us to see some things as they really are.

Then there is the issue of how to define, label, and classify all the kinds and varieties of states of the mind (for a discussion of folk classifications of states of mind see D'Andrade 1983). Every state of mind (e.g., believing that ___, wishing that ___, perceiving that ___, remembering that ___, dreaming that ___) carries us through the here-and-now appearance of a "symbolic" form (e.g., the verbal utterance: my garden populated with unicorns) into the exteriorized framework (the reality or conceivable world) to which the posit refers.

But what states of mind are there, and how are they interrelated? Some argue, for example, that imagination is in contrast to perception, and that it is bad to confuse one with the other. Some argue that perception is a form of imagination (for example, that visual perception is a "construction," etc.), while others argue that imagination is a form of perception (for example, dreaming as the witnessing of a plane of reality). Still others argue both ways, and dialectically, for imaginative perception and perceptive imagination.

Finally there is the issue of how to identify, interpret, and translate the particular state of mind (wishing that ___, knowing that ___, believing that ___, pretending that ___, imagining that ___, etc.) suggested by any particular symbolic form, for example, to select a random illustration, the reality-posit "I am a witch."

What state of mind should we attribute to our neighbor in the sixteenth century when she confesses she is a witch? Is it a case of knowing that ___ ? Or is it a case of believing ___? Or pretending ___? Or wishing ___? Or dreaming ___? Or is it a case of knowing that ___ because of dreaming that ___? Or perhaps believing that ___ because of wishing that ___? And should that attribution, a sixteenth-century attribution about a sixteenth-century state of mind, be any different from the twentieth-century attribution we should make today about that twentieth-century state of mind? What if the reality-posit ("I am a witch") came in the form of a confession from our neighbor living today, and we had to make a twentieth-century attribution about a twentieth-century state of mind? Should that attribution be any different, and why?

The illustration, of course, is hardly random, for there has been within anthropology much controversy over the famous "witch question," and not surprisingly the issue remains unresolved. The question can be put this way: Cross-culturally and historically, why have so many accused witches confessed, even without torture, and why have so many of them appeared convinced of their own guilt?

Cultural anthropology will probably come to an end when it comes up with an incontestable answer to the witch question. Later in this essay I will develop a postpositivist rationalistic conception of so-called super-natural beliefs, which promotes the idea of reality-testing as a meta-physical (= super-natural) act and which implies that we consider answering the witch question (see above) this way: because they were witches. Perhaps that answer will help keep cultural anthropology alive for at least another generation.

So much for preliminaries. That crosscutting issue concerning the degree of rationality or realism of the states of mind associated with "symbolic" forms divides anthropological relativists into two camps.

There are the ontological atheists (subjectivist, emotivist, nonrationalist, "God is dead") who believe that symbolic forms or reality-posits are not uniform or homogeneous around the world because realities are creatively fabricated, invented, or "made up." Culture is interpreted as a case of imagining that ___. Like other products of the imagination it is "free" to vary.

Then there are the ontological polytheists (objectivist, cognitivist, rationalist, realist) who think that reality-posits are not uniform or homogeneous around the world because reality is not uniform or homogeneous. Culture is interpreted as a case of perceiving that ___ or understanding that ___ or appreciating that ___. According to the ontological polytheists the framework of reality is multiplex in disjoint planes, and it makes sense to interpret diversity as though there is more than one objective world.

Of course a third possibility exists. That third possibility is that reality is uniform or homogeneous, and that symbolic forms and reality-posits are not uniform and homogeneous around the world because not everyone is equally in touch with reality (see Spiro 1982, 1984; Gellner 1985). Thus, some peoples, it might be argued, cannot always tell the difference between wishing and believing or between imagining and perceiving, and in certain intellectual domains they confuse fantasy with reality and permit primary process thinking to become a prominent feature of their mental functioning.

It is the search for an alternative to that third hypothetical possibility (and its developmental and monistic implications) that unites relativists, spanning the divide between the ontological atheists ("God is dead"; reality is a fabrication) and the ontological polytheists ("monotheism is dead"; cultural variety illuminates the multiplicity of objective worlds). The aim of relativism is, after all, to find defensible ways, if there are any, to give permission to diversity.

To write the slogan "God is dead" is to invoke the very much alive spirit of Friedrich Nietzsche, and it is with Nietzsche that any story about ontological atheism ought to begin. Nietzsche was not a *cultural* relativist. He was too much of an existentialist and individualist for that. And one should not forget that it was Nietzsche who once described Asia as a "dreamy" place where they still do "not know how to distinguish between truth and poetry." Nevertheless, it is Nietzsche's conception of the nature of cultural things that has set the agenda for "modern" interpretations of the states of mind associated with symbolic forms. According to Nietzsche's conception reality-posits or symbolic forms have null-reference, for the realities they posit do not exist. Thus spake Zarathustra. Ontological atheism was born.

Thus Spake Nietzsche

Friedrich Nietzsche is not an acknowledged founding father of cultural anthropology, yet, far more than is realized, his way of thinking propagated and took over in modern anthropology (on the Nietzschian foundations of modern social and political consciousness see MacIntyre 1981). Around 1882 Nietzsche thought he had the answer to the "witch question." Many contemporary cultural anthropologists think he was right.

Nietzsche not only suspected (and regretted?) that God was dead. As a protopositivist, Nietzsche had doubts about the realism or rationality of all unperceived or unseen things (including God, witches, souls, sin, necessity, rights, values, and morality).

Positivism is empiricism, in its purest form. At the risk of oversimplification, it might be stated that the central doctrine of positivism is that only seeing is believing, and that, therefore, one should stick with appearances or experiences, for they are the only reality, while any other claim to knowledge is either tautology or metaphysical nonsense.

In his work *Human, All Too Human* Nietzsche, who flirted with positivism at various points in his writings, put it this way: "And what magnificent instruments of observation we possess in our senses. . . . Today we possess science precisely to the extent to which we have decided to *accept* the testimony of the senses—to the extent to which we sharpen them further, arm them, and learn to think them through. The rest is miscarriage and not-yet-science—in other words, metaphysics, theology, psychology, epistemology—or formal science, a doctrine of signs such as logic and that applied logic that is called mathematics. In them reality is not encountered at all, not even as a problem."

Nietzsche's answer to the witch question flows from his no-nonsense positivism: "Although the most acute judges of the witches, and even the witches themselves, were convinced of the guilt of witchery, the guilt nevertheless was non-existent." He goes on to say, shockingly, "It is thus with all guilt."

Nietzsche gives what might be called a "null-reference" answer to the witch question. While the reality-posit "I am a witch" has reference to an externalized frame containing "witches" as its content, the reality it posits is associated with a state of mind known as imagination and does not exist. Nietzsche then generalizes his null-reference argument to each and every case where the following two conditions hold: (a) a supposed objective-external yet invisible entity is invoked (e.g., natural rights) and (b) with respect to that unseen thing the self is supposed to be subordinate, bound, or guilty.

The gist of a null-reference argument goes something like this: when it comes to God, sin, morality, necessity, and witchery, there is nothing real "out there" in the nature of things to be guilty of or to be bound by. Thus, no objective basis exists for the subjective sense of being commanded by God; or for a feeling of sin; or for a pang of conscience; or for a perception of inevitability and necessity; or for the conviction that one is a witch. Such senses, feelings, pangs, perceptions, and convictions tell us nothing about the external world but much about phantoms that haunt the human mind.

Nietzsche reasons on. Moral obligations are phantoms, not objective facts out there waiting to be discovered through positive inquiry. As he puts it in one of his witty aphorisms: "being moral means being highly accessible to fear."

Similarly, belief in the God-phantom, sin-phantom, conscience-phantom, necessity-phantom, and witch-phantom is little more than slavish susceptibility to custom, suggestion, indoctrination, conformity, reward, or social pressure. At best, we believe the things we believe because the expression of those beliefs produces agreeable feelings in powerful or significant others who are the upholders of the phantom order. We certainly do not believe them because they are true, for there is nothing out there for them to be true of.

Enter the *Übermensch* (sometimes translated as "overman"; mocked by George Bernard Shaw as the "superman"), Nietzsche's ideal of the fully developed and mature autonomous individual. "Behind your thoughts and feelings, my brother, there stands a mighty ruler, an unknown sage—whose name is self. In your body he dwells; he is your body."

Thus spake Zarathustra. The self strives to realize its essential, objective, or inherent nature, which is to be self-caused or free. To be self-caused or free is to resist all external constraints, especially phantoms of the imagination disguised as cold necessity or objective truth.

The liberated individual (the *Übermensch*) seeks to rid its self of phantoms. It strives to manifest its deepest nature, the self's will to possess the power of total autonomous self-control (the so-called "will to power"). The *Übermensch* (who, ironically, in Nietzsche's account seems to be quite God-like) realizes that it is only it who is necessary and real, the creator through reification and projection of what it previously mistook for the discovery of the external constraints of reality.

Thus, according to Nietzsche, men and women are the makers of the reality before which they bow down as its slave. If the self is to authenticate its self and fully realize its nature (essential autonomy or self-creative freedom), apparent realities must be permanently transcended or, at least, repeatedly remade. Just as a "snake that cannot shed its skin perishes," so too perishes the self who cannot shed the "received wisdom" of the past and, so to speak, make its own mind up, for its self.

The *Übermensch* attains this-worldly transcendence. Looking through and penetrating the shroud of tradition, it sees and recognizes a terrible truth. At once aware that much that was supposed to be natural and real is merely a reified phantom of mind, it discards the shackles of convention, unencumbers itself of the yoke of tradition, and sets itself free. There in Nietzsche's conception of the *Übermensch* is born, perhaps reborn, existentialism's ego, the idea of a really real plane of ultimate self-determination existing prior to or outside of society, the idea of the creative source behind the phantom of custom-bound constraint. Later I will have more to say about Nietzsche's existentialism, and about his positivism, for he used them reciprocally to define one another.

God Is Dead: The Nietzschian Anthropology of Phantomlike Culture

Nietzsche's answer to the witch question has become, ironically, the "conventional wisdom" of modern anthropology. Prominent theorists of culture, who are in dispute about almost everything else, share with each other the Nietzschian assumption that tradition-based reality-posits are imaginary phantoms of mind. In general, "supernatural" entities, moral obligations, and society itself are presumed to have standing only as imposed or projected mental representations or symbolic forms (reality-posits); and the realities that are posited are viewed as either unreal, irreal, nonreal, or as real only as reality-posits.

Murdock (1980:54), for example, expresses the now common contemporary Nietzschian view when he states: "There are no such things as souls, or demons, and such mental constructs as Jehovah are as fictitious as those of Superman or Santa Claus (it is not Nietzsche's

Übermensch he has in mind, but rather the Superman who is able to bend steel in his bare hands). Neither ghosts nor gods exert the slightest influence on men and their behavior."

That Nietzschian null-reference argument is also forcefully reiterated by Schneider (1965:85-86): "There is no supernatural. Ghosts do not exist. Spirits do not in fact make storms, cause winds, bring illness or effect cures. The gods in the heavens do not really make the stars go around and neither do they decide each man's fate at his birth. Since there are no real ghosts, spirits, gods, and goddesses, it follows logically . . . that their real and true nature cannot decisively shape man's beliefs about them or the social institutions related to them. Man's beliefs about ghosts and spirits must be wholly formed by man himself. Whatever unity there is to man's beliefs about the supernatural derives, therefore, from the nature of man himself and not from the nature of the supernatural."

Of course, as Schneider was well aware in 1965, that news had not yet arrived in all circles, and over the centuries, in most circles where the news that God is dead had arrived, it had been strenuously resisted. That fact continues to lend great fascination to the problem of interpreting the state of mind associated with so-called supernatural reality-posits and symbolic forms.

Peoples whose symbolic forms posit gods, ghosts, spirits, or witches appear to live under the impression that there is something there for them to be mindful of. Their reality-posits have, thus, often been interpreted as instances of "believing that ___." Indeed, in those cultures where such symbolic forms exist the native who posits spirits does not seem indifferent to external reality referencing questions such as: What makes spirits angry? Can they invade a person's body? How can invading spirits be exorcised? (see Nuckolls 1986; Obeyesekere 1981; Shweder 1986, 1987). And if we go back not so far in the English and American historical traditions, those who believed in witches went out hunting for them in external reality, where they sometimes found them, occasionally roasting them alive when they had.

In Nietzsche's *Prologue* Zarathustra comes to a forest where he meets "an old man who had left his holy cottage to look for roots in the woods." " 'And what is a saint doing in the forest?' asked Zarathustra." The old man answered: "I make songs and sing them; and when I make songs I laugh, cry and hum: thus I praise God. With singing, crying, laughing and humming, I praise the god who is my god. But what do you bring us as a gift?"

The text goes on as follows: "When Zarathustra heard those words he bade the saint farewell and said: 'What could I have to give you? But let me go quickly lest I take something from you!' And thus they separated, the old man and the man, laughing as two boys laugh. But when Zarathustra was alone he spoke thus to his heart: 'Could it be possible? This old saint in the forest has not yet heard anything of this, that *God is dead.'* "

God is dead for contemporary anthropologists. The major measure of his fate is that almost all theory in contemporary anthropology designed to explain the origin and function of other people's reality-posits is made possible by a Nietzschian null-reference assumption.

Murdock and Schneider have already been quoted. You can tell that you are dealing with assumptions very deep within the anthropological worldview, very central to its web of belief, when George Peter Murdock and David M. Schneider end up in agreement. When it comes to the existence of gods, ghosts, witches, and demons, there is agreement.

Spiro (1982:53-55, 63; 1984), to cite one other leading culture theorist, also a Nietzschian spirit, adopts Murdock's and Schneider's identical line of reasoning and, with characteristic clarity, follows it to its logical limit. Spiro argues that it is precisely because ghosts, spirits, gods, and witches do not exist, the main significance of those ideas is that they are fanciful states of mind analogous to dreams-as-dreamt and other hallucinations in which "stimuli originating in the inner world are taken as objects and events in the outer world," and mental constructs or symbolic forms are taken for external reality. He wonders (1982:55) why it is that "the religious believer does not (like the awakened dreamer) awaken from his religious slumber and recognize that the mythico-religious world exists not in some external reality, but rather in the inner reality of the mind."

As Murdock's, Schneider's, and Spiro's arguments suggest, the "received wisdom" of the day in anthropology is founded on Nietzsche's null-reference solution to the problem of interpreting the state of mind associated with symbolic forms. Indeed, so commonplace is Nietzschian thinking among anthropologists that it has made its mark on anthropology's central concept, the concept of "culture."

According to that Nietzschian conception of "culture," posited realities exist outside or external to us only to the extent we misperceive them as such. Such reality-posits (for example, of a world where the ill-will of others can make you sick or the spirit of a dead ancestor is a force to be contended with or where it is objectively wrong to carry any object more than six feet on the sabbath day) are interpreted as mystifying or delusive reifications of our own projections.

In that contemporary conception of "culture," reality-posits are theorized to be "constituted" or "constructed" from within a mental zone occupied by such states of mind as imagining, pretending, or wishing. It is that mental zone where subjectivity predominates over objectivity and where the realities we posit do not exist except as reality-posits. In that Nietzschian conception of culture, nothing is objectively or factually good or bad, right or wrong; only falsely believing that it is so makes it seem that it is so.

Contemporary anthropology is very contemporary, without being self-conscious about it or assuming much responsibility for it. Being contemporary, most anthropologists are Nietzschian individualists; and being Nietzschian individualists and anthropologists, they are prone to analyze other people's posits about reality, constraint, and obligation as though "reality," "constraint," and "obligation" ought to be put in quotation marks. The received anthropological view of things is that a traditional culture's view of "things" consists of meanings (aspects of subjectivity) imposed or projected by human beings onto the world, imposed meanings first dignified by each generation as "objective knowledge" about the world and then passed off as "received wisdom" one generation to the next. Although, according to some contemporary theorists of culture, there is always a small elite of philosopher-kings (for example, contemporary theorists of culture) who know that the whole thing is "made up" or a necessary sham or the innocence of Nietzsche's forest saint.

Indeed, I would speculate that one of the appeals of theory in anthropology is that theory in anthropology is atheistic by assumption. One does not have to spend your time arguing whether there exists God, sin, or sorcery. They are presumed to be fabrications of the mind, figments of the imagination, or imposed meanings whose origin (from within the subject) and ontological status (as a null-reference category) are never in doubt.

Much debate in cultural anthropology thus starts on a common ground of null-reference reasoning—for example, gods and witches (and sin and evil eye, etc.) do not exist. The common ground then gets divided, often passionately, over a secondary question: Is the native really aiming or intending through his reality-posits and symbolic forms (the idea of a witch) to say something true about states of the world? Is the native's state of mind really a matter of belief?

Those who answer Yes to the secondary question (for example, the Marxists or the Freudians) interpret the reality-posits and symbolic forms of other peoples as primary process thinking or irrational consciousness (false objectivity or reified subjectivity). They are Nietzschian in their interpretation of symbolic forms, but they are not relativists, for their aim is to educate or "enlighten" out differences rather than permit them.

Those who answer No (e.g., the so-called "symbolic" anthropologists) interpret other people's reality-posits and symbolic forms as some form of poetics or stylistics or drama or pretend or "performative" devoid of any reality-finding intent (or function) vis-à-vis an objective world. They are Nietzschian ontological atheists, and they are relativistic as well.

In either case the reality-posits of the other (e.g., the idea of a witch) are assumed to refer to imaginary worlds that do not exist except as reality-posits. In either case the Nietzschian null-reference assumption of the modern liberated individual qua anthropologist goes unquestioned and unexamined as it is put to work, but at a great cost.

The Cause That Triumphed: The Cost of Victory

Nietzsche advised: part from your cause as soon as it triumphs; hold suspect all "received wisdom" and cross-examine it as a prejudice from the past. At this historical moment in the West our received wisdom, obvious truths, and innocent suppositions are Nietzschian: the things to which Gods, ghosts, souls, witches, and demons refer do not exist; gods, ghosts, souls, witches, and demons exist solely as elements in a fictive or imaginary reality; they are posits that human beings impose on the world.

As Nietzsche knew, it is never easy to argue against received wisdom. One always runs the risk of being dismissed as passion-driven, as nihilistic, as ridiculous. Yet, if you are a Nietzschian, there is always good reason to try, even when the received wisdom is Nietzschian. In this case there are two good reasons. A null-reference, God-is-dead, phantoms-of-mind conception of culture has two notable consequences, which seem unacceptable to the oversoul I know the best, and which, perhaps, will be judged unacceptable by other oversouls like mine.

The first consequence of a null-reference conception of culture is the degrading of other peoples once the symbolic forms (reality-posits) and states of mind of the other are viewed as alien to the symbolic forms and states of mind of the self. The second consequence is the degrading of society (tradition, custom, ways of life) once society is viewed as alien to nature and to the objective world.

Among anthropologists, just as among all thoughtful people, there are those who feel obliged to go wherever they are led by their preconceptions, while others (and in this case I am one of them) become

suspicious when their preconceptions lead them where they do not want
to go.

The Other Made Alien to the Self

Because of the prevalence of null-reference reasoning, a characteristic feature of theory in anthropology is the unilateral degrading of
other people's (apparently) supposed truths about nature and the world.
Specially targeted for unilateral degrading are those beliefs about natural law that other peoples view as most noteworthy and significant,
reality-posits associated with beliefs about wandering or reincarnating
souls, witchcraft and sorcery, spirit possession and exorcism, pollution
and purity, illness and health, karma and sin, gods and their goddesses,
and so on.

The anthropologist, often acting unwittingly or with noble or even
"liberal" intentions, degrades other peoples posits about natural law by
approaching and analyzing them as though they were "super"-natural,
rhetorical, imaginary, or phantastic. Indeed, it is noteworthy, and perhaps reminiscent of Nietzsche's positivism, that in anthropological theory the notion "super"-natural comes close to meaning null-reference,
which, if you are a positivist, means "meta"-physical, which in the
language of positivism is a synonym for "nonsense."

It is striking how much the contemporary anthropologist's conception of the native resembles the positivist's conception of the metaphysician. One witty definition of a metaphysician goes like this: "A metaphysician is a man who wanders into a dark cellar, at midnight, without
a light, looking for a black cat, that isn't there." How reminiscent of the
metaphysical native, on his knees, searching in the inner sanctum of
some decrepit temple for a beneficent god.

The received view, then, is that culture consists of received meanings or reality-posits that human beings impose on the world, where the
emphasis is on the *imposition* of meaning. The meanings that get imposed are assumed to have null-reference, even when, perhaps especially when, the native is adamant that his ideas about nature and the world
are not simply creations or phantoms of mind, but rather conceptions of
reality that illuminate experience and take you beyond yourself to reality.

The more stubborn the native's commitment to his culture's
"phantastic" or "meta"-physical or "super"-natural beliefs, the greater
the feeling of confidence for the Nietzschian null-reference reasoner.
The Nietzschian all along assumed that culture, custom, and tradition
exercise their phantom grip over the human mind in direct proportion

to the underdevelopment in our species of full and exclusive rationality and individual autonomy. What better evidence of a failure of reality-testing or a confusion of fantasy with reality than the adamant reiteration of the accusation that one's neighbor is a witch, or, worse yet, the neighbor's confession that the accusation is correct!

Accordingly, anthropological theory under the influence of Nietzschian thinking and his philosophy of science has been designed to explain the origin and function of ideas prejudged through positivist null-reference reasoning to be phantom-like, hallucinatory, or fictive.

Not surprisingly, the explanations offered are typically Nietzschian. Hypothesized is some irrational or extrarational or nonrational process, defined by a diminution or displacement of complete, exclusive, autonomous rational functioning. That irrational or extrarational process is then invoked in order to help explain how so many phantom-like, meta-physical, super-natural, delusionary, and arbitrary reality-posits could have gotten themselves lodged and stuck inside people's heads.

One type of explanation (culture as conditioned response) argues that human beings impose meanings on the world because human beings are slaves of their culture who believe what they are told. A second type of explanation (culture as defensive mechanism) argues that human beings believe what they wish to be true, and culture is a massive projective system put out there to satisfy their wishes. A third type of explanation (culture as symbolic) argues that human beings, masters of rhetoric, play, sham, and drama, do not, after all, really believe the things we think they believe, or if they do believe them, they do not literally believe them but rather comprehend them as metaphors or tropes or as imaginative creations.

Spiro (1982), for example, only one step removed from Nietzsche through Freud, explains "mythico-religious" reality-posits (e.g., the idea of God) as the reified and emotionally motivated projection of one's childhood images and fantasies concerning parents and parental figures. Indeed, the concept of God is interpreted as a need-driven, mixed-up idea of a parent ("Entirely helpless from birth, and absolutely dependent on these beings, young children form highly distorted, exaggerated and even bizarre representations of these parenting figures," which then provide a basis for mental representations of the "superhuman figures of the religious world" [1982:59, 62]), and so-called "super"-natural beliefs are glossed as primary process failures of reality-testing, wherein "fantasy is taken for reality" (1982:52-53).

Murdock (1980:89), who argues Nietzsche-like that the ethical doctrines of other peoples are often arbitrary and devoid of objective justification (he has in mind the fact that among the Semang it is, for example, a sin to comb your hair during a thunderstorm or to tell a joke to your mother-in-law), thinks Nietzsche-like that ethics has its origin in fear of the sanctioning power of a phantom called God—a learning process by which one phantom (God) begets another phantom (sin).

Others point to the weight of "history" or "tradition" or "social-class position" to explain the origin of reality-posits. People believe the phantastic things they believe about the way the world actually is because that is what their "teachers" told them to believe. And why did their "teachers" believe it? Because that is what their "teachers" told them to believe. And why did the first "teacher" to believe it believe it? Irrational projection. Fear of sanction. To serve class interest. Wish fulfillment. Long in advance of research, the Nietzschian anthropologist has ruled out, by presupposition, at least one possibility: that some aspect of experience is actually illuminated by placing it under the description of a god, or a witch, or an invading demonic spirit, or pollution, or karma, or original sin!

Thus, in the end it is a consequence of the Nietzschian anthropology of phantom culture that, wittingly or unwittingly, it represents the "other," the native, the alien, under the aspect of the innocent, the romantic, the bizarre, the comic, the burlesque, the theatrical, or the absurd, as the history of culture becomes the record of mankind's sometimes staged, sometimes passionate positing of, and pursuit after, things that do not exist.

Tradition Made Alien to Nature

Besides the unilateral degrading of other people's ideas about reality, a second consequence of a Nietzschian null-reference conception of culture is the degrading of society, custom, and tradition once they are alienated from nature and set in contrast to the objective world. The history is perhaps well known of attempts by theorists to equate customary practice with "convention" and thereby radically separate society from nature. Here I allude to only one incident in a much longer story.

Anthropology became the study of phantom reality-posits, in part, because a more general transformation was taking place in our culture's idea of an objective world governed by natural law. Since about the time of the "Enlightenment" our culture became obsessed with stripping "Mother Nature" of her animus and reinterpreting the concept of what is natural, or a law of nature, as equivalent in meaning to what is mindless, involuntary, and mechanical, without feeling, intention, or plan.

In that "Enlightened" world the designation "natural" science and the predicates "real" and "objective" science came to be restricted to those physical and biological disciplines that conceive of nature or the objective-thing-world as a force field of external causal constraints, devoid of any mental or subjective life. Social "science," now a decidedly suspect category, got a reputation for being "soft" and unreal, and for talking in tongues or "jargon."

By the time anthropology first got to know them, society, tradition, and custom had already suffered humiliation through exposure to the "Enlightenment." Within the terms of the emerging Western dualism of mindless nature and self-determined minds, physical nature and the natural environment had a legitimate place in the scheme of things, as did individuals, and jointly they typified the really real—but not society, tradition, and custom. It was an achievement of the "Enlightenment" to cast them out of reality as the heteronomous (i.e., authoritarian and arbitrary) impositions of ancient and disposable regimes.

It would seem to have been the fate of modern anthropology that she (the discipline of anthropology) was first introduced to society, tradition, and custom only after they (society, tradition, and custom) had been denied a rightful and important place in the modern Western scheme of things. Some will say that it is a black and terrible fate, and they will say it with some reason.

That "Enlightenment" thesis—mindless nature devoid of subjectivity—not surprisingly produced its hypothetical (and romantic) antithesis—mindful persons devoid of natural law or objective constraint, for whom "social" constraints were unnatural, hence unreal, and unreal, hence repressive. One hundred years into the "Enlightenment," Nietzsche was quite prepared to play both sides of the dualism against any middle.

We have seen how Nietzsche did it: null-reference reasoning pressed to its "Enlightened" positive science limit, beyond which there is said to exist a realm of ideal existential freedom. By now the argument is familiar. Nature is mindless, objective, and visible. It is empty of such unseen, unobservable, meta-physical things as god, sin, obligation, value, morality, and so on. If such things exist at all, they exist only as reality-posits in the mind. And if they exist only in the mind, they are not objective and thus ought not be allowed to be constraining. If human beings feel constrained by such things, it is only because, not yet realizing their essential nature (self-determination), they do not distinguish between truth and poetry, confusing, quite irrationally, external reality with what exists nowhere else but in their minds.

Nietzsche is thereby led by his flirtation with positivism to the anticipation of Sartre and many other existentialists, who later try to implement his individualistic and liberationist agenda. Freedom and self-creation are identified as the essential features of self. A finger is pointed at custom, convention, and tradition, which stand accused of being little more than bad faith and self-deception persisting over time, a self-deception founded on the spurious belief that man-in-society is bound by necessary external constraints.

Today, not surprisingly, with our contemporary and now popular Nietzschian consciousness of free individuals and mindless nature, tradition-bound folks are widely apprehended as curious or exotic or innocent leftovers from some dark age who have not yet seen the light. The modern Nietzschian individualist has available a discriminating and impressive vocabulary (innocent, childlike, quaint, simple, primitive, exotic, undifferentiated, misguided, ignorant, uneducated, pious, sentimental, dogmatic, conformist, cultist, brainwashed, authoritarian, fanatical, neurotic, strange, superstitious, etc., etc.) for bracketing or for stigmatizing or for keeping at a distance all those who would insist that it is precisely the strictures and disciplines of their tradition that put them in touch with reality.

To us "moderns" they (e.g., the Amish or the Hassidim, or members of the Hare Krishnas "cult," etc.) seem "out of it," lost in their (quaint or passionate or mindless) illusions off on the peripheries of the modern world we know; whereas the modern world, we know, sits right on top of the pulse of the really real, or, at least, pretty close to it.

The moral of this little parable of "the history of tradition made alien to nature" repeats a central thesis of the essay: anthropology assumed its modern form by stepping into the shadow of a protopositivist, protoexistential Nietzschian vision of reality. Quite naturally, all too naturally, anthropology became, in that Nietzschian world, the discipline for the systematic study and critique of the apparent self-deception and bad faith that is tradition—people hunting for witches that never existed, praying to gods that are dead, sacrificing animals to an empty sky, tormenting themselves with guilt over sins no more substantial than a dream or hallucination, "searching in the dark, without a light, for a black cat, that isn't there."

An "Enlightened" anthropology just kept things going. Society, tradition, and custom became the objects of a richly elaborated Nietzschian (read "modern") scholarly rhetoric of degradation or displacement. Armed with ever more sophisticated versions of that antisocietal rhetoric, custom became "mere convention" (obligations for which no rational justification can be offered); and it was redefined as either dogma, or thoughtless habit and routine, or as a quaint relic of outdated ways of doing things, or, perhaps, in romantic response, as a somewhat cryptic symbolic code designed to give surreptitious expression to imaginary or fanciful or wistful posits about the world.

As for tradition, it got redescribed in some quarters as arbitrary and oppressive injunction. Arbitrary because the content of its injunctions (e.g., no driving of cars on the sabbath day) seemed difficult for reflective individuals to justify through appeals to logic or scientific evidence. Oppressive because, after reason was put aside, the injunction still remained, backed only by power. (" 'Shut up!' my father explained," as Ring Lardner put it) and sustainable only by "virtue" of terrifying or, at least, unpleasant sanctions.

Anthropology is no innocent in the "modern" world. It has played its proper Nietzschian parts in a reality consisting of (and exhausted by) free individuals and mindless nature, in which tradition has become problematical and has been turned into something burdensome to be overcome or as something fanciful or fashionable to be marketed with "arts and leisure."

Today, anthropology's favorite Nietzschian role is the "ghost buster," the "Enlightened" critic who steps outside of and transcends his own tradition. Indeed, many anthropologists spend their time promoting free individualism (rebellion and liberation) through the criticism of social institutions and customary practices and by means of the revelatory unmasking of received wisdom, dramatically exposed as phantom culture. Many phantoms have been added to the modernist's list of things that do not exist except in the minds of their beholders: not only the obvious phantoms like God, sin, sorcery, witches, and the evil eye but also other phantoms such as childhood, mental illness, sex roles, kinship, sacredness, authority, and even ethnographic writing itself (see, e.g., Schneider 1985; Foucault 1965; Clifford and Marcus 1984).

Another favorite Nietzschian role is the "psyche analyst." The "God is dead" presupposition presents anthropologists with the apparent problem of having to explain the imaginary reality-posits, primary process thinking, and phantom culture of others. Hence the intellectual agenda of the psyche analysts in anthropology: to develop a science of other-than-rational or less-than-rational states of mind (e.g., wishing, fantasizing, fearing, the motivational integration of culture) to account for the perplexing worldwide distribution of slavish susceptibility to custom and tradition (see, e.g., Whiting and Child 1953; Whiting 1967; Spiro 1965, 1982, 1983).

Even those anthropologists who pride themselves on sticking to the study of mindless nature adopt the Nietzschian line about tradition as phantom culture, renouncing as "soft" or "humanistic" the study of society, custom, and tradition, while promoting the "hard" study of genuine external constraints through neurology, biology, demography, or even computer science.

It seems highly likely that occasions exist when the best way to make sense of another person's apparently alien reality-posits is to attribute to him false beliefs, or deficient reasoning, or false consciousness, or to view the reality-posits of the other as intendedly ironical, or hyperbolic, or metaphorical, or comic, or fanciful, or theatrical, or imaginary, and so on. And I am fairly confident there are cases (for example, the development and dissemination by the American Psychiatric Association of the diagnostic categories listed in their widely used "DSM-3" manual) where power and self-interest have played a notable part in conferring a sense of realism on imaginary reality-posits.

The "God is dead" school of anthropology has experimented with all of those interpretive possibilities, tracing with much care and sophistication the implications of some seemingly innocent suppositions: the supposition that notions like god, witch, sorcery, soul, or sin refer to nothing in reality; the supposition that gods, ghosts, souls, and such exist solely as fictive or imaginary elements in psychic (subjective) reality (only "in the head") or as cultural meanings *imposed* by human beings on a constructed world.

To this point in the essay I have described the pervasive influence of those Nietzschian suppositions in anthropology, and I have identified some of the consequences of Nietzschian reasoning, especially the degrading of custom and tradition, thrown out of the natural world, and the derogation of the other people's ideas and practices, made alien to the self and treated as unreal or made up or illusory.

In this section I outline a post-Nietzschian approach which, it is to be hoped, can avoid those consequences. There are two requirements which must be fulfilled if that hope is to be realized: the substitution of an alternative philosophy of science for Nietzsche's positivism and the restoration of dignity to a much maligned ancient role (the "casuist" and his casuistry), rescripted to be played out on center stage next to the "ghost buster" and the "psyche analyst."

Post-Nietzschian Anthropology

A Postpositivist Philosophy of Science

Nietzsche probably never realized that he was held prisoner by the phantom of positivism. Through its famous (and somewhat notorious) "verifiability principle" and its demand for "operational definitions," the phantom holds that only seeing is believing and that only the data of the senses should be treated as real. With the wave of its antimetaphysical and atheistic hand the phantom of positivism rejects all unseen postulated forces or entities as nonsense that ought never to play a part in our knowledge of the world. The first commandment of positivism is the prohibition on transcendent entities (Gellner 1984), and the first transcendent entity to go is the idea of a reality hidden behind appearances. (Hence the great risk in positivism that it will devolve into solipsism, for how can I ever know for certain if my appearances-sensations-experiences are the same as yours?)

Bewitched by the phantom, yet faithful to its modernist spirit, Nietzsche reasoned himself into a corner. He forced upon himself, within the terms of positivism's conception of objectivity, a rather unfortunate dichotomous choice.

According to positivism either postulated forces and entities are directly verifiable through observation or experience, or else they are unreal. Nietzsche's forced and unfortunate choice was as follows: either classify people's reality-posits about Gods, ghosts, witches, and sin as objective, and hence, in principle, directly accessible to the senses of any (reliable? trained? normal?) observer; or else classify people's reality-posits as subjective or imaginary entities with null-reference, projected onto the world.

The rub with the first choice is obvious. To argue that God, ghosts, witches, and sin are objective in *that* sense (directly perceptible) is, in the modern world, to run the risk of being branded an enemy of reason and common sense, dismissed, denounced, committed, or forced to recant.

With sufficient qualification (and ingenuity) that rub can perhaps be smoothed out. But it would require a good deal of other-than-modern and antidemocratic confidence in the fidelity or veracity of the visions, testimonials, and mystical or miraculous experiences of a self-privileging minority who claim to have special or superior powers to see or experience what no one else is able to observe.

That first choice will, of course, seem both plausible and attractive to those who believe in "seers" and in the extra-ordinary sightedness of "experts" or "virtuosos" credited with a unique ability to make "contact" and to peer into reality as it really is. The rest of us, however, a diverse collection of modern and postmodern scholars and scientists, admittedly have great difficulty with the idea that knowledge of reality should be established on the basis of "revealed" truths or from the reports of a seer recording his visions. Nietzsche's *Übermensch* was not someone with better eyesight, nor was he someone with keener ears, able to listen carefully to voices that no one else could hear.

The second choice, the "God is dead" alternative, was discussed above. As we have seen, it is not difficult to understand what it means to claim that other people's reality-posits have null-reference or exist "only in their heads." In evaluating the cogency of the claim the issue is not one of coherency but rather of the plausibility and acceptability of the consequences of certain presuppositions about the reality-posit of the "other."

In the cases with which I am most familiar (e.g., orthodox Hindu conceptions of karma and reincarnating souls: Shweder 1985, 1986; Shweder and Miller 1985; Shweder, Mahapatra, and Miller 1987) all of the following seems to be true of the reality-posits of the other: (a) the other does not view his own ideas as arbitrary, conventional, consensus-based, or as emotive expressions of imagination, desire, or will; (b) the other believes his reality-posits express significant insights into what the world is like and that the reality posited can be used to illuminate or interpret the facts of experience; (c) the other remains convinced that his reality-posits are a form of knowledge about the world, even after we explain that he is suffering from a deluded false consciousness or that it is all imaginary or made up; and (d) the other does not reason irrationally with his ideas (see, for example, Malleus Maleficarum, a closely reasoned treatment of the theory of witchcraft, originally published in 1489; also Shweder 1986).

The idea is, of course, a familiar one in the modern world that under certain kinds of circumstances certain classes of people may be highly motivated to resist disillusionment and to deny that their consciousness is false. That idea is not incoherent either, and it may even be true in certain fascinating cases. Yet what is the justification for using that idea axiomatically to interpret the long-term refusal of most peoples around the world to abandon their so-called super-natural, phantom-like, meta-physical beliefs (about gods, witches, spirits, fate, etc.)? At this point in the history of modern social science such irrationalist accounts have yet to establish their inherent plausibility through firm empirical backing, and for the most part they have consisted of provocative and sometimes quite spectacular handwaving and much speculation about unseen forces.

Modern thought is also rich in labels ("reification," "naturalization," "naive realism") for the supposed error of taking your "symbols" or reality-posits too directly or too literally, for the supposed mistake of treating your representational scheme as a part of the reality it describes, and for the supposed confusion of conflating the sign with the signified and apprehending your own subjective creation as an objective discovery. Yet, while there are many names for those supposed blunders, there is no convincing explanation for their near universal occurrence. There may even be good reasons to think that the "blunders" themselves are not always blunders (see, e.g., Goodman 1968).

Faced with the two unacceptable alternatives posed by positivism's phantom—directly perceivable, hence real versus unobservable, hence unreal—a third alternative is to reject them both. Or, in this case to try to struggle free of the phantom's quite special preconception of the idea of objectivity (reality directly observable by means of the senses) found hovering over the alternatives. It should be possible to get free, or in this case to reconstitute a bond, perhaps an indissociable link, between objectivity and subjectivity without totally destroying either term of their supposed opposition.

Forty years of postpositivist reflection have prepared the way for an understanding of some of the ways objectivity and subjectivity may need each other and can live together without either pushing the other out, although it may well be an irony in the history of the philosophy of science that, as Michael Friedman (n.d.) has argued, much of postpositivist reflection (Kuhn, Hanson, Toulmin, Feyerabend, Lakatos, Hesse, Goodman) has recapitulated ideas already available in positivist circles (for example, the relativistic conclusions of the Marburg School and the doctrine of "logical idealism").

The main thing that needs to be drawn on in postpositivist reflection is a two-sided idea which can be expressed in variant ways as follows. While (side 1) nothing *in particular* exists independent of our theoretical interpretation of it (the principle of subject-dependency) and while all theories are inherently underdetermined by the facts (the principle of cognitive undecidability), there still does exist (side 2) the reality and accomplishment of "normal science": operating within the subject-dependent, cognitively undecidable terms of a "paradigm." While, as Toulmin has put it, (side 1) facts are not self-describing, (side 2) neither are theories self-confirming. While (side 1) "paradigms" may not be fully commensurate or intertranslatable (the principles of holism and incommensurability), (side 2) rationality and a sound reality orientation may not require uniformity or convergence of belief across competent observers. And, by extension, when it comes to the tradition-based reality-posits of the peoples studied by anthropologists, it is the native's success at reasoning with his reality-posits and using them to organize and make sense of certain of his experiences that lends those theories their authority as accounts of what is natural, real, or objective.

Those, of course, are "big ideas." I cannot argue them here, nor can I undertake, on this occasion, to review revisions in the concept of objectivity in contemporary philosophy of science (see Putnam 1981). I cannot even attempt a full-blown explication, much less a systematic defense of the relevant core aphorism for a post-Nietzschian anthropology: reality-testing is a metaphysical (i.e., "super" natural) act, for *every* account of reality is built up out of assumptions not directly checkable against observable evidence or deducible from undeniable first principles.

In brief, however, the basic line of argument goes something like this. The postulation of our own internal mental constructs as external forces lending intelligibility to the data of the senses seems to be a central and indispensable feature not only of imaginary, fanciful, hallucinatory, and delusional thinking but of scientific thought as well. What Derrida (1977) calls the "metaphysics of presence," consisting of all those essential asymmetrical contrasts of the signifier to the signified, the sensible to the intelligible, the immediate to the hidden, the apparent to the real, is not something we can do without, for, as Derrida (1977:13) notes all too briefly in a passing remark, "nothing is conceivable" without it. While reality is not something we can do without, neither can it be reached (for it is beyond experience and transcends appearances) except by an act of imaginative projection implicating the knower as well as the known.

Horton (1967), in effect arguing that there is an indissociable link between science and the metaphysics of presence, aptly makes the point that to construct a scientific theory is to elaborate "a scheme of forces or entities operating 'behind' or 'within' the world of common-sense observation." Except for the radical and flawed attempt by positivists to proselytize a scientific atheism, in which everything unseen, hidden, or beneath the surface is eliminated from scientific discourse, Horton's definition does seem to capture a characteristic feature of reality-finding science.

And, as almost all postpositivists now seem to recognize, the postulation of a world of unseen and unseeable forces or entities operating behind the apparent world of our reality-posits is not only an indispensable act of interpretation but also a highly discretionary one, only weakly constrained by the content of the reality-posit itself.

An interpretive or hermeneutic or projective element (call it what you will) has long since been incorporated into philosophical conceptions of objectivity-seeking science. Any science must address with great respect all our reality-posits, but it would utterly fail as a science if it ever tried to let all those appearances-sensations-experiences speak entirely for themselves, or if it ever let them by their own authority establish themselves as "observations" or "facts" about reality.

Objectivity-seeking science portrays for us a really real external world so as to explain our reality-posits, but it does so by making use of our reality-posits in a selective, presumptive, and partial way. One reason for this is that there is no authoritative feature of a reality-posit per se that can certify it as a perception or a witnessing rather than an illusion, or guarantee, for example, that dreaming or imagining is not a form of witnessing or that any particular reality-posit is a fact about the world rather than a feature of our state of mind or an artifact of our measuring instruments.

Were one to judge that a particular reality-posit represented a genuine fact about reality one might be led, if it were an anomalous fact, to alter a conception of the world. Yet, were one to judge that that same reality-posit really represented measurement error, one might dismiss it as insignificant and not treat it as sign or indicator of the world outside our symbolic forms.

Since no reality-finding science can treat all appearances-sensations-experiences as revelatory of the objective world, and since, at least for the moment, no infallible way exists to decide which reality-posits are signs of reality and which are not, much is discretionary in every portrait of the objective world out there beyond our symbolic forms. Reality, after all, for all we can ever really know, may be far away, or deep within, or hidden behind, and thus only viewable "as if through a glass darkly"; or perhaps the really real really is only available through a privileged state of mind (e.g., deep meditation) attainable only by a privileged few. Perhaps, as some peoples around the world have long suspected, the royal road to reality is through the reality-posits that appear before us while asleep or in reverie. The idea certainly has a noble and common lineage that dreaming or imagining is a form of witnessing or perceiving illuminating deeper truths.

Many postpositivist accounts of the history of scientific knowledge conclude that there may not exist self-validating methods or procedures for establishing the realism of the picture one has painted of the unseen and unseeable entities and forces controlling appearance-sensation-experience. Those historical accounts typically, and quite reasonably, treat the institutionalized sciences of our own society as relatively good examples, or at least as the best examples we have got, of reality-finding, objectivity-seeking reality-positing. The accounts try to demonstrate that the notable accomplishments of those sciences are not produced by accumulating a vast corpus of directly observable facts (perceiving that __, in contrast to imagining that __), nor are they the products of some standardized or automated rules and procedures for gaining knowledge.

For example, the rule of "parsimony" or "simplicity" has often been pointed to as a formal standard for assessing the relative realism or veracity of alternative accounts of what the world is like and for deciding which reality-posits correspond more closely to reality. Yet, as Michael Friedman (n.d.) has pointed out, that standard suffers from deep inadequacies, for "we have no clear account of what such 'simplicity' really comes to nor, more importantly, any assurance that 'simplicity'— whatever it is—is a reliable guide to truth."

The same story seems to hold again and again in the history and philosophy of science. There have been many proposed criteria (reliability or consensus, confirmation through the prediction of other reality-posits, survival through repeated attempts at disconfirmation, parsimony) for assessing the degree of correspondence or realism of a reality-posit to the unseen objective world it purports to represent. Whatever the criterion, there seems to be no way to guarantee that it is a realistic test of similitude. In that regard there is a unity to science, for the "natural" sciences and the "human" sciences do not differ in standardized or automated methodology—they both lack one.

The story of postpositivist philosophy of science seems to have two themes, although it is the first theme that has gotten most of, and certainly too much of, the attention. That first theme, the celebrated one, is about the retreat from the idea of a method (the scientific method), which if diligently and systematically applied is guaranteed to paint for you a realistic portrait of the unseen entities and forces controlling the regularities reported through a reality-posit. That theme is about the impossibility of defining, in the abstract, the borders between good science, bad science, nonscience, and imaginary nonsense.

At times the retreat from generalized scientific methodism has had an intoxicating effect. As a consequence of the retreat there has appeared in the minds of some thinkers the specter that objectivity-seeking reality-finding science itself may be false consciousness, totally imaginary, fictive, or delusional, a Nietzschian phantom of mind (see Campbell 1986 and Gergen 1986).

There is, I think, as hinted at earlier, a more fruitful path of interpretation to follow, which I shall now describe in a bit more detail. It is a path less cluttered with Nietzschian (protopositivist) prejudgments and far less debunking of the meta-physical or super-natural in science.

At least two responses are possible if you accept the postpositivist claim that physics is indissociable from meta-physics, nature indissociable from super-nature, and science indissociable from religion. If you are a positivist, you will respond, "So much the worse for physics, nature, and science." Those Nietzschians who analyze science as ideology or false consciousness make manifest that positivistic response. The second possible response is "So much the better for meta-physics, super-nature, and religion," a response that might serve as a post-Nietzschian's post-positivist retort.

Hence the second theme of postpositivist thinking, the one that deserves far more attention. That theme is about the idea that it is not really cause for alarm that good reality-finding science has important elements that are inextricably subjective or discretionary. Only in a world founded on the presuppositions of positivism will it sound face-tious, nihilistic, or ironical to argue that out of respect for Darwin (or Freud) disconfirmability ought to be dropped as a necessary feature of good science, or to argue from the history of successful science that it is not always advisable for scientists to stick to the presumed facts or to strive for agreement on the meaning of core concepts.

In a postpositivist world, or at least in a defensible postpositivist world, that same argument ought to be construed in quite a different way. Postpositivists are no less concerned with what is real than are the positivists, and among sensible postpositivists it is understood that science is good and successful. Yet in a postpositivist world it is also understood that it is possible for us to have important knowledge of the world, even if the objective world is subject-dependent and multiplex and even if we give up trying to describe the world independent of our involvement with it or reactions to it or conceptions of it. Hence, the continental chorus singing with Kuhnian overtones that it is our prejudices and partialities that make it possible for us to see, if not everything, then at least something.

Accordingly, it is a core aphorism for the post-Nietzschian position advocated here that the objective world is incapable of being represented completely if represented from any one point of view, and incapable of being represented intelligibly if represented from all points of view at once.

The real trick and the noble challenge for the post-Nietzschian is to view the objective world from many points of view (or from the point of view of each of several prejudices), but to do it in sequence. The proper aim within each point of view is to adopt the stance of (what Putnam has called) an "internal realist" ("normal science" operating within the terms of some paradigm), seeing as best one can with the received "dogma" of the moment. The challenge is to always feel eager to move on to some other worldview, in hot pursuit of the echo of Nelson Goodman's (1984) siren song: "One might say there is only one world but this holds for each of the many worlds."

Mary Hesse (1972), who in an essay entitled "In Defense of Objectivity" has tried to inform subjectivists and other hermeneutic critics of science that their conception of objectivity-seeking science is about a century out of date, has some stimulating and provocative things to say about divergences in thinking in "modern" physics.

She points out that the description of real-world essences in modern physics has been neither cumulative nor convergent: "The succession of theories of the atom, and hence the fundamental nature of matter, for example, exhibits no convergence, but oscillates between continuity and discontinuity, field conceptions and particle conceptions, and even speculatively among different typologies of space." Other philosophers (e.g., Nelson Goodman) have recommended for modern physics a policy of "judicious vacillation" between "a world of waves and a world of particles as suits one's purposes." With judicious vacillation one gains access to multiple objective worlds.

There are three implications, as I understand them, to Hesse's observation about divergences in thinking in physics, and none of them is that modern physics has been impeded in its progress or that scientific thinking is a whimsical or nihilistic or ideological process.

One implication is that convergence in imaginative projections about the unseeable or "hidden" forces lurking behind the evidence of the senses is not an essential element of mature scientific thinking. A second implication is that any established and successful vision of what is real is indissociably linked to judgments that are discretionary and presumptive, and that, thus, there is legitimate scope for disagreement or divergence in world pictures among quite "hard-nosed" reality-seeking scientists, lay or professional. A third implication is that one of the great challenges for any science is to find some way to represent, describe, and explain the multiplicity of the objective world. Of what does that multiplicity consist?

The message of all this for dedicated Nietzschians is that it is time to shed one's skin and adopt a new philosophy of science. It is time to move from the modern into the postmodern era. In a post-Nietzschian world informed by postpositivist conceptions, objectivity, truth, and reality are inextricably associated with, and are not possible without, something prior contributed by the subject. Nothing intelligible remains of reality once you have "corrected" for all the possible prejudgments or "biases" of the observer, for all conceptions of reality are, in some measure, irrepressible acts of imaginative projection across the inherent gap between appearance and reality.

In that post-Nietzschian world God is not dead; only positivism and monotheism are dead. Polytheism is alive and well. Its doctrine is the relativistic idea of multiple objective worlds, and its commandment is participation in the never-ending process of overcoming partial views.

Quite rightly there are those moderns who will worry about the subordination of the individual with that return of the gods. Yet, in that polytheistic post-Nietzschian world there still remains reason not to be a slave to the received wisdom of your tradition. That reason, however, is not that tradition is unreal or phantastic or fictive or empty in its reference. The real reason is that any single tradition is partial, for each tradition is only one piece of reality brought out into high consciousness and enshrined in local doctrine or dogma. The aim for the post-Nietzschian, then, is identical to one of the aims of good anthropology, to be the student and beneficiary of all traditions, and the slave to none.

Perhaps that is a new thing for Nietzschians: transcendence without superiority, scorn, or cynicism, and without the degrading of tradition; and perhaps it is that newness that should recommend it if you are a Nietzschian.

Transcendence without scorn is the kind of transcendence that comes from constantly moving from one objective world to the next, inside and then out, outside and then in, all the while standing back and trying to make sense of the whole journey. It is a state of mind in which there is a detached engagement with each of several traditions, which promotes an engaging detachment from each of one's many selves.

To orthodox Nietzschians that state of mind of detached engagement will, no doubt, seem far too involved with, and constrained by, the mundane practices of the everyday world, especially in comparison to the state of mind contemplated by Nietzschian ascetics (the ecstatic otherworldliness of the transcendence into pure spirit) or the state of mind contemplated by Nietzschian nihilists (the this-worldly freedom of the transcendence into pure individualism).

Yet, in a postpositivist world that is what an "Enlightened" and noble anthropology ought to be about, at least in part—going to some far away place where you honor and take "literally" (as a matter of belief) those reality-posits so alien in order to discover other realities hidden within the self, waiting to be drawn out into consciousness. The transcendent and the immanent are, in reality, not that far apart, as polytheistic relativists (and mystics, I am told) come to know.

As for those who fear that if truth is not unitary, then nihilism will reign and that polytheism is merely a code word for anarchy, it is comforting to remind oneself, again and again, that just because there is no one uniform reality (God, foundation, truth) does not mean there are no realities (Gods, foundations, truths) at all.

RICHARD A. SHWEDER

The Ancient Role of the Casuist

To be a Nietzschian ascetic or liberationist is to be suspicious of pious devotion to tradition or custom. Held hostage, historically, to a positivist conception of reality (only seeing is believing) and a null-reference (phantom) conception of culture, it has not been legitimate for a Nietzschian to provide a rational justification for custom or to take seriously the substance or content of other peoples so-called "super-" natural or "meta-"physical beliefs.

The scope for a Nietzschian anthropology is broadened in a post-postivist world, as the rationalization of custom and tradition becomes a legitimate objective, and as there emerges a type of relativist doctrine (ontological polytheism) in which realism and rationality are compatible with the idea of multiple worlds.

For if there is no reality without "meta"-physics and each reality-testing meta-physic (i.e., each culture or tradition) is but a partial representation of the multiplicity of the objective world, it becomes possible to transcend tradition by showing how each tradition lights some plane of reality but not all of it. Since each is but a partial representation, it must be transcended. Since each is a representation of reality, it lends itself to a process of rational reconstruction through which it may become an object of respect.

The art of rational reconstruction is an ancient one, sometimes referred to as casuistry, and it is a modern role for the "casuist"—the adroit rationalizer—that a post-Nietzschian anthropology needs to reconstruct.

It is ironical that in postmodern times the practice of casuistry has retained its medieval stigma of disrepute, connoting a degenerate and deceptive ability through adroit rationalization to justify anything or to defend any exotic practice, act, or point of view. It is ironical because what the medieval church saw as the corruption in casuistry is, in the contemporary world, no longer a sinful thing.

It was in the late middle ages that casuistry first got a bad reputation, and ever since that time casuistry has had terrible press. Pascal described casuistry as the sophistical evasion of the word of God, and it is not too difficult to understand why.

During the late middle ages there was a point of view according to which "sadness" was thought to be a cardinal sin, as though to be "dispirited" was an insult to God. In a world with a God so prone to take offense, the practice of casuistry was naturally at great risk. For what could be more irritating to a superior being, confident of his own omniscience, than to have some casuist intent on the corrosion of dogma step forward with a nimble defense of some alternative point of view. The supposed corruption in casuistry is its corrosion of dogma, which today, at least in the democracies of the world, ought to be an idealized rather than vilified thing. Apparently it takes a long time to overcome the effects of a reckless press.

In fact, the much maligned casuists of the middle ages were serious scholars at medieval universities who had the temerity to try to come up with a rational justification for tradition and for those seemingly arbitrary ritual observances and ecclesiastical rules that others slavishly accepted on faith or church authority. What made the casuists such a pain in the neck for the medieval church was that eventually the casuists got so good at rationalization that they were even able to come up with compelling rational justifications for opposition to authority, for disrespect of fixed or formal rules, and for the adoption of alternative traditions and practices.

Perhaps the most famous casuist of the middle ages was Peter Abelard (the so-called "Socrates of the Gauls"), the twelfth-century theologian, logician, and canon of Notre Dame, whose passionate life has been immortalized in the love letters of Heloise. The young Abelard, a master at rationalization, not only talked Heloise into the virtue of giving up her virginity; he also reasoned his way into several heresies.

Abelard had a knack for infuriating the authorities and promulgators of dogma in the medieval church. He wandered around France wondering out loud how to reconcile divine oneness with the existence of a trinity, and embarrassing his superiors and teachers with puzzles about the one and the many, uniformity and multiplicity, the same and the different, the universal and the particular. He compiled for himself a collection of authoritative, yet diametrically opposed, opinions on points of church doctrine, with the implication that the discrepancies in interpretation could not be reconciled into a single homogeneous truth. Distrustful of any attempt to canonize morality as a set of fixed and general principles, such as "it is wrong to lie," he kept coming up with exceptional cases that did not fit the rule. He reasoned himself to the view that there could be no culpability for sin if you did not intend to transgress; good intentions and personal conscience, he argued, take precedence over deeds and external observances. He nearly turned the church into a debating club, with adversaries outdoing each other with ingenious justifications for the sometimes baffling and seemingly pointless rules and prohibitions set forth in scripture.

Not surprisingly many people in the twelfth century hated Abelard, with a passion. He was persecuted by St. Bernard, who saw madness as the outcome of Abelard's methods—a calculus for heresy. To his critics, Abelard, the apparent nihilist, seemed to be saying that if your conscience does not bother you, you can do whatever you want. As the church viewed it, by the time Abelard finished an exegesis of a sacred text, the words of God had been erased through interpretation. In 1121 his book on *Divine Unity and Trinity* was burned at an ecclesiastical council. The pope condemned him and kept him quiet by issuing an injunction against his lecturing. And, as we all know with amazement and perhaps with horror, Heloise's uncle, a canon of the church, took care of Abelard's manhood—divine emasculation on behalf of an exasperated and tongue-tied God.

It would seem from the example of Abelard that casuistry, at its very best, is antidogmatic and quite risky, surprising and distractive of habitual ways of seeing, agile and on the move against any single fixed point of view or frame of reference. It presses irreverence into the service of reality, in recognition of the idea that it is only by constantly switching frames that we honor the multiplex world.

Abelard, of course, was not the first casuist, for it is an ancient role. There is casuistry in the Talmudic commentaries, where for every letter of the law there are always two or more spirits, or rabbis, with quite alternative views of what it all means.

And the Stoics and the Sophists knew of casuistry. I once was told a story (perhaps apocryphal) about an ancient Greek philosopher who was invited to Rome to give two lectures to the imperial elite. Weary of the single-mindedness, smugness, and absolutism of Roman domination, our speaker anticipated Abelard's tactics.

In the morning he expounded the thesis that human society is analogous to the societies of ants and bees and other animal societies, and that even monkeys have a military hierarchy and chain of command. A brilliant lecture shedding much light on human behavior that was well received.

In the afternoon, refusing to let any one viewpoint of reality reign, he expounded the contrary thesis that human society and animal society are not analogous, and that animals are fundamentally different from people. After all, animals have no language or conscience, and they certainly do not know how to cook. The philosopher, a Greek, and obviously a casuist at heart, found himself imprisoned for irreverence.

It is perhaps fortunate for contemporary anthropologists that irreverence is the first commandment of the postmodern world, and that once again the jester has become an admired role, as we have remembered at long last the importance of living ironically and by our wits. Thus, there was no church injunction against lecturing, indeed it was by invitation, when in 1983 Clifford Geertz delivered the annual "Distinguished Lecture" (entitled "Anti Anti-Relativism") to the American Anthropological Association. One point of the lecture was to rally anthropologists to the task of challenging the received and unquestioned assumptions and classifications of our own contemporary empire. [I tried my hand at it in this essay.] Unlike Abelard, Clifford Geertz walked off the stage unharmed, to applause. What used to be a medieval heresy is now one of several currents in a contemporary discipline called anthropology, where, barring the reappearance of a St. Bernard, casuists can now practice their art or alchemy without stigma on the same stage as the ghost busters and psyche analysts.

References

Campbell, D. T. 1986. "Science's Social System of Validity-Enhancing Belief Change and the Problems of the Social Sciences." In *Metatheory in Social Science*, ed. D.W. Fiske and R.A. Shweder. Chicago: University of Chicago Press.

Clifford, J., and G. E. Marcus, eds. 1986. *Writing Culture*. Berkeley and Los Angeles: University of California Press.

D'Andrade, R. G. 1983. A Folk Model of the Mind. Unpublished manuscript. Dept. of Anthropology, University of California, San Diego. La Jolla, California 92093.

Derrida, J. 1977. *Of Grammatology*. Tr. Gayatri C. Spivak. Baltimore: Johns Hopkins University Press.

Fiske, D., and R. Shweder, eds. 1986. *Metatheory in Social Science: Pluralisms and Subjectivities*. Chicago and London: The University of Chicago Press.

Foucault, M. 1965. *Madness and Civilization*. New York: Mentor.

Friedman, M. n.d. Scientific Objectivity in Historical Perspective. Unpublished manuscript.

Geertz, C. 1984. "Anti Anti-Relativism." *American Anthropologist* 86:263-278.

Gellner, E. 1985. *Relativism and the Social Sciences*. Cambridge: Cambridge University Press.

Gergen, K. J. 1986. "Correspondence Versus Autonomy in the Language of Understanding Human Action." In *Metatheory in Social Science*, ed. D. W. Fiske and R. A. Shweder. Chicago: University of Chicago Press.

Goodman, N. 1968. *Languages of Art*. New York: Bobbs-Merrill.

Goodman, N. 1984. "Notes on the Well-Made World." *Partisan Review* 51:276-288.

Hesse, M. 1972. "In Defense of Objectivity." *Proceedings of the British Academy* 58:275-292.

Horton, R. 1967. "African Traditional Thought and Western Science." *Africa* 37:50-71 (part 1), 159-187 (part 2).

Hollis, M., and S. Lukes. 1982. *Rationality and Relativism*. Cambridge, MA: The MIT Press.

MacIntyre, A. 1981. *After Virtue: A Study in Moral Theory*. Notre Dame, IN: University of Notre Dame Press.

Malleus Maleficarum. 1928. John Rodker Publisher (originally 1489).

Murdock, G. P. 1980. *Theories of Illness*. Pittsburgh: University of Pittsburgh Press.

Nuckolls, C. 1986. *Culture and Causal Thinking*. Unpublished Ph.D. Dissertation. Department of South Asian Languages and Civilization. University of Chicago.

Obeyesekere, G. 1981. *Medusa's Hair: An Essay on Personal Symbols and Religious Experience*. London and Chicago: University of Chicago Press.

Putnam, H. 1981. *Philosophical Papers: Reason, Truth and History* Vol. 3. Cambridge: Cambridge University Press.

Schneider, D. M. 1965. "Kinship and Biology." In *Aspects of the Analysis of Family Structure*, ed. A.G. Coale *et al.* Princeton: Princeton University Press.

———. 1985. *What Is Kinship?* Ann Arbor: University of Michigan Press.

Shweder, R. A. 1985. "Menstrual Pollution, Soul Loss and the Comparative Study of Emotions." In *Culture and Depression: Towards an Anthropology of Affects and Affective Disorders*, ed. A. Kleinman and B. J. Good. Los Angeles: University of California Press.

———. 1986. "Divergent Rationalities." In *Metatheory in Social Science: Pluralisms and Subjectivities*, ed. D. W. Fiske and R. A. Schweder. Chicago: University of Chicago Press.

———. 1987. "How to Look at Medusa without Turning to Stone." *Contributions to Indian Sociology* 21: 37-55.

Shweder, R. A., and E. J. Bourne. 1982. "Does the concept of the person vary cross-culturally?" In *Cultural Conceptions of Mental Health and Therapy*, ed. A. J. Marsella and G. White. Dordrecht, Holland: Reidel. (Reprinted in *Culture Theory: Essays on Mind, Self, and Emotion*, ed. R. A. Shweder and R. A. LeVine. New York: Cambridge University Press, 1984.)

Shweder, R. A., and R. A. LeVine, eds. 1984. *Culture Theory: Essays on Mind, Self, and Emotion*. New York: Cambridge University Press.

Shweder, R. A., and J. G. Miller. 1985. "The Social Construction of the Person: How Is It Possible?" In *The Social Construction of the Person*, ed. Kenneth J. Gergen and Keith Davis. International Series in Social Psychology. New York: Springer Verlag.

Shweder, R. A., M. Mahapatra, and J. G. Miller. 1987. "Culture and Moral Development." In *The Emergence of Moral Concepts in Young Children*, ed. J. Kagan and S. Lamb. Chicago: University of Chicago Press.

Shweder, R. A., and N. C. Much. 1987. "Determinations of Meaning: Discourse and Moral Socialization." In *Social Interaction and Socio-moral Development*, ed. W. Kurtines and J. Gewirtz. New York: Wiley.

Spiro, M. 1965. "Religion as a Culturally Constituted Defense Mechanism." In *Context and Meaning in Cultural Anthropology*, ed. M. Spiro. New York: Free Press.

———. 1982. "Collective Representations and Mental Representations in Religious Symbol Systems." In *On Symbols in Anthropology*, vol. 3, ed. J. Maquet. Los Angeles: University of California Press.

———. 1983. *Oedipus in the Trobriands*. Chicago: University of Chicago Press.

———. 1984. "Some Reflections on Cultural Determinism and Relativism with Special Reference to Emotion and Reason." In *Culture Theory: Essays on Mind, Self, and Emotion*, ed. R. A. Shweder and R. A. LeVine. New York: Cambridge University Press.

———. 1986. "Cultural Relativism and the Future of Anthropology." *Cultural Anthropology* 1:259-286.

Whiting, J. 1967. "Sorcery, Sin and the Superego." In *Cross-Cultural Approaches*, ed. C. S. Ford. New Haven: HRAF Press. (Originally in *Nebraska Symposium on Motivation*. University of Nebraska Press, 1959.)

Whiting, J., and I. Child. 1953. Reprint edition: *Child Training and Personality*. New Haven: Yale University Press, 1967.

Wilson, B. R. 1970. *Rationality*. Oxford: Basil Blackwell.

Three Kinds of Incommensurability[1]

DAVID B. WONG

There are three versions of the thesis that there are theories of the world incommensurable with our theory. These versions correspond to three kinds of incommensurability. One version involves incommensurability with respect to translation and says that terms in at least some other theories cannot be equated in meaning and reference with any terms in our theory. A second version involves incommensurability with respect to justification and says that at least some other theories differ from our own with respect to fundamental premises about the nature of the world or fundamental forms of reasoning. A third version involves incommensurability with respect to evaluation and says that we cannot make a judgment of superiority between our own theory and at least some other theories. Now a common move of authors who argue for incommensurability is to derive this third kind of evaluative incommensurability from incommensurability of translation or of justification.

I will suggest in this paper that arguments from the first kind of incommensurability do not establish anything interesting about the third kind, and that the furor over untranslatability has obscured the most interesting case for evaluative incommensurability. This case arises precisely from an understanding of what is believed in other cultures and from an appreciation of why it is believed. It is based on the second kind of incommensurability, but it is not based in the usual way. The usual way is to argue that we run out of justifications for our most basic premises and forms of reasoning, and that when others hold different premises and forms, all the ways of showing that we are superior end up being circular. The usual way, therefore, depends on skeptical worries arising from our foundationless epistemology. I will sketch an argument that is compatible with granting that our premises are truer and forms of reasoning more reliable than those of others. I conclude by explaining why the argument is inconclusive, even though it has substantial power.

I begin with the debate over arguments for evaluative incommensurability that are based on untranslatability. The extreme case of untranslatability would be the discovery of a language of which no significant range of sentences could be translated. If there were such a case, no judgment of superiority could be made with respect to beliefs expressed in the other language and our own beliefs. Donald Davidson is well known for his argument that there could be no such case. The problem, he says, lies in making sense of the idea that we could recognize something both as a *language* and as untranslatable. It, furthermore, has been noted by both Davidson and Hilary Putnam that there is something exceedingly odd in what some advocates of incommensurability do: claiming that another theory is so alien to ours that there can be no translation and then arguing for this by giving lengthy explanations of the theory in question.[2] Even if there were a radically untranslatable language, its existence would support the claim for evaluative incommensurability only in a weak sense. It would be impossible to judge between the beliefs expressed in the other language and our own only in the sense that we could not know what those other beliefs were. There would be no basis for a claim of superiority only because we would not have one of the terms that must stand in the comparative relation.

Alasdair MacIntyre has sketched a more subtle and realistic case for evaluative incommensurability that is based on incommensurability of the first two kinds. He points to the possibility of partial untranslatability between two languages. Though speakers of each langauge may be able to translate phrases from the other language when these phrases are uttered in certain types of situations, they may lack the power to extrapolate to new uses of these phrases. The power to extrapolate, he says, depends on an ability to refer and allude to a particular common stock of canonical texts. The inability to translate certain parts of the language will be a barrier to knowledge of the canonical texts, but lack of knowledge of the texts will be a barrier to getting any further in the task of translation.[3]

MacIntyre thinks that speakers of modern European languages are *not* in this fix. We are able to represent an indefinite variety of systems of beliefs by means of a variety of devices such as paraphrase and scholarly gloss. The conditions that give rise to translatability, however, also give rise to incommensurability of the second kind. We have many texts that were canonical for cultures that have contributed to our heterogeneous heritage. The variety of these texts allows us to represent an indefinite variety of systems of beliefs, but it also prevents us from regarding any coherent set of texts as canonical for us. We have become aware of the wide range of varying and conflicting types of justificatory argument used to support various types of contending belief, and of the varying and conflicting theoretical accounts of rational justification. Incommensurability as untranslatability is no longer the problem at this point in MacIntyre's story. It is precisely our understanding of other languages and other cultures that persuades us of the existence of incommensurability with respect to fundamental premises or forms of reasoning. And awareness of this kind of incommensurability makes it difficult for us to accept claims for the superiority of any single system of belief. The possibility of evaluative incommensurability arises precisely when untranslatability is overcome.[4]

There is much that seems readily acceptable in MacIntyre's story. Undoubtedly there are many instances of the partial untranslatability he describes. His claim that it can be overcome by speakers of modern languages is plausible and so is his claim that the accurate translation of a belief system held by others may raise issues about incommensurability of the second and third kinds. In fact, it seems to me that the most powerful evidence for evaluative incommensurability arises, not when we fail to make another culture intelligible to us, but precisely when we make it intelligible enough to realize that their fundamental concepts, beliefs, and modes of justification are different from ours.

On the other side, MacIntyre rightly rejects the tendency of some contemporary antirelativists to hold that we necessarily inhabit our own conceptual schemes and that we necessarily translate the conceptual schemes of others through rendering their concepts and beliefs similar to our own in all or most important respects. Davidson, for instance, argues that the principle of charity is necessarily presupposed in translation because all we have to start with is a set of sentences the speaker holds true. To gain a foothold in translation, he argues, we must assume the speaker generally agrees with us in our beliefs. We then are in a position to attribute explicable disagreement between the speaker and us in *some* cases, but we could not judge that others had concepts or beliefs radically different from our own because of the underlying methodology of translation. This picture mistakenly assumes that it is unproblematic to speak of *our* beliefs. It neglects the diversity and ambiguities present in our own conceptual scheme, and furthermore neglects the fact that in rendering a scheme intelligible to ourselves we often draw from the diverse and conflicting possibilities of belief and modes of justification that are contained within our own tradition.

Good examples of this are found in Peter Winch's and Charles Taylor's comments on the dispute over the interpretation of Zande magical rites. On one side of the dispute are those who would view the rites as misguided attempts to control nature, a kind of prototechnology.

Peter Winch represents the other side when he argues that we cannot project our own purposes onto the Azande. The rites constitute a "form of expression" that provides an Azande the opportunity to reflect on how "the life he lives, his relations with his fellows, his chances for acting decently or doing evil, may all spring from his relation to his crops." The rites express a recognition that

> life is subject to contingencies, rather than an attempt to control these. . . . We have a drama of resentments, evil-doing, revenge, expiation, in which there are ways of dealing (symbolically) with misfortunes and their disruptive effect on a man's relations with his fellows, with ways in which life can go on despite such disruptions.[5]

To illuminate the expressive function of Zande rites, Winch refers to the Judaeo-Christian conception of "If it be thy Will," as developed in the story of Job. Christian prayers of supplication are like the Zande rites, not in the content of the attitudes expressed, but in the respect that they do express such attitudes. Winch, therefore, is making the rites intelligible by drawing on a way that language is used for expressive purposes within our own tradition.

Charles Taylor finds some plausibility in Winch's interpretation but ultimately presents another, drawing from his own tradition in presenting and clarifying it. The problem with Winch's interpretation, he argues, is that the Azande cannot be described as expressing an attitude toward contingencies in their rites, *as opposed* to trying to gain control of these contingencies. There is evidence that the Azande have this latter purpose in mind, even if they use their rites to accomplish the former as well. The right thing to say about the Azande is that they make no distinction between these purposes. To understand better the lack of what seems to be a fundamental distinction, we must grasp a way of understanding the world that has not been purged of its symbolic and expressive aspects. We must grasp an older conception of rationality that makes no distinction between understanding the world and coming into attunement with it:

> We don't understand the order of things without understanding our place in it, because we are part of this order. And we cannot understand the order and our place in it without loving it, without seeing its goodness, which is what I want to call being in attunement with it. Not being in attunement with it is a sufficient condition of not understanding it, for anyone who genuinely understands must love it; and not understanding it is incompatible with being in attunement with it, since this presupposes understanding.[6]

Taylor's idea is that the absence of a distinction between expressing and controlling must be understood in the context of the absence of a distinction between understanding the world and becoming attuned to it. Expressing the recognition that life is subject to contingencies is a mode of attunement to the world. And since attunement is intertwined with understanding, expressing is intertwined with the modes of understanding that make control possible. Taylor believes that the European cultural tradition embodied this connection until the advent of modern science, when the world ceased to be a possible object of attunement. We severed the connection between understanding and attunement, dismissing it as mere projection onto the world the order of things we find meaningful or flattering.

One point I want to emphasize about Taylor's interpretation is that it was reflection on the roots of his own tradition that led him to propose a useful way of looking at Zande magical rites. Another point I want to emphasize is that his interpretation has much resonance for the understanding of other cultures. It sheds light, for example, on a dominant theme within the premodern Chinese intellectual tradition. This theme asserts a kind of attunement between humankind, heaven, and earth, and it attributes moral qualities to heaven and earth. Taylor's description also helps us to understand the Mbuti of Central Africa, hunter-gatherers who regard the forest as the source of their existence and indeed of all goodness, who talk, shout, whisper, and sing to the forest.[7] Taylor has hit upon a way of thinking that is frequently congenial to the human mind, that appears in the cultural past of European languages, and that at the same time differs significantly from a dominant way of thinking in the modern West.

There are plenty of other examples in which we draw on the richness and ambiguities of our own tradition in rendering intelligible another language and tradition. These examples put into question Davidson's arguments against the possibility of alternative conceptual schemes. But coming to terms with his arguments requires that we acknowledge the seed of plausibility in them. His arguments depend on the idea that in understanding others we must render them like ourselves, and it must be admitted that this idea is supported to a certain extent by a plausible picture of translation. Richard Grandy has claimed that we should translate a speaker's utterances in such a way that the imputed pattern of relations among beliefs, desires, and the world be as similar to our own as possible. Grandy derives this "principle of humanity," as he calls it, from the assumption that the ultimate purpose of translation is to enable the translator to make the best possible predictions and offer the best explanations of the speaker's behavior. We predict and explain by translating verbal behavior into our own language, using the translation to fix the content of the speaker's beliefs, desires, and other propositional attitudes. Then we combine this information with a psychological model of the speaker to turn out predictions and explanations. Grandy suggests, plausibly enough, that we use ourselves as models. We consider what we would do if we had the relevant beliefs, desires, and so on. The success of the simulation depends on the similarity of the speaker's belief and desire network to our own.[8]

This picture pushes us in the direction of attributing our own basic forms of practical reasoning and inferential patterns to other speakers, because doing so would seem to be a minimal condition for making sense of the connections within their systems of beliefs and desires. This picture also pushes us, to a certain extent, in the direction of attributing the contents of our belief and desires to theirs. But this picture allows us to interpret others as differing significantly from us in their beliefs and desires too. And that is because the psychological model we use in understanding them is a collective "us"—we who have a certain range of desires and beliefs. If we each used only our individual selves in predicting and explaining the behavior of others, we would be much poorer predictors and explainers than we in fact are. In growing up we learn and are taught that people differ from us in what they desire and what they believe. We learn that differences in belief cannot always be explained on the basis of some demonstrable error in reasoning by someone, nor can they always be explained by saying that people have different evidential bases. We, therefore, have a conception of the normal *range* of desires and beliefs that comes with being recognizably human.

We can agree that we must make others like us in order to interpret and translate them, as long as we recognize that already implicit in our conception of "us" is a diversity of belief and desire. When we eventually come to understand the beliefs of another culture that initially look bizarre, we draw from our conception of the range of possible human desire and belief. We draw analogies between those beliefs and others that already lie within the range of the recognizably human (between notions of attunement in our own past and the beliefs of the Azande; between Christian prayer and magical rites), and we understand better. But we can still recognize difference, for even though there will be overlap between the range of human desire and belief as we conceive it and the beliefs we end up attributing to speakers of other cultures, it is quite possible for us to attribute to them beliefs that not many of "us" hold, or ones that do not dominate our view of the world as these beliefs dominate the others' view of the world, or ones that most of us no longer hold, or ones that are somewhat familiar to us by analogy but elaborated in unfamiliar or novel ways. Translation is based on a prior conception of what human beings desire and believe, but at the same time this conception is subject to expansion and modification as a result of the translation itself.

Davidson might reply to this criticism by reminding us of his claim that we could not judge others to have beliefs *radically* different from ours. He might allow for many of the differences in concept and belief I have pointed out, perhaps dismissing differences in evaluative and metaphysical beliefs as nonradical differences, while insisting on uniformity of belief, say, concerning midsize objects of the human environment.[9] Now this defense makes Davidson's claim against partial incommensurability less striking than they appear when he is speaking generally and not giving examples of what he would and would not allow. Furthermore, even if there is general agreement on the existence of things such as rocks, trees, and people, there certainly seem to be striking differences in beliefs about other entities that exist and have their effects on the "commonsense" entities. The anthropologist Joanna Overing, for instance, describes the Piaroa's belief in the beings of dreams who are capable of causally interacting with the beings of wakefulness.[10] Furthermore, there seems to be striking difference in beliefs about the causal connections between the entities of the "commonsense" world. The Azande seem genuinely to expect the ritual poisoning of a cock to tell them whether all sorts of events in the past and future have happened or will happen. This possible defense of Davidson's, then, both diminishes the significance of his claim against incommensurability and fails to eliminate the possibility of significant difference. More importantly, however, this defense unjustifiably assumes that we can say a priori that we must model others after ourselves in all or most important respects. How can we rule out the possibility that some lesser degree of overlap would suffice for making them intelligible to us?

So far I have supported MacIntyre's story of how the issue of evaluative incommensurability becomes a real one for us. However, there needs to be further discussion of one point in MacIntyre's story of how rendering another language intelligible *necessarily* raises the possibility of incommensurability of the third kind. His story assumes that we can represent the beliefs expressed in the other language only if our own language is free of commitment to those beliefs or to *any other beliefs* that are rivals to them. It is not obvious why this should be so. The mere presence of a variety of texts from different parts of the cultural past, and even of fundamentally different beliefs about the world and modes of justification, does not entail absence of commitment to a certain set of texts, beliefs, and modes of justification. Nor does the commitment thereby prevent a grasp of other texts, beliefs, and modes. There seems nothing in the requirements of overcoming partial untranslatability that *entails* that the speakers of modern languages are forced to accept evaluative incommensurability.

Perhaps MacIntyre's point is that the kind of awareness of diverse belief systems and modes of justification that is necessary for being able to translate the languages of cultures very different from one's own is just the sort of awareness that tends to undermine commitment to any one system of beliefs and of modes of justification. When we find diversity on the most fundamental levels, we despair of finding any genuinely neutral and independent standard of justification that will allow us to say which of the many conflicting systems is the best, and not being able to say which is the best tends to erode any commitments we may have or to inhibit the formation of new ones. So put, the issue comes down to the threat of skepticism at a time when a foundationless epistemology seems to be our most viable alternative. Indeed this way of understanding MacIntyre's argument seems the most natural way to construe all arguments from the second to the third kind of incommensurability. It might be thought that all such arguments rely, at least implicitly, on the idea that a neutral and independent standard is needed for judging between two theories of the world.

When arguments for evaluative incommensurability are construed in such a manner, they involve us in the very difficult question of whether such a standard is indeed needed. After having set out the argument described above, MacIntyre goes on to describe a way in which the case for evaluative incommensurability may be overcome, and this way does not involve reference to an independent and neutral standard. What I would like to argue in this essay is that even if judgments of superiority do not require a neutral and independent standard, a substantial argument for evaluative incommensurability can be made, starting with a recognition of some actual cases of incommensurability with respect to premises and forms of reasoning.

Ian Hacking, drawing from the work of A.C. Krombie, has pointed to the possibility of different *styles* of scientific reasoning, many of them discernible within the Western tradition, emerging at definite points, sometimes dying out, others still going strong.[11] Neither induction nor deduction are "styles" in Hacking's sense, because they are merely devices for passing from truth to truth. They do not determine the class of sentences that assert possibilities of truth or falsehood, and that is what styles of reasoning do. Hacking believes that in Renaissance medicine, alchemy, and astrology the way that propositions are defended and proposed are entirely alien to us. To understand what was taken to be legitimate candidates for truth or falsity (for example, that mercury salve might be good for syphilis because mercury is signed by the planet Mercury, which signs the marketplace, where syphilis is contracted), we must learn the chains of reasoning that went into proposing and defending these propositions.

Now it seems to me that Hacking's concept of "styles of reasoning" encompasses material rules of inference. By "material rules" I mean rules that are not rules of formal logic or of induction, but rules that determine what facts count as evidence and that determine the ways in which facts can weigh in favor of claims. For example, the material rules of inference in Renaissance medicine prescribe that the associations between mercury, the planet Mercury, the marketplace, and syphilis count as evidence for the claim that mercury salve is good for syphilis. If there are differences in forms of reasoning or modes of justification, they are likely to be focused around differences in material rules of inference that constitute a style of reasoning.

I suggest that a family of styles of reasoning is clustered around the conception of understanding and attunement described by Taylor. I say a "family" because there surely are important differences between the styles exhibited by the Azande, premodern European scientists, and the premodern Chinese. One difference between the styles lies in the attitudes toward the world that attunement involves. Taylor's characterization of attunement as involving *love* of the world seems best suited to Platonic Christianity. Chinese versions of attunement involve acceptance and appreciation rather than anything we could characterize as love.

Common to different versions of attunement, however, is the theme that the world operates in certain patterns or according to certain principles. Also the common theme exists that human beings become attuned to the world by "replicating" in some sense the same patterns in their relations to other human beings and to the natural world. This is the idea of finding one's place in the order of things, which Taylor mentioned in the passage quoted above. And finally, the different styles share the characteristic of making attunement both a necessary and sufficient condition of understanding. I want to focus on the Chinese style of reasoning, sketch how the common themes are fleshed out, relate why I think it really is a distinctive style of reasoning, and finally explain why the nature of its distinctiveness raises questions about evaluative incommensurability. I pick the Chinese case because we have so much knowledge about their theories of the world and because it arises from such a highly developed and sophisticated intellectual tradition that the question of evaluative incommensurability with modern European culture arises naturally and immediately.

In the premodern Chinese tradition "the order of things" was partly defined by a theory of the two fundamental forces in the universe. The two forces are yin and yang. One dominates for a time, then the other, in wavelike succession. Yin is associated with coldness, cloudiness, rain, femaleness, and that which is inside and dark. Yang is associated with sunshine and heat, with spring and summer, and maleness. In his classic study of Chinese science and civilization Joseph Needham quotes from a Han Confucianist text that points out certain correlations in the yin operations of Heaven with events in human affairs. When Heaven is about to make the yin rain fall, for example, people feel sleepy. The theory is that when the yin force in Heaven and Earth begins to dominate, the yin force in people responds by taking the lead.

Another major theory in the tradition that partially defined the order of things was that of the five elements. These elements were not so much five sorts of matter but five sorts of processes. The element of water, for example, stood for soaking, dripping, and descending; fire stood for heating, burning, and ascending; and earth stood for the production of vegetation and nutritivity. During the Han dynasty it was believed that each of the elements dominated in a yearly cycle, and the order of succession was, in part, an order of conquest. Fire conquers the element of metal, for example, because fire can melt metal; earth conquers water because it can dam it up and constrain it.[12] All sorts of things in the universe were correlated with the five elements, and the corresponding principle of conquest was applied. The dog is associated with the earth, while the tiger is associated with the wood, so as wood conquers the earth, the tiger conquers the dog.

Sinologists such as Joseph Needham, Hellmut Wilhelm, and Marcel Granet have named the kind of thinking illustrated above as "coordinative or associative thinking," and they see in it a distinctive causality and logic, a characteristic thought form.[13] Needham describes the style in the following way:

> The symbolic correlations or correspondences all formed part of one colossal pattern. Things behaved in particular ways not necessarily because of prior actions or impulsions of other things, but because their position in the ever-moving cyclical universe was such that they were endowed with intrinsic natures which made that behavior inevitable for them. If they did not behave in those particular ways they would lose their relational positions in the whole (which made them what they were),

and turn into something other than themselves. They were thus parts in existential dependence upon the whole world-organism. And they reacted upon one another not so much by mechanical impulsion or causation as by a kind of mysterious resonance.[14]

Needham contrasts this style of thought with "primitive thinking," as Levy-Bruhl characterized it:

> Chinese coordinative thinking was *not* primitive thinking in the sense that it was an alogical or pre-logical chaos in which anything could be the cause of anything else, and where men's ideas were guided by the pure fancies of one or another medicine-man. It was a picture of an extremely and precisely ordered universe. . . . But it was a universe in which this organisation came about, not because of fiats issued by a supreme creator-lawgiver, which things must obey subject to sanctions imposable by angels attendant; nor because of the physical clash of innumerable billiard-balls in which the motion of the one was the physical cause of the impulsion of the other. It was an ordered harmony of wills without the ordainer; it was like the spontaneous yet ordered, in the sense of the patterned, movements of dancers in a country dance of figures, none of whom are bound by law to do what they do, nor yet pushed by others coming behind, but cooperate in a voluntary harmony of wills.[15]

Not all instances of "coordinative thinking" were committed to the rather curious correlations between animals and elements described above. Chu Hsi, who wrote much later in the tradition, and who is considered one of the most influential of Chinese philosophers, carried this thinking to an extremely high level of abstraction. For him the universe was composed of "ch'i," a term with no real correlate in English, but which is sometimes translated as "matter-energy" or "material force." The point of these translations is to indicate that ch'i is not inert material substance but closer to matter as now conceived under subatomic physics: convertible to energy and formed from energy. Chu Hsi posited a principle of cosmic organization that governed the transformations of ch'i—"li." The principle of cosmic organization pervaded everything, such that right order in human affairs, as described by such moral qualities as righteousness, propriety, and love, were high manifestations of that single principle. For Chu Hsi, and this holds generally of the premodern tradition, moral instruction is of one piece with description of the cosmic organization.[16] To carry out successfully that instruction is to find one's place in the order of things.

Reflecting on the consistent way in which this type of thought recurs throughout the Chinese intellectual tradition, we may conclude that understanding the universe was closely associated with achieving attunement with it. So closely, in fact, that attunement had become a necessary and sufficient condition of understanding. This conclusion fits with several major features of the Chinese tradition. For one thing, the intertwining of attunement and understanding is present in all sorts of philosophies in ancient and medieval China. These philosophies give many different sorts of views about the nature of the world to which we can become attuned, along with different views as to the manner in which we are to become attuned. Taoism gives a very different view of understanding the world and becoming attuned to it than Confucianism does, but both do intertwine understanding and attunement. The intertwining is consistent with another, oft-remarked feature of Chinese thought—that it has a consistently practical focus. The point of thinking well is to live well. We rarely find an appreciation for discovering the way things *really* are, divorced from all questions of how such a discovery would fit into a desirable way of life. There is no correlate to the Aristotelian doctrine that *theoria* is a good in itself and in fact the highest good for humankind. Another feature of the tradition that fits with the intertwining of attunement and understanding is lack of a clear or prominent distinction between what is true on the one hand and what it would be good for us to believe on the other.

That is why I find unconvincing a possible objection to the claim that the association of understanding and attunement we find in the tradition is part of a distinctive style of *reasoning*. The objection is that there is no distinctive style here, just a distinctive set of basic premises about the world: the universe is organized according to a pattern such that the human moral qualities are in some way reflections and instances of that overall pattern, for instance. Given the truth of such a premise, and given sufficient clarification of its content, we could understand that if it were true, we would reason like them. So the rejoinder goes.[17] But even if we were to accept that the view of the world described above *can* be set out like premises of a theory, it is still possible that the premises are *treated* as constants within a tradition, to the extent that they become incorporated into the conception of understanding. These constants result in material rules of inference that determine what facts count as evidence and in what ways they count. They determine, for instance, that the association between yin and rain counts as evidence for increased sleepiness among people.

We make intelligible another cultural tradition by determining what interpretations make for the best explanation of important features of that tradition. This is how we decide on the hypothesis that certain beliefs have been incorporated into the conception of under-

standing in such a way that a distinctive style of reasoning arises. I have
indicated what features in the premodern Chinese tradition weigh in
favor of this hypothesis but have not offered conclusive evidence for it.
Such a hypothesis needs to be confirmed through much more investigation and reflection on a long and complex tradition. In the rest of this
paper I want to explore the implications of assuming that it is true.
Assume that attunement did become a necessary and sufficient condition of understanding in the Chinese tradition. What implications for
the issue of evaluative incommensurability follow from that?

A good case for evaluative incommensurability follows straightforwardly from a "criterial conception of rationality," as Hilary Putnam
calls it. A criterial conception holds that institutionalized norms define
what is, and is not, rationally acceptable.[18] If the association of attunement and understanding had become institutionalized, it would follow
that the Chinese not only accepted as rational things that are not so for
us, but that these things *were* rational for them. This seems to be a
strong form of evaluative incommensurability, but the criterial conception is wrong.

The Chinese themes described above, even at their most dominant
within the tradition, always had their skeptics, and I take it that this will
hold true of any tradition that is long enough and which allows debate
and reflection. The Han philosopher Hsün Tzu, for instance, denied the
usual correlations made between heaven, earth, and human affairs, and
urged instead the investigation of nature for the sake of controlling it.[19]
The fact that this prototechnological attitude failed to take hold within
the tradition does not render his criticisms meaningless, nor does it
obscure the fact that he was offering to his contemporaries a conception
of understanding nature that was a radical alternative to the dominant
conception. Criterial conceptions of rationality overlook the richness
and diversity of actual intellectual traditions, and even if certain criteria
of rationality gain a dominance in such traditions, the presence of
dissent indicates the meaningfulness of challenge to those criteria.

To see how the dominant conception of understanding in the
Chinese tradition could weigh in favor of evaluative incommensurability, we must first recognize that even though what is rationally acceptable is not definable by accepted criteria, it does not follow that whatever is rationally acceptable in different cultures is the same. And I am
not making the mundane point that what is rational to believe depends
on the available evidence, which may vary from culture to culture, and
on the known methods for evaluating evidence and testing claims.
There may be relativity in rational acceptability, even if we hold such
factors constant.

That is because the rationality of belief is in part determined by the values of a culture if these values are not irrationally held. If the goal of attunement to nature is highly valued in a culture, it may be that what is rational to believe in this culture is different from what it is rational to believe in a culture that does not place a high value on this goal. To put the point in another way: we must grant that the rationality of belief can never be reduced to the criteria that are dominant within a culture, and while the rationality of belief takes the form of a normative ideal that we may never fully grasp, there still may be significant differences in the ways that ideal is legitimately satisfied as we move from culture to culture; the differences may depend on differences among primary values held.

In this way we may defend the possibility of evaluative incommensurability, independently of the issue of skepticism about our ability to make judgments on other theories when there is no independent and theory-neutral standard for making such judgments. Suppose that we have a correspondence theory of truth, and that our beliefs are true if and only if they map onto a world that exists independently of those beliefs. Further, suppose that the modern divorce between understanding and attunement does result in a truer understanding of nature. We still could distinguish the *epistemic warrant* for holding a belief and the *rationality* of holding that belief. We may do so by tying epistemic warrant to an external criterion, as in causal or reliabilist theories of knowledge,[20] while tying rationality to the achievement of what is desirable for us. In this way the issue of whether it is rational to conjoin understanding and attunement remains open, even after we assume that it results in a less reliable style of reasoning. The costs of accepting a divorce between understanding and attunement may be too high if the goal of attunement is valued highly enough.

Now we must consider whether it is rational to value attunement so highly. The case for evaluative incommensurability should not depend on the adoption of a purely instrumentalist view of practical reasoning that permits no criticism of the rationality of our ultimate ends but only of our means. But it seems to me that the burden of proof lies on those who would declare the high value placed on attunement to be irrational, given that we can understand the satisfactions of a life in which attunement is in great measure achieved. It is interesting to note in this regard that the anthropologist Robin Horton, who conducted an extensive comparison of traditional African and modern Western thought that was in many respects unfavorable to African thought, chose to live in "still-heavily traditional Africa" because of his "discovery of things lost at home," including an "intensely poetic quality in

everyday life and thought, and vivid enjoyment of the passing moment"
that have been driven out of sophisticated Western life by "the faith in
progress."[21]

It may be objected that traditional conceptions linking understanding and attunement will never result in as great a control over
nature, and that people of all cultures have an interest in having some
degree of control. It does not follow, however, that the degree of control
afforded by modern science and technology is to be bought at any cost.
The obvious reply to this move would be to point out that the ideal
thing would be to have a form of life in which attunement and greater
control over nature are combined and reconciled. William Wainwright
declares that "it is by no means clear but that a comprehensive theory
would be better if it not only provided accurate and precise explanations of the quantitative aspects of natural phenomena and a plausible
account of the nature of natural forces, but also provided the sort of
illumination associated with attunement."[22] It certainly must be admitted that such a synthesis is not only a logical possibility but would be
highly desirable as well.

Yet to point to the possibility when we have no idea of how to
realize it is not a sufficient reply to the case for evaluative incommensurability, not when the actual history of traditional and modern cultures
indicates that the divorce of understanding and attunement tends to
undermine the belief in larger natural forces that "resonate" in response
to human values and ideals. Wainwright's suggestion does weigh in
favor of refraining from making a *final* judgment on the existence of
evaluative incommensurability. It is fair to say that there is no *proof* of
evaluative incommensurability because of the possibility that there is
some third form of life superior to both a form of life premised on the
connection between understanding and attunement and a form premised on their divorce. On the other hand, we have no reason to think
that the third possibility is realizable. We furthermore can see great
value in the two forms of life we know to be realizable, and we cannot
see why one form has priority over the other. Provisional acceptance of
evaluative incommensurability seems reasonable.

I want to stress the fact that I am not making the argument for
incommensurability from a skeptical position. I am assuming that we
know our own "style" of reasoning is more reliable. But I am also
assuming that our knowledge and experience of other cultures and of
the diversity of our own cultural roots has had a broadening effect on
our notion of what a good human life is. We may reject the notion that
all forms of life are equally good and accept the notion that there is
more than one form of life that is best. We need not be skeptical about

the objectivity of value judgments to introduce a reasonable amount of pluralism into those judgments.

To reinforce this point, let me sketch a spectrum of differences between forms of life that raise issues of evaluative incommensurability. Suppose that a woman is trying to decide between the life of a musician and the life of a philosopher. We want to say in this case that the rationality of her accepting one or the other "form of life" essentially depends on factors such as her temperament, her most important desires, her talents, and her circumstances. We would be most reluctant to say that one or the other form was *generally* superior. We do not think that our inability to prescribe a general choice is evidence for skepticism about value judgments. This sort of case is at one end of the spectrum. Now consider the difference between life under an absolute dictator who has rigid ideas as to what races are superior and life as we know it in a modern Western democracy. Most of us think there are objective and general reasons for preferring one form over the other. If there were no such reasons to be given, the skeptical issue legitimately arises. This sort of case is at the other end of the spectrum.

Finally, consider the contrast between a form of life focused around the connection between understanding and attunement and a form focused on the severance of that connection. This is a case that falls somewhere between the two ends. Argument and discussion of the case could make us locate it closer to one or the other end of the spectrum. I have been trying to move it closer to the musician-philosopher end. My argument has relied not merely on our inability to show why the form of life focused around severance is superior or inferior to the other form. It has relied on what I believe to be our genuine appreciation of the potential satisfactions of both forms. If a person is not able to see these satisfactions, then it is possible that nothing more in the way of argument or demonstration could be given to her. But there still could be fact of the matter.

Some forms of life may be so far from a person's experience and dominant propensities that she is unable to see what satisfactions they could yield. That may be a reflection on her and her limitations rather than on the forms of life. Sometimes becoming better acquainted with a form of life induces a new appreciation of it. Perhaps Horton went through such a learning experience, and perhaps some anthropologists who vigorously defend the possibility of evaluative incommensurability do so from field experiences that are learning experiences in this sense. It may not be practical or desirable for our skeptic to go out into the field, but she must allow for the possibility of conversion, especially since others have been so converted.

I hope that I have provided some support for the conclusion that the most interesting and substantial cases for evaluative incommensurability arise, not from our inability to make sense of another people's beliefs, but precisely from those situations in which we understand and see how different their beliefs are from our own. The question of evaluative incommensurability arises, not because their beliefs appear bizarre to us, but because we can understand how they are tied to a life that people would want to live. And we can understand because we can relate features of our own traditions to theirs in such a way that we become aware of what is gained from that sort of life and what we have lost. These cases for evaluative incommensurability need not arise from skepticism about the lack of an independent and neutral standard for judging between theories, but rather from a solid sense of what is satisfying in alternative forms of life. To close this essay, however, I want to raise the one factor that somewhat undermines the case for evaluative incommensurability. This factor involves a lack of understanding of ourselves and of what we are striving for.

To explain this factor I begin with a possible objection to the argument as set out so far. Recall that in making that argument I assumed that we have a correspondence theory of truth. The possible objection can be put in terms of a question: "Since the premodern Chinese valued attunement so highly and did not sever understanding and attunement, perhaps they did not even have a notion of truth as correspondence; and if they did not, in what sense can we say they believed anything to be true (in our correspondence sense of truth)?"

The answer to the question of whether the premodern Chinese had a correspondence notion of truth must be determined through investigation of the tradition. I think a case for the lack of such a notion could be made, based on the lack of a distinction between what is true and what it would be good to believe. But even if they did not have such a notion, we still can intelligibly attribute beliefs to them. And the reason is again rooted in the richness and diversity of our own tradition. Truth within our own tradition has been subject to different interpretations. We have listened to those who argue that we can never make good on the vague notion of correspondence truth, that we shall never cash it out by specifying the right relation between true propositions or statements and whatever it is they purport to be about. We know about coherence notions as rivals to the correspondence interpretation. And we have heard Hilary Putnam repudiate the correspondence interpretation and propose that our notion of truth is value-laden (coherence, simplicity, instrumental efficacy) and that the relevant cognitive values are arbitrary, considered as anything but a part of the holistic conception of human flourishing.[23]

At this point we have come round in a full circle. We find within our own tradition the notion of truth that may belong to the premodern Chinese. We may not even be able to say that our own beliefs and forms of reasoning were truer and more reliable (in the correspondence sense) than theirs. There still would be the question of whether their notion of flourishing was better or worse than ours. Finding the answer would depend on formulating the notion of flourishing that we have and then comparing it with that of the premodern Chinese.

The main point, in any case, is that once we stop supposing for the sake of argument that we have this or that notion of truth, the position we take on the issue of evaluative incommensurability depends on the extent to which we understand *ourselves* and our most fundamental normative ideals, such as truth and flourishing. That we do understand ourselves sufficiently to make a judgment is not at all clear. This seems the most serious challenge to the advocates of evaluative incommensurability. In fact, this is a challenge both to those who want to say that once we understand people in other cultures, they turn out to be essentially like us and to believe essentially as we do, and to those who say that there are worlds incommensurable with our own. Both sides make too easy an assumption about what we are like and what we believe.

Notes

1. Work on this essay was in part made possible by a fellowship from the American Council of Learned Societies. I gratefully acknowledge its support. I also owe a great deal to Amélie Rorty, Eli Hirsch, and Jerry Samet, who gave me many helpful comments on a previous version of this essay.

2. See Davidson on Whorf's claims about the incommensurability of Hopi metaphysics and on Kuhn's descriptions couched in postrevolutionary idiom of what things were like before the scientific revolution: "On the Very Idea of a Conceptual Scheme," Presidential Address delivered before the Seventieth Eastern Division meeting of the American Philosophical Association, 1973, *Proceedings and Addresses of the APA* 47 (1974): 6. Putnam makes a similar point concerning claims about the incommensurability asserted to hold between Galileo's theory and our current scientific theory: see *Reason, Truth and History* (Cambridge: Cambridge University Press, 1981).

3. Alasdair MacIntyre, "Relativism, Power, and Philosophy," Presidential Address delivered before the Eighty-first Eastern Division Meeting of the American Philosophical Association, 1984, *APA Proceedings* 59 (1985): 9.

4. Ibid., pp. 13-17.

5. Peter Winch, "Understanding a Primitive Society," in *Rationality*, ed. Bryan R. Wilson (New York: Harper, 1979), pp. 100, 104-105.

6. Charles Taylor, "Rationality," in *Rationality and Relativism*, ed. Martin Hollis and Steven Lukes (Cambridge: MIT Press, 1982), pp. 95-96.

7. Colin M. Turnbull, *The Human Cycle* (New York: Simon and Shuster, 1983), pp. 30-31.

8. See Richard Grandy, "Reference, Meaning, and Belief," *Journal of Philosophy* 70 (1973): 439-452.

9. I am indebted to Eli Hirsch for bringing this possible reply to my attention.

10. Joanna Overing, "Today I shall call him 'Mummy': multiple worlds and classificatory confusion," in *Reason and Morality*, ed. Joanna Overing (London and New York: Tavistock, 1985), pp. 152-179.

11. Ian Hacking, "Language, Truth and Reason," in *Rationality and Relativism*, pp. 48-66.

12. Joseph Needham, *Science and Civilisation in China* (Cambridge: Cambridge at the University Press, 1956), vol. 2, pp. 275-276.

13. See ibid., pp. 280-281; Hellmut Wilhelm, *A Short History of Chinese Civilisation*, tr. J. Joshua (London: Harrap, 1929), esp. p. 35; Marcel Granet, *La Pensee Chinoise* (Paris: Albin Michel, 1934).

14. Needham, *Science and Civilisation in China*, p. 281.

15. Ibid., p. 287.

16. See Chu Hsi, *Chu Tzu ch'uan-shu* (Complete Works of Chu Hsi), sections 1-37, 100-113.

17. W. Newton Smith makes such a rejoinder to Charles Taylor's claim that the pre-Galileans had a conception of rationality that associates understanding with attunement. See his "Relativism and the Possibility of Interpretation," in *Rationality and Relativism*, especially pp. 111-112.

18. See Putnam's *Reason, Truth and History*, p. 110.

19. See *The Hsün Tzu*, chapter 17, "On Nature."

20. Peter Railton makes this point in "Moral Realism," *Philosophical Review* 95 (1986): 163-207.

21. Robin Horton, "African Thought and Western Science," in *Rationality*, ed. Bryan Wilson, p. 170.

22. See William Wainwright, "Does Disagreement Imply Relativism?" *International Philosophical Quarterly* 26 (1986): 58.

23. Putnam, *Reason, Truth and History*, p. 136.

The Myth of the Subjective

DONALD DAVIDSON

This is an essay on an old topic, the relation between the human mind and the rest of nature, the subjective and the objective as we have come to think of them. This dualism, though in its way too obvious to question, carries with it in our tradition a large, and not necessarily appropriate, burden of associated ideas. Some of these ideas are now coming under critical scrutiny, and the result promises to mark a sea change in contemporary philosophical thought—a change so profound that we may not recognize that it is occurring.

The present essay, while clearly tendentious, is not designed primarily to convert the skeptic; its chief aim is to describe, from one point of view, a fairly widely recognized development in recent thinking about the contents of the mind, and to suggest some of the consequences that I think follow from this development.

Minds are many; nature is one. Each of us has one's own position in the world, and hence one's own perspective on it. It is easy to slide from this truism to some confused notion of conceptual relativism. The former, harmless, relativism is just the familiar relativism of position in space and time. Because each of us preempts a volume of space-time, two of us cannot be in exactly the same place at the same time. The relations among our positions are intelligible because we can locate each person in a single, common world and a shared time frame.

Conceptual relativism may seem similar, but the analogy is difficult to carry out. For what is the common reference point, or system of coordinates, to which each scheme is relative? Without a good answer to this question the claim that each of us in some sense inhabits his own world loses its intelligibility.

For this reason and others I have long held that there are limits to how much individual or social systems of thought can differ. If by conceptual relativism we mean the idea that conceptual schemes and moral systems, or the languages associated with them, can differ massively—to the extent of being mutually unintelligible or incommensurable, or forever beyond rational resolve—then I reject conceptual relativism.[1] Of course there are contrasts from epoch to epoch, from culture to culture, and person to person of kinds which we all recognize and struggle with; but these are contrasts which, with sympathy and effort, we can explain and understand. Trouble comes when we try to embrace the idea that there might be more comprehensive differences, for this seems (absurdly) to ask us to take up a stance outside our own ways of thought.

In my opinion we do not understand the idea of such a really foreign scheme. We know what states of mind are like, and how they are correctly identified; they are just those states whose contents can be discovered in well-known ways. If other people or creatures are in states not discoverable by these methods, it can be, not because our methods fail us, but because those states are not correctly called states of mind—they are not beliefs, desires, wishes, or intentions. The meaninglessness of the idea of a conceptual scheme forever beyond our grasp is due not to our inability to understand such a scheme or to our other human limitations; it is due simply to what we mean by a system of concepts.

Many philosophers are not satisfied with arguments like these because they think there is another way in which conceptual relativism can be made intelligible. For it seems that we could make sense of such relativism provided we could find an element in the mind untouched by conceptual interpretation. Then various schemes might be seen as relative to, and assigned the role of organizing, this common element. The common element is, of course, some version of Kant's "content," Hume's impressions and ideas, sense data, uninterpreted sensation, the sensuous given. Kant thought only one scheme was possible, but once the dualism of scheme and content was made explicit, the possibility of alternative schemes was apparent. The idea is explicit in the work of C. I. Lewis:

> There are, in our cognitive experience, two elements; the immediate data, such as those of sense, which are presented or given to the mind, and a form, construction, or interpretation, which represents the activity of thought.[2]

If we could conceive of the function of conceptual schemes in this way, relativism would appear to be an abstract possibility despite doubts about how an alien scheme might be deciphered: the idea would be that different schemes or languages constitute different ways in which what is given in experience may be organized. On this account there would be no point of view from which we could survey such schemes, and perhaps no way we could in general compare or evaluate them; still, as long as we thought we understood the scheme-content dichotomy, we could imagine the unsullied stream of experience being variously re-worked by various minds or cultures. In this way, it may be held, conceptual relativism can be provided with the element to which alter-native schemes are related: that element is the uninterpreted given, the uncategorized contents of experience.

To a large extent this picture of mind and its place in nature has defined the problems modern philosophy has thought it had to solve. Among these problems are many of the basic issues concerning knowl-edge: how we know about the "external world," how we know about other minds, even how we know the contents of our own mind. But we should also include the problem of the nature of moral knowledge, the analysis of perception, and many troubling issues in the philosophy of psychology and the theory of meaning.

Corresponding to this catalog of problems or problem areas is a long list of ways in which the supposed scheme-content contrast has been formulated. The scheme may be thought of as an ideology, a set of concepts suited to the task of organizing experience into objects, events, states, and complexes of such; or the scheme may be a language, per-haps with predicates and associated apparatus, interpreted to serve an ideology. The contents of the scheme may be objects of a special sort, such as sense-data, percepts, impressions, sensations, or appearances; or the objects may dissolve into adverbial modifications of experience: we may be "appeared to redly." Philosophers have shown ingenuity in finding ways of putting into words the contents of the given; there are those strange, verbless sentences like 'Red here now' and the various formulations of protocol sentences over which the logical positivists quarreled.

Putting the matter, or content, into words, however, is not neces-sary, and according to some views, not possible. The scheme-content division can survive even in an environment that shuns the analytic-synthetic distinction, sense-data, or the assumption that there can be thoughts or experiences that are free of theory. If I am right, this is the environment provided by W. V. Quine. According to Quine's "natural-ized epistemology" we should ask no more from the philosophy of knowledge than an account of how, given the evidence we have to go on, we are able to form a satisfactory theory of the world. The account draws on the best theory we have: our present science. The evidence on which the meanings of our sentences, and all our knowledge, ultimately depend is provided by stimulations of our sense organs. It is these stimulations that provide a person with his only cues to "what goes on around him." Quine is not, of course, a reductionist: "we cannot strip away the conceptual trappings sentence by sentence." Nevertheless, there is according to Quine a definite distinction to be made between the invariant content and the variant conceptual trappings, between "report and invention, substance and style, cues and conceptualization." For,

> we can investigate the world, and man as a part of it, and thus find out what cues he could have of what goes on around him. Subtracting his cues from his world view, we get man's net contribution as the difference. This difference marks the extent of man's conceptual sovereignty—the domain within which he can revise theory while saving the data.[3]

Worldview and cues, theory and data: these are the scheme and content of which I have been speaking.

What matters, then, is not whether we can describe the data in a neutral, theory-free idiom; what matters is that there should be an ultimate source of evidence whose character can be wholly specified without reference to what it is evidence for. Thus patterns of stimulation, like sense-data, can be identified and described without reference to "what goes on around us." If our knowledge of the world derives entirely from evidence of this kind, then not only may our senses sometimes deceive us; it is possible that we are systematically and generally deceived.

It is easy to remember what prompts this view: it is thought necessary to insulate the ultimate sources of evidence from the outside world in order to guarantee the authority of the evidence for the subject. Since we cannot be certain what the world outside the mind is like, the subjective can keep its virtue—its chastity, its certainty for us—only by being protected from contamination by the world. The familiar trouble is, of course, that the disconnection creates a gap no reasoning or construction can plausibly bridge. Once the Cartesian starting point has been chosen, there is no saying what the evidence is evidence for, or so it seems. Idealism, reductionist forms of empiricism, and skepticism loom.

The story is familiar, but let me continue in my breathless way through one more chapter. If the ultimate evidence for our schemes and theories, the raw material on which they are based, is subjective in the way I have described, then so is whatever is directly based on it: our beliefs, desires, intentions, and what we mean by our words. Though these are the progeny of our "view of the world"—indeed, taken together, they constitute our view of the world—nevertheless they too retain the Cartesian independence from what they purport to be about that the evidence on which they are based had: like sensations, they could be just as they are, and the world be very different. Our beliefs purport to represent something objective, but the character of their subjectivity prevents us from taking the first step in determining whether they correspond to what they pretend to represent.

Instead of saying it is the scheme-content dichotomy that has dominated and defined the problems of modern philosophy, then, one could as well say it is how the dualism of the objective and the subjective has been conceived. For these dualisms have a common origin: a concept of the mind with its private states and objects.

I have reached the point to which I have been leading, for it seems to me that the most promising and interesting change that is occurring in philosophy today is that these dualisms are being questioned in new ways or are being radically reworked. There is a good chance they will be abandoned, at least in their present form. The change is just now becoming evident, and its consequences have barely been recognized, even by those who are bringing it about; and of course it is, and will be, strongly resisted by many. What we are about to see is the emergence of a radically revised view of the relation of mind and the world.

Let me describe what I take to be some of the portents of this change.

The action has centered on the concept of subjectivity, what is "in the mind." Let us start with what it is we know or grasp when we know the meaning of a word or sentence. It is a commonplace of the empirical tradition that we learn our first words (which at the start serve the function of sentences)—words like 'apple', 'man', 'dog', 'water'—through a conditioning of sounds or verbal behavior to appropriate bits of matter in the public domain. The conditioning works best with objects that interest the learner and are hard to miss by either teacher or pupil. This is not just a story about how we learn to use words: it must also be an essential part of an adequate account of what words refer to and what they mean.

Needless to say, the whole story cannot be this simple. On the other hand, it is hard to believe that this sort of direct interaction between language users and public events and objects is not a basic part of the whole story, the part that, directly or indirectly, largely determines how words are related to things. Yet the story entails consequences that seem to have been ignored until very recently. One consequence is that the details of the mechanisms that constitute the causal chains from speaker to speaker, and spoken-of object to speaker to language learner, cannot in themselves matter to meaning and reference. The grasp of meanings is determined only by the terminal elements in the conditioning process and is tested only by the end product: use of words geared to appropriate objects and situations. This is perhaps best seen by noticing that two speakers who "mean the same thing" by an expression need have no more in common than their dispositions to appropriate verbal behavior; the neural networks may be very different. The matter may be put the other way around: two speakers may be alike in all relevant physical respects, and yet they may mean quite different things by the same words because of differences in the external situations in which the words were learned. Insofar, then, as the subjective or mental is thought of as supervenient on the physical characteristics of a person, and nothing more, meanings cannot be purely subjective or mental. As Hilary Putnam put it, "meanings ain't in the head."[4] The point is that the correct interpretation of what a speaker means is not determined solely by what is in his head; it depends also on the natural history of what is in the head. Putnam's argument depends on rather elaborate thought experiments which some philosophers have found unconvincing. But as far as I can see, the case can best be made by appealing directly to obvious facts about language learning and to facts about how we interpret words and languages with which we are unfamiliar.[5] The relevant facts have already been mentioned above; in the simplest and most basic cases words and sentences derive their meaning from the objects and circumstances in which they were learned. A sentence which one has been conditioned by the learning process to be caused to hold true by the presence of fires will be true when there is a fire present; a word one has been conditioned to be caused to hold applicable by the presence of snakes will refer to snakes. Of course very many words and sentences are not learned this way, but it is those that are that anchor language to the world.

If the meanings of sentences are propositions, and propositions are the objects of attitudes like belief, intention, and desire, then what has been said about meanings must hold true of all of the propositional attitudes. The point can be made without recourse to propositions or other supposed objects of the attitudes. For from the fact that speakers are in general capable of expressing their thoughts in language, it follows that to the extent that the subjectivity of meaning is in doubt, so is that of thought generally.

The fallout from these considerations for the theory of knowledge is (or ought to be) nothing less than revolutionary. If words and thoughts are, in the most basic cases, necessarily about the sorts of objects and events that cause them, there is no room for Cartesian doubts about the independent existence of such objects and events. Doubts there can be, or course. But there need be nothing we are indubitably right about for it to be certain that we are mostly right about the nature of the world. Sometimes skepticism seems to rest on a simple fallacy, the fallacy of reasoning from the fact that there is nothing we might not be wrong about to the conclusion that we might be wrong about everything. The second possibility is ruled out if we accept that our simplest sentences are given their meanings by the situations that generally cause us to hold them true or false, since to hold a sentence we understand to be true or false is to have a belief. Continuing along this line, we see that general skepticism about the deliverances of the senses cannot even be formulated, since the senses and their deliverances play no central *theoretical* role in the account of belief, meaning, and knowledge if the contents of the mind depend on the causal relations, whatever they may be, between the attitudes and the world. This is not to deny the importance of the actual casual role of the senses in knowledge and the acquisition of language, of course.

The reason the senses are of no primary theoretical importance to the philosophical account of knowledge is that it is an empirical accident that our ears, eyes, taste buds, and tactile and olfactory organs play a causal role in the formation of beliefs about the world. The causal connections between thought and objects and events in the world could have been established in entirely different ways without this making any difference to the contents or veridicality of belief. Philosophy has made the mistake of supposing that because it is often natural to terminate the defense of a particular claim to knowledge with "I saw it with my own eyes," all justification of empirical knowledge must trace back to sensory experience. What is true is that certain beliefs directly caused by sensory experience are often veridical and therefore often provide good reasons for further beliefs. But this does not set such beliefs apart in principle or award them epistemological priority.

If this is right, epistemology (as apart, perhaps, from the study of perception, which is now seen to be only distantly related to epistemology) has no basic need for purely private, subjective "objects of the mind," either as uninterpreted sense data or experience on the one hand, or as fully interpreted propositions on the other. Content and scheme, as remarked in the quotation from C. I. Lewis, came as a pair; we can let them go together. Once we take this step, no *objects* will be left with respect to which the problem of representation can be raised. Beliefs are true or false, but they represent nothing. It is good to be rid of representations, and with them the correspondence theory of truth, for it is thinking there are representations that engenders thoughts of relativism. Representations *are* relative to a scheme; a map represents Mexico, say--but only relative to a mercator, or some other, projection.

There is an abundance of puzzles about sensation and perception, but these puzzles are not, as I said, foundational for epistemology. The question of what is directly experienced in sensation, and how this is related to judgments of perception, while as hard to answer as it ever was, can no longer be assumed to be a central question for the theory of knowledge. The reason has already been given: although sensation plays a crucial role in the causal process that connects beliefs with the world, it is a mistake to think it plays an *epistemological* role in determining the contents of those beliefs. In accepting this conclusion we abandon the key dogma of traditional empiricism, what I have called the third dogma of empiricism. But that is to be expected: empiricism is the view that the subjective is the foundation of objective empirical knowledge. I am suggesting that empirical knowledge has no epistemological foundation and needs none.[6]

There is another familiar problem that is transformed when we recognize that beliefs, desires, and the other so-called propositional attitudes are not subjective in the way we thought they were. The problem is how one person knows the mind of another. Perhaps it is obvious that if the account I have sketched of our understanding of language, and its connection with the contents of thought, is correct, the accessibility of the minds of others is assured from the start. Skepticism about the *possibility* of knowing other minds is thus ruled out. But to recognize this is not to answer the question what conceptual conditions do we place on the pattern of thought that make it possible for an interpreter to progress from observed behavior to knowledge of the intentional attitudes of another. That this question *has* an answer, however, is guaranteed by the fact that the nature of language and thought is such as to make them interpretable.[7]

It should not be assumed that if we cease to be bullied or beguiled by the scheme-content and subjective-objective dichotomies, all the problems of epistemology will evaporate. But the problems that seem salient will change. Answering the global skeptic will no longer be a challenge, the search for epistemological foundations in experience will be seen as pointless, and conceptual relativism will lose its appeal. But plenty of questions of equal or greater interest will remain, or be generated by the new stance. The demise of the subjective as previously conceived leaves us without foundations for knowledge and relieves us of the need for them. New problems then arise, however, that cluster around the nature of error, for error is hard to identify and explain if the holism that goes with a nonfoundational approach is not somehow constrained. It is not problematic whether knowledge of the world and of other minds is possible; it remains as much a question as ever how we attain such knowledge, and the conditions belief must satisfy to count as knowledge. These are not so much questions in traditional epistemology as they are questions about the nature of rationality. They are questions that, like the epistemological questions they replace, have no final answer; but unlike the questions they replace, they are worth trying to answer.

Familiarity with many of the points I have been making is fairly widespread among philosophers today. But only a few among these philosophers, as far as I know, have appreciated the scope of the entailed revolution in our ways of thinking about philosophy. At least part of the reason for this failure may be traced to certain misunderstandings concerning the nature of the new antisubjectivism (as we may try calling it). Here are three of the misunderstandings.

1. People have been persuaded of the dependence of meanings on factors outside the head by examples rather than by general arguments. There is, therefore, a strong tendency to suppose that the dependence is limited to the sorts of expressions that recur in the examples: proper names, natural kind words like 'water' and 'gold', and indexicals. But in fact, the phenomenon is ubiquitous, since it is inseparable from the social character of language. It is not a local problem to be solved by some clever semantic trick; it is a perfectly general fact about the nature of thought and speech.[8]

2. If mental states like belief, desire, intention, and meaning are not supervenient on the physical states of the agent alone, then, it has been argued, theories that identify mental states and events with physical states of and events in the body must be wrong. This is suggested by Putnam's claim that "Meanings ain't in the head," and it is explicitly claimed by Tyler Burge and Andrew Woodfield.[9] The argument assumes that if a state or event is identified (perhaps necessarily, if it is a mental state or event) by reference to things outside of the body, then the state or event itself must be outside the body, or at least not identical with any event in the body. This is simply a mistake: one might as well argue that a sunburned patch of skin is not located on the body of the person who is sunburned (since the state of the skin has been identified by reference to the sun). Similarly, mental states are characterized in part by their relations to events and objects outside of the person, but this does not show that mental states are states of anything more than the person or that they are not identical with physical states.

3. A third misunderstanding is closely related to the second. It is

thought that if the correct determination of an agent's thoughts depends, at least to some degree, on the causal history of those thoughts, and the agent may be ignorant of that history, then the agent may not know what he thinks (and, mutatis mutandis, what he means, intends, and so on). The "new antisubjectivism" is, thus, seen as a threat to first person authority—to the fact that people generally know without recourse to inference from evidence, and so in a way that others do not, what they themselves think, want, and intend. A natural, if unjustified, reaction is to resort to maneuvers designed to insulate mental states once more from their external determiners.

The maneuvers are not needed, and surely not wanted if knowledge is to be defended, for first person authority is not threatened. I may not know the difference between an echidna and a porcupine; as a result I may call all echidnas I come across porcupines. Yet, because of the environment in which I learned the word 'porcupine', my word 'porcupine' refers to porcupines and not to echidnas; this is what I think it refers to, and what I believe I see before me when I honestly affirm, "That's a porcupine." My ignorance of the circumstances that determine what I mean and think has no tendency to show that I don't know what I mean and think. To suppose otherwise is to show how strongly we are wed to the idea of subjective mental states that might be just as they are independent of the rest of the world and its history.

Another reaction to the imagined threat to our real inner lives is to concede that beliefs and other mental states as we normally identify them are not truly subjective, but at the same time to hold that there are similar inner mental states that are. The idea might be, for example, that since nothing in my inner state or my behavior distinguishes between porcupines and echidnas, what I really believe when I see an echidna (or a porcupine) is that what is before me is an animal with certain general characteristics—characteristics that are in fact shared by porcupines and echidnas. The trouble is that since my *word* 'porcupine' refers only to porcupines, I apparently do not know what I mean when I say, "That's a porcupine." This unattractive solution is unnecessary, for it is based on a confusion about what is "inner." Since there is no present *physical* difference between my actual state and the state I would be in if I meant "echidna or porcupine" or "animal with such and such properties" rather than "porcupine" and believed what I would then mean, it does not follow that there is no *psychological* difference. (There may be no physical difference between being sunburned and being burned by a sunlamp, but there is a difference, since one state was, and the other was not, caused by the sun. Psychological states are in this respect like sunburn.) So nothing stands in the way of saying I can know what I mean when I use the word 'porcupine' and what I believe when I have thoughts about porcupines, even though I cannot tell an echidna from a porcupine. The psychological difference, which is just the difference between meaning and believing there is a porcupine before me, and meaning and believing there is a creature with certain common features of porcupines and echidnas, is exactly the difference needed to insure that I know what I mean and what I think. All that Putnam and others have shown is that this difference does not have to be reflected in the physical state of the brain.

Inventing a new set of truly "inner," or "narrow," psychological states is not, then, a way of restoring first person authority to the mental; quite the contrary. There remains the claim, however, that a systematic science of psychology requires states of the agent that can be identified without reference to their history or other connections with the outside world. Otherwise, it is said, there would be no accounting for the fact that I, who may refer only to porcupines by my word 'porcupine', can no more tell the difference between a porcupine and an echidna than if (physically unchanged) I meant instead "porcupine or echidna."

The prospects for a scientific psychology are not directly relevant to the topic of this paper, and so we may disregard the question whether there are inner states of agents which might explain their behavior better than ordinary beliefs and desires. But it is relevant to consider whether there are states of mind which have a better claim to be called subjective than the propositional attitudes as these are usually conceived and identified.

Two suggestions have been made. The more modest (to be found in the work of Jerry Fodor, for example) is that we might take as the true inner or solipsistic states selected states from among the usual attitudes and modifications of these. Thoughts about porcupines and echidnas would be eliminated, since the contents of such thoughts are identified by relations to the outside world; but admissible would be thoughts about animals satisfying certain general criteria (the very ones we use in deciding whether something is a porcupine, for example).[10]

Such inner states, if they exist, would qualify as subjective by almost any standards: they could be identified and classified without reference to external objects and events; they could be called on to serve as the foundations of empirical knowledge; and the authority of the first person could plausibly apply to them.

It seems clear, however, that there are no such states, at least if they can be expressed in words. The "general features" or "criteria" we use to identify porcupines are such as having four feet, a nose, eyes, and quills. But it is evident that the meanings of the words that refer to these features, and the contents of the concepts the words express, depend as much on the natural history of how the words and concepts were acquired as was the case for "porcupine" and "echidna." There are no words, or concepts tied to words, that are not to be understood and interpreted, directly or indirectly, in terms of causal relations between people and the world (and, or course, the relations among words and other words, concepts and other concepts).

At this point one can imagine a proposal to the effect that there are inexpressible phenomenal criteria to which the publicly expressible criteria can be reduced; and here it is to be hoped that memories of past failures of such reductionistic fantasies will serve to suppress the thought that the proposal could be carried out. But, even aside from nostalgic musings about phenomenalistic reduction, it is instructive to find the effort to make psychology scientific turning into a search for internal propositional states that can be detected and identified apart from relations to the rest of the world, much as earlier philosophers sought for something "given in experience" which contained no necessary clue to what was going on outside. The motive is similar in the two cases: it is thought that a sound footing, whether for knowledge or for psychology, requires something inner in the sense of being nonrelational.

The second, and more revolutionary, suggestion is that the mental states needed for a scientific psychology, though roughly propositional in character, bear no direct relation to common beliefs, desires, and intentions.[11] These states are, in effect, stipulated to be those that explain behavior, and they are therefore inner or subjective only in the sense of characterizing a person or similar subject and being beneath the skin. There is no reason to suppose that people can tell when they are in such states.

In summary, I have made five connected points about the "contents of the mind."

First, states of mind like doubts, wishes, beliefs, and desires are identified in part by the social and historical context in which they are acquired; in this respect they are like other states that are identified by their causes, such as suffering from snow blindness or favism (a disease caused by contact with the fava bean).

Second, this does not show that states of mind are not physical states of a person; how we describe and identify events and states has nothing directly to do with where those states and events are.

Third, the fact that states of mind, including what is meant by a speaker, are identified by causal relations with external objects and events is essential to the possibility of communication, and it makes one mind accessible in principle to another; but this public and interactive aspect of the mind has no tendency to diminish the importance of first-person authority.

Fourth, the idea that there is a basic division between uninterpreted experience and an organizing conceptual scheme is a deep mistake, born of the essentially incoherent picture of the mind as a passive but critical spectator of an inner show. A naturalistic account of knowledge makes no appeal to such epistemological intermediaries as sense-data, qualia, or raw feels. As a result, global skepticism of the senses is not a position that can be formulated.

Finally, I have argued against the postulation of "objects of thought," whether these are conceived on the model of sense-data or as propositional in character. There are the many states of mind, but their description does not require that there be ghostly entities that the mind somehow contemplates. To dispense with such entities is to eliminate rather than solve a number of vexing problems. For we cannot ask how such objects can represent the world if there are no such objects, nor can we be puzzled by the question of how the mind can directly be acquainted with them.

What remains of the concept of subjectivity? So far as I can see, two features of the subjective as classically conceived remain in place. Thoughts are private, in the obvious but important sense in which property can be private, that is, belong to one person. And knowledge of thoughts is asymmetrical, in that the person who has a thought generally knows he has it in a way in which others cannot. But this is all there is to the subjective. So far from constituting a preserve so insulated that it is a problem how it can yield knowledge of an outside world or be known to others, thought is necessarily part of a common public world. Not only can others learn what we think by noting the causal dependencies that give our thoughts their content, but the very possibility of thought demands shared standards of truth and objectivity.

Notes

1. I have argued for this in "On the Very Idea of a Conceptual Scheme," reprinted in *Inquiries into Truth and Interpretation* (The Clarendon Press, 1984).

2. C. I. Lewis, *Mind and the World Order* (Scribner's, 1929), p. 38. Lewis declares that it is the task of philosophy "to reveal those categorical criteria which the mind applies to what is given to it." (p. 36)

3. This passage, and the quotations that precede it, are from W. V. Quine, *Word and Object* (M.I.T. Press, 1960). In fairness it should be noted that Quine has often stated explicitly that he is not a conceptual relativist.

4. Hilary Putnam, "The Meaning of 'Meaning'," reprinted in *Philosophical Papers*, vol. 2: *Mind, Language, and Reality* (Cambridge University Press, 1975), p. 227.

5. Donald Davidson, "Knowing One's Own Mind," *Proceedings and Addresses of the American Philosophical Association*, 1986 (forthcoming).

6. Donald Davidson, "A Coherence Theory of Truth and Knowledge," in *Kant oder Hegel*, ed. D. Henrich (Klett-Cotta, 1983).

7. Donald Davidson, "First Person Authority," *Dialectica* 38 (1984).

8. Tyler Burge, "Individualism and the Mental," in *Midwest Studies in Philosophy*, vol. 4, ed. Peter French, Theodore Uehling, and Howard Wettstein (University of Minnesota Press, 1979).

9. Ibid., p. 111, and Andrew Woodfield, *Thought and Object*, ed. Andrew Woodfield (Clarendon Press, 1982), p. viii.

10. Jerry Fodor, "Methodological Solipsism Considered as a Research Strategy in Cognitive Psychology," *The Behavioral and Brain Sciences* 3 (1980).

11. This idea has been promoted by Steven Stich, *From Folk Psychology to Cognitive Science: The Case against Belief* (M.I.T. Press, 1983).

Truth and Convention:
On Davidson's Refutation
of Conceptual Relativism

HILARY W. PUTNAM

The "internal realism" I have defended[1] has both a positive and a negative side. Internal realism denies that there is a fact of the matter as to which of the conceptual schemes that serve us so well—the conceptual scheme of commonsense objects, with their vague identity conditions and their dispositional and counterfactual properties, or the scientific-philosophical scheme of fundamental particles and their "aggregations" (i.e., their mereological sums)—is "really true." Each of these schemes contains, in its present form, bits that are "true" (or "right") and bits that will turn out to be "wrong" in one way or another—bits that are right and wrong *by the standards appropriate to the scheme itself*—but the question "which kind of 'true' is really Truth" is one that internal realism rejects.

A simple example[2] will illustrate what I mean. Consider "a world with three individuals" (Carnap often used examples like this when we were doing inductive logic together in the early nineteen fifties), x_1, x_2, x_3. How many *objects* are there in this world?

Well, I *said* "consider a world with just three individuals" didn't I? So mustn't there be three objects? Can there be nonabstract entities which are not "individuals"?

One possible answer is No. We can identify "individual," "object," "particular," and so on and find no absurdity in a world with just three objects which are independent, unrelated, "logical atoms." But there are perfectly good logical doctrines which lead to different results.

Suppose, for example, like some Polish logicians, I believe that for

Reprinted from *Dialectica* 41:1-2 (1987): 69-77.

every two particulars there is an object which is their sum. (This is the basic assumption of "mereology," the calculus of parts and wholes invented by Lesniewski). If I ignore, for the moment, the so-called "null object," then I will find that the world of "three individuals" (as Carnap might have had it, at least when he was doing inductive logic) actually contains *seven* objects:

World 1	World 2
x_1, x_2, x_3	$x_1, x_2, x_3, x_1 + x_2,$
	$x_1 + x_3, x_2 + x_3, x_1 + x_2 + x_3$
(A world á la Carnap)	("Same" world á la Polish logician)

Some logicians (though not Lesniewski) would also say that there is a "null object" which they count as a part of every object. If we accepted this suggestion and added this individual (call it 0), then we would say that Carnap's world contains *eight* objects.

Now the classic metaphysical realist way of dealing with such problems is well known. It is to say that there is a single world (think of this as a piece of dough) which we can slice into pieces in different ways. But this "cookie-cutter" metaphor founders on the question "What are the 'parts' of this dough?" If the answer is that $x_1, x_2, x_3, x_1 + x_2,$ $x_1 + x_3, x_2 + x_3, x_1 + x_2 + x_3$ are all the different "pieces," then we have, not a *neutral* description, but rather a *partisan* description—just the description of the Warsaw logician! And it is no accident that metaphysical realism cannot really recognize the phenomenon of conceptual relativity—for that phenomenon turns on the fact that *the logical primitives themselves, and in particular the notions of object and existence, have a multitude of different uses rather than one absolute "meaning."*

An example which is historically important, if more complex than the one just given, is the ancient dispute about the ontological status of the Euclidean plane. Imagine a Euclidean plane. Think of the points in the plane. Are these *parts* of the plane, as Leibniz thought? Or are they "mere limits," as Kant[3] said?

If you say, in *this* case, that these are "two ways of slicing the same dough," then you must admit that what is a *part* of space, in one version of the facts, is an abstract entity (say, a set of convergent spheres—although there is not, of course, a *unique way* of construing points as limits) in the other version. But then you will have conceded that which entities are "abstract entities" and which are "concrete objects," at least, is version-relative. Metaphysical realists to this day continue to argue about whether points (space-time points, nowadays, rather than points in the plane or in three-dimensional space) are individuals or properties, particulars or mere limits, and so on. My view is that God himself, if he consented to answer the question "Do points really exist or are they mere limits?" would say, "I don't know"; not because his omniscience is limited, but because there is a limit to how far questions make sense.

One last point before I leave these examples: *given* a version, the question "How many objects are there?" has an answer, namely, "three" in the case of the first version ("Carnap's World") and "seven" in the case of the second version ("The Polish Logician's World"). Once we make clear how we are using "object" (or "exist"), the question "How many objects exist?" has an answer that is not at all a matter of "convention." That is why I say that this sort of example does not support cultural relativism. Of course, our concepts are culturally relative, but it does not follow that the truth or falsity of what we say using those concepts is simply "determined" by the culture. But the idea that there is an Archimedean point (or a use of "exist" inherent in the world itself) from which the question "How many objects *really* exist?" makes sense is an illusion.

Nor does it help, in general, to talk about "meanings" or "truth conditions." Consider again the two sentences (I am referring to the same example as before)

(1) There is an object which is partly red and partly black.
(2) There is an object which is red and an object which is black.

Observe that (2) is a sentence which is true in both the Carnapian and the Polish logician's version if, say, x_1 is red and x_2 is black. (1) is a sentence which is true in the Polish logician's version. What is its status in the Carnapian version?

Let me introduce an imaginary philosopher whom I will call "Prof. Antipode." Professor Antipode is violently opposed to Polish mereology. He talks like this: "I know what you are talking about if by an object you mean a car, or a bee, or a human being, or a book, or the Eiffel Tower. I even understand it if you refer to my nose or the hood of my car as 'an object'. But when philosophers say that there is an 'object' consisting of *the Eiffel Tower and my nose,* that is just plain crazy. There simply is no such object. Carnap was talking just fine when he said to you 'consider a world with just three objects'—I ignore Carnap's regrettable tendency to what he called 'tolerance'—and it is crazy to suppose that every finite universe contains all the objects those Poles would invent, or, if you please, 'postulate'. You cannot create objects by 'postulation' any more than you can bake a cake by 'postulation'."

Now, the language Carnap had in mind (we were working together on inductive logic at the time, and most often the languages we considered had only one-place predicates) probably did not contain a two-place predicate for the relation "part of," but even if it did, we can imagine Professor Antipode denying that there is any object of which x_1 and x_2 are both "parts." If there were such an object, it would have to be different from both of them," he would say (and here the Polish logician would agree), "and the only object different from both of them in the world you showed us is x_3. But x_3 does not overlap with either x_1 or x_2. Only in the overheated imagination of the Polish logician is there such an additional object as $x_1 + x_2$." If we add "Part Of" to Carnap's little language, so that sentence (1) can be expressed in it, thus:

3) (Ex)(Ey)(Ez) (y is Part Of x & z is Part Of x & Red(y) & Black(z)),

then, true to his anti-Polish form, Professor Antipode will say that this sentence is false. "Whether you say it in plain English or in fancy symbols," he growls, "if you have a world of three nonoverlapping individuals, which is what Carnap described, and each is wholly red or wholly black, which is what Carnap said, then there cannot be such a thing in that world as an 'object which is partly red and partly black'. Talking about the 'mereological sum of x_1 and x_2' makes no more sense than talking about 'the mereological sum of my nose and the Eiffel Tower'."

Professor Antipode, it will be seen, is a staunch metaphysical realist. He *knows* that only some objects are parts of other objects, and that to say that for *every* pair of objects there is an object of which they both are parts (which is an axiom of mereology) is just "rubbish". (In the world Carnap imagined (1) is false and (2) is true, and there is the whole story.)

Carnap himself would have taken a very different attitude, Carnap was a conceptual relativist (that is, in part, what his famous Principle of Tolerance is all about), and he would have said that we can choose to make (1) false (that is, we can choose to talk the way Professor Antipode talks) *or* we can choose to make (1) true—to talk as the Polish logician talks. There is even—and this is very important—a way in which we can have the best of both worlds. We keep Carnap's version as our official version (our "unabbreviated language"); we refrain from adding Part Of as a new primitive, as we did before, but we introduce Part Of as a *defined* expression (as "abbreviated language," or, as Quine often puts it, as a *façon de parler*). This can be done, not by giving an *explicit* defintion of Part Of, but by giving a scheme which translates the Polish logician's language into Carnap's language (and such a scheme can easily be given in a recursive way, in the case of the kind of first order language with finitely many individuals that Carnap had in mind). Under such a scheme (1) turns out to say no more and no less than (2).

[To verify this, assuming that "red" and "black" are predicates of Carnap's language, observe that the only way a Polish logician's object—a mereological sum—can be partly red is by containing a red atom, and the only way it can be partly black is by containing a black atom. So if (1) is true in the Polish logician's language, then there is at least one red atom and at least one black atom—which is what (2) says in Carnap's language. Conversely, if there is at least one black atom and at least one red atom, then their mereological sum is an "object" (in the Polish logician's sense) which is partly red and partly black.]

While the formal possiblity of doing this—of "interpreting" the Polish logician's version in Carnap's version—is easy to establish as a result in mathematical logic, the philosophical significance of this fact, of the interpretability of the second language in the first, is more controversial. An objection—an objection to the idea that this kind of interpretability supports conceptual relativity in any way—might come from a philosopher who pursues what is called "meaning theory." Such a philosopher might ask, "What is the point of treating (1) as an abbreviation of (2) if it does not, in fact, have the same *meaning* as (2)?" Meaning theorists who follow Donald Davidson might argue that while (1) and (2) are "mathematically equivalent" (if, like the Polish logician, and unlike Professor Antipode, we are willing to count the axioms of mereology as having the status of logical or mathematical truths), still, sentence (2) is not a sentence one would ordinarily offer as an explanation of the truth-conditions of sentence (1); or at least doing so would hardly be in accordance with what is called "translation practice." And a "meaning theory," it is said, must not correlate just *any* extensionally or even mathematically correct truth-conditions with the sentences of the language the theory describes; the sentence used to state a truth condition for a sentence must be one that might be correlated with that sentence by "translation practice." Whatever one is doing when one invents reductive definitions that enable one to explain away talk about "suspicious" entities as a mere *façon* de parler, it obviously is not simply "radical translation."

One suggestion as to what one *is* doing comes from a classic article by Quine. In "On What There Is" he suggested that the stance to take in a case such as the one I have been describing—in a case in which one language seems more useful than another, because it countenances entities which (although philosophically "suspicious") enable us to say various things in fewer words, and in which the at first blush "richer" language is formally interpretable in the at first blush "poorer" language—might be to say (a stance Professor Antipode might adopt): "Sentence (1), asserting as it does the existence of mereological sums, is literally false. But if one wants to go on talking like the Polish logician while rejecting his undesirable ontological commitments, one can do that. One can responsibly take the view that the Polish logician's story is only a useful make-believe, and yet employ its idioms, on the ground that each of the sentences in that idiom, whatever its 'meaning', *can* be regarded—by fiat, if you like—as merely a convenient abbreviation of whatever sentence in the 'unabbreviated language' it is correlated with be the interpretation scheme."

To give another example, one long familiar to students of mathematical philosophy, Frege and Russell showed that number theory is interpretable in set theory. This means that if one wants to avoid ontological commitments to "unreduced numbers" (to numbers as objects over and above sets)—and if one does not mind commitment to *sets!*—one can treat every sentence of number theory, and, indeed, every sentence in the language which uses a number word, as a mere abbreviation for another sentence, one which quantifies over sets, but not over any such entities as "numbers." One need not claim that the sentence of number theory and its translation in set theory have the same "meaning." If they do not, so much the worse for our intuitive notion of a "number"! What this kind of interpretation—call it *reductive interpretation*—provides is evidence against the real existence of the unreduced entities, as anything over and above the entities countenanced by the language to which we are doing the reducing. The moral we should draw from the work of Frege and Russell is not that there is a conceptual *choice* to be made between using a language which countenances only sets and one which countenances set *and* numbers, but that—unless the numbers are in fact identical with the set with which we identified them—there is no reason to believe in the existence of numbers. Talk of numbers is best treated as a mere *façon de parler*. Or so Quine maintains.

It is easy to see why Professor Antipode should like this line. In the case of the two versions we have been discussing, the reductive interpretation is syncategorematic, that is, it interprets sentence (1) (and likewise any other sentence of Carnap's language) as a whole but does not identify the individual words in (1) with individual words and phrases in (2); nor does it identify "mereological sums" with any objects in the language to which the reducing is being done. (1) as a whole is "translated" by (2) as a whole, but the noun-phrase "object which is partly red and partly black" has no translation by itself. In this case the moral of the translation—the moral if Professor Antipode imitates Quine's rhetoric—is slightly different. We cannot say *either mereological sums are identical with the entities with which we identified them or they do not really exist* (because the "translation," or relative interpretation of the

Polish logician's language in Carnap's language, did not identify "mereological sums" with *anything,* it just showed how to translate sentences about them syncategorematically). The moral is rather, *mereological sums do not really exist, but it is sometimes useful to talk* as if *they existed.* Of course Professor Antipode would be delighted with *this* moral!

I do not mean to give the impression that the possibility of reducing entities away by a formal translation scheme is always decisive evidence that they do not really exist according to Quine. Sometimes we have the choice of either doing without one batch of entities, call them the A entities, or doing without another batch, call them the B entities—the reduction may be possible in either direction. In such a case Occam's Razor does not know who to shave! Or the reducing language may itself seem suspicious (some people think *sets* are very suspicious entities). But when the reducing language (the prima facie "poorer" language) is one we are happy with , and the reduction does not go both ways, it is clear that Quine regards this as very strong evidence for denying the real existence of the unreduced entities.

Carnap, on the other hand, rejected the idea that there is "evidence" against the "existence" of numbers (or against the existence of numbers as objects distinct from sets). He would, I am sure, have similarly rejected the idea that there is evidence against the "existence" of mereological sums. I know what he would have said about this question: he would have said that the question is one of a choice of a language. On some days it may be convenient to use what I have been calling "Carnap's language" (although he would not have *objected* to the other language); on other days it may be convenient to use the Polish logician's language. For some purposes it may be convenient to regard the Polish logician's language of mereological sums as "primitive notation," in other contexts it may be better to take Carnap's language as the primitive notation and to regard the Polish logician's language as "abbreviations," or defined notation. And I agree with him.

It will be seen that there are a number of different stances one could take to the question of the *relation* between (1) and (2). One could say:

(a) The two sentences are mathematically equivalent.
(b) The two sentences are logically equivalent.
(c) The two sentences are neither logically nor mathematically equivalent.
(d) The first sentence is false and the second true (Professor Antipode's position).

(e) The two sentences are alike in truth value and meaning.

(f) The two sentences are alike in truth value and unlike in mean-
    ing.

(g) The second sentence can be used as an abbreviation of the first,
    but this is really just a useful "make believe."

My own position—and my own internal realism—is that there is
no fact of the matter as to which of *these* positions is correct. Taking the
original dispute up into the "metalevel" and reformulating it as a dispute about the properties—mathematical or logical equivalence, synonymy, or whatever—of linguistic forms does not help. None of these
notions is well defined enough to be a useful tool in such cases. Suppose, for example, I follow the apparently innocent route pioneered by
Donald Davidson and say that the test for meaning is to see what we get
when we construct a theory of language which is (1) recursively presented (in the style of a Tarskian truth-definition) and (2) in accord with
translation practice. Obviously I shall have to admit that it violates
standard translation practice to give (2) as a translation of (1).[4] This
settles the truth-value of (e) above: (e) is false whether the sentences be
alike or unlike in truth-value, since they are not the same in meaning.

Suppose we follow Davidson farther and accept the central Davidsonian tenet that if I regard a sentence in an "alien language" as meaningful (and I claim to know what it means), then I must be able to give
(or would be able to give if I were sufficiently self-conscious about my
knowledge) a *truth condition* for that sentence in my "own" language.
(One which follows from a "meaning theory" which is in conformity
with the "constraints on translation practice." If my "own" language is
Carnap's, and we accept it that *no* "truth condition" for (1) stateable in
Carnap's language will satisfy the constraints on translation practice any
better than (2) did, then the conclusion is forced: the Polish logician's
language is *meaningless*. We have arrived at a strong metaphysical
result from what looked like a bit of ordinary language philosophizing
(aided with a bit of Tarskian semantics) about the notion of "meaning"!

Of course we might simply adopt the Polish logician's language as
our own language to begin with. But what we cannot do, according to
Davidson, is regard both choices as genuinely open.

It seems to me that the very assumption that there is such a thing
as the radical interpreter's "own" language—*one* language in which he
can give the truth conditions for *every* sentence in *every* language he
claims to be able to understand—is what forces the conclusion. As long
as one operates with this assumption, conceptual relativism will seem
unintelligible (as it does to Davidson[5]). But if one recognizes that the

radical interpreter himself may have more than one "home" conceptual scheme, and that "translation practice" may be governed by more than one set of constraints, then one sees that conceptual relativity does not disappear when we inquire into the "meanings" of the various conceptual alternatives: it simply reproduces itself at a metalinguistic level!

Notes

1. Cf. H. Putnam, *Reason, Truth, and History*.

2. This example comes from H. Putnam, *The Many Faces of Realism*.

3. "dcm mathematischen Punkte, der einfach, aber kein Teil, sondern bloss die Grenze eines Raumes ist." *Kritik der reinen Vernunft* B470; note also the flat statement "Nun besteht der Raum nicht aus einfachen Teilen, sondern aus Räumen" (ibid., B463). Both remarks occur on the "Antithesis" side of the Second Antinomy.

4. For example, even the truth-functional connectives are not preserved if we "translate" (1) as (2).

5. Cf. D. Davidson, "The Very Idea of a Conceptual Scheme."

References

Davidson, D. 1974. "The Very Idea of a Conceptual Scheme." In David son's *Truth and Interpretation*.

Davidson, D. 1984. *Truth and Interpretation*. Oxford University Press.

Putnam, H. 1981. *Reason, Truth and History*. Cambridge University Press.

Putnam, H. 1987. *The Many Faces of Realism* (Carus Lectures). Open Court.

Quine, W. V. 1953. "On What There Is." In Quine's *From a Logical Point of View*. Harvard University Press.

Relativism, Power, and Philosophy

Alasdair MacIntyre

1

It was Anthony Collins, the friend of John Locke, who remarked that, had it not been for the Boyle Lecturers' annual demonstrations of the existence of God, few people would ever have doubted it.[1] It may have been a similar spirit of argumentative contrariness that led me to begin to appreciate fully both the strength and the importance of the case to be made out in favor of at least one version of relativism only after reading some recent philosophical root-and-branch dismissals of relativism as such.[2] But of course I ought not to have been such a latecomer to that appreciation. For relativism, like skepticism, is one of those doctrines that have by now been refuted a number of times too often. Nothing is perhaps a surer sign that a doctrine embodies some not-to-be-neglected truth than that in the course of the history of philosophy it should have been refuted again and again. Genuinely refutable doctrines only need to be refuted once.

Philosophical doctrines that are not susceptible of genuine refutation fall into at least two classes. There are some to which, in the light of the rational justification that can be provided for them, we owe simple assent. But there are others to which our assent is or ought to be accorded only with a recognition that what they present is a moment in the development of thought which has to be, if possible, transcended; and this even although we may as yet lack adequate grounds for believing ourselves able to transcend them. Skepticism is one such doctrine, and relativism is another. But no doctrine can be genuinely transcended until we understand what is to be said in its favor. And a first step

Presidential Address delivered before the 81st Annual Eastern Division Meeting of the American Philosophical Association in New York City, New York, December 29, 1984; reprinted with permission from *Proceedings and Addresses of the American Philosophical Association*, American Philosophical Association, 1985, pp. 5-22.

toward understanding this in the case of relativism must be to show that the purported refutations have largely missed its point and so been misdirected.

It is not that there is nothing to be learned from them. From them we can certainly learn how to formulate relativism in a way that does not gratuitously entangle it with error. So we can learn from Socrates' encounter with the formulations of Protagoras in the *Theatetus*[3] that relativists must be careful not to allow themselves to be trapped into making some type of universal self-referential claim. Such a claim, by denying to all doctrines whatsoever the predicates 'is true' and 'is false', unless these are radically reinterpreted to mean no more than 'seems true to such and such persons' and 'seems false to such and such persons', turns the interesting assertion that relativism is true into the uninteresting assertion that relativism seems true to relativists. And we can learn from Hegel's critique of Kant[4] that relativists must be careful to avoid framing their theses in a way that presupposes the legitimacy of some version of what has come to be called the scheme-content distinction, that is, the distinction between some concept or conceptual scheme on the one hand and on the other an entirely preconceptual world or given waiting to be rescued from in one version blindness, in another nakedness, by being conceptualized.

Yet it is important to be precise about what we have to learn from these refutations of particular formulations of relativism; and it is important therefore not to abstract for formulaic use what we take to be the essence of some refutation from the context in which such as Plato or Hegel embedded it and from which it drew its peculiar force. So we are perhaps entitled to express a certain polite surprise when a contemporary philosopher who has shown both assiduity and ingenuity in trying to make credible the view that 'is true' says no more than is said by 'seems true to such and such persons, namely *us*' asserts that if there were any contemporary relativists, one could use against them some variant of what he calls the "arguments Socrates used against Protagoras."[5] The surprise derives from our remembering that the premises from which Plato derived Socrates' refutation of Protragoras' version of relativism also entailed the necessary failure of any reinterpretative reduction of 'is true' to 'seems true to such and such persons.' From these premises the one conclusion is not available without the other.

The same kind of polite surprise is warranted when another distinguished contemporary philosopher, having repeated the substance of Hegel's demonstration of the illegitimacy of any dualism which tears apart conceptual schemes on the one hand and the world on the other, concludes to the necessary incoherence of the very idea of a conceptual scheme.[6] It was, after all, Hegel who gave its canonical form both to the idea of a conceptual scheme and to that of alternative and incompatible conceptual schemes, and he did so without ever violating his own ban on the illegitimate dualist scheme/content and scheme/world distinctions.[7] Nor was Hegel alone in this; the same could be said of his predecessor, Vico,[8] and of his successor, Collingwood.[9]

We need, then, in order to capture the truth in relativism, a formulation of that doctrine which has learned from both Plato and Hegel: it must avoid Protagorean self-trivializing by giving its due to the Platonic distinction between 'is true' and 'seems true to such and such persons'; and in any appeal that it makes to the idea of alternative conceptual schemes, it must be careful to follow Hegel in leaving no opening for any scheme/content or scheme/world distinction.

2

'Relativism', as I am going to use that expression, names one kind of conclusion to enquiry into a particular class of problems. Those questions arise in the first place for people who live in certain highly specific types of social and cultural situation, but this is not to say that they are not distinctively philosophical questions. They are indeed examples of questions which *both* are inescapable for certain ordinary agents and language-users *and* have the characteristic structure of philosophical problems. It is perhaps unsurprising that they have been overlooked by those recent philosophers who want to make a sharp dichotomy between the realm of philosophical theorizing and that of everyday belief because they suppose both that it is philosophers themselves who largely generate philosophical problems by their own misconceptions and that everyday life cannot be apt to suffer from types of disorder which require specifically philosophical diagnosis. This attitude is perhaps a symptom of a certain lack of sociological imagination, of too impoverished a view of the types of social and institutional circumstances which generate philosophical problems. What then are the social and institutional circumstances which generate the cluster of problems to which some version of relativism can be a rational response?

They are the social and institutional circumstances of those who inhabit a certain type of frontier or boundary situation. Consider the predicament of someone who lives in a time and place where he or she is a full member of two linguistic communities, speaking one language, Zuni, say, or Irish, exclusively to the older members of his or her family and village and Spanish or English, say, to those from the world outside, who seek to engage him or her in a way of life in the exclusively Spanish- or English-speaking world. Economic and social circumstance may enforce on such a person a final choice between inhabiting the one linguistic community and inhabiting the other, and in some times and places this is much more than a choice between two languages, at least in any narrowly conceived sense of "language." For a language may be so used, and both Irish and Zuni have in some past periods been so used, that to share in its use is to presuppose one cosmology rather than another, one relationship of local law and custom to cosmic order rather than another, one justification of particular relationships of individual to community and of both to land and to landscape rather than another. In such a language even the use of proper names may on occasion have such presuppositions.

If, for example, I speak in Irish, even today, let alone three hundred years ago, of Doire Colmcille—of Doire in modern Irish—the presuppositions and implications of my utterance are quite other than if I speak in English of Londonderry. But, it may be asked, are these not simply two names of one and the same place? The answer is first that no proper name of place or person names any place or person *as such*; it names *in the first instance* only *for* those who are members of some particular linguistic and cultural community by identifying places and persons in terms of the scheme of identification shared by, and perhaps partially constitutive of, that community. The relation of a proper name to its bearer cannot be elucidated without reference to such identifying functions.[10] And second that 'Doire Colmcille' names—embodies a communal intention of naming—a place with a continuous identity ever since it became in fact St. Columba's oak grove in 546 and that 'Londonderry' names a settlement made only in the seventeenth century and is a name whose use presupposes the legitimacy of that settlement and of the use of the English language to name it. Notice that the name 'Doire Colmcille' is as a name untranslatable; you can translate the Gaelic expression 'doire Colmcille' by the English expression 'St. Columba's oak grove'; but that cannot be the translation of a place name, for it is not itself the name of any place. And what is true of the relationship of 'Doire Colmcille' in Irish to 'Londonderry' in English holds equally of the relationship of the names of the Zuni villages in the sixteenth century, such as 'Itwana', to the Spanish name for them as the Seven Cities of Cibola.[11]

To this the response may be that although there may as a matter of contingent historical fact be certain kinds of association attaching to the use of 'Doire Colmcille' rather than 'Londonderry' or vice versa, the use of the name merely *qua* name carries with it no presuppositions concerning political or social legitimacy. And it might be thought that this could be shown by appeal to the fact that some ignorant stranger might use the name 'Londonderry' in order to ask the way and in identifying the place on the map at which he or she wished to arrive would have shown that one *can* use the name for purposes of identification without any such presupposition. But such a stranger is only able now to use a name which has indeed been made available to those outside its primary community of use because the members of the primary community use or used it as they do, and that stranger's secondary use of the name is therefore parasitic upon its uses by the primary community. Moreover, such secondary nonpresupposition-laden uses do not thereby become names freed from any specific social context of use. They are very specifically names-as-used-by-strangers-or-tourists. Philosophers of logic have sometimes treated the way in which such names are used by strangers or tourists as exemplifying some essential core naming relation, a concept about which I shall have to say something later on in the argument; for the moment I note only that in so doing such philosophers have obscured the difference between the type of natural language in which the standard uses of a variety of expressions commit the user to an expression of a shared, communal belief and the type of natural language in which this is so minimally or not at all.

In the type of frontier or boundary situation which I have been describing both languages—the Irish of, say, 1700 and the English of the plantation settlements of the same date, or the Zuni Shiwi language of, say, 1540 and the Spanish of the *conquistadores*—are at the former end of this spectrum of natural-languages-in-use. Thus what the bilingual speaker in both members of one of these pairs is going to have to choose between, in deciding to spend his or her life within one linguistic community rather than the other, is also to some substantial degree alternative and incompatible sets of beliefs and ways of life. Moreover each of these sets of beliefs and ways of life will have internal to its own specific modes of rational justification in key areas and its own correspondingly specific warrants for claims to truth.

It is not that the beliefs of each such community cannot be represented in any way at all in the language of the other; it is rather that the outcome in each case of rendering those beliefs sufficiently intelligible to be evaluated by a member of the other community involves characterizing those beliefs in such a way that they are bound to be rejected. What is from the one point of view a just act of war will be from the other theft; what is from the one point of view an original act of acquisition, of what had so far belonged to nobody and therefore of what had remained available to become only now someone's private property, will be from the other point of view the illegitimate seizure of what had so far belonged to nobody because it is what *cannot* ever be made into private property—for example, common land. The Spaniards brought alien concepts of ownership deriving from Roman, feudal, and canon law to their transactions with the Indians; the English brought concepts of individual property rights recognized by English common-law decisions to Ireland at a time when there was certainly a translation for the Latin *'jus'* in Irish, but none for the expression 'a right' (understood as something that attaches not to status, role, or function, but to individuals as such).

It will not at this point be helpful to remark either that in both these pairs of linguistic communities a great many other beliefs were of course shared by members of both communities or that in particular no one had ever had any difficulty in translating 'Snow is white' from one language to the other. There are indeed large parts of every language that are translatable into every other, and there are types of routine or routinizable social situations which are reproduced in many—some perhaps even in all—cultures. And the project of matching types of sentence-in-use to types of routinizable situation reproduced in many cultures, and of both to the habits of assenting to or dissenting from the uses of such sentences, will doubtless, if actually carried through rather than merely projected, lay bare the relationship between these facts and the type and range of translatability that hold in consequence of that relationship. But the suspicion which I have gradually come to entertain about this type of project is that what can be expected from it is perhaps not so much an adequate semantics for natural languages or a theory of truth in such languages as a series of excellent Phrase Books for Travelers. For it is precisely those features of languages whose mastery *cannot* be acquired from such phrase books which generate untranslatability between languages.

What are those features? They include a power to extrapolate from uses of expressions learned in certain types of situations to the making and understanding of new and newly illuminating uses. The availability of this power to the members of a whole linguistic community of the type which I have been characterizing depends in part upon their shared ability to refer and allude to a particular common stock of canonical texts, texts which define the literary and linguistic tradition which members of that community inhabit. For it is by allusion to such texts that linguistic innovation and extrapolation proceed; what those texts provide are both shared exemplars from which to extrapolate and shared exemplars of the activity of extrapolation.

It is characteristically poets and saga reciters who in such societies make and continually remake these at first oral and then written texts; only poetic narrative is memorable in the required way, and, as we should have learned from Vico,[12] it is the linguistic capacities and abilities provided by poetry and saga which make later forms of prose possible. Concepts are first acquired and understood in terms of poetic images, and the movement of thought from the concreteness and particularity of the imaged to the abstractness of the conceptual never completely leaves that concreteness and particularity behind. Conceptions of courage and of justice, of authority, sovereignty and property, of what understanding is and what failure to understand is, all these will continue to be elaborated from exemplars to be found in the socially recognized canonical texts. And this will still be the case when prose supplements poetry, when law books are added to myth and epic, and when dramatic works are added to both. The consequence is that when two such distinct linguistic communities confront one another, each with its own body of canonical texts, its own exemplary images, and its own tradition of elaborating concepts in terms of these, but each also lacking a knowledge of, let alone linguistic capacities informed by, the tradition of the other community, each will represent the beliefs of the other within its own discourse in abstraction from the relevant tradition and so in a way that ensures misunderstanding. From each point of view certain of the key concepts and beliefs of the other, just because they are presented apart from that context of inherited texts from which they draw their conceptual life, will necessarily appear contextless and lacking in justification.

Here we confront one more instance of the hermeneutic circle. The initial inability of the members of each linguistic community to translate certain parts of the language of the other community into their own is a barrier to knowledge of the tradition embodied in the uses of that language; but lack of knowledge of the tradition is itself sufficient to preclude accurate translation of those parts of the alien language. And once again the fact that certain other parts of the two languages may translate quite easily into each other provides no reason at all for skepticism about partial untranslatability. The sentences-in-use which are the untranslatable parts of this type of language-in-use are not in fact capable of being logically derived from, constructed out of, reduced to, or otherwise rendered into the sentences-in-use which comprise the translatable part of the same language-in-use. Nor should this surprise us. One of the marks of a genuinely adequate knowledge of two quite different languages by one and the same person is that person's ability to discriminate between those parts of each language which are translatable into the other and those which are not. Some degree of partial untranslatability marks the relationship of every language to every other.

Notice that this recognition of untranslatability never entails an acknowledgment of some necessary limit to understanding. Conversely, that we can understand completely what is being said in some language other than our own never entails that we can translate what we understand. And it is this ability both to understand and to recognize the partial untranslatability of what is understood which combines with the specific social, conceptual, and linguistic characteristics of the type of boundary situation which I have identified to create the predicament of the bilingual speaker who in that type of situation has to choose between membership in one or other of the two rival linguistic communities.

Remember that the contingent features of that speaker's situation make this not only a choice between languages, but one between two mutually incompatible conceptualizations of natural and social reality; and it is not only a choice between two mutually incompatible sets of beliefs, but one between sets of beliefs so structured that each has internal to it its own standards of truth and justification. Moreover, this choice has to be made with only the limited linguistic and conceptual resources afforded by the two languages in question. What constraints do these limits impose?

They exclude the possibility of appeal to some neutral or independent standard of rational justification to justify the choice of one set of beliefs, one way of life, one linguistic community rather than the other. For the only standards of truth and justification made available within the two communities are those between which a choice has to be made. And the only resources afforded for the members of each community to represent the concepts, beliefs, and standards of the other ensure that from the point of view of each its own concepts, beliefs, and standards will be vindicated and those of its rival found wanting.

Here then two rival conceptual schemes do confront one another. For those culturally and linguistically able to inhabit only one of them no problem arises. But for our imagined person who has the abilities to understand both, but who must choose to inhabit only one, the nature of the choice is bound, if he or she is adequately reflective, to transform his or her understanding of truth and of rational justification. For he or she will not be able to find application for the concepts of truth and justification which are independent of the standards of one community or the other. There is no access to any subject matter which is not conceptualized in terms that already presuppose the truth of one set of claims rather than the other. Hegel's proscription of any appeal to an extraconceptual reality is not being infringed. Each community, using its own criteria of *sameness* and *difference*, recognizes that it is one and the same subject matter about which they are advancing their claim; incommensurability and incompatibility are not incompatible.

The only way to characterize adequately the predicament thus created for our imaginary person is in the idiom which Plato provided. For that person will now have to reinterpret the predicates 'is true' and 'is justified' so that to apply them will in future claim no more than would be claimed by 'seems true to this particular community' or 'seems justified to this particular community'. Rational choice will have transformed our imaginary person into a relativist. But why call this a predicament? Because in so reinterpreting these predicates our imaginary Zuni or Irish person will have, without in the least intending to, separated him or herself effectively from both contending communities. For no sixteenth- or seventeenth-century community was able to understand itself relativistically.

To all this the reply may well be: So what? Even if it is conceded that I have provided a defensible version of relativism, and even if it is allowed that our imaginary person did in certain times and places have real counterparts, Irish or Zuni or whatever, what of it? That kind of relativism was imposed by the contingencies of their historical, social, and linguistic circumstances, contingencies which deprived our imaginary person and his or her real counterparts of the linguistic and conceptual resources necessary to avoid or refute relativism. But *we*, it may be suggested, do have those resources, so what is the relevance of your philosophical figment to *us?*

Just this is, of course, the question. Is it indeed the case that if we were to specify the linguistic and conceptual resources that would have to be provided to enable our imaginary person to overcome the particular contingent limitations of his or her situation, we should have shown how relativism can be avoided or refuted? If we succeed in transforming this imaginary person, so that he or she becomes just like us, will the relativization of the predicates of truth and justification no longer be forced upon him or her, or indeed ourselves? To these questions I therefore turn, but before turning I want to enquire briefly what will be at stake in giving one kind of answer to them rather than another.

3

The same considerations which ensure that someone compelled to choose between the claims of two rival linguistic communities, in the type of circumstance that I have described, will be unable to appeal to any neutral, independent standard of rational justification by which to judge between their competing claims also ensure that more generally the members of any two such communities will have to conduct their relationship with members of the other community without resort to any such appeal. But where there is no resort to such standards, human relationships are perforce relationships of will and power unmediated by rationality. I do not mean that where there is no resort to such standards, each of the contending parties in such communal relationships will necessarily act unreasonably, that is unreasonably from its own particular point of view as to what constitutes unreason. But it is just that point of view that in their transactions each community will be trying to impose upon the other. And when it becomes reasonable from the point of view of one of the contending parties to impose their will by force upon the other in the name of their own idiosyncratic conception of reasonableness, that is what they will do.

So it was with the Spanish in their relationships with the Zuni; so it has been with the English in their relationships with the Irish. And one instrument of such force is the imposition of one's own language at the expense of the other's. But can it ever be otherwise? Only if the relativism which emerged as the only rational attitude to the competing claims of two such antagonistic communities turns out not to be the last word on all relationships between rival human communities; only, that is, if linguistic and conceptual resources can indeed be supplied so that that relativism can be avoided or circumvented. For only in cases where that relativism does not have the last word does the possibility open up of substituting, for a politics in which the exercise of power is unmediated by rationality, a politics in which the exercise of power is both mediated and tempered by appeal to standards of rational justification independent of the particularism of the contending parties.

I am not of course suggesting that the identification and formulation of such nonrelativist standards of truth and justification is ever by itself sufficient to overcome a politics of unmediated will and power in the conflicts that occur within communities, let alone in the conflicts that occur between communities. And I am not suggesting that force may not on occasion be used to serve the purposes of genuine practical rationality as well as those of idiosyncratic and one-sided reasonableness. I *am* claiming that it is only in those forms of human relationship in which it is possible to appeal to impersonal standards of judgment, neutral between competing claims and affording the best type of rational justification both relevant and available, that the possibility opens up of unmasking and dethroning arbitrary exercises of power, tyrannical power within communities and imperialist power between communities. Plato was once again right: the argument against the tyrant and the argument against relativized predicates of truth and justification require the same premises.

This would of course be denied by our contemporary post-Nietzschean anti-Platonists. But even they on occasion inadvertently provide support for this thesis. Perhaps the most cogent, because the most systematic, exposition of the view that all attempts to appeal to would-be impersonal standards of truth and rational justification must fail to provide any effective alternative to established distributions of power, just because every such attempt and appeal itself operates according to the laws of some institutionalized distribution of power, is that of Michel Foucault in his earlier writings. So Foucault can write about the politics of truth and the political economy of truth in a way that treats all appeals to truth and to rational justification as themselves particularist forms of power inextricably associated with other forms of imposition and constraint.[13] But Foucault cannot articulate this view either generally or in his detailed institutional studies without presupposing a radical incommensurability thesis, a thesis that indeed only seems to emerge as a conclusion from his studies because it *was* presupposed from the outset. And that thesis is entitled to our assent if and only if the version of relativism which I have described does have the last word.

So it turns out that how we understand the politics of power depends in crucial part upon the answers that we give to certain philosophical questions. Janice Moulton[14] and Robert Nozick[15] have both recently suggested that philosophy has been damaged by an excessive use of adversarial and antagonistic idioms. We speak too readily, they think, of winning and losing arguments, of others being forced to acknowledge our conclusions and so on; and insofar as such idioms obscure the need for the cooperative virtues in philosophical activity, they are certainly right. Nonetheless, the language of antagonism has one important positive function. It signals to us that philosophy, like all other institutionalized human activities, is a milieu of conflict. And the conflicts of philosophy stand in a number of often complex and often indirect relationships to a variety of other conflicts. The complexity, the indirectness, and the variety all help to conceal from us that even the more abstract and technical issues of our discipline—issues concerning naming, reference, truth, and translatability—may on occasion be as crucial in their political or social implications as are theories of the social contract or of natural right. The former no less than the latter have implications for the nature and limitations of rationality in the arenas of political society. All philosophy, one way or another, is political philosophy.

Sometimes philosophy fares better by our forgetting this, at least temporarily, but we can scarcely avoid bearing it in mind in returning to the question to which the present argument has led: What other resources would our imaginary person in his or her sixteenth- or seventeenth-century boundary situation have had to possess, what resources that he or she lacked would we have to possess, if we are to be able to appeal to standards of judgment in respect of truth and rational justification which do not relativize these predicates to the conceptual scheme of one particular cultural and linguistic community?

4

A necessary first step out of the relativistic predicament would be the learning of some third language, a language of a very different kind from the two available to our imaginary person so far. Such a third language, if it was to provide the needed resources, would have to be a language with two central characteristics. First, its everyday use must be such that it does *not* presuppose allegiance to either of the two rival sets of beliefs between which our imaginary person has to choose or indeed, so far as possible, to any other set of beliefs which might compete for allegiance with those two. And second, it must be able to provide the resources for an accurate representation of the two competing schemes of belief, including that in the tradition of each community which provides that background for its present beliefs, without which they cannot be fully intelligible or their purported justification adequately understood. What kind of language-in-use would this be?

One central feature that it would have to possess, if it were to satisfy the first of these two conditions, can be illustrated by considering how its use of proper names, for example of place-names, would contrast with that of the languages in terms of which the problem has so far been framed. For in this third language the relationship of a name to what is named will have to be specifiable, so far as possible, independently of any particular scheme of identification embodying the beliefs of some particular community. Names in consequence will have to have become detached from those descriptions which, within some given and presupposed context defined by the beliefs of some particular community, uniquely identify person or place. Particular proper names will have ceased to be equivalent to and, in virtue of that loss of equivalence, will have ceased to have the same sense as particular definite descriptions. Names of places will have become equally available for any user to employ whatever his or her beliefs. Names having been Fregean will have become by a process of social change Kripkean.[16]

The immediate response of most philosophical logicians will once again be to say that I have in so characterizing these changes confused the essential function of naming with its merely contingent accompaniments. But it is just this notion of a single essential naming relationship or function that I reject; just as we have learned that meaning is not a unitary notion, so we ought also to have learned that there are multifarious modes of identifying, picking out, referring to, calling toward, in, or up and the like, all of which connect a name and a named, but there is no single core relation of name to named for theories of reference to be theories of. Or rather, if there were to be such a relation, it would be what Russell said it was, and it is notorious that Russell's characterization of that relation entails that there is indeed a class of proper names, but that none of the expressions which we have hitherto called names are among them.[17]

A second feature of this type of language will be the absence of texts which are canonical for its common use. Allusion and quotation will have become specialized devices, and the literate will have been divorced from the literary. For texts, whether oral or written, embody and presuppose beliefs, and this type of language is, so far as possible, *qua* language-in-use, neutral between competing systems of beliefs. What it will provide are resources for the representation of an indefinite variety of systems of beliefs, most of them originally at home in very different types of linguistic community by means of a variety of devices which enable those who construct such representations to do so in a way that is quite independent of their own commitments. What kind of devices are these? Where the text is in a foreign language, translation will be supplemented both by paraphrase and by scholarly gloss.[18] Words as common as *'polis'* and *'dikaiosune'* in fifth-century Attic Greek cannot be translated in any strict sense into twentieth-century English or French or German—examples, it will have been obvious at once, of this type of language—but their use can be quite adequately elucidated. The traditions that appealed to canonical texts can now become matter for successful historical enquiry, and the relevant texts embodying those traditions can be established, edited, and translated or otherwise elucidated. The belief-system of any and every culture, or of almost any and every culture, can thus be accurately represented within our own. But certain features of the resulting stock of representations need to be taken into account.

One concerns the asymmetry of this representation relation. From the fact that we in modern English or some other modern language, with our academic resources, can accurately represent the belief-system or part of the belief-system of another culture, it does not follow that the corresponding part of our belief-system can be represented in the language-in-use of that other culture. Using modern English, Charles H. Kahn has shown how the Homeric uses of the verb *eimi* can be accurately and adequately represented.[19] But his explanation of why certain types of translation or paraphrase would be a misrepresentation—namely, that, for example, the English verb 'exist' has emerged from a history whose first stage was the transition to classical Greek and which was then informed successively by classical Latin poetic usage, by medieval Latin philosophical usage, and finally by some essentially modern preoccupations, so that we just cannot use 'exist' to translate or to explicate the characteristic and varying features of Homeric uses of *eimi*—has as a consequence that it would not have been possible within the Homeric linguistic community to represent accurately the modern English uses of 'exist'. And what is true of the relationship of archaic Greek to modern English would be equally true of the relationship to modern English of seventeenth-century Irish or sixteenth-century Zuni. But from this fact we might be tempted to draw a mistaken conclusion.

Return to the condition of our imaginary person once poised between sixteenth-century Zuni and Spanish or seventeenth-century Irish and English, but now, presumably some three hundred years older, considering whether to address his other problems instead in twentieth-century English or French or whatever. Since such a person can provide him or herself with such an adequate degree of neutral representation of both systems of belief in a modern language, but cannot represent adequately or neutrally in either of his or her earlier languages either the systems of belief of the rival linguistic communities who spoke those languages or the standpoints afforded by twentieth-century English or French for the provision of such representation, it might seem that the only rational course for such a person is to conduct his or her enquiry from now on in one of the modern languages, thus escaping from some at least of the limitations imposed on his or her earlier condition, the very limitations which enforced relativist conclusions. But it is just at this point that a second feature of the representations of schemes of belief in specifically modern natural languages presents a crucial difficulty.

The only way in which our frustrated relativist can hope to transcend the limitations which imposed that relativism is by formulating in the language that he or she can now speak, one of the languages of modernity, an impersonal and neutral standard of rational justification in the light of which the claims of the competing belief-systems can be evaluated. But what he or she will in fact learn from acquiring this new language is that it is a central feature of the culture whose language it is that rationally founded agreement as to the nature of the justification required is not to be obtained. Rational justification within the context of such cultures becomes an essentially contested concept, and this for a number of distinct, but related, types of reason.

One arises from the nature of the historical process which made the language of modernity what it is. A central feature of that process had to be, I have already argued, the detachment of the language-in-use from any particular set of canonical texts; and an early stage in that history was the gradual accumulation in the culture of so many different, heterogeneous, and conflicting bodies of canonical texts from so many diverse parts of the cultural past that every one of them had to forego any exclusive claim to canonical status and thereby, it soon became apparent, any claim to canonical status at all. So the accumulation of Greek, Hebrew, and Latin texts at the Renaissance proved only a prologue not only to the annexation of Chinese, Sanskrit, Mayan, and Old Irish texts, and to the bestowal of equal status upon texts in European vernacular languages from the thirteenth to the nineteenth centuries, but also to the discovery of a wide range of preliterate cultures, the whole finally to be assembled in that modern liberal arts college museum of academic culture, whose introductory tour is provided by those Great Books courses which run from Gilgamesh to Saul Bellow via Confucius, Dante, Newton, *Tristram Shandy*, and Margaret Mead.

What the history that culminates in this kind of educational gallimaufry produced along the way was a large and general awareness of the wide range of varying and conflicting types of justificatory argument used to support various types of contending belief, and also of the wide range of varying and conflicting theoretical accounts of rational justification available to support their use. The consequence was a multiplication of rival standpoints concerning a wide range of subject-matters, none of them able to provide the resources for their own final vindication and the overthrow of their competitors. So within philosophy foundationalists war with coherentists and both with skeptics and perspectivists, while conceptions of truth as empirical adequacy contend against a variety of mutually incompatible realisms and both against truth conceived as disclosure. Within the academic study of literature controversies over the nature of interpretation and about the justification not only of particular interpretations of particular texts but even of what it is that such interpretations are interpretations of, parody philosophical debate in both idiom and interminability. And psychology has happily accommodated numbers of mutually incompatible schools of thought, each with its own idiosyncratic account of justification, ever since it became an independent academic discipline.

Where the dominant institutions and modes of thought in our larger political society sanction and even encourage disagreement, as upon theological questions, it is widely accepted that in the debates between contending modes of justification there can be no rational conclusion. But even where those same institutions and modes of thought prescribe a large measure of agreement, as in the natural sciences, not only do nonscientific modes of thought such as astrology (which happens to have its own well-organized and far from unsophisticated standards of justification) continue to flourish alongside the sciences, but it remains impossible to secure agreement on why the key transitions in the past history of our culture from prescientific thought to scientific, and from one mode of scientific thought to another, were or are rationally justified. So incommensurability as a feature of the history of the natural sciences has continually been rediscovered and recharacterized from a variety of justificatory standpoints: by Gaston Bachelard in the context of the French debates of the 1920s; by Michael Polanyi in such a way as to warrant a blend of fideism and realism; by Thomas Kuhn in a way designed to undermine logical empiricism; by Paul Feyerabend in an anarchist mode; and by Ian Hacking in an historical thesis about 'styles of thought'.

The multiplicity of mutually irreconcilable standpoints concerning justification is one that each of us tends to recognize easily and even scornfully in other academic professions. But from within our own profession each of us characteristically views and describes the situation only from the specific point of view of his or her own commitments, judging the success and failure of other points of view from the standpoint afforded by standards of justification internal to our own; and by so doing we render our overall cultural situation invisible, at least for most of the time. That this should be the case, that we should tend to be guilty of this kind of one-sidedness, is scarcely surprising. It says no more about us than that we are, sociologically at least, normal human beings. The danger of contemporary antirelativism, however, is that it suggests that what is in fact a contingent social condition whose limitations it is important for us to overcome is in fact a necessary condition of rational social existence. For antirelativism pictures us first as necessarily inhabiting our own conceptual scheme, our own *Weltanschauung* ("*Whose* conceptual scheme, whose *Weltanschauung* but our own could we be expected to inhabit?" is the rhetorical question that is sometimes posed), and second as necessarily acquiring whatever understanding we may possess of the conceptual schemes and *Weltanschauungen* of others by a process of translation so conceived that any intelligible rendering of the concepts and beliefs of the others must represent them as in all central respects similar to our own.

What I have tried to suggest by contrast is that when we learn the languages of certain radically different cultures, it is in the course of discovering what is untranslatable in them, and why, that we learn how not only to occupy alternative viewpoints but in terms of those viewpoints to frame questions to which under certain conditions a version of relativism is the inescapable answer. And in so doing we are also able to learn how to view our own peculiarly modern standpoint from a vantage point outside itself. For consider now the view of that modern standpoint afforded to our imaginary person who had hoped to remedy the deficiencies of his or her particular type of premodern language by learning to speak one of the languages of modernity.

Where in his or her premodern language he or she was unable to free him or herself from the limitations of the justificatory schemes built into and presupposed by each particular language-in-use, and so was unable to discover a set of neutral and independent standards of rational justification, by appeal to which his or her choice of allegiance to the beliefs and way of life of one community rather than the other could be made, he or she now speaks a language the use of which is free from such commitments. But the culture which is able to make such a language available is so only because it is a culture offering for the relevant kinds of controversial subject matter, all too many heterogeneous and incompatible schemes of rational justification. And every attempt to advance sufficient reasons for choosing any one such scheme over its rivals must always turn out to presuppose the prior adoption of that scheme itself or of some other. For without such a prior prerational commitment no reason will count as a good reason.

Hence our imaginary person whose acquisition of one of the natural languages of modernity—twentieth-century English or French or whatever—was to rescue him or her from the relativism imposed by his or her previous condition cannot find here any more than there, albeit for very different reasons, any genuinely neutral and independent standard of rational justification. And it remains only to recognize that if our imaginary sixteenth- or seventeenth-century person, knowing both the languages that he or she then knew and subsequently learning our own, would be unable to avoid relativistic conclusions, then we in turn by learning his or her languages, or languages like them, and so learning both to imagine and to understand ourselves from the standpoint of such an external observer would have to reach the same conclusions. Relativism after all turns out to be so far immune to refutation, even by us.

5

It does not follow that relativism cannot be transcended. We may be tempted to think so by noticing that the version of relativism which resists refutation is itself a relativized relativism, since what my arguments show, if they succeed, are that relativism is inescapable from certain particular points of view—one of which happens to be that which most people in modern societies such as ours take to be their own. And this may seem to provide additional confirmation, if such is still needed, that there is after all no mode of thought, enquiry, or practice which is not from some particular point of view, and whose judgments do not therefore take place on the basis of what Edmund Burke called prejudices, prejudgments. But it does not follow, as we might suppose if we did concede the last word to relativism, that we are thereby condemned to or imprisoned within our own particular standpoint, able to controvert that of others only by appealing to standards which already presuppose the standpoint of our own prejudices. Why not?

Begin from a fact which at this stage can be little more than suggestive. It is that those natural languages in which philosophy became a developed form of enquiry, so later generating from itself first the natural and then the social sciences, were in the condition neither on the one hand of sixteenth- and seventeenth-century Zuni and Irish nor in that of the natural languages of modernity. The Attic Greek of the fifth and fourth centuries, the Latin of the twelfth to fourteenth centuries, the English, French, German, and Latin of the seventeenth and eighteenth centuries were each of them neither as relatively presuppositionless in respect of key beliefs as the languages of modernity were to become, nor as closely tied in their use to the presuppositions of one single closely knit set of beliefs as some premodern languages are and have been. Consider in this respect the difference between Attic and Homeric Greek or that between mature philosophical Latin after Augustine and Jerome and the Latin that had preceded the discoveries by Lucretius and Cicero that they could only think certain Greek thoughts in Latin if they radically neologized. Such languages-in-use, we may note, have a wide enough range of canonical texts to provide to some degree alternative and rival modes of justification, but a narrow enough range so that the debate between these modes is focused and determinate. What emerges within the conceptual schemes of such languages is a developed problematic, a set of debates concerning a body of often interrelated problems, problems canonical for those inhabiting that particular scheme, by reference to work upon which rational progress, or failure to achieve such progress, is evaluated. Each such problematic is of course internal to some particular conceptual scheme embodied in some particular historical tradition with its own given starting point, its own prejudices. To become a philosopher always involved learning to inhabit such a tradition, a fact not likely to be obvious to those brought up from infancy within one, but very obvious to those brought up outside any such. It is no accident for example that for Irish speakers to become philosophers they had first to learn Greek and Latin, like Johannes Scotus Eriugena in the ninth century.

The development of a problematic within a tradition characteristically goes through certain well-marked stages—not necessarily of course the same stages in every tradition—among them periods in which progress, as judged by the standards internal to that particular tradition, falters or fails, attempt after attempt to solve or resolve certain key problems or issues proves fruitless and the tradition appears, again by its own standards, to have degenerated. Characteristically, if not universally, at this stage contradictions appear that cannot be resolved within the particular tradition's own conceptual framework: that is to say, there can be drawn from within the tradition equally well-grounded support for incompatible positions; at the same time enquiries tend to become diverse and particularized and to lose any overall sense of direction; and debates about realism may become fashionable.[20] And what the adherents of such a tradition may have to learn in such a period is that their tradition lacks the resources to explain its own failing condition. They are all the more likely to learn that if they encounter some other standpoint, conceptually richer and more resourceful, which *is* able to provide just such an explanation.

So it was, for example, when Galilean and Newtonian natural philosophy turned out to provide a more adequate explanation by its own standards not only of nature than scholasticism had afforded but also of why late medieval scholastic enquiries had been only able to proceed so far and no further. Scholasticism's successes and more importantly its frustrations and limitation, judged by scholasticism's own standards of success and failure rather than by any later standards, only became intelligible in the light afforded by Galileo and Newton.

That the theoretical standpoint of Galileo or Newton may have been incommensurable with that of the scholastics is not inconsistent with this recognition of how the later physical tradition transcended the limitations of the earlier. And it is of course not only within the history of natural philosophy that this kind of claim can be identified and sometimes vindicated. Such a claim is implicit in the relationship of some of the medieval theistic Aristotelians to Aristotle in respect of theology and of Dante's *Commedia* to the *Aeneid* in respect of poetic imagination.

These examples direct our attention to a central characteristic of theoretical and practical rationality. Rationality, understood within some particular tradition with its own specific conceptual scheme and problematic, as it always has been and will be, nonetheless requires *qua* rationality a recognition that the rational inadequacies of that tradition from its own point of view—and every tradition must from the point of view of its own problematic view itself as to some degree inadequate—may at any time prove to be such that perhaps only the resources provided by some quite alien tradition—far more alien, it may be, than Newton was to the scholastics—will enable us to identify and to understand the limitations of our own tradition; and this provision may require that we transfer our allegiance to that hitherto alien tradition. It is because such rationality requires this recognition that the key concepts embodied in rational theory and practice within any tradition which has a developed problematic, including the concepts of truth and rational justification, cannot be defined exclusively in terms of or collapsed into those conceptions of them that are presently at home within the modes of theory and practice of the particular conceptual scheme of that tradition, or even some idealized version of those conceptions: the Platonic distinction between 'is true' and 'seems true to such and such person' turns out within such traditions to survive the recognition of the truth in relativism.

It is only from the standpoint of a rationality thus characterized, and that is to say from the standpoint of a tradition embodying such a conception of rationality, that a rejoinder can be made to those post-Nietzschean theories according to which rational argument, enquiry, and practice always express some interest of power and are indeed the masks worn by some will to power. And in this respect there is a crucial difference between rationality thus understood and the rationality characteristic of the Enlightenment and of its heirs. Ever since the Enlightenment our culture has been far too hospitable to the all too plainly self-interested belief that whenever we succeed in discovering the rationality of other and alien cultures and traditions, by making their behavior intelligible and by understanding their languages, what we will also discover is that in essentials they are just like us. Too much in recent and contemporary antirelativism continues to express this Enlightenment point of view and thereby makes more plausible than they ought to be those theories which identify every form of rationality with some form of contending power. What can liberate rationality from this identification is precisely an acknowledgment, only possible from within a certain kind of tradition, that rationality requires a readiness on our part to accept, and indeed to welcome, a possible future defeat of the forms of theory and practice in which it has up till now been taken to be embodied within our own tradition, at the hands of some alien and perhaps even as yet largely unintelligible tradition of thought and practice; and this is an acknowledgment of which the traditions that we inherit have too seldom been capable.

Notes

1. "An Answer to Mr. Clarke's Third Defence of his Letter to Mr. Dodwell," p. 883 in *The Works of Samuel Clarke, D.D.*, vol. III (London, 1738).

2. Most notably by Richard Rorty, "Pragmatism, Relativism, and Irrationalism," *Proceedings and Addresses of the American Philosophical Association,* 53 (1980): 719-738, reprinted in *Consequences of Pragmatism* (Minneapolis, 1982), pp.160-175, and by Donald Davidson in "On the Very Idea of a Conceptual Scheme," *Proceedings and Addresses of the American Philosophical Association, 47* (1974): 5-20, reprinted in *Inquiries into Truth and Interpretation* (Oxford, 1984), pp.183-198, and in *Expressing Evaluations,* The 1982 Lindley Lecture at the University of Kansas.

3. *Theatetus* 152a-179b, and especially 170e-171c.

4. See for example in the first part of the *Enzyklopädie der philosophischen Wissenschaften* (1817) translated by William Wallace as *The Logic Of Hegel* (Oxford, 1873), section 44, and "Remark: The Thing-in-itself of Transcendental Idealism" appended to chapter 1, A(b) of section two, of book two of Hegel's *Science of Logic* (London, 1969), which is A. V. Miller's translation of the *Wissenschaft der Logik* (1812).

5. Richard Rorty, "Pragmatism, Relativism, and Irrationalism," in *Consequences of Pragmatism*, p.167.

6. Donald Davidson argues in "On the Very Idea of a Conceptual Scheme" that the scheme-content distinction involves the notion of a relationship between a language or conceptual scheme on the one hand and on the other "something neutral and common that lies outside all schemes" (p. 190) and that the only relationships possible between a language or conceptual scheme and such a something are those of the scheme organizing, systematizing, or dividing whatever it is, or of it fitting or accounting for whatever it is. Davidson then shows that spelling out these relationships involves characterizing what was allegedly neutral and common, so that it is neither, but a subject matter which "we will have to individuate according to familiar principles," so that any language which enables us to speak of it "must be a language very like our own" (p. 192). Hegel argues conversely in the passages cited in note 4 that if we deny to such a something or other those characteristics that it must lack if it is to be genuinely prior to all categorization, as what is "neutral and common" (Davidson's expression) must be, it will turn out to be nothing at all. And in the context of a different discussion, after pointing out that what is alleged to be beyond all conceptualization by reason of its particularity "*cannot be reached* by language. . . . In the actual attempt to say it, it would therefore crumble away . . ."

(Phanomenologie des Geistes [1807], paragraph 110, A.V. Miller's translation in *Phenomenology of Spirit* [Oxford, 1977]) he points out that in characterizing the whatever it is, we find ourselves individuating according to familiar principles, anticipating Davidson very precisely. The page references to Davidson are to *Inquiries into Truth and Interpretation.*

7. One example of Hegel's treatment of rival conceptual schemes is found in the *Phanomenologie,* VI, B, II a *"Der Kampf der Aufklarung mit dem Aberglauben."*

8. For Vico who gave us the first genuinely historical treatment of conceptual schemes, see especially book IV, sections I-XI, of the *Principi di Scienza Nuova* (1744), translated by T. G. Bergin and H. Fisch as *The New Science of Giambattista Vico* (Cornell, 1948).

9. It was of course Collingwood's antirealism, already spelled out in *Speculum Mentis* (Oxford, 1924), that committed him to the rejection of any version of the scheme-context distinction. For his treatment of alternative conceptual schemes see especially the *Essay on Metaphysics* (Oxford, 1940).

10. Paul Ziff in "About Proper Names" (*Mind* 86, July 1977) draws attention to the importance of attending "to the relevant anthropological and linguistic data." An exemplary study is Robin Fox, "Structure of Personal Names on Tory Island" (*Man,* 1963) reprinted as "Personal Names" in *Encounter with Anthropology* (New York, 1973).

11. On the first encounters of the Zuni with the Spaniards see F. H. Cushing, "Outlines of Zuni Creation Myths" in *13th Annual Report of the Bureau of Ethnology* (Washington, D.C., 1896), pp. 326-333, and on the way places are located and the middle place named, pp. 367-373.

12. Vico, *Principi di Scienza Nuova,* paragraphs 34-36, for example.

13. See for an introduction chapter 5 and chapter 6 (both originally in *Microfisica del Potere* (Turin, 1977) of *Power/Knowledge* (New York, 1980). Chapter 5 is translated by Kate Soper; chapter 6 by Colin Gordon.

14. Janice Moulton, "A Paradigm of Philosophy: the Adversary Method", in *Discovering Reality* (Dordrecht, 1983), edited by S. Harding and M. B. Hintikka.

15. Robert Nozick, *Philosophical Explanations* (Cambridge, Mass.), 1981, pp. 4-8.

16. What has to be supplied here is an account of how one and the same proper name can be used in a variety of ways which connect it to one and the same bearer.

17. Bertrand Russell, "The Philosophy of Logical Atomism," pp. 200-203 in *Logic and Knowledge,* ed. R. C. Marsh (London, 1956), originally published in *The Monist,* 1918.

18. See John Wallace, "Translation Theories and the Decipherment of Linear B," *Theory and Decision II* (1979).

19. *The Verb 'Be' and its Synonyms,* ed. J. W. M. Verhaar, part 6: *The Verb 'Be' in Ancient Greek* by Charles H. Kahn (Foundations of Language Supplement Series, vol. 16 [Dordrecht, 1973]).

20. Neither realism nor antirealism should be thought of as mistakes (or truths) generated by philosophers reflecting upon the sciences from some external standpoint. They are in fact primarily moments in the self-interpretation of the sciences. And the growth of debates about realism characteristically is a symptom of the inability of scientists to give a cogent account to themselves of the status of their enquiries.

Acknowledgments

My colleagues John Compton, John Post, Charles Scott, and Harry Teloh subjected an earlier version of this essay to rigorous and constructive criticism. A different kind of debt is to Brian Friel's play *Translations* (Faber & Faber, 1981) and to my former colleague Dennis Tedlock's translations of narrative poetry of the Zuni Indians *Finding the Centre* (University of Nebraska Press, 1978), which threw a very different light on problems of translation from that afforded by most recent philosophical writing.

The Horizon of Reason

GORDON C. F. BEARN

MOTTO

One human being can be a complete enigma to another. We learn this when we come into a strange country with entirely strange traditions; and what is more, even given a mastery of the country's language. We do not *understand* the people. (And not because of not knowing what they are saying to themselves.) We cannot find our feet with them. [Wir koennen uns nicht in sie finden.]
　　　　　Wittgenstein, *Philosophical Investigations*, page 223e.

In this essay I argue that the powerful considerations brought by Davidson against epistemological relativism should not be seen as demonstrating that there is no truth in relativism. His arguments should be seen rather as defining the limits within which we can intelligibly speak of an epistemic practice at all. This suggests that Davidson's views could house two distinctively relativistic observations. The first is simply that there are limits to what we can intelligibly suppose to be an epistemic practice, and the second is that within these limits there is room for a diversity of epistemic practices which could with justice be described as revealing the truth in relativism. On this account Davidson's transcendental argument against the very possibility of epistemological relativism only reveals the horizon of relativism: the horizon of reason.

1. Relativism, Realism, and Reason

Epistemological relativism is sometimes motivated by a particular problem: to understand the existence of radical discontinuities between artistic, religious, political, medical, scientific, or other traditions. It is, of course, possible to offer a relativistic treatment of some domains and not others. Imagine a dispute between two persons who do not accept the same considerations as being relevant to determining which of them is right and which of them is wrong. Such a dispute could not be resolved by appeal to relevant evidence without begging the question against one or the other disputant. Where two traditions are in this way discontinuous, I shall say they are incommensurable. At least at the time the discontinuity appears, the two traditions share no standards of epistemic appraisal which could resolve the dispute without begging the question against one or the other disputant. However, I do not mean to imply that members of the two traditions are unable either to understand each other or to evaluate the epistemic virtues of the other tradition. The fact that traditions can be incommensurable in this way is a familiar feature of some discussions of moral and aesthetic evaluation, and has been argued to have been implicit in the history of science by Hanson, Toulmin, Feyerabend, and most famously by Kuhn. My own view is that a correct understanding of that fact requires us to acknowledge the truth in relativism.

This motivation is subject to the following very natural realist objection: even if there were discontinuities of this sort between various traditions, this could never show that *truth* was relative to tradition but—at best—that rationality or being a good reason was relative. This natural objection assumes that truth is a *nonepistemic notion.* That is to say: there is no relation of entailment between there being excellent reasons for believing that p is true and p's actually being true.[1] It seems as if truth's being nonepistemic would steal the thunder from relativism. There could be no dramatic announcement that truth was relative, only the announcement that different groups of people have not always agreed about what was a good reason for thinking that, for example, eating walnut meat would cure headaches. And this, so the objection goes, is hardly worth a dramatic announcement.

In response to this natural objection, the relativist may find herself trying to appropriate a modified notion of truth for her own purposes. Realizing that if truth were an epistemic notion, and thus there would be a relation of entailment between reason's being relative and truth's being relative, the relativist will set about arguing for two claims: first, that truth may coherently be taken to be an epistemic notion and, second, that the radically nonepistemic notion of truth is (somehow) incoherent. Perhaps, following Dewey, she will replace truth with warranted assertability.

I do not think that this is the most satisfactory response to the realist objection to relativism. For suppose the relativist is successful in both of these projects, then the fact of incommensurability presents us with the representative of one tradition asserting that p is true-according-to-his-standards and the representative of another tradition asserting that p is not true-according-to-her-standards. On this account the conflict between our two representatives would have been explained away. Our representatives would not be disagreeing over the application of one predicate to p; they would be choosing to apply different predicates. The *urgency* of the fact of incommensurability would have evaporated.

On some accounts this kind of domestication of incommensurability is the goal of relativism; B.A.O. Williams is giving voice to a widespread opinion when he suggests that "the aim of relativism is to *explain away* a conflict," for example, to explain away the fact of incommensurability.[2] My own aims are different; they are not to undermine but to understand the conflict exhibited by that fact. The hope is that this search for understanding might teach us something about what Emerson called the "mysteries of human condition," about the fact that our knowledge is fated to be human.[3]

When we are actually involved in a dispute with another, and even when we imagine that dispute to be with the representative of an incommensurable tradition, we nevertheless find the following thought unavoidable: EITHER the dispute is superficial, affecting the application of predicates much weaker than truth such as "polite," in which case conflict can be either explained away or lived with,[4] OR the dispute is not superficial, and only one of the disputants can be correct, in which case we may be more or less secure in the thought that we have truth on our side. The most natural way to accommodate this thought, and the experience it records, is to accept the viability of the nonepistemic notion of truth. But now we must ask: If it is conceded that such a notion of truth would give urgency to the fact of incommensurability, would it drain the interest from incommensurability? To ask the question is to answer it: urgent issues hold our interest.

Acceptance of the coherence of the nonepistemic notion of truth, and even acceptance of the further possibility of the future universal agreement of all inquirers, is not the death knell of relativism.[5] It would be if these ideas guaranteed that dialog would at some time end in a mutually acceptable reasonable resolution. But it should come as no surprise that commitment to the *hope* of such a resolution does not guarantee the *existence* of such a resolution. The proper conclusion to draw from this connection between relativism and our commitment to the nonepistemic notion of truth is this. If there seems no way to resolve, by appeal to reasons, a dispute between ourselves and others without begging the question against ourselves or our fellow conversationalists, then our commitment to the nonepistemic notion will support in these circumstances the feeling that our hopes have been frustrated, or worse, dashed. We will want to continue the dialog to attempt a resolution. But our commitment gives us no guarantee that we will, in fact, reach one. It does not even guarantee the ethereal existence of a resolution in logical heaven. It only guarantees that we will try to reach one, and it guarantees that we will try *for a time,* but not for *all* time. There are more important things than talk.

As for relativism, I think this entails that we will never accept a purported proof that there is no possible way to resolve an incommensurable dispute. Even if epistemological relativism can prove itself coherent, it will never prove itself true, because it could never make itself welcome. What our acceptance of the nonepistemic notion of truth may mean is that we cannot experience the fact of incommensurability in the Derridean spirit of gaiety and play, but in the spirit of something like intellectual tragedy. Nietzsche reached this point in his first book, when he wrote:

> The periphery of the circle of science has an infinite number of points; and while there is no telling how this circle could ever be surveyed completely, noble and gifted men nevertheless reach, ere half their time and inevitably, such boundary points on the periphery from which one gazes into what defies illumination. When they see to their horror how logic coils up at these boundaries and finally bites its own tail—suddenly a new form of insight breaks through, *tragic insight.*[6]

In this section I have argued that if we advance on epistemological relativism by means of an epistemic reduction of the concept of truth, the excitement of relativism would evaporate. A more promising way to advance would be to concede the coherence of the nonepistemic conception of truth and focus one's attention on the concept of *reason;*[7] one might even say, on a critique of reason. Although the nonepistemic notion of truth regulates our quest for a solution to any intellectual dispute, it can play no particular role in any particular dispute. Accepting the coherence and relevance of a nonepistemic conception of truth will not affect the existence of the fact of incommensurability, but it will affect our experience of that fact. The exposure of human knowledge to the possibility of incommensurable conflict is our exposure to the possibility of something akin to intellectual tragedy.

Having sketched an approach to the motivation of relativism and blocked out the interaction between relativism and realism, I will now consider in detail a conspicuous attempt to demonstrate that the relativist's thesis is fundamentally incoherent.

2. Davidson's Anti-Relativism

Davidson used the occasion of his December 1973 presidential address to the Eastern Division of the APA to present a vigorous critique of the work of Kuhn, Feyerabend, Whorf, and Quine. As he read them, these quite different authors shared a commitment to what he called the third dogma of empiricism and a consequent concern with underdetermination relativism, the view that two incompatible systematizations of experience might be equally reasonable to believe. The second version of what became his presidential address was called "The Third Dogma of Empiricism," and the aim of that address was first of all to refute that dogma and only secondly to refute all forms of epistemological relativism.[8] I shall argue that there is a truth in relativism which can survive the defeat of the dogma.

In "Two Dogmas" (1951) Quine summarized his opposition to the twin dogmas of the analytic and of verificationism:

> My present suggestion is that it is nonsense, and the root of much nonsense, to speak of a linguistic component and a factual component in the truth of any individual statement. Taken collectively, science has its double dependence upon language and experience; but this duality is not significantly traceable into the statements of science *taken one by one.*[9]

This passage reveals Quine's commitment to the remaining third dogma: the dualism of a domain of meaning (conceptual schemes) and a domain of experience (empirical content) which, although not applicable to sentences taken one by one, is nevertheless applicable to our language as a whole. In his presidential address Davidson explains:

> In place of the dualism of the analytic-synthetic we get the dualism of conceptual scheme and empirical content. . . . I want to urge that this second dualism of scheme and content, of organizing system and something waiting to be organized, cannot be made intelligible and defensible. It is itself a dogma of empiricism, the third dogma.[10]

There is a connection between the third dogma and underdetermination relativism: because if we may separate scheme and content, it might be empirically possible for there to be a number of incompatible but empirically adequate schemes for organizing the subjective basis of our knowledge of the world. Quine's various attempts to make sense of the possibility of empirically equivalent but incompatible systems of the world constitute a presently unfinished story whose moral, according to recent Quine, is said to be that, given an accepted set of observation sentences and one or two logician's tricks, any apparently equivalent but incompatible systems of the world can be shown to be if equivalent, compatible.[11]

Davidson's attack strikes at a deeper level than Quine's. Instead of demonstrating the difficulty of showing that two empirically equivalent systems are indeed incompatible, Davidson attacks the picture which sets Quine's predicament: the picture of a conceptual scheme organizing or fitting our perceptual experience. If Davidson's arguments are successful, it is not even logically possible for there to be two radically different empirically equivalent systems of the world. Originally Davidson's strategy was to argue that the very idea of a conceptual scheme was incoherent; recently he has presented the complementary considerations which are designed to show that the very idea of subjective experiential evidence is incoherent.[12] Since my sketch of how one might try to motivate epistemological relativism made use of differing judgments about what it would be reasonable to believe, and since this might be described as disagreement about different concepts of rationality, I will concentrate on the first strategy.

This approach can be conceived as a generalized argument that is then directed at two different degrees of alternativeness in conceptual schemes. The generalized argument[13] is this:

(1) Conceptual schemes are not odd platonic entities; they are languages.
(2) Intertranslatability establishes sameness of conceptual scheme.
(3) Translatability into *our* language is the criterion for something's *being* a language.
So (4) An "alternative conceptual scheme" would have to be *BOTH*
    (a) a conceptual scheme, hence, (by 1) a language, and hence (by 3) translatable into our own language; *AND*
    (b) an alternative to our conceptual scheme, hence (by 2) not translatable into our own language.
So (5) The idea of an alternative conceptual scheme is in contradiction with itself.
But (6) "If we cannot intelligibly say that schemes are different, neither can we . . . say that they are one."[14]
So (7) The very idea of a conceptual scheme is unintelligible.

In considering this argument I will follow Davidson in distinguishing two different possibilities. (i) The possibility that there could be radically alternative conceptual schemes which, by (2) above, would be completely untranslatable. And (ii) the more reasonable possibility that there could be moderately alternative conceptual schemes which, again by (2), would be moderately resistant to translation.

(i) Radically Alternative Conceptual Schemes

The case against radical alternatives, against the existence of a language which was entirely untranslatable, is very strong indeed. It would be especially strong if we accepted (3), the view that nothing can *be* a language unless it is translatable into our own language. Those who would defend the existence of radically alternative schemes will, therefore reject (3) and propose a different criterion for being a language. Quite aware of this, Davidson devotes more than half his address to a consideration of two alternatives to (3):

(3*o) Organizing (systematizing, dividing up) the stream of experience is the criterion for being a language (conceptual scheme).

(3*f) Fitting (predicting, accounting for, facing) the tribunal of experience is the criterion for being a language (conceptual scheme).[15]

The defender of radically alternative conceptual schemes plans to use the fact that (3*o) and (3*f) are independent of questions of translatability to thwart Davidson's anti-relativist argument. Davidson argues that they are not separable from the demand that languages be translatable into our own.

Against (3*o) Davidson simply says that whereas it makes sense to say that one is organizing a group of things, it does not make sense to say that one is organizing a single thing, such as experience. However, if (3*o) is to be of service as a criterion for being a language, then it must make sense to speak of organizing one single thing; so it cannot perform that service. What has happened is that a concept (organizing) is being asked to do a job which it is singularly unable to do. The mistake, if we may call it such, is of a piece with what Kant would have called a dialectical illusion: the deceptively significant use of concepts, whose proper use presupposes a domain of objects, to describe what it is to be an object at all, what Kant calls *Gegenstaende ueberhaupt*.[16]

Davidson's argument against (3*f) is more elaborate. First, he notes that the sense of "fitting" experience or "coping with" experience which the defender of radically alternative conceptual schemes needs is rather special. Describing this opponent, he writes: "what is in view here is not just actually available evidence; it is the totality of possible sensory evidence past, present, and future." [17] But it is not clear that each of Davidson's official targets is committed even to the coherence of such a totality, let alone to a substantive use of it in the defense of their version of relativism.

To take just one example, a Kuhnian defense of the incommensurability of problems, solutions, and standards (not of concepts or worlds) need take no stand on whether or not "all possible evidence" would be unable to bridge the incommensurability.[18] The only claim is that at some time rational appeal to the evidence available—at that time—was unable to bridge the gap. This weaker claim would be sufficient to demonstrate that science actually moves forward in something less than an ideally rational manner. And it is sufficient to deliver at least one kind of relativity to scientific traditions. Hence, it can be seen that although Davidson claims to be addressing a position common to Whorf, Feyerabend, Kuhn, Quine, and others, his arguments are in fact primarily designed to engage one: Quine. It is Quine's underdetermination relativism that will lose its philosophical interest if theory is not underdetermined by all possible data past, present, and future, because it is Quine who uses all possible data in setting up his underdetermination problem.

Suppose that what our hypothetically untranslatable language-like entity had to "cope with" were not only all available, but all possible, evidence. Suppose further, as Davidson argues in another essay, that there is no more to the concept of fitting the facts than is captured by the concept of being true.[19] Then (3*f) will only help us make sense of radically alternative conceptual schemes if we can make sense of a language-like entity being both completely untranslatable and true. Against this possibility Davidson notes that Tarski's Convention T means that there is no way to make sense of truth without appealing to translation. Hence (3*f) will not manage to stay free of translatability, and it will not be able to circumvent the argument against radically alternative schemes.

Another way of putting this point is that nothing which is completely untranslatable can even seem to be the sort of thing that can be true or false. We forget this when we consider the language-like activity as the speech of strangers we have *yet* to translate, we should rather think of it as sounds—whether made by humans or waterfalls—which have completely resisted every attempt at translation. There is no temptation to call those noises untranslatable languages.[20] No doubt, there are other alternatives to (3) that Davidson has not canvassed. [21] Nevertheless, a consideration of what our actual response would be to the complete frustration of all our efforts at translating language-like sounds is sufficient to extinguish the confident hope of progress in the endeavor to find a form of (3) entirely free from a commitment to translatability into our language.

(ii) Moderately Alternative Conceptual Schemes

Moderately alternative schemes would merely be moderately resistant to translation. Given the way I have set up the possibility of relativistic treatment of some domains and not others, this second part of Davidson's attack on the possibility of relativism will more directly engage the strategy for a defense of relativism outlined in section 1.

Davidson suggests that if we are to make sense of moderately alternative conceptual schemes (of partial failure of translation), we will need "a theory of translation or interpretation that makes no assumptions about shared meanings, concepts, or beliefs."[22] However we evaluate his final position, we might immediately suspect that Davidson has made things too difficult for his opponent. If one were trying to make sense of the possibility of partial failure of translation, then why could one not defend a theory of translation or interpretation which makes some assumptions about the *partial* sharing of meanings, concepts, and beliefs? If Davidson thought that if two languages shared any beliefs or meanings, then they would of necessity share them all, one could make sense of his stringent constraint. But that would require a commitment to a particularly exaggerated form of holism. As it happens, Davidson's own theory of interpretation permits what we can recognize as two languages to share some but not all their conceptual resources. My interpretive strategy will therefore be to determine the consequences for the sharing of beliefs that follow from Davidson's theory of interpretation.

With Quine, Davidson approaches the problem of translation via a consideration of radical interpretation, and with Quine, he assumes that even before we can translate what the strangers are saying, we can recognize when they hold what they are saying true. [23] When the stranger holds a sentence-like entity true, that behavior is a "vector of two forces," first what the stranger means by the sentence and second what he believes about the world.[24] The logical puzzle which the radical interpreter faces is to solve for both unknowns at once. The apparently extreme difficulty of this puzzle is exhibited in this passage from one of Davidson's more recent articles: "If he [the radical interpreter] knew the meanings, he would know the beliefs, and if he knew the beliefs expressed by the sentences assented to, he would know the meanings. But how can he learn both at once, since each depends on the other?" [25]

Davidson's solution to this puzzle is predicated on the purposes of interpretation. We want to understand what the strangers are saying with the hope of predicting and explaining their behavior. Given our desire to understand the strangers, Davidson notes that "the only possibility at the start is to assume general agreement on beliefs. . . . Charity is forced on us; whether we like it or not, if we want to understand others, we must count them right in most matters."[26] This principle of charity would fix the beliefs of the strangers, and we could solve for the remaining unknown—the meaning of their utterances—in a fairly mechanical manner. As Davidson puts it, "from a formal point of view, the principle of charity helps solve the problem of the interaction of meaning and belief by restraining the degrees of freedom allowed belief while determining how to interpret words."[27]

Given this approach to interpretation, it is clear that any strangers whose speech was recognizable as a partially translatable language would share *many* beliefs and concepts with us, but they would not necessarily share *all* our beliefs and concepts: "the method is not designed to eliminate disagreement, nor can it." [28] They would necessarily share those of our beliefs that are, as Davidson variously puts it, "basic" or held "most stubbornly" or are "most central" to our whole system of beliefs about the world.[29] Unless these beliefs were shared, we would not have been able to translate the stranger's speech at all. But will this defeat every form of epistemological relativism?

3. The Foundation of Charity

The central point of the strategy I used in section 1 to motivate epistemological relativism was that different people or groups of people might disagree about what was a good reason for what. In such a case it would be impossible to resolve their dispute without begging the question against one or the other disputant. It would be easy to defend this motivation while agreeing with Davidson's rejection of the possibility of *radically* alternative conceptual schemes. It is more difficult to determine whether anything Davidson says against the possibility of *moderately* alternative conceptual schemes would also damage the strategy of section 1.

At least half of this difficulty derives from its not being clear what Davidson wants to say about the moderate form of relativism. This is because, as I have emphasized, Davidson's target is only incidentally the possibility of a defensible form of relativism. First of all, his target is the third dogma of empiricism. According to the third dogma, at the level of entire languages it makes sense to speak of a difference between a realm of meaning and a realm of experience. In his discussion of moderate relativism Davidson argues that the task of radical interpretation forces charity upon us, and he draws a negative conclusion about the third dogma. Where interpretation reveals that—as he puts it—"others think differently from us," Davidson suggests that there is no general way of assigning the difference to the realm of meaning or the realm of belief.[30] The procedures of radical interpretation have reinforced the thought that our access to different ways of thinking is not such as to be able to support a clean distinction between a realm of meaning and a realm of experience. Let us grant, therefore, that the third dogma is dead and let it lie, but what of moderate relativism?

Davidson conceded, in passing, that it is possible to discover people who think differently from ourselves, and this is surely one of the points relativists have been eager to make. Might it be possible to accept Davidson's victory over the very idea of the third dogma, while denying that he has thereby eliminated the very idea of epistemological relativism? In order to defend the remaining possibility of relativism, we must gain a deeper appreciation of the principle of charity than I have yet provided.

The first reaction to Davidson's appeal to charity is likely to be that he is merely reading our beliefs (and desires) into the stranger's mind. But since it appears to be a contingent matter whether the stranger shares our beliefs, it also appears we might be mistaken in interpreting the stranger charitably. Davidson's reply is simple: "Since charity is not an option . . . it is meaningless to suggest we might fall into massive error by adopting it."[31]

There are two senses of "nonoptional" that may relevantly be in play here. (1) The sense of "nonoptional" presented by a valid argument: given the truth of the premises, the conclusion is nonoptional—call this the logical sense of "nonoptional." (2) The sense of "nonoptional" presented by the fact that it is not optional whether I will see with my eyes or with my ears—call this the empirical sense of "nonoptional." Both senses of "nonoptional" were at play in Hume's discussion of the authority of experience. Although Hume concedes that "none but a fool or madman" would ever dispute the authority of experience, he nevertheless denies that that authority can be philosophically grounded.[32] The authority of experience is on Hume's account logically optional but empirically nonoptional.

It might appear that Davidson thinks that the appeal to charity is nonoptional in the logical sense. This interpretation is encouraged by his offering charity as a solution to the formally described puzzle of solving for two unknowns at once: the stranger's beliefs and the meaning of the stranger's words. We are told that charity is forced on us as the only way to proceed with finding a solution to this problem. But looked at as a question of logic, this is not true. Suppose that it were logically necessary to fix the stranger's beliefs and solve for the meaning of the words. We would still have an option about what beliefs to attribute to the stranger. As a matter of logic, there is nothing more to recommend the principle of charity than the principle of barbarity, the principle that we should make as many as possible of the stranger's beliefs not true, but false.[33] The principle of charity is not logically nonoptional.

Davidson's defense of the principle of charity is consistent with his recognition of this fact. He observes, for example, that the "point of the principle of charity is to make the speaker intelligible."[34] But what we find intelligible is nonoptional in the empirical sense: we can no more decide what we find intelligible than we can decide to see with our eyes; we find out. The foundations of Davidson's argument against moderate forms of relativism is not finally the principle of charity; it is what that principle rests on. We are charitable, because by being charitable we remain faithful to our judgments about what is and is not intelligible. Davidson says:

> The aim of interpretation is not agreement but understanding. My point has always been that understanding can be secured only by interpreting in a way that makes for the right sort of agreement. The "right sort" however is no easier to specify than to say what constitues a good reason for holding a particular belief.[35]

In spite of appearances, even on Davidson's own account the foundation of our interpretive practice is provided, not by a solution to a decision problem, but rather by the fact that we find this and not that to be an intelligible reason for believing that *p*.

If charity is nonoptional, then it is nonoptional in the empirical sense. As a matter of the logic of the predicament of the radical interpreter, there is no more to be said on behalf of charity than there is to be said on behalf of barbarity. What charity really means is that in interpreting others we have no choice but to find them intelligible, and the limits of intelligibility are set by the brute fact that we find some things and not others intelligible. Since intelligibility is a constraint on any empirical description of the world, I am tempted to say that the fact that we find this and not that intelligible is not really empirical or logical at all, but transcendental. However that may be, we may now ask: In this context what remains of epistemological relativism?

4. The Fate of Human Knowledge

(i) Davidson and Wittgenstein

In the corridors of the academy one often hears it said that Davidson's approach to language recalls Wittgenstein's. There is much to
make this seem surprising: Davidson's commitment to the importance
of the situation of the radical interpreter, his commitment to extensionalism, his hunch that the way to gather an understanding of meaning is
to construct a Tarskian truth-theory for a given language. But we are
now in a position to understand at least two dimensions of Davidson's
work which do indeed recall the mature Wittgenstein: the foundations
of the principle of charity and the opposition to the third dogma.

My interpretation of the foundations of charity reveals that principle to rest on the brute fact that we find some things and not others
intelligible. When we attempt to understand an other, we are attempting
to make their linguistic and other actions intelligible. What we can find
intelligible is not so much *grounded* on our judgments that this and not
that is an intelligible reason for asserting that *p* as it is *exhibited* in these
judgments. Suppose we tried to ground these judgments. If the judgments were really basic, then this putative grounding would presuppose
just those basic judgments about what was an intelligible reason for
what that we were trying to ground. As Wittgenstein puts it: "we keep
on finding ourselves on the old level."[36] The judgments which are the
foundations of charity do not support our conception of intelligibility,
as it were from the outside; they exhibit a part of that very conception.

It will be clear that I am trying to bring to the reader's mind those
paragraphs of Wittgenstein's *Philosophical Investigations* which conclude with the passage:

> 242. If language is to be a means of communication there must be
> agreement (Uebereinstimmung) not only in definitions but also (queer as
> this may sound) in judgments.[37]

What is the force here of "judgments"? If we are to communicate with
each other by means of a system of concepts, then even if we both
accept the same expressions as definitions of other expressions, we
would be unable to communicate unless we also agreed in judging that a
given expression applied to a given object. If we agree to follow the rules
on the back of the box but cannot manage to agree on how to apply
them, then we will be unable to play that game. Agreement on the
definition of "the end of the game" will not be enough to permit playing
of the game. The judgments that we must share—in addition to sharing

the definitions—are judgments such as *this* is the end of the game or *this* is a chair. It is this sort of judgment that we must share (agree in making) if language is to be a means of communication or, what comes to nearly the same thing, if radical interpretation is to be possible.

Why does this sound queer? One reason is that we so easily fall in with the third dogma of empiricism, with the idea that there is a realm of conceptual truth which is completely autonomous with respect to the facts of the world, including the fact of our being human. It sounds queer because if Wittgenstein is right, then it will not make sense to speak of there being an autonomous realm of concepts which organizes experience. It will only make sense to attribute a system of concepts to another if we can understand those concepts, and we will only be able to understand them if we agree in judging that *this* is a good reason for that. The principle of charity rests on our agreement in judgments: "it is essential for communication that we agree in a large number of judgments."[38]

(ii) Wittgenstein's Anti-Relativism: Security and Insecurity

We are now in a position to assess the effect of Davidson's antirelativistic arguments on the motivation of relativism sketched in section 1. Our question becomes: Is it conceivable that the stranger not share with us those basic judgments (about what is and is not an intelligible reason for a belief) which I have argued represent the foundation of the principle of charity? My answer will turn on there being two different kinds or levels of such basic judgments. Given that Wittgenstein has turned his back on the third dogma, is it still true that Wittgenstein's mature philosophy is relativistic? Yes and no.

Many of Davidson's antirelativistic conclusions will survive this Wittgensteinian translation. However, since what must be accepted, if we are to find others intelligible, has turned out to be particular judgments, we will not, as philosophers, be able to decide what kinds of thinking are possible apart from the hard, lonely, grey work of actual confrontation with old books or other creatures. But what room is left here for relativism? Ironically, Wittgenstein was kept from realizing the relativistic consequences of his investigations by focusing on too narrow a range of examples.[39] He draws his examples from elementary arithmetic and from ordinary objects familiar to us all, from objects Cavell refers to as generic objects.[40] In each case these are examples about which we are all experts or, better, about which in the appropriate sense there are no experts. There are mathematicians who study the natural numbers and art historians who study chairs, but $2+2$'s equalling 4 or this object being a chair are judgments we all share.

When my explanations and reasons run out, in the face of persistent questioning by a child, or in the face of the fact of incommensurability, then I may find that I am content to say with Wittgenstein that this is simply what I do or this is how it strikes me (not us).[41] I may find myself content to accept my own views as correct even though I am unable to begin to move my interlocutor. My guess is that we will feel this way, secure in our judgments, when the subjects are those about which—because of near-universal familiarity—there are no experts. Helping myself to Cavell's translation of "Uebereinstimmung" as attunement (not Anscombe's as agreement), I will call these judgments our *secure attunements*. They are particular judgments, and we will naturally read them into the speech of others unless something indicates that it would be mistaken so to do. The other side of reason here is, not an alternative way of thinking, but not thinking at all. And if those who do not think at all are, for all the world, human this is madness.[42] In *On Certainty* Wittgenstein notes that there are some propositions about which it is not possible to be mistaken, but only possible to reveal a "mental disturbance."[43] Perhaps this thought is what prompted him to write: "if in the midst of life we are in death, so in sanity we are surrounded by madness."[44]

These considerations are perfectly opposed to relativism. They deny the possibility of a way of thinking radically different from our own. This was the first conclusion reached by Davidson, and I have all along accepted it. We are now considering whether these Wittgensteinian foundations of the principle of charity exclude the possibility of a moderately different way of thinking. To answer this question we must understand the nature and extent of the secure attunements we share. I will approach this obliquely by considering how secure attunements differ from ones which we might call insecure.

Our secure attunements are those concerning which—without for a moment doubting the correctness of our judgments—we would be willing to cut off debate saying: this is what I do. The insecurity of *insecure attunements* consists in the fact that we cannot escape the doubt that what we just do is nothing more than what we do. We cannot escape the doubt that we might be wrong. It is characteristic of some recent art that it brings into question the limits of what we would be willing to call a serious aesthetic statement. Consider for example Rauschenberg's 1953 piece called "Erased de Kooning Drawing," which is just what it says it is. For some of us our judgments about the aesthetic seriousness of this work are insecure: our acceptance of it as a serious aesthetic statement is not strong enough to turn away doubts about its authenticity, nor are these doubts strong enough to secure the judgment that it is a complete fraud. In debate with a defender of the view that the

Rauschenberg is a plain fraud we are at least willing to agree that we might be wrong and our opponent correct, so we may be willing to agree to disagree. Our willingness to agree sincerely that our judgment might be wrong may provide a rough criterion for whether to class a judgment as secure or insecure. (We are not willing to agree that we might be wrong about whether this essay is printed in Chinese.)

For the purposes of this essay I shall also include in the class of insecure attunements those judgments which—like judgments of etiquette—we are not so much willing to agree that we might be wrong about as we are willing to agree that slurping and sipping hot liquids are, at some level, equally valid ways of drinking tea. Here we are willing to agree not that we might lose the race but that it might be a dead heat.

The mere fact that there are others who do not share an attunement with us is not sufficient to render that attunement insecure. Tribes with strange ways of justifying the judgment that witches cause illness do not share all of our attunements with us, but we are not willing to agree that we might be wrong about the nonexistence of witches. For whatever reasons—broadminded or tyrannical—we may not want to interfere with their practice, but we do not for a minute think that their practice is correct and ours incorrect, or that they are equally valid. Diversity alone does not bring insecurity in its wake.

Neither is it the case that the distinction between secure and insecure attunements can unproblematically be mapped onto the distinction between judgments within ethics and aesthetics on the one hand and the sciences on the other, the so-called fact/value distinction. Many ethical judgments provide examples of just the sort of judgment which I have called secure: judgments about which we are not willing to agree that we might be mistaken. Consider, for example, the judgment that rape is not a good thing. On the side of science the underdetermination of theory-choice by available evidence would provide an example of a situation where scientists' judgments in favor of one theory or another would be insecure. Consider, for example, the situation of physical scientists in the early 1920s when Einstein's and Whitehead's theories of relativity were all but empirically equivalent.

I do not believe that any of the usual ways of distinguishing different parts of the field of knowledge—mathematical, empirical, ethical—reproduces the distinction I am trying to draw here between those of our attunements which are secure and those which are insecure. This distinction seems to reappear not at the boundaries but within each domain of knowledge. I am, however, reasonably happy about allowing our willingness to agree that we might be mistaken (or that our view and our opponent's view might be equally valid) to determine which of our attunements are secure, which are insecure, and which are hard to classify as one or the other. It is probably fair to say that our secure attunements were the subject of Wittgenstein's investigation in *On Certainty* of what in the system of our beliefs "stands fast [fest-steht]."[45]

Is there any way to predict which of my judgments are secure and which are insecure? I do not think so. This would be like predicting whether I will enjoy the taste of raw fish; I have to find out. Which judgments are secure and which are not depends on what is *natural* for me. The limits of our practice of giving and accepting reasons for our beliefs, what Wittgenstein sometimes refers to as the limits of empiricism, "are not assumptions unguaranteed, or intuitively known to be correct: they are ways in which we make comparisons and in which we act."[46] This raises the question of how "our concepts, the use of our words, are constrained by a scaffolding of facts [Geruest von Tatsaechlichen]" without being *justified* by those facts and without being *about* those facts: the question of the role of the transcendental in the mature Wittgenstein.[47] I cannot here begin to defend my hunch that our secure attunements might be viewed as playing a role analogous to the role played by tautologies and contradictions in the *Tractatus*. Our secure attunements do not explain or justify; they exhibit, they show, they make manifest the transcendental logic of the world.[48]

(iii) A Wittgensteinian Relativism: Securities of Second Nature

The sense that all humans have at all times shared the same secure attunements suggests that if there were any truth in relativism, it would have to apply to the domain of insecure attunements, the only domain where there appear to be diverging attunements. However, there are also differences between groups of people about judgments which I shall class as secure attunements, although they share features with both our secure and our insecure attunements. At this intermediate level, as with secure attunements, we are unwilling to agree that we might be mistaken; we are secure in our judgment that they are correct. At this level, as with insecure attunements, there are or have been people who did not share these judgments with us. Wittgenstein appears to be describing this intermediate level when he writes: "I am sure, *sure*, [*sicher*], that he is not pretending; but some third person is not. Can I always convince him? And if not is there some mistake in his reasoning?"[49] I can be slightly more concrete.

Michel Foucault's investigation of the history of various sorts of disciplines presents us with an attempt to uncover what *could be said* at various times about people we, today, consider insane, criminal, or perverse. The attempt is helpfully viewed as a grammatical investigation in the manner of Wittgenstein's writings on very elementary mathematics but directed rather at objects about which there are experts, not at objects about which there are no experts. Foucault's investigations are investigations, not of the grammar of our discourse about generic objects, but of the grammar of our discourse about what Cavell would call specific objects.[50] Foucault's first approach to a collection of old books and papers is to attempt to discern unities in the discourse, to determine the kinds of things that can and cannot be said. Foucault:

> The analysis of the discursive field is oriented in a quite different way; we must grasp the statement in the exact specificity of its occurrence; determine its conditions of existence, fix at least its limits, establish its correlations with other statements that may be connected with it and show what other forms of statements it excludes. We do not seek, below what is manifest, the half silent murmur of another discourse.[51]

The discursive relations that Foucault attempts to unearth are not, he says, internal to discourse in the way a justification of the claim that the battery is dead is internal to discourse about cars, nor are they external to discourse in the way that sex bias is external to discourse about the internal combustion engine. Discursive relations are

> In a sense, at the limit of discourse: they . . . determine the group of relations that discourse must establish in order to speak of this or that object, in order to deal with them, name them, analyse them, classify them, explain them, etc. These relations characterize not the language [langue] used by discourse, nor the circumstances in which it is deployed, but discourse itself as a practice.[52]

The first of these passages is clearly in the same spirit as this one from Wittgenstein's writings on mathematics of around 1933-34:

> Time and again I would like to say: What *I* check is the *account books* of mathematicians; their mental processes, joys, depressions and instincts as they go about their business may be important in other connections, but they are no concern of mine.[53]

And again, explicitly linking this investigation to what he called grammar, Wittgenstein wrote: "grammar is the account books of language. They must show the actual transaction of language."[54]

Further, the connection between grammar and the limits of discourse is at least as clear as the connection between Foucault's discursive relations and the limits of discourse. Wittgenstein wrote in 1930:

> What belongs to the essence of the world simply *cannot* be said. . . . But the essence of language is a picture of the essence of the world, and philosophy as custodian of grammar can in fact grasp the essence of the world, only not in the propositions of language, but in the rules for this language which exclude nonsensical combinations of signs.[55]

These transcendental concerns of the maturing Wittgenstein endured even into the last year of his life when he wrote: "Am I not getting closer and closer to saying that logic cannot be described. You must look at the practice of language, then you will see it."[56] Here it may be seen why one will be tempted to recall the *Tractatus* by saying that the transcendental logic of the world shows inself in our secure attunements. If Foucault could uncover the fact that different groups of people do not necessarily share all the same secure attunements, then he would have uncovered a phenomenon Kant would not have thought possible: the phenomenon of transcendental conflict.[57]

Although I have not seriously defended my hunch that Foucault and Wittgenstein can best be understood as being engaged in the same style of investigations but in different domains, I hope that these strikingly similar passages are sufficient to motivate my Foucauldian extension of Wittgenstein's grammatical investigations. If Wittgenstein was kept from seeing the relativistic dimension of his work, it might be because he did not think of the possibility of a grammatical investigation not of the everyday but of the scientific. Foucault's historical investigations fill this lack. Foucault is famous for one result of his analysis of the specific limits of discursive practices, namely, that quite suddenly things that it was (grammatically) impossible to say can become possible to say. Because it was his first attempt at charting this sort of rupture, the most well-known example of this sort of change is the creation of a class of persons we would recognize as the insane. It was only at the end of the eighteenth century that the insane were isolated from a motley assortment of undesirables including the poor, the unemployed, and prisoners, in a barely articulated pool of folk including those we today would describe as the mentally ill.[58]

What I take this sort of empirical or historical discovery to reveal is the intermediate level of judgments that I mentioned above. In addition to our insecure attunements there are two kinds of secure attunements. Let me draw together my attempt at classifying these various types of judgments. First, secure attunements which are natural: (1a) we are so secure in our judgment that they are correct that we are unwilling to agree that we might be wrong about them, and (1b) as a matter of fact these are shared by all human beings. Second, secure attunements which are, as it were, second nature: (2a) again we are so secure we are unwilling to agree that we might be mistaken, but (2b) here, as a matter of fact, there are or have been peoples who have not shared them with us. Third, insecure attunements: (3a) here we are sometimes willing to agree that we might be mistaken, and (3b), as a matter of fact, there are people who have not shared them with us. I take it to be an empirical matter whether or not there do exist any examples of judgments meeting these descriptions, but I will proceed on the assumption that there are examples of each of these types.

Total Relativism. Our natural secure attunements are those of our judgments which it is inconceivable for a human being not to share, those of our judgments which Davidson's principle of charity takes for granted. These judgments make radically alternative modes of thinking literally inconceivable, they make total relativism unimaginable, and they make radical translation as easy as it is.[59] Davidson's primary conclusion is retained.

Effortless Relativism. Our insecure attunements which, like our judgments about etiquette, we think are no better and no worse than those apparently competing judgments made by people from other cultures, these insecure attunements open the door to an effortless form of relativism. Where people disagree over the application of predicates much weaker than truth, such as politeness, there we may agree that the conflict can be explained away or lived with. But there is more to learn from the challenge of relativism: the fact of incommensurability teaches a deeper, more difficult lesson about the fate of human knowledge.

Moderate Relativism. Those of our secure attunements which are only second nature help us make sense of the possibility of there being moderately different ways of thinking even while we reject the third dogma of empiricism. This will happen when different groups of people do not share all the important judgments of the form: this is a good reason for that belief. That people have not always and everywhere shared judgments of that form and that they have not always been willing to agree to disagree about the correctness of those judgments has been shown in detail by historians such as Foucault and Kuhn. Even if scientists share a commitment, for example, to increasing the coverage of their theories, they may not always share the judgment that this is a more important problem to have solved than that. At such a time they will be disagreeing about what is a good reason for accepting or rejecting a given theory. As Kuhn puts it, "when scientists must choose between competing theories, two men fully committed to the same list of criteria for theory choice may nevertheless reach different conclusions."[60] This is the fact of incommensurability: scientists disagreeing, not over those of their secure attunements which are natural, but over those of their secure attunements which have become second nature. This is not the fact that anything goes, or that one tradition is unable to evaluate the other. It is the fact that there is sometimes no way to resolve an epistemic dispute without begging the question against one or the other or both disputants.

Our natural secure attunements mark the horizon of relativism, the horizon of what we will accept as an epistemic practice at all, but within this horizon there can exist a diversity of epistemic practices which may with justice be described as revealing the truth in relativism. That our epistemic practices are open to the possibility of incommensurable conflict—transcendental conflict—is what I have meant to speak of as the fact that our knowledge is fated to be human: the fate of human knowledge.

I have already suggested that madness marks the rupture between ourselves and those who do not share all of our natural secure attunements. As a last hypothesis, let me suggest that something like humor be taken as a criterion for there being a rupture between second nature attunements. Why is it that we smile or laugh when we hear that walnuts were once thought to cure headaches because walnut meat resembles brain meat? Foucault says the *The Order of Things* arose out of the laughter that was forced from him by the reading of a bizarre system of classification imagined by Borges:

> Animals are divided into: (a) belonging to the emperor, (b) embalmed, (c) tame, (d) suckling pigs, (e) sirens, (f) fabulous, (g) stray dogs, (h) included in the present classification, (i) frenzied, (j) innumerable, (k) drawn with a very fine camelhair brush, (l) *et cetera,* (m) having just broken the water pitcher, (n) that from a long way off look like flies.[61]

Why does this make us laugh? This is not laughter as at a humorous joke. It is not cruel laughter at someone's misfortune or ignorance: not even our own ignorance. It has been suggested to me that this is not so much laughter as giddiness.[62] But why should our head be set swimming on reading a list such as Borges'?

Perhaps we are possessed by this giddy feeling because the fact of incommensurability brings us face to face with the fate of human knowledge: that our own practices of classification and of giving and accepting reasons are without grounds. Perhaps our giddiness results from our obscure realization that there is no more grounding for our natural secure attunements than for those that are only second nature. Using an expression Nussbaum employs when describing ethical life, we might say that our epistemic practices are essentially fragile: exposed to the possibility of intellectual tragedy.[63] If the epistemic practices of two traditions (happily) do not fall apart, this is no less a matter of fate than when (tragically) they do. Our giddiness, our nervous laughter, reveals the fact that our epistemic practices are the groundless ground of our knowledge of objects in the world.[64] Our giddiness reveals what Heidegger, in a darker mood, thought to be revealed by anxiety [Angst], the fact that "human existence can relate to beings only if it holds itself out into the nothing."[65] Even Wittgenstein (who may not have been unaware of this Heideggerian text) could write that were he so much as to begin to doubt his natural secure attunements, he should find himself standing before what he calls the nothing, vor dem Nichts.[66]

Conclusion

Davidson's primary conclusion charts the limits of relativism; it does not erase it from the charts altogether. It points to the natural limitations on the amount of diversity we can tolerate concerning what is a good reason for what. Davidson's primary conclusion marks the horizon of relativism: the horizon of reason.

Our natural secure attunements mark the horizon of what may intelligibly be said to be an epistemic practice at all. But our experience of the fact of incommensurability shows that there are secure attunements which are only second nature. We may understand the incommensurability between some epistemic practices as manifesting the fact that their participants do not share all of their second nature secure attunements. The fact that our epistemic practices are exposed to the possibility of incommensurable conflict is the truth in relativism. It is the fate of human knowledge.

But what supports our most natural secure attunements? On the one hand nothing; they are the groundless grounds of our epistemic practices. Yet this can be put in another way. Without being grounded or justified by facts about our being human, these most secure attunements would not exist were it not for certain "extremely general facts of nature . . . [which] are hardly ever mentioned because of their extreme generality."[67] I have suggested that the horizon of relativism is the horizon of reason; it now appears that the horizon of reason is the horizon of the human. Knowledge is a fragile accomplishment, fated to be human.[68]

Notes

1. The terminology is Putnam's. He calls a commitment to a nonepistemic conception "metaphysical realism." See his "Realism and Reason" (December 1976) in *Meaning and the Moral Sciences* (London: Routledge and Kegan Paul, 1978), p. 125.

2. B. A. O. Williams, *Ethics and the Limits of Philosophy* (Cambridge: Harvard University Press, 1985), p. 156.

3. R. W. Emerson, "Fate" (1860) in *Ralph Waldo Emerson: Essays and Lectures* (New York: The Library of America , 1983), p. 966. My attention was drawn to the significance of this phrase by S. Cavell's essay "Genteel Responses to Kant?" *Raritan,* Fall 1983, pp. 34-61, esp. pp. 46-47.

4. Compare: J. Margolis, *Pragmatism without Foundations* (Oxford: B. Blackwell, 1986), chapter 1.

5. *Pace* Eddy Zemach's critique of Rorty in "Truth and Some Relativists," typescript 1985/86.

6. F. Nietzsche, *The Birth of Tragedy* (1872), tr. W. Kaufmann (New York: Vintage Books, 1967), paragraph 15, pages 97-98. The reference to "gaiety" is of course a gesture to Nietzsche's *The Gay Science* of 1882 and 1887; among many references to Nietzsche and play see: J. Derrida, "Differance," (1968) in his *Margins of Philosophy* (Chicago: University of Chicago Press, 1982), p. 27.

I may seem to have implied that as Nietzsche matured, he gave up tragedy for gaiety. Although this is a familiar description of Nietzsche's development, it is not unproblematic. Even in the 1887 edition of *The Gay Science,* part 5, 382, and in the 1888 *Twilight of the Idols,* ch. 10, #5, there is a sense of the enduring significance of this "tragic insight."

For more equivocal thoughts on intellectual tragedy see S. Cavell, *The Claim of Reason* (New York: Oxford University Press, 1979), pp. 19 and 454.

7. Putnam has recently tried to turn our attention away from truth to reason by arguing that the only coherent notion of truth is the epistemically reduced notion of "idealized rational acceptability." *Reason, Truth, and History,* p. 55. What I am suggesting is that even if the nonepistemic conception of truth survives his attacks, it should be of little concern to epistemologists. See M. Williams, "Do We (Epistemologists) Need a Theory of Truth?" *Philosophical Topics* 14, 1 (Spring 1986): 223-242.

8. The Presidential Address was called "On the Very Idea of a Conceptual Scheme" and now appears in D. Davidson, *Inquiries into Truth and Interpretation* (Oxford: Clarendon Press, 1984). Hereafter referred to as: D. Davidson, "On the Very Idea. . . ." See p. xi for 1970 title.

9. W. V. Quine, "Two Dogmas of Empiricism" (1951), in *From a Logical Point of View,* second edition (New York: Harper Torchbooks, 1961), p. 42, my emphasis.

10. D. Davidson, "On the Very Idea . . . ," p. 189; in a recent lecture Davidson argues that the third dogma of empiricism is familiar as the Cartesian

assumption that knowledge is based on something subjective: "The Myth of The Subjective," Selfridge Lecture, Lehigh University, September 24, 1986.

11. See, for example, W. V. Quine, *Theories and Things* (Cambridge: The Belknap Press, 1981), pp. 29-30. Also see: W.V. Quine, "Relativism and Absolutism," *Monist* 67, 3 (July 1984): 293-296. M. Dummett anticipated this conclusion in his *Frege: Philosophy of Language* (1973) (Cambridge: Harvard University Press, second edition 1981), p. 617n.

12. The idea of a conceptual scheme is attacked in Davidson's "On the Very Idea . . ." (1974). The idea of subjective experience is attacked in D. Davidson, "A Coherence Theory of Truth and Knowledge" (1983) and "Empirical Content" (1982), both in E. LePore, ed., *Truth and Interpretation* (Oxford: B. Blackwell, 1986).

13. This version of Davidson's argument is built on N. Rescher's two-premise version in his "Conceptual Schemes" (1980), now chapter 2 of his *Empirical Inquiry* (London: Athalone Press, 1982).

14. D. Davidson, "On the Very Idea . . . ," p. 198.

15. Ibid., p.191.

16. See I. Kant, *Critique of Pure Reason,* A63 = B88.

17. D. Davidson, "On the Very Idea . . . ," p. 193.

18. For this distinction between incommensurability (1) of problems and standards, (2) of concepts, and (3) of worlds see G. Doppelt, "Kuhn's Epistemological Relativism . . ." (1978), reprinted in M. Krausz and J. W. Meiland, eds., *Relativism: Cognitive and Moral* (Notre Dame: University of Notre Dame Press, 1982).

19. D. Davison, "True to the Facts" (1969), in his *Inquiries into Truth and Interpretation* (Oxford: Clarendon Press, 1984), especially p. 42. This is the argument that Barwise and Perry refer to as the slingshot in "Semantic Innocence and Uncompromising Situations," *Midwest Studies in Philosophy,* vol. 6 (Minneapolis: University of Minnesota Press, 1981), pp. 387-403.

20. A similar conclusion is reached by Wittgenstein in *Philosophical Investigations* (Oxford: B. Blackwell, 1976), #207.

21. One possibility suggested by Davidson's own theory of interpretation (see below) would be to make the behavior of holding a sentence true the criterion for being a language. Davidson follows Quine in suggesting that this could be discerned even before we can translate a single word of the stranger's language, so it looks like just what, at this point, the relativist needs. But if we found ourselves completely unable to translate the stranger's "language," we would, I think, lose our confidence in having discerned the holding true behavior. This suggestion, therefore, must be rejected along with (3*o) and (3*f).

22. D. Davidson, "On the Very Idea . . . ," p. 195.

23. Recently Davidson has argued that desiring true is more basic than holding true, because on its basis we can determine the stanger's desires as well as his meanings and his beliefs. But for my purposes this is not important.

24. D. Davidson, "On the Very Idea . . . ," p. 196.

25. D. Davidson, "A Coherence Theory of Truth and Knowledge" (1983),

reprinted in E. LePore, ed., *Truth and Interpretation* (Oxford: B. Blackwell, 1986), p. 315. (Hereafter: D. Davidson, "A Coherence Theory. . .")

26. D. Davidson, "On the Very Idea . . . ," p. 196 and p. 197.

27. D. Davidson, "A Coherence Theory. . . ," p. 316.

28. D. Davidson, "On the Very Idea . . . ," p. 196.

29. D. Davidson, "A Coherence Theory. . . ," p. 319 and p. 316.

30. D. Davidson, "On the Very Idea . . . ," p. 197.

31. Ibid., p. 197.

32. D. Hume, *An Enquiry on Human Understanding* (1748) (Indianapolis: Hackett, 1977), sec. 4, part 2, p. 23.

33. Compare: C. McGinn, "Charity, Interpretation, and Belief," *Journal of Philosophy* (1977): 523.

34. D. Davidson, "A Coherence Theory. . . ," p. 316.

35. D. Davidson, Introduction to *Inquiries into Truth and Interpretation* (Oxford: Clarendon Press, 1984), p. xvii.

36. L. Wittgenstein, *Remarks on the Foundations of Mathematics,* third edition (Oxford: B. Blackwell, 1978), part vi, p. 333.

37. L. Wittgenstein, *Philosophical Investigations,* #242.

38. L. Wittgenstein, *Remarks on the Foundations of Mathematics,* third edition, vi, #39, p. 343.

39. This irony was suggested to me by F. Zemach. (Recall: L. Wittgenstein, *Philosophical Investigations,* #593.)

40. S. Cavell, *The Claim of Reason,* chapter 2, esp. p. 52.

41. L. Wittgenstein, *Philosophical Investigations,* #s 217 and 219, and S. Cavell, *The Claim of Reason,* pp. 124-125.

42. R. Hanna has reminded me that, except in severe cases, madness is not properly described as the complete absence of thought. More frequently the psychotic should be described as not sharing all of our most secure attunements. This is how one might describe a person who says that he is dead.

43. L. Wittgenstein, *On Certainty* (New York: Harper and Row, 1972), ##71, 155, 195, and 281.

44. L. Wittgenstein, *Remarks on the Foundations of Mathematics,* first edition (Cambridge: MIT Press, 1956), IV, #53, p. 157. As far as I can determine, this remark has been silently eliminated from the third edition.

45. L. Wittgenstein, *On Certainty,* #144, and throughout. I was surprised to notice that in these notes Wittgenstein is more likely to be found writing about *Sicherheit* than about *Gewissheit.* Perhaps the editors should have published the notes under the title *Ueber Sicherheit/On Security.*

46. L. Wittgenstein, *Remarks on the Foundations of Mathematics,* third edition, VII, #21, 387.

47. L. Wittgenstein speaks of the scaffolding of facts in his *Remarks on the Philosophy of Psychology* vol. 2 (dictated 1948) (Chicago: University of Chicago Press, 1980), #190. He speaks of "logical scaffolding" in his *Tractatus* (1921), 3.42.

For more on the role of the transcendental in the later Wittgenstein see

B. A. O. Williams "Wittgenstein and Idealism" (1974), in his *Moral Luck* (Cambridge: Cambridge University Press, 1982); J. Lear, "Leaving the World Alone" *J. Phil.* 79 (1982); and my "Relativism as *Reductio" Mind* v. 94 (1985).

48. L. Wittgenstein, *Tractatus Logico-Philosophicus* (1921) (London: Routledge and Kegan Paul, 1977), 6.13: "Logic is transcendental"; 6.22: "The logic of the world . . . is shown in tautologies by the propositions of logic. . . ."

49. L. Wittgenstein, *Philosophical Investigations,* page 227.

50. S. Cavell, *The Claim of Reason,* chapter 2, esp. p. 52.

51. M. Foucault, *The Archaeology of Knowledge* (1969) (New York: Harper Torchbooks, 1980), p. 28.

52. Ibid., p. 46.

53. L. Wittgenstein, *Philosophical Grammar* (Berkeley: University of California Press, 1978), p. 295.

54. Ibid., p. 87.

55. L. Wittgenstein, *Philosophical Remarks* (Chicago: University of Chicago Press, 1980), p. 85.

56. L. Wittgenstein, *On Certainty,* #501.

57. R. Hanna put me onto the expression "transcendental conflict."

58. M. Foucault, *Madness and Civilization* (1961) (New York: Vintage Books, 1973), p. 39.

59. G. H. von Wright also suggests a connection between the idea of a Weltbild which appears in *On Certainty* and the ease with which we manage to understand others in his "Wittgenstein on Certainty" (1970), in his *Wittgenstein* (Minneapolis: University of Minnesota Press, no date), p. 176.

60. T. S. Kuhn, "Objectivity, Value Judgment, and Theory Choice" (1973), in his *The Essential Tension* (Chicago: University of Chicago Press, 1977), p. 324. This essay brings to mind the second paragraph of Hume's "Of the Standard of Taste" (1757).

61. J. Borges in M. Foucault, *The Order of Things* (New York: Vintage Books, 1973), "Preface, 1966," p. xv.

62. "Giddy" was suggested by M. Raposa. This word for being light-headed or incapadable of serious thought seems to be derived from an expression meaning madness caused by being possessed by a God.

63. M. Nussbaum, *The Fragility of Goodness* (Cambridge: Cambridge University Press, 1986).

64. "Groundless ground *[abgruendigen Grunde]"* is an expression used by Heidegger in his 1929 lecture "What Is Metaphysics?" in *Basic Writings* (New York: Harper and Row, 1977), p. 112. It appears to be the ancestor of J. Derrida's "fonds sans fond" in "Plato's Pharmacy" (1968), in *Dissemination* (Chicago: University of Chicago Press, 1981), p. 127.

65. M. Heidegger, "What Is Metaphysics?" *Basic Writings.* p. 111.

66. L. Wittgenstein, *On Certainty,* #370. For Wittgenstein's discussion of Heidegger and his probable awareness of the lecture cited in the previous two notes see Wittgenstein "On Heidegger" (Dec. 30, 1929) and the "Editor's Commentary" in M. Murray, ed., *Heidegger and Modern Philosophy* (New Haven: Yale University Press, 1978), pp. 80-83, esp. 81.

67. L. Wittgenstein, *Philosophical Investigations,* p. 56e.

68. An early version of this paper was read at Lehigh in December 1986, and I am thankful for what I learned from the discussion which took place at that time. I am even more thankful to have been able to use the detailed, written responses this essay has received from John Hare, Norman Melchert, and Robert Hanna.

The Truth about Relativism

Joseph Margolis

Any would-be defense of relativism must make its way against ingrained prejudice, ignorance of logical options not often exercised, the fatal support of historically hopeless theories that monopolize the popular sense of the label, and the sheer difficulty of fixing the full significance of what a viable account would entail. It requires a good dose of patience and a sense of what is missing in standard accounts of truth-claims. The bare bones of every relativism that has survived all the charges of self-contradiction, conceptual anarchy, nihilism, irrelevance, palpable falsehood, and even recovery within an ampler antirelativism features two essential doctrines: (1) that, in formal terms, truth-values logically weaker than bipolar value (true and false) may be admitted to govern otherwise coherent forms of inquiry and constative acts, and (2) that substantively, not merely for evidentiary or epistemic reasons, certain sectors of the real world open to constative inquiry may be shown to support only such weaker truth-values. That is all.

It is true that doctrines (1) and (2) do not exhaust all potentially interesting forms of relativism—for example, relativisms confined to the management of truth-claims under various contingent limitations regarding the state of knowledge. But such theories, like theories of probabilistic judgments relativized to shifting evidentiary concessions, are easily reconciled with strongly antirelativistic accounts of empirical truth-claims. It is also true that (1) and (2) cannot by themselves define a full-blooded relativism. Given the unfavorable climate of opinion, however, it would not be a bad idea to introduce a rationale for supporting (1) and (2)—or for supporting either one alone—to encourage the development of all sorts of relativisms that are needlessly battered by the usual charges mentioned. Our strategy, therefore, will be confined to showing (section I) a lacuna regarding bivalence and *tertium non datur* (in effect, alternative views regarding the scope of excluded middle) essential to the defense of (1); to showing (section II) how the application of one of the most influential analyses of the predicate "true," the application of a Tarskian-like theory of truth to natural language or to the language of natural inquiry, obscures both the lacuna charged and the need for an independent analysis of the nature of the empirical domain to which a Tarskian-like (or any other similarly extensional) account is to be applied (bridging [1] and [2]; and to showing (section III) what is involved in distinguishing relativisms that depend on substantive views of the nature of particular sectors of reality (domains suited to empirical inquiry) from those merely confined to cognitive limitations of one sort or another (the distinctive feature of [2]).

The account that follows is essentially strategic, therefore. It lays the ground for relativistic theories distributed over particular empirical domains, but it does not pretend to supply any single such theory. It cannot even pretend to have established doctrines (1) and (2).[1] It is meant primarily to offer a defense of the viability of relativistic theories and to indicate the direction in which the most ramified theories are bound to go. It is certainly not meant to advance the most radical forms of relativism that have been advocated. It would be impossible in any case to assess the prospects of such theories within the span of this paper. The burden of what follows is, then, no more than the thesis that standard views of a realist inquiry and science cannot convincingly preclude versions of the moderate relativism here espoused. Whether more radical options would also be defensible is a question left unanswered. But the intended gain, if confirmed, would certainly be a handsome one.

I

In Robert Stalnacker's recent account of propositions and of their role in developing an adequate theory of beliefs and of intentionality in general, the following thesis is advanced: "A proposition is a function from possible worlds into truth-values." Stalnacker goes on to say, by way of explanation: "There are just two truth-values—true and false. What are they: mysterious Fregean objects, properties, relations of correspondence and noncorrespondence? The answer is that it does not matter what they are: there is nothing essential to them except that there are exactly two of them."[2] Stalnacker does not pause to link truth-values to the processes of actual inquiry or the resolution of scientific and metaphysical questions: he says, "these questions are concerned less with truth itself than with belief, assertion, and argument, and with the relation between the actual world and other possible worlds."[3] Perhaps.

But might it not be a substantive matter regarding truth-values that: (a) their number cannot be determined independently of particular inquiries into particular sectors of the world, and (b) relative to particular such inquiries, their number cannot convincingly be fixed as two?

In fact, Stalnacker nearly concedes the point in an extremely candid and telling way in attempting to strengthen a realism with regard to counterfactuals, context-dependence, and a possible-worlds reading of intentionality—against the encroachments of antirealism. We shall shortly be able to trade very profitably on his careful remarks in this regard. So let us have them before us:

> The interests, projects, presuppostions, culture, and community of a speaker or writer provide resources for the efficient expression of content, but they also provide something more fundamental: they provide resources which contribute to the construction of content itself. Content, I have been suggesting, can be represented as a subset of some set of possible states of the world. . . . But if the space of possible states of the world itself, the way it is possible to distinguish one possible state from another, is influenced by the situations and activities of the speakers (or more generally, the agents) doing the distinguishing, then we have a kind of context-dependence that infects content itself and not just the means used to express it. . . . I think this is right. . . . But it is no retreat from a reasonable realism to admit that *the way we describe the world*—the features and aspects of reality that we choose to focus our attention on—is not entirely dictated by the reality we purport to describe. However we arrive at *the concepts we use to describe the world,* so long as there is something *in* the world in virtue of which our descriptions are true or false, the realist will be vindicated.[4]

Here we must notice that Stalnacker means to *restrict* the "constructive" feature of descriptions or knowledge to the "content" of such descriptions (or to the way we "express" them), but he nowhere frontally considers that the real world as we inquire into it cannot be disjunctively segregated from our would-be descriptions of it. It is true that he criticizes Bas van Fraassen's thesis that "scientific *propositions* are not context-dependent in any essential way." But at that very point Stalnacker remarks that he himself assumes "that context-dependence is a matter of the relation between expressions and their content."[5]

Now, this is simply unsupported and quite arbitrary, peculiarly so in the context, for instance, of attempting to offset Michael Dummett's antirealism (regardless of the merits of Dummett's position). For *if* there is no way to support a pertinent realism except *within* the framework of the indissolubility of realist and idealist elements, or of something like a minimal Kantianism (without Kant's "objectivist" claims), or of some form of antirealism in the sense of admitting concessions in the direction of decidability (though not necessarily Dummett's extreme view of that), or of something like what Hilary Putnam has recently dubbed the "internalist" view of science (again, without subscribing to Putnam's many variant themes), then Stalnacker *could* not restrict context-dependence to descriptive *expressions:* context-dependence would affect *what we take the real world to be,* and in that case the naive assurance "so long as there is something in the world in virtue of which our descriptions are true or false" would not hold at all.

To concede this much is *not* (necessarily) to retreat from realism or to endorse any extreme version of antirealism. But it is certainly to concede either that it is not the case that "there are just two truth-values—true and false" or that it is the case that we are unable to say how many we will *need* without prior attention to what we take *the world we are able to inquire into* to be like. It is essential to relativism, it should be said, that we cannot always reasonably claim that there are just two truth-values and that, in particular sectors of inquiry, it is more reasonable to claim that the truth-values or truth-like values we need are logically weaker than the bipolar pair—but not merely (if we are to hold to realism) because of limitations restricted to the cognitive resources of human investigators.[6]

Michael Dummett's antirealism is a little surprising, once this distinction is in place. For Dummett opposes what *he* calls the "realist" view: "the belief [bivalence, excluded middle] that for any statement there must be something in virtue of which either it or its negation is true: it being only on the basis of this belief that we can justify the idea that truth and falsity play an essential role in the notion of the meaning of a statement, that the general form of an explanation of meaning is a statement of the truth-conditions."[7] Since the antirealist interprets "capable of being known" as "capable of being known *by us*," the antirealist is himself a realist (and the realist may be conceded to hold a defensible position) just insofar as both restrict the "realist interpretation" to "those statements [only] which are in principle effectively decidable."[8] The upshot is that Dummett only appears to retreat from a bipolar pair of truth-values in giving up bivalence. For he gives up bivalence in order to disqualify realism (or what Putnam has dubbed "metaphysical realism"[9]), but he is not at all prepared to give up *tertium non datur*—"the principle that, for no statement, can we ever rule out both the possiblity of its being true and that of its being false, in other words, the principle that there can be no circumstances in which a statement can be recognized as being, irrevocably, neither true nor false [excluded middle restored after deciding decidability]."[10] In effect, this is to draw Stalnacker and Dummett closer to one another's sense of realism (though not necessarily to one another's specific views about the realist import of given kinds of statements, for instance, counterfactuals). In a way, therefore, the same weakness noted in Stalnacker's account reappears in Dummett's—in a different guise. For Dummett never explains *why,* if the realist view of truth (in effect, bivalence) fails because it is "spurious," because it supposes that the truth-values of *any* statement may (for all we know) be decidable by beings whose cognitive capacities exceed our own, the serious *antirealist* objection might not, relative to a particular domain, extend to bipolar truth-values themselves—to the equally "spurious" assurance that *tertium non datur* will always (may we say "irrevocably"?) obtain. Clearly, Dummett (not unlike Stalnacker) must segregate the question of decidability and the question of reality. But that is an illicit, unmotivated maneuver: illicit, because it must be open to discovery *what* the actual conditions are on which claims *are* decidable; unmotivated, because the antirealist scruple has not been brought to bear on *tertium non datur* itself.

Finally, and very simply, Dummett had objected to F. P. Ramsey's "redundancy theory of truth," that is, the thesis that "is true" is "an obviously superfluous addition" to an asserted proposition.[11] Dummett's objection, however, focuses only on the fact that Ramsey has left no room for the antirealist complaint. But there is a deeper reason Ramsey's thesis is inadequate: it may just be that for a particular sector of inquiry the redundancy theory is actually false; the truth-like values it will support may be logically weaker than the bipolar pair.

There you have the charge. Neither Stalnacker nor Dummett nor Ramsey has actually bothered to consider that the viable *claims of determinate sectors of inquiry* may not support—*anywhere along a continuum from realism to antirealism*—*bipolar truth-values (or, effectively, tertium non datur or an adjusted version of excluded middle).*

Relativism obliges us to retreat from bipolar truth-values or *tertium non datur*—but *not* globally, not indiscriminately, not on an all-or-nothing basis. Relativism is a logical thesis, an alethic thesis, applied piecemeal. It could not be a reasonable thesis if it did not resist the kind of disjunctions Stalnacker and Dummett favor (Stalnacker: between "reality" and our expressed descriptions of reality; Dummett: between the decidability of our statements and what, apart from their decidability, decidability cannot fail to reveal about "reality" thus addressed). In a word, a serious relativism fitted to the actual inquiries of the sciences, ontology, methodology, interpretation, appraisal and evaluation, and more, *cannot fail to presuppose that in no respect is the world distribu-*

tively, cognitively transparent, sufficiently transparent, either in advance of or subsequent to establishing decidability, to be able to install bipolar values everywhere.

II

There are two very large substantive constraints on all seriously engaged speculations regarding the truth-values (or truth-like values) suited to a given domain of inquiry. They are of rather different sorts, but they must be brought to bear jointly on such strong claims as those of Stalnacker, Ramsey, and Dummett. One stems (in our own time) from Alfred Tarski's *metameta*theoretical discussion of truth; the other, from the generally convergent finding of recent Western philosophy repudiating all cognitive transparency. Relativism is the beneficiary of the intersection of these two currents. The convergence intended yields the protean finding that there is no realism suited to rigorous inquiry that can escape the limitation that the world we inquire into is not *cognitively* accessible in any way that would support a disjunction between *it* and whatever *we* identify as the world we inquire into. That is the idealist face every realist torso must expose if it cannot claim perfect transparency. It is also in a way the important theme of nearly every contemporary philosophy of science: we may inquire into an independent world, but we cannot state its nature as it is independently of our inquiries.[12]

This is what is implicitly denied or unacknowledged in Stalnacker's and Dummett's disjunctions: we cannot relegate the open, unsystematizable consequences of context-dependence to the mere cultural *expressions* of our science without affecting the demarcation of the structures of the world we examine; and we cannot encumber the claims of our science in the name of *decidability*, while assuring ourselves in advance that no decidable claims can fail to accord with the formal features of bipolar truth-values. We cannot convincingly support the cognitively blind assurance that the real world cannot but accord with certain logical doctrines—largely formal, largely uninterpreted, largely untested—that assure us *a priori* that only research programs congruent with those doctrines could possibly be viable or productive.

In an intriguing sense these and related claims are due, perhaps a little indirectly, to a misreading or misapplication of Tarski's well-known account of truth or of similar purely formal theories of truth. Certainly, both Stalnacker's and Dummett's disjunctions are loosely analogous with Tarski's distinction between the concept of logical consequence and the criterion of deducibility.[13] But Tarski addresses the issue only in formal terms suited to the arithmetic of natural numbers, and himself admits the material difficulty of adequately sorting disjunctively logical and extralogical terms. Without the extension of Tarski's kind of analysis to the whole of that part of natural language that is needed in the pursuit of the empirical sciences (if that makes sense), it would be quite impossible to vindicate either Stalnacker's or Dummett's disjunctions. Tarski quite openly concludes: we may be "compelled to regard such concepts as 'logical consequence', 'analytical statement', and 'tautology' as relative concepts which must, on each occasion, be related to a definite, although in greater or less degree arbitrary, division of terms into logical and extralogical. The fluctuation in the common usage of the concept of consequence would—in part at least—be quite naturally reflected in such a compulsory situation."[14] Correspondingly, Tarski was quite convinced that his semantic conception of truth was not, in general, suited to the "whole" of the language used in the empirical sciences.[15]

It has been said, for instance by Hilary Putnam, that "true" on Tarski's theory "is, amazingly, a *philosophically neutral* notion. 'True' is just a device for 'semantic ascent': for 'raising' assertions from the 'object language' to the 'meta-language', and the device does not commit one epistemologically or metaphysically."[16] But the fact is that Tarski's complete conception *fits* certain formalized languages only. Either, then, Putnam has prized apart the "bare" concept from its "application" or else he has divided Tarski's theory pointlessly and against Tarski's own purpose. One *can* distinguish between Tarski's bare "definitional" notion of "true" and the actual "structural-descriptive" rule or canon for determining the truth of distributed object-language sentences. But doing that would deprive the definitional element itself of any substantive bearing on *the actual sentences* of a functioning science. For instance, one could hold (on Dummett's summary) that, "for any sentence A, A is [materially] equivalent to $\ulcorner$ It is true that A $\urcorner$, or to $\ulcorner$ S is true $\urcorner$, where S is a [metalinguistic] ('structural-descriptive') name for A."[17] But *if* we separate the two notions, Putnam would be right in treating Tarski's equivalence thesis as "philosophically neutral" only in the undesirably strong sense that it had no philosophical bearing at all in an *epistemically* pertinent regard; for what would be the point of introducing provision for a structral-descriptive name for A if, in doing so, we had to concede no information about the nature of the relevant descriptions of such distributed sentences? On the other hand, *if* such descriptions did conform with what Tarski offers as the extensionally regimented descriptions suitably fitted *to* the interpreted formal languages he actually examines, then: first of all, the notion would no longer be philosophically neutral (it obviously would favor a global extensionalism), and, secondly, it (the complete notion) would require, to be theoretically vindicated, an independent argument about the properties of the pertinent language of science—which Tarski, confessedly, nowhere provides. It is Dummett's point that "Rejection of the principle of bivalence [every statement is either true or false] when not accompanied by rejection of *tertium non datur* [no statement is neither true nor false] does not lead to any conflict with the equivalence thesis." But it is also Dummett's point (against Ramsey's redundancy thesis) that since the Tarskian truth-definition "is *not* an expansion of the object-language," we cannot *apply* the predicate 'true' to the sentences of an object-language (any object-language)—in accord with the truth-definition—"if we do not yet understand the object-language . . . [that is, if we do not have] a grasp of the meaning of each such sentence" in virtue of which 'true' can be distributively applied.[18]

The point is that *if* Tarski's conception of truth—that is, the entire conception, including provision for the metalinguistic structural description of distributed object-language sentences—fits the formalized languages Tarski claims it fits, then it does so on the strength *of an actual analysis of such languages*. It is not construed by Tarski to be an *a priori* matter. Hence, if it is to be extended to natural languages, then, on Tarski's view, it must be suitably justified by an analysis of those languages as well. *If* the Tarskian defintion of truth (without the structural-descriptive account) is "philosophically neutral," then it is neutral because it is vacuous, *because it affirms no object-language/metalanguage relationship and because it imposes no constraint on any material equivalence between object-language and metalinguistic sentences.* It may well capture some profound common intuition about truth, but it could hardly (then) be said to capture such an intuition along the lines of the equivalence thesis. Anyone who supposed it would automatically do that would have to be extraordinarily sanguine about extensionalism—and would in any case be open to empirical challenge and possible defeat. Hence, it does not really matter that Tarski's definition invokes bipolar truth-values, for it was meant all along for languages that conformed sufficiently closely to the formal languages that serve as Tarski's paradigms, and there it *is* the appropriate choice. Therefore, no incompatibility exists between subscribing to Tarski's conception and insisting that, for particular domains of inquiry, we should (should have to) introduce truth-values logically weaker than the bipolar pair.

In fact, if theories of truth are viewed empirically, then there are at least two distinct sources of contention vis-à-vis Tarski's conception:

first, that truth-values logically weaker than bipolar values may be required in particular domains (the formal concession essential to relativism), and, second, that for either bipolar or logically weaker values or both, sentences true or justified with regard to the actual features of a given domain of inquiry may not satisfy Tarski's provisions for their "structural" description (an ontological claim that, however minimal in other respects, is not in the least inhospitable to relativism).

Donald Davidson (the effective custodian of all efforts to extend Tarski's account to empirical diciplines) is quite explicit about "treating theories of truth as empirical theories," though he obviously means this more in terms of (what he calls) "Convention T," the "structural-descriptive" account, than in terms of the suitability of restricting the range of bipolar values.[19] Thus he says, answering one of his critics: "Of course my project does require that all sentences of natural languages can be handled by a T-theory, and so if the intensional idioms resist such treatment, my plan [the grand plan of Davidson's philosophy] has foundered. It seems to be the case, though the matter is not entirely simple or clear, that a theory of truth that satisfies anything like Convention T cannot allow an intensional semantics, and this has prompted me to try to show how an extensional semantics can handle what is special about belief sentences, indirect discourse, and other such sentences."[20]

Davidson's admission shows very nicely the underground linkage between limiting extending the scope of bipolar truth-values by analogy with Tarski's analysis of certain formal languages and supporting an ontology that eschews all cognitive transparency, along lines favoring a pragmatized holism and the indissoluble symbiosis of realist and idealist elements.[21] For there can be no doubt that the prospects of a sturdy and substantive relativism positively depend on such philosophical policies as: (a) rejecting transparency, (b) advocating scientific holism, and (c) acknowledging the indissolubility of realist and idealist themes within the scope of (a) and (b). If we continued along these lines, emphasizing, for instance, (d) the historical contingency of inquiry itself and (e) the context-dependence of inquiry under the condition of being unable to fix the absolute context of all context-dependence (relative to all possible worlds, say, or to synthetic *a priori* truths)—if we continued thus— we should have admitted just the conditions under which "an intensional semantics" would be least likely to be suppressed or eliminated. Projects like Davidson's would then "founder" (as Davidson admits), and a robust relativism would either be required or strongly favored. The irony is that Davidson *is* quite well committed to (a)-(e), and yet he comes extraordinarily close to advocating on *a priori* grounds the extension of Tarski's strategy to the empirical disciplines (in fact, to the whole of natural language). The issue is a tricky one, but its resolution definitely bears on rescuing relativism. For in demonstrating the impossibility of vindicating on purely formal grounds a bipolar model for all empirical domains—in particular, in demonstrating that no formalism of Tarski's sort (as Tarski himself clearly foresaw) could vindicate either the universal applicability of bipolar values or a thoroughly extensional treatment of every empirical domain (which would entail bipolarity)—we effectively demonstrate that the relativistic account cannot be precluded for particular inquiries. So the issue invites a bit of patience regarding Davidson's important attempt to extend a Tarskian-like model to natural languages.

Davidson's would-be extension is actually not easy to defend. Its weakness, in fact, serves to expose a characteristic double prejudice against relativistic truth-values and a strong intensionalism that would be hospitable to relativism.

But that extension is not easy to defend. There is, in fact, a certain conceptual slippage in Davidson's argument—that cannot fail to recall Putnam's hearty claim about the "amazing" philosophical neutrality of Tarski's conception of truth. For consider that when he sketches the extension of "Convention T" to natural languages, Davidson candidly observes:

> I suggest that a theory of truth for a language [as we want a theory to do] does . . . give the meanings of all independently meaningful expressions on the basis of an analysis of their structure. And . . . a semantic theory of a natural language cannot be considered adequate unless it provides an account of the concept of truth for that language along the general lines proposed by Tarski for formalized languages.[22]

Here Davidson advocates Convention T as a *criterion* of the adequacy of theories of truth. The point of his proposal is, however, not entirely clear. It definitely risks being equivocal. For there is a sense in which the appeal to Tarski is merely an appeal to *some* (as yet unspecified) metalinguistic description of the structural properties of object-language sentences, in virtue of which the truth of such sentences can be shown to depend on the structure and structural relations among their constituent parts. It is, perhaps, in this sense that Davidson warns us that "to seek a theory that accords with Convention T is not, in itself at least, to settle for Model T logic or semantics [that is, Tarski's own full strategy]. Convention T, in the skeletal form I have given it, makes no mention of extensionality, truth functionality, or first-order logic. It invites us to use whatever devices we can contrive appropriately to bridge the gap between sentence mentioned and sentence used. Restrictions on ontology, ideology, or inferential power find favor, from the present point of view, only if they result from adopting Convention T as a touchstone. "What I want to defend is the Convention as a criterion of theories, not any particular theories that have been shown to satisfy the Convention in particular cases [Tarski's own application, say], the resources to which they may have been limited."[23] On this first line of advocating Convention T, then, emphasis is placed on preferring or favoring structural-descriptive ways of linking the extension of the truth of particular (object-language) sentences to those very sentences rather than on relying (hence, on giving their meanings thereby) on any other approach to managing that relationship. Davidson does not (here) deny the power of Tarski's example: it is only that he does not trade on its own particular strategies; on the contrary, here he proposes a more general overview by means of which to demonstrate the superiority of Tarski's full account over all others. But how does he do this?

The apparent argument is simplicity itself. "Let someone say [Davidson observes], 'There are a million stars out tonight' and another reply, 'That's true', then nothing could be plainer than that what the first has said is true if and only if what the other has said is true. . . . We have learned to represent these facts by sentences of the form: 'The sentence "There are a million stars out tonight" is true if and only if there are a million stars out tonight'. Because T-sentences (as we may call them) [sentences of the biconditional form just illustrated] are so obviously true, some philosophers have thought that the concept of truth, at least as applied to sentences, was trivial. But that's not so. T-sentences don't . . . show how to live without a truth predicate; but taken together, they do tell what it would be like to have one. For since there is a T-sentence corresponding to each sentence of the language for which truth is in question, the totality of T-sentences exactly fixes the extension, among the sentences, of any predicate that plays the role of the words 'is true'. From this it is clear that although T-sentences do not define truth, they can be used to define truth predicatehood: any predicate is a truth predicate that makes all T-sentences true."[24]

Look at this a little more carefully, however. When T-sentences are constructed to capture the sense of narratives like the story of the million stars—when they "are so obviously true"—they are meant to be trivially true; they are *not* meant to affirm a material equivalence between object-language sentences and metalinguistic sentences formed by any (as yet unspecified) structural analysis of those sentences, that thereby gives "the truth conditions of the described sentence[s]."[25] On that reading (the second reading of the equivocation remarked) T-sentences are hardly "obviously true." Putnam's (and Davidson's) claim could only refer to the vacuous thesis ("obviously true") that *if,* in stories like the million-stars story, in asserting "There are a million stars out tonight" one is affirming that there are (that it is true that there are), then the corresponding T-sentence is ("obviously") true as well. But that is to say that in the original irresistible vignette *nothing is said or intended regarding relations between object-language and metalanguage,* certainly not anything regarding any (specified or unspecified) structural-descriptive analysis of object-language sentences in virtue of which their truth-conditions are given.

No. The irresistible vignette *may* capture a profound intuition about truth. Such a vignette *is* "philosophically neutral." It *may* reasonably be said to be the intuition on which Tarski constructs his account. But the latter (the strong extensionalized account suited to certain formalized languages), *and* its extension to natural languages (Davidson's project), *and* the import of using Tarski's (so-called) Convention T as a *criterion* of the adequacy of theories of truth (without yet invoking Tarski's own strongly extensionalized program) *are definitely not philosophically neutral.* The statement of these three theses is certainly not obviously true. So Davidon shifts ground considerably when, with all his cautions, he finally affirms: "The reason Convention T is acceptable as a criterion of theories is that (i) T-sentences are clearly true (preanalytically)—something we could recognize only if we already (partly) understood the predicate 'is true', and (ii) the totality of T-sentences fixes the extension of the truth predicate uniquely. The interest of a theory of truth, viewed as an empirical theory of a natural language, is not that it tells us what truth is in general, but that it reveals how the truth of every sentence of a particular L [a particular language] depends on its structure and constituents."[26] Here it is obvious that Davidson must be equivocating on the meaning of "T-sentences" in giving his reasons for supporting Convention T: in (i)"T-sentences" must, to be "clearly true (preanalytically)," take the trivial form of the first reading of Tarski's strategy; and in (ii) "T-sentences" must accord with an extension of Tarski's own strategy (which Tarski never intended and actually believed unworkable) or else must involve some suitably strong analogue of Tarski's own strategy (recalling Davidson's caveat about not adopting prematurely "Model T logic or semantics"). In any case, it is certainly not clear that either in general (by some as yet unspecified structural-descriptive canon fitted to Convention T) or specifically as an extension of Tarski's own canon, the criterion offered in (ii)—that *"the totality of T-sentences fixes the extension of the truth predicate uniquely"*—could be shown to be true, could be shown to be sufficiently promising to support an empirically responsible claim that it is true, or could be so characterized that we would even have a reasonable sense of *how to proceed to show that it was true*—or to show, for that reason, that the truth-values logically weaker than the bipolar pair could never be empirically vindicated (on doctrine 1).

This is the sense in which Davidson's claim is effectively, must be, an a priori claim, despite all his insistence on treating the theory of truth as an empirical question. Apart from his own frank admission of numerous details that we cannot yet be sure would support the extension of Tarski's strongly extensionalized canon,[27] there is the stunningly plain fact that to the extent Davidson subscribes (as he apparently does) to Quine's holism, to the extent he admits the historicized and contextualized nature of natural language, to the extent he subscribes to our constraints (a)-(e), it is simply impossible for him to profess (ii) *on empirical grounds.*[28]

Davidson actually calls a theory of truth, that is, "a theory that satisfies something like Tarski's Convention T" (where he simply appeals to "a canonical description of a sentence of L"without insisting on Tarski's own canon—but also without refusing its use), "absolute": "to distinguish [it, he says] from theories that (also) relativize truth to an interpretation, a model, a possible world, or a domain. In a theory of the sort I am describing, the truth predicate is not defined, but must be considered a primitive expression."[29] But in the *empirical* sense in which the theory proposed is to be fitted to natural language, subscribing to (a)-(e), or even to a good part of that set, effectively commits one to relativizing determinations of truth-conditions, even if the predicate 'true' is not itself treated relationally. Davidson himself makes the essential admission: " 'absolute' truth goes relative when applied to a natural language."[30] But it does so, surely, in just that sense in which criterion (ii) regarding testing the adequacy of any theory of truth cannot be shown to be effective, cannot eliminate an "intensional semantics," and cannot preclude the need to retreat (in particular domains of inquiry) from bipolar truth-values to logically weaker values. In this sense no extension of a Tarski-like strategy could, *empirically,* disallow a substantive relativism. This, then, confirms the sense in which relativism is favored by the intersection of neutralizing Tarskian-like programs for the empirical sciences and exploiting the ramified import of the developing philosophical repudiation of all forms of cognitive transparency. But it also prophesies increasing concessions regarding intentional complications in the analysis of any theory of science and serious inquiry. That is, the failure of Davidson to vindicate a Tarskisn-like program for natural languages is not Davidson's fault. It is merely a symptom of the impossibility of settling a priori, by formal means alone, the adequacy of (a) an extensional model for natural languages and (b) the adequacy of a bipolar model of truth-values for any particular sector of inquiry (whether in accord with bivalence or *tertium non datur*).

III

There is no need for a developed relativism if transparency obtains. On that condition any relativism signifies merely provisional limitations in the cognitive powers of human investigators. A substantive relativism requires that the scientific description of the "independent" physical world (that is, the real world as it is independent of human inquiry) be an artifact of a cognitive competence that is at once justifiably realist in its claims about that independent world and incapable in principle of being extricated from the preformative conditions of the historical existence of human investigators—whether conceptual, doxastic, conative, institutional, praxical, ideological, tacit, programmatic, or critical conditions. It must, in short, manifest—symbiotically—both realist and idealist aspects. It may be that Kantianism in its strict form preserves a version of transparency (or what effectively functions as a surrogate for transparency); at the same time it fuses the realist and idealist features of an apt science. That, presumably, is what Husserl objected to in Kant, in charging Kant with "objectivism."[31] An analogous charge has been leveled of course against Husserl as well, given his obsessive search for the apodictic, his transcendental solipsism, and his sense of the apparent privilege of the phenomenological method.[32] In that spirit we may employ the pejorative epithet "logocentrism" for any theory that fixes, in the absence of, or even specifically in opposition to, pretensions of transparency, a privileged constraint on any reasonably productive (or realist) science within the bounds of a realist/idealist fusion. Thus, in the analytic tradition there can be no doubt that Quine's extreme extensionlism—particularly its a priori repudiation of intentionality (and consequent intentional complications)[33] must count as a most influential form of logocentrism in the absence of (in opposition to, in fact) all forms of transparency. This is the same sense in which the global a priori insistence on bipolar truth-values, in Stalnacker and Dummett, and the union of that thesis, *via* Tarski, with a subtle version of Quine's extensionalism, as in Davidson, are here construed as forms of logocentrism. The fact is that doctrines of these sorts preclude any substantive relativism. It is an irony, therefore, as well as a clear sign of a profound incoherence, that Quine is the champion both of a draconian extensionalism that precludes an empirically exploratory relativism along intentional lines and of a pragmatized holism that entails a pervasive relativism.

The principle benefit, as far as the fortunes of relativism are concerned, of the realist/idealist symbiosis under conditions precluding transparency and logocentrism is simply that relativism can no longer be restricted to the contingencies of cognitive accident and limitation. That is, the contribution of relativism cannot be exhausted by considerations of probabilizing evidence, or of ambiguity, or vagueness, or of deliberately heuristic or idiosyncratically constructed schemata, or interpretations, or the like. On the argument, relativism, a robust or substantive relativism, answers to the general finding that *we cannot uniquely fix the structures of reality just at the point at which we are reasonably justified in treating our cognitive claims in realist terms.* There are many ways in which this charge could be fleshed out. But the following may serve as the barest hints of substantive possibilities going beyond (but hardly precluding) mere epistemic limitations. For example, ontic commitment, construed in accord with Quine's holist insistence on indeterminacy of translation and inscrutability of reference, cannot fail to support relativism.[34] Again, if cultural phenomena are real and exhibit intensionally complex intentional features, despite Quine's repudiation of intentionality, [35] then it becomes impossible to disallow interpretive complexities from affecting our being able to identify descriptively unique, or at least convergent and compatible, real structures within the cultural world—for reasons that cannot be confined to mere evidentiary considerations. Again, if cultural phenomena, artworks for instance, actually possess intentional structures, then we cannot draw a principled demarcation between the properties such phenomena possess and properties that can only be imputed to such phenomena. [36] Again, if high-level theories in the physical sciences are radically underdetermined by observational data, if there are good reasons (causal reasons involving strategic experiments or technological inventions) for regarding as real theoretical entities postulated in ways that also serve to explain observed regularities, and if explanatory laws are idealizations from, even distortions of, phenomenological regularities or laws, then, for reasons that exceed epistemic worries, there can be no way of precluding relativistic accounts of such entities.[37] These four lines of inquiry, all concerned with determining what there (really) is or what the properties of what there is (really) are, are certainly among the more salient options that a moderate relativism would claim to accommodate. They indicate that a merely formal extensionalism, even a formal physicalism, could not convincingly preclude the relativistic option, and that any enrichment of such an account by admitting the intentional complexities of the cultural world is bound to strengthen its hand. But our concern here is to indicate, without actually elaborating, the full sense in which the question of relativism is a substantive and not merely a formal matter (the point of our having distinguished, at the start of this paper, between doctrines 1 and 2).

Notice that the physical sciences are themselves enterprises that, precisely in positing an "independent physical world," fall within the inquiries of culturally encumbered human investigators. Clearly, the social and historical world of man cannot intelligibly be construed as separable, even in principle, from the investigative aptitudes of reflexive inquirers; although to say that is not to preclude pertinent notions of objective confirmation and validity with regard to the human sciences; it is only to insist that in the space of human culture there can be no initial disjunction between the epistemological and the ontological. There is none in the physical sciences either; but there is often said to be one (extensionalism), and there *is* a systematic function assigned the notion of an "independent physical world" *within* the space of the other that cannot even in principle (or at least so we are here claiming) be matched in the human sciences.[38] Relativism, then, is nothing less than the attempt to recover within realist terms whatever forms of objectivity may be secured for any science or comparable inquiry in which, for reasons affected by the impossibility of uniquely fixing the real structures of this or that sector of things, we are obliged to retreat to truth-like values logically weaker than bipolar values.

Nevertheless, relativism has a bad name. Its ancient form, Protagoreanism, is a philosophical scandal: not, let it be said, because Protagoras' thesis cannot be given a coherent reading, but because almost no one wishes to. Paul Feyerabend offers these tantalizingly brief sentences in introducing his collected *Philosophical Papers:* "The reader will notice that some articles [included] defend ideas which are attacked in others. This reflects my belief (which seems to have been held by Protagoras) that good arguments can be found for the opposite sides of any issue."[39] Feyerabend associates this belief with what he calls "democratic relativism," which to many may suggest only a sense of conceptual thrift and an unwillingness to lose potential contributions made by fringe or minority groups. But Feyerabend's view is actually closer to attacking the logocentrism of privileged traditions (under what, notably, as in Putnam's criticisms,[40] are would-be idealist constraints on scientific realism). Hence, when, subverting the hegemony of Western science (Western "rationalism"),Feyerabend observes, *"They simply take it for granted that their own traditions of standard construction and standard rejection are the only traditions that count,"*[41] he is speaking not merely of intellectual tolerance but surely also as a relativist committed to the thesis we have just formulated—the structures of reality cannot be fixed either in terms of transparency or logocentric privilege (a priori, privileged traditions)—and as one committed as well to the thesis that *that* is a reasonable reading of Protagoras.

This may be a way of understanding sympathetically the ancient report that Protagoras "was the first to say that there were two contradictory arguments about everything."[42] It suggests regarding his famous maxim, "Of all things the measure is Man, of the things that are, that they are, and of the things that are not, that they are not,"[43] that Protagoras should be construed as anticipating modern forms of incommensurabilism (or a retreat from bipolar truth-values) rather than as merely subscribing to the anciently assigned doctrine that every opinion is true and every opinion false. The latter is usually pressed even today, as, for instance, quite straightforwardly by W. H. Newton-Smith.[44] In that form it is simply a hopelessly stupid thesis. We may then identify "ancient" relativism *(Protagoreanism)* as the stupid doctrine that any and every statement is both true and false, while at the same time we reserve for ourselves the right to construe Protagoras' own view as requiring a retreat from the global adequacy of bipolar values and a shift, under that constraint, toward a form of incommensurabilism.

The pity is we have lost Protagoras' work. There is an ancient report that the Athenians destroyed all the copies of Protagoras' book; Plato's *Protagoras* is certainly at least in part a parody for his own purpose; and Aristotle's refutation of Protagoras in the *Metaphysics could,* on the standard argument regarding the law of contradiction, be offset if Protagoras had meant to retreat from bipolar values. (So read, Protagoras' maxim would afford a nice counter to that of Parmenides.[45]) In any case there is a way of attempting to salvage even the ancient form of relativism. (Also, to put matters this way helps, as we shall see, to give form to the notion that relativism is much more flexible than ordinarily admitted.)

The principle modern form is, suprisingly, almost as inexplicit as Protagoreanism. It is usually termed *incommensurabilism* and is formulated chiefly (and disadvantageously) by the opponents of those said to advance the thesis—in particular, against Thomas Kuhn and Paul Feyerabend. Incommensurabilism *begins* at least with the conceptually innocuous truism that not all measures are mutually commensurable (in the sense, for instance, in which the hypotenuse of an isosceles right triangle is incommensurable with its side), although that is no reason for believing that incommensurable measures are not, severally, capable of being successfully applied *and* of being jointly intelligible, even comparable, to the same rational agent.[46] Incommensurabilism acquires color as a form of relativism only when, one way or another, it extends to what may be called "conceptual relativity," that is, accords with the thesis that—under the preformational conditions of historical existence or under the conditions of adhering to different theories, different research projects, different paradigms, different modes of training, orientation, and the like (or both)—different investigators (located either synchronically or diachronically) are, on the available evidence, often unable to incorporate an adequate and coherent picture of one another's conceptions within the terms of reference of their own. The emphasis here is on distinctly finite, real-time constraints in attempting to effect such coherence. But it emphatically is not skeptical about the intelligibility of such divergent conceptions.

So construed, incommensurabilism is not a principled position but an empirical phenomenon that yields a certain relativity of inquiry and the results of inquiry that, over time, may in principle be overtaken distributively. The opponents of incommensurabilism, however, take its contemporary advocates to be advancing a very strong principled thesis—a thesis, in fact, that is either incoherent or unnecessarily (and unconvincingly) skeptical. As with Protagoreanism, therefore, it is the better part of strategy to seek to recover a viable form of incommensurabilism from the excesses of its overzealous opponents.

Two lines of argument have been pursued. One distinctly treats incommensurabilism as the "new relativism" and takes it to be tantamount to "skepticism, historicism, and nihilism" (as notably by Richard Bernstein[47]); the other treats incommensurabilism as flatly incoherent and self-defeating (as notably by Donald Davidson[48]). On Bernstein's view the objectivist is committed to "some permanent, ahistorical matrix or framework" for resolving all cognitive questions; the relativist denies that there is such a framework and *thereupon* draws the skeptical conclusion.[49] The incommensurabilist thesis is therefore the denial of objectivism construed as disallowing the adjudication of all truth-claims. Bernstein does *not* advocate returning to objectivism. He means merely to urge either that the rejection of that doctrine does not lead to relativism or skepticism or that there may be a form of incommensurabilism that does not lead to the relativist or skeptical conclusion. But he never exlains how this is possible, and the relativist, sympathetic with incommensurabilism, *may* simply retreat from the global adequacy of bipolar values *and thereby seperate relativism from skepticism.*[50] Bernstein himself apparently believes that the ongoing "tradition" of inquiry somehow preserves the path by means of which unique or very strongly convergent resolutions of contending truth-claims can be counted on to be effected. But this itself is an obvious form of logocentric assurance—one we may christen "traditionalism," one in fact strenuously advocated (but not seriously defended or methodologically specified) by Hans-Georg Gadamer (whom Bernstein professes to follow) and by Charles Taylor.[51]

The second counterstrategy (Davidson's) leads us to consider the tenability of "conceptual relativism," the thesis (on Davidson's reading) that *we* are able to individuate plural conceptual schemes different from our own because of *their* partial or total untranslatability into *our* conceptual scheme.[52] The argument is intended as a *reductio* specifically against Kuhn and Feyerabend. But the truth of the matter is that we have no clear idea how to establish untranslat*ability* (nor does Davidson) when we have merely encountered an actual failure of translation of a suitably stubborn and pervasive kind. So "conceptual relativism" may well be an excessive and incoherent claim, as Davidson avers. But a *moderate* incommensurabilist (certainly Kuhn in his more careful moments, possibly even Feyerabend despite his deliberate provocations) may affirm no more than "conceptual relativity" (as characterized above: sustained failure of translation under real-time conditions). He may then go on to reject "conceptual relativism" (Davidson's impossibly difficult untranslatability thesis) and to lead the first option in the direction of a principled argument, as by: (a) denying (what Bernstein terms) the objectivist thesis (which, in an obvious sense, Davidson is logocentrically committed to, by way of his reading of Tarski's semantic conception); (b) affirming some form of the realist/idealist symbiosis; and (c) concluding that, under the actual contingencies of historical inquiry and existence, we can never ensure escaping some range of (moderate) incommensurability. This is all the relativist needs to ensure the recovery of the incommensurabilist thesis as a valid form of relativism not in the least skewed toward skepticism or nihilism. That thesis is certainly not internally incoherent. Within the analytic tradition of the philosophy of science perhaps Ian Hacking is as reasonable an advocate of this sort of relativism as any,[53] though it is also fairly assigned to Kuhn and Feyerabend.

Nevertheless, relativism does not achieve its strongest formulation in Protagoreanism and incommensurabilism, though it may avail itself of their resources. What we may now characterize as a *robust* or moderate relativism is a substantive thesis about constraints on truth-values in distributed sectors of inquiry due to (what may be generously construed as) empirical evidence that those sectors (but not necessarily every sector) cannot reasonably support truth-claims in terms of bipolar values. On the argument we must fall back to logically weaker, many-valued claims (as of plausibility, reasonableness, aptness, and the like) if we are to salvage a measure of objectivity with respect to the inquiries of those sectors. Such a retreat may be required, for instance, in advancing claims about explanatory theories and laws in the physical sciences,[54] or about reference to theoretical entities through changing theories,[55] or about ontological schemes of "what there is"[56] If the concession is required here, it is a foregone conclusion that it will be required in historical studies, in interpretation, in the social and human sciences, in criticism, and in appraisal and evaluation as well.

The skeleton of the relativist argument, then, is extraordinarily simple. It posits the nearly trivial (but not unimportant) thesis that we may introduce by fiat any consistent logical constraints we care to admit on the truth-values or truth-like values particular sets of claims or claims in particular sectors of inquiry may take. We may, by fiat alone, deny to a given sector the power of pertinent claims or judgments to take bipolar truth-values (or, acknowledging an asymmetry between "true" and "false," the power to take the strong value "true"); and then, by introducing logically weaker values, we may admit claims or judgments to be evidentially supported or supportable even where, on a bipolar model of truth-values but not now, admissible judgments would yield incompatible or contradictory claims. We may simply abandon excluded middle or *tertium non datur*. On the new model such judgments could be said to be "incongruent," and a suitable discipline could be provided for their confirmation and disconfirmation. At the same time, on the strength of relevance considerations certain other logically undesirable possibilities could easily be precluded (in probabilistic contexts, for instance, it would be undesirable to deny that "Nixon probably knew about Watergate in advance and did not know about Watergate in advance" was a contradiction, even though "There is a probability that Nixon knew about Watergate in advance and a probability that Nixon did not know about Watergate in advance" would normally not be construed as self-contradictory).[57]

The essential point is that the formal (relativistic) characterization of truth-like values *appropriate* to particular sectors of inquiry (i) need not be logically incoherent or self-contradictory, (ii) effectively captures the salvageable themes of Protagoreanism and incommensurabilism and more, and (iii) may be formulated so as to accommodate the salient philosophical convergences of our own time. The rest of the argument really concerns how to show, in given sectors of inquiry, that a relativistic thesis is as reasonable as, or more reasonable than, any program of scientific *objectivity*—not committed to transparency or logocentric privilege—that still insists (in the manner of Stalnacker, Dummett, and

Davidson, and so many others) that "there are just two truth-values."[58]

The strongest substantive reason for advocating relativism rests, as we have seen, with the finding that we cannot uniquely fix the structures of reality just where we are justified in insisting on the objective and realist import of our cognitive claims. That finding draws strength from arguments in favor of the realist/idealist symbiosis of science, a pragmatized holism, a moderate incommensurabilism, a historicized context-dependent sense of human inquiry and existence, the impossibility of totalizing the conditions of cognition, and the general rejection of transparency and logocentrism. It needs to be said as well that since relativism is to be promoted in a piecemeal and distributed way, there is no incompatibility in managing, within one science, both bipolar claims and the logically weaker claims here advocated; for it is certainly clear that inquiries that promote relativistic values depend on a *theory* of bipolar values even where they retreat from the use of such values. Also, of course, there is no reason to deny that relativistic programs readily accommodate comparative judgments of merit or force, notions of progress, rigorous evidence, and the like. In short, relativism is expressly opposed to skepticism and nihilism. There are no areas of inquiry usually cast in bipolar terms that are adversely affected by replacing such values with relativistic values. The reason for the substitution, wherever applied, would rest with an argument that the bipolar model was too strict for the domain in question; in effect, the evidence would itself be straightforwardly empirical.

It is extraordinary, therefore, how little must be adjusted in order to make room for a viable relativism—and how extensive its scope may arguably be. It may take a limited evidentiary form if one insists, but its principal force rests with substantive claims about the real structure of this or that sector of inquiry. Any latitude regarding that structure—in physical as well as cultural terms—along, say, the four lines of reasoning sketched just above or in accord with the realist/idealist symbiosis, the rejection of cognitive transparency, the artifactual nature of whatever, within inquiry, we take to be real, or the impossibility of closure in realist terms, is bound to favor the pertinence of relativistic claims.

Relativism, then, is the thesis, at once alethic and metaphysical, that particular sectors of reality can only support, distributively, incongruent claims, that is, claims that on a bipolar model but not now would confirm incompatible or contradictory judgments and claims. To forestall misunderstanding, it may be mentioned again that relevance constraints may always be introduced to disallow unwanted contradictions even within the space of relativistic truth-values; that relativism itself is fully compatible with extensionalism and physicalism but is also hospitable to the intentional complexities of human culture; that no bona fide inquiries are adversely affected merely by introducing relativistic values; that the use of relativistic values is entirely reconcilable with the use of bipolar values; and that judgments of scientific progress or of the comparative force of opposed claims, or judgments of comparative value, are entirely eligible within the space of relativistic values. Where applicable, bipolar values quite understandably take precedence over relativistic values. But relativistically, judgments of greater or lesser epistemic force need not be disjunctively construed.

So relativism is clearly coherent and viable and, on the strength of substantive arguments, may well be favored in one domain or another.

Notes

1. The ramified account on which the present argument depends is given in Joseph Margolis, *Pragmatism without Foundations: Reconciling Realism and Relativism* (Oxford: Basil Blackwell, 1986) and *Science without Unity: Reconciling the Human and Natural Sciences* (Oxford: Basil Blackwell, 1987).

2. Robert C. Stalnacker, *Inquiry* (Cambridge: MIT Press, 1984), p. 2.

3. Ibid.

4. Ibid., pp. 152-153; italics added.

5. Ibid., p. 151; see Bas C. van Fraassen, *The Scientific Image* (Oxford: Clarendon, 1980), pp. 134-137.

6. The full argument regarding realism and antirealism is given in *Pragmatism without Foundations,* pt. 2, especially with regard to van Fraassen, Dummett, and Putnam.

7. Michael Dummett, "Truth," *Truth and Other Enigmas* (Cambridge: Harvard University Press, 1978), p. 14.

8. Ibid., p. 24; I have italicized "realist."

9. See Hilary Putnam, *Meaning and the Moral Sciences* (London: Routledge and Kegan Paul, 1978).

10. Dummett, Preface to *Truth and Other Enigmas,* p. xxx.

11. F. P. Ramsey, "Facts and Propositions," *Foundations of Mathematics,* ed. Richard B. Braithewaite (London: Routledge and Kegan Paul, 1931), p. 143.

12. See Thomas S. Kuhn, *The Structure of Scientific Revolutions,* 2nd ed. enl. (Chicago: University of Chicago Press, 1970), Postscript, 1969.

13. Alfred Tarski, "On the Concept of Logical Consequence," *Logic, Semantics, Metamathematics,* tr. J. H. Woodger, 2nd ed. John Corcoran (Indinapolis: Hackett, 1983).

14. Ibid., p. 120.

15. See Alfred Tarski, "The Concept of Truth in Formalized Languages," *Logic, Semantics, Metamathematics*; also Alfred Tarski, "The Semantic Conception of Truth," reprinted in Leonard Linsky, ed., *Semantics and the Philosophy of Language* (Urbana: University of Illinois Press, 1952).

16. Hilary Putnam, "Reference and Truth," *Philosophical Papers,* vol. 3 (Cambridge: Cambridge University Press, 1983), p. 76.

17. Dummett, Preface to *Truth and Other Enigmas,* p. xx.

18. Ibid., xx-xxi.

19. Donald Davidson, *Inquiries into Truth and Interpretation* (Oxford: Clarendon, 1984), Introduction, p. xiv.

20. Donald Davidson, "Reply to Foster," *Inquiries into Truth and Interpretation,* p. 176.

21. That is, of course, always conceding that "ontologies" need not be committed to transparency—contrary to the fashionable charge in Richard Rorty, *Philosophy and the Mirror of Nature* (Princeton: Princeton University Press, 1979).

22. Donald Davidson, "Semantics for Natural Languages," *Inquiries into Truth and Interpretation,* p. 55. Cf. "Truth and Meaning," ibid., p. 35.

23. Donald Davidson, "In Defense of Convention T," *Inquiries into Truth and Interpretation,* p. 68.

24. Ibid., p. 65.

25. One of the most recent formulations of "Convention T" is given by Davidson in "Reality without Reference," *Inquiries into Truth and Interpretation,* p. 215.

26. Donald Davidson, "Reality without Reference," p. 218.

27. See, for instance, "Truth and Meaning," pp. 35-36.

28. See the perceptive remarks of Ian Hacking, *Why Does Language Matter to Philosophy?* (Cambridge: Cambridge University Press, 1975), pp. 154-155.

29. "Reality without Reference," pp. 215-216.

30. "In Defense of Convention T," p. 75.

31. See Edmund Husserl, *Phenomenology and the Crisis of Philosophy,* tr. Quentin Lauer (New York: Harper and Row, 1965).

32. This marks a substantial part of the thrust of Derrida's early work, though it is as much addressed to Kant as to Husserl. See Jacques Derrida, *Speech and Phenomena,* tr. David B. Allison (Evanston: Northwestern University Press, 1973).

33. W. V. Quine, *Word and Object* (Cambridge: MIT Press, 1960), §45.

34. Ibid., §15-16.

35. Ibid., §15.

36. This is an issue on which both Monroe Beardsley's New Critical conception and E. D. Hirsch's romantic hermeneutic conception of literature utterly fail to exclude relativism. See, for instance, Monroe C. Beardsley, *The Possibility of Criticism* (Detroit: Wayne State University Press, 1970), esp. "The Authority of the Text"; and E. D. Hirsch, Jr., *The Validity of Interpretation* (New Haven: Yale University Press, 1967); also, Joseph Margolis, *Art and Philosophy* (Atlantic Highlands, N.J.: Humanities Press, 1980), ch. 6.

37. See, for instance, Nancy Cartwright, *How the Laws of Physics Lie* (Oxford: Clarendon, 1985); Ian Hacking, *Representing and Intervening* (Cambridge: Cambridge University Press, 1985).

38. See Carl G. Hempel, "Studies in the Logic of Explanation," *in Aspects of Scientific Explanation* (New York: Free Press, 1965), p. 263.

39. Paul K. Feyerabend, *Realism, Rationalism and Scientific Method,* Philosophical Papers, vol. 1 (Cambridge: Cambridge University Press, 1981), p. xiv.

40. See Hilary Putnam, "Two Conceptions of Rationality," *Reason, Truth, and History* (Cambridge: Cambridge University Press, 1981).

41. Paul K. Feyerabend, "Historical Background: Some Observations on the Decay of the Philosophy of Science," *Problems of Empiricism,* Philosophical Papers, vol. 2 (Cambridge: Cambridge University Press, 1981), pp. 28-29.

42. Kathleen Freeman, *Ancilla to the Pre-Socratic Philosophers* (Oxford: Basil Blackwell, 1948), p. 126.

43. Ibid., p. 125.

44. W. H. Newton-Smith, *The Rationality of Science* (London: Routledge and Kegan Paul, 1981), pp. 34-37.

45. See Mario Untersteiner, *The Sophists,* tr. Kathleen Freeman (Oxford: Basil Blackwell, 1954), p. 50, n. 18; also Untersteiner's effort at reconstructing Protagoras, ch. 3, pt. 3.

46. Perhaps the clearest expression of this view is given in Thomas S. Kuhn, "Theory-Change as Structure-Change: Comments on the Sneed Formalism," *Erkenntnis* 10 (1976), where the triangle case is given.

47. Richard J. Bernstein, *Beyond Objectivism and Relativism* (Philadelphia: University of Pennsylvania Press, 1983), pp. 79, 2f.

48. Donald Davidson, "On the Very Idea of a Conceptual Scheme," *Inquiries into Truth and Interpretation.*

49. Bernstein, *Beyond Objectivism and Relativism,* p. 8.

50. This is the argument of Margolis, *Pragmatism without Foundations,* ch. 3.

51. See Charles Taylor, "Philosophy and Its History," in *Philosophy in History* ed. Richard Rorty *et al* (Cambridge: Cambridge University Press, 1984).

52. Davidson, "On the Very Idea of a Conceptual Scheme," pp. 197-198.

53. Ian Hacking, "Language, Truth, and Reason," in *Rationality and Relativism* ed. Martin Hollis and Steven Lukes (Cambridge: MIT Press, 1982).

54. See Cartwright, *How the Laws of Physics Lie.*

55. See Hilary Putnam, *Meaning and the Moral Sciences,* Lecture 2, The John Locke Lectures, 1976.

56. This is surely the essential point of Quine's notion of "ontological relativity." See W. V. Quine, "Ontological Relativity," in *Ontological Relativity and Other Essays* (New York: Columbia University Press, 1969).

57. See Margolis, *Pragmatism without Foundations,* pt. 1.

58. It is fashionable but completely unjustified to construe relativism as committed to treating "truth or rational acceptability as *subjective*," as Putnam does, "Two Concepts of Rationality," p. 123. At best it is the result of a conventional reading of Protagoras; at worst it is a cryptic reference to the arbitrary skepticism of incommensurabilism.

Contra Relativism:
A Thought-Experiment[1]

Thomas McCarthy

In recent Anglo-American philosophy impulses to relativism have come not only from such internal developments as the growing influence of postempiricist perspectives but also from developments in such areas as the history of ideas, cultural anthropology, and the sociology of knowledge. In this essay I shall be concerned with the brief for relativism advanced by proponents of a "strong program" in the sociology of knowledge. This choice is motivated by the observation that philosophical arguments for relativism frequently rest on a certain misreading of the interpretive practices involved in empirical studies of belief systems, and this same misreading is explicitly advanced by Barry Barnes and David Bloor as the justification for their strong program.[2]

Eschewing any concern with the epistemic status of the collectively accepted systems of belief under investigation, they recommend treating all beliefs "on a par with one another as to the causes of their credibility." On this approach "the incidence of all beliefs without exception calls for empirical investigation and must be accounted for . . . without regard to the status of the belief as it is judged and evaluated by the sociologist's own standards."[3] There is an explicitly philosophical rationale behind this abstinence:

> The relativist, like everyone else, is under the necessity to sort out beliefs, accepting some and rejecting others. He will naturally have preferences and these will typically coincide with those of others in his locality. The words 'true' and 'false' provide the idiom in which those evaluations are expressed and the words 'rational' and 'irrational' will have a similar function. . . . The crucial point is that the relativist accepts . . . that none of the justifications of his preferences can be formulated in absolute or context-independent terms. In the last analysis, he acknowledges that his

justifications will stop at some principle or alleged matter of fact that only has local credibility. . . For the relativist there is no sense attached to the idea that some standards or beliefs are really rational as distinct from merely locally accepted as such. Because he thinks that there are no context-free or super-cultural norms of rationality he does not see rationally and irrationally held beliefs as making up two distinct and qualitatively different classes of things. They do not fall into two different natural kinds which make different sorts of appeal to the human mind, or stand in a different relationship to reality, or depend for their credibility on different patterns of social organization. Hence the relativist conclusion that they are to be explained in the same way.[4]

This undercuts the rationalist distinction between validity and credibility and the accompanying claim that whereas the latter might be explained by "contingent determinants," the former can be accounted for only by an appeal to reasons. There is nothing, Barnes and Bloor insist, so contingent and socially variable as what counts as a reason for what. Something is evidence for something else only in a certain context, and thus this relation is itself a "prime target for sociological inquiry and explanation."[5]

Here the symbiosis between empirical research program and philosophical viewpoint is evident. It is also typically involved, though seldom so explicitly, in the philosophical defense of relativism. There it is assumed that historians, sociologists, and ethnographers supply us with the purely descriptive accounts of the diversity of belief systems that furnish the empirical background to the philosophical argument. Any doubts about one partner in this intimate association will affect our confidence in the other. If philosophical relativism were to prove indefensible, we might want to give the validity/credibility distinction some play in the sociology of knowledge; if strictly neutral descriptive accounts of systems of belief proved to be impossible in principle, we might well come to doubt some of the usual arguments for philosophical relativism. In what follows I want to argue that something like the latter situation does in fact obtain, in particular, that the strong program in the sociology of knowledge rests on a misconception of this point.

The keystone of my argument will be a certain *Gedankenexperiment* involving an imagined dialogue between proponents of a mode of thought loosely characterized as "modern-scientific" and proponents of another mode just as loosely characterized as "magico-mythical." I should make clear at the start that I am not interested here in praising or criticizing either of these for its own sake, but only in the *logic* of the thought-experiment, and this stands out the more clearly the greater the cultural distance between the dialogue partners. My suggestion will be that this *Gendankenexperiment* has something essential to add to that perennial favorite of the philosophers, the field linguist involved in radical interpretation.

Let me begin by following out a few clues from the first round of debate about the sociology of knowledge sparked by Karl Mannheim's launching of his program in the 1920s. In his 1930 review of Mannheim's *Ideology and Utopia* Max Horkheimer argued that the historically conditioned character of a belief is not *per se* incompatible with its being true: only against the background of traditional ontological-theological conceptions of eternal, unchanging truth could this seem to be the case.[6] But there is no need, he went on, of any absolute guarantee in order to distinguish meaningfully between truth and error. Rather, what is required is a concept of truth consisent with our finitude, with our historicity, with the dependence of thought on changing social conditions. On such a concept failure to measure up to absolute, unconditioned standards would be irrelevant. To regard this failure as leading directly to cognitive relativism is just another version of the "God is dead, everything is permitted" fallacy of disappointed expectations. As Horkheimer put it: "That all our thoughts, true and false, depend on conditions which can change is just as certain as that the idea of an eternal truth outliving all knowing subjects is unfulfillable. This in no way affects the validity of science . . . Anyone who is concerned about the correctness of his judgments about innerworldly objects has nothing to hope and nothing to fear from a decision on the problem of absolute truth . . . It is not clear to me that the fact of *Seinsgebundenheit* (existential determination) should affect the truth of a judgment—why shouldn't insight be just as *seinsgebunden* as error?"[7] In short, there is no *direct* route from finitude and historicity to relativism, though there may well be a longer path. In the first instance the challenge is to deabsolutize the notion of truth.

In his 1935 essay "On the Problem of Truth" Horkheimer attempted to do just that.[8] He argued against the equation of fallibility with relativity. To grant that there is no final and conclusive theory of reality of which we are capable is not at all to abandon the distinction between truth and error. We make this distinction in relation to "the available means of cognition."[9] The claim that a belief is true must stand the test of experience and practice *in the present*. Knowing that we are fallible, that what stands the test today may well fail to do so in the next century, does not prevent us, or even exempt us, from making and defending claims to truth here and now. Consider the following: A claims that S is p. B disputes his claim. They resort to "experience and practice," the "available means of cognition," to settle the matter. This shows that S is indeed p. A was right. But B points out that there is no absolute warrantee of truth. Experience and practice are historically variable. If the past is any guide, the means of cognition available in the next century will be different from those presently available. Therefore, B concludes, A should withdraw his claim to truth. I think it is clear that this conclusion does not follow. A's claim stands unless and until it is actually defeated. If B's argument carried, it would entail the withdrawal of all truth claims, that is, the end of speech as we know it or even can imagine it. Or perhaps we should just attach the rider "As far as we know" to every statement. But then it would not be doing any work at all. The practices of separating truth from error would continue undisturbed. What it was reasonable to accept before adding the explicit reminder of our finitude and fallibility it would be reasonable to accept thereafter. The abstract recognition that all our beliefs are open to correction does not make a rationally warranted belief any less warranted, any less rational. As Horkheimer put it: "A later correction does not mean that a former truth was formerly untrue."[10]

This way of putting the point is somewhat misleading. As a first step toward a more adequate formulation, consider Hilary Putnam's characterization of "truth" in terms of rational acceptability: "To reject the idea that there is a coherent 'external' perspective, a theory that is simply true 'in itself,' apart from all possible observers, is not to identify truth with rational acceptability. Truth cannot simply *be* rational acceptability for one fundamental reason; truth is supposed to be a property of a statement that cannot be lost, whereas justification can be lost . . . Truth is an *idealization* of rational acceptability. We speak as if there were such things as epistemologically ideal conditions, and we call a statement true if it would be justified under such conditions."[11] There have been numerous attempts to capture this idealizing moment in our conception of truth—for example, Kant's notion of a regulative idea, Peirce's notion of the opinion fated to be agreed upon at the end of inquiry, Habermas' notion of a consensus arrived at in unconstrained rational discourse—but this way of approaching the matter also leads to trouble.

Any attempt to *identify* truth with assertibility under ideal conditions, to *define* it as idealized rational acceptability, takes us to the edge of a naturalistic fallacy, if not over.[12] But there is no need for us to put the point in that way. For our present purposes what is important is the nature of the *internal relation* between truth and rational acceptability that is embedded in our *practices* of truth-telling—of affirming and denying, asserting and contesting, stating and criticizing and so on. My claim is that our uses of 'true' include not only a "disquotational use"

and an "endorsing use" but other normative uses as well, including, but
not limited to, what Rorty calls its "cautionary" uses, such as "reminding ourselves that justification is relative to, and no better than, the
beliefs cited as grounds for S, and that such justification is no guarantee
that things will go well if we take S as a 'rule for action.' "[13] Thus an
adequate account of our practices of truth will have to capture not only
the immanence of our appeals to warranting reasons—their socially
conditioned character—but their "transcendence" as well. While we
have no idea of standards of rationality wholly independent of historically concrete languages and practices, it remains that "reason" also
serves as a "cautionary" idea with reference to which we can criticize
the standards we inherit; though not divorced from social practices of
justification, it cannot be reduced to any particular set thereof. Correspondingly, the notion of truth, while essentially related to warranted
assertability by the standards or warrants of this or that culture, cannot
be reduced to any particular set of such standards or warrants.

To put this yet another way, we can, and typically do, make
historically situated and fallible claims to unconditional truth. As a
consequence, the idea of truth can be turned around in a critical way to
call such claims into question by, for instance, arguing that a given
statement of the case is not final, that there is a need to push further to
get at unacknowledged conditions, background presuppositions, and the
like. Of course, we can never arrive at any wholly unconditioned truth,
but the idea of it is a driving force behind our critical-reflective practices. This is not to say that we have a substantive conception of "the
Truth" or even an explanatory theory of truth. But we do have an
understanding-in-use of "true" which enables, sometimes even requires,
us to call into question accepted beliefs and practices. This is not a
metaphysical point. As Wittgenstein might say, it is what we do: we treat
truth claims as involving some "transcendent," "regulative," normative
surplus of meaning beyond "what we happen to agree upon at this
particular time and place."

Applying this to Horkheimer's argument, we would have to alter
his statement "A later correction does not mean that a former truth was
formerly untrue" to read "A later correction does not mean that a
formerly warranted belief was formerly unwarranted" or, alternatively,
"A later correction does not mean that a formerly justified claim to
truth was formerly unjustified." That is, the belief, which we now know
to be untrue, was warranted, justified, rationally acceptable in previous
circumstances—but not ideally. We now have to take a second look at
this notion of "ideally," and from a different angle.

Can "ideally" here mean anything more than "from our point of view," "according to our standards and criteria"? If we surrender, as Horkheimer does, the Hegelian notion that "we" can ever occupy the position of absolute knowledge, our judgment of "their" beliefs as rationally acceptable in those circumstances but not ideally can, it seems, *effectively* amount only to saying that what was acceptable to them is not to us. As Barnes and Bloor put this point, the distinction between validity and credibility is not an absolute but a "local" distinction relative to the accepted methods and assumptions of the evaluator's own group. To pretend otherwise, they argue, is merely to suppose that credibility and validity are identical in one's own case.[14] So we seem to have gone round in a circle and come back to the very point at which we first encountered relativism.

Horkheimer's way of breaking out of this circle was to insist that the for us/for them relation is a dialectical one.[15] The invocation of "dialectic" here serves as a reminder that the relation of social investigators to the belief systems they investigate is not at all the relation of neutral observers to phenomena they describe from some Archimedean point outside of the world; nor is it a relation of empathetic identification with subjects whose world can then be faithfully reexperienced. It is rather analogous to a dialogue relation between two subjects, "we" and "they," which allows not only for differences in point of view but also, in principle, for discussion of these differences. "For them" p is rationally acceptable: it is warranted by their experience and practice in light of their canons of reason and criteria of truth. "For us" it is not rationally acceptable: we detect conditional and limited aspects of their practices and standards. We attempt to criticize and relativize their beliefs from our putatively more adequate point of view. It is important to keep in mind, however, that we may be mistaken as well as they. Thus, while we are convinced that p is not rationally acceptable and are prepared to make the case to that effect, we have to remain open to possible counterarguments from them as well as from others.

This model of critical dialogue corrects a certain imbalance in the treatments of the interpretive situation inspired by the recently very influential "principle of charity in interpretation." In an understandable reaction to the ethnocentric biases of Victorian anthropology, contemporary interpretation theorists have stressed the obligation of the interpreter to broaden his or her horizon so as to make place for the very different concepts and beliefs, standards and practices, of alien cultures and bygone epochs. Thus, to take an early example, Peter Winch, in his much discussed essay on "Understanding a Primitive Society," argued that "the onus is on us to extend our understanding" rather than "insist on seeing (things) in terms of our own ready made distinction(s)."[16] As a corrective to ethnocentrism Winch's promotion of the charity principle was all to the good. But as a guide to the logic of cross-cultural encounter it too was one-sided.

If there is initial disagreement in beliefs and practices, concepts and criteria, and if there is no extramundane standpoint from which neutrally to adjudicate the differences, and if neither side is justified in assuming without further ado the superiority of its own way of looking at things, then a discussion of the differences is the only nonarbitrary path open for weighing the pros and cons of the divergent outlooks. If this discussion is to be symmetrical, then "their" views will have to be given equal consideration with "our" views. *We* shall have to try to appreciate how things look from *their* point of view. And this will require expanding the horizon of our own, as Winch points out. What he fails to consider is that symmetry requires the same of them. That is, *they* would, correspondingly, have to learn to see things from *our* point of view as well if discussion of the differences in belief and practice is to proceed without unduly privileging the one or the other side. As I shall soon argue, this description of the logical—or, in this case, dialogical—situation has far-reaching consequences for the whole discussion of relativism. [17] The view I am recommending can be thought of as a kind of *Gedankenexperiment:* faced with a question about the relative merits, in this or that regard, of two fundamentally different ways of looking at things, we try to imagine a dialogue between proponents of them, such that each side is under the obligation to do everything possible to understand how things look from the other side.

It might seem that this is merely to substitute a hermeneutic model of dialogue or conversation for the sociologist of knowledge's attitude of neutral description—and without having solved our original problem, for there are hermeneutic versions of relativism as well. On such accounts interpretation is viewed as necessarily situation-bound, an understanding from a point of view, on the same level as what is understood. Thus social inquirers are not, as we may mistakenly suppose, neutral observers, explainers, predictors; neither are they sovereign critics who may safely assume their own cognitive superiority. They are, however virtually, partners in dialogue, participants in a conversation about the common concerns of human life.

Critics of relativism need not, I think, deny this, but they would have to resist the relativistic implications that are usually drawn from it. To grant that every point of view is historically situated is not *ipso facto* to surrender all claims to validity, to drop any claim that one view is better than another. For example—and this is only an example—in the context of debating the relative merits of prescientific and scientific accounts of natural processes, the technological advances connected with the former could count as *one* argument in their favor. As embodied, active beings, our ordinary prescientific understandings of the world are, as Charles Taylor has recently put it, "inseparable from an ability to make one's way around in it and deal with the things in it," that is, from "recipes for action." Technological advances, as "more far-reaching recipes," cannot but force the issue between scientific and prescientific theories, for they "command attention and demand explanation" not only from our point of view but from theirs as well, that is, from the point of view of any group that has to reproduce its existence in active exchange with the environment—that is, from the point of view of any human group.[18] Thus in our transcultural dialogue we might want to take the position that there has been a learning process in regard to our *technical* understanding of natural processes, that we have learned how to pursue the common human interest in prediction and control more effectively by differentiating out its pursuit from other— moral, emotional, symbolic, aesthetic, and such,—concerns. In short, while the open-ended "conversation of humankind" rules out the assumption that our point of view is absolute, it does not require us simply to drop notions of cognitive advance or learning from experience.

On the other hand, it does not give us any general license to apply these notions wherever "their" views are different from "ours." We have to be prepared to learn from them in areas where their experience has taught them things we do not know, or know less well, or once knew but have since forgotten. Logically speaking, we have to allow for regression as well as progression in any given domain, as well as for straightforward differences in approach and differentials of development. While they may have something to learn from us regarding science and technology, we may have something to learn from them about alternative attitudes toward and conceptions of nature. While they may have something to learn from us about individualistic conceptions of self and personality, we may have something to learn from them about the limits to such conceptions.

There are, however, some important respects in which the learning situation may not be symmetrical. Consider the case of magico-mythical worldviews in tribal societies. If it is true, as many anthropologists claim, that they are typically characterized by the lack of a developed awareness of alternatives to the established body of beliefs, and that this accounts in part for such phenomena as the sacredness of beliefs, taboo avoidance reactions in the face of challenges to them, and the magical power of words (which are regarded as having a unique and intimate relation to things)—then the very process of their coming to understand how we see things (apart from any discussion of relative merits) could have far-reaching implications for their views. For one thing they would have to understand in understanding us is our historically, sociologically, and anthropologically schooled view of the diversity of systems of belief and practice. To put what could be a very long story in a nutshell: the symmetry of the dialogue situation would require that they try to understand our beliefs and practices—as we must theirs—including the reasons why we hold the beliefs we do, the justifications we offer for accepting the practices we do, as well as the criticisms we have developed in rejecting other alternatives in our past—some of them rather similiar to those obtaining in their society. I think it is clear that this very attempt to find a common language for discussing relative merits might well lead, independently of any specific discussions, at the very least to a more qualified acceptance of those aspects of the tribal culture that depend precisely on *not* having had certain experiences—for example, of cultural change and cultural pluralism—we have had, and on *not* having learned certain things we have learned—for example, about the historical and social variety of systems of belief and practice.

The same sort of consideration applies to other structural features (and I am here confining my remarks to such features) of what they would have to come to understand in coming to understand our point of view—for instance, to the differentiations we make between the concerns of science and religion, art and morality, and so forth. It is typical of tribal and traditional systems of belief that they do not differentiate in the same way, that they address simultaneously what we would describe as religious, scientific, moral, emotional, and aesthetic concerns. They are, in Alasdair MacIntyre's phrase, "poised in ambiguity," such that the very posing of such questions as Is this science or theology, symbolic expression or applied technique, or all at once? can permanently upset the balance—as it did in our own past.[19] And again, to understand much of what we believe, they would have to understand the type of reflective, second- and higher-order activities in which we engage—explicating and evaluating basic categories, assumptions, aims and criteria, considering alternatives and justifying choices—coming to understand which might itself bring with it irreversible changes in outlook. We too often forget, I think, that in some situations it is difficult not to learn, and difficult often to ignore what one has learned.

Furthermore, once the discussion got underway, they would have to face other deep-seated disadvantages. In making the case for the rational superiority of a view to its rivals, one very important consideration is its ability to explain the accomplishments and failures of its rivals, to incorporate their strengths and transcend their limitations. While this tactic may lead in the case of contemporary debates to a situation in which, as Richard Rorty has put it, everyone goes around applying an *Aufhebung* to everyone else, its consequences in the case at hand are far more one-sided. For offering an alternative account of our science and technology, law and morality, art and religion, and so on incorporating their accomplishments and transcending their limitations is evidently going to be more of a problem for them than the corresponding task is for us—for our culture has been involved in doing just this sort of thing for some time now. For them, however, this would be, in a way, to cease being who they are. This is not to say that we are always right and they are always wrong. But it is to suggest that the concept of learning has its application at the sociocultural level as well, and that as a result the conversation of humankind does *not* place each system of beliefs on a par with every other. Some differences are more than mere differences, precisely because they can best be understood as the results of learning.

Here the advocates of a strong program in the sociology of knowledge might take a different tack, namely, grant this point and argue that while nothing *prevents* an interpreter from adopting the attitude of a participant in dialogue or argumentation, nothing *requires* him or her to do so. They might thus propose a division of labor between the sociologist of knowledge who neutrally describes and explains belief systems and the humanist or critic who evaluates and criticizes them, that is, between investigators who adopt the objectivating attitude of the noninvolved and those who adopt the performative attitude of participants.

Against a similar proposal by Mannheim, Horkheimer argued that the social investigator was unavoidably "involved" in the object he or she was studying, that the sociologist of knowledge's claim to strict neutrality was a prime instance of self-misunderstanding. Arguments to this effect have turned up in the contemporary relativism debates as well. It has been argued, for instance, that in explaining actor's beliefs the sociologist cannot avoid at least implicitly endorsing or rejecting the reasons they would give for them.[20] For instance, if he or she is pursuing a strong program in the manner of Barnes and Bloor, then he or she offers explanations in terms of such "contingent determinants" as processes of socialization and class membership, social integration and cultural transmission, influences of authority, roles, institutions, group interests, and so forth. The variety of candidates for "contingent determinants of belief" is obviously very wide. There does not appear to be any property they possess in common, except perhaps that they are *not* the sorts of evidencing *reasons* actors themselves would give for their beliefs.

It is important at this point in the argument to note that Barnes and Bloor want to avoid opposing social determinants, on the one side, to epistemic factors or evidencing reasons, on the other. (It is difficult to imagine how the "incidence of belief" in this or that scientific theory could be explained without reference to reasons in any form.) Instead, they argue that evidencing reasons *are a species of* social determinant. "It would be difficult," they write, "to find a commodity more contingent and more socially variable than . . . evidencing reasons."[21] In short, in the relation "x is a reason for y," what counts as a good reason for holding a belief or performing an action, is socially variable and socially explicable. Their point then is not that reasons cannot figure in the sociologist of knowledge's accounts, but that they are referred to descriptively and not normatively, that they are mentioned but not used.[22] No beliefs are explained, they claim, in a way that presupposes a normative evaluation of them. In particular, the sociologist's own evaluations play no role in his explanations. Explanation is perfectly symmetrical in respect to true and false beliefs, rational and irrational practices—as he would judge these things from his own socially situated point of view.

It is this claim, the sociologist of knowledge's putative neutrality, that I want to consider in the remainder of this paper. I shall suggest, as Horkheimer did fifty years ago, that this is a subtle instance of self-misunderstanding, that the sociologist of knowledge's evaluations do play a role, however implicitly, in his or her explanations. The argument, which I can only sketch here, runs as follows. Everyone seems agreed, finally, that we have to understand beliefs and practices in their settings and uses. The very indentification of what is to be explained is an interpretive enterprise, and this inevitably lands us in a hermeneutic circle. For my purposes it is not important whether this circle is explicated in terms of Gadamer's *Vorgriff auf Vollkommenheit,* Winch's principle of charity in interpretation, Davidson's "transcendental" version thereof (according to which "we must assume that by and large a speaker we do not yet understand is consistent and correct in his beliefs—according to our own standards, of course"[23]), or the weaker "principle of humanity" to the effect that whether we regard their beliefs as true or false, *their being held* must be intelligible.[24] What interests me here is the common point that meaning and validity are inseparable, that the identification and interpretation of beliefs is possible only under certain *pragmatic constraints* to the effect that we view what we are interpreting as largely reasonable in its context. Most relativists are only too happy to grant this notion of "reasonableness in context," for it appears to be just the sort of local notion they favor. But they fail to see that there is a dialectical pitfall here, which Alasdair MacIntyre pointed out some time ago in his critique of Winch.[25] For, *to whom* must the behavior be shown to be intelligible or reasonable in its context? To the interpreter of course (not to the natives, surely). And this means: by the light of standards of intelligibility and rationality amenable to her. The interpreter must come to see how a certain belief or practice could appear reasonable in a certain context. If the belief is one her culture does not hold, she will look for differences of context to account for the differences of belief. That is, she will note features present in their context and absent from ours, or present in our context and absent from theirs, such that these presences and absences make the differences intelligible. Notice that all of this is required in the very attempt to understand alien systems of belief. Notice also that ascertaining the *what* of belief has also and inescapably involved us in grasping the *how* and *why* of belief. Notice finally that the interpreter's involvment in this process is such that her evaluations do play a role, albeit a tacit role, in her account of alien beliefs. It is her standards that are at work in her sense of what might reasonably be believed in a given context, of what might be accounted for by what she regards as normal processes of perception, cognition, and reasoning, and of what can be accounted for only by pointing to special circumstances.

The dialectical point is that our explication contains, at least implicitly, an evaluation. It says, in effect, that a given belief might make sense and reasonably be held in a given context—for example, in the context of a preliterate, relatively stable and homogenous, relatively isolated culture, in the absence of a developed science, philosophy, historiography, and so forth—and this amounts to saying that it is a belief which could no longer reasonably be held. Or we may find that what we have to abstract from in our setting, or notice in their setting, in order to make a difference in belief understandable makes us aware for the first time of the peculiarities of certain aspects of our context, and thus of the deficiencies in the beliefs that we now see to be limited by them.[26]

My point in all this is *not* that it is always wrong to approach beliefs in a descriptive mode, bracketing any *explicit* considerations of questions of validity. I am not arguing that the sociology of knowledge and intellectual history are intrinsically illegitimate enterprises which should be eliminated. What I am concerned with is a certain *lack of self-consciousness* that can and often does lead to serious misunderstandings. Even while bracketing questions of validity, the position of the sociologist of knowledge is not that of the ideally neutral spectator. She is implicitly involved in evaluating beliefs even as she is trying merely to describe and to explain them.[27] For meaning and validity are intertwined, and both are internally connected with reasons. In interpreting we cannot but move in the space of reasons. And in coming to understand "their" beliefs and how they reason about them the question of whether or not they have come to hold them for reasons "we" can accept cannot but play a role in how we proceed. Futhermore, when we offer an account of their beliefs which differs from their own account, we have *ipso facto* criticized them, implied that we are right and they are wrong.

Critical social science has the merit of making this implicit dialectic explicit. It openly addresses the question of the validity of the belief systems it studies. And thus it avoids the self-misunderstanding that still—fifty years later—plagues relativist versions of the sociology of knowledge and those philosophers who draw uncritically upon them.

Notes

1. An earlier version of this paper was read at a conference on "The Shaping of Scientific Rationality," held at the University of Notre Dame in April 1986. The proceedings of that conference were published under the title *Construction and Constraint: The Shaping of Scientific Rationality,* edited by Ernan McMullin (Notre Dame, 1988).

2. I shall be concentrating on the statement of their position in "Relativism, Rationalism and the Sociology of Knowledge," in *Rationality and Relativism,* ed. M. Hollis and S. Lukes (Cambridge, Mass., 1982), pp. 21-47. See also B. Barnes, *Interests and the Growth of Knowledge* (London, 1977); D. Bloor, *Knowledge and Social Imagery* (London, 1976); and the discussion of their program in J. R. Brown, ed., *Scientific Rationality: The Sociological Turn* (Dordrecht, 1984).

3. Barnes and Bloor, "Relativism, Rationalism and the Sociology of Knowledge," p. 23.

4. Ibid., pp. 27-28.

5. Ibid., p. 29.

6. M. Horkheimer, "Ein neuer Ideologiebegriff?" *Archiv für die Geschichte des Sozialismus und der Arbeiterbewegung* 15 (1930), reprinted in *Der Streit um die Wissenssoziologie,* 2 vols., ed. V. Meja and N. Stehr (Frankfurt, 1982), vol. 2, pp. 474-496, here p. 485.

7. Ibid., pp. 485-486.

8. M. Horkheimer, "On the Problem of Truth," in *The Essential Frankfurt School Reader,* ed. A. Arato and E. Gebhardt (New York, 1978), pp. 407-443.

9. Ibid., p. 421.

10. Ibid., p. 422.

11. H. Putnam, *Reason, Truth and History* (Cambridge, 1981), pp. 54-55. In a subsequent piece, "Why Reason Can't Be Naturalized," *Synthese* 52 (1982): 1-23, reprinted in *After Philosphy*, ed. K. Baynes, J. Bohamn, T. McCarthy (Cambridge, Mass., 1987), pp. 222-224, Putnam offers an interesting view of cultural relativism as a kind of naturalism that replaces philosophy's traditional deference to the natural sciences with a deference to the social, cultural, and/or historical sciences, and an interesting argument to the effect that, consistently thought through, cultural relativism implies a kind of cultural imperialism: If reason, justification, truth, and so on are whatever the norms of the local culture determine them to be, the utterances with which I interpret other cultures can claim truth only as determined by the norms of my culture. "Other cultures become, so to speak, logical constructions out of the procedures and practices of American culture" (p. 232); thus it makes no sense for the cultural relativist to add that they are in a symmetrical situation with respect to us. It is symmetry of this sort that I am trying to preserve with the dialogue model presented below.

12. I am indebted to Arthur Fine and Michael Williams for making this clear to me, though neither is likely to agree with the tack I take below. For their own views of the matter see Arthur Fine, "And Not Anti-Realism Either," *Nous* 18 (1984): 51-65; Michael Williams, "Coherence, Falsification, and Truth," *Review of Metaphysics* 34 (1980): 243-272; and "Do We (Epistemologists) Need a Theory of Truth?" *Philosophical Topics* 14 (1986): 223-242.

13. Richard Rorty, "Pragmatism, Davidson and Truth," in *Truth and Interpretation: Perspectives on the Philosophy of Donald Davidson*, ed. Ernest LePore (New York, 1986), pp. 333-355, here pp. 334-335. Rorty would not approve of the particular twist I give to his terminology.

14. Barnes and Bloor, "Relativism, Rationalism and the Sociology of Knowledge," p. 30.

15. I do not claim to be faithful to Horkheimer's understanding of dialectic in what follows. While the "for us/for them" terminology is intended to remind the reader of Hegel's dialectical approach in the *Phenomenology of Spirit,* in crossing it with the terminology of "dialogue" I am giving it a Gadamerian twist.

16. P. Winch, "Understanding a Primitive Society," in *Rationality,* ed. Bryan Wilson (New York, 1971), pp. 78-111, here p. 102.

17. Note that this is meant to be an account of certain aspects of the *logic* of the encounter between different worldviews and forms of life. In actual fact, of course, understanding alien cultures usually takes the form of a monologue, with imperialist overtones, in which "they" can gain a voice only to the extent that they learn to speak the hegemonic language, that is, become "modernized." Moreover, as I am concerned here to undercut relativism, I accentuate the negative: what we cannot accept; and neglect the positive: the suggestive possibilities from which we can learn. The importance of these qualifications on my argument were brought home to me by Carlos Thiebaut.

18. Charles Taylor, "Rationality," in *Rationality and Relativism*, pp. 87-105, here pp. 101-103. Compare Habermas's account of basic, species-wide, cognitive interests in *Knowledge and Human Interests* (Boston, 1971).

19. A. MacIntyre, "Rationality and the Explanation of Action," in A. MacIntyre, *Against the Self-Images of the Age* (London, 1971), pp. 244-259, here p. 252.

20. See, for instance, J. Habermas, *The Theory of Communicative Action I: Reason and the Rationalization of Society* (Boston, 1984), pp. 102-136.

21. Barnes and Bloor, "Relativism, Rationalism and the Sociology of Knowledge," p. 28.

22. On this point see Gary Gutting, "The Strong Program in the Sociology of Knowledge," in *Scientific Rationality*, pp. 95-112.

23. D. Davidson, "Psychology as Philosophy," in *Essays on Actions and Events* (Oxford, 1980), pp. 229-244, here p. 238. In "A Coherence Theory of Truth and Knowledge," in *Truth and Interpretation*, pp. 307-319, he characterizes this as a "methodological necessity" of correct interpretation (p. 316), an idea that I render below in terms of the "pragmatic constraints" on interpretation.

24. Steven Lukes runs through some of these different versions in "Relativism in Its Place," in *Rationality and Relativism*, pp. 261-305.

25. A. MacIntyre, "Is Understanding a Religion Compatible with Believing?" in *Rationality*, pp. 62-77.

26. A similar point, that there can be no absolute separation between understanding past systems of belief and relating them to present concerns and criteria, is argued by Richard Rorty, J. B. Schneewind, and Quentin Skinner in their editors' introduction to *Philosophy and History* (Cambridge, 1984), pp. 1-14. On p. 8 they write: "The idea of 'the truth about the past, uncontaminated by present perspectives or concerns' . . . is a romantic ideal of purity which has no relation to any actual inquiry which human beings have undertaken or could undertake." In his own contribution to the volume "The Historiography of Philosophy: Four Genres" (pp. 49-75) Rorty puts the point as follows: "Ayers overdoes the opposition between 'our terms' and 'his terms' when he suggests that one can do historical reconstruction first and leave rational reconstruction for later. The two genres can never be *that* independent, because you will not know much about what the dead meant prior to figuring out how much truth they knew. These two topics should be seen as moments in a continuing movement around the hermeneutic circle, a circle one has to have gone round a good many times before one can begin to do *either* sort of reconstruction" (p. 53). In the same essay Rorty explicitly invokes a dialogue (or "conversation") model to capture the relation between the historian of philosophy and "the mighty dead" (p. 51). But it does not play the same role in his argument as it does in mine, since he applies it only to the case of rational reconstruction, and since even this application is presented in a one-sided manner: the point of such conversation, he tells us, is "to assure ourselves that there has been rational progress in the course of recorded history—that we differ from our ancestors on grounds which

our ancestors could be led to accept" (ibid.). Like Gadamer, I want to allow for the possibility, indeed the certainty, that conversation with the past can also show us where we went wrong. As his discussion of another genre, *Geistesgeschichte*, suggests, Rorty would probably not disagree with this; but he takes such observations as automatically supporting the relativist, whereas I construe them as placing the interpreter, at least implicitly, in the position of one arguing about which beliefs are warranted or rationally acceptable.

27. This is a modification of the position I defended in "Reflections on Rationalization in *The Theory of Communicative Action,*" in *Habermas and Modernity,* ed. R. Bernstein (Cambridge, Mass., 1985), pp. 177-191, esp. 183-186. While I also argued there that the interpreter is not an ideally neutral spectator, I did not see this as entailing implicit evaluations of the others' beliefs and their reasons for holding them.

Relativism, Value-Freedom, and the Sociology of Science

Russell Keat

I

Since its inception in the work of the classical social theorists the sociology of knowledge—or as some would prefer, of belief—has generated an extensive array of debates about relativism. A central question has been whether the very existence of social determinants for beliefs makes it impossible to regard them as true or rational in any absolute sense, and this has proved especially contentious in the case of scientific beliefs, at least for the many who, whilst happily conceding some form of relativism for moral and political beliefs, are loath to accept a relativist view of science. Hence, if the social determination of beliefs does entail relativism, and scientific or cognitive relativism is to be avoided, definite limits must be placed upon the legitimate domain of inquiry for a sociology of belief. It must confine itself to the study of the nonscientific beliefs, among which may perhaps also be included the results of quite clearly defective or spurious attempts at science.

In rejecting this "limitation thesis" (LT) a number of different arguments have been invoked by those who insist on pursuing the project of an unrestricted sociology of scientific knowledge. Some have declared the question of relativism an exclusively philosophical one: if the discovery of social determinants for scientific beliefs causes difficulties for (nonrelativist) philosophers, so be it—let them deal with their own problems. Others have argued that if the social determination of scientific beliefs entails cognitive relativism, then, since such determinants can in fact be identified, this should simply be taken to provide support for relativism—"philosophical" objections notwithstanding. Others again have similarly been unconcerned by the relativistic implications of their work, but for the additional reason that they believe

272

cognitive relativism to be justified anyway on independent grounds.

Just such a variety of attitudes can be discerned among advocates of the "strong programme" (SP) for the sociology of science, initially developed in the work of David Bloor and Barry Barnes in the mid-1970s and subsequently providing the methodological rationale for the empirical research of the so-called 'Edinburgh School.'[1] Opposed to the LT in any form, the SP's advocates have often focused their criticisms upon one especially influential version of it. According to this no sociological (causal) explanations are permissible for *rational* scientific beliefs, which are instead to be noncausally "explained" by the procedure of rational reconstruction: by demonstrating how their acceptance satisfies the requirements of some philosophically preferred conception of rationality.[2] By contrast, proponents of the SP have tended to regard the concept of rationality as having no place in a properly scientific study of science. Their program commits them, instead, to identifying the social determinants of all "scientific" beliefs—defined merely as whichever are regarded as such by relevant social groups—irrespective of their truth or falsity, rationality or irrationality, or conformity to any philosophical prescriptions for genuine scientificity; and for good measure the SP asserts that sociological enquiries conducted in its name are likewise subject to social determination.

Both critics and advocates of the SP have largely agreed that the program entails some form of cognitive relativism.[3] For some critics, admittedly, it is the substantive character of the research performed under the SP's auspices that has chiefly been faulted, the program's relativism being merely noted *en passant.* For others, however, it is precisely the SP's relativism that has been seen as providing the main grounds for rejecting it; and among these are some who have viewed the program as especially vulnerable to a version of the self-refutation argument against relativism. In response to the charge of relativism the SP's advocates have displayed either mild embarrassment, studied indifference, or open celebration—so that by some, indeed, it has actually been called "The Empirical Programme of Relativism."[4]

It is this widely shared belief in the SP's relativism that I shall contest. The program, I shall argue, neither implies nor necessarily assumes any form of cognitive relativism. Undeniably, most of its proponents in fact subscribe to some such view. But this is due either to their regarding it as entailed by the SP itself or to their being convinced of it on independent grounds. I shall thus be providing a defense of the program against criticisms based on its supposed relativism—though this defense will hardly be welcomed by many of its proponents. Nor will they be likely to welcome my further claim that, partly through misconceptions about the SP's relativism and what this would imply, the research inspired by the program is subjected to unfortunate and unnecessary theoretical limitations. Ultimately, I shall suggest, these involve a failure to explore just those issues that would be most relevant to a properly, sociologically, informed discussion of cognitive relativism itself. More obviously, they remove from the program's agenda a range of politically significant questions about the social organization of scientific practice—such as what, if any, are the cultural conditions which support or undermine the process of rational scientific enquiry. Such questions, according to the SP's proponents, cannot be addressed by a strictly scientific sociology of scientific beliefs, since they employ normative concepts of "rationality" and hence require the sociologist to make a certain kind of (intrinsically unscientific) "value-judgment."

It is by exploring this (at least implicit) idea of a value-free sociology of science that I shall criticize the view that cognitive relativism is entailed by the SP and attempt to free it from its advocates' self-imposed limitations. Working from a general consideration of value-free social science, in which the relevant normative concepts are traditionally of a political or moral nature, I shall outline a conception of value-freedom according to which the claims of such a science can and should be assessed independently of value-judgments employing the concepts of "justice," "freedom," and the like. But, I shall argue, this doctrine of value-freedom need not rely upon a relativist view of values, and neither does it require the elimination of such concepts in framing or answering legitimate theoretical questions. Analogously, I shall suggest, the descriptive and explanatory claims of a value-free sociology of science, for which the relevant normative concepts are those of "rationality," "scientificity," and so on, are independent of value-judgments employing these concepts. But this does not require the assumption of cognitive relativism, nor does it rule out the use of specific conceptions of rationality or scientificity in identifying and resolving theoretical problems.[5]

More generally, I shall suggest, the question of cognitive relativism should be seen to bear a similar, and similarly complex, relationship to the assumptions and findings of the sociology of science as that of moral relativism does to sociological investigations that deal with moral and political beliefs. In both cases a properly value-free sociology may well produce results· that are relevant in various ways to the philosophical issue of relativism. But relativism is neither directly implied nor necessarily assumed by the possibility of a scientific sociology of beliefs.

I shall proceed in the following manner. After some preliminary remarks in section II about the formulation of the SP and the concepts of relativism and scientific rationality, I turn in section III to examine the idea of value-freedom in the social sciences and to show that certain further doctrines often associated with this are not in fact entailed by it. In section IV I present the main features of a value-free sociology of science, giving particular attention to the place within it of conceptions of scientific rationality; and in section V I offer some possible diagnoses for the SP's having been thought to entail certain views which—understood as (cognitively) value-free sociology of science—it does not, including cognitive relativism. I conclude, in section VI, by indicating how the possible results of sociological inquiries about scientific beliefs might bear upon the problem of cognitive relativism.

II

The basic features of the SP are normally taken to be defined by the following four tenets:

1. *Causality:* It would be causal, that is, concerned with the conditions which bring about belief or states of knowledge. Naturally there will be other types of causes apart from social ones which will cooperate in bringing about belief.
2. *Impartiality:* It would be impartial with respect to truth and falsity, rationality or irrationality, success or failure. Both sides of these dichotomies will require explanation.
3. *Symmetry:* It would be symmetrical in its style of explanation. The same types of cause would explain, say, true and false beliefs.
4. *Reflexivity:* It would be reflexive. In principle its patterns of explanation would have to be applicable to sociology itself. Like the requirement of symmetry, this is a response to the need to seek for general explanations. It is an obvious requirement of principle because otherwise sociology would be a standing refutation of its own theories.[6]

Critical discussions of the program have identified a number of issues concerning the precise sense of each tenet and the logical relationships between them.[7] I shall comment briefly on some that will prove relevant at various points later on.

The first set of problems concern tenet 1. From this it seems clear that the SP does not assert that all scientific beliefs are determined exclusively by social factors: within its overall commitment to complete causal determination some possible explanatory power is allowed to nonsocial factors. This raises the question of how "strong" the SP actually is,[8] and indeed of whether the program is genuinely testable without further specification of the relative significance to be ascribed to social and nonsocial determinants. More important, for my purposes, is the question of how the distinction between these is itself to be drawn.

In implicit answer to this, advocates of the SP have cited some or all of the following as paradigmatically nonsocial determinants: biological, or biologically grounded, factors such as innate features of the human species' sensory mechanisms, or forms of "natural rationality"—that is, any genetically programed capacity for, or tendency toward, certain modes of reasoning; psychological characteristics of individuals which are not themselves amenable to sociological explanation; and "external reality" itself. I shall focus on just one question of the many raised by this: Are what may be termed "accepted norms of scientific rationality" to be regarded as social or as nonsocial determinants?

At least prima facie, members of scientific communities typically endorse various principles of argumentation and reasoning as properly governing the acceptance or rejection of one another's scientific claims. To what extent, if any, these norms of reasoning actually influence their beliefs is an empirically open question. But whether these are deemed "social" or "nonsocial" will significantly affect both the content and the plausibility of specific SP-explanations for scientific beliefs. Unlike, it seems, many proponents of the SP, I can see little reason to deny a social status to such norms of rationality—unless, of course, they are largely explicable in biological terms, and hence belong to the category of "natural" rationality.[9]

The second set of problems concern tenets 2 and 3. In support of the former, proponents of the SP have sometimes claimed that it is impossible to distinguish, for example, rational from irrational (scientific) beliefs. But I shall take it that this is not entailed by tenet 2 itself, which commits one only to regarding such distinctions as *irrelevant* to the explanation of beliefs—the precise nature of this (ir)relevance can be left unspecified for the moment. In the case of tenet 3 two related problems may be noted. First, there is an apparent ambiguity in the sense to be given to "the same types of cause." Does the "sameness" here consist in there being *social* determination in both cases, or in there being the same *types* of social determinants for both? Whichever answer is given, a second problem arises: Should tenet 3 be taken to assert that there are *in fact* "the same types of cause" for, for example, both rational and irrational beliefs; or only that one should not, in advance of empirical research, assume that the two necessarily differ in this respect? The former is perhaps the more plausible reading of tenet 3; the latter, I shall argue later, is the more plausible view.[10]

Finally, some remarks about tenet 4. To those who are impressed by self-refutation arguments against relativism it might seem that this assertion of "reflexivity" makes the SP peculiarly vulnerable. But as some commentators have noted, tenet 4 is effectively entailed by tenet 1, so that if there are difficulties of this kind for the SP, they are not generated by tenet 4 itself. However, since I shall be arguing that the program (with or without tenet 4) does not entail relativism, such issues will not require attention.

What now needs clarification is the nature of the SP's supposed relativism. I shall focus upon what has been the main concern of both advocates and critics, namely, relativism with respect to scientific rationality. Adopting the customary (though by no means unproblematic) distinctions between moral and cognitive relativism,[11] and within the latter between ontological and epistemological relativism, this can be located as a particular form of the last of these. I shall ignore the question of whether epistemological relativism can be defended without commitment to ontological relativism, merely noting that at least some proponents of the SP are apparently happy to espouse the former whilst continuing to talk of "external reality"—for instance, as a nonsocial (though only partial) determinant of scientific beliefs.

Relativism concerning scientific rationality can be understood in the following manner. The work of, for example, inductivist or hypothetico-deductivist philosophers of science may be regarded as an attempt to specify certain rules or standards by which the truth or falsity of scientific theories and, hence, the rationality or otherwise of their acceptance are to be judged. Such proposals thus involve both the articulation of a specific conception of scientific rationality and the claim that this is the proper basis upon which scientific beliefs should be assessed.[12] By contrast the relativist maintains that there are a number—perhaps an indefinite number—of actual and possible conceptions of rationality, but that no one of these can be shown to be superior to all others. Hence, although one can determine whether, and to what extent, the acceptance of a scientific belief is "rational" with respect to some particular such conception, one cannot show that it is rational in any absolute sense, since no one conception of rationality can itself be justified and thereby shown to be correct. (For convenience I shall from now on refer to this specific form of epistemological relativism simply as "cognitive relativism.")

A similar characterization can be given for the kind of *moral* relativism which will figure significantly in what follows. Assuming such relativism is applicable to political as well as moral values, I shall indicate its nature in the case of justice—in particular, justice concerning the distribution of social goods. One can find within political philosophy a number of distinct and competing conceptions of justice: egalitarian principles; desert-based principles invoking criteria such as skill, output, or effort; need-based principles; Rawls' difference principle; Nozick's noncoercive transfers; and so on. Defenders of such conceptions typically maintain that a society's actual distribution of social goods should be judged by reference to their preferred criteria: "justice requires that . . . ," and hence the distribution is legitimately criticized to the extent that these requirements are not met. By contrast, then, the moral relativist will assert that although one can show that a society's distribution of social goods is just or unjust relative to a particular conception of justice, there is no way of showing that one such conception is itself uniquely preferable or correct. Hence, no absolute judgments of the justice or injustice of particular distributions can be rationally justified: nothing is just or unjust *tout court.*

Two further points about both forms of relativism can be noted here. The first concerns the fact that in making judgments such as "X is rational" or "Y is unjust" one is normally taken to be (among other things) expressing some kind of approval or disapproval, support or criticism, praise or condemnation, of the item concerned. This can be termed the "appraising force" of the judgment, and its presence is at least partly constitutive of something's being a *value-judgment.* (To talk of value-judgments in this way does not, of course, commit one to an expressivist metaethics.) I shall assume that this feature of such judgments is preseved in a relativist account, but I shall leave open the question whether the relativist's rejection of "absolute" justifications undermines also any justification for a value-judgment's appraising force.

The second point is this. In support of these forms of relativism claims of one or both of the following kinds may sometimes be made: (i) that different conceptions of rationality/justice have in fact been endorsed by different scientific communities/social groups at different times; (ii) that sociological explanations can be provided for such variations. What degree of support is provided for relativism by (i) and (ii)—themselves often, though misleadingly, termed "sociological relativism"—will be addressed briefly in section VI: they will not be taken as constitutive elements of either cognitive or moral relativism in the ensuing discussion.

III

The central thesis involved in the idea of a value-free social science can be presented as follows: The truth or falsity of descriptive and explanatory claims in the social sciences is logically independent of the acceptance or rejection of any value-judgments about what is referred to in such claims.

I shall not here attempt to defend this thesis—henceforth, VF— since my main concern is to show that certain further theses often associated with VF are not entailed by it, and the implications of this for the nature of a value-free sociology of science.[13] But before doing so, some remarks are necessary about this formulation of the doctrine of value-freedom.

First, although VF is presented here in a realist vocabulary, both for convenience and from conviction, it could easily be translated into a form compatible with at least several versions of instrumentalism or pragmatism. Second, the formulation is somewhat narrower in scope than is usual, in that the range of value-judgments is restricted to those directed at items referred to in the relevant descriptive and explanatory claims. This is a convenient limitation that could be removed if necessary. Third, VF does not straightforwardly support a practical maxim of the form "Do not allow your assessment of a (social) scientific claim to be influenced by your commitment to any value-judgments." Such an implication would obtain only if the maxim were modified so as to read "*improperly* influenced," as a result of which it might become vacuous.

Finally, whilst VF clearly depends upon some version of the dichotomy between "facts and values" (or better, perhaps, between "the world and its evaluation"), it is compatible with a considerable variety of metaethical positions concerning the cognitive status of value-judgments, including both those which allow, and those which deny, the ascription of truth-values to such judgments. (My use, in VF, of the phrase "acceptance or rejection" in relation to value-judgments is intended to mark this neutrality.) Hence, as will now be briefly argued, VF does not entail the following:

NVF (1): no rational justification can be provided for value-judgments.

Undeniably, NVF (1) can be used to support an argument for VF, and indeed many proponents of VF, such as Weber, have done just this. The argument runs along the following lines: social science must produce rationally justifiable knowledge-claims; value-judgments are not rationally justifiable; *ergo* social science must be value-free. But the question remains of whether VF *requires* the assumption of NVF (1)— of whether there are alternative arguments for VF which do not rely on such skepticism about value-judgments.

That there are is supported by the following considerations. All the advocates of VF need maintain is that the acceptance or rejection of value-judgments about the objects of inquiry are *irrelevant* to the truth or falsity of its descriptive and explanatory claims. The criteria of validity for these claims must be logically distinct from those governing value-judgments. But there is no need to assert that value-judgments lack any such criteria, and are hence not rationally justifiable. (To put this point another way: VF does not require the assumption of scientism, that is, of the view that science is the only genuine form of human knowledge.) Hence, for example, both Kantian and subjectivist views of the cognitive status of value-judgments are equally consistent with the doctrine of value-freedom. A fortiori, VF does not require the assumption of moral relativism, and there is no need to spell out here the relativist's somewhat complex attitude toward NVF (1) itself.

Similarly brief consideration can now be given to a further thesis, sometimes thought to be implied by the doctrine of value-freedom, namely:

> NVF (2): no reference can be made in a social science to the (moral and political) values of those whom it investigates.

It is rare to find explicit arguments aimed at showing that NVF (2) is implied by VF: more often the claim that it is seems due to simple misunderstanding. It may, perhaps, be thought that value-free descriptions of the values which other people accept—that is, of their moral and political beliefs—are particularly difficult to achieve. But it is far from clear why this should be so, and to support such optimism, one might reasonably note that the truth or falsity of statements reporting beliefs is independent of the truth or falsity of the reported beliefs. Hence, for example, the claim that members of a certain social group endorse some particular view of justice is itself neutral with respect to the merits of that view.[14]

More worthy of attention, however—since it raises issues that will prove important later on—are the relationships between both VF and NVF (2), and the substantive claims of what may broadly be termed *materialist* social theories, such as Marxism. One can define such a theory as maintaining both

(i)   that the values accepted by social groups have little if any explanatory power, and

(ii) that the acceptance of these values can itself be explained primarily by reference to "material" conditions—"material" being taken to exclude, at the very least, any processes of a ratiocinative or reflective nature.

Clearly, the truth of these claims neither implies nor is implied by NVF (2): indeed they could not be established without rejecting this thesis, since the ascription of what is basically an epiphenomenal status to "accepted values" requires that descriptive statements can be made about them. But whether these materialist claims are correct is itself a substantive theoretical question, contested for example in Weber's disagreement with Marx in his (nonmaterialist) account of the Protestant ethic's role in the historical emergence of modern capitalism. What the doctrine of value-freedom maintains is that the significant differences between Marx's and Weber's political values are irrelevant to the resolution of this explanatory dispute, like any others.

More complex issues, however, are raised by a further thesis often thought to be implied by VF, namely:

NVF (3): social science must not employ any normative concepts in its descriptive and explanatory claims.

Without attempting a strict definition of "normative concept," I shall take it that justice, freedom, alienation, exploitation, and so on are paradigmatic instances of this kind, and that this is so by virtue of their typically being understood to (at least partly) indicate the appraising force expressed in the value-judgments which employ them.

To show that NVF (3) does not follow from VF it will be convenient to proceed by considering some hypothetical examples of social scientific claims involving the concept of justice. The first involves its possible use in providing explanations for some social phenomenon. Suppose that the collapse of a political regime is said to have been due to its injustice, in particular the injustice of its pattern of economic distribution. (This explanation is, of course, to be distinguished from one which refers instead to the distributive pattern's being perceived or regarded as unjust by certain social groups.) Such an explanation, I shall argue, is compatible with the doctrine of value-freedom provided that the concept of justice is being employed in what may be termed a *purely characterizing* manner: namely, one in which both the "correctness" or justifiability of the concept(ion) of justice involved, and the appraising force of its normal use, are put aside or "suspended."[15]

For example, suppose that the specific conception of justice involved in the claim "the regime fell because of its injustice" is egalitarian. Then the truth of this explanatory claim can be assessed independently of whether economic equality *is* "what justice requires," that is, independently of whether the egalitarian conception of justice is correct or rationally justified; and the question of whether the unequal pattern of distribution caused the regime's downfall can be answered without either endorsing or rejecting the appraising force normally expressed by statements employing the concept of justice.

Some further comments need now to be made about this. First, in

using the concept of justice in this purely characterizing manner it is
essential that one indicates clearly the specific conception of justice
involved; otherwise fruitless debates may be generated through mere
ambiguity. Second, any such conception must be operationalizable, that
is, it must meet the standard requirements imposed upon scientific
concepts with respect to the testability of statements which employ
them. (To accept such requirements does not commit one to a verificationist or operationalist theory of meaning, however.) The egalitarian
conception of justice, fairly obviously, meets this condition; so too, it
could be argued, does Nozick's transfer principle, Rawls's difference
principle, and many others. It will, of course, be no easy matter to
determine whether a pattern of economic distribution meets, for example, the difference principle, since this will depend on answering counterfactual questions about the effects of alternative distributions on the
amounts of goods possessed by various social groups. But such epistemic difficulties are hardly peculiar to conceptions of justice: they are a
commonplace of scientific enquiry.

Third, this characterizing use of normative concepts is compatible
not only with the doctrine of value-freedom but also with moral relativism. Indeed, what the moral relativist says about concepts such as
justice fits very well with the account so far given of their characterizing
use. For the relativist will maintain that while one cannot rationally
justify any particular conception of justice, and hence cannot show that
a state of affairs is just or unjust *tout court,* one *can* determine its justice
or injustice relative to the criteria specified in some particular such
conception. But it is precisely this possibility which the purely characterizing use of normative concepts depends upon, together with the
suspension of the appraising force typically implied by their employment in making value-judgments. The characterizing claims of a value-
free science can thus be assessed independently of the correctness of, for
example, the specific conception of justice involved, and, hence, also
independently of whether rational justifications of such conceptions are
possible—that is, of the question of relativism itself. So value-freedom
does not entail either NVF (3) or moral relativism, and moral relativism
is, like value-freedom, consistent with the denial of NVF (3).

Similiar points apply to the use of normative concepts in specifying a domain of inquiry or in posing explanatory questions, as distinct
from their use in making explanatory claims of the kind indicated
earlier. Thus the doctrine of value-freedom does not rule out posing
such questions as: What explains the injustice (or the unjust character)
of some society's pattern of economic distribution; to what extent was
this determined by the nature of its political system; and so on? Like-

wise, a value-free social science may legitimately address more general theoretical questions such as: What, if any, are the necessary and/or sufficient conditions (political, cultural, economic, and so on) for distributive justice; is the capitalist mode of production intrinsically incompatible with distributive justice—and if so, what exactly is it about capitalism that explains this; and so on? These questions can be both asked and answered consistently with VF, provided that the conditions noted above for the characterizing use of normative concepts are fully met.

The view of value-freedom and its implications that is being defended here may be illuminated by contrasting it with two mutually oppposing attitudes often adopted toward Marxist social theory. According to one, Marxism is to be rejected as unscientific because it addresses such issues as: What are the determinants of alienated human activity, or what are the effects upon political systems of exploitative relations of production? The very terms in which these questions are posed, it is argued, show that Marxist theory is not properly value-free. According to the other, however, it is the doctrine of value-freedom itself that is at fault, since it prohibits investigation of precisely those issues which Marxism rightly addresses. Marxist social theory is thus to be applauded for rejecting the straightjacket of value-free "scientificity."

But both these attitudes should themselves be rejected, since they assume that VF entails NVF (3). A social theory which refused to ask and answer the kinds of questions which Marxism addresses would indeed be politically impoverished. But there is no need for a value-free social theory to suffer this. Nonetheless, as will now be argued, in refusing the unnecessary limitations which would be imposed by NFV (3), the work of social theorists becomes vulnerable to a certain kind of normative criticism which cannot straightforwardly be dismissed by invoking the doctrine of value-freedom.

Suppose that one has put forward some theoretical explanation of why it is that capitalism necessarily generates, or tends to generate, distributive injustice. Two kinds of objection may be raised: first, that the proposed explanation is false, or at least insufficiently well supported to render even its provisional acceptance rational; and second, that the conception of justice involved is itself objectionable—that there is no good reason to employ this particular conception since, for example, it gives insufficient attention to the requirements of desert, property rights, or such like.

The two kinds of criticism are, of course, entirely distinct: the theory's explanatory claims may perfectly well be true, despite the failings of its conception of justice; and vice versa. This much is ensured by the idea of value-freedom. But value-freedom does not protect social theorists from the latter kind of criticism, which concerns, one might say, the normative significance of their theoretical work rather than its scientific credibility. An analogy may be helpful here. One can—and should—distinguish between the adequacy of a solution and the significance of the problem it is intended to resolve. There can be good solutions to insignificant problems and bad solutions to significant ones. The doctrine of value-freedom requires one to recognize this distinction, but it does not absolve one from normative criticism of the concepts employed in specifying theoretical problems.[16]

IV

The preceding account of value-freedom in the social sciences can now be used to articulate the nature of a value-free sociology of science. The basic move is to apply what has been said about moral and political values, such as justice, to cognitive "values": in particular, to (scientific) rationality. By doing so, I will argue, one can see that a value-free sociology of science does not require the assumption of cognitive relativism with respect to rationality; that it does not rule out the possibility of nonmaterialist explanations which refer to the conception(s) of rationality accepted by members of a scientific community; and that it allows the characterizing use of specific conceptions of rationality in the identification of legitimate theoretical questions about its domain of enquiry.

First, then, how will the doctrine of value-freedom itself apply in the case of a value-free sociology of science? VF will now read as follows:

> The truth or falsity of descriptive and explanatory claims about scientific beliefs is logically independent of the acceptance or rejection of any value-judgments concerning the rationality of those beliefs.

Drawing upon what has been said earlier about the use of normative concepts in making value-judgments, one can regard such judgments about the rationality of a scientific belief as expressing some favourable or unfavourable appraisal of the belief by virtue of its meeting or failing to meet some preferred conception of rationality. So the descriptive and explanatory claims of a value-free sociology of science are to be independent both of the endorsement or rejection of such appraisals and of the correctness or justifiability of the conception(s) of rationality they employ.

One can now go on to consider in turn the implications for a value-free sociology of science of VF's not entailing any of NVF (1)–(3). First, since VF does not entail that value-judgments cannot be rationally justified (NVF [1]), it does not entail that no justification can be provided for value-judgments about the rationality of scientific beliefs. That such judgments cannot be rationally justified would, of course, provide a possible reason for insisting upon value-freedom in the sociology of science. But it is not a necessary one: all that VF requires to be assumed is that these judgments are irrelevant in assessing the sociology of science's claims about scientific beliefs. Further, since VF does not entail NVF (1), it is perfectly compatible with both relativist and nonrelativist views of scientific rationality. Thus a value-free sociology of science need not, at least on these grounds, involve commitment to cognitive relativism.

Next, since VF does not imply NVF (2), a value-free sociology of science is not barred from making descriptive and explanatory claims about the conceptions of rationality that may actually be accepted by the members of a scientific community or of other social groups. The truth or falsity of claims made about these "accepted values" is to be assessed independently of endorsing or rejecting these values. Further, what degree of explanatory power such accepted values may have, and what are the determinants of their *being* accepted, are to be regarded as essentially open substantive theoretical questions to be answered in a value-free manner. Hence, for example, it might be the case that a broadly materialist social theory of science is correct. But the basic project of a sociology of science cannot assume this a priori, and certainly it is not implied by its proper commitment to value-freedom. (The question of whether a scientific community's accepted conception of rationality is rightly regarded as a *social* determinant will be discussed later.)

Finally, since VF does not imply NVF (3), a value-free sociology of science is not prohibited from employing the normative concept of scientific rationality, provided that this is used in a purely characterizing manner. This means that the particular conception of rationality involved, which should itself be appropriately operationalizable, must be clearly specified; that the appraising force of the concept's use in (cognitive) value-judgments be suspended; and that likewise suspended is any claim to the effect that this particular conception of scientific rationality is itself correct or justifiable. These characterizing uses of the concept of rationality are thus compatible with both relativist and nonrelativist views about scientific rationality. Further, the possibility of such uses is itself supported by the relativist's claim that while no scientific belief can be shown to be rational *tout court,* what can be determined is whether a belief is rational with respect to some specified conception of rationality.[17]

Thus a value-free sociology of science may legitimately address questions such as the following: What are the effects of different forms of organization within scientific communities on their ability to generate rational scientific beliefs; what kinds of political and economic systems either favor or undermine these forms of organization, and hence their respective likelihoods of success in producing such beliefs; what, if any, are the cultural preconditions for the practice of rational scientific belief-formation; and so on?[18] Such questions—like their counterparts concerning the relationships between economic systems and distributive justice—are clearly of some political significance. A sociology of science which refused to address them would be considerably impoverished, but fortunately the doctrine of value-freedom does not impose this self-denying ordinance.

Yet neither does it protect the sociologist of science from criticism which is directed against the conception of scientific rationality that has been employed in asking such questions, and which thereby also challenges whatever political conclusions might otherwise be drawn from the suggested answers. If the theory proposed has used a conception of rationality that the critic regards as defective or unjustifiable, then the significance of its results may legitimately be challenged. The sociology of science is as vulnerable as any other area of social theory to the charge of providing excellent solutions to pseudoproblems or poor solutions to genuine ones. One can construct a successful science of pseudoscience or an unsuccessful science of genuine science. What the doctrine of value-freedom insists is only that the two kinds of failure be kept distinct.

However, the reference here to the ideas of genuine and pseudoscience raises two further issues about value-freedom in the sociology of science which somewhat complicate the preceding account. The first is this. It might be argued that the concept of rationality is so central to what is meant by calling something a (genuine) science, or by terming a belief (genuinely) scientific, that sociologists of science must employ *some* reasonably plausible conception of rationality in identifying their domain of inquiry. Otherwise, their work simply would not deserve the title of a sociology of "science." So the characterizing use of conceptions of rationality is not merely permissible, as has so far been maintained; rather, it is essential.

This line of argument has sometimes been offered as a criticism of the SP, whose proponents have generally claimed that the program *must* define its object-domain only as consisting of whatever has been *regard-*

ed as scientific by the members of relevant social groups—apparently on the grounds that any "epistemologically" based definition would fall foul of the program's own commitment both to (cognitive) value-neutrality and to relativism. I have already argued that neither of these provides grounds for prohibiting the characterizing use of conceptions of rationality, and hence that sociologists of science are perfectly at liberty to define their object-domain in ways that make use of such conceptions. However, what of the claim that this is not merely optional but required?

While this view has certain merits, its critical implications are less far-reaching than may initially appear. First, those who are disinclined—for whatever reason—to accept this requirement can respond by allowing that their work is to be taken "only" as a sociology of what are regarded as scientific beliefs by certain social groups, and by retitling their inquirers accordingly. Next, it may in any case turn out that the set of beliefs they thereby investigate more or less coincides extensionally with those that satisfy the conception of genuine scientificity insisted upon by their critics. Finally, the actual explanatory claims made by the sociologist concerning "beliefs that are merely regarded as scientific" are not themselves rendered defective by the possible failure of those beliefs to satisfy an epistemologically preferred criterion of scientificity.

The second, and partly related, issue is this. I have so far assumed, for the sake of convenience, that conceptions of scientific rationality involve only the specification of what standards have to be met by a belief for its possible acceptance to be rational. But it may be argued that for someone's actual acceptance of a belief to be rational it is not sufficient that the belief meets the specified standards. What is also necessary is that the person's acceptance of the belief is actually due to, or determined by, their regarding it as meeting those standards. Likewise, "genuinely scientific beliefs" are those which not only meet such criteria but are accepted because of their being thought to do so. That there are good reasons for a belief does not by itself make its acceptance by someone rational; the reasons must, as it were, be causally operative.

I shall call a conception of scientific rationality which includes this additional causal requirement, a "type-(2)" conception, to distinguish it from the "type-(1)" conceptions so far considered. There is no question here of debating their respective merits: they are designed for different purposes and are not in competition with one another. But it is worth noting briefly some implications of employing type-(2) conceptions of rationality in the kinds of characterizing use of normative concepts previously discussed. In particular, suppose that such a conception were employed in specifying the overall object-domain for a sociology of science. Then, in effect, a good deal of empirical investigation would be necessary before such a sociology could even begin: enough would have to be known about the determinants of "scientific" beliefs to ensure that they qualified as type-(2) rational beliefs.

There is nothing intrinsically objectionable in this—in adopting, that is, a theory-loaded criterion for domain-specification. Nonetheless, there are some persuasive pragmatic reasons against such use of type-(2) conceptions of rationality in the sociology of science. In particular, an unnecessarily cumbersome terminology would be required in asking, as a substantive theoretical question, whether a scientific community's acceptance of type-(1) conceptions of rationality was in fact causally operative in determining their "scientific" beliefs, as distinct from other possible determinants. It is surely more convenient to be able to ask, as a question *within* the sociology of *science,* to what extent beliefs that are type-(1) rational have also been type-(2) rational. In what follows, therefore, I shall continue to use "rational" to mean type-(1) rational unless otherwise indicated.

V

It was noted at the outset that both advocates and critics of the SP generally agree that the programme entails cognitive relativism. By contrast I have been arguing that to the extent at least that the program is taken simply to specify the basic features of a properly scientific, and hence (cognitively) value-free, sociology of science there are no good grounds for thinking this. I have also argued that neither value-freedom nor cognitive relativism would justify the exclusion of conceptions of rationality from the theoretical vocabulary of such a "science of science"; nor would it rule out in principle the ascription of explanatory power to the conceptions of rationality accepted by members of a scientific community.

I shall now suggest some possible reasons which might lead an advocate of the SP to make these (in my view) mistaken claims, and thereby also potentially to confuse its critics. In doing so I shall return at times to various problems in the formulation of the program noted earlier. I begin by considering the program's "origins" in its opposition to the limitation thesis (LT) and suggest how mistakes about the SP's commitment to relativism could be generated by this.

According to what is in this context the relevant version of the LT, neither causal explanations in general, nor sociological explanations in particular, are to be provided for rational scientific beliefs, which are

instead to be noncausally explained by the procedure of rational reconstruction. This basically consists in showing how they satisfy the requirements of some conception of rationality, and are hence such that it
would be rational for members of the relevant scientific community to
accept them. (Clearly, only a type-(1) conception of rationality would be
suitable for this task.) For reasons by now familiar, the operation of this
procedure requires at least that the conception of rationality be suitably
operationalizable, so that it can be used to make purely characterizing
claims about whether a particular belief is or is not rational. Such
characterizing claims do not, of themselves, involve commitment to
either a relativist or a nonrelativist view of scientific rationality. But it
can plausibly be argued that any advocate of the LT in this rational
reconstructionist version *is* committed, at least for all practical purposes, to rejecting cognitive relativism concerning scientific rationality.

This can be seen from the following considerations. Advocates of
the LT are concerned to put boundaries upon the legitimate object-
domain for a sociology of belief—to identify what can and cannot be
subject to sociological explanation. But if a relativist view of scientific
rationality were accepted, then either the boundaries drawn would, as it
were, be constantly shifting in relation to each "equally (un)justifiable"
conception of reality; or it would have to be admitted that, in drawing a
single determinate boundary by reference to just one such conception, a
purely arbitrary decision was being made. Clearly, the central purpose of
the LT would be undermined by these consequences of cognitive relativism.

Thus, while the procedure of rational reconstruction can be oper-
ated without commitment to nonrelational, its employment in the service of the LT does involve such commitment. Imagine, now, someone
considering the merits of the LT, who is already convinced of the virtues
of cognitive relativism—a person, say, who had been favorably impressed by the various broadly relativist views which emerged in the
postpositivist epistemology of the 1960s and 70s, or who had indeed
contributed to these. Such a person would legitimately regard the LT as
absurd—as presupposing an archaically objectivist philosophy of science. Their opposition to the LT—and hence, also, their potential support for the SP—would thus be "based" upon their cognitive relativism,
and quite reasonably so, in that relativism would indeed provide good
grounds for rejecting the LT.

It might then be tempting for such a person to conclude that the
SP *itself* requires the assumption of cognitive relativism and that the LT
can only be rejected on this basis. But this conclusion could only be
drawn if there were no other grounds for rejecting the LT—grounds

which did not themselves entail cognitive relativism.

That there are such alternative grounds might plausibly be argued in the following way. The procedures of rational reconstruction and causal explanation are not mutually exclusive. They can both be applied to the same set of beliefs, since they are concerned with distinct questions—the former with justification, the latter with explanation. To show that a belief is justifiable one must show (at least) that it is reconstructible by reference to some particular conception of rationality. But success in so doing does not entail that the belief's acceptance has no causal determinants. Nor, conversely, does the existence of such determinants entail that the belief is not justifiable, let alone that the very question of its justifiability is misplaced or illegitimate.

In other words, the LT could be rejected on the grounds that it misconceived the relationships between justification and explanation, and hence without assuming cognitive relativism. So although cognitive relativists may reasonably deploy their relativism in supporting the SP against the LT, they would be wrong to conclude from this that support for the program requires commitment to relativism. And the same would hold for the program's espousal of (cognitive) value-freedom, expressed—albeit ambiguously—in the tenets of impartiality and symmetry (that is, tenets 2 and 3).[19]

How far this account of the hypothetical relativist's support for the SP is true of the program's *actual* proponents I shall not discuss here: its main purpose is heuristic, in clarifying the relationships between relativism, the LT, and the SP.[20] A similar point now applies in considering how it might be that advocates of the SP have mistakenly taken it to rule out any significant use of conceptions of rationality. I shall do this by commenting on the following passage from one of its actual proponents, but without claiming that this is strictly representative:

> "The programme's endorsement of relativism means that it must seek to explain the content of scientific knowledge as far as possible in social terms. *Rationality* (whatever that means) must play little part in explaining how the world comes to appear as it does. Thus beliefs that seem less rational should be explained in the same way as those that seem more rational. Relativism is thus translated into symmetry and impartiality, in Bloor's terms.[21]

The first question to raise is what exactly is meant by saying that "rationality" has little explanatory power with respect to scientific beliefs. If the rationality of a belief consists in its meeting the requirements of some (type-1) conception of rationality, then quite clearly this feature of the belief cannot (causally) explain its acceptance by anyone: to think that it could, would involve confusing the task of justification with that of causal explanation. But this cannot be the point being made here, since what is claimed is that rationality has *little* explanatory power, not that it (necessarily) has none at all.

Perhaps, then, what is meant by "rationality" is instead the conception(s) of rationality actually accepted by the members of a scientific community, and it is these that are being said to play a minor role in explaining scientific beliefs. But if so, it is difficult to understand why this should be thought either to follow from, or to be necessarily assumed by, the SP—nor would the program's supposed relativism add plausibility to the thought. For the claim that "accepted values" have little explanatory power is basically an assertion of sociological materialism, and there seems nothing in the definition of the SP that would commit its proponents to this substantive theoretical position.

But there is a complication here. Perhaps it is being assumed in this passage that "accepted conceptions of rationality" are not properly categorized as *social* determinants, and that therefore the SP can ascribe little explanatory power to them simply because of its exclusive concern with the *social* determination of scientific beliefs. But there are two difficulties with this. First, it seems both highly implausible and unduly restrictive to adopt a definition of 'sociality' according to which accepted values turn out to be nonsocial.[22] If one considers what has been suggested throughout to be the analogous case of "accepted moral and political values," then such a definition would entail that significant modes of "social" theory are not *social* at all—for instance, the Weberian theory of the origins of capitalism. It would surely be preferable to regard the disputes between Marxists and Weberians as substantive matters *within* social theory rather than between social and nonsocial theories.

The second difficulty is this. Even if so unduly restrictive a definition of sociality were accepted, the minor explanatory role of accepted conceptions of rationality would be entailed by the SP only if it were itself formulated in a very "strong" manner. It was noted earlier (in II above) that the program's first tenet does not specify the relative importance of social, as compared with nonsocial, determinants of beliefs. If tenet 1 is taken to claim only that social factors always play at least *some* significant part in the determination of scientific beliefs, then the question of whether this is a predominant part is left open. If, alternatively, tenet 1 is taken as claiming that nonsocial determinants never exercise more than a minor influence, then certainly it would follow that accepted conceptions of rationality (if deemed to be nonsocial) have little explanatory power. It should be noted, however, that several critics of the empirical research conducted in the name of the SP have argued that there is little if any evidence to support the substantive truth of tenet 1, interpreted in this way.[23]

Hence, the claim that accepted conceptions of rationality have little explanatory power is entailed by the SP only if one adopts both a strong reading of tenet 1 and a restrictive definition of sociality, neither of which are especially plausible. But this is not the only point at which lack of clarity or actual ambiguity in the SP's tenets may give rise to the illusion that certain substantive theoretical claims about the determinants of scientific beliefs can be established merely by the methodological requirements of a scientific sociology of science. Similiar problems may afflict tenets 2 and 3, especially the latter—the symmetry thesis. Understood as an attempt to express the requirement of (cognitive) value-freedom, tenet 3 should be read in the following way: the question of what determines the acceptance of scientific beliefs is to be answered independently of any judgments about their rationality, that is, independently of any favorable or unfavorable appraisals of those beliefs based upon their meeting or not meeting the requirements of some preferred conception of scientific rationality.[24] And this, of course, rightly makes the assessment of explanatory claims about the social determinants of scientific beliefs independent of the question of cognitive relativism, and more generally of what if any justication can be provided for such conceptions of rationality.

It is, nonetheless, quite tempting for the symmetry thesis to be understood in a significantly different way, namely, as asserting that the causal determinants of "rational" beliefs are in fact precisely the same as those of "nonrational" beliefs. Further, suppose that what is meant by "the same types of cause" is "in both cases predominantly social," and that the concept of sociality is taken to exclude accepted conceptions of rationality. Then tenet 3 would be claiming that both rational and nonrational scientific beliefs have in common the absence of any major degree of causal determination by a scientific community's accepted cognitive values. No doubt it is just conceivable that this is true. But it seems strange to insist that anyone endorsing the legitimacy of a scientific sociology of science must thereby assent to this apparently contentious substantive hypothesis.

Of course, most proponents of the SP would, in any case, not allow the formulation of any hypothesis of this kind, since they would regard its use of the concept of rationality as offending their, or their program's, commitment to cognitive relativism and/or value-freedom. I have already argued that these objections are misconceived. But in the concluding remarks which follow I shall suggest that *unless* the SP is understood so as to legitimate the investigation of such hypotheses, the potential contribution of its empirical research to the issue of cognitive relativism will be greatly impoverished.

VI

To deny, as I have, that the SP either implies or necessarily assumes relativism may seem to presuppose a certain view of the relationship between the philosophy and the sociology of science, namely, that the former is a strictly autonomous enterprise to which the latter is entirely irrelevant. More specifically, according to this view the question of cognitive relativism (with respect to scientific rationality) is a purely philosophical one, to the resolution of which nothing can be contributed by the empirical results of a sociology of science. But this view is not thus presupposed, nor is it correct. For, although the philosophy and sociology of science are indeed distinct and mutually irreducible forms of inquiry,[25] neither are likely to be well conducted in isolation from the other—any more than are moral philosophy and the sociology of moral beliefs and practices. I shall now indicate briefly some of the possible, and complex, relationships between the two in the case of cognitive relativism.

First, sociological investigations might reveal one or both of the following: that the theoretical beliefs of various scientific communities do not conform to the conception(s) of rationality prescribed by certain philosophers of science, or that there is considerable diversity in the conceptions of rationality endorsed by members of different scientific communities. Concentrating here on the latter possibility, what would be the significance of such diversity for the preferred conception of rationality of a nonrelativist philosophy of science? Clearly this cannot be a matter of simple refutation: the actual diversity of accepted cognitive values no more entails cognitive relativism than the diversity of accepted moral values entails moral relativism. (It is, incidentally, curious how willing some cognitive relativists are to invoke an inappropriately refutationist logic in this context, while elsewhere deriding the absolutist pretensions of hypothetic-deductivist philosophy of science.)

Hence, there is nothing logically to prevent the nonrelativist philosopher of science simply proceeding to criticize those scientific communities for endorsing defective cognitive values. Yet, to do this without pause for thought would be unwise. For, surely, these alternative conceptions of rationality should be treated with some respect—with at least as much respect, indeed, as the views of other philosophers of science whose conceptions of scientific rationality likewise differ from that which is being defended. The cognitive values endorsed by scientists are not *ipso facto* philosophically insignificant: one may, as it were, learn as much from arguing with Newton or Einstein about scientific rationality as from arguing with Mill or Popper.

Second, the sociology of science might not only discover the existence of such diversity but also propose certain explanations for this, for why it is that these varying conceptions of rationality have in fact been accepted by different scientific communities. But the bearing of such explanations on the question of cognitive relativism will depend at least partly on their actual character—on the kinds of (social) determinants supposedly identified. In particular, as argued earlier, one should not assume that any sociological explanation is necessarily materialist. Hence, for example, it might be that a scientific community's acceptance of certain cognitive values was largely due to the influence of broader philosophical or intellectual movements or traditions. If so, the problems thereby posed for the nonrelativist philosopher of science would be no different from those posed more generally for philosophy by the historical and cultural diversity of such forms of thought.

But suppose instead that the proposed explanations were of a materialist nature. The analogy with moral relativism may again be helpful here. Consider the case of Marx's materialist explanations for the acceptance of dominant moral and political values. It is at least arguable that the truth of these explanations is consistent with a nonrelativist position, and that Marx was himself, therefore, consistent in distinguishing between ideological and nonideological values and in adopting a normatively critical standpoint toward the former. If so, the same might be true in the case of cognitive relativism and materialist explanations of accepted cognitive values. The significance of such explanations would not be that they directly establish relativism, but that they should make the nonrelativist philosopher of science *suspicious* of the apparent attractiveness and superiority of their preferred conception of scientific rationality—suspicious that its till-now unacknowledged material determinants have imbued it with various elements of ideological distortion. But to be on one's guard is one thing; to think there is nothing to be guarded is quite another.

Finally, sociological studies of science might reveal that while the conception(s) of rationality endorsed by particular scientific communities generally conformed to the preferred conception(s) of nonrelativist philosophers of science, the theoretical beliefs held by members of those communities cannot be fully explained by their acceptance of those cognitive values. It might further be argued that *had* the scientists concerned relied exclusively on the considerations dictated by those standards of rationality, they would have been unable to make the necessary—albeit provisional—decisions that faced them in assessing the merits of possible theoretical beliefs: they would, as it were, have been forced into a situation of immobilizing agnosticism.

Now this possible conclusion of sociological inquiries would not straightforwardly support cognitive relativism. The nonrelativist could still maintain that there were universally applicable "absolute" standards of scientific rationality. But what might have to be accepted is that by themselves these do not provide a complete basis for the kinds of cognitive decisions that have to be made in scientific practice, and that such decisions will always also require various informal, and in certain ways context-specific, modes of argumentation.[26] This does not, of course, imply that the philosophy of science is at this point simply replaceable by the sociology of science; rather it suggests that philosophical reflection on the concept of rationality must be informed by the practices of reasoning.

But what is also apparent, both from this and the previous cases considered, is that the significance of sociological investigations for the problems of relativism depends, not upon the mere existence of social determinants for scientific beliefs, but upon the specific character of those determinants; and that a sociology of science, whose results might contribute to the resolution of these problems, must not inhibit itself from deploying conceptions of scientific rationality in its theoretical work.

Notes

(I am grateful to my colleague John O'Neill for discussion of the issues addressed in this paper.)

1. See David Bloor, *Knowledge and Social Imagery* (London: Routledge and Kegan Paul, 1976); Barry Barnes, *Scientific Knowledge and Sociological Theory* (London: Routledge and Kegan Paul, 1974), and *Interests and the Growth of Knowledge* (London: Routledge and Kegan Paul, 1977). For a review of the Edinburgh School's research see S. Shapin, "History of Science and Its Sociological Reconstruction," *History of Science* 20 (1982). The Edinburgh School's approach can be broadly distinguinshed from that of the "social constructionists" such as Bruno Latour and Steven Woolgar, *Laboratory Life: The Social Construction of Scientific Facts* (London: Sage Publications, 1979): see Paul Tibbetts, "The Sociology of Scientific Knowledge: The Constructivist Thesis and Relativism," *Philosophy of the Social Sciences* 16 (1986). The disagree-

ments emerge strongly in the exchanges between Woolgar and Barnes in *Social Studies of Science* 11 (1981).

2. As, e.g., in Larry Laudan, *Progress and Its Problems* (Berkeley: University of California Press, 1977), and Imre Lakatos, *The Methodology of Scientific Research Programmes,* ed. J. Worrall and G. Currie (Cambridge: Cambridge University Press, 1978); but I shall not restrict the concept of rational reconstruction to the particular standards of rationality endorsed by Laudan or Lakatos.

3. For criticisms of the SP see, e.g., W. H. Newton-Smith, *The Rationality of Science* (London: Routledge and Kegan Paul, 1981), ch. 10; Larry Laudan, "The Pseudo-Science of Science?" *Philosophy of the Social Sciences* 11 (1981); Roger Trigg, *Reality at Risk* (Brighton: Harvester Press, 1980), ch. 5; Martin Hollis, "The Social Destruction of Reality," in *Rationality and Relativism,* ed. M. Hollis and S. Lukes (Oxford: Basil Blackwell, 1982); Ray Pawson and Nicholas Tilley, "Monstrous Thoughts: Weaknesses in the Strong Programme of the Sociology of Science," *Occasional Papers in Sociology,* no. 14 (Department of Sociology, University of Leeds, 1982); Ernan McMullin, "The Rational and the Social in the History of Science," in *Scientific Rationality: The Sociological Turn,* ed. R. Brown (Dordrecht: D. Reidel, 1984). For defenses see, e.g., Mary Hesse, "The Strong Thesis of the Sociology of Science," in *Revolutions and Reconstructions in the Philosophy of Science* (Brighton: Harvester Press, 1980); David Bloor, "The Strengths of the Strong Programme," *Philosophy of the Social Sciences* 11 (1981); Barry Barnes and David Bloor, "Relativism, Rationalism and the Sociology of Knowledge," in *Rationality and Relativism*; Peter T. Manicas and Alan Rosenberg, "Naturalism, Epistemological Individualism and 'The Strong Programme' in the Sociology of Knowledge," *Journal for the Theory of Social Behaviour* 15 (1985). (The voluminous literature on the SP can usefully be approached through the pages of *Social Studies of Science* and *Philosophy of the Social Sciences* from the late 1970s.)

4. For example, H. M. Collins, "Stages in the Empirical Programme of Relativism," *Social Studies of Science* 11 (1981).

5. There may be grounds for believing that the SP entails a relativism which would remain unaffected by my arguments concerning value-freedom. Nonetheless, confusion about the issues I address here underlies a good deal of the debate about the program's supposed relativism.

6. As presented in Bloor, *Knowledge and Social Imagery,* pp. 4-5.

7. See especially Laudan, "The Pseudo-Science of Science?" and Bloor's reply, "The Strengths of the Strong Programme."

8. On this see Hesse, "The Strong Thesis," and G. Freudenthal, "How Strong Is Dr. Bloor's Strong Programme?" *Studies in the History and Philosophy of Science* 10 (1979).

9. On Barnes' use of the concept of natural rationality see Manicas and Rosenberg, "Naturalism, Epistemological Individualism and 'The Strong Programme'."

10. On the interpretation of tenets 2 and 3, and for a revised formulation offered later by Bloor, see Newton-Smith, *The Rationality of Science,* pp. 247-252.

11. As, e.g., in the Introduction to Jack W. Meiland and Michael Krausz, eds., *Relativism: Cognitive and Moral* (Notre Dame and London: University of Notre Dame Press, 1982). I make no attempt to justify the specific formulations of relativism adopted in what follows, assuming merely that they are well recognizable as such: for instance, my account of "relativism with respect to scientific rationality" corresponds closely to the way Hollis and Lukes define "relativism of reason" in their Introduction to *Rationality and Relativism*. But my later use of the phrases 'cognitive values' and 'cognitive value-freedom' suggests that at least the *terminology* of the "cognitive v. moral" distinction is misleading.

12. Many conceptions of scientific rationality are, of course, a good deal more complex than the two noted here—e.g., Lakatos' sophisticated methodological falsification. Most involve rules relating "evidence" to "theory," and some also "theory" to "theory"; and distinctions may be drawn between "ideal" and "available" evidence. Those which refer to "empirical data" may be subject to problems connected with other forms of epistemological relativism, but I shall not consider these here. I shall also ignore distinctions between conceptions which allow for "degrees of rationality" and those which do not.

13. For an attempt to support the claims about value-freedom made here see the opening chapters of Russell Keat, *The Politics of Social Theory* (Chicago: Chicago University Press, 1981), which develops further the position defended in chapter 9 of Russell Keat and John Urry, *Social Theory as Science* (London: Routledge and Kegan Paul, second edition, 1982).

14. Here as elsewhere in the paper I leave aside problems concerning the criteria for correct interpretations of beliefs, which raise issues quite distinct from those with which I am directly concerned.

15. The distinction here between characterization and appraisal derives partly from E. Nagel, *The Structure of Science* (London: Routledge and Kegan Paul, 1961), pp. 491-494.

16. Nor is this the only respect in which scientific work is always necessarily more than an exclusively cognitive enterprise and must therefore be judged accordingly.

17. Indeed, proponents of the SP sometimes defend themselves against the charge that their relativism undermines their own scientific claims by saying that these meet the requirements of "local" standards of rationality. In doing so, they implicitly accept what they elsewhere deny, namely, that scientific beliefs can be "characterized" as rational or irrational.

18. These are the kinds of questions addressed by "Mertonian" sociology of science—see, e.g., Robert K. Merton, *The Sociology of Science* (Chicago: University of Chicago Press, 1973). Proponents of the SP, in rightly asserting the possiblity of social determination for the specific content of scientific beliefs as distinct from the institutional requirements for the practice of "good science," have wrongly concluded that questions about the latter must be excluded. On the opposition of the Edinburgh School to the Mertonians see H. M. Collins, "The Sociology of Scientific Knowledge: Studies of Contemporary Science," *Annual Review of Sociology* 9 (1983).

19. Here, as throughout, I assume that tenets 2 and 3 are best understood

as an (admittedly confused) attempt to express the idea of cognitive value-freedom. Certainly I can see no other legitimate rationale for them, and that Barnes, at least, has this idea in mind is indicated by his comment that "as a methodological principle we must not allow the evaluation of beliefs to determine what form of sociological account we put forward to explain them" *(Interests and the Growth of Knowledge,* p. 25).

20. See Collins, "The Sociology of Scientific Knowledge," for useful information on the prior intellectual commitments of various proponents of the SP. In the case of Bloor the influence of a certain interpretation of Wittgenstein and Durkheim is evident and further developed in his later *Wittgenstein: A Social Theory of Knowledge* (New York: Columbia University Press, 1983). It is, I believe, unfortunate that the SP has been so closely associated by both advocates and critics with the broadly relativistic tendencies in recent philosophy of science, since neither of the two actually has much to do with the other.

21. Collins, "The Sociology of Scientific Knowledge," p. 272; while not altogether representative, this passage illustrates some quite widespread confusions in the literature on the SP.

22. Hence I am unhappy with the *terms* used by McMullin, in "The Rational and the Social," to distinguish what he calls "epistemic" and "social" factors: the former correspond closely to my "accepted (cognitive) values." But the difference is mainly terminological, since he regards both as legitimately occurring in causal explanations of scientific beliefs and rightly criticizes proponents of the SP for what is, in my terms, their a priori materialism.

23. See, e.g., McMullin, "The Rational and the Social," and Pawson and Tilley, "Monstrous Thoughts."

24. Here as throughout I consider tenet 3 in relation only to rationality/irrationality, and not to truth/falsity; but similar arguments could be developed to deal with the latter also. I therefore disagree with, e.g., Newton-Smith, who argues in *The Rationality of Science,* pp. 252-253, that in the case of simple perceptual beliefs the explanation of true beliefs *necessarily* differs from that of false ones. Whether there are such differences is, in my view, an empirically open question, and hence not one whose answer depends on prior assessements of truth and falsity.

25. Much of the SP's supposed relativism is due to some of its proponents' commitment to the reduction of philosophical to sociological enquiry. But no such reduction is required by the program itself; nor do I find attractive the revival of nineteenth-century positivistic scientism which this reductionism often implicitly involves (see *The Politics of Social Theory,* ch. 1). For example, when Barnes and Bloor proclaim that "Far from being a threat to the scientific understanding of forms of knowledge, relativism is required by it," they seem to assume that science provides the only kind of knowledge one could have about science: see "Relativism, Rationalism and the Sociology of Knowledge," p. 21.

26. And hence, also, that scientific rationality is not algorithmic. The apparent relativism of "social constructionists" such as Woolgar and Latour (see note 1 above) seems often to rely on the mistaken assumption that scientific rationality must be algorithmic, together with a curious espousal of Bridgmanesque operationalism in a new, sociological guise.

Internal Criticism and
Indian Rationalist Traditions

MARTHA C. NUSSBAUM AND AMARTYA SEN

1. Introduction

This paper has two closely related aims. The first is to diagnose some problems of emphasis and interpretation that have arisen in attempts to describe the values of a particular society, namely, India. The second is to investigate some general methodological and philosophical issues that are raised by any attempt to describe and assess the values of a traditional society. Both projects were originally motivated by the desire to find a philosophical and conceptual framework within which to discuss some urgent problems that arise in the course of "development," especially economic development. It was originally prepared for a project at the World Institute for Development Economics Research (WIDER) that was concerned with analyzing the relationship among value, technology, and development. The project was based on the important recognition that values cannot be treated, as they often are in the literature on "economic development," as purely instrumental objects in promoting development. Indeed, the very idea of "development"—whether seen from within a culture or in the stylized impersonal context of development economics—is inevitably based on a particular class of values, in terms of which progress is judged and development is measured.

There are two distinct issues involved in recognizing the importance of the "value-relativity" of the concept of development. The first is the elementary but far-reaching fact that without some idea of ends that are themselves external to the development process and in terms of which the process may be assessed, we cannot begin to say what changes are to count as "development." In judging development in the context of a culture the values that are supported and are sustainable in that culture provide an essential point of reference. The need for internal criticism and rational assessment of the values of a culture—to be discussed presently (section 4)—does not undermine the essentiality of the cultural reference or eliminate the fact of the value-relativity of the concept of development.

The second issue concerns the possible undermining of traditional values that may result from the process of change. The WIDER project has been particularly concerned with the impact of imported technology on traditional values, but the problem is, of course, relevant in many other contexts as well. This "undermining" may take two rather different forms, which have to be distinguished. It could be the case that the *objects of valuation* that a particular traditional value system treasures—such as a particular lifestyle—may become more difficult to obtain and sustain as a result of material change. The other way that the values may be "undermined" is a weakening of the hold of those *values themselves* on the subjects.

To illustrate the difference, the use of modern technology may make it hard to lead a life of free, unrouted work, and this would, in one sense, "undermine" a traditional value that attaches importance to spontaneity of the kind rejected by the use of the new technology. The other sense of "undermining" the value in question is to make people turn against valuing that type of spontaneity altogether. The two processes, which we may respectively call "object failure" and "value rejection," are undoubtedly related to each other (for one thing, "sour grapes" are common enough[1]), but they raise rather different evaluative problems, neither of which can subsume the other.

When values are unchanged but the objects valued (such as states of affairs, activities, and so on) become unachievable (that is, when there is "object failure"), there is a clear and palpable loss *within* the unchanging frame of reference. The importance that is attached to that loss cannot be independent of the assessment of that value, but there is no denial of the immediacy of the loss, In the case, on the other hand, of "value rejection" the frame of reference itself ceases to be stationary, and whether there is any loss in this or not cannot be ascertained automatically on the basis of *either* the subsequent *or* the antecedent values. The *process* of rejection is important here. Was the rejection based on, or would it be supported by, a reasoned and involved internal critique? A reasoned critical rejection of old values on the basis of, say, new facts or new knowledge or new understanding of old facts must command respect. Indeed, such value rejection may often show the power and reach of an appropriate internal critique (see sections 4 and 5).

Aside from the conceptual and evaluative complications involved in this problem, there are also difficult substantive issues in characterizing the values of a culture. The identification of values may itself be difficult, and there is, in addition, the further problem of determining what values are to be regarded as central. The lives of human beings are guided by a variety of valuational presumptions and attitudes, and some things are valued more fundamentally than others. Indeed, some values are basically instrumental to achieving other valuable things, and this instrumentality may either be immediately seen or be ascertainable on the basis of probing and deliberative analysis.[2] The undermining of some values subscribed to in a community may be a matter of great moment in a way the undermining of some other—more instrumental or less deeply held—values need not be.

The problem of identification of values and diagnosis of central values is further compounded by the diversity that may well exist within a community. Various divergent traditions may survive side by side within the same country and indeed even in the same locality. Determining what the "basic" traditional values are (the undermining of which, especially through object failure, would involve a loss) may not be a trivial, or even a simple, question. Since no culture is fully static, there is also the problem of valuational dynamics and evolution, and the issue of centrality is not independent of that problem either.

The substantive issue with which our discussion is concerned relates to certain standard diagnoses of the fundamental nature of Indian culture and the identification of the central values in that tradition, the undermining of which is particularly feared by cultural conservationists (section 2). This essay will examine some biases in the common reading of Indian traditions and cultures in this context (section 3), arguing, in particular, that there has been an overemphasis on the mystical and religious aspects of Indian society and a relative neglect of the more "rationalistic" and "analytical" features.

Much of our discussion, however, is concerned with methodological rather than substantive issues (sections 4-5). Understanding a culture and its central values is a demanding exercise, raising difficult problems of observation and evidence, on the one hand, and of interpretation and assessment, on the other. Indeed, the paper's substantive propositions regarding the nature of Indian culture and its misdescriptions are put forward here with some hesitation and tentativeness in recognition of difficulty of these methodological problems. We shall say little here about problems of evidence and description, which are plain enough from the paper's substantive sections. But we shall describe an approach to rational critical assessment, one that has Aristotelian roots, and we shall examine its power and reach.

2. Religion, Mysticism, and the Nonrational

The importance of religion in Indian society can scarcely be denied. Religious values and practices differ between groups. Furthermore, given the nature of Hinduism, the majority religion in India, the religious beliefs are frequently of a kind that can be described as being more mystical than corresponding religious beliefs in many other cultures, though the ranking of mysticism is an inherently ambiguous exercise.

In understanding the values of a culture it is tempting to take a rapid jump from one aspect of the lives that many people lead to a characterization of the "essence" of that culture. What may be called the "more mystical than thou" interpretation of the nature of Indian culture undoubtedly draws part of its strength from such an exercise. The interpretation is, however, also much assisted by a particular reading of the intellectual contributions of India to the world of thought, imagination, and creativity. The sheer volume of religious literature in India far exceeds that of all other countries, perhaps even all of them put together. Given the religious interpretation of Indian philosophy (on which more presently), the massive contribution of philosophical ideas coming from India is also typically seen in a very special light, emphasizing their nonanalytical aspects.

There are, of course, many scholarly studies of other aspects of Indian civilization, and there is no dearth of expertise on other areas of Indian culture and thought, but as a broad generalization of how India is widely viewed in terms of its alleged values and culture there is much truth in this "more mystical" imaging. Aside from the role of this image in the assessment of Indian culture, it also has a clear bearing on the alarm with which the "undermining" of "traditional" Indian values is often viewed in the context of economic development. Modern technology and science tend to be hostile to mysticism, and to that extent it might well be thought that something exceptionally valuable is being threatened by the expansion of modern technology and science occurring in India. The issue, thus, relates directly to the central question in the WIDER research project on technology and values.[3]

The special imaging of India is not new. In the last few centuries, with the so-called "expansion of Europe," the common Western perception of India has been, to a great extent, based on looking for contrasts, with differences, rather than similarities, tending to be emphasized in the Western "discovery of India." This has gone hand in hand with recognizing certain very elementary points of similarity on basic and gross matters (rather than those involving sophistication of emotions or thought). For example, Rudyard Kipling could unhesitatingly assert, "Oh, East is East, and West is West, and never the twain shall meet," and in the same verse go on to say, "But there is neither East nor West, nor Border, nor Breed, nor Birth,/ When two strong men stand face to face, though they come from the ends of earth!" *(The Ballad of East and West).* The "macho" values may, thus, be shared between the "East" and the "West," which for Kipling did not really differ much from India and Britain respectively, but on less elementary matters Kipling would not accept any diminution of the East-West gulf.

The image of the "mystical East," and specifically India, is not a matter only of popular conception but has a good deal of following in the typical Indologist's summary view of Indian intellectual history. In this respect there is also no real gulf between the things that the Western scholars have typically tended to emphasize in Indian culture and what Indian Indologists have themselves most often highlighted. This close correspondence may not, however, be particularly remarkable, since approaches to "cultural summarizing" are generally quite "infectious," and, no less importantly, modern Indian scholarship is greatly derivative from the West. There is nothing odd in the fact that this dependence extends even to the understanding of the "essence" of Indian culture itself. It is nevertheless a matter of some descriptive importance to recognize that the "more mystical" overall view of Indian traditions is largely *shared* in Western and Indian professional perceptions.

In their eminently useful "sourcebook" of Indian philosophy Radhakrishnan and Moore give expression to the standard view of Indian philosophy when they say, "the chief mark of Indian philosophy in general is its concentration upon the spiritual."[4] This is not based on ignoring nonspiritual parts of Indian thinking altogether (indeed Radhakrishnan and Moore include in their sourcebook extensive excerpts from the atheistic and materialistic "Cārvāka" school).[5] It is based rather on seeing these departures as aberrations, which are "relatively minor."[6]

This simple view of the nature of Indian philosophy is rather rarely challenged. Bimal Matilal, one of the few major challengers, puts the problem thus in answer to the criticism that he has been "leaning over backwards" to "show the analytic nature of Indian philosophy": "Too often the term Indian philosophy is identified with a subject that is presented as mystical and non-argumentative, that is at best poetic and at worst dogmatic. A corrective to this view is long overdue."[7]

In fact, the origins of the dominant view of Indian philosophy go back many centuries. For example, already in 1690 John Locke felt rather superior on this score in his *Essay Concerning Human Understanding:*

> Had the poor Indian Philosopher (who imagined that the earth also wanted something to bear it up) but thought of this word substance he needed not to have been at the trouble to find an elephant to support it, and a tortoise to support his elephant; the word substance would have done it effectively.[8]

> The Indian before mentioned who, saying that the world was supported by a great elephant, was asked what the elephant rested on; to which his answer was, a great tortoise; but being again pressed to know what gave support to the broad-backed tortoise, replied, *something he knows not what.*[9]

The parable does, of course, come from an old religious myth in India, but as Matilal notes, "it would be impossible to find a text in classical Indian philosophy where the elephant-tortoise device is put forward as a philosophical explanation of the support of the earth."[10]

3. Pluralities and Divisions

There is, in fact, a peculiar contrast between the enormous variety in traditional Indian culture and the simple concentration on mysticism and nonrationality in the typical image of India. The contrast is not, however, one of nonintersecting contrariness. The mystical and the nonrational do, in fact, exist plentifully in Indian intellectual history and social practice. The problem relates, not to the *inclusion* of these elements in the conventional image of India, but to the almost total *exclusion* of all other elements which also belong to the Indian traditions.[11]

It is arguable that the systematic bias in the reading of Indian culture relates to ignoring—or downplaying the importance of—some of the urban and urbane parts of the Indian heritage. The intellectual activities coming from these parts of the society have historically included many critical features that simply do not fit into the mystical image.

Matilal has emphasized the importance of controversies on the theory of knowledge in classical Indian philosophy flourishing between 100 AD and 1400 AD and has distinguished between the "skeptical," "phenomenalist," and "realist" positions.[12]

These and many other contributions in philosophy and logic belong at least as much to Indian intellectual history as do popular myths about the earth, the elephant, and the tortoise.

Similarly, the achievements of Indian mathematics—neither particularly spiritual nor especially mystical—were substantial enough to rival Indian contributions to the world of religion and spirituality.[13] In particular, the development of the decimal system (and the related numerical representation) in India had a major impact on the flourishing Arab civilization in the Middle Ages and through the Arabs reached Europe early in this millennium. By around 1400 AD they began what Alexander Murray describes as "an effective conquest of all literal culture."[14]

Other areas of major achievements include *inter alia* such subjects as political analysis and statecraft (including some of the earliest discussions of economics, by Kautilya in particular), linguistic and grammatical studies (including the pioneering contributions of Panini), and medicine (including the classic *Suśruta-saṁhitā)*.

Similarly, the pursuit of pleasure and fulfillment in sexual activities (including the *Kāma-sutra* and *Anangaranga),* the teaching of practical wisdom and shrewdness through the literary medium of fables (including *Hitopadésa* and *Pancatantra),* invention and analysis of various games of skill and chance (including chess), development of sampling procedures for personal and business calculations (discussed in the epic *Mahābhārata* among other places), and other such "practical" activities obviously cannot be fitted easily into the mystical mould. The groups of people who were led to these activities clearly had a great deal of "earthly" concerns, which influenced their values and living styles, and which they pursued in straightforwardly "rational" ways.[15]

The nature of Indian literary contributions also point toward a deep-seated plurality of concerns. Whether we look at the epics, the *Ramayana* and the *Mahābhārata* (especially the latter), or at fiction or poetry, it will be hard to take the view that mystical concerns and spirituality have been the dominant influences. Some of the ancient plays are straightforwardly social (e.g., *Mrcchakatikam,* which also happens to be deeply skeptical of religious pretensions), while others are more mixed, but altogether the insight that they give about the lives of the people involved can scarcely be seen as one of unrelieved spirituality.

If these substantial and powerful parts of Indian traditions are simply ignored, the view that we would get of Indian culture and thought will be extremely biased and distorted. The volume and variety of Indian contributions to religious thinking, impressive as they are, cannot obliterate these *other* features in Indian history. As it happens, even in religious discussions not everything went in the direction of nonrationality and myticism. In fact, the most important religious leader produced in India, namely, Gautama Buddha, not only preached an agnostic religion but also gave rationalistic reasons as to why this is the only acceptable position.[16]

Straightforwardly atheistic positions were taken by the Cārvāka school and the Lokāyata, producing some highly antispiritual and anti-mystical—and incidentally rather hedonistic—philosophical arguments in the field of religion. Radhakrishnan and Moore may describe these latter schools as "relatively minor," but they have been traditionally viewed as important enough to figure as a major part of Indian philosophical tradition. For example, in *Sarvadarśanasaṁgraha* (literally, "the collection of all philosophies"), produced by Mādhava Acārya in the fourteenth century, the Cārvāka school was sympathetically described in the first chapter, which consisted in fact only of this presentation.[17] In the light of the nature and force of such evidence a nonpluralistic interpretation of the basic Indian traditions would be hard to sustain.

It is, of course, possible to close one's eyes to the totality of all this—and similar—evidence and take a view of "true India" that is separated from these intellectual and sophisticated concerns, for example, to base one's view of the "real" Indian philosophy on studying popular myths rather than philosophical writings. This would be something like an opposite prejudice to one that has tended to dominate much of the writing of social and economic history in India, concentrating almost exclusively on the upper classes and the elite.[18] It would amount to viewing Indian culture and tradition in more compartmentalized terms than can be reasonably defended. The transmission of knowledge, literature, lifestyle, and so forth from one part of the society to another is too general a phenomenon to be left out in trying to understand any part of the society in depth. As it happens, various features that we firmly associate with traditional Western civilization had also been, for long stretches of time, confined to certain limited parts of the society. Indeed, the issue of "elitist bias" in the interpretation of Western cultures, going all the way back to understanding ancient Greece, is far from trivial, and the problem can scarcely be resolved in the Indian case by insisting on the opposite "nonelite bias," excluding from the reckoning of Indian culture the achievements and concerns of the intellectual elite. A clearer recognition of variety in Indian traditions, with active links as well as deep divisions, can help us to get a more balanced view of the nature of Indian culture.

4. Cultural Values and Rational Criticism

In order to attempt a proper reappraisal of Indian culture and values we have to draw on evidence of many types, and we have to pay serious attention to the methodological problems involved in such an appraisal. We have only begun to confront these problems. But in speaking of the need to do justice to the culture's own capacity for internal criticism and evaluative reflection, we have arrived at a deep philosophical problem. Indeed, it is one of the most complex and urgent problems faced by any study of development and technological transformation in traditional societies. Scientific and technological change can modify and even undermine tradition. But it is difficult not to feel that some of these changes are beneficial to the societies that undergo them. In fact, the very concept of "development" as it is most often used in the discourse that surrounds it has an evaluative dimension. A change that is not thought to be in some way beneficial would not usually be described as a part of "development." But then in order to know which changes count as development, that is, as beneficial alterations, we need to have not only a description of the practices and the values of a culture but also some sort of evaluation *of* those practices and values: which ones are, in fact, the most valuable? Which are central—the ones that it would be especially unwise to undermine? Which accepted values and practices, on the other hand, might well be modified, and on what grounds?

The first step toward answering these questions is, as we have already indicated, to get a rich, broad, and deep description of the culture in question, one that is not limited—as many studies in development economics tend to be—to a narrow sphere of "economic" values. But once we have done this—and especially, once we have noticed tensions and oppositions *among* the values and practices of the culture itself—we shall need to do some further evaluative reflection if our description is to have any practical value. We could try to avoid the appearance of evaluation by adopting some trivial or mechanical evaluative criterion: for example, by saying that the values to be preserved at all costs are the ones that are shared by the greatest *number* of the society's people. But this procedure does not really avoid evaluation and ranking; it simply does the job in a particularly mindless and insensitive way. Such a way out would be especially inappropriate for a heterogeneous society like India.

On the other hand, overall evaluations of a particular tradition are nearly always full of peril—especially when they involve (as they can hardly help doing, given the conflicting and plural nature of the values involved) going against some group's deeply held beliefs. It is frequently felt that any modification of tradition, especially through scientific and/or urban rational criticism, must be an unacceptable external imposition upon traditional culture. This feeling is nourished by the belief that rational criticism is always detached and external—that the only vantage point from which statements like the ones we have quoted from the guidelines *can* be made is that of a detached observer. In fact, such a person, because of his or her detachment, is bound to be insufficiently respectful of cultural integrity.

This problem is a deep one, and it lies at the heart of a lot of the most interesting recent work in ethical and political theory. Not much hope exists that we can solve it to anyone's satisfaction here. Nonetheless, we can at least get started on the problem by sketching a method for the evaluation and criticism of tradition that responds both (a) to the need for criticism and (b) to the worries about external imposition. This method has to satisfy various criteria of appropriateness. It must be *internal,* using resources inside the culture itself in order to criticize certain aspects of the culture. Second, it must be *immersed rather than detached* (i.e., its norm of objectivity should not be one that involves the detachment of the judging subject from the practices, the perceptions, even the emotions, of the culture), stressing, instead, that objective value judgments can be made from the point of view of experienced immersion in the way of life of a culture. And yet, third, it will have to be *genuinely critical,* subjecting traditional beliefs and practices to critical examination. At this point we shall again turn to ancient Greece—in this case, to Aristotle, whose account of how to proceed seems to us an especially suggestive and promising one.

Aristotle's highly critical works on ethics were intended to have a practical and not merely theoretical value.[19] Like the WIDER project, they were supposed to have a bearing on social and political choice; and like the project, they were openly critical of approaches to social planning that isolated economic values from a deeper and fuller description of the values of a society. He holds that any good account of development must be rooted in this sort of deep description and in a dialectical evaluation of the traditions described. Aristotle's search is for an account of value that will be genuinely rooted in the experience of the people and genuinely practical, and yet also be evaluative in such a way as to help leaders structure things for the best, enabling people to live as good and flourishing a life as possible.

He describes his method in the following way:

Here, as in all other cases, we must set down the appearances and, first working through the puzzles, in this way go on to show, if possible, the truth of all the traditional beliefs about these experiences; and, if this is not possible, then truth of the greatest number and the most basic. For if the difficulties are resolved and the traditional beliefs are left in place, we will have done enough showing.[20]

This all requires comment. But we shall approach that job indirectly. There is no better way to get an idea of what Aristotle is offering us here than to understand the view it opposes. This view is Plato's. When Aristotle says that a critical study of values (a recommendation of the best values for a culture) should limit itself to a sifting of "appearances," a word that he uses to designate traditional opinions about values,[21] he is making positive use of a term that Plato had used pejoratively, opposing it to "truth" and to "what really is so." For Plato the opinions of finite and imperfect people, as embodied in their traditions, are hardly a sufficient basis for an account of what is really good, even *good for* those very same people. People stop short with traditional opinion only "out of laziness," says Glaucon to Socrates in Book 6 of the *Republic*. Socrates replies, "Laziness, however, is a quality that the guardian of a city and of laws can do without." A good inquiry into what the good life is should not, in this view, allow itself to be distorted by the antecedent beliefs and values of the interested parties. It should be a dispassionate search for truth, conducted as a mathematician, say, would conduct an inquiry as to whether a certain conjecture was true or not true. The mathematician must not allow his *wish* that the conjecture should turn out true, or false, to influence his enquiry into its status or his choice of methods of proof. Just must it be so for the enquirer whose aim is to recommend certain values as best for the development and flourishing of a people. It must resolutely exclude, in this view, any influence from the beliefs of those people as to what lives are best to live, or from wishes as to the sort of lives they want to live.

In the *Phaedrus* Plato's Socrates creates a moving image to express this idea. The philosopher's soul walks out to the rim of the heavens, apart from all traditions, all concrete ways of life, "whole and unblemished . . . in the pure light." And there the soul, looking with the pure eye of reason, understands the truth of value as it really is in itself: "It sees justice itself, it sees moderation, it sees knowledge—not that knowledge that changes and varies with the various objects that we now call beings—but the genuine knowledge seated in that which truly is." In other words, the truth about the best life might turn out any way at all, so far as *we* and *our* lives are concerned. The best life and values (the best account of the ends of development) are what they are, and our thoughts and wishes cannot make them be otherwise. The best life might turn out to be a life that no one in our community could even attain. Or again, it might turn out to be a life that is so out of line with the traditions of the community, and the values of the people in it, that these people would find it repugnant, or base, or so impoverished that they would die rather than live it. Such results would indeed be unlucky for that community, but they would not constitute any reason to call the inquiry itself, or its methods, into question. Plato stresses, furthermore, that the relationship between our cognitive processes and the true good is contingent. It happens that we have faculties such that we (or some of us) are able to grasp the good and, having grasped it, live by it. But we might have been otherwise. (Some of us *are* otherwise.) And the true values would still have been just the same.[22]

This is one very powerful and deeply rooted picture of ethical inquiry and ethical truth. It has played a big part in the Western scientific tradition, and it is certainly one view that people frequently have in mind when they speak (well or ill) of "Western rationality." As it happens, it is prominent in Indian philosophy as well, where it has been both defended *and* challenged, as Bimal Matilal has shown in his recent book *Perception*.[23] This is the picture that Aristotle wants to undermine. Ethical inquiry, he insists, must be what we might call "value-relative." That is, they are not "pure" inquiries conducted in a void; they are questions about living asked by communities of human beings who are actually engaged in living and valuing. What will count as an appropriate, and even a *true,* outcome of such inquiry is constrained, and appropriately constrained, by what human beings antecedently value and need. He develops the point by using an analogy between ethics and medical science. We will develop the point here as analogy, but we can also understand it literally at the same time, since medical values are a part of our concern.

The point seems to be as follows. Think of medical inquiry conducted on the rim of heaven, by pure souls without any knowledge of the feelings, the needs, the pleasures and pains of actual living creatures. Think of these heavenly doctors trying to come up with an account of health and the healthy life, and with procedures to bring about health, apart from a detailed and "inside" understanding of the creatures whom they are going to treat. These doctors would probably turn out to be very poor doctors indeed. Heavenly mathematics is one thing, but medicine seems paradigmatic of an art that is immersed, engaged, working in a pragmatic partnership with those whom it treats. It must take very seriously their pains and pleasures, their own sense of where health and flourishing lie. Its aim is to help, and that aim can never be completely separated from a concern for the patient's own sense of the better and the worse. Suppose the heavenly doctor comes down from the rim of heaven and announces, "See this condition of body which you, poor old women, find intolerably painful and crippling? Well, that's what health is, as I have discovered by consulting the sort of knowledge that resides in true being. You children here: you say that you are hungry; you cry. But this too is health; and you will be making cognitive progress if you learn to see things this way." Our first reaction may be that this "doctor" is sadistic and callous. But the important point here is that he *cannot be right.*

Health does not have an existence in heaven, apart from people and their lives. It is not a being apart from becoming. People can indeed go wrong about their health in many ways. They can think they are doing well when they are not. They can also think they are doing badly when they are really well. But the *sense* of that claim is that the scientist or doctor could *show* them something about their condition which, were they to listen and eventually to understand, would convince them—in terms of a general idea of health and human activity about which they both agree—that their initial judgment had been wrong. Perhaps not all actual individuals will be convinced by the medical truth, but for it to *be* medical truth it seems to be necessary, at the least, that individuals who are in some way representative, attentive, who have scrutinized the alternatives in the right way, should be convinced. This does not, of course, mean that the therapist cannot alter people's ideas concerning what health *is* at the level of more concrete specification. One of her main tasks will frequently be to produce a concrete specification of this vague end, telling us its elements; and this specification may well clash with the patient's prereflective specification. But the challenge of medicine always is to come back to people's desires and needs and sense of value. It must deliver to them a life that will in the end be accepted as a flourishing existence, or else nothing has been accomplished.

So much, Aristotle claims, is true of ethical value. We do not inquire in a vacuum. Our conditions and ways of life, and the hopes, pleasures, pains, and evaluations that are a part of these, cannot be left out of the inquiry without making it pointless and incoherent. We do not stand on the rim of heaven and look "out there" for truth; if we did we would not find the right thing. Ethical truth is in and of human life; it can be seen only from the point of view of immersion. He illustrates the point with an example. Some people have suggested that the good life comes to human beings simply by luck or by nature; our own voluntary striving and activity contribute nothing. But, says Aristotle, if we hold this view up against the deepest values and beliefs of the people with whom we are concerned, we are entitled to reject it—and to reject it *as false*—on the grounds that its acceptance would clash so deeply with these values that we would consider such a life to be not worth the living. Here, as in the medical case, we want to say not only that we would be pragmatically justified in rejecting the dismal proposal. We want to say that it must be false as a view of value for these people—just as the view must be false that an intolerable crippling condition of body is what human health is. The ethical good, like health, is a notion whose meaning cannot be understood except in relation to the creature in question, *and* in relation to the nature of their antecedent values and ways of life.[24]

Are we, then, entitled to speak of "truth" here? John Rawls, developing a somewhat similar account of ethical inquiry,[25] has concluded that we are not. We ought to jettison the notion of truth, once we see that the search for the best account in ethics has these pragmatic elements. Aristotle does, however, speak of truth, and for good reason. Rawls is deeply impressed by a contrast between the human sciences and the natural sciences; and he refers sympathetically to a view like Plato's about truth in the natural sciences. Aristotle holds that *all* truth is in some sense internal and value-laden. And recent work in the philosophy of sciences has given support to his position. Detachment in any area yields not objectivity but incoherence. All truth is seen from somewhere; if we try to see from outside of human life, we see nothing at all. Supporting this position, Hilary Putnam has recently argued that once we have the correct understanding of scientific truth, we will see that there is just as much, and the same sort of, truth and objectivity in ethics as in science. And he argues, with Aristotle, that this really is *truth,* and an "internal realism," not a collapse into idealism or subjectivism.[26]

Aristotle has further arguments defending the claim that an internal inquiry can yield truth and objectivity. He gives us an account of the practical achievements of an internal inquiry that show us how it can in fact achieve a degree of clarity, ordering, and societal consensus that entitle us to claim that we have moved beyond the superficial desires of the participants to a deeper and more objective level. That movement, he holds, is what truth in ethics is all about. He does not dispute Plato's claim that many desires that people feel are bad guides to ethical truth—because they can be deformed by conditions of injustice and deprivation, because they frequently express superficial interests that are at odds even with a deeper level of need and value in that same person. But he thinks that the way to circumnavigate these obstacles is not Plato's way of disregarding the people's values altogether; it is to conduct a reflective dialectical examination that will take the people's views very seriously and then move them toward the recognition and the clarification of what actually are, for them, the most central values. Most of the time we talk carelessly and somewhat "randomly" about our values. And yet it may sometimes be very important to us (as it is in connection with many of our practical purposes) to become clearer about our values and also to reach some sort of societal agreement about them. Aristotle insists that these two goals—individual clarification and communal attunement—can be achieved together by a cooperative critical discourse that insists upon the philosophical virtues of orderliness, deliberateness, and precision:

> Concerning all these things we must try to seek conviction through arguments, using the traditional beliefs as our witnesses and standards. For it would be best of all if all human beings could come into an evident communal agreement with what we shall say, but, if not, that all should agree in some way. And this they will do if they are led carefully until they shift their position. For everyone has something of his own to contribute to the truth, and it is from these that we go on to give a sort of demonstration about these things. For from what is said truly but not clearly, as we advance we will also get clarity, always moving from what is usually said in a jumbled fashion to more perspicuous view. There is a difference in every inquiry between arguments that are said in a philosophical way and those that are not. Hence we must not think that it is superfluous for the political person to engage in the sort of reflection that makes perspicuous not only the 'that' but also the 'why': for this is the contribution of the philosopher in each area.[27]

Here again Aristotle insists, against the Platonist approach, on the fundamental internality of the reflective process that assesses values: the "witnesses" and "standards" of the process are the "appearances," or the shared beliefs, and each participant has something to contribute to the truth. And yet the process does not give us back a simple repetition of what each person thought at the start. This is so because when we scrutinize what we think, we will notice inconsistencies and unclarities that we do not notice when we simply talk and act without reflecting. When the deliberative process confronts the reflecting participant with all of the alternative views on a topic, leads him or her through a thorough imaginative exploration of each, and shows how each choice bears on many others that this person wishes to make in a consistent way—then many unconsidered positions may be modified. And yet this modification, if it takes place, will take place, not as imposition from without, but as a discovery about that person's own values that are the deepest and the most central. This is self-discovery and discovery of one's own traditions.

Aristotle believes that agreement *among* people will be enhanced by this self-clarifying procedure. For much disagreement results from ambiguous and vague statement of positions, and much more from a pressing of one idea to the neglect of other related considerations. The effort to develop a position that is consistent over many issues frequently leads to the dropping of immoderate claims on a single issue. But his method also relies upon the fact that the parties engaged in the procedure identify themselves as social beings (not as isolated units)—beings connected to one another by a network of relations, political, cognitive, emotional (and the political relation is best understood, he believes, as having emotional dimensions). Thus they conceive of the goal of the reflective process as the finding of a view according to which they can live together in community—a shared and shareable view of value. And so they are frequently willing to move away from a personal claim, even when narrow consistency does not force them to do so, in order to bring themselves into harmony with the views and claims of others—achieving the larger sort of self-consistency that is the internal harmony of the political and relational self.

This process is viewed not in any simple way as the transcending or sacrificing of self; it is a further part of the discovery of self, since the self is understood in its very nature to be a relational entity, and its own ends are understood as shared ends. We emphasize this, since it seems clear that to conceive of the person as fundamentally relational does transform the way in which numerous familiar problems of social and political choice will be stated. And it offers a promising way of reformulating the goals and procedures of the reflective process—one that will also harmonize well with conceptions of selfhood, individuality, and community that are in fact held by many people in developing nations. In Western society they are less widely held, and it has been forcefully argued that they are held by women far more frequently than by men.[28] So we are saying that the most promising account of the reflective assessment of values may be one that departs from *some* traditional norms of "Western rationality" (though this departure is suggested by Aristotle's criticisms of Plato, therefore by an internal criticism of this tradition by other aspects of itself).

In three other important ways the Aristotelian process departs from the norms that are frequently defended in contemporary ethical and social theory. This is not the place to go into these in detail, but they need to be mentioned, or the relationship of our process to its political aim will be misunderstood.[29]

i. Noncommensurability

The procedure insists on treating each of the values involved as a qualitatively distinct item, not reducible to any other item, not conceivable as simply a certain quantity of something else. This commitment to the qualitative integrity of each value is one of the greatest advantages of this procedure over other approaches that might be used (e.g., in some of the literature on development economics) in assessing traditional cultures.[30]

ii. Essentiality of the particular

This procedure insists that evaluative choices cannot be well made unless we confront contexts of choice, and the items in them, as particulars (in this connection, one of us has spoken of "the priority of the particular").[31] Universal rules and other ethical generalizations have worth only insofar as they correctly summarize particulars; they are rules of thumb and cannot, in general, take precedence over concrete perceptions. Correct choice is understood, not as the application of rules that have independent validity to cases, but as an improvisatory perceiving, guided by rules but responsible above all to what is newly seen. This seems to us, again, to have considerable importance for the issues involved in the WIDER project. For if reflection and choice are understood in this way, it becomes vastly more difficult to overlook the complex and individual history of a culture and its people. These historical idiosyncrasies become of high ethical relevance and must be confronted. And they will best be confronted, the procedure tells us, by a person who is experienced in that culture, immersed and not detached. For only that sort of person will be in a position to *see* all the particular factors that bear upon choice in a complex and historically rich context.

iii. Essential role of emotions and imagination

The procedure is immersed in another way: it insists that intellect cannot work well apart from the emotions and the imagination. Many conceptions of rationality, including Plato's, regard these elements of the personality as intrusions and not aids in the valuational process. This means, among other things, that it is vastly easier for them to commend a reflection that is detached and lacking in concrete experience of the culture being evaluated. The Aristotelian insists that a correct "perception" of value cannot be reached at all by the intellect acting alone—and, therefore, not without the kind of experienced connectedness that would enable the person to feel and respond to, as well as intellectually apprehend, the values with which he or she is confronted. Their meaning can be seen only through and in such responses. The emotions are cognitive; they indicate to us where importance is to be found.

We want to put the problem of rational assessment of the values of a culture in this general perspective. In understanding what types of problems are involved in assessing various effects of economic development and in appraising different kinds of social change we cannot simply assume that there are given lists of "good" changes and "bad" ones, as is often taken for granted (e.g., "modernizing" is good, or—alternatively—"preserving tradition" is desirable). We have to see the nature of that identification as itself a dynamic process requiring internal and immersed critical appraisal and involving emotional and imaginative responses to the challenges involved.

Given the nature of this evaluative process, it might look as if such critical work can never come from people who do not belong to that culture. This is not quite correct, but it is important for an outsider to get enough understanding of the culture in question to be able to satisfy the requirement that the critique be internal and immersed in the ways discussed earlier. The problem of understanding can be a serious one even for members of that culture itself, since even they may not have direct experience of all the relevant alternatives. The Aristotelian procedure would recommend various ways of closing this gap as a part of the critical exercise. There are, of course, very many different means of acquiring knowledge and understanding of a traditional culture. It is particularly important in this context to emphasize the relevance of turning to history, and also to literature, including stories—formal and informal. In stories a traditional culture tells about itself. By studying them the "critical subject" not merely discovers the values that are cherished in that culture but is also initiated into an activity of imagination and emotion that can enable her to *see* these values.[32] The discussion in the two preceding sections has pointed to some of the issues involved in this inquiry and to some types of literature that might be particularly relevant. The important additional point to emphasize here is that a valid procedure calls for the use of literature, not so much for detached intellectual judgment, but primarily for involved and responsive understanding and evaluation.

The critical process discussed here, though internal, can frequently lead to criticism of traditional values, and indeed to the rejection of some of them. There are contradictory beliefs entertained, and reflection may lead to reassertion of some and rejection of others. There is also recognition of the beliefs held by others and an understanding of their values, aims, and predicaments. Deeper reflection may lead to the rejection of many things people superficially believe and say. Even an internal critique—not only an external one—can go against practices that may give the appearance of uncompromising conviction.

Many different types of unsustainable values can be illustrated. To take but one example, consider the following example from Aristotle himself. He records—accurately enough—that in traditional Greek thought such great importance is attached to honor and to the avoidance of shame that people frequently say, and at some level think they believe, that honor is the main end in human life. He argues very persuasively that a deeper and broader survey of beliefs will reveal that honor actually is not valuable apart from excellent action: that honor won by bad deeds or by erroneous attribution of good deeds is not prized at all, and that when honor *is* prized, it is so as the fitting cultural sign that an excellent action has been performed. This seems to be, in fact, a perceptive and deep reading of tradition—more correct *as description* than many ancient (and modern) descriptions of Greek values. In a certain sense, however, it is also a genuine criticism of tradition, in that people really did say these things and did act on them in social life. This is the way in which an inquiry that is descriptive—but reflectively descriptive—can also have real critical force.

5. Limits and Reach

There are some special features of the outlined view of a valuational procedure that should be noted as being potentially problematic. In this section two of them are taken up. First, human beings are seen in a particular way in this approach. They are seen essentially as social creatures whose deep aim is to live in a community with others and to share with others a conception of value. This belief plays a regulative role in the entire process and is clearly at a different level from the values that are assessed by the process described (using the regulative value). Another regulative value is the commitment to a tradition of rational argumentation—especially to standards of consistency and clarity. These are, in fact, among the deepest held traditional values in ancient Athenian culture. But they need not be always accepted. (The latter requirement is, for example, not so clearly accepted even in all parts of ancient Greek culture, for example in Sparta, though the Athenian endorsement was largely shared by some others, say, Ionians.)

Those who see the Indian tradition as geared to unreasoned mysticism and uncritical synthesizing (a view that is commonly held but was challenged in earlier sections of this essay) would possibly see in the role of these regulative values—especially in the assumption of a rational tradition—a proof of the inappropriateness of the Aristotelian procedure for Indian use. But the tradition of rational argument is, in fact, one part of the Indian heritage also and has a long history of strong endorsement (see section 3). The difficulty that might have to be faced concerns the existence of some traditions within the plurality of Indian culture which would seem to have no such commitment. But even in those cases it is not obvious that a reasoned *defense* can be sustained any more than a reasoned *criticism* can be made. Indeed, as Aristotle has argued elsewhere, a good case can be made for considering a commitment to noncontradiction to be constitutive at a very basic level of *all* human thought and speech.[33] The absence of this commitment in the culture would be problematic not merely for the procedure discussed here but for any kind of critical procedure—except a purely "external" one in which the values of that culture are rejected or endorsed by critical ("rational") commentators *from outside.* The regulative values are, thus, rather crucial for the entire exercise of internal assessment, to which the motivation underlying the WIDER project in question is committed (no less than we are).

Second, we have a very important set of issues to face about the boundaries of the cultural unit that is to be described in each case. We have spoken of a rational criticism of culture that proceeds by utilizing material internal to the culture itself. But what, after all, is "a culture"? Does all of India have a single culture, and, if so, in what sense? (Does all of the United States?) It is quite easy to see why a member of a certain *part* of a culture could feel resentful of a criticism that comes from another part—from, for example, another religious tradition with different ethical beliefs. Members of two subgroups may well not agree on what are the deepest values. Will not a procedure that decides in favor of one or another set of values seem arbitrary and unfair? We all know in our own political lives the sense of indignation that comes when one discovers that the values of a group whose entire way of life seems completely alien to us have been imposed upon all by a procedure that pretends to fairness. It takes extreme goodwill and long traditions of respect for the deliberative procedures involved not to refuse the result directly. Will not India raise comparable and far greater problems? The Aristotelian procedure says nothing about the value of toleration or about protection of the right to diverse choices of good. These values need to be incorporated into the procedure as regulative, and it will take a lot of thought to decide exactly how and where to do this.

There is a similar problem at the other end. Suppose the culture under survey shows widespread agreement—traditionally and now—on certain value or values. Does this really suffice to make the value or values justified according to our procedure? Or are we entitled to appeal to a larger community—a plurality of related societies, say—for a rational criticism of that entire culture? This is often an urgent question, especially where issues of sexism, racism, and religious intolerance are concerned. We can identify many groups at many times in human history who have held beliefs about female inferiority. Sometimes these views are lightly held, so that they would not survive the process of reflective scrutiny. Frequently they are opposed by other internal values, such as belief in the equal rights of each human individual. And frequently it is true that a richer and more imaginative (and correspondingly more involved or compassionate) look at women's lives will go far to alter perceptions and engender internal criticisms. But this need not invariably happen.[34]

However, the limits of internal criticism are not always easy to define. Any culture is a part of a bigger plurality to which it belongs. The values and traditions of the others may be known and discussed (or *can be* known and discussed) without making criticism based on that understanding in any sense "external." An internal critique cannot ignore internal facts but does not preclude response to other societies and to an extended plurality of cultures. Values of one part of that plurality can, thus, enter in an integral way in an internal critique in another part, since the knowledge of culture A by culture B is as much a part of the internal reality of culture B—indeed more directly so—as it is of culture A.

It is this admissibility of cross-cultural reference that makes the scope of internal critiques a good deal wider than might be at first imagined. It also makes the phenomenon of "value rejection," which was discussed in the first section of this essay, have a more inclusive class of possible causal antecedents than responses to changes occurring primarily inside the economy or society in question. Sustainability of values in a world not cut up into self-contained bits is a more exacting critical test—within the general structure of *internal* criticism—than it is in a world within which information or influence does not travel. While it should not be taken for granted, as Elster has rightly argued (in *Sour Grapes),* that subsequent values are necessarily more important than antecedent values, it is nevertheless difficult not to have respect for subsequent values that are arrived at on the basis of an internal critique in response to enhanced information and understanding (including *inter alia* those about the workings and achievements of other societies and cultures).

Cross-cultural linkages have importance in several different ways. The coverage of principles of justice and equality defended in a society can leave out some groups within that society when it stands largely in isolation, but the same society may find that exclusion to be unviable when less exclusive formats in other societies are known and understood here. The exclusion of slaves in one society, untouchables in another, and women in still another may be much harder to sustain when other societies show the way to different types of social arrangements. This genesis of value rejection can be seen to be a part of an internal process in which facts of knowledge, understanding, and response play a crucial part.

Another respect in which cross-cultural links may be important is in the terms of the requirements of well-being of each person whose interests may command attention. It is possible to think of the well-being of a person as being a matter of his or her ability to do this or be that—what has been called the person's "capabilities."[35] It has been argued that there is some basic similarity in the list of capabilities sought in different parts of the world, even when the commodity bundles associated with the same capabilities may differ (e.g., the ability to appear in public without shame, which may be valued in different cultures in much the same way, may nevertheless have quite different commodity or action requirements in one culture vis-à-vis another).[36] Intercultural linkages help, on the one hand, to identify and endorse the valuation of these basic, *generally* formulated, capabilities, and, on the other, they may also tend to reduce the differences of *specific* forms of commodities and actions needed for the realization of those capabilities in the respective culture.

Coming back to the question of the position of women, which is important both as an illustration and as a case on its own, the issue of linkages is important in several distinct respects. First, linkages make it hard for women to be excluded from consideration of justice and equality in one society when they are not so excluded in others.[37] Second, in highlighting the congruence in valuing certain basic capabilities (e.g., the ability to be well nourished, to be free from avoidable morbidity or premature mortality, to be free to occupy positions of power and influence) the more "open" perspective places certain parameters inescapably in the focus of attention, and they have to be taken into account in judging the position of women as well (rather than judging their well-being or advantage in some specially limited way, such as by the test as to whether women are "happy" with their place in life).[38] Third, as the *forms* of free actions of women in one society influence what is accepted in another, even the differences in the specific *forms* of free action may be revised.

These issues, which may be practically quite important, are to be seen, not as matters of external critique, but as parts of an internal critique when the influences operate *through* internal response to things learned from elsewhere. For example, in criticizing the position of women in, say, today's Iran, reference to freedom enjoyed by women elsewhere is no more "external" than reference to the position of women in Iran's own past if the challenge to the present arrangements comes through criticisms from within, based on responding to conditions at another time or at another place.

The limits of an internal critique can be as wide as the varieties of information that affect the reflection and aspirations of members of the culture in question. The demand for internality of criticism insists that criticism cannot come altogether from outside, but it need not insist on a narrow or exclusive list of the influences that can "count" in the dynamics of a society's internal critique. Internal criticism can have a long reach.

6. Concluding Remarks

In this paper we have been concerned with both substantive and methodological issues. On substantive matters our general conclusion regarding the often-aired conservationist worries about the "undermining" of Indian culture due to the spread of modern science and technology is that they may well be, to a great extent, seriously misleading. It is arguable that these worries are based on drawing alarmist inferences from an overly narrow and biased view of the nature of Indian culture, and also on ignoring the legitimacy, power, and reach of possible internal criticism of parts of the old tradition in the light of new information and understanding. The descriptive and evaluative problems raised by the phenomenon of "value rejection" (as opposed to "object failure") call for a reexamination of the nature of Indian culture and of the requirements of internal criticism.

Notes

1. See Jon Elster, *Sour Grapes* (Cambridge: Cambridge University Press, 1983).

2. On this see Amartya Sen, *Collective Choice and Social Welfare* (San Francisco: Holden-Day, 1970; republished Amsterdam: North-Holland, 1979), chapter 5.

3. See Stephen A. Marglin and Frédérique Apffel Marglin, "Project Guidelines: Development and Technological Transformation in Traditional Societies, Alternative Approaches" (Helsinki: WIDER, 1986).

4. S. Radhakrishnan and S. A. Moore, eds., *A Sourcebook in Indian Philosophy* (Princeton: Princeton University Press, 1957), p. xxiii. Among the other characteristics that Radhakrishnan and Moore identify are: "the intimate relationship of philosophy and life"; "the introspective attitude to reality"; the alleged feature that "most Indian philosophy is idealistic in one form or another"; that "intuition is accepted as the only method through which the ultimate can be known"; "acceptance of authority"; and a "synthetic approach" (pp. xxiii-xxviii).

5. Ibid., pp. 227-249.

6. Ibid., p. xxiii.

7. B. K. Matilal, *Perception: An Essay on Classical Indian Theories of Knowledge* (Oxford: Clarendon Press, 1986), pp. 4-5. Among the earlier disputations there are the Marxist critiques by Debiprasad Chattopadhyaya, *Lokāyata: A Study of Ancient Indian Materialism* (New Delhi: People's Publishing House, 1959) and *Indian Atheism: A Marxist Analysis* (Calcutta: Manisha, 1959).

8. John Locke, *An Essay Concerning Human Understanding* (1690), book 2, chapter 13, 19.

9. Locke, book 2, chapter 23, 2.

10. Matilal, *Perception,* p. 4.

11. The specifically "Hindu" form of much of the interpretation of Indian culture is itself a very serious limitation, both because of the size and importance of other religious communities—especially Islam—in undivided India (and indeed even in India *after* the partition) and also because of the influence of Islamic civilization and values on Hindu culture. The latter has been extensively discussed in Kshiti Mohan Sen's *Hindu O Mushalmáner Jukto Shādhonā* (in Bengali; Calcutta, 1950). See also his *Hinduism* (Harmondsworth: Penguin Books, 1960), especially the chapters on "Medieval Mysticism in India" and "The Bāuls of Bengal."

12. Matilal, *Perception*; see also B. K. Matilal and J. L. Shaw, eds., *Analytical Philosophy in Comparative Perspective: Exploratory Essays in Current Theories and Classical Indian Theories of Meaning and Reference* (Dordrecht: Reidel, 1985).

13. As a matter of some interest, as far as influence abroad is concerned, the two main religions that India helped in spreading abroad were *Buddhism*

(through the efforts of Aśoka and later ones) and *Islam*, which went to South-east Asian countries (such as Indonesia), not from the Arab world, but from India (in particular Gujarat).

14. A. Murray, *Reason and Society in the Middle Ages*, revised edition (Oxford: Clarendon Press, 1985), p. 168. Murray's own analysis is concerned with showing that "the pattern of the numerals adoption will reflect, not any foreign technological bombardment, but native aspirations and pressures" (p. 168). It is arguable that this perspective may be relevant not merely in under-standing the impact of Eastern technology on the West but also the converse. See also section 5.

15. Ian Hacking relates the development of sampling and probability theory in India to the presence of "an advanced merchant system"; see *The Emergence of Probability* (Cambridge: Cambridge University Press, 1975), p. 8.

16. Buddha's critical views of "personal identity" have also received some serious philosophical analysis and support recently; see Derek Parfit, *Reasons and Persons* (Oxford: Clarendon Press, 1984), chapters 12 and 13, and appendix J.

17. See Madhava Acharya, *The Sarva-Darsana Samgraha Or Review of Different Systems of Hindu Philosophy,* tr. R. B. Cowell and A. E. Gough (New Delhi: Cosmo Publications, 1976). Radhakrishnan and Moore also provide partial translations of some other documents related to this tradition, in particu-lar *Sarvasiddhāntasaṁgraha* by Saṁkara, the seventh-century treatise *Tattvopa-plavasiṁhā* (highly polemical "against all of the other schools of Indian Philos-ophy"), and the ancient play *Prabodha-candrodaya* (literally translated, "the moonrise of intellect") with characters expounding materialist views.

18. On this see Ranajit Guha, "On Some Aspects of Historiography of Colonial India," in *Subaltern Studies* 1, ed. R. Guha (New Delhi: Oxford University Press, 1982).

19. See Nussbaum, "Therapeutic Arguments: Epicurus and Aristotle," in *The Norms of Nature,* ed. M. Schofield and G. Striker (Cambridge: Cambridge University Press, 1986); also "Nature, Function, and Capability: Aristotle on the Basis of Political Distribution," read to the Oberlin Philosophy Colloquium, April 1986, and to be published in the proceedings of the 12th Symposium Aristotelicum (1987) and *Oxford Studies in Ancient Philosophy,* 1988.

20. On this passage *(Nicomachean Ethics,* 1145 b 1ff.) and Aristotle's method in both science and ethics see Nussbaum, *The Fragility of Goodness* (Cambridge: Cambridge University Press, 1986), chapter 8 (which is much the same as her "Saving Aristotle's Appearances," in *Language and Logos,* ed. M. Schofield and M. Nussbaum [Cambridge: Cambridge University Press, 1982]).

21. See Nussbaum, *The Fragility of Goodness,* chapter 8, and G.E.L. Owen, *"Tithenai ta Phainomena"* in Owen, *Logic, Science, and Dialectic: Col-lected Essays on Greek Philosophy* (London, 1986).

22. This contrast is developed at greater length in Nussbaum, *The Ther-apy of Desire* (The Martin Classical Lectures, 1986), forthcoming. For the account of Plato see also *The Fragility of Goodness,* chapter 5.

23. Oxford: Clarendon Press, 1986.

24. Again, this argument is developed with full textual references in Nussbaum, *The Therapy of Desire.*

25. J. Rawls, "Kantian Constructivism in Ethical Theory: Dewey Lectures 1980," *Journal of Philosophy* 77 (September 1980). See also his *A Theory of Justice* (Cambridge, Mass.: Harvard University Press, 1971), pp. 46-53.

26. See H. Putnam, *Reason, Truth, and History* (Cambridge: Cambridge University Press, 1981) and especially *The Many Faces of Realism,* The Carus Lectures, 1985, forthcoming. For a more detailed development of some aspects of Aristotle's position see Nussbaum, "Non-Relative Virtues: An Aristotelian Approach," a WIDER Working Paper, in *Midwest Studies in Philosophy,* vol. 13, *Ethical Theory: Character and Virtue,* ed. Peter A. French, Theodore E. Uehling, Jr., and Howard K. Wettstein (Notre Dame, IN: University of Notre Dame Press, 1988).

27. Aristotle, *Eudemian Ethics,* 1216a 26-39; see Nussbaum, "Therapeutic Arguments."

28. See, for example, Carol Gilligan, *In a Different Voice* (Cambridge: Harvard University Press, 1985).

29. All these points are given a detailed discussion in Nussbaum, "The Discernment of Perception: An Aristotelian Conception of Private and Public Morality," in *Proceedings of Boston Area Colloquium in Ancient Philosophy* (1985), pp. 151–201.

30. See Nussbaum, "The Discernment of Perception" and also "Plato on Commensurability and Desire," *Proceedings of the Aristotelian Society, Supplementary Volume,* 84 (1984), pp. 55-80; and Amartya Sen, "Plural Utility," *Proceedings of the Aristotelian Society,* 80 (1980).

31. Nussbaum, "The Discernment of Perception" and *The Fragility of Goodness,* chapter 10. Also her "Perceptive Equilibrium: Literary Theory and Ethical Theory," forthcoming in *Critical Projections,* ed. R. Cohen (London: Methuen, 1987), and also "Moral Attention and the Moral Task of Literature," in *Philosophy and the Question of Literature,* ed. A. Cascardi (Baltimore: Johns Hopkins University Press, 1987); a shorter version of the latter was previously published as " 'Finely Aware and Richly Responsible': Moral Attention and the Moral Task of Literature," *Journal of Philosophy* 82 (1985): 516-529.

32. See Nussbaum, "Moral Attention and the Moral Task of Literature."

33. See Nussbaum, *The Fragility of Goodness,* chapter 8 (= "Saving Aristotle's Appearances"), and also H. Putnam, "There Is at Least One a priori Truth," *Erkenntnis* 13 (1978): 153-170, reprinted in Putnam, *Realism and Reason: Philosophical Papers,* vol. 3 (Cambridge: Cambridge University Press, 1983), pp. 98-114.

34. Aristotle's infamous remarks concerning women and slaves are a case in point, though their superficiality shows some evidence of lack of reflection.

35. The position argued in Amartya Sen, "Equality of What?" in *Tanner Lectures on Human Values,* vol. 1, ed. S. McMurrin (Cambridge: Cambridge University Press, 1980), reprinted in his *Choice, Welfare and Measurement*

(Oxford: Blackwell, 1982) and in his "Well-being, Agency and Freedom: The Dewey Lectures 184," *Journal of Philosophy* 82 (1985).

36. The point goes back to Adam Smith, *An Inquiry into the Nature and Causes of the Wealth of Nations* (1776). On this see Amartya Sen, *Resources, Values and Development* (Oxford: Blackwell, 1984), and in some form to Aristotle himself, on which (and for some further explorations of the Aristotelian perspective) see Martha Nussbaum, "Nature, Function, and Capability: Aristotle on the Basis of Political Distribution."

37. One could certainly ask whether Aristotle's views on women could have survived critical reflection armed with the information and understanding of social arrangements that have emerged since his times.

38. On this see Amartya Sen, *Commodities and Capabilities* (Amsterdam: North-Holland, 1985); also his "Well-being, Agency and Freedom: The Dewey Lectures 1984" (1985).

Phenomenological Rationality and the Overcoming of Relativism*

Jitendra N. Mohanty

Instead of first developing the phenomenological concept of rationality, and then applying that concept in the task of overcoming relativism, I will, in this article, follow the reverse order: I will first show that relativism can be overcome from within phenomenology and then draw some morals about the type of rationality this procedure of overcoming relativism illustrates.

I turn now to the first task.

1. Phenomenology and Relativism

In the early years of the phenomenological movement it appeared as though relativism had been, once for all, overcome. The elaborate and widely ramified critique of psychologism was also taken to be, by implication, a critique of all relativism and a defense not merely of the idea of pure logic but also of the possibility of arriving at essential, and so nonrelative, truths about all sorts of things: religion, law, art, and society, to mention only some.

Such is, however, the fate of phenomenology that relativistic implications appear to disrupt its essentialism from within. This occurs in various way, some of which I will recall.[1] First of all, the purely descriptive, nonreductionist approach to phenomena inevitably led to a pluralism which refused to be rounded off within, or for the sake of, a system. Consider, for example, space: purely descriptively, you have sacred space and profane space,[2] space as experienced in a familiar setting, and space

*An early version of this paper was read at the meetings of The German Phenomenological Society in Trier, June 1985, and has appeared in German in *Vernunft und Kontingenz,* ed. Wolfgang Orth (Freiburg/München: Karl Alber, 1986).

that is threatening and strange (in an unfamiliar setting), space as experienced in walking or in dancing, in listening to music, or in looking at a painting.[3] How are you to bring these data under a common "essence"? All those ethnological data which seemingly promote relativisms would find their places within such a descriptive phenomenology. The very idea of one objective world, of one moral theory, even of one life-world would be threatened by such descriptive phenomenology.

Second, as essentialism in phenomenology imperceptibly yielded to meaning-constitution, and as the given data for descriptive research were found to have been preconstituted by meaning-conferring, and thus interpretive, acts, the possibility of very different, often radically different, interpretations of the same hyletic data, and so of the constitution of incommensurable objectivities, came to the fore. The transition to the relativism of alternate conceptual frameworks did not require a long step. In fact, all that was needed was another premise: namely, that every interpretive act presupposes, and is already embedded in, an interpretive framework (a step Husserl, perhaps, never could take).

Third, as phenomenology, in its attempt to be *radical,* reached the seemingly ultimate ground of the *life-world* that is prior to, and also the point of departure for, all theoretical constituting acts, it also found itself confronted with the same specter of relativism which it had faced early during the purely descriptive program. For if life-world is truely to be *life*-world and not a theoretical posit, then one must recognize that there is not one life-world, but in fact there are many life-worlds. Here, again, ethnology finds itself useful for phenomenology. A primitive tribal community of New Guinea certainly does not have the same life-world as the present-day New Yorker. Whose life-world was Schutz describing?

I believe that a sound philosophy, phenomenological or not, must be able to overcome relativism. But I also believe that the early phenomenologist's optimism that relativism had been disposed of was too hasty. If relativism is to be overcome, one cannot just begin by "refuting it"; one must be able to "go through" it as far as one can and *then* go beyond it. In other words, the journey has to be long and understanding, and the overcoming has to be from within relativism. In this essay I will briefly follow such a path, in its barest outline, and toward the end indicate its bearing on moral philosophy.

2. "Alternate Conceptual Frameworks"/ "Radically Different Worlds": Some Attempts at Refutations

If Husserl rejected relativism as incoherent, Donald Davidson in a well-known paper[4] has sought to demonstrate that the talk of alternate conceptual frameworks (which, as I pointed out, emerges from within descriptive as well as constitutive phenomenology) is unintelligible. But Davidson's aim is not merely to show that the idea of a conceptual scheme as alternate to ours makes no sense but also to prove the far more radical thesis that the very talk of a conceptual framework is unintelligible. As a consequence, he insists, the very distinction between conceptual scheme and uninterpreted data must also be given up. To give up that distinction would amount to giving up all transcendental arguments, and so all foundationalist transcendental philosophies—to give up, in other words, the project of legitimizing the application of a conceptual framework, the *quaestio juris* of the Kantian philosophy.

I will not presently comment upon the claim that Davidson has given a transcendental argument to prove the impossibility of all transcendental arguments. My present concern is to what extent he succeeds in showing the impossibility of a radical relativism of conceptual frameworks or of their correlative worlds. Davidson's argument runs somewhat like this. To speak of alternate conceptual schemes is to speak of *radically* different schemes in the sense that they must have to be mutually untranslatable. If there are alternate conceptual schemes, they must be embodied in languages which are not translatable to ours. But it is this claim which Davidson finds unacceptable, especially because any such conceptual scheme could be true without making any sense to us. For Davidson a theory of meaning is indeed reducible to a theory of truth, so that the notion of truth cannot be divorced from that of translation (if the Tarskian convention T embodies our best intuitions about "truth"). It therefore could make no sense to speak of a conceptual scheme as being true but untranslatable. Now, of course we are not obliged to accept Donaldson's premise that the Tarskian convention T does indeed embody our best intuition about truth, or his other assumption that a theory of meaning is reducible to a theory of truth (which is consequent upon denying the Frege-Husserl semantics to which I am committed). Nevertheless, we have to take into account Davidson's point that an alternate conceptual scheme or talk about a radically different world, being untranslatable to our home language, would make no sense. In order to bring out the nature of this argument and assess its value I will compare it with an argument by Husserl which seemingly is to the same effect, that is, a denial of radically different worlds.

The argument occurs in Husserl's writings at various places. I will recall three such places.

First, in §48 of the *Ideas* I Husserl writes:

What is perceivable by *one* Ego must *in principle* be conceivable by *every* Ego. And though as *a matter of fact* it is not true that everyone stands or can stand in a relation of empathy of inward understanding of every other one, . . . yet in point of principle there exist *essential possibilities for the setting up of an understanding.* . . . If there are worlds or real things at all, the empirical motivations which constitute them must be *able* to reach into my experience, and that of every single Ego.[5]

In §60 of the *Cartesian Meditations* Husserl asks: "Is it *conceivable* (to me, . . .) that two or more separate *pluralities of monads, i.e.,* pluralities *not in communion,* coexist, each of which accordingly constitute *a world of its own,* so that together they constitute two worlds . . . ?" To this question he answers: "Manifestly, instead of being a conceivability, that is a pure absurdity. . . the two worlds are then necessarily mere 'surrounding worlds', . . . and mere aspects of a single objective world, which is *common* to them. For indeed, the two intersubjectivities are not absolutely isolated. As imagined by me, each of them is in necessary communion with me . . . as the constitutive primal monad relative to them." "Actually therefore," Husserl concludes, "there *can* exist only a single community of monads."[6]

Finally, in a fragment dating from 1921, now included in the second intersubjectivity volume,[7] Husserl discusses the same issue in greater detail. He sets out to prove that if there are several subjects, they must necessarily be able to be in a possible communicative state (*Kommerzium*) and therefore constitute a common world. By the common world he means one spatiotemporal world in which the subjects as corporeal beings apprehend each other as "other" subjects. Apprehension of the other subject's body *(Leib),* which is necessary for apprehending the other as a subject, requires being in the same spatiotemporal system. Furthermore, if there is to be a plurality of subjects, this plurality must be, in principle, experienceable as a plurality. Every experience or presentation of such a plurality points to a possible subject. Such a subject must be in an *Einfühlungszusammenhang* (i.e., belong to an interconnection of empathetic understanding with the others). Therefore, such a subject and the others, that is, the plurality of subjects we hypothesized, must belong to one common world.

These arguments are in part intended to prove that there must be one space and time, that is, one spatiotemporal world for all subjects, although each subject may have its own *Mit-Welt.* For otherwise (i) these subjects would not apprehend each other as subjects; (ii) the plurality of subjects that is hypothesized will not be apprehended *as a plural-*

ity by any possible subject, and so the hypothesization would be mean-ingless; and (iii) the positing of a world that is for only one subject will be meaningless for another unless the latter can experience the world as his. The argument can be generalized to prove the unity of the world in a sense that goes beyond the thesis of one space and one time.

Compare Husserl's arguments with Davidson's. Davidson's argu-ment insists on translatability, for the ideas of translatability, meaning-fulness, and truth cannot be separated. If there is to be another concep-tual framework, or talk of another world, any such must be translatable to mine, our home language; if it is, then it is not an alternate conceptu-al scheme, not a description of another radically different world. Hus-serl's argument insists on "Vorstellbarkeit." The other subject must be presentable along with his body to any of the others, to me, to start with. The other's world (regarded initially as being radically different) must be experienceable by me. And the plurality of subjects (each *ex hypoth-esis* with its own world) must be presentable to someone as a plurality. Otherwise each of these locutions (that there is another subject, another world, a plurality of subjects) would make no sense to me but so also to any of the others. Both Davidson and Husserl are making a similar demand upon the relativist: The talk of alternate schemes or worlds can make sense only if such a scheme is translatable to ours, that is, home language; the talk of a world would make sense only if it is *experiencea-ble* by me or by us (who already share a common world). It might appear that the idea of translatability is free from that subjectivism which attaches to the idea of experienceability, but the fault of subjectiv-ism is mitigated to the point of being totally harmless when what is required is experienceability by any subject whatsoever. Likewise, the requirement of translatability to *our* home language may appear to be chauvinistic, but this is removed by requiring that all alternate schemes should be mutually translatable.

What is dissatisfying with this way of overcoming relativism— Davidson's or Husserl's—is that *it again takes a short cut.* It is impatient with relativism, even as an initial truth. In fact, one suspects whether the "refutation" does not beg the issue. What I, on the other hand, want to begin with is a recognition of the fact that a certain cultural pluralism (and an associated thesis of pluralism of worlds) is one of the desiderata of modern ways of thinking. An unadulterated monistic conception of the world—be it the conception of the world of antiquity or of modern science—has simply no future. Richard Rorty has complained that transcendental philosophies have sought to legitimize a favored repre-sentation of the world.[8] We simply cannot start today with any such favored representation in the same way as Kant started from the world of which Euclidean geometry and Newtonian physics held good. If we are to find a way out of relativism, it can only be *after* the phenomenon of relativism has been granted its initial recognition. But where can we go from there? What path lies open for us?

3. Another Husserlian Path

Two suggestions of Husserlian thinking have been mentioned by me and then set aside. One was to insist on essence of "world," even if there are many worlds. This essence, which is to be a "formal essence" after all, is given by a formal ontology. What was threatened at the level of contents is thereby gained only at the level of form. The other was to tie the significance of any locution about alternate worlds to experienceability by *me*, and, in the long run, by any and every ego. This delivers a common intersubjective world at the level of contents, but, not unlike Davidson's, appears to beg the issue, and is no less impatient with the phenomenon of relativism than the first, the eidetic move.

But the same Husserlian thinking provides us with another, and to my mind, more promising lead: this is the famed principle of noesis-noema correlation. In order to bring out how this can help us here let me recall a distinction that Davidson draws in the paper referred to earlier. The talk of many different worlds, Davidson points out,[9] is ambiguous as between (i) talking about the many possible worlds from the same point of view and (ii) talking about them as though they are but the same world seen from many different points of view. "Strawson's many imagined worlds are seen (or heard)—anyway described—from the same point of view, Kuhn's one world is seen from different points of view." Davidson has no quarrel with the former sort of concept, and so with the Leibnizian talk of many possible worlds. Nor does Husserl have anything against such locution. "Naturally Leibniz is right," Husserl writes, "that infinitely many monads and groups of monads are conceivable, that it does not follow that all these possibilities are compossible; and, again, when he says that infinitely many worlds might have been 'created', but not two or more at once, since they are incompossible."[10]

What Davidson wants to rule out is the possibility of describing the same world from radically different points of view, where these points of view are mutually incommensurable, and their descriptions mutually untranslatable. In fact, what he ends up by proving—what was the ruling intention all along—is that there is *no point of view* on the world, no conceptual scheme by which it is interpreted. There can only be different languages in which to describe the world, and these languages are mutually translatable.

Obviously, Husserl's rejection of relativism in the sense of the thesis that there are mutually incommensurable worlds can amount neither to the thesis that we cannot speak of many possible worlds any two of which are jointly incompossible, nor to the thesis that we cannot describe the same world from many different points of view. The notion of point of view, of interpretive framework, is not ruled out by Husserl. What he is rejecting is the *actuality* (not possibility) of many incommensurable worlds. So although it appeared a little while ago as though both Husserl and Davidson were attacking the same thesis, it indeed now seems that Husserl does in fact envisage that the same world must be describable from many different points of view. What he was rejecting is the thesis that each of these descriptions is *a* world. It is rather a world-noema. The different world-noemata can nevertheless be of one and the same world and therefore must be, in the long run, commensurable.

I do not think anyone would want to deny that there are different points of view from which one and the same thing can be perceived, thought of, talked about. But to say that there are *radically* different points of view such that the descriptions they generate are totally incommensurable is quite another thing, and I deny this. Between the view that there are such incommensurable worlds (or, untranslatable languages, totally unintelligible conceptual schemes) and the view that all talk of possible nonactual worlds involves nothing more than "redistribution of truth-values" over sentences in our present languages "in various systematic ways" there must be an intermediate position which I want to adopt. In order to formulate such a position I will proceed through several steps. First, I will indicate how the principle of noesis-noema correlation applies to the problem at hand. Second, I will distinguish between two levels of discourse: internal and external. I will, in effect, insist upon the relevance of the idea of transcendental ego to this issue. Finally, I will make a distinction between "person" and "subject."

(a) Let us view each world as a noematic structure. To each such structure there would correspond an entire nexus of interpretive acts on the part of the community for which such a world obtains. We may then speak of a noesis-noema correlation that is itself nonrelativistic. If the essentialism was a shortcut and also too formalistic a step, and the tying of all meaningfulness to experienceability by *any* ego too liberal (inasmuch it permits every one to be an insider to every world), the present manner of isolating invariant noesis-noema correlation structure overcomes relativism by taking seriously the phenomena on which relativism is founded. The next step would be this: just as the identity of an object is constituted by the system of noemata through which "one and the same" object is presented, so also in the case under consideration the one world—not in the sense of the totality of all worlds, but in the sense of that whose versions they all are—may be looked upon as that regulative concept which not only orders the various quasi-incommensurable worlds but also delineates the path that shall lead us out of a possibly hopeless chaos toward communication and understanding.

On the intermediate position I am seeking to formulate, each world-noema is different from any other, it embodies a unique point of view, but it also "overlaps" and "intersects" some other world-noemata—thus making transition from one to the other *theoretically* possible. (Although W^1 and W^3 would appear to be utterly distinct, their distinction is mediated by W^2 with which both "overlap.") Translatability is a deceptive concept in any case. If you can adhere to a very strict concept of translatability, no "radical translation" between any two languages is possible. And yet with a less strict concept we do translate. Every language can say—as Gadamer has stated—what is said in any other, *but in its own way.* This "way" alone is what is untranslatable.

(b) To get clear about the situation, let us distinguish between two levels of discourse: the internal and external. At the internal level there are "radically" different worlds, conceptual frameworks, languages, such that for the *person* who naively lives *within* his own, the others are "bare others," at most "interesting," but still "do not make sense." Translatability and intelligibility are at most ideals, but they were never meant to work out. Translation, understanding, and communication take place within a common, shared world. At this level there is a home language and a home "life-world."

However, if I am to be able to speak of alternate conceptual schemes, I must be able to translate the others into mine, or mine into the others'. Languages (and schemes) must be mutually translatable. But when I assert this, I am taking, not the "internal" standpoint, but rather the "external" standpoint, from which stance any language is as good as any other; none is *mine.* All possible worlds are then spread out before my gaze; none is more my own than any other. I am then a transcendental ego. The transcendental ego is no standpoint: all possible standpoints are arraigned before his look. The transcendental ego has no *home* language.

Thus the empirical person living in his world, speaking his language, using his conceptual scheme, sharing in his tradition, is subject to a point of view of his own, of his community. But he does not, in his prereflective naivity, know that he sees the world from a standpoint. He lives in, perceives, knows the world, the only world that is there for him. That, however, he is subject to a perspective, a standpoint, a conceptual framework, is brought out by reflection (and the reflection may be occasioned by a great variety of circumstances). But to be able to survey all possible points of view, conceptual frameworks, languages objectively—as making sense to each other; therefore, as commensurable and mutually translatable—one needs to take up a stance, which is none other than that of a transcendental ego.

The thesis of relativity of worlds is an initial response of reflection. But this thesis of relativity has to be limited by the thesis of the common horizon within which these standpoints are after all possible. The *one* world is not the common *content* to which the different world-noemata provide different conceptual schemes. The many worlds are then neither gotten by "redistribution of truth-values" for sentences in the home language, nor are they different conceptualizations of one and the same preexistent world. They are noemata *of* one world, but the one world is also *being* constituted through them—always under the threat of being broken down.

4. 'The World of Physics'

It is not my intention to identify this concept of one world of which the many worlds are noemata with the world of physics or the Kantian Nature. There is no doubt, though, that the world of physics does indeed lay claim to this status. For me it is but another such noematic structure. The expression 'world of physics' is ambiguous. For one thing it means the world of scientific entities. In another sense it means the world of experienceable things and events determined and governed by laws of physics, and for whose explanation the scientific entities are posited as theoretical constructs. Nature, as Kant understood it, is the world of physics in the second sense. Kant, as is well known, regarded Nature in this sense as constructed out of simple, atomic, discrete sense impressions. I basically agree with the Kantian point of view. However, since I reject the Humean-Kantian conception of "impression," I regard the Kantian Nature as constructed rather out of the many prescientific *worlds* in which we, with our prescientific interests, find ourselves. Any such world is a sedimented structure of meanings inherited from the past. I will not in this essay develop the broad stages of the process by which the scientific-objective world emerges, with its imperious claim to be the world-in-itself, out of the prescientific worlds. It claims to be the world as it is in itself, when all human subjectivity is removed from the scene. Paradoxically, however, science itself gives rise to a new tradition, and like all traditions, this one also is constituted by sedimentation of meaning structures. What is important for my present concern is that in my view the world of physics is a higher order noematic structure, founded upon prescientific noemata, claiming to supersede their validity-claims, but with no more than its own validity-claim. The appeal to science, then, with a view to overcome relativism is futile.

5. Two Clarifications

In my attempt to find a way out of relativism I have made use of two strategies. One of them is the idea of overlapping of noemata. The other is that of translatability. In this section I will briefly clarify these two as I want them to be understood.

(a) The basic idea of overlapping of noemata is Husserl's, but my present use of it was first *suggested* to me by Michael Dummett's use of the principle of "conservative extension" with a view to make communication possible between classical and intuitionistic logics. Let W and W^1 be two world-noemata such that they are furthest removed from each other in the sense that any communication between them seems impossible. In such a case what I postulate is that there will always be a series of Ws such that (i) every succeeding member of the series overlaps the preceeding member and (ii) the first member of the series will overlap W and the final member will overlap W^1.

W W^1

Nothing in this guarantees that there is only one such series. There may be in fact many different ways of linking W and W^1. But in any case the result would be the same: there would be in principle a way of establishing communication between W and W^1. In conceiving of such a series of overlapping noemata I am of course assuming that each W is *not* a fully holistic system; if it were so, it would just be impossible for it to share part of its contents with another W.

(b) By insisting that any language is translatable to any other I may be taken to be begging the issue. However, that would be the case only if we take "translatability" in a static sense. In this static sense we ascribe translatability or the lack of it to two languages L^1 and L^2 when each is regarded as a completed totality. We freeze the growing process that a language is and want to find out if one such frozen system is translatable or not to another such. It is in this sense that I take Davidson to be insisting on translatability. My use of it, however, is different. I take it that as L^1 is translated into L^2, or vice versa, in this process both L^1 and L^2 undergo transformation. They both end up enriched. Translation in this sense changes both the languages. One cannot arrest L^1 at its present stage of growth and demand L^2 to be translated into it, or vice versa. Like interpersonal communication, translation enriches both. In this sense, then, mutual translatability is a regulative ideal that we can hardly dispense with: languages have to grow toward its realization.

6. The "Transcendental Ego," Impersonality, and Objectivity

Since I have characterized the point of view of the transcendental ego as that of an outsider, a few words need to be added to avoid misunderstanding on this score. It has wrongly been held by many that the point of view of transcendental ego yields a fully objective, and objectively determinate, world, such as the world of physics. However, it is not without significance that in Husserl's thinking the idea of transcendental ego and the idea of noesis-noema correlation are closely interlinked. From the stance of the transcendental ego, all are not objects, but rather all objects are meaning-structures. What we have then is not one impersonal description of the world in which personal or communal interpretations do not figure at all. What we have is rather an array of noesis-noema correlations, an array of worlds and morals, each having its own validity-claim and its origin in interpreting and evaluating acts. Thus the transcendental ego is antimonistic: it respects pluralism and is tolerant of diversities. In this sense transcendental thinking, instead of being committed to a favored representation of the world, shall respect limitless diversities of interpretations.

The overcoming of relativism that phenomenology should espouse cannot consist in that *violent* act by which one validity-claim imperiously supersedes all others but shall rather consist in that gentle and tolerant view which recognizes that unity is always in the process of being achieved by communication and is just too fragile to be sustained by any violence. The world-in-itself is rather a regulative idea that guides communication and translation. To elevate any world, scientific or religious, to the status of absolute is to fall into the trap of relativistic arguments: the "other" would remain unconvinced, and communication and internal criticism would be closed off.

After indicating how phenomenology can overcome relativism, I propose to use the preceeding argument as a case study for eliciting a few lessons about the peculiar nature of phenomenological rationality.

First of all, it is clear that phenomenological rationality is *not* the formal-mathematical rationality which finds expression in the formalism of logic, semantics, formal ontology, and mathematics. The formal-mathematical rationality is empty, the universality that is accomplished pays the price of abstracting from all contents. But while not eschewing this empty formalism, phenomenology does not simply turn away from it. Rather, it recognizes its role as an incipient formal ontology and proceeds to the concrete domain of consciousness wherein these forms come into being through a constructive and constitutive rationality.

At the other end from formal-mathematical rationality is the anthropological, local, cultural rationality which sustains relativisms of all sorts and which resists attempts to impose universality *ab extra*. There is an initial validity of the claim of each such "system" of the local standpoint, the conceptual framework of each culture, to be autonomous, refusing absorption into a larger scheme of things.

But the phenomenological rationality rejects as much that empty formal universality as this concrete particularity. Using a Hegelian jargon, one may say that what phenomenology is after is rather a concrete universality.

The search for essences and essential structures—so inalienably linked with the idea of phenomenology—holds out hopes for reaching such a concrete universality. The rationality that manifests itself in essential structures of phenomena is not however typically phenomenological; it is rather basically Greek, and to the extent phenomenology exhibits it, it is a participant in the grand tradition inherited from the Greeks. Two serious difficulties vitiate the quest for essences: for one thing, the method employed—construed as a method for discovering essences—is hopelessly circular; for another, an essence characterizes a thing only under a certain description and not under another (recall Quine's famous example of a bicyclist mathematician).

The truly phenomenological rationality, then, exhibits itself in the next move from here onward: in the suspension of the first-order truth claims and in transforming the concern with essences (formal or material) to concern with *meanings*. The local anthropological systems, then, reveal themselves as meaning-structures, or complex noemata. Universality is *not* imposed *ab extra* on the plurality of such noemata but is permitted to emerge through the process of overlapping among such noemata. It is in this idea of "overlapping" and "emergence" of identity, rather than its imposition through a metaphysical essentialism (as through political absolution), that rationality is seen in operation.

I will conclude by drawing attention to two features of this process. Here, in the first place, there is no opposition between diversity and unity. Unity is being worked out rather than being a preexistent metaphysical entity. The process is gentle and tolerant rather than violent and imperious. In the second place, the rationality that underlies this process is a reconciliation between the perceptual and the communicative models. In perception we find the origin of the idea of overlapping noemata; in conversation we find the origin of the idea of "conservative extension." Phenomenological rationality lies perched between the two.

Notes

1. David Carr has shown this well in his unpublished essay with the same title as my present essay.

2. Mircea Eliade has emphasized this distinction in his numerous studies on the phenomenology of religion.

3. Cp. E. Straus, *Phenomenological Psychology* (New York, 1968).

4. D. Davidson, "On the Very Idea of Conceptual Scheme," in *Proceedings of the American Philosophical Association,* 19 (1973/74), pp. 5-20.

5. *Husserliana,* vol. III/1, p. 102f.

6. *Husserliana,* vol. I, p. 166f.

7. *Husserliana,* vol. XIV, pp. 91-101.

8. R. Rorty, *Philosophy and the Mirror of Human Nature* (Princeton, 1980).

9. Davidson, "On the Very Idea," p. 9.

10. *Husserliana,* vol. I, p. 167.

Ethical Relativism and Confrontation of Cultures

Bimal Krishna Matilal

1. Moral Relativism Revisited

I shall argue that the culture-relativity of moral norms is usually ill-conceived and generally indefensible.[1] Whether there are culture-invariant principles of morality or not is a question that will inevitably arise, but to this I shall give only some suggestive answers. There are various strands in our texture of the controversy over moral relativism. I isolate the following positions:

1. Ethical standards found in different cultures are only in apparent conflict with each other. This plurality exists only at the surface. At some deeper level there is only one set of moral standards to which everybody should conform, and it is possible to discover this singular standard of universal morality through rational means. I shall call it moral monism or singularism.

2. Intercultural plurality of moral standards is reflected also in the intracultural plurality of norms (which is witnessed by the pervasive presence of moral conflicts in persons). "My country before my family" is a classic example of a practical resolution of such a conflict. The diversity of goods in a single moral domain demands an assessment of their priorities and relative importance leading presumably to a single coherent ordering of goods. This goal may be ever elusive, but a constant effort to order priorities is desirable. I shall call this pluralism.

3. Genuine plurality exists, and some are more right than others, but there is no way to decide or know which ones are better or worse than others. Despite the air of Orwellian cliché, this can be a seriously held position. I shall call it agnosticism. Moral conflicts on this view would be ineliminable.

4. Among the many moral norms available across culture it is

impossible to judge objectively some as better or worse than others, for although they may be mutually comprehensible, there is no transcultural standard of evaluation. Culture-bound norms are neither good nor bad. This is what I shall call soft relativism.

5. Culture-bound moral norms are both incommensurable and mutually incomprehensible, and hence one may say that one norm is just as good or as bad as the other. This I shall call hard relativism.

I believe there are formidable objections to all these positions. Of these, 4 and 5 are clearly relativistic, 3 is in the twilight zone, while 1 and 2 seem to be compatible with realism. I shall try to support a modified version of 2 and argue that while 1 or even 2 may encourage the risk of what is called "moral jingoism," both 4 and 5 (and to some extent 3) encourage and sustain a sort of moral insouciance that was regarded as a "virtue" by some liberal colonialists. I further believe that if morality is to be a domain of ultimate importance, then both must be avoided, jingoism and insouciance.

Although we are bound to talk about cultural relativism, our concern here is with ethics. Ethical or moral realism has notoriously been on the firing line, more so than cognitive realism by any reckoning. The controversy about the so-called gap between fact and value is only too familiar. But one can still be an ethical realist while believing the gap to exist. J. L. Mackie has described ethics as "Inventing Right and Wrong" and categorically denied that there can be any *objective* values (*Ethics,* Penguin, 1977). It may be possible to distinguish between two kinds of nonobjectivism: moral relativism and subjectivism. A significant point about subjectivism is what we can call Hamlet's maxim: neither is good or bad, but thinking makes it so. Relativism insists, not on the individual thinking, but on the fact that there are alternative (irreducible) norms imbedded in different culture-groups, and hence what is good for one group may not be so for the other. Further it claims that there is no rational basis for choice between such alternative norms. Relativism could be intracultural (as distinct from one derived from cultural relativism), for moral conflicts and moral disagreements are proverbially widespread within a culture or a group, and there seems to be very little scope for rational choice to be made among rival moral theories. Our main target, however, will be intercultural moral relativism.

Some philosophers distinguish between cognitive or metaphysical realism and moral realism and seriously argue in favor of the former while rejecting the latter. There are also those who find it hard to stomach metaphysical realism today (regard it as a sort of a vestige of bygone ages, a dogma of Western science). These philosophers are also apt to argue willynilly for relativism in ethics. It is a rather curious phenomenon that the metaphysical realist's distrust for moral realism has been rather pervasive. A relevant point has been made by H. Putnam on this issue. He says that the modern tendencies to be too realistic about physics—and too subjectivist about ethics—are in fact "interlinked," for both seem to be connected with the not fully examined, but widespread, consensus among people about physics furnishing us with one True Theory (truth independent of all observers) and ethics offering us a variety of moral norms, culture-relative or group-relative, and/ or a number of irreconcilable and irreducible (conflicting) moral theories. However, recent discussion on the nature of science or scientific theories as well as on the nature of truth and objectivity has slackened our faith in such a conception of science (as Science providing us with a perfectly "transparent" description of reality). Thus, it may be contended that the so-called truths of science cannot be entirely "value-free," and by the same token the truths of ethics cannot be entirely "fact-free."

An uncritical version of ethical relativism is current among people. Bernard Williams has called it "the anthropologist's heresy," also "vulgar relativism," which he has convincingly shown to be absurd and inconsistent (1981, 132–143). This muddled doctrine was once popular with some "liberal" colonialists. It asserts that there are ultimate moral disagreements among societies such that moral adjudication of right and wrong is always relative to a given society, and then it goes on to say that we are required to be equally well-disposed to everyone else's ethical beliefs, for it is wrong to condemn the moral values of others. While we might recognize its beneficial effect in the past, during the history of colonization, we need not be blind to the weakness of its theoretical foundation. It is sometimes claimed that we should not upset the essential value-structure of an underdeveloped or developing society by an imposition of the standards or norms of a developed Western society even if such imposition is required for the sake of economic progress, to implement, for example, a speedy transfer of modern technology. Whatever truth there may be in this claim, it seems to be not entirely unrelated to the relativism of the old "liberal" colonialists. The liberal idea here is connected with the recognition (and fear) of oppression and violence, inflicted usually upon a third-world society in the name of progress, and in view of certain unwelcome results brought about by the modern technocrats in such societies, this may have some *moral* justification. The newly gained ecological consciousness would consider it a good thing not to destroy the environment in thoughtless urgency. But at a theoretical level this kind of ethical relativism has repugnant consequences, for it is not entirely free from the reflexes of colonialism. I shall argue that this is not just true of what Williams has dubbed "vulgar relativism." It is in general true of any significant form of ethical relativism. For even if some version of ethical relativism is shown to be coherent or free from inconsistency, it does not establish it as a (nonrelatively) true doctrine. Coherence is the first step toward such establishment, but it is not the only step.

It has generally been argued that some version of relativism in ethics is not only coherent but also *true*. For example, we may refer to a version given by Bernard Williams (1981: 132-173). Gilbert Harman has formulated another coherent version (1975). These versions seem to avoid traditional and standard errors of relativism.

For Williams the truth in relativism lies in the view that there may be two societies with divergent moral systems which will have only what he called "notional confrontation" between them, one not being a "real option" for the other, and hence the vocabulary of appraisal ("true-false," "right-wrong," etc.) will have no genuine application. Unlike "vulgar relativism," this version is free from inconsistency because the concept of "notional confrontation" allows a form of thought for thinking about the moral concerns of different societies, but disallows any substantive relation of such concerns to our own concerns "which alone can give any point or substance to the appraisal." As long as confrontation stops short of being a "real option," questions of appraisal, according to Williams, "do not *genuinely* arise" (my emphasis). This seems to be an approximation of what I have called "soft relativism," which allows incommensurability only as a limiting case. Williams, however, is well aware that there may be some nonstandard errors in this view. For example, it is wrong to think today of a culture as completely individuated and self-contained *vis-à-vis* another comparable culture. In his own words, "social practices could never come forward with a certificate saying that they belonged to a genuinely different culture, so that they are guaranteed immunity to other judgments and reactions" (1985: 158).

In his recent writings Williams (1985: 220), having dismissed the anthropologist's point that a nonrelativistic doctrine of universal toleration can be based upon the incommensurability of cultural moral codes, has given a heavily qualified account of "relativism of distance." This theory envisions notional confrontation between past and present societies, as well as between future and present, and hence can justify the *epoché* of ethical evaluation only in this limited sense. But even this may seem inappropriate, as William concedes, under the historical pressure of a nonrelativistic notion of social justice. This "relativism of distance" seems to be flawless as a theoretical construct, but the nonrelativistic notion of justice and equality may over time force an unjust caste-orientated or slave-orientated society to be transformed into a comparatively just one. I wish to comment here on one minor point raised by Williams. This concerns the asymmetrically related options.

It has been pointed out (by Williams) that while some version of modern technological life is a real option for members of surviving traditional societies, their life is not a real option for those belonging to modern technological societies, and this is true "despite the passionate nostalgia of many." This asymmetry seems to be simply the asymmetry of time or history, which is usually expressed in such clichés as "we cannot re-create the past" or "we can have only one-directional travel through time." It is certainly true that we cannot live the life of a Greek Bronze Age chief. But it is not clear why Williams thinks that the option to "go native" culturally is unavailable to modern Western people. Let us pursue this thought a little further. A so-called "traditional" society today opts for technology along with understandable resistance from many sections, and thus constant readjustment or ongoing reassessment of traditional values (including value-rejection) is called for. When the dust settles down, it would be correct to say that for a member of a "traditional society" of the third world the modern Western society has been a "real option" (in Williams' sense). But that does not settle the question why for a member of the latter the former cannot be a real option. For if the member of a third-world traditional society can (if it is possible for him or her to do so) opt for modern Western life, it is as much possible (there is no theoretical barrier a priori for a modern Western man or woman to opt for a life in the traditional society as long as such a society exists somewhere on this globe and knowledge about its value-structure and such is a matter of public knowledge. The "nostalgia" of a Westerner that Williams refers to needs to be discouraged. For it is undoubtedly a form of neurotic behavior. But it needs to be emphasized that there is no asymmetry of options here (except, of course, the asymmetry of time). It is also important to realize that when a "traditional" society develops technology, it becomes a *new* society, not a replica or a blueprint of the so-called "Western technological" society. It would be, to use Williams' own argument to fortify this point, "too early or too late" for an Indian to be a Westerner and vice versa. It would be too early when thought of an alternative has not penetrated the consciousness of the Indian, and too late when he is already confronted with the new situation.

Another source of uneasiness in this "soft" version of relativism is the fact that even a purely notional confrontation of two cultures can give substance to the vocabulary of appraisal. Short of circularity, it is difficult to see why a notional confrontation, which is a situation of confrontation between two cultures without one being a "real option" for the other, must resolve into rendering the vocabulary of appraisal totally pointless. For we can use *substantially* such vocabulary where there are objective criteria or some other methods, and this possibility cannot be written off in any kind of confrontation.

I shall now examine another version of moral relativism propounded and defended by Harman. Harman talks about what he calls "inner moral judgment" that underlies the agent's motivating reasons to do what he does, and this motivational attitude concerns primarily intuitions of the agent and his peers to keep an agreement. The inner moral judgment is relative to such a tacit agreement. Harman distinguishes moral "oughts" from other types of "oughts," and separates the "right" from the "good" by focusing upon the agent's moral frame of reference: what he ought or ought not to have done (not what is or would have been a good or desirable act). The argument *seems* impeccable. But one can think of at least two serious flaws that lurk behind it. First, it has a very repugnant consequence. For, it implies that people like Hitler or the Martians or a member of Murder, Incorporated, can *only* be called *evil* in our vocabulary; they cannot be *judged* to be wrongdoers. This consequence is openly admitted by Harman, and, indeed, he thinks this feature to be partly supportive of the correctness of this position (psychologically speaking, so the argument goes, it is more satisfying for us to call Hitler evil than simply state that what he was doing was wrong!). But what is psychologically satisfying may not be a good evidence for a correct doctrine. How can we separate the concept of evil from that of wrongdoing?

The argument here partly depends upon a sort of (indefensible) dogma about what is actually the correct linguistic intuition. It also lacks a practical content. It becomes necessary to conceive first of all the bizarre creatures coming from outer space and then declare the incomparability of the set of "morals" or standards accepted in their bizarre society with that of ours. Such argument seems to be a priori, if not circular. As far as description of Hitler is concerned, what happens to be part of the rhetoric is assigned a literal meaning here. "Hitler was a monster" becomes "Hitler belongs to the society of monsters." First we must be forced to assume that "their" standards are entirely opposite to "ours" (the "alien creatures" must not be like us humans), and then it is an a priori argument to show that vocabularies of appraisals, which must get their meaning in relation to such "agreed" standards, do not make sense across such different sets of standards. The worth of linguistic intuition can be stretched too far. It does not seem too odd to say in English that Hitler, being a rational human being, turned into a madman and committed most serious crimes against humanity, while it would be counterintuitive to say that Hitler reached an inner "moral" judgment following his *own* set of "moral" principles and did those terrible things which he did. The latter part would be an affront to our usual feeling about morality. It is not clear here whether this is "hard relativism" or "soft relativism," whether the Martian good is incomprehensible to us or whether our standard simply does not apply there. It seems that Harman would prefer the second alternative. Then the point about psychological satisfaction in Harman's argument can be made to stand on its head. It is because we judge Hitler by our standard that we can condemn him as a wrongdoer (evil).

While Williams is well aware of the difficulties involved in clearly individuating cultures (he gets around this by talking about past and present and future societies), Harman uses science fiction (Martians), common fictions (Murder, Inc.), and "fictionalized" history (Hitler) to individuate group moralities. Our point is, not that such groups or persons do not exist in our midst (with the exception of the Martians), but that unless we "fictionalize" or imagine them to be *entirely beyond our pale,* that is, entirely unlike us, the argument loses its substance. These creatures have to share with us only a narrow form of rationality (to make the so-called "inner moral judgment" possible), but nothing much else. We may decide to call them monsters (Hitler), mentally deranged or impaired persons (Murder, Inc.), or subhumans, but then we have already judged them, that is, excluded them from our moral domain. We cannot expect the "subhumans" to be moral.

There seem to be an undue assumption that these familiar figures—Hitler, members of Murder, Inc.—must be beyond the pale, like the outer-space creatures, and would feel no moral compunction (no inner conflict) in deciding to act in the way they act. This might have led Harman to construe moral relativism in the way he did. It seems that the problem of translation is not the issue here. For we can presumably interpret the Martian activity, or the act of the member of Murder, Inc., by following generally the attribution of beliefs to the Martian and by the Davidsonian hermeneutical triangle of meaning, belief, and action (Davidson, 1980, 1984). But if termination of one's life in a particular way is believed to be *murder* by both, the Martians and us, then one cannot stop short of calling the agent murderer or morally condemning both the agent and the act. If we can attribute other factual beliefs to the Martians, by the same token we would have to attribute to them some of our basic beliefs about values. But on Harmanian theory we simply attribute a sort of rationality (conscious reasoning to reach the inner judgment) to them but not anything else. The point again is not that such persons do not exist but that in the context of moral judgment either we allow them the honor of belonging to the human race and then morally condemn them for their deeds or, as in the case of mentally impaired persons, we may treat them as subhuman, which will be also a (moral) judgment, and relativism will thus lose much of its purchase. Otherwise there seems to be in Harmanian *epoché* an uncanny resonance of the role of the "tolerant" liberal colonialists or the old confusion of the anthropologists. The "unconscious" of such liberal colonialists nurtures contempt for the "savage" practices of the natives, while outwardly there is exemplary unconcern: "they are not like US!" Once again relativism becomes (mistakenly) a plea for so-called universal tolerance, but in reality one suspects it to be a hedge for a "put-down" of the alien society.[2]

A classic example of the conflict situation is offered at the beginning of the celebrated Hindu text, the *Bhagavad-Gītā,* and the solution therein offers a striking but not entirely unjustified parallelism with Harman's version of moral relativism. Arjuna, the warrior, is torn by conflict on the eve of the battle of Kuruksetra whether he ought to fight or not, whether he ought to kill his relatives including his honorable grandfather and his teacher in order to recover his kingdom, or quit the battlefield and accept a more modest form of life (a recluse, cf. *bhaiksyam apīha loke)* to avoid the moral consequences of his impending act of violence. Lord Kṛṣṇa (i.e., somebody like Hare's "archangel" or even Arjuna's own alter ego) advised to fight. The chief among Kṛṣṇa's arguments was an appeal to the *agreed upon* moral code of the Kṣatriya caste to which Arjuna belonged. One might say that this was an ideal case (instantiation) of the Harmanian notion of inner moral judgment. For here someone S (Kṛṣṇa) says that A (Arjuna) *morally* ought to do D (fighting, killing of relatives), and Kṛṣṇa assumes that Arjuna intends to act in accordance with an agreement (moral code of the Kṣatriya caste or group), and thus Arjuna has reasons to fight (reasons endorsed by Kṛṣṇa and other members of the Kṣatriya caste).

Some critics, both traditional and modern, have repeatedly pointed out that this is a morally dubious position. Arjuna wanted to be a moral hero and not answer the call of his vocation as an actual hero. His vocation was to kill and conquer everybody in the battlefield. He wanted to avoid the morally repugnant consequences of the war by his last-minute decision of withdrawal. In this move he wanted to respond to the pressure of *dharma* of a different kind. As a human being, as a member of the royal family, as a devoted grandson, as a student, and so on he was responding, temporarily at least, to another (different) set of *dharma,* ideals, or standards. Arjuna's dilemma was genuine, for he was both a member of Kṣatriya caste (one *dharma*) and a member of the (royal) family with filial and brotherly duties (another *dharma*). But rṣna's advice was that the ethical code of the Kṣatriya caste (which was arguably not very different from that of Murder, Inc., of Harman) must take precedence in this case over other *dharmas*. Within the narrow confines of the caste duties the logic seems impeccable. However, one feels irresistibly that something is morally amiss here. If the story of the *Gītā* were a single episode and the larger background of Mahābhārata were forgotten, then Arjuna's dilemma would not seem to be very different from the same of that young man (in Sartre's much discussed example) who, in an occupied country, has to decide whether to join the resistance movement and thereby bring punishment upon his family or remain with the family and protect his parents.

The member of Murder, Inc., in Harman's description does not have to be a mentally deranged person, but some sort of lobotomy should be performed by Murder, Inc., on its designated member to make him immune to any moral compunction toward his decision to kill not only the innocent bank manager but also, say, his father or son or wife or his beloved, simply at "duty's" call. (Remember that he has to *kill*, not simply terminate the life-motion of a human body.) The Harmanian assumption is that one through rational choice has to be exclusively and solely a member of a group, that is, simply a Kṣatriya or a Murder, Inc., member, not anything else, not a father, or a son, or a lover. The recent case of Nezar Hindawi sending his unsuspecting pregnant girlfriend to blow up the El-Al plane is also a case in point. Here we meet the familiar "fanatic" of Hare, who might have had a "mental" lobotomy through strict indoctrination.

The Harmanian version of relativism shifts our attention from the act to the agent, and in this sense the theory is agent-dependent: we cannot morally condemn the person but only the acts. The argument is sound, but is this plausible? If an alternative explanation of the phenomenon on which Harman's argument essentially depends—the agent's apparently conflict-free conviction about his own moral commitment to which he would not subject others—can be made equally plausible, such argument for relativism will have very little significance. Harman's argument seems to depend upon an implicit appeal to our *felt* sense of unfairness of morally condemning a person (for doing something) using standards that are not his own or about which he is unaware or to which he is uncommitted. But this may be a "false" feeling. How can we write off the commitment of a responsible human being to protect life rather than destroy it? Even Arjuna felt that he was committed to a set of norms other than the *dharma* of a Kṣatriya. Multiple-group membership or multiplicity of commitments is a well-attested phenomenon, but this cannot be a sufficient ground for any significant form of relativism. Pluralism is not relativism. Conflict does not prove relativism.

The case of the *Gītā* may be analyzed differently. Although I have disapprovingly referred above to Kṛṣṇa's argument to persuade Arjuna to fight in the *Bhagavad-Gītā,* in order to show my disapproval of moral relativism that may be implicit in Kṛṣṇa's initial argument, I do not maintain that Kṛṣṇa's final advice to fight would not have any nonrelativistic moral justification. In the larger context of the epic Mahābhārata, of which the *Gītā* is only a part, this does have a justification. In the tally of wrongdoings of both sides, the Kauravas and the Pāṇḍavas, Duryodhana (of the Kauravas) certainly exceeded Pāṇḍavas in malignity by deliberately inflicting unforgivable humiliation upon Draupadī, the rather innocent daughter-in-law of the family. By claiming similarly that what Nezar Hindawi did (even if he did it without any compunction or inner conflict, in which case he is mentally deranged in our terminology) was morally wrong, I do not claim nor do I imply in any other way that the Palestinian cause is unjust or morally wrong. They are decidedly different issues. But this point is not relevant here.

We may distinguish between the anthropologist's claim of moral relativism across culture and the sort of (intracultural) relativism forced upon us sometimes due to either the alleged noncognitive conception of ethical discourse or persistent disagreement (presumably irresoluble) in valuings within a community. One is, however, intimately connected with the other, but we are concerned here directly with intercultural moral relativism. There is a tendency among philosophers to conflate the two. Although sometimes it is harmless, this slide between intercultural variety of norms and intracultural disagreements about moral principles or moral theories (such as Kantian or utilitarian or egoistic) is, to say the least, confusing. Whether different moral theories (or principles) recognized and well-respected within a given culture are reconcilable or not is decidedly a different issue from cultural (ethical) relativism which is arguable on the basis of such notions as incomprehensibility, incommensurability, and untranslatability. It is, however, possible to see intracultural *variation* in valuing as something that is to be explained as reflecting "ways of life," not as reflecting variable perceptions of objective values. In that case, as we will see in the next section, we have reason to believe that intracultural (moral) relativism is only a special case of cultural relativism.

2. The Anthropologist's Dilemma

Ethical systems are believed to rest on basic axiomatic constructions of reality that are ingrained in different worldviews or cosmologies. Therefore, the anthropologists have argued, relativism is inescapable, for such axiomatic constructions of reality are irreducibly varied, being part and parcel of different cultures.

These culture-relative axiomatic constructions are presumably conditioned by human cognitive ability, their capacity to synthesize sensory inputs, to process them in order to formulate their informational content and to abstract from them generalities. Our anthropologists argue that they have empirical evidence for showing that these cognitive abilities vary from culture to culture, group to group. The Eskimos, for example, have a large number of words in their vocabulary for "snow," for they can certainly perceive more features of the "snow" phenomenon to which we are presumably blind. Here the premise of the anthropologists is not in dispute; the conclusion is. For the premise does not entail mutual incomprehensibility of cultural constructs, nor even the incommensurability of the standards of valuing across culture. What it proves is pluralism. There is, however, another component of the anthropologists' argument, a *reductio ad absurdum,* which makes relativism a plausible and attractive hypothesis. Some of the alien's beliefs or his alleged standards of valuings *appear* to be irrational by our own reckoning. Since it would be "absurd" to attribute irrationality to the alien, we contend that these standards (or "beliefs") are rational when interpreted within the context of his own worldview, which is different from ours. Hence relativism saves the embarrassment of the liberal anthropologist who finds the ever-yawning gap between "we" and "they" and cannot find comfort in the thought that of course "we" are superior beings (rational) while "they" are not.

There is another way of arguing the same point. Different norms need not be incommensurable. Two systems are incommensurable when they not only have different constitutive rules but also are rivals such that in the Quinean sense there is "no fact of the matter" to decide in favor of either. Thus, different cultural constructs may or may not entail the thesis of incommensurability. But the anthropologist can still argue that even commensurability may not give rise to "real confrontation" or to a "real option" in Williams' sense. The core values of a culture, the relativist insists, are immanent in its collective activities, in its myths, rituals, kinship systems, customs, in standard interpersonal behavior, and they account for our motivation for action. The culture's ethical system is not available externally for real confrontation with another separately. So we have relativism. This seems to be akin to Quinean indeterminacy thesis where too many acceptable but conflicting translations are possible among schemes (there being "no fact of the matter" to decide in favor of any). To wit: the imbeddedness of ethical norms defies piecemeal options. Internally coherent worldviews as wholes are competitors; there is no Archimedian point from which to choose one over the other. Moreover, prospect for any change or option for such imbedded norms would necessarily require destruction of the culture as a whole.

This picture is in accord with the social scientist's conception of ethical relativism. It rejects ethical absolutes in a way that is reminiscent of the Athenian skeptics (Sextus), who obtained quietude and abstained from the rashness of dogmatism through consideration of comparative ethnography (Needham, 1985: 35). I believe such skepticism cannot be easily dismissed.

Modern ethnographers, however, would allow that a conscious "individual" belonging to a particular culture may self-consciously be able to articulate explicitly and discursively the ethical norms embedded in his or her culture. In the process she would have to distance herself from her culture or community and develop an internal critique for looking across boundaries in order to have the *real* options derivable from her knowledge and acquaintance of other cultures. But the doings of such an individual cannot seriously affect relativism. The individual who chooses to be "outcast" in this way may be regarded as a new community with perhaps only one member, but then his ethical norms would be imbedded in his changed, or thoroughly modified, worldview or cosmology. They would be, in other words, part and parcel of his own axiomatic constructions of reality. To cite an example, in a traditional Indian society the highly Westernized people formed without difficulty and perhaps unconsciously a distinct and distinguishable separate community of their own vis-à-vis the old traditional society, and we can witness the possibility of "peaceful" coexistence and not real confrontation or conflict between such distinct cultural groups or subgroups.

We may make further concession to vindicate relativism and refuse to accept the "gap" between cultures, between "we" and "they." Cultures, as indeed we have noted above, are never found completely individuated and self-contained vis-à-vis other cultures. But during contacts and confrontation traits are borrowed freely and then integrated into the borrowing culture's worldview or cosmology. The core of the culture, however, shows resilience and resistance to any radical change. Hence, traits or new values that cannot be integrated with the core are ignored or rejected. A cultural anthropologist observes such resilience and resistance and hence concludes that there is cultural continuity, and therefore the sets of ethical norms ingrained in such cultures, or ways of life, with their priorities among virtues and their dependent moral rules, are also preserved in tact, precluding any real option through real confrontation.

This is another powerful argument. It would, if true, uphold the sort of relativism that is not obviously incoherent. It does not depend upon mutual incomprehensibility, or completely on incommensurability. A culture is compared with a language (Wittgensteinian "language-game"). This analogy, for the relativists, has a deep consequence. A culture, like a natural language, apart from satisfying some common need of the people, has to grow within the constraints of a particular history and geography over a period of time, developing its particular norms and vocabulary. The recognition of the "particularity" in the study of cultures, as well as awareness of diversity in ideals for a complete life and in standard patterns of admired activity, naturally makes room for a sort of ethical relativism wherein values of different cultures cannot be assessed against each other, moralities cannot be compared or criticized, much in the same way the grammatical peculiarities of one language cannot be evaluated against those in another language. It is a good analogy, but can this analogy be sustained?

I shall now argue that this is not quite right. (1) Noticing that a culture resists drastic changes in norms, we may unconsciously be driven to a belief in the immutability of the norms or the central core of a culture—a belief that may well amount to a sort of "essentialism." Arguably, during violent interface between cultures (and it does not matter whether confrontation is real or notional), if there is asymmetry in power and richness, either the central core of the weaker culture is destroyed or it maintains a very precarious and mutilated existence. This empirical fact, however, does not show that the essentialist dogma is well-founded. Once we give up the "essentialist's" dogma, we would find it natural to talk about not mutilation or destruction but mutation and change. Violence or aggression would still be present due to alleged asymmetry, but that is a different issue. Any form of oppression is repulsive, and insouciant relativism may be a veil for negative oppression or neglect. In a dynamic world, however, cultural norms cannot remain immutable. In the context of ongoing mutation and change the reinforcement of peculiarities in the pursuit of a distinguishing ideal will have its trade-offs, will entail a sacrifice or suppression of some other dispositions that were previously admired or are now admired in other ways of life. Such value trade-offs are features of any living and growing culture. A culture is like a living organism: it grows and changes and adapts itself to the ever-changing environments. In this process "sour grapes" are many. But by contrast, if an organism loses this behavior of *adaptive preference formations* (Elster, 1982: 219-238), it becomes a piece of dead wood to be preserved in a museum. Everything has a cost, even growth or survival. Therefore, if a culture modifies itself over a period of time vis-à-vis another culture, the ethical norms imbedded in it must take the same route.

Particularly during an interface both sides (weak and strong) go through a "conversion" procedure, the asymmetry is only in degrees of modification. This fact seems to conflict with the assumption of any significant form of relativism. There may not be any real appraisal by someone standing apart using transcultural standards of evaluation, but internal forces of both cultures, which make interaction possible, would make the possibility of such appraisal at least compatible.

(2) This modified relativism still seems to be open to the David-sonian objection against conceptual relativism: "Different points of view make sense, but only if there is a common coordinate system on which to plot them; yet the existence of a common system belies the claim of dramatic incomparability" (Davidson, 1984: 67). The phrase "axiomatic constructions of reality" obviously presupposes the scheme-content duality. This duality is unintelligible, for we cannot find an intelligible basis on which it can be said that schemes are different. However, "looseness of fit" (that no doubt exists) between the common-ly shared world or the broad base of humanity on the one hand, and the different interesting things people want to do and/or talk about on the other hand, may give some content to the supposition of different conceptual schemes, for this seems to bypass the Davidsonian objec-tion. But even this alleged Davidsonian lack of concern for alternative interests (Hacking, 1982: 61-62) need not frighten the liberalists, for the Davidsonian dismissal of the third dogma (of the duality of scheme and content) is compatible with the open-endedness of certain types of dia-logue or statements which may accommodate alternative interests. But this does not support ethical relativism in any "exciting" form. Accept-ance of plurality of interest does not amount to relativism, as we have noted already. Among music lovers, for example, there will always be those that are for the latest pop music, while others will prefer Mozart.

(3) Stuart Hampshire has argued that there are "two faces of morality" (1983: 2-3)—the rational side and the less than rational, the historically and geographically conditioned, the less than fully articulate side. This distinction seems to coincide with the intuition which led the Indian ethicists to champion group-relative *dharmas,* on the one hand,

and distinguish between, on the other hand, what they called *sādhāraṇa dharma* and *viśeṣa dharmas.* These two aspects of morality, the "universalizing and the particularizing" aspects, underline the distinction between two modes of understanding and explaining—one is more natural in natural sciences and the other in social sciences, in linguistics and historical studies. Social science may emulate natural science, but the gap will always be there as long as it has one foot rooted in humanistic studies, and if this is uprooted, social science would not be social science. What the cultural anthropologists notice, the imbeddedness of a certain set of values in a given culture, may indeed be true, but in accepting this we should not overlook another layer of values, another aspect of moral norms, those that relate to the abstract and universal, species-wide requirements derived from basic human necessities. This is sometimes reflected in our talk about a distinction between mores and morality. Our supposition is that there may indeed be some sort of incommensurability, or "undercommensurability," and hence a sort of relativism among cultural norms as far as the "particularizing," the historically conditioned, and therefore in some sense contingent, side of morality, is concerned (cf. *viśeṣa dharma*). This side naturally offers the strongest resistance to change during confrontation and interaction, although in a dynamic world nothing that is "a particular" or a "concrete" object is totally immune to mutation. But there is also that more general side of morality, those aspects that respond to man's need as a biological creature, and of which only he himself is aware and capable of doing something about, not the other creatures.

To articulate this culture-neutral side of morality is not an easy task. These values or value-experiences may not be totally immutable across cultures or over time, but there is some sort of constancy in them to make them enduring and invariant. Being pressed on further, one may provide a list of (invariant) moral virtues, something like what the Indian ethicists called the set of *sādhāraṇa dharma.* Granted that the exact definition of these virtues would be debatable, moral philosophers, surprisingly, have seldom spent time over the articulation of such basic virtues. Alternatively, one may develop a thesis that pleasure and pain in some basic (but specific) sense provide such reasons for action as is agent-neutral (Nagel) or even culture-neutral. Or one may investigate whether the Rawlsian notion of "primary goods" which include liberty and opportunity, income and wealth, the bases of wealth, and so on or Sen's notion of "basic capabilities," need for nutritional requirements, for participation in social life, and so on, which are recognizably culture-dependent, can be sharpened and modified to provide a basis for articulating culture-transcendent (culture-neutral) values.[3] Or, one may develop a viable concept of human need. As Phillipa Foot has said (p. 164),

> Granted that it is wrong to assume identity of aims between peoples of different cultures: nevertheless there is a great deal that all men have in common. All need affection, the cooperation of others, a place in a community, and help in trouble.

It may be that the Martians, if they exist, are differently constituted. But we are talking of human need and want. It is important to realize that the Martian culture is deemed to be "alien" in one sense, but a third-world culture or a tribal culture is "alien" in a different, much less exaggerated sense. To call them human is to attribute to them certain dispositions, certain patterns of beliefs and propensities to desire things, and dispositions to act so as to avoid excessive pain and suffering and to want pleasures. Attribution of beliefs, desires, and want is a "package deal"; certain modes of valuings cannot be separated from it.

3. Diversity and Relativity

The lesson from comparative ethnography need not engender universal skepticism about moral values. The problem cases, the irrational beliefs, or bizarre ethical principles of alien cultures may be given alternative explanation without assuming relativism. If we take their apparent bizarreness or irrationality to be coming from the fact that they are judged by the standards of a modern Western worldview, we veer toward relativism. It satisfies the "liberal conscience, wary of ethnocentrism." As Charles Taylor (1982: 99) has remarked, "It takes the heat off; we no longer have to judge whose way of life is superior." But if instead we shift our attention from the property "apparent bizarreness" to the locus of that property, the principles or moral beliefs, and examine whether they really qualify as moral principles or beliefs in the strict sense that we tend to attach to them, we might be in for a surprise. False starts are many. It may be that what we take to be the moral or factual belief of the alien vis-à-vis our own (contrary) moral or factual belief is simply a (wrong) construal by us of the alien's behavior from what he apparently says and does, in which case we need not christen it as a moral or factual belief and a fortiori need not attribute irrationality or bizarrerie to such mental states. Inferential errors are very common.

The anthropologists usually christen such dubious, unexamined, and hence irrational mental states as full-fledged beliefs and then turn to explain their alleged bizarrerie with recourse to symbolism, metaphors, or nonliteral interpretation. But symbolism has its own problems. Relativism becomes a smooth doctrine to get rid of the rough edges of such symbolism (Sperber, 1982).

Alternatively, we may be content with the attribution of beliefs and values to the alien and follow the Davidsonian line (1980) that such beliefs and wants cause action. But irrational human action or behavior may be furnished with a number of psychological explanations, wishful thinking, adaptive preferences, self-deception, rationalization, and so on. Thus, I believe, a view of human irrationality (rather than a *separate* worldview conceived by the relativist) can often offer causal explanation of the genesis of the alien's irrational beliefs and values and the actions prompted by them. Sometimes social historical explanation of bizarre behavior is in order.

Despite the so-called "culture shocks," quaintness, and sometimes a bizarre feeling which a member of one culture experiences when confronted with an "alien" culture (for those interested, I refer to a poem by Craig Rains, *A Martian Sends a Postcard Home* [London, 1979]) a cross-cultural assessment[4] of certain central ethical issues is not only possible but also probable. As E. Gellner (1982: 185-186) has pointed out, the anthropologists seldom report complete *failure* coming back from a field trip; they often report success or partial failure.[5] Yet

> On the often rather *a priori* reasoning of relativist philosophers, who start out from doctrines such as ultimacy and self-sufficiency of 'forms of life', we might have expected such failure to be much more common. It is *success* in explaining culture A in the language of culture B which is, in the light of such a philosophy, really puzzling.

Admission of diversity resulting from normal, postenlightenment humility, as well as open-mindedness to learn "what else" is there, does not amount to any exciting form of relativism which may be objected to by a realist. The enlightened, self-conscious modern citizen thinks (with some justification) that if his own right to recommend a moral norm for another person (his neighbor) is as thorny a question as the justification of morality itself, more so it must be to recommend a moral norm to a distant culture-group. This may induce humility and tolerance, and perhaps it demands—rightly I believe—patience, care, and caution lest we prejudicially judge, when we try to understand and interpret the alien's ethical code. When the so-called code becomes sufficiently *transparent* to us, so that we can also rank it, the "excitement" of relativism subsides. One may of course decide, despite transparency, to refrain respectfully from ranking or judging it, as, in Harman's example, the pacifist who has conscientious objection to war may, with respect, refuse to judge others who do not have such objection. But this refusal of the pacifist, *pace* Harman, does not support any interesting kind of relativism. It can be explained in terms of the lack of interest on the part of the pacifist to analyze the situation any further or to make any comparative value judgment. What is politically expeditious may not be ethically relevant. The point is whether recognition of *difference* can always be morally neutral.

Cultural relativism is actually a recommended hypothetical construct, being in fact instrumental to our understanding of a culture from the internalist's viewpoint. In practice, however, cultures and subcultures do *flow* into one another. They are rarely like *dead* watertight compartments. We may reassert the earlier point about the improbability of finding two fully individuable, clearly self-contained and self-sufficient cultures for an effective theoretical contrast. In the interaction both sides get modified, though sometimes subtly and imperceptibly. Side by side there are many cases of irrational formation of mental states, wishful thinking, possible self-deception, and adaptive preferences. People do react and respond under confrontation, and by then it is *too late* for the *epoché* of the relativists. If, however, we talk about the preconfrontation period, ethical relativism then should either remain unformulated or be only an idle hypothetical construct to be formulated in the postconfrontation period.

Much has been made of the Wittgensteinian notion of "forms of life" or even that of his "language-game." But, as Williams has argued, the issue here was not really relativism (1981: 160), for otherwise, if the relativist element is added to the notion, we face "the gravest difficulty" in the philosophy of social sciences. We have to posit the existence of culturally distinct groups with different worldviews and hold at the same time that our access to them is inescapably and nontrivially conditioned by our own worldview. And this cannot stop short of what Williams calls "aggregative solipsism" (1981: 158). The relativist story about the plurality of "forms of life" should therefore be taken with a pinch of salt. As Paul Seabright has recently argued (1987: 27), the social scientist's explanation of "forms of life" (even in the Wittgensteinian sense) is not only possible but necessary, and sometimes this explanation will be directly causal in nature. One might similarly argue that transcultural criticism of ethical norms is equally possible. Just as the causal explanation cannot by itself require us to alter our practices, transcultural criticism may similarly be not enough to effect the value-rejection. But it can certainly illuminate our understanding of ethical norms, ours as well as theirs.

4. Confrontation and Convergence

Introducing a contrast between nature and convention, some philosophers maintain that ethical norms are based mostly or entirely upon convention or cultural underpinnings and not upon "the naked man" (as Hampshire once put it, 1983: 142). But man is not only a cultural creature but also a natural biological creature. It is "the naked man" whose needs, pleasures, pains, and wants would have extreme relevance to many basic issues of ethics. The description of man is not exhausted by a complete enumeration of properties that result from his cultural underpinnings alone. If we strip him or her of all cultural underpinnings, we reach "the naked man." It is generally easy to ascertain that the group heritage or the collective personality is sometimes glorified by such expressions as "national character." But most of what are presumed to constitute the "national character" of a group may simply be some persisting peculiarities that distinguish a group of people from their neighbors as well as determine the set of responses they make to various situational questions. An ethical code determined by such contingencies would *ex hypothesi* be culture-relative, and the anthropologist's point about imbeddedness would be true of such codes. But this does not affect our argument in favor of a set of basic values concordant with the value-experiences of the "naked man." The common dispositions, constitutive of the concept of "the naked man," may be recognized as numerous simple facts about needs, wants, and desires, for example, removal of suffering, love of justice, courage in the face of injustice, pride, shame, love of children, delight, laughter, happiness. In other words, the connotation of our "naked man" need not be some intractable human essence. The suggested commonness of responses and emotions does not presuppose the essentialist dogma.

There is a substantive ethical insight in the modern discussion of both contractualism and utilitarianism—it is the universal attribution of moral personality. On this assumption we regard that other human agents, including agents in the so-called "alien" culture which is confronted by us or which confronts us, are, as subjects of practical reasoning, on the same footing as ourselves. Such basic insight into the nature of moral thinking itself is derived as much from Kant as from other ethical philosophers. This insight, when it is properly comprehended, may require us to transcend the practical problems presented by the bewildering variety of ethical codes across cultures and to assess the intercultural valuings. In ultimate analysis, or as a sequel to a series of confrontation and interaction, one may imagine the possibility in the future of a convergence of certain basic, culturally invariant ethical norms. The question arises whether there is any substance to this thought at all.

We have distinguished, à la Hampshire, between moral norms that are local and culture-relative and those that are culture-invariant. It is not unthinkable that a partial convergence, if not a full one, is possible through proper confrontation and clash between culture, a convergence, not necessarily of local moral norms, but of course of the basic ethical norms, to the extent these norms and ideals are responses to the needs of the "naked man." Some local norms may be more deeply entrenched in a desired and respected way of life in a given society. Preference for this way of life would have to be "perfectly prudent preference" (to use a phrase from Hare), that is, it has to be what someone would desire if fully informed and unconfused. To exclude the slave-society or the caste-society we have to banish "antisocial" and "irrational" preferences from this set of preferences, and then we can justifiably apply the term 'moral' to such norms. Such parochial moral norms may remain non-convergent even when confrontation of cultures takes place. The internal dynamism (within a culture) looks beyond the cultural boundaries (and unconsciously toward a sort of convergence where singularism may be a guiding principle). Since today's world is not cut up into self-contained bits, this internal dynamism seems to be enhanced, leading to value-rejection or value-acceptance or both, and this need not always be "sour grapes."

The claim of the nonrelativist is minimum: certain basic moral principles are neither agent-relative nor contingent upon any specific type of social order. These principles are sometimes claimed to flow from the "nature" of human needs. One may understand this as an attempt to uncover a core of shared rationality that is reached by gradually peeling off or stripping down the overlay of distinctive cultural mores, local customs, and individual idiosyncrasies. It may be that the vision of convergence foresees the existence of One World and hence is little more than an idle pipedream. But the nonrelativist may say in reply that there is already One World for us to share, although we neither have, nor do we need, *one kind of man* to share that One World. All that the liberalism of postenlightenment or even the post-Second World War period wants to preserve and maintain as valuable, and for fear of whose loss the liberal philosophers are prone to embrace relativism, would remain unthreatened by our admission of the singularity of the world alongside diversity of peoples. Although the prospect for convergence is necessarily foreseen by one kind of person, one special group perhaps, it is accessible, to be sure, to all kinds of people, without its being the case now (or even in some foreseeable future) that all do accept it. If this position is akin to moral singularism, it is at such a basic level that it does not encourage moral jingoism, or an attitude of "holier-than-thou" toward an "alien" culture. Our theory is, however, that an alien culture cannot remain totally "alien" after confrontation and interaction. In this context we decry the talk of relativism that is often used as a ploy (or a pseudophilosophical defense) for keeping the culture of a subdued group completely separated in a protected area as a museum piece or an "endangered" zoological species. For it becomes a modern version of liberal colonialism caught on the wrong foot. There seems to be an echo of this point in Dan Sperber's not so popular comment:

> In pre-relativist anthropology, Westerners thought themselves as superior to all other people. Relativism replaced this despicable hierarchical gap by a kind of cognitive apartheid (1982: 119-180).

The position which I am defining is sensitive to the liberalist's worries but avoids his blunder in being too sympathetic to relativism. It is mildly optimistic about convergence and mildly predictive of singularism at a certain basic level. But it accommodates pluralism (and regards it as a contingency) with respect to the *viśeṣa dharma* or culture-relative (local or parochial) norms. It may at the same time be compatible with such pluralism as would assume that a single coherent ordering of goods is not only desirable but also possible. Rather it would endorse a sort of agnosticism (though not skepticism) about the possibility of resolving conflicts of (intercultural as well as intracultural) moral principles through only rational means. It only allows that there would be certain contingent factors (alongside reason) which could resolve (causally) many "practical" ethical conflicts. This position also concedes that while some principles may be objectively better than others, we may recognize only this much without exactly recognizing which ones. (There is a limit to human capacity at any time.) To return to Putnam, "belief in a pluralistic ideal is not the same thing as belief that every ideal of human flourishing is as good as every other's" (1985: 148). In recommending clearer understanding among humans for convergence of certain vital interests and goals, we do not recommend elimination of all different natural languages, or a return to the pre-Tower-of-Babel period. Clearer and unambiguous understanding does not necessarily require use of only *one* natural language by all.

The significant, and perhaps the central, issue in relativism is that the moral principles are culture-relative in a way that we can either apply the predicate "neither right nor wrong" or "neither true nor false" to such principles or judgments reached thereby, or we can say "such questions do not arise." In this sense this is reminiscent of the last alternative (*koṭi*) of the Buddhist or Nāgarjunian tetralemma: "Is it? Is it not? Is it both? Is it neither?" I shall conclude with a comment on Nāgarjuna. We should remember that Nāgarjuna rejected all the alternatives including the "neither-nor." This will show that the description of Nāgarjuna's Mādhyamika philosophy as relativism is entirely wrong. I believe "The Middle Way" is not relativism in any significant sense. If the Buddhist tetralemma is not just a puzzle presented to confound our intellect, the lesson to be learnt here may be that the doctrine is closer to nonrelativism than what is ordinarily assumed. By rejecting the previous alternatives Nāgarjuna no doubt rejected the forms of realism that were current during his time. But by rejecting the fourth alternative he did reject relativism too and perhaps hinted by his *upaya-kausalya* that a return to realism without dogma is not only possible but also advisable. This may bring us back to reality but not to the original *construction* of reality that was refuted already by Nāgarjuna; it is a new openended way of dealing with reality without the usual dogmas of empiricism. The Mādhyamikas do not give up the world.

Notes

1. I am grateful to R. Needham, G. A. Cohen, J. Lipner, M. Nussbaum, A. Chakrabarti, G. Spivack, M. Krausz, and A. K. Sen for their comments on an earlier draft of this essay. Another version of this essay was presented at the Plenary Session of Extraordinary World Congress of Philosophy held at Cordoba, Argentina, September 20-26, 1987. Some comments on the anthropologist's dilemma was inspired by a letter from F. Marglin.

2. It should be admitted that Harman's defense of relativism is logically faultless. The problems that we have mentioned lie with the assumptions or premises. For example, he insists on the notion of agreement in intuitions and answers a point about a slave-society. There, after insisting that "this society was to be one in which no aspects of the moral understanding shared by the masters spoke against slavery" (p. 203), he concedes, "in fact that is unlikely, since there is *some* arbitrariness in the idea that people are to be treated in different ways depending on whether they are both slave or free" (his emphasis). I have simply insisted upon this arbitrariness, once we accept the agents as people.

3. I say this with much trepidation and recognize that neither the protagonists (Rawls and Sen) described these notions as culture-neutral. It is arguable whether these notions will have transcultural validity in any significant sense, for they have been developed in a culture-specific manner. But I believe they may be given culture-neutral significance and still retain their substantive moral values to the extent that they respond to the needs of the "naked man."

4. Ethnocentrism is, however, a state of mind. The members or some members of an ethnic group could be so ethnocentric, and therefore so blind to anything admirable—even comprehensible—in other peoples' culture, that they can really be identified with the ethnocentric inhabitants of Escher's "different worlds" in his famous painting *Relativity.* Contacts between these inhabitants of different worlds (though they may make use of the same staircase) are in Escher's conception out of the question. The utterly ethnocentric person cannot even make the first move to comprehend that there are "other worlds," much like the celebrated frog (in the Indian parable of "the Frog and the Well") who, living all his life in the well, never comprehended that there was a world outside. There may be a possible paradox here. Relativism is the suggested way to overcome ethnocentrism, while (extreme) ethnocentrism provokes hard relativism. The first significant step to overcome such ethnocentrism is not only to recognize that there are others but also to comprehend that their beliefs and acts may to some extent be incommensurable with ours. But then they may also be, under certain circumstances, real options for us. Thus, even soft relativism may dissolve. The reference to Craig Rains is thankfully received from P. Mitter.

5. A comment made by B. Scharfestein in private correspondence may be relevant here. "Each of the relativist philosophers seems to have a front door that opens on lonely incommensurables, relatives too distant to be sure they understand anything of one another, but a back door that opens on a common world, in which neighbours talk companionably across their fences."

References

Davidson, D. 1980. (1) *Essays on Actions and Events.* Oxford: Clarendon Press.
———. 1984. (2) *Truth and Interpretation.* Oxford: Clarendon Press.
Elster, J. 1982. (1) "Sour Grapes—Utilitarianism and the Genesis of Wants." In *Utilitarianism and Beyond*, ed. Sen and Williams. Cambridge: Cambridge University Press.
———. 1982. (2) "Belief, Bias and Ideology." In *Rationality and Relativism,* ed. Hollis and Lukes. Oxford: Blackwell.
Gellner, E. 1982. "Relativism and Universals." In *Rationality and Relativism.*
Hacking, I. 1982. "Language, Truth and Reason." In *Rationality and Relativism.*
Hampshire, S. 1983. *Morality and Conflict.* Oxford: Blackwell.
Hare, R. M. 1981. *Moral Thinking.* Oxford: Clarendon Press.
Harman, G. 1982."Moral Relativism Defended." In *Relativism,* ed. Meiland and Krausz. Notre Dame: University of Notre Dame Press.
Mackie, J. L. 1977. *Ethics.* Middlesex: Pelican Book.
Needham, R. 1985. *Exemplars.* Berkeley: University of California Press.
Putnam, H. 1981. *Reason, Truth, and History.* Cambridge: Cambridge University Press.
Quine, W. V. 1960. *Words and Object.* Cambridge, Mass.: M.I.T. Press.

Rawls, J. 1972. *A Theory of Justice.* Oxford.
Seabright, P. 1987. "Explaining Cultural Divergence: A Wittgensteinian Paradox." *Journal of Philosophy* (January 1987).
Sen, A.K. 1979. "Equality of What?" Tanner Lectures.
Sperber, D. 1982. "Apparently Irrational Beliefs." In *Rationality and Relativism.*
Taylor, C. 1982. "Rationality." In *Rationality and Relativism.*
Williams, B. 1981. (1) *Moral Luck.* Cambridge: Cambridge University Press.
———. 1985. (2) *Ethics and the Limits of Philosophy.* London: Penguin Books.
Wittgenstein, L. 1958. *Philosophical Investigations.* Oxford: Blackwell.

Is There A Single True Morality?

Gilbert Harman

Confession

I have always been a moral relativist. As far back as I can remember thinking about it, it has seemed to me obvious that the dictates of morality arise from some sort of convention or understanding among people, that different people arrive at different understandings, and that there are no basic moral demands that apply to everyone. For many years, this seemed so obvious to me that I assumed it was everyone's instinctive view, at least everyone who gave the matter any thought "in this day and age."

When I first studied philosophical ethics (in the 1950s), I was not disabused of this opinion. The main issue at the time seemed to be to determine exactly what form of "noncognitivism" was correct. (According to noncognitivism, moral judgments do not function to describe a moral reality but do something else—express feelings, prescribe a course of action, and so forth.)

It is true that many of the philosophers I studied seemed for some reason to want to avoid calling themselves "relativists." This was usually accomplished by defining moral relativism to be an obviously inconsistent position; for example, the view both that there are no universal moral truths and also that everyone ought to follow the dictates of his or her group, where this last claim is taken to be a universal moral truth. I wasn't sure what this verbal maneuver was supposed to accomplish. Why would anyone want to give such a definition of moral relativism? Moral relativism was obviously correct, and the philosophers I was

Reprinted from David Copp and David Zimmerman, eds., *Morality, Reason and Truth: New Essays on the Foundations of Ethics* (Rowman and Allanheld, 1984), pp. 27-48.

studying seemed all to be moral relativists even if they did not want to describe themselves in that way.

In the 1960s I was distressed to hear from various people teaching ethics that students in their classes tended to proclaim themselves moral relativists until they had been shown how confused they were about ethics. I suspected that what confusions there were were not confusions of the students, but were confusions of their teachers, due perhaps to a faulty definition of moral relativism. It seemed to me that the obvious solution was to show that moral relativism can be consistently defined as a plausible view and that standard objections to moral relativism are mistaken.

So, I eventually wrote and published an essay about this (Harman, 1975), naively thinking it would clear things up and end worries about moral relativism. I was surprised to discover that this did not happen. I was also startled to find that many students in my own ethics courses resisted my attempt to make clear what I thought they instinctively believed. After some study I concluded that in fact only some of the students in my courses were instinctive moral relativists; a significant number of them were instinctive absolutists.

I had known of course that there were philosophers and friends of mine who were not moral relativists. For a long time I attributed this to their perversity and love of the bizarre and attached no significance to it. But then I discovered that some of them thought moral relativism was the perverse view, a kind of philosophical folly like skepticism about other minds or the external world (for example, Nagel, 1980). I was stunned! How could they think that when they knew so many moral relativists (like me) and no epistemological skeptics (at least none who took such skepticism seriously in ordinary life)? It then occurred to me to wonder how I could think of moral absolutism as such a perverse view when I knew so many moral absolutists.

The Issue

It turns out to my surprise that the question whether there is a single true morality is an unresolved issue in moral philosophy. On one side are relativists, skeptics, nihilists, and noncognitivists. On the other side are those who believe in absolute values and a moral law that applies to everyone. Strangely, only a few people seem to be undecided. Almost everyone seems to be firmly on one side or the other, and almost everyone seems to think his or her side is obviously right, the other side representing a kind of ridiculous folly. This is strange since everyone knows, or ought to know, that many intelligent people are on each side of this issue.

Two Approaches

In this essay I want to suggest that part of the explanation for this mutual incomprehension is that there are two different ways to do moral philosophy. If one approach is taken, moral relativism, noncognitivism, or skepticism may seem obviously correct and moral absolutism may seem foolish. If the other approach is taken, absolutism may seem clearly right and skepticism, relativism, and noncognitivism may seem foolish.

The difference in approaches is, to put it crudely, a difference in attitude toward science. One side says we must concentrate on finding the place of value and obligation in the world of facts as revealed by science. The other side says we must ignore that problem and concentrate on ethics proper.

Of course, both sides agree that we must begin at the beginning with our initial beliefs, both moral and nonmoral, and consider possible modifications that will make these beliefs more coherent with each other and with plausible generalizations and other explanatory principles. Eventually, we hope to arrive at a "reflective equilibrium" (Rawls, 1971) when no further modifications seem called for, at least for the time being. This process will inevitably leave many issues unresolved; in particular, we may find ourselves with no account of the place that value and obligation have in the world of facts. This will not dismay someone who is willing to leave that question unanswered, but it will be disturbing to someone who, on the way to "reflective equilibrium," has come to think that the basic issue in moral philosophy is precisely how value and obligation fit into the scientific conception of the world.

I will use the term "naturalism" for an approach to ethics that is in this way dominated by a concern with the place of values in the natural world. I will call any approach that is not so dominated an instance of "autonomous ethics," since such an approach allows us to pursue ethics internally. Of course, autonomous ethics allows that science is relevant to ethics in as much as ethical assessment depends on the facts of the case. But unlike naturalism, autonomous ethics does not take the main question of ethics to be the naturalistic status of values and obligations.

Naturalism

I hope the terms "naturalism" and "autonomous ethics" will not be too misleading. The term "naturalism" is sometimes reserved for the thesis that moral judgments can be analyzed into or reduced to factual statements of a sort clearly compatible with the scientific world view. I am using the term "naturalism" more broadly in a more traditional and accurate sense. Naturalism in this sense does not have to lead to naturalistic reduction, although that is one possibility. Another possibility is that there is no way in which ethics could fit into the scientific conception of the world. In that case naturalism leads to moral nihilism, as in Mackie (1977). Mackie supposes that ethics requires absolute values which have the property that anyone aware of their existence must necessarily be motivated to act morally. Since our scientific conception of the world has no place for entities of this sort, and since there is no way in which we could become aware of such entities, Mackie concludes that ethics must be rejected as resting on a false presupposition. That is a version of naturalism as I am using the term.

Naturalism can also lead one to a noncognitive analysis of moral judgments. In this view, moral judgments do not function to describe the world, but to do something else—to express one's attitudes for and against things, as Stevenson (1963) argues—or to recommend one or another course of action or general policy, as Hare (1952, 1981) proposes. Or a naturalist may decide that moral judgments do make factual claims that fit in with the claims of science. This can be illustrated by some sort of naturalistic reduction. One example would be an analysis that takes moral claims to be claims about the reactions of a hypothetical impartial observer as in Hume (1739) or Firth (1952).

More complex positions are possible. Mackie (1977) argues in Chapter 1 that ethics rests on a false presupposition, but then he goes on in later chapters to discuss particular moral issues. It is almost as if he had first demonstrated that God does not exist and had then gone on to consider whether He is wise and loving. Presumably, Mackie believes that ethics as normally conceived must be or can be replaced with something else. But he does not indicate exactly what sort of replacement he has in mind—whether it is an institution of some sort, for example. Nor does he say how moral claims made within this replacement fit in with the claims of science. I suspect he would accept some sort of noncognitivist account of the judgments that are to replace the old moral judgments.

It is possible to be both a naturalist and an absolutist, although this is not very common. Firth (1952) defends an absolutist version of the ideal-observer theory and Hare (1981) defends an absolutist version of noncognitivism. But I will argue that the most plausible versions of naturalism involve a moral relativism that says different agents are subject to different basic moral requirements depending on the moral conventions in which they participate.

Autonomous Ethics

Naturalism tends toward relativism. What I am calling autonomous ethics, on the other hand, can have a very different tendency. In this approach, science is relevant, since our moral judgments depend on what we take the facts to be; but we attach no special importance to saying how obligations and values can be part of the world revealed by science. Rather, we do ethics internally. We begin with our initial moral beliefs and search for general principles. Our initial opinions can be changed to some extent so as to come into agreement with appealing general principles and our beliefs about the facts, but an important aspect of the appeal of such principles will be the way in which they account for what we already accept.

This approach normally (but not always) involves an initial assumption of moral absolutism, which in this context is of course not the thesis that there are simple moral principles that hold absolutely without exceptions, but rather the thesis that there are basic moral demands that apply to all moral agents. Autonomous ethics tends to retain that absolutist thesis. It may also involve some sort of intuitionism, claiming that each of us has immediate insight into the truths of certain moral principles. It sometimes leads to a fairly conservative morality, not much different from one's initial starting point. That is not surprising given the privileged position assigned to our initial moral beliefs.

But let me stress that conservatism is not inevitable, and autonomous ethics can and often does lead to more radical moralities too. It leads some philosophers to a radical utilitarianism, for example. It leads Rawls (1971) to principles of social justice that appear to be considerably more egalitarian than those most people accept. And Nozick (1974), using the same general approach, comes out at a very different place, in which he ends up denying that any sort of egalitarian redistribution by governments is ever morally justified. (However, the moral theory in Nozick, 1981, as contrasted with the political theory in Nozick, 1974, insists on the moral requirement of helping others.) Indeed, there are many different ways in which ethics can be pursued as an autonomous discipline with its own principles that are not reducible to the principles of any science. I can illustrate this variety by mentioning a few of the many other contemporary philosophers who accept some form of autonomous ethics: Baier (1958), Darwall (1983), Donagan (1977), Frankena (1976), Fried (1978), Gewirth (1978), Grice (1967), Nagel (1970, 1980), and Richards (1971). Each of these philosophers has a somewhat different approach, although all are absolutists who rely on some form of autonomous ethics.

I should say that it is possible to believe in autonomous ethics without being an absolutist. One might be impressed by the variety of views held by those who accept autonomous ethics and so be led to allow for relativism while continuing to accept the method of autonomous ethics, believing that naturalism must be rejected. A possible example is McDowell (1978, 1979, 1981). But the tendency of autonomism in ethics is toward absolutism. In what follows I will restrict my discussion to absolutist versions of autonomous ethics and to relativistic versions of naturalism.

Teachers of Ethics

I might also mention that ethics pursued internally, as in autonomous ethics, is more interesting to many people than ethics as pursued by naturalism. That is because autonomous ethics allows one to spend more of one's time thinking about interesting complicated moral puzzles than naturalistic ethics does, and many people find moral puzzles more interesting than "abstract" questions about the objectivity of value and its place in nature. Philosophers attracted by naturalism tend not to find ethics as interesting a subject as do philosophers attracted by autonomous ethics. So, relativists tend to be less interested in ethics than absolutists are. For example, logicians, philosophers of science, and philosophers of mathematics, who tend toward naturalism, are usually not moral absolutists and are not very interested in ethics as a philosophical subject. Philosophers who are relatively interested in ethics tend to be those who favor autonomous ethics and therefore tend to be absolutists. This is why teachers of ethics tend more than their students to be absolutists. It is not merely, as they sometimes suppose, that ethics teachers have seen through confusions that affect their students. A more important factor is that relativists tend not to become teachers of ethics.

Why Do We Believe What We Believe?

Autonomous ethics and naturalism represent very different attitudes toward the relation between science and ethics. Consider, for example, the question of what explains our believing what we in fact believe. Naturalists see an important difference between our factual beliefs and our moral beliefs. Our ordinary factual beliefs provide us with evidence that there is an independent world of objects because our having those beliefs cannot be plausibly explained without assuming we interact with an independent world of objects external to ourselves, objects we perceive and manipulate. But our having the moral beliefs we have can be explained entirely in terms of our upbringing and our psychology, without any appeal to an independent realm of values and obligations. So our moral beliefs do not provide us with evidence for such an independent realm of values and obligations, and we must choose between skepticism, noncognitivism, and relativism (Harman, 1977, chapter 1).

Autonomists disagree with this. They claim we often believe that something is good or right or obligatory in part because it *is* good or right or obligatory. They accuse naturalists of begging the question. When naturalists say that a belief cannot be explained by virtue of something's being right, unless that thing's being right consists in some psychological or sociological fact, they simply assume that all explanatory factors are part of the world revealed by science. But this is the point at issue. Autonomists argue that it is more obvious that we sometimes recognize what is right than that naturalism is correct. True, we may be unable to say how a given "moral fact" and someone's recognition of it fit into the world of facts as revealed by science. But there are always unanswered questions. To jump from our current inability to answer this question to skepticism, relativism, or noncognitivism is to make a more drastic move than this puzzle warrants, from the point of view of autonomous ethics.

Explanation and Reduction

The naturalist seeks to locate the place of value, justice, right, and wrong, and so forth in the world in a way that makes clear how they might explain what we take them to explain. A naturalist cannot understand how value, justice, right, and wrong might figure in explanations without having some sense of their "location" in the world. We can say that this involves "naturalistic reduction," but it need not involve reductive definitions of a serious sort. Indeed, reduction rarely (if ever) involves serious reductive definitions. We identify tables with clusters of atoms in a way that allows us to understand how tables can hold up the things they hold up without having to suppose the word *table* is definable using only the concepts of physics! Similarly, we identify colors with dispositional properties of objects, namely, their tendencies to look in certain ways to certain sorts of observers in certain conditions, without having to suppose there is a satisfactory definition in these terms. Similarly for temperatures, genes, and so on. What a naturalistic wants is to be able to locate value, justice, right, wrong, and so forth in the world in the way that tables, colors, genes, temperatures, and so on can be located in the world.

What is at issue here is understanding *how* moral facts might explain something, how the badness of someone's character might explain why that person acts in a certain way, to take an example from Sturgeon's essay. It is not sufficient that one be prepared to accept the counterfactual judgment that the person would not have acted in that way if the person had not had a bad character, if one does not see how the *badness* of the person's character could have such an effect. A naturalist believes one can see that only by locating badness of character in aspects of the world which one sees can have that effect.

Notice that a "naturalist" as I am here using the term is not just someone who supposes that all aspects of the world have a naturalistic location in this way, but rather someone who takes it to be of overriding importance in doing moral philosophy actually to attempt to locate moral properties. My claim is that, when one takes this attempt seriously, one will tend to become skeptical or relativistic. Sturgeon is not a naturalist in my sense, despite his insistence that he takes moral facts to be natural facts.

Moral Absolutism Defined

I now want to be more specific about what is to count as moral absolutism. Various things might be meant by the claim that there are absolute values and one true morality. Moral absolutists in one sense might not be moral absolutists in other senses. We must be careful not to mix up real issues with purely verbal issues. So let me stipulate that I will take moral absolutism to be a view about the moral reasons people have to do things and to want or hope for things. I will understand a belief about absolute values to be a belief that there are things that everyone has a reason to hope or wish for. To say that there is a moral law that "applies to everyone" is, I hereby stipulate, to say that everyone has sufficient reasons to follow that law.

It is true that many philosophers pursue something that resembles autonomous ethics when they ask what principles an "ideal" moral code of one or another sort would have, quite apart from the question whether people now have any reason to follow that code. Depending on what sort of idealization is being considered, there may or may not be a unique "ideal" code of that sort. But I am not going to count as a form of moral absolutism the claim that there is a unique ideal moral code of such and such a type. Relativists and absolutists in my sense might very well agree about this claim without that having any effect at all on what I take to be the basic issue that separates them, since this claim has no immediate relevance to questions about what reasons people actually have to hope for certain things or do certain things.

Similarly, I am not going to count as a form of moral absolutism the claim that there is one true morality that applies to everyone in that everyone ought to follow it, if this is not taken to imply that everyone has a sufficient reason to follow it. I am not sure what *ought* is supposed to mean if it is disconnected in this way from reasons to do things. If what is meant is that it ought to be the case that everyone followed the one true morality—in other words that it would be a good thing if they did—then this is a version of the view that there is a unique "ideal" moral code. I am not sure what else might be meant, although a great deal more could be said here (Harman 1978a). Rather than try to say it, however, I simply stipulate that this sort of claim is not a version of what I am counting as moral absolutism.

I should note that, of the contemporary philosophers I have identified as absolutists, Baier, Darwall, Donagan, Frankena, Gewirth, Grice, Nagel, and Richards, clearly advocate moral absolutism in this sense. They all think that there are basic moral demands that in some sense every competent adult has reasons to adhere to. I *believe* the others I mentioned—namely Rawls, Nozick, and Fried—also agreed with this, although they do not explicitly say so in the works I have cited.

Does a Single Moral Law Apply to Everyone?

Consider the issue between absolutism and relativism concerning reasons people have for doing things. According to moral absolutism about this, there is a single moral law that applies to everyone; in other words, there are moral demands that everyone has sufficient reasons to follow, and these demands are the source of all moral reasons. Moral relativism denies that there are universal basic moral demands and says different people are subject to different basic moral demands depending on the social customs, practices, conventions, values, and principles that they accept.

For example, a moral absolutist might suppose there is a basic moral prohibition on causing harm or injury to other people. This prohibition is in one sense not absolute, since it can be overridden by more compelling considerations and since it allows exceptions in order to punish criminals, for instance. But the prohibition is supposed to be

universal in the sense that it applies to absolutely all agents and not just
to those who happen to participate in certain conventions. The absolutist claims that absolutely everyone has sufficient reasons to observe this
prohibition and to act as it and other basic moral requirements dictate.

A moral relativist denies this and claims that many people have no
reasons to observe this prohibition. Many people participate in moralities that sharply distinguish insiders and outsiders and do not prohibit
harm or injury to outsiders, except perhaps as this is likely to lead to
retaliation against insiders. A person participating in such a morality
has no reason to avoid harm or injury to outsiders, according to the
relativist, and so the general prohibition does not apply to that person.
Such a person may be a member of some primitive tribal group, but he
or she need not be. He or she might also be part of contemporary
society, a successful professional criminal, say, who recognizes various
obligations to other members of a criminal organization but not to
those on the outside. According to the moral relativist, the successful
criminal may well have no reason at all not to harm his or her victims.

An Argument for Relativism

Let us concentrate on this case. The moral absolutist says the
demands of the one true morality apply as much to this successful
criminal as to anyone else, so this criminal does have a reason not to
harm a given victim. The relativist denies the criminal has any such
reason and so denies the relevant moral demand is a universal demand
that applies to everyone. Here naturalism tends to support relativism in
the following way.

Consider what it is for someone to have a sufficient reason to do
something. Naturalism requires that this should be explained in terms
congenial to science. We cannot simply treat this as irreducibly normative, saying, for example, that someone has a sufficient reason to do
something if and only if he or she ought to do it. Now, presumably,
someone has a sufficient reason to do something if and only if there is
warranted reasoning that person could do which would lead him or her
to decide to do that thing. A naturalist will suppose that a person with a
sufficient reason to do something might fail to reason in this way to
such a decision only because of some sort of empirically discoverable
failure, due to inattention, or lack of time, or failure to consider or
appreciate certain arguments, or ignorance of certain available evidence, or an error in reasoning, or some sort of irrationality or unreasonableness, or weakness of will. If the person does not intend to do
something and that is not because he or she has failed in some such

empirically discoverable way to reason to a decision to do that thing, then, according to the naturalist, that person cannot have a sufficient reason to do that thing. This is the first premise in a naturalistic argument in support of the relativist.

The other premise is that there are people, such as certain professional criminals, who do not act in accordance with the alleged requirement not to harm or injure others, where this is not due to inattention or failure to consider or appreciate certain arguments, or ignorance of certain evidence, or any errors in reasoning, or any sort of irrationality or unreasonableness, or weakness of will. The argument for this is simply that there clearly are people who do not adhere to the requirement in question and who do not *seem* to have failed in any of these ways. So, in the absence of special theoretical reasons, deriving, say, from psychology, to think these people must have failed in one of the specified ways, we can conclude they have not done so.

From these two premises it follows that there are people who do not have sufficient reasons, and therefore do not have sufficient moral reasons, to adhere to the general prohibition against harming or injuring others. In particular, a successful criminal may not have a sufficient reason not to harm his or her victims. The moral prohibition against harming others may simply fail to apply to such a person. It may fail to apply in the relevant sense, which is of course not to say that the principle makes an explicit exception for criminals, allowing them but not others to injure and harm people without restraint. Rather, the principle may fail to apply in the sense that the criminal in question may fail to have sufficient reason to act in accordance with the principle.

An Absolutist Reply

Moral absolutism must reject this argument. It can do so by invoking autonomous ethics at the place at which moral relativism invokes naturalism. Autonomous ethics does not suppose that we must give some sort of naturalistic account of having a sufficient reason to do something, nor does it suppose that only a science like psychology can discover the conditions under which someone has failed to reason in a certain way because of inattention, irrationality, unreasonableness, or any of the other causes of failure mentioned in the relativistic argument.

Autonomous ethics approaches this issue in the following way. We begin with certain beliefs. Presumably these imply that everyone has a sufficient reason to observe the prohibition against harm to others, including, in particular, the successful criminal who does not participate in or accept any practice of observing this general prohibition. At the start we therefore believe that the criminal does have sufficient reason not to harm his or her victims. Following autonomous ethics, then, we should continue to believe this unless such continued belief conflicts with generalizations or other theoretical principles internal to ethics that we find attractive because they do a better job at making sense of most of the things we originally believe. Taking this approach, the absolutist must claim that the relativistic argument does not provide sufficient reason to abandon our original absolutism. It is more plausible, according to the absolutist, that at least one of the premises of the relativistic argument is false than that its conclusion is true.

Assessing the First Premise

The first premise of the relativistic argument is that for someone to have a sufficient reason to do something there must be warranted reasoning available to that person that leads to a decision to do that thing, so that if the person fails to intend to do that thing it must be because of inattention, lack of time, failure to consider or appreciate certain arguments, ignorance of relevant evidence, an error in reasoning, irrationality, unreasonableness, or weakness of will. The absolutist might object that this is oversimplified. If a person with sufficient reason to do something does not do it, then something has gone wrong, and it might be one of the things the relativist mentions, but it might be something else as well. There might be something wrong with the *person* in question. That person might be bad, immoral. The failure might simply be a failure not to care enough about other people. A person ought to care about others and there is something wrong with a person who does not care, even if that person is not inattentive, ignorant, rushed, or defective in any other of the particular ways the relativist mentions. So, even if some people fail to observe the prohibition against harming others not because of inattention, lack of time, and so forth, but simply because of lack of concern and respect for others, such people still do have sufficient reason not to harm others. (This response on behalf of absolutism was suggested to me by Thomas M. Scanlon.)

This response to the relativistic argument is a response within autonomous ethics. It does not explain having a sufficient reason to do something in terms that are acceptably factual from a naturalistic perspective. It appeals also to the notion of something's being wrong with someone, where what might be wrong is simply that the person is bad or immoral. It is like saying one has a sufficient reason to do something if and only if one ought to do it, or if and only if it would be wrong not to do it.

The relativist claims that the only plausible accounts of these normative notions are relativistic ones. There is no prohibition on harm to outsiders in the criminals' morality. There is such a prohibition only in some other morality. In that other morality something is wrong with a person who has no compunction about injuring someone else; but nothing is wrong with such a person with respect to the criminal morality, as long as those injured are outsiders. But how can it be a sufficient reason for the criminal not to harm his or her victims that this is prohibited by somebody else's morality? How can its being bad, immoral, or wrong in this other morality not to care about and respect others give the criminal, who does not accept that morality, a sufficient reason to do anything.

The absolutist's answer is that failure to respect others is not just wrong according to some morality the criminal does not accept; it is also wrong, period. Something is really wrong with lack of respect and concern for others. It is not just wrong in relation to one or another morality. Of course, the relativist will not be satisfied with this answer and, appealing to naturalism, will ask what it is for something to be wrong in this way. The absolutist supposes that the failure to care about and respect others does involve something the absolutist points to by saying this failure is wrong. But what is this thing that is true of such a failure to care and that can give the criminal a sufficient reason not to harm and injure others? The relativist can see no aspect of such a failure that could provide such a reason. This of course is because the relativist, as a naturalist, considers only aspects of the failure that are clearly compatible with a scientific world view. The relativist disregards putative aspects that can be specified only in normative terms. But the absolutist, as an autonomist, can specify the relevant aspect of such a failure to care about others: It is bad, immoral, wrong not to care; the criminal ought to have this concern and respect and so ought not to harm and injure others, and therefore has a sufficient reason not to harm and injure them.

Assessing the Second Premise

We have been discussing an argument for relativism concerning moral reasons. We have seen that naturalism supports the first premise of this argument and that autonomous ethics allows the rejection of this premise. The same thing is true of the second premise, which says that there are people, such as the successful criminal, who do not observe the alleged requirement not to harm or injure others and this is not due to inattention, failure to consider or appreciate certain arguments, ignorance of relevant evidence, errors in reasoning, irrationality, unreasonableness, or weakness of will. Naturalism supports this because there do seem to be such people, and no scientifically acceptable grounds exist for thinking this is an illusion. On the other hand, autonomous ethics allows other grounds, not reducible to scientific grounds, for thinking this is an illusion. In autonomous ethics we begin by supposing that we recognize the wrongness of harming others, where this is to recognize a sufficient reason not to harm others. If that is something we recognize, then it must be there to be recognized, so the successful criminal in question must be failing to recognize and appreciate something that is there.

The absolutist might argue that the criminal must be irrational or at least unreasonable. Seeing that a proposed course of action will probably cause serious injury to some outsider, the criminal does not treat this as a reason not to undertake that course of action. This must be irrational or unreasonable, because such a consideration simply is such a reason and indeed is an obvious reason, a basic reason, not one that has to be derived in some complex way through arcane reasoning. But then it must be irrational or at least unreasonable for the criminal not to care sufficiently about others, since the criminal's lack of concern for others is what is responsible for the criminal's not taking the likelihood of harm to an outsider to be a reason against a proposed course of action. This is one way an absolutist might argue.

The relativist's reply to such an argument is that, on any plausible characterization of reasonableness and unreasonableness (or rationality and irrationality) as notions that can be part of the scientific conception of the world, the absolutist's claim is just false. Someone can be completely rational without feeling concern and respect for outsiders. But of course this reply appeals to naturalism. The absolutist who rejects naturalism in favor of autonomous ethics relies on an unreduced normative characterization of rationality and irrationality (or reasonableness and unreasonableness).

Now the argument continues as before. The relativist argues that, if rationality and irrationality (or reasonableness and unreasonableness) are conceived normatively, they become relative notions. What one morality counts as irrational or unreasonable, another does not. The criminal is not irrational or unreasonable in relation to criminal morality, but only in relation to a morality the criminal rejects. But the fact that it is irrational or unreasonable in relation to this other morality not to have concern and respect for others does not give the criminal who rejects that morality any reason to avoid harming or injuring others. The absolutist replies that relative irrationality or unreasonableness is not what is in question. The criminal is irrational or at least unreasonable, period. Not just irrational or unreasonable in relation to a morality he or she does not accept. Since it is irrational or unreasonable for anyone not to care sufficiently about others, everyone has a sufficient reason not to injure others, whether he or she recognizes this reason or, through irrationality or unreasonableness, does not recognize it.

The naturalist is unconvinced by this because the naturalist can find no aspect of the criminal the absolutist might be referring to in saying the criminal is "irrational" or "unreasonable," if this aspect is to give the criminal any reason to care about others. This of course is because the naturalist is considering only naturalistic aspects of the criminal, whereas the absolutist, as an autonomist, is thinking about an unreduced normative aspect, something the naturalist cannot appeal to.

So, as was true of the first premise of the relativistic argument about reasons, the second premise depends on an assumption of naturalism. By appealing to autonomous ethics, an absolutist can reject this premise.

An absolutist may in fact actually accept one or the other of the premises of the relativistic argument (although of course not both). A given absolutist might reject either the first premise or the second or both premises. An absolutist might even be undecided, holding merely that one or the other premise must be rejected, without saying which. There is nothing wrong with being undecided about this. Reflective equilibrium leaves many issues unresolved.

Are There Absolute Moral Values?

The situation is similar in the theory of value. Naturalism tends to support the conclusion that all value is relative and that something is always good for one or another person or group of people or in relation to a specified set of purposes or interests or aims. Autonomous ethics allows also for absolute values, things that are good, period, and not just good for someone or some group or for some purpose.

The issue here concerns the goodness or value of a possible state of affairs, not the goodness or value of something as a thing of a given sort. The issue is not what it is for something to be a good thing of a kind, a good knife, a good watch, a good backswing, a good apple, a good farmer, a good poem. The issue is rather what it is for an event or situation to be a good thing; what is it, for example, to be a good thing that it is raining or that Egypt and Israel signed a peace treaty.

It is uncontroversial that this sort of goodness is sometimes relational. A situation is good for someone or some group of people, good from a certain point of view, in relation to certain purposes or interests. That it is raining is a good thing for the farmer, but not for the vacationer. That Egypt and Israel signed a peace treaty might be good from their point of view, but not from the point of view of the PLO. Given a fixed point of reference, we can evaluate states of affairs as better or worse. The value of a state of affairs in relation to that reference point represents the degree to which someone with the relevant purposes and interests has a reason to try to bring about, or want, or at least hope for that state of affairs.

Now it can be argued that there is also a kind of absolute value. The claim is that states of affairs can be good or bad, period, and not merely good or bad for someone or in relation to given purposes or interests. On hearing of pointless painful experiments on laboratory animals, for example, one immediately reacts with the thought that this is bad and it would be good to eliminate such practices. Clearly, one does not simply mean that these tortures are bad for the animals involved and that these animals would benefit if such experiments were ended. A heartless experimenter might agree that what he does is bad for the animals without having to agree that it would be a good thing to eliminate this sort of experimentation. Similarly, it seems intelligible to suppose that it would be better if there were no inequalities of wealth and income in the world even though this would not be better for everyone, not for those who are now relatively wealthy, for instance. And this seems to say more, for example, than that the average person would be better off if there were no such inequalities, since an elitist might agree with that but not agree that the envisioned state of affairs would be better, period, than our present situation. Again, we can consider which of various population policies would lead to the best resulting state of affairs even though these policies would result in different populations, so that we cannot be simply considering the interests and purposes of some fixed group. It may seem, then, that we can consider the absolute value of a possible state of affairs.

Skepticism about Absolute Values

The relative value of a possible state of affairs in relation to given purposes and interests is a measure of the extent to which someone with those purposes and interests has a reason to try to bring about, or want, or hope for that state of affairs. The absolute value of a possible state of affairs is a measure of the extent to which anyone, apart from having a personal stake in the matter, has a reason to try to bring about, or want, or hope for that state of affairs. Naturalism leads to skepticism at this point. How could we ever be aware of absolute values? How could we ever know that everyone has a reason to want a certain possible state of affairs?

Further reflection along naturalistic lines suggests that apparent absolute values are often illusory projections of one's personal values onto the world. Sometimes this sort of projection yields plausible results, but usually it does not. To begin with the most plausible sort of case, in hearing about the pain involved in animal experimentation, our sympathies are immediately and vividly engaged; we immediately side with the animals against the experimenters. In saying "That is awful!" we are not just saying "That is awful for the animals," since our remark expresses our sympathetic identification with the point of view of the animals. We do not merely state a fact; we express our feelings and we expect an awareness of this state of affairs to call forth the same feelings of dismay in everyone. This expectation seems reasonable enough in this case, since it may well be, as Brandt argues, that everyone has a sympathetic reaction to suffering (1976, p. 450).

But plausibility vanishes as soon as the case becomes even a little complex. Suppose the animal experiments are not pointless but are an essential part of a kind of medical research that promises to alleviate a certain amount of human suffering. Or suppose that, although the experiments promise no practical benefit of this sort, they are relevant to a theoretical issue in psychology. A given person may still feel that it is bad that the experiments should occur and that it would be good if they were not done, the gain not being worth the cost. Again, the person is not just saying that the experiments are bad for the animals, something to which everyone would agree. He or she is also expressing overall disapproval of the experiments, expecting others also to disapprove if they consider the issue in an impartial way. The trouble is that people react differently to these cases.

Consider the question whether it is good or bad to experiment painfully on animals in order to resolve certain theoretical issues in psychology. The extent to which this is (absolutely) good is the extent to which everyone (apart from any personal stake in the matter) has a reason to try to bring it about that such experiments are done, or to want them to be done, or hope that they are done. The extent to which this is (absolutely) bad is the extent to which everyone (apart from any personal stake) has a reason to try to end the experiments, or want them

to end, or hope they end. But naturalism suggests that there is no
unique answer here and that what a person has a reason to want will
depend on the relative value he or she attaches to animal suffering, to
using animals as means, and to theoretical progress in psychology. Different people attach different values to these things without having
overlooked something, without being irrational or unreasonable, and so
on. So it seems that some people will have reason to be in favor of the
experiments and others will have reason to be opposed to the experiments, where this is determined by the personal values of those people.
If we suppose that our answer is the right answer, we are merely projecting our own values onto the world.

The Issue Joined

Of course, autonomous ethics sees nothing wrong with projecting
our own values onto the world, holding in fact that that is exactly the
right method! We should begin with our initial valuations and modify
them only in the interests of theoretical simplicity. If we start out believing in absolute values, we should continue believing this until forced to
believe otherwise.

Clearly the controversy over absolute values parallels the controversy about reasons to do things. The argument against absolute values
has the same structure as the relativistic argument about reasons to do
things. Its first premise is that a person has a reason to want or hope for
or try to bring about a particular state of affairs only to the extent that
he or she would be irrational or unreasonable not to want that state of
affairs unless he or she was unaware of some relevant consideration, was
confused, or had some other specified defect. Its second premise is that,
except for the simplest cases, a person can fail to want a given state of
affairs without being irrational or unreasonable or ignorant or whatever.
The conclusion is that, except possibly for simple cases, where, for
example, the only thing relevant is that a creature suffers, there are no
reasons everyone has to want or hope for or try to bring about a given
state of affairs. So there are no nontrivial absolute values.

As before, the two premises are defended in each case by an appeal
to naturalism: We must give a naturalistic account of reasons and we
must give empirical grounds for supposing someone to be irrational or
unreasonable. The absolutist rejects the argument as before by invoking
autonomous ethics, perhaps by rejecting the naturalistic account of
reasons, perhaps by rejecting the requirement that scientific grounds

must be given for a judgment of irrationality or unreasonableness, possibly remaining undecided between these alternatives.

Naturalism Versus Autonomous Ethics

So the issue between relativism and absolutism comes down to the dispute between naturalism and autonomous ethics. Which is the best approach in moral philosophy? Should we concentrate on the place of values and reasons in the world of scientific fact, as naturalism recommends, or should we start with our initial moral beliefs and look for general principles and moral theories that will eventually yield a reflective equilibrium, not putting too much weight on the question of the place of value in the world of facts.

Religious Beliefs

In thinking of the issue between naturalism and autonomous ethics, it is useful to consider analogous issues that arise in other areas. Consider religious beliefs. Our scientific conception of the world has no place for gods, angels, demons, or devils. Naturalists hold that there is no empirical evidence for the existence of such beings nor for any sort of divine intervention in human history. Naturalists say that people's religious beliefs can be explained in terms of their upbringing and psychology without any supernatural assumptions, so these beliefs provide no evidence whatsoever for the truth of religious claims. Naturalists therefore incline toward skepticism and atheism, although naturalism might also lead to a kind of religious noncognitivism which supposes that religious language makes no factual claims about a supernatural realm but has a different function, for example, in religious ritual.

Another approach to religion is for a believer to start with his or her initial religious beliefs, including beliefs in the authority of certain writings, and then to develop general principles and theories that would accommodate these beliefs, allowing modifications in the interest of more plausible general principles. This will continue until no further modifications seem useful in improving the organization and coherence of that person's views. Inevitably, many questions will remain unanswered, and these will include issues concerning the relation between that person's religious views and his or her scientific views, for example, as regards creation. But this is not a serious worry for autonomous religion, which will say this shows merely that science is not everything, or at least that there are things we do not know and perhaps never will understand.

Naturalists say there is no reason to accept religious claims, because the fact that people have the religious beliefs they have can be explained without any supernatural assumptions. Religious autonomists say there is reason to accept religious claims, at least for someone who begins with religious beliefs, since the process of generalization, systematization, and theory construction internal to religion will give that person no reason to abandon more than a few, if any, of those religious beliefs. Furthermore, certain supernatural events might be part of the correct explanation of the appearance of sacred texts, the occurrence of miracles, and particular religious experiences. There is at present no way to say how these religious explanations mesh with ordinary scientific conceptions, but that by itself is no more an objection to religion than it is an objection to science.

Naturalists in ethics might urge this religious analogy as an *ad hominem* argument against those defenders of autonomous ethics who are not willing to take the same line with respect to religion.

Beliefs about the Mind

There is another sort of issue in which an autonomous position comes off looking rather good, even in an irreligious age, namely, the so-called mind-body problem. Here the naturalistic position corresponds to the thesis of physicalism, according to which all real aspects of mind must be features of the physical brain and central nervous system, its atomic or neural structure, or some more complex structure that the brain and nervous system instantiate. This may involve behaviorism or some sort of functionalism that treats the brain as an information-processing system like a computer in a robot. A few defenders of this approach, like Skinner (1974), conclude that there are no mental events, no mind, no consciousness, no sensation. (Rorty, 1965, sympathetically describes a similar view, "eliminative materialism.") But most physicalists suppose that mental events and other aspects of mind do exist and can be identified with certain physical or structural or functional aspects of the brain and central nervous system.

On the other side is autonomous mentalism, which holds that the physicalist hypothesis clearly leaves something out. In this view we clearly know we are conscious, can initiate action, and have experiences of a distinctive phenomenological character and feeling. The physicalist hypothesis does not account for this. A computer or robot is not conscious. Although a robot can move, it does not *act* in the way people can act. And a robot has no sensuous experience. Indeed, something could have exactly the functional structure of the human brain and nervous system without being conscious. Block (1978) describes a case in which one billion people in radio communication with each other model a particular brain for an hour, each person corresponding to a particular neuron in the brain. Block takes it to be absurd to suppose that this vast collection of people would have a group consciousness that was phenomenologically the same as the consciousness of the person whose brain and central nervous system was being modeled. Nagel (1979) observes that we might know everything there was to know about the neurophysiological structure and functioning of the brain and central nervous system of a bat without knowing what the experience of the bat was like. Defenders of autonomous mentalism agree that this leaves a mind-body problem, since they are unable to say how consciousness, free will, and sensory experience can be part of the world described by physics. But they deny that this means we must stop believing in consciousness or must identify it with some aspect of physical or functional structure. For they claim, with considerable plausibility, that it is much more reasonable to believe in consciousness, free will, and sensory experience, and to believe that these are not aspects of neurophysiological functional structure, than it is to believe in physicalism.

I am not saying that autonomous mentalism *is* more plausible than physicalism. After all is said and done, I find a physicalistic functionalism more plausible than autonomous mentalism. My point is that autonomous mentalism is a perfectly respectable philosophical position.

A defender of autonomous ethics might even argue that naturalism in ethics loses much of its plausibility once autonomous mentalism is recognized as plausible. For that casts doubt on the universal applicability of the naturalistic approach and therefore casts doubt on the naturalist's argument that a belief that something is right cannot be explained by that thing's being actually right unless that thing's being right consists in some psychological or sociological fact. The naturalist's only argument for this, it might be said, depends on accepting the general applicability of naturalism. But it is not obvious that this approach is generally applicable, since it is not obviously correct as compared with autonomous mentalism. There is at least some plausibility to the claim that one's awareness of what red looks like is to be explained by appeal to an experience of redness that does not consist entirely in some neurophysiological event. It might be said that the naturalist has no argument against autonomous ethics, since the naturalist cannot take for granted the general applicability of naturalism.

Ethics

Defenders of autonomous ethics argue that their approach represents the only undogmatic way to proceed. They say that naturalism begs the question in supposing that everything true must fit into a scientific account of the world and by supposing that the central question about morality is how, if at all, morality fits into such a scientific account.

Defenders of naturalism reply that naturalism itself is the result of following the method of reflective equilibrium, and that autonomous ethics begs the question by assigning a specially protected status to initial moral beliefs as compared, say, with initial beliefs about the flatness of the earth or the influence of the stars on human history. Naturalists say that, starting with our initial beliefs, we are led to develop a scientific conception of the world as an account of everything there is. In doing so, we also acquire beliefs about how we learn about the world and about how errors can arise in our thinking. We come to see how superstition arises. We begin to worry about our moral views: Are they mere superstitions? We note certain sorts of disagreement in morality and extreme differences in moral customs. We observe that some people are not much influenced by what we consider important moral considerations. All this leads us to raise as a central question about morality how morality fits in with our scientific conception of the world. Naturalism is no mere prejudice in favor of science; it is an inevitable consequence of intelligent thought. This, at least, is what a defender of naturalism will say.

A defender of autonomous ethics will reply that moral disagreements, differences in custom, and the behavior of criminals prove nothing. All these things are compatible with moral absolutism.

The naturalist retorts that any view can be made *compatible* with the evidence; astrology, for example, is perfectly compatible with the evidence. The issue is not what is compatible with the evidence, but what best accounts for it. The naturalist argues that relativism accounts for the evidence better than absolutism does, since relativism is able to say how reasons and values are part of the world science describes, whereas absolutism is not able to do that.

The defender of autonomous ethics replies that such an argument is no better than the corresponding argument for behaviorism. Behaviorism is able to say how mental states (as it conceives them) are part of the world physics describes and autonomous mentalism is not able to say how mental states (as *it* conceives them) are part of the world physics describes; but one should not for this reason alone abandon one's initial view that one is conscious, makes decisions, has feelings, and so on, where this is not just being disposed to act in various ways (since something could have the dispositions without being conscious and could be conscious without having the dispositions). Similarly, one should not accept the naturalistic argument and give up one's belief in absolute values and universal moral reasons.

I see no knockdown argument for either side. A question of judgment is involved, "Which view is more plausible, all things considered?" To me, the relativistic naturalist position seems more plausible. Others find the absolutist position of autonomous ethics more plausible. I have not tried to show that one side is correct. I have tried to bring out the central issue.

References

Baier, Kurt. 1958. *The Moral Point of View.* Reprint edition: Ithaca, NY: Cornell University Press, 1965. Abridged edition: Random House, New York.

Block, Ned. 1978. "Troubles with Functionalism." In *Perception and Cognition: Issues in the Foundations of Psychology,* ed. C. Wade Savage. Minnesota Studies in the Philosophy of Science, vol. 9. Minneapolis: University of Minnesota Press.

Brandt, Richard B. 1976. "The Psychology of Benevolence and Its Implications for Philosophy." *The Journal of Philosophy* 73: 429-453.

Darwall, Stephen L. 1983. *Impartial Reason.* Ithaca, NY: Cornell University Press.

Donagan, Alan. 1977. *The Theory of Morality.* University of Chicago Press.

Firth, Roderick. 1952. "Ethical Absolutism and the Ideal Observer." *Philosophy and Phenomenological Research* 12: 317-345.

Frankena, William. 1976. In *Perspectives on Morality,* ed. K. E. Goodpaster, Notre Dame, IN: University of Notre Dame Press.

Fried, Charles. 1978. *Right and Wrong.* Cambridge, MA: Harvard University Press.

Gauthier, David. 1967. "Morality and Advantage." *The Philosophical Review* 76: 460-475.

Gewirth, Alan. 1978. *Reason and Morality.* University of Chicago Press.

Grice, Geoffrey Russell. 1967. *The Grounds of Moral Judgment.* Cambridge, MA: Cambridge University Press.

Hare, R. M. 1952. *The Language of Morals.* Oxford: The Clarendon Press of Oxford University Press.

———. 1981. *Moral Thinking: Its Levels, Method and Point.* Oxford: The Clarendon Press of Oxford University Press.

Harman, Gilbert. 1973. *Thought.* Princeton, NJ: Princeton University Press.
————. 1975. "Moral Relativism Defended." *The Philosophical Review* 84: 3-22.
————. 1977. *The Nature of Morality: An Introduction to Ethics.* New York: Oxford University Press.
————. 1978a. "Relativistic Ethics: Morality as Politics." In *Midwest Studies in Philosophy,* vol. 3, *Studies in Ethical Theory,* ed. Peter A. French, Theodore E. Uehling, Jr., and Howard K. Wettstein, pp. 109–121. The University of Minnesota, Morris.
Hume, David. 1739. *Treatise of Human Nature.* Edited edition: ed. L. A. Selby-Bigge. Oxford: The Clarendon Press of Oxford University Press, 1978.
Mackie, John L. 1977. *Ethics: Inventing Right and Wrong.* Harmondsworth, England: Penguin.
McDowell, John. 1978. "Are Moral Requirements Hypothetical Imperatives?" *Proceedings of the Aristotelian Society, Supplementary Volume* 52: 13-29.
————. 1979: "Virtue and Reason." *The Monist* 62: 331-350.
————. 1981: "Noncognitivism and Rule Following." In *Wittgenstein: To Follow a Rule*, ed. Steven H. Holtzman and Christopher M. Leich, pp. 141-162. London: Routledge and Kegan Paul.
Nagel, Thomas. 1970. *The Possibility of Altruism.* Oxford: Oxford University Press.
————. 1979. "What Is It Like to Be a Bat?" In *Mortal Questions*, pp. 165-180. Cambridge: Cambridge University Press.
————. 1980. "The Limits of Objectivity." In *The Tanner Lectures on Human Values,* ed. Sterling M. McMurrin, pp. 77-139. Salt Lake City: University of Utah Press; Cambridge: Cambridge University Press.
Nozick, Robert. 1974. *Anarchy, State and Utopia.* New York: Basic Books.
————. 1981. *Philosophical Explanations.* Cambridge, MA: Harvard University Press.
Rawls, John. 1971. *A Theory of Justice.* Cambridge, MA: Belknap Press of Harvard University Press.
Richards, David A. J. 1971. *A Theory of Reason for Action.* Oxford: Oxford University Press.
Rorty, Richard. 1965. "Mind-Body Identity, Privacy, and Categories," *Review of Metaphysics* 19: 24–54.
Skinner, B. F. 1974. *About Behaviorism.* New York: Alfred A. Knopf.
Stevenson, Charles L. 1963. *Facts and Values.* New Haven, CT: Yale University Press.

The "Self" as a Theoretical Concept

Rom Harré

1. Persons and Selves: The Duality of Social and Personal Being

Mead and Vygotsky shared the view that "mental" processes are organized in ways that derive from the manner in which social interactions unfold. Since most social interactions are mediated through linguistic or quasi-linguistic processes, the structures of conversation offer themselves as obvious and convenient candidates for the sources of the organization of those activities we naively ascribe to mind. Conversing is a public and collective activity into which every individual human being must be drawn, eventually, as a competent speaker and listener. I shall call the organization of conversation the "primary structure."

In the primary structure people appear as locations for speech acts. As such they are metaphysically simple, without internal structure. Real human beings, however, are not mere locations: they are "internally" complex. The modes of organization of this internal complexity I will call the "secondary structure."

By virtue of the existence of individually located secondary structures the speech acts of the human conversation can be represented as grounded in mental activity and treated as the product of expressions of personal intention. The strong social constructivist thesis, that each secondary structure is a variously imperfect reflection of the primary structure, will turn out to be true only in a limited way. The properties of the primary structure of a social world, once appropriated by an individual as a secondary structure, are then modified to a greater or lesser degree by intrinsic personal processes. Action within the primary structures, the public and collective social world, is attributed in our culture to unitary persons. Detailed consideration of the formal properties of secondary structures, including the organization of experience,

The material for this essay is drawn from my *Personal Being* (Oxford: Blackwell, 1983).

thought, and action as mine, required, I hope to show, a second centering in another unity which I shall call a "self." The status of this "unity"
is problematic.

I propose to amplify a tendency noticeable in recent philosophical
writing to work toward a distinction between the individuality of a
human being as it is publicly identified and collectively defined, and the
individuality of the unitary subject of experience. Recent arguments
about the basis of personal identity have turned on the relative weight to
be given to public bodily continuity and maintenance of behavioral style
as against the continuity or discontinuity of some felt unity of experience.

I hope to justify the introduction of a new duality into the metaphysics of psychology, a duality between person and self. Persons as
social individuals are locations in the primary structure and so are
identifiable by public criteria. The intentionality of their actions and
speeches is interpreted within a social framework of interpersonal commitments. Selves are Cartesian egos, the inexperienceable subjects of all
subjective predications, manifested in the unified organization of perceptions, feelings, and beliefs of each human being with regard to their
own experience of themselves and which typically appear in the forms
of self-description. There may be human beings whose belief systems,
imaginary anticipations, and so on are organized in some nonunitary
way. Necessarily all human beings who are members of moral orders are
persons, social individuals, but the degree of their psychological individuality, their personal being, I take to be contingent. The distinctions to
be drawn out in this essay as founding hypotheses for personal psychology are but the empirical counterparts of the oppositions displayed in
Strawson's stern warning: "The concepts of pure individual consciousness—the pure ego—cannot exist as a primary concept in terms of
which the concept of a person can be explained or analysed. It can exist,
if at all, as a secondary non-primitive concept, which itself is to be
explained, analysed in terms of the concept of a person" (Strawson,
Individuals, p. 102). Why should this distinction be introduced to play
so fundamental a role? I shall support it by demonstrating its power to
resolve certain persisting philosophical issues and by its utility in making intelligible a dimension of intercultural differences brought out by
comparative anthropology. The duality of person and self is thus fitted
to be the conceptual foundation of a program of psychological research.

At this point it will be well to distinguish social constructivist
theories of self from the social-learning theories of such as Bandura
(1973). Social-learning theorists claim (no doubt correctly) that certain
traits, dispositions, and the like are the result, not of native develop-

ment, but of the acquisition in social contexts of beliefs and habits. The social constructivist, however, goes much further, asking whether the self-"centered" structure of our system of beliefs, or any other structure personal systems of belief may be found to have, such as the triple-agency structure proposed by Freud, is itself a belief of social origin. For those who answer this question in the affirmative, not only the content but the form of mind is socially acquired.

Finally, I want to emphasize that my concern is not with the "self-concept" as it is currently understood in psychology. As Rogers introduced the term in "A Theory of Therapy," it is clearly to be taken to refer to a belief system: "The organized, consistent gestalt composed of the characteristics of the 'I' or 'me' and the perceptions of the relationships of the 'I' or 'me' to others and to various aspects of life, together with the values attached to these perceptions" is the self-concept. It is also usually taken to include what a person thinks they would like to be. However, self-concept is often carelessly spoken of as "self." For instance, in *Personality* Liebert and Spiegler remark, "The person defends himself from . . . impending danger by a process of defence which maintains the self *[sic]* as it exists at that time." Sometimes there is a correlated concept of "identity" which treats the belief systems of each person as their identity. This is a qualitative concept presuming the grasp by each of his or her own numerical identity. In a word, identity crises are not crises of identity. To be troubled as to who I am, in the sense of what kind of person I am, requires that I know that I am.

My concern is with the origin and nature of the structure of a person's belief system, and the relation of that structure to the generally "centered" structure of experience I shall refer to throughout this work as the "sense of self." It is that which, as Doris Lessing has put it, is "kept burning" behind our many roles.

2. Philosophical Issues Concerning Persons as Selves

The quest for the true bases of the sense of individuality and continuous self-identity of human beings is a persistent theme in philosophy. I shall somewhat artificially separate my treatment into grammatical and metaphysical investigations.

Grammatical Investigations

The philosophical grammar of proper names and personal pronouns should throw some light on the nature of the beings to which they are used to refer. For my purposes in this chapter I need consider only the first person pronoun "I," whose modes of use one might think are closely related to conceptions of personhood and self. Some philosophers have argued that "I" is nonreferential; others that it does denote something, though there have been great differences in their views as to the nature of the referent, roughly whether it is body or mind (soul).

Referentialists differ further as to whether the referent is a collection or bundle of properties, states, and so on, or an entity. Hume's bundle of perceptions' view of personal psychological unity, set out in *A Treatise of Human Nature,* stands in the strongest possible contrast to McTaggart's claim that "I" is a logically proper name, that is, a name used referentially for speaking of a being of which one has immediate acquaintance *(The Nature of Existence).* In McTaggart's view (recently endorsed by Mandell in *The Identify of Self),* to be aware of the referent of "I" is not to know that some particular cluster of properties has been realized. It is to be aware of the being to which those properties are ascribed. McTaggart's argument turns on the alleged point that I could not know that some description applied to me unless I was acquainted not only with the property ascribed but the "myself" to which it is ascribed.

There are various ways to make the step to the nonreferential theory, but the basic thought is simple. After all the properties—physical, mental, dispositional, and so on of a human being—have been enumerated, the claim that I am that person expresses an additional piece of information not included among either the corporeal or mental attributes of the person in question. A person could, for example, imagine him or herself to be of a different nation, culture, sex, or time, and yet think that *he* or *she* was that person without contradicting any current facts true of that person. But what is the force of the extra element in the first-person statements? First-person assertions such as "I am here" and "It's me" are nonempirical in the sense that there are no conditions under which their utterance would be false. According to nonreferentialists like Vesy *(Personal Identity),* Anscombe ("The First Person") or Coval *(Scepticism and the First Person)* the irreducible extra element such statements introduce into the discourse is the display or indication of uniqueness, the feature I have called "location in the primary structure," the logical property of indexicality. Anscombe's conclusion that "there is no subject to which 'I' refers, there are just 'I'-thoughts" is obviously true for the primary structure in which "I" functions as a person label by pinning speech-acts to speaker. Her argument (and indeed I think the arguments of all nonreferentialists) supports the view that there is no *given empirical* subject to which "I" refers in the declaration and ordering of thought. Thoughts are also unified in personal experience, and that unification is not as the set of properties observed to characterize an observable being, the ego. Contrary to McTaggart's claim in *The Nature of Existence*, I do not believe that we are acquainted with our psychological "centers." But it does not follow that because there is no empirically given unifying *entity* that there is no unifying *concept.*

I must certainly have the concept of myself as a subject of experience to be able to order my beliefs, memories, and plans the way I do. Ostensive definition is not the only way a concept can be acquired. So "awareness of myself" is not a necessary condition for me to have the concept of myself. As in physical sciences, so in this case, a concept can be acquired by a semantic displacement. I propose the hypothesis that "I" as self is a concept acquired by semantic displacement of the concept of "I" as a person.

I believe that no resolution of the antithesis between referential and nonreferential uses of "I" is possible through generalizing one of the alternatives in an attempt to provide a unified account by subsuming the other. The reasons for identifying each of these uses of "I" in current English, each with its appropriate metaphysical theory, seem to be sound. In each case the counterarguments can be treated as demonstrations of the need to admit the viability of the other concept somewhere in our socio- and psycholinguistic practices.

A passage from Mandell's *The Identity of Self* (p. 29) cries out for a dualist resolution. In commenting on the view that "I" is used indexically to indicate or display the speaker as the person committed to an utterance he says:

> Even if the arguments that 'I'm here' or 'It's me' is some sort of truth valueless indication were successful, the suggestion that we could then go on to generalize this and claim that, even in assertions like 'I am increasingly aware of the difficulty of this topic', 'I' is being used as some sort of indicator, without awareness of a subject, looks thoroughly implausible.

Indeed it does. An awareness of one of my own states as mine is certainly presupposed in that remark, and so is the knowledge that it is mine, and with it is presupposed the concept of myself. There is the difficulty that is being experienced, and the location of that difficulty within an ordered framework of experience that is mine. The most elegant resolution of the irreducibility of this kind of sentence to an indexical (nonreferential) form is to come to accept that for subjective ascriptions to make sense no more than the self as a theoretical concept need be invoked. In this sort of context "I" refers to an entity without empirically given properties. It lacks such properties, not because it is not given in immediate experience, contra Hume, Ryle, and others, but because it is of the same kind as the familiar hypothetical entities that are the referents of nominal expressions in deep physical theories. The mystery is resolved once one sees that the "inner self" is in many ways like the "gravitational field" invoked to explain the regularities of free fall as the products of an underlying being, the gravitational field. This innovation breaks the chain of McTaggart's argument in *The Nature of Existence*. Just as I can ascribe properties to the gravitational field without experience of it, so too I can ascribe properties to myself without an empirical acquaintance with my "inner being." Persons are indexed (indicated) as speakers; selves are referred to as organizing principles of the psychological unities that confer subjective individuality. But the unity is that of an imposed structure, not that of a common substantial core. These distinctions can be associated with the fact of personal identity germane to the individuality of persons, and the sense of personal identity germane to the individuality of selves.

Since the dualism sketched in this section will play such a large role in the theory of personal being, it is worth elaborating the theory of indexical expressions a little further. It is clear that the pronoun "I" cannot be understood along the same lines as we understand proper names. Its referential function is dependent upon context and use. In indexical uses a pronoun is used to locate speech acts of various kinds, such as avowals, commitments, and so on, at a particular location in the array of persons. This feature can be brought out by comparing "I" with other indexicals. "I" is to Rom Harré as "here" is to Binghamton. "Here" is the space indexical I would use to refer to wherever I happen to be at the moment of speaking or writing, whereas Binghamton is the proper name of a location in space where I am only occasionally. It is true that "here" and "Binghamton" sometimes pick out the same spot. But "here" is always close to where I am speaking, while Binghamton is not. It is worth noticing that since the indexicals in the pronoun system are used by speakers in the first person, then the indexical system cannot function to refer reflexively to possible persons. These features of the use of pronouns are very well known and have been investigated in considerable detail.

However, there has been considerable controversy over the logical grammar of indexicals. On one account the pronouns have been treated as ambiguous proper names, terms without content whose function is just to refer or point to that which they currently name. But so far as my intuitions go, "I" is never ambiguous. It is not an ambiguous proper name because it is not a proper name at all. By turning to the way indexicals are used a more plausible model emerges. To use a pronoun is to mark or label an utterance with a person location just as to use a space-time indexical is to mark an utterance with the space-time location of the act of utterance. Part of the temptation to treat "I" as a kind of name is a misunderstanding about the metaphysical standing of people in the primary array. I have suggested that they are like locations, not like things.

Metaphysical Investigations

Both philosophers and psychologists, for instance Kant and Kelly, have seen the need for the concept of a self, a concept other than that of the socially defined "person" who is the bearer of the indexical force of the pronoun "I." Each human being's conception of oneself is more elaborate than could be explained solely by invoking the hypothesis that he or she believes him or herself to be a person among an array of persons, each of whom is a publicly observable being. We are familiar in physics with concepts introduced to refer to transcendental, nonobservable realities, belief in which enables us to order experience in various ways. For instance, a concept like gravitational field or electric or magnetic potential is of this kind. In learning to use the concept "gravity" I acquire a way of organizing my experience of falling bodies, hot-air balloons, earth satellites, and so on into a single coherent framework.

The structure of the gravitational field enables us to understand the apparently unique and differentiated motions of bodies in proximity to the earth. The organizing power of the concept is independent of whether we treat gravitational potentials as real-world entities or mere fictions. I want to suggest that "I," the first-person pronoun, in addition to its role as a speaker-indexical, does have a referential force to a hypothetical entity, "the self," in much the same way that the gravitational term g refers to a hypothetical entity, the gravitational field. Possession of the theoretical concept "self" permits just the kind of organization of a person's experience that Kant called "synthetic unity." Suppose for the moment that these are indeed the functions of "I" and that this dual use of the language of self-reference enables us to locate speech acts in the array of persons and permits each person to organize his or her experience with the help of a powerful theoretical concept acquired by coming to believe the theory that they are selves, that is, psychologically unitary beings, we can ask how is the dual function of "I" acquired by a speaker.

The concept of "person" does not need, but does not run counter to, the possibility that the being to which it is applied has private experiences. Such a being may not know that those experiences are his or hers, perhaps because of the lack of appropriate conceptual resources with which to construct such a thought. The remark "I am tired" could have force in the interpersonal conversation without the speaker being able to formulate the explicit reflection "I know that I am tired." In following Strawson (in *Individuals*) in identifying persons through capacities for self and other ascriptions of experiences, thoughts, and feelings in *public* discourse, I do not want to exceed the public and collective contexts of avowals and expressive remarks. Speech acts are part of the *expression* of feeling, opinion, intentions, and so on. To say "I'm tired" is part of what it is to be tired.

For Strawson "person" is (a) a primitive concept, (b) such that a person can attribute experiences to him or herself in exactly the same sense as experiences are attributed to other persons. The same concept of "tiredness" informs "I am tired" and "You are tired," though there are all sorts of differences between typical uses of and grounds for these statements. For example, they can be used for quite different speech acts. A use of the former could be an excuse, while an utterance of the latter could be an accusation. The grounds on which I make a public declaration of my condition (tiredness), my moral feelings (anger), my intentions, and so on are systematically different from those upon which I describe, accuse, or commiserate with you or you do the like with me. In order to maintain the identity of meaning of a basically constant psychological predicate, in all of these diverse uses, it is necessary to subscribe to a theory of the meaning of predicates which does not reduce that meaning to the evidence or grounds, if any, upon which they are ascribed. Though I will not be defending any particular theory of the meaning of psychological predicates, I shall be working with the presumption that any form of verificationist theory which reduces meaning to grounds of assertion must be rejected. It is widely agreed among philosophers that there are many psychological predicates which are properly self-ascribed without evidence, while grounds are needed for the ascription of those predicates to others.

Does it follow from this condition on the meaning of predicates that the referents of the "person"-referring expressions in a conversation are just the publicly identifiable beings, persons, in the sense I have marked out for the purpose of this discussion? Strawson *(Individuals)* makes a good deal of the central place that action predicates have in routine practices of ascriptions to persons. So for him and for Hampshire *(Thought and Action)*, "digging the garden" in "I'm digging the garden," "You're digging the garden," and "He's digging the garden" must have, indeed obviously just does have, the same meaning. And the three subjects of this attribution are severally publicly identified persons. As I hope to show, our local cultural and linguistic practices involve a secondary formation in the organization of belief and experience, so that these referring expressions are dual. Among these practices are a range of queries of the form "Does he know he is digging the garden?" which we might ask of someone with an obsessive/compulsive neurosis, or who we thought was sleepwalking or under the influence of drugs.

Action predicates are centrally located in a spectrum of adjectives, verbs, and adverbs appropriate for persons. There are the corporeal "fat, red-faced, and sweating," and then there are those used for intentional actions, such as "running for the bus"; there are also "natural compounds," such as "flopping down feeling exhausted" and, finally, predicates used in private acts of self-description and self-admonition, for instance, "I must try to control my irritation with him" or "I really must lose some weight." Notice that both "irritation" and "weight" appear in attributions in the primary structure, thus being guaranteed a public meaning.

Strawson's proposal (in *Individuals*) is presented as an analysis of the concept of person in everyday use. Whether this exercise in descriptive metaphysics is adequate as a study in psycholinguistics is a question needing research. For my purposes his analysis provides further support for my proposal to treat "person" as an elementary "location" in the primary structure, remarks emanating from which can be understood without reference to the truth or falsity of complementary descriptions of inner states.

While Strawson's account is defensible for predication in the primary structure, I do not believe it is adequate for predication in the secondary structures appropriated from it. To appreciate this one needs to look more closely at first-person predication. Consider again the remark "I am tired." It can be uttered as a complaint, as a move in the primary structure of persons in conversation. No particular organization of the speaker's experience and system of beliefs, memories, and so on is required as a necessary condition for the effective production of that speech act. The speaker may treat his actions, including his speechacts, as performed in obedience to the commands of the gods. (Jaynes has suggested this was the case with pre-Homeric Greeks.) He may think of himself as an independent agent. But if the utterance is read as a report of an experience, then not only is it a move in the primary structure of the conversing group—say, a complaint—it is also a description of a condition located somehow in the secondary structure of that person. Tiredness as an experience is to be fitted in with other experiences, memories, beliefs, plans, and so on. Of what is it then a property?

The way the secondary structure is organized, and particularly the way it is unified by the theory of selfhood entertained by the being in question, will determine how that experience can be located within the secondary structure. There may be great differences in the way certain experiences—say, the realization that one has the solution to a problem—are fitted into the secondary structure. Those Greeks who believed in inspiration from the Muses would have taken no personal responsibility for the thought of the key to a proof. It would have been located in a typical thought pattern rather differently from the way we, post Freud, locate such things.

Moral considerations are strikingly absent from Strawson's account, but the emphasis on action at least provides a place for their natural introduction. If actions are ascribed to persons, the evaluation of actions can be transferred to persons if we can introduce the concept of "responsibility." To put it in psychological terms, persons are those beings who act intentionally. Much philosophical work needs to be done to link acting intentionally with the foundations for ascriptions of responsibility in the claim that a person on a particular occasion could have done other than one did. I believe that the link is conceptual rather than empirical, but the establishing of this point must await a detailed analysis of the concept of agency. At least one can say moral responsibility comes into being in a society by way of the people coming to believe that they are agents.

Anthropological and historic evidence will be presented to demonstrate that what every society recognizes as human individuality in the form of persons is the Strawsonian sense of embodied agent, that is, there is a common primary stucture. But there are very wide variations in secondary structure, that is, in the degree of singularity with which persons organize their experienced thoughts, feelings, premonitions, and plans as their own. The most important evidence of all would be the discovery of a tribe of persons without selves.

3. Anthropological Evidence to Demonstrate the Analytical Separability of Indexical and Theoretical Aspects of Self-Reference

Though it would be hard to prove that there was a tribe quite without selves, there is enough diversity in the ways people conceive of themselves to support my case for a dualism between public-collective and private-individual concepts of human individuality. In this section I will sketch two case studies of "psychologies" which are distinctive enough to support the tentative dualism of concepts of human individuality that is suggested by the philosophical analysis just attempted. If one could find cultures with well-established institutions of individual and reflexive personal reference as part of public discourse, but which have very different ways of organizing the structure of thought, emotion, consciousness, agency, and so on as these are displayed in forms of talk, then one would have established in principle the distinctiveness of these two main aspects of reflexive reference.

To conceive of myself as a person, I must conceive of others as persons, a thought expressed by Strawson in the terms of the capacity of a person to ascribe psychological and other person attributes to self and others. But Strawson quite fails to explain how I come to conceive of myself as a self, an "inner" unity. The idea that there is no such inner unity is a philosophical doctrine that can be dispelled by the anthropological case to be made in this section.

The "I" theory sketched in the last section requires a mode of reflexive reference to persons ubiquitous to all mankind insofar as the fact of social responsibility is a feature necessary for the maintenance of any society whatsoever. In addition, there appear to be distinctive modes and degrees of private and individual self-attribution and self-criticism dependent on different concepts of psychological unity.

The first-person pronouns in use in a culture could all even be plural, locating commitments at the obligated group. Such a culture might have no use for the concept of individual self and simply have *no* organized unity for a consistent subject of psychological predication. If we could find or even imagine such a culture, it would support the hypothesis of the logical independence of a theory based on a concept of the self, belief in which enables self-attributive discourse to be organized in a practical and satisfactory fashion, from the beliefs and conventions supporting public-collective indexical reference; this could be proved if different societies could be shown to use different self-theories, while capable of similar public acts of personal commitment such as promising or resigning. Anthropological research supports this conjecture. Our Western self-theory seems to be located somewhere toward a midpoint of a spectrum of self-theories distinguished by the degree of emphasis on individual uniqueness, independence, and power. The anthropological material demonstrates the cultural relativity of the way in which European languages influence the construction of personal theories of self-reference. I want to illustrate this by taking two cases, one where the self-theory is weaker than the Western European and one where it is stronger. Eskimos, though sharing a concept of identity of persons with ourselves, do not use a concept of "inner" unity of self comparable to ours. Maoris, on the other hand, seem to have a stronger sense of distinctiveness, inviolability, and power of self-activation than we do. The evidence to be cited in this section is a mere sketch of what would be required for a fully conclusive demonstration. The fact of individual identity of each person as a social being is well recognized among the Eskimos. They deploy a system of personal names and make assessments of each other within a moral order, though in ways markedly different from ours. An economical way of revealing the differences in the personal centering of thought and feeling between the Eskimos and ourselves is to look at their indigenous psychology of the emotions and, by way of further evidence, their psychology of art and the premises of their moral theory.

The idea that linguistic forms determine psychological structures (the Sapir-Whorf hypothesis) is now widely agreed to be too simplistic. Nevertheless, it seems reasonable to suppose that distinctive linguistic forms facilitate distinctive modes of psychological organization, as the preconditions for the possibility of certain kinds of talk. Linguistic evidence can be telling only if it is accompanied by the ethnographic reports describing the practices and setting out the theories of the folk which point to the same distinctive features that are hinted at in the way the language works.

Eskimo is a polysynthetic language with only minor variations over the vast area in which it is spoken. It is built up of complex word-sentences, by the addition of suffixes and infixes to bases. Qualification of a base continues until the utterance is disambiguated relative to context. There are strict positional rules governing the order of infixes and suffixes, both with respect to morphology and to sense. The system of personalizing suffixes should give us what linguistic evidence there might be for the resources available for expressing a sense of personal identity.

The personalizing suffixes form two groups. The "-ik" group locates something at the speaker, and these I take to be functionally equivalent to the indexical uses of "I." The "-tok" group locates matters at someone other than the speaker. Colin Irwin (personal correspondence) describes "-tok" as having a directive function, diverting attention away from the speaker to some other. Thus "indignation" is "peu-gu-sungi-tok," not a feeling of the speaker, but annoyance directed at another. Further, where in English a referential form of the pronoun would be used as in "I am," say, uttered in reply to "Who (i.e., which person) is preparing dinner?" Eskimo would render this with the possessive suffix "-nga," as in "uva-nga," "the being here mine." These and other features of the language suggest very strongly that while the uses of English favor a theory of the person conceived not only as a location but as a substance, qualified by attributes, in Eskimo persons are rendered as qualifications (for instance, as locations) of substantialized qualities and relations. Similarly, according to Birket-Smith in *The Eskimos* the content of "I hear him" would be expressed in Eskimo by "tusurp-a-ra," literally "his making of a sound with reference to me."

Insofar as vocabulary and grammatical form can be cited as evidence, Eskimos seem to be perfect Strawsonians, distinguishing the emotions of themselves and others by referring them to locations in the array of embodied persons, the grammatical forms emphasizing public display. For instance, anger, much disapproved of according to ethnographers, is almost always ascribed in the third person, the "target," "ningaq-tok." Virtues are similarly identified in terms of public display. Colin Irwin quotes an informant as explaining that wisdom is used to describe "someone who has not said his or her thought for a long period of time."

Languages radically defective in explicit vocabularies can usually be found to have the resources to convey a thought or express a feeling for which there is no specific lexical item. Conversely, it may even be, as Robert Heinlein once remarked, that English can describe emotions that the human organism is incapable of experiencing. To complete the case for Eskimo psychology, as a counterexample to a claim for the strict universality of thought forms, one must turn to characteristic social patterns, to the social expression of emotions, and to the patterns of moral judgment and the Eskimo conception of action.

Many travelers have reported the extraordinary degree to which an Eskimo's emotions seem to be influenced by his or her fellows. When one weeps, they all weep; when one laughs, they all laugh. Jennes (1922) remarks, "The Copper Eskimo, as a rule, displays very little independence in either thought or action. . . . He follows the multitude, agrees to whatever is said, and reflects the emotions of those around him." At least with respect to a large and varied catalog of public performances, individual feelings, intentions, and reasonings play a very minor role.

Important aspects of the Eskimo conception of action are revealed in their theory of art. Carpenter (1966) has emphasized the degree to which Eskimos hold that "man is the force that reveals form." Riesman (1966) says, "a work of art is conceived of as the bringing forth, the releasing of a meaning, which was latent in the material itself." First-hand descriptions of Eskimo practices are alike in describing the trouble the artist takes in brooding on the question of what form is latent in the material. According to Carpenter no Eskimo equivalents exist for our concepts of "making" and "creating"; carving, for instance, is described in terms of releasing or revealing what is already there. The concept of active individual agency plays scarcely any role in their theory of art.

Eskimo morality is centered on a sharp distinction between communal matters and personal and private matters. Only the former are appraised as good or bad. The social virtues of cooperativeness, peacefulness, and so on are highly praised. Fair dealing in an individualistic person-to-person sense or truth-telling are at best secondary virtues. Theft from persons, as one might expect, is not conceived as a serious misdemeanor. According to Jennes "the majority of natives merely look foolish if caught in the act of stealing, and repent their clumsiness." The overriding force of communal considerations in Eskimo ethics is emphasized by Jennes:

> To the Copper Eskimo goodness means social goodness, that and no more. Whatever affects the welfare of the community as a whole is morally good or bad. . . . The foremost virtues therefore are peacefulness and good-nature, courage and energy, patience and endurance, honesty, hospitality, charity towards both the old and the young, loyal cooperation with one's kin and providence in all questions relating to the food supply.

Colin Irwin has taken this a step further to demonstrate that the practical virtues are based, not on a concept of enlightened self-interest, but on a rational appreciation of the social conditions that will support the next generation. According to Irwin "the primary interest of the Inuit is the future generation. They use every part of their physical and intellectual abilities in the advancement of that end."

Maori Psychology of Personal Power

Maori psychological theory is centered on a system of active principles for which there are corresponding material representations. Their "ways of thought" are dominated by a social psychological theory based on the concept of *tapu* which is embedded in their general psychology of active principles and powers. A Maori's injunction "Do not touch his head; it is *tapu*" has something of the force of "Do not touch that bare wire; it is electrified." An apparently harmless and quiescent thing is charged with power; in our terms it has potential energy.

Maori psychological theory, according to Best (1922), is based on the hypothesis of three active principles:

(1) *Wairua:* a principle of being.

Each particular has a distinctive *wairua.* The Maori system is non-Cartesian (there is no duality of material and mental substance);

mental and most other functions of a particular human are all within the scope of the *wairua* of that being. As a principle of being-in-general there are *wairua* too for inanimate particulars. The *wairua* of a being is substantial. It can leave the body and travel in space and time. Its condition is variable. When *toi-ora,* it lends well-being to its proper particular, but if interfered with by magic, it can decline in tone, inducing *pawera,* a generalized condition of dread of impending evil. Each *wairua,* being particular, must have its own essence, *aiwe.*

(2) *Mauoi:* the physical life principle.
(3) *Hau:* vitality, zest, or activity.

Both *mauoi* and *hau* are capable of material representation. An inanimate thing can represent the *hau* of an animate being. For my purpose *mauoi* is the most important of these powers. As *mauoi* is not the abstract social expressive property of *amour propre,* dignity, and so on, but can be materially represented, it can be materially defiled. Threat to personal standing can come from insult and from violation. It is violation, not as a bearer of insult (as it might be in Spain), but violation as a physical encroachment on the untouchable.

If the psychology of man is conceived in terms of active powers, it is easy to see how socially powerful people might be thought to be especially highly charged, and given the Maori view that powers are realized in material substrates, how dangerous it might be to touch such a being. The practices around the notion of *tapu,* such as *rahui*— putting some charged thing as a marker on some piece of property like a *kumera* (sweet-potato) garden—has the same rationality as surrounding a prison or a storehouse of valuables with an electric fence. The obvious explanation of *tapu,* then, is reached by embedding an indigenous psychology of active powers in a cosmology or general theory of nature, which is based on a substantialization of energy potentials, the Western parallel being the ether theories of electricity. Charge in this sense is the property called *mana,* which, as a substantialized power, is present in varying degrees in different persons in different substances, depending upon the actual power which they have.

In sharp contrast to this is Freud's theory of *tapu.* Freud (1955) argued, in effect, that *tapu* is not a unique psychological phenomenon but is a manifestation of the same psychological mechanisms as he observed in the genesis and maintenance of obsessional neuroses. In both the practices of *tapu* and the ways that obsessional neurotics behave there is a displacement of the prohibition on touching, from one thing to another. On this view *tapu* could not be a feature of an indigenous psychology since it is no more than a series of local manifestations of a universal psychological process. Freud bases his argument on the analogy that *tapu* is to obsessional behavior what the indigenous practices of such as the Maori are to the behavior of neurotics. In accordance with this line of reasoning he says, "But one thing would certainly follow from the persistence of the taboo, namely that the original desire to do the prohibited thing must also still persist among the tribes concerned." In short, they would like to do the thing, but their fear is stronger. "The desire is unconscious, however, in every individual member of the tribe, just as it is in neurotics." To explain the transfer of *tapu* from one person or object to another Freud says, "Anyone who has violated a taboo becomes taboo himself, because he possesses the dangerous quality of tempting others to follow his example."

The weaknesses of this theory are apparent. First of all, as Freud himself is willing to concede, the argument from the personal history of an obsessional individual to the social history of a tribe would be unconvincing without the parallels that are presumed to be observed in the behavior of members of a tribe practicing *tapu* and an obsessional neurotic. The difficulty with Freud's view is revealed in this passage: "Dead men, new born babies . . . stimulate desire by their special helplessness." One might well ask how that sort of "stimulation of desire" (whatever that might mean) can be compared with the desire to overthrow the king because of his special power, envied by lesser persons, the explanation Freud offers for the *tapu* character of the king's body. If, on the other hand, one were to treat Maori psychology as a unique theory, then a dead man would be a danger because of the likely presence of a malevolent power. Within the cosmology of the Maoris, as within the cosmology of many nineteenth-century physicists, powers must be realized in material substances. Thus a dead man is highly charged with the material carrier of the malevolent power that killed him. It would be as unwise to touch a dead man as it is to touch a bare wire.

Relative to the collectivist psychology of the Eskimo, Maori culture exhibited as extreme a form of individualism as found in the courtly Middle Ages of Europe. Though social givens such as birth determine the scope for individual achievement, as indeed it did in medieval Europe, *mana* was amplified by personal accomplishment. And it is individuals, who, above all, become so charged with power that their dignity-preserving sanctity is treated as something physical. A test for the degree of individualism within the ranks of an ordered collective is the treatment of proper names. So dear did a Maori hold his personal honor that elaborate games were devised to deal with the problems of the arrival of a stranger. To ask a man for his honor-bearing name would have been to demonstrate publicly that his personal fame had not reached his hosts, and this would humiliate him. Nor could he directly reveal it without humiliating himself.

4. Animate Beings to Selves

There are three main theories current to explain how people acquire minds.

Contemporary innateness theorists are careful to avoid any claims involving innate cognitive contents. Chomsky's well-known theory of an inborn language-acquisition device proposes an organ preprogrammed to pick out language from all other environing happenings. Much recent work in the study of very young children suggests a preprogramming of actions that provoke from the mother the kind of performances and displays that are "just right" as a foundation for acquisition of person-engendering beliefs and skills. While it is fair to say that the language-acquisition device is not held in much favor by developmental psycholinguistics, the preprogrammed prompting theory is becoming well-grounded empirically.

Two rather different brigades make up the noninnateness or early experience camp. Freudian developmentalists look for the structuring of mind into the familiar Freudian form as a product of inevitable interactions with and relations to the mother and father. The third theory appears as an outgrowth of critical attention to Piaget's stages-development conception, contributed to by various hands, notably Bruner (1976) and the Shotter-Newson partnership (1974). Like the Freudian theory, it directs attention to the social processes and relations in which an infant is engaged. The attention is focused particularly on the linguistic environment, which appears in the form of speech-in-a-situated-practice, the type of activity Wittgenstein called a language game. Various such games have been seen to be involved in the acquisition of the wherewithal for acquiring personal being, but those in which psychological symbiosis occurs—that is, routine supplementation of the incomplete cognitive, emotional, and intentional repertoire of one being by another through speech—are the most potent. It is in the language games of psychological symbiosis that the transformation of animate beings into persons is accomplished. Those principles that Wittgenstein called the grammar of such ways of talk can appear as the metaphysics of distinctive ways of personal being.

Some measure of programming can be accommodated in the psychological symbiosis theory in that the infant prompts the mother to produce the kind of performances that supplement the infant's current

deficits. Furthermore, if the particular forms that belief-systems take are
determined by the language-games thus played, local differences in such
mutual activities could be cited to explain the actual distribution of
structures approximating those identified by Freudians, neo-Freudians,
and others.

I now take up the problem of how to represent the transformation
of animate beings into persons. The basic thesis of this paper is that
animate beings are fully human if they are in possession of a theory—a
theory about themselves. It is a theory in terms of which a being orders,
partitions, and reflects on its own experience and becomes capable of
self-intervention and control. In the span of human kind there may be
many such person-engendering theories. The ordering and partitioning
as it is carried on in our social and historical conditions is dependent on
a belief that the three unities involved in the structuring of consciousness, agency, and history, namely, point of view, point of action, and life
trajectory, are manifestations of a more fundamental unity, something
like the Cartesian ego or Kantian noumenal self. The theory of the
unity of unities, so to speak, should appear in characteristic ways, in
particular how a person talks and is talked to by those who take him or
her to be a person, and in the degree to which a person believes him or
herself to be autonomous. This is not merely a philosophical theory
about the necessary conditions for personhood as we live it and conceive
it. Since I have offered a hypothesis about how these conditions are met
in a particular culture, namely, ours, there are empirical consequences.
For instance, the fact that the theory is supposed to be effective on
actual occasions of talk suggests a project in developmental psychology.
It would make sense to look for conversational practices in which a
theory of the appropriate kind could be acquired by an animate being
who is, thereby, transformed into a being whose conversational practice
reveals (because it *is)* mentation organized in a strong unitary fashion.

Why should this account of the transformation of an animate
being be taken seriously? Might it not be that by a process of biological
maturation an individual develops in such a way that it can discover
empirically, by a certain kind of observation, prompted perhaps by
others, that it is a psychological unity: that there is an "I" and a "Thou";
that there are some states of affairs (and so a world) which are independent of any of his or her plans and best attempts to realize them and
some that are not; that, by and large, human sensibility extends roughly
as far as the bodily envelope; and so on. Why could these not be
empirical discoveries made by virtue of growing powers of discernment
as a result of the natural process of maturation? Two objections can be
made to a maturation theory. First, one could try to specify the kind of
experience which would have to be possible if the "inner" unity of one's

own personhood were to be a possible object of empirical discovery. Even the most dedicated of all the many explorers of the psyche, Husserl, failed to find an entity at the center of experience. In developing his idea of the transcendental reduction of experience, in what he calls the first and second "*epochés,*" he takes us through an intellectual exercise by progressively examining experience, looking for the characteristics, labels, or markings which would identify items in that experience as belonging to that individual. He claimed that there is an ultimate stage of transcendental reduction, where experience is reduced to a "primordial sphere" of phenomenon, in which no labels of ownership remain. It cannot be through an empirical discovery that experiences are marked as mine that I become aware of my own "objectivity." The ego itself, if it exists, is never presented in experience. Even if one is obliged to concede that the "primordial sphere" is organized from "here and now," that that sphere has a center, so to speak, there is no way of partitioning the primordial experience of the world into "mine" and "other than mine" by reference to given empirically distinguishable features of that experience. According to Husserl such distinction must be *constituted.* Interestingly, yoga psychology, with its emphasis on techniques of self-discovery, is based on the thesis that the "self" to be discovered is without content.

A different but complementary argument starts with Hume's skeptical doubts about the self. He pointed out that "the self" itself can never be presented in experience. "When I turn my reflection on *myself,* I never can perceive this *self* without some one or more perceptions; nor can I ever perceive anything but perceptions. It is the composition of these, therefore, which forms the self." Instances of thinking, feeling, and so on are not related to a central being experienced in just the same way as they are, and to which they could thereby be seen to be related. That which unifies them as *my* thoughts, processes of reasoning, and so on is not an empirically manifested individual substance. According to Hume the mere composition of thoughts and feelings into sequences is the real referent of the concept of self, the impression from which we gain the idea.

5. Kant: Creation of the Self in the Syntheses of Experience.

Personal Unity

Kant's introduction of the concept of the transcendental unity of apperception could be thought of as filling the gap Hume drove between the apparent substantial referent of the *cogito* of Descartes and the "plain facts of experience." It suggests a nonempirical referent for "I" which is not a mere composition. For Kant the unity of experience that is given in experience is an orderliness which is the product of a synthesis. As he says in the *Critique of Pure Reason,* "I am conscious of myself not as I am in myself, but only that I am. The representation is a *thought* [that is, has the status of a theory] not an intuition [that is, it is not an experience]" (B157).

To formulate a theory one requires not only the thought of an object in general but an intuition to determine it, to make the representation concrete, that is, thinkable, so "I require . . . besides the thought of myself [which I shall be arguing is a socially engendered theory] in intuition of the manifold in me, the unified field of consciousness, in time etc. by which I determine the thought" *(Critique of Pure Reason).* So Kantian synthetic unities in experience are to be treated, not as inductive evidence for the theory of transcendental self (and unity of apperception), but as concrete manifestations of personhood, that is, as representations they provide the grounding for the sense of self.

Kant's account of determination of this kind is by reference to the temporal properties of inner experience. In another passage from the *Critique of Pure Reason* Kant elaborates this idea: "But it [the "I think"] can have no special designation, because it serves only to introduce all our thought, as belonging to consciousness" (p. 329). In short, the "I" in "I think" is not a referring expression in the demonstrative sense, that is, it does not denote a possible object of experience, but identifies (indexically) or labels a collection of expressions of thought as belonging to one person. Unlike the constructivist position which takes the basic role of *"cogito"*-type expressions to be in the primary structure, that is, the public conversation, anchoring expression of opinion to their proper persons, Kant asks us to think of the "cogito" as a label by whose use both public and private discourse about experience becomes an expression of the unified experience of a being. But the experience of that being as to its form(s) of order is just the awareness of that unity.

Three Syntheses of Mind and How They Make a Possible Sense of Self

By its synthesizing powers a human being creates order and unity both in the flux of sensations engendering an empirical world as experienced and in the experiences which are of that world. Both "outer sense" and "inner sense" are unified by an active synthesizing of experiential fragments. The self emerges for each of us in a complex interweaving of complementary syntheses, which are necessary, Kant believes, to give form to experience as we have it. Our experience has three prominent structural features: it is organized as a spatiotemporal manifold; it presents a world of causally interacting objects; and it is unified as a field of consciousness. The self-unity appears in the syntheses which produce the two latter. To produce the given unities three syntheses are required.

(1) To show that the unity of apperception, that is, conscious awareness of a unified field of conscious experiences, is the product of a synthesis: according to Kant there is "the necessity of a synthesis of the manifold given in intuition, without which the thoroughgoing identity of self-consciousness cannot be thought" (B135). The argument has the form: "The identity of self-consciousness is given. What makes it possible?" The answer: "Only a synthesis." According to Walker (1978) this argument is successful because the synthesis involved in self-descriptions must be transcendental, that is, involve the application of a concept. "It could hardly be held to be governed by an empirical concept, learned by abstraction from experience"; hence it must involve an a priori category.

(2) To show that the transcendental affinity of appearances, that is, the physical world of which I am aware, must be a unity because consciousness is a unified field:

I must think of myself as a unity;
therefore,
I must think of my experiences as a unity;
therefore,
I must think of them as forming a unified objective world
(to paraphrase the argument of A113f).

Even if these arguments were successful (and [2] looks implausible), neither goes to show that conscious experience must have the particular form of unity that we mean when we talk of "self," that is, as an asymmetrical centralized structure that has properties of a single substance.

(3) To show that inner sense must be synthesized according to a concept, the same line of argument is brought to bear on the explication of a person's subjective sense of self as the nodal point of his or her structured mode of experience. According to Kant whatever concept it is must be the application of some a priori category. The arguments of the transcendental deduction take the personal unities as given. Can we find in Kant any further observations on how they emerge?

I believe Kant's view to be that the personal unities as experienced do not emerge in a special synthetic act but are engendered in the course of synthesizing the sensory flux into the spatiotemporally ordered dualistic world of things (outer sense) and thoughts (inner sense). To demonstrate this I examine one of the syntheses involved in engendering the "transcendental unity of apperception." In B133 Kant says:

> Only so far, therefore, as I can unite a manifold of given representations in *one consciousness* is it possible for me to represent to myself the *identity of the consciousness in (that is throughout) these representations.* In other words, the *analytic* unity of apperception is possible only under the presupposition of a certain *synthetic* quality.

This is second-order synthesis, so to speak, operating upon the groundwork of primary synthesis in which space, time, and objects are created. One could look on Kant's observation in B133 as a statement of a key feature of the deep grammar of expressions like "I think." The proper use of this expression, to mark the contents of one consciousness, does not require that a substantial referent be secured for the "I." To suppose that it does is to be guilty of the fallacious reasoning Kant exposes in the Paralogisms.

Strawson (1966) takes the central Kantian point to be the duplicity of aspects of experience. "On the one hand, it cumulatively builds up a picture of the world" in which things and events are presented as having an objective order. "On the other hand, it possesses its own order as a series of experiences" (p. 106). This duality is related to self-consciousness, according to Strawson, by the treatment sketched above. A glance at that treatment reveals that, far from bypassing the doctrine of synthesis, it presupposes it. In the duality of world and experience "it (experience) possesses its own order as a series of experiences" (perhaps ultimately as a series of judgments). But only if that series is experienced as a series could it serve as a basis for self-ascription, for it is only by virtue of the unity of the sequence of experiences as a series that the singularity of an experiencing self is presented since we are all agreed that it is not presented *in* itself. Admittedly, Kant does not give an account of what sort of intellectual activity synthesizing might be, but the clue lies in the passage in which the synthetic unity of apperception is presented as a *thought*. By this remark Kant means what I believe we would mean by saying that it is a theoretical concept. Kant's theses concerning synthesis are the essential core of a psychological theory.

The treatment I offer differs from Kant's in two important respects. Kant thinks that a transcendental object "can contain nothing but transcendental properties," but this is so only if we stick to inner sense. One way of putting the great advance made by social constructivists is that they see that *social* predicates can serve in the discussion of the transcendental conditions and forms of mind. Kant also thinks that the ultimate referent of the concept of "active self" is a real, singular, but necessarily hidden being, the final source of the activity by which minds and empirical worlds are created in complementary synthetic acts. I have tried to show that the latter proposal multiplies entities beyond necessity.

The outcome of this is the conclusion that to know that I am is not to have a special reflexive experience in which I am presented to myself as an object. Rather it is to have accepted a special kind of theory in terms of which experiences are categorized as "of myself" and "not of myself," and actions are taken as "mine" and "not as mine," the central theoretical concept being that of an organizing, experiencing, and active self, the hypothetical entity corresponding to which is the putative referent of "I" ("my," "mine," and so on). The same theory allows us to categorize some reflections as memories, that is, as representations of incidents in *my* life, and so create the possibility of an autobiography. In short, to have a unified mind is to use a special kind of theory, not to have access to an inner being through a special kind of experience. Of course, being in possession of a theory as a working hypothesis for categorizing and ordering experience does indeed make available to a human being the possibility of new kinds of experience, that is, the experiences as of being in the world as a person, that is, a being not only defined as singular by the social practices of others of his or her collective but as conceiving of itself as a self and so organizing its experience in certain ways. The question of whether there is a referent for the theoretical concept of "the self" other than the unity of the unities of experience need never be raised in psychology. Since I shall be arguing that its aetiology begins for each of us with the public concept of a person, any metaphysical or noumenal self, pulsing away beyond all possible experience, is redundant. But this I have yet to prove.

6. Status of the Hypothetical Entity to Which "I" as a Theoretical Concept Might Be Taken to Refer

Some transcendental concepts in the physical sciences are strongly referential, and most right-thinking persons believe that their referents are real, even though they are ordinarily not observable with the unaided senses. Most chemists believe, I suppose, in the reality of ions. Some theoretical concepts do not refer to real things. The skin of a falling drop is not a real entity, although there are pseudoreferential concepts in the theory of droplet formation which seem to refer to it. The referential aspects of the use of "I" as a theoretical term must be examined as seriously as one would the putative claim to denote something of important concepts in physics or chemistry. There are three obvious possibilities: the "self" which has no referent; its referent is the same as that of the public-collective concept "person"; or it refers to structural and dynamic features of organization of experience.

One might treat "gravitational potential" as a convenient fiction, that is, as a theoretical concept which serves to order our experience of falling bodies and planetary systems within the one frame of thought. Taking this case as a model would suggest that by the use of "I," "my," and so on each of us can order our experience into mine and not mine, into a public and private sphere, into present experience and memories of the past by reference to a fictional psychic entity which confers a deep unity on all these aspects of our life, all "mental" because they are taken to be attributes or states of it. In Kantian terms one could say that provided we synthesize our experience into a unified structure, we do not need the hypothesis of a noumenal self, a unity beyond experience. Recognizing the dual role of "I believe . . . ," "I undertake to . . . ," and "I'm sorry . . . ," and so on, they need not be read as predications of properties to an individual psychic substance, some mysterious self, but social acts proper for a *person* of my sort. In its social use, "I" would have the major self-referential function of indexically locating the speaker in the array of persons. However, there are other possibilities.

Perhaps persons are the referents of both indexical and theoretical aspects of reflexive reference. Thus construed persons would be exhaustively accounted for as social beings. However, although I want to emphasize that the most plausible account of the origins of the theoretical concept of myself that I use in ordering my experience is that it is to be found in social practices in which persons as social beings are referred to, it would be a mistake to identify self as an organizing concept with the public-collective or social concept of person without further ado. As I argued, the theoretical concept of the self is required to give an account of the synthetic unities in experience, the organization of our fields of consciousness, the hierarchical organization of our mastery of lower desires in the service of higher aspirations, and all the other features of our mental life that in Kant's phrase "determine the thought I am a transcendental ego."

However, the variations in "I" theories, some of which I have used to illustrate the argument and which are typical of different cultures, leave room for more specific distinctions within each culture, in the form in which individuality of personhood is displayed in the public-collective arena. The general, the culturally relative and social concept of a person can become more highly differentiated within a culture by the spread of conceptions about what it is to be a proper or fashionable kind of person, and what sort of capacities are needed to be able to illustrate that one is such a being. Nicknaming systems provide a nice example. Social norms are represented by pejorative uses of nicknames which highlight ways in which proper persons in closed societies are *not* meant to be. For example, "Dumbo" and "Brainbox" identify levels of intelligence which are either too low or too high for the norm sustained in that group. "Piggy" identifies a bodily form that is generally unacceptable. The effect of a nicknaming system is not merely to describe the existing range of ways of social being in that society; it also creates distinctions among persons. A person is given a nickname primarily to illustrate a social norm. The individual whose idiosyncracies have marked him or her out may not violate the norm very much, but the behavior and even the appearance of the bearer are often pushed further along in the dimension in which that nickname lies. Someone who is only a bit grubby but is stigmatized as "Stinker" can be required to exemplify the sin of uncleanliness in a more florid fashion than he did originally. The Brainboxes are required to be cleverer, the Dumbos more stupid, than their natural endowment would demand. The system of nicknames is a *représentation sociale* which actively creates distinctions among persons in the real world. It is not confined to the autonomous worlds of childhood, for wherever nicknaming flourishes, in prisons, in jazz bands, and so on, this phenomenon is clearly identifiable.

In like manner a person's self (the supposed private-individual referent of the "I" around which, according to the Cartesian picture, experience is organized as mine) is a conjunction of a generic element, that determined by the rules for using "I" and its cognates, and a specific element, local folk theories of how a self is supposed to be. For example, Western societies differ greatly in the amount of self-attention regarded as proper. What a person will be capable of will depend, in part, on the particular form of generic self-theory they acquire, because it is in terms of that theory that they will construe themselves as more or less autonomous, determined, and so on. These more specific theories are, I believe, also encapsulated in *représentations sociales* and the associated linguistic practices in terms of which cognitive capacities are legitimately displayed, just as variants of public-collective ways of being a person are determined.

To illustrate the power of a *représentation sociale,* let me quote from David Ingleby's paper "Ideology and the Human Sciences" (1970):

> [A] reifying model of human nature, by definition, presents men as less
> than they really are or could be. To the extent that society requires men,

or a certain proportion of them, to be thing-like in their work, orientation and experiencing, such a model will constitute both a reflection and a reinforcement of that society, reinforcing because men tend to become what they are told they are. . . . Above all, he is confronted in the possibility of being understood as a species of thing with the threat of ultimate finality, denied the facility to transcend in any way the material out of which he is made; all value must lose value for him.

7. Sources of Our Person Theories

There are a great many different ways in which a local "I am centered round a self" theory could be acquired, and no doubt several are involved in its actual acquisition in the course of any human development. I shall concentrate on only one by examining the possibility that learning the pronoun system, and in particular the rules for the use of "I," is in part the learning of a theory. Bruner's work (1976) suggests that the rules for the use of personal pronouns are learned through a sequence of language games. Midway in the sequence is the language game of indexicality, that is, the use of "I" to locate all sorts of matters at a certain point (individual) within the array of persons. These include the point of view from which the world is being perceived, which person has made a commitment, who wishes to be seen as contrite, who has performed some action, and so on. Since social practices such as blame, commitment, describing from a point of view, and so on essentially involve both speech and action, it would be reasonable to look for the key occasions in Wittgensteinian language games. I believe that only some of these key occasions and their typical practices have been described. Bruner has begun in a very prescient way to identify the key language games involved in the acquisition of linguistic competence in the management of individual desires. I want to show, from the theoretical point of view, where his researches fit into the investigation of how we each acquire the theory that we are persons like the others.

Learning to Think as a Self

What sociolinguistic practices (language games) are there in the course of which competence in the use of personal pronouns is acquired? We can control our researches with the help of the following hypotheses.

Points of View

We might look for occasions of address which imply a standpoint other than that of another person. Contrary to the mythology of "moral development" psychology, the idea of multiple points of view is grasped very early. In "Early Rule Structure," Bruner's pioneering analysis (with Sherwood) of the peek-a-boo game, we find a study of one of the many sociolinguistic practices in whose course the connection between personhood and point of view is established. Two ideas are acquired in playing this game: (a) there are distinct points of view from which the world takes on a different cast, and (b) those points of view are located at persons. It now seems likely that these ideas are acquired in the course of six or seven months. From a developmental psycho-linguistic viewpoint it could be said that in mastering this language-game a child begins to grasp the indexical properties of self-referring speech. In such practices we learn to locate our speech acts in the array of persons, *including ourselves.* This is all part of the foundation of deixis, the capacity to direct attention to one thing from the standpoint of a point of view in an array of other things. A number of psychologists, in particular E. V. Clark, have studied the development of deixis in infants. However, her work merely catalogs ascending degree of mastery of the deictic and indexical uses of referring expressions, including pronouns. So far as I have followed her studies, she has paid little attention to the language-game features of deictic activities, and none at all to the kind of talk in which a mother embeds the whole business of making requests. Bruner's investigations of deixis have used the idea of "request formats" as part of the development of reaching, following line of sight and so on, and such formats are indeed language-games.

Point of Action

Our second hypothesis draws attention to the effects of those occasions in the practical and moral orders in which speech acts of accusations, praise, blame, justification, excuse, attribution of intentions, wants, and so on are involved. It is in these language-games that the child is introduced to the idea of itself as an autonomous actor. Believing itself to be the author of many of its actions permits a consequential expansion in its capacity to order its experience and control its actions. A research program parallel to Bruner's on deixis should be undertaken to explore the sequences of language-games in the course of which the acquisition of the full sense of self-activation is acquired.

The argument so far suggests that the process of transformation from animate to human being follows two steps. In one, the concepts of point of view and point of action are acquired. In the second, the capacity to contemplate oneself reflexively as the unifying principle of these "origins" implies the separation of the use of indexicals from the deployment of a theoretical concept of self. Only thus, it will emerge, can one explain how it is that self-consciousness, self-intervention, and autobiography are possible. Self-consciousness on this view is not a new kind of consciousness but rather a new way of partitioning that of which one is aware by reference to a theory, one's theory of oneself.

Psychological Symbiosis

If selfhood is learned, how is it learned? The processes by which merely animate beings become self-conscious agents must be looked for in social episodes in which certain kinds of language games are played, engendering talk with appropriate cognitive properties, for instance, expression of feelings and intentions. All this is to be found in the phenomenon of psychological symbiosis. The idea of psychological symbiosis comes from Spitz (1965) but has been developed by Shotter and Newson (1974) in the study of the kind of talk in which mothers embed their infant offspring. Psychological symbiosis is a permanent interactive relation between two persons, in the course of which one supplements the psychological attributes of the other as they are displayed in social performances, so that the other appears as a complete and competent social and psychological being. The general definition does not specify the relationship between the two persons who form a symbiotic dyad. There are many possibilities. For example, there are cases of considerable practical importance where, though the supplementations are mutual, the power relations in the dyad are asymmetrical. The symbiotic dyad is to be conceived as a single social being. There is evidence that the dyad as a social being may interact socially with one of its own constituent persons, who displays individually proper attributes and powers.

The relevant characteristics of mother-talk have been noticed by psychologists other than Richards and Shotter and Newson, but not correctly described. Snow (1978) notes, "Mothers constantly talked about the child's wishes, needs and intentions." The use of "about" in this sentence misconstrues the relationship as it is seen from the standpoint of psychological symbiosis. In psychological symbiosis mothers do not talk *about* the child's wishes and emotions: they *supply* the child with wishes, needs, intentions, wants, and the like and interact with the child as if it had them. Psychological symbiosis is a supplementation by one person of another person's public display in order to satisfy the criteria of personhood with respect to psychological competencies and attributes in day-to-day use in a particular society in this or that specific social milieu. A mother may undertake to supplement her daughter's psychology differently in a medical consultation from the way she does it for a visiting relative. I want to extend the idea of psychological symbiosis beyond the context for which it was originally introduced, namely, for the ways mothers publicly supplement the psychology of their children. I shall use the term for every case in which a group of people complete inadequate social and psychological beings through public symbiotic activity, particularly in talking for each other. There may be several persons involved in the supplementation process.

Why do these practices exist? I believe that the answer can be found by reference to the requirements of moral orders, as they are defined and sustained in particular collectives. By a "moral order" I understand a collectively maintained system of public criteria for holding persons in respect or contempt and the rituals for ratification of judgments in accordance with these criteria. The moral value of persons and their actions are publicly displayed by such a system. It is realized in practices such as being deferential to someone or censuring someone by trials, by punishments, by insults, by apologies, and so on. Psychological supplementation of another may be required if a display of personal incompetence or deficiency is routinely taken as a reason for unfavorable moral assessment. Goffman (1969) adds the thought that support of this sort may be forthcoming, not so much on behalf of the moral standing of the one who is supplemented, as in defense of the reputations of those with whom he or she is seen to be consorting.

The crucial person-engendering language-games involving the indexical and referential features of the uses of pronouns—and all sorts of other devices by which concept pairs like "self and other," "agent and patient," complementary points of view, continuity and discontinuity of experience, and so on are shared with an infant—take place in conditions of psychological symbiosis. One who is always presented as a person, by taking over the conventions through which this social act is achieved, becomes organized as a self. That is the main empirical hypothesis which I believe to be a consequence of the considerations so far advanced, and in the testing of which the limits of the conceptual system from which it springs can be discovered.

What lessons can be drawn from the foregoing study that might bear on the issue of relativism? The considerations advanced in this essay have been supported both by conceptual analysis and by the findings of linguists and anthropologists. Taken together, their effect is to drive a wedge between the concept of a person as a being whose identity consists in the unity of an embodied perceiver with a relatively continuous spatiotemporal point of view and the concept of a person centered on an identity as the one author of that beings' thoughts and actions. As matters of individual experience, these identities are mediated by the public practices of address in which such issues as the proper assignment of personal responsibility are resolved on a day-to-day basis. In our culture the working metaphysics of persons encoded in our practices imposes a unity on these unities of point of view and of the authorship of action. But I hope to have gained some support for the idea that there are cultures in which, *at most,* the unity of a person as an embodied perceiver is routinely maintained. This minimal form of unity ties in with the idea of people-space locations which are occupied from time to time by speech-acts.

But the notion of "person" is both a moral and an ontological concept. Insofar as moral responsibility is not tied to a one-to-one correspondence with the embodied beings that *we* call persons, a cultural diversity of moral orders is revealed. And this diversity is significant for claims about the psychology of the species *homo sapiens.* I have proposed the explanatory hypothesis that one's sense of self is modeled on one's role as a person in this or that society, a role realized in all sorts of language-games. To think of oneself as an atomic individual, all of whose attributes are properties of an inner entity, is as culturally specific as it is to think of oneself, as some Africans do, as the spokesperson for a real collective of beings, some ancient and some yet to be manifested in bodily form, each of whom is itself but a nexus in that very network.

References

Anscombe, G. E. M. 1975. "The First Person." In *Mind and Language,* ed. S. Guttenplan. Oxford: Clarendon Press.

Bandura, A. 1977. *Social Learning Theory.* Englewood Cliffs, N.J.: Prentice Hall.

Best, E. 1922. *Spiritual and Mental Concepts of the Maori.* Wellington, N.Z.: Dominion Museum.

Birkett Smith, G. 1922. *The Eskimos.* London: Longmans.

Bruner, J.S. 1976. "Early Rule Structure: The Case of 'Peek-A-Boo'." In *Life Sentences* ed. R. Harre. Chichester: Wiley.

Carpenter, E.E. 1976. *Eskimo Realities.* New York: Holt, Rinehart and Winston.

Coval, S. 1977. *Scepticism and the First Person.* Cambridge, MA: Harvard University Press.

Freud, S. 1955. *Totem and Taboo.* London: Hogarth Press.

Goffman, E. 1969. "On Face Work." In *Where the Action Is.* London: Allen Lane.

Hampshire, S. 1959. *Thought and Action.* London: Chatto and Windus. Reprint edition: Notre Dame: University of Notre Dame Press, 1983.

Hume, D. 1739. *A Treatise of Human Nature.* London.

Ingleby, D. 1970. "Ideology and the Human Sciences," *Human Context* 2:159-180.

Jennes, D. 1922. *The Copper Eskimos.* Ottawa: The Government Printer.

Kant, I. 1781. *Critique of Pure Reason.* Riga.

Liebert, R. M., and M. D. Spiegler. 1974. *Personality.* London: Irwin Dorsey.

McTaggart, J. M. E. 1927. *The Nature of Existence.* Cambridge: Cambridge University Press.

Mandell, G. 1981. *The Identity of Self.* Edinburgh: The University Press.

Riesman, R. 1966. "Eskimo Discovery of Man's Place in the Universe." In *Sign, Image and Symbol*, ed. S. Kepes. London: Studio Vista.

Shotter, J., and J. Newson. 1974. "How Babies Communicate," *New Society* 29:345-347.

Spitz, R. A. 1965. *The First Year of Life.* New York: International Universities Press.

Strawson, P. F. 1959. *Individuals.* London: Methuen.

Strawson, P. F. 1966. *The Bounds of Sense.* London: Methuen.

Vesey, G. 1973. *Personal Identity.* Open University Press.

Walker, R. C. S. 1978. *Kant.* London: Routledge and Kegan Paul.

Relativism, Persons, and Practices

Amélie Oksenberg Rorty

I

To put it bluntly, the controversy over cultural relativism, whether it be construed as a controversy about cross-cultural interpretation or about cross-cultural evaluation, is the kind of dispute that gives intellectuals a bad name among sensible people. Both sides are so bent on exaggeration that they seem to be displacing the real issues that divide them. The claims of relativists and their opponents are, when sanely and modestly construed, each plausible and mutually compatible. When those claims are globally extended and exaggerated —with relativists denying the possibility of cross-cultural understanding and their opponents denying the possibility of systematic untranslatability— they are indeed incompatible; but then they are also wildly implausible. Any sensible, widely traveled, multilingual person knows that in matters of translation, as in other practical matters, there is nothing resembling certainty or proof: the correctness or adequacy of an interpretation cannot be conclusively or uncontrovertibly established. Sometimes there is unexpectedly subtle and refined communication across radically different cultures; sometimes there is unsurmountable bafflement and systematic misunderstanding between relatively close cultures. For the most part, however, we live in the interesting intermediate grey area of partial success and partial failure of interpretation and communication. That grey area is to be found at home among neighbors as well as abroad among strangers, and it is to be found between the self of yesterday and the self of tomorrow.

What, if anything, is really at stake in the controversy? And why do the parties to the dispute energetically inflate their claims beyond plausibility, deflecting attention from what might really divide them?

First, relativists are quite right to insist that even such dramatically basic activities as birth, copulation, and death, such basic processes as eating and sleeping, physical growth and physical decay, are intentionally described in ways that affect phenomenological experience. Events and processes are encompassed and bounded, articulated and differentiated, within the web of a culture's conceptual and linguistic categories; their meaning is formed by its primary practices and sacred books, songs and rituals. Even the conceptions of social practices and meaning are sufficiently culturally specific so that it is tendentious to refer to conceptions *of* culture practices, as if *culture* or *practice* were Platonic forms, waiting to be conceptualized this way or that. Indeed the very practices of interpretation and evaluation are themselves culturally variable.

But nothing follows from this about the impossibility of cross-cultural interpretation, communication, or evaluation, particularly among cultures engaged in practical interactions with one another. The core truth of relativism —the intentionality of practice and experience— does not entail that successful communication and justified evaluation require strict identity of meaning. There are, furthermore, basic culturally invariant psychophysical and biosocial salience markers that set the focus and boundaries of attention, however variously these foci may be identified, interpreted, or evaluated.

Second, antirelativists with a strong realist bent rightly insist that there are events and facts —some of them intentionally described by reference to social practices— whose truth is not culturally determined. However they may be articulated or conceptualized, radical changes take place at birth and death; however they may be evaluated or integrated with other activities, eating and sleeping have specific organic effects. Shylock's plaintive "If you cut me, do I not bleed?" must be acknowledged, even if the connotations of the Elizabethan expressions "cut" and "bleed" cannot be captured in Ladino or Italian. Though there are dramatic variations in the criteria for, and the evaluation of, health and illness, and even in the experience of pain, specific chemicals tend on the whole to produce specific bodily changes, some impeding and others enhancing vital bodily functioning.

Realist-minded antirelativists are also right to claim that in the nature of the case, social life has certain crucial nodes or foci of attention and concern: a society establishes patterns or modes of governance, of decision making and arbitration; it has patterns and modes of producing food and raising children; it has ways of dealing with transitions between life and death, with growth and aging. Since we are the sorts of creatures for whom everything is significant, creatures who also attempt to find regularities, if not laws, we endow these nodes and foci of social concern with meaning. It is an open empirical question —one which cannot be settled to everyone's satisfaction— whether these social nodes exhibit significant regularities.

But it doesn't follow from this that there are basic culturally neutral referential expressions or that distinctive cultures must in the end assign the same significance to cross-cultural facts or events. The core truths of antirelativism do not entail that there is a reductive foundational basis for interpretation, or universal standards for all types of evaluation. Antirelativists can acknowledge that the significance of social life —and sometimes even the determination of what is important to a culture's life— is so culturally specific that it is sometimes difficult to identify such foci or nodes across cultures. (If the "legal system" of a culture is entirely absorbed in what another culture would regard as "religious life" it is tendentious to compare legal systems as if one were comparing different varieties of the same species or variations on the same theme.) Empirical investigation determines whether —or how— specific kinds of intentional descriptions of such nodal foci are phenomenologically, and sometimes even physiologically, self-fulfilling.

Third, relativism and antirelativism are, when modestly formulated, perfectly compatible. Relativism need not foreclose the possibility of successful cross-cultural interpretation, communication, or evaluation; antirelativism need not foreclose the possibility of radical cross-cultural incomprehension and misinterpretation.

Sometimes it is helpful to remind ourselves of obvious, banal, Philistine truths.

1. Most cultures are composed of intersecting networks of subcultures, each with distinctive practices, forming linguistic subcommunities. The directness of interpretation and evaluation among a culture's subcultures is, like that between cultures, partly a function of the extent to which their practices and experiences overlap. "Sharing a history" is not sufficient for direct interpretation and communication: the length and indirectness of an interpretive chain depend on the extent to which subcultures share experiences and perspectives on that history. (Did Southern slaves share a history with their owners in 1860? Did Manchester mill hands share a history with factory owners?) When tasks and practices are radically differentiated by gender, status, age, or roles, interpretation and communication are correspondingly attenuated. The evaluation of practices and performances across groups becomes increasingly perspectivally slanted.

2. The success of difficult, subtle interpretation and communication often depends on the temperament, the talent, and the preoccupations of the individuals involved. To be sure, everything —including hostility— is grist for the interpreter, but on the whole a nonthreatening demeanor is more likely to elicit cooperative, culturally typical speech

and behavior than an intrusive one. Though gestures, intonation patterns, silences, and facial expressions themselves differ culturally, talented and skilled observers of such expressive behavior are advantaged in interpreting and communicating. Besides the interpretive advantages of temperament and talent there are those of experience. A recently bereaved anthropologist might, without sentimental projection, be in a better position to give a subtle explanation of culturally variable mourning behavior that an angry adolescent boy who shares the mourner's language.

3. There are distinctive types, levels, and degrees of communication, each with distinctive criteria for success.

(a) "Good enough" communication for interactive situations and practices does not require strict identity of connotative meaning. In political negotiations and mercantile exchange, for instance, it is enough that the parties recognize the suitability of the other's contributions to be willing to continue the exchange. Such communication can be practically successful without being subtly shaded.

(b) "Good enough translation" —even of highly allusive poetry— does not require a word-by-word or phrase-by-phrase synonymy. The sense and meaning can be conveyed to the satisfaction of bilingualists by a network of analogous connotative associations. Sometimes this is achieved by indirection, sometimes by verbosity. Here, as elsewhere, there are trade-offs for distinctive criteria of success. The poignant sense of untranslatability —of lost meaning— does not argue for incomprehensibility: a translator might be able to fabricate a "missing verse" good enough to fool a discerning native literary critic.

(c) "Good enough explanation" need not involve elegant or precise translation. An interpreter's explanation of the etiology and function of native speech and practice can sometimes require lengthy, elaborate, and sometimes indirect translation into the original language.

5. Our own neighbors are often the true but opaque audience for cross-cultural evaluation. In condemning or praising the practices of cultures that do not interact with our own, we are often implicitly considering whether to adopt analogous practices ourselves. In evaluating the practices of cultures with which we are interacting, our concerns are directed largely to their effects on the area of intersection. In a way most evaluations are not intended to hit their direct objects: they are presented as considerations in a practical deliberation rather than as contextless conclusions to be registered in the Book of the World. Their declarative form is meant to enhance their rhetorical force.

Since the core truths of relativism are compatible with those of its alleged opponents, what is at stake in keeping the debate alive? The electrical charge of controversy carries the baggage of personal and cultural psychology, with both parties speaking to central but archaic desires and convictions. One item on the hidden agenda is the horror of being judged or evaluated, mixed with the pleasure of judging and evaluating. The relativist voices our conviction that only our intimates have the right to evaluate us, along with the certainty that those who judge us harshly have failed to understand us. The antirelativist voices our conviction that we could, given time and cooperation, understand anybody, and that anybody should be able to understand us, if he would but take the time and if we choose to help him. (So if he doesn't understand us, either he didn't try hard enough or we chose to remain opaque.)

There is another, more philosophically respectable philosophic issue at stake. It is not surprising that the relativism controversy should have arisen in the wake of logical positivism. Strong versions of relativism have their roots in the seed bed that hybridized, cross-fertilized theories of truth with theories of meaning. The antirelativist reaction is, in part at least, an attempt to secure an independent ground for the evaluation of truth-claims. It rests on the view that while meaning points to the direction for verification, it cannot determine truth. It is for this reason that a good deal of the relativism controversy centered on two related issues: whether there are culture-neutral referential expressions and whether radical translation is susceptible to verification.

One of the reasons that generalized debates about relativism are ill conceived is that they treat cross-cultural interpretations and evaluations as reports of speakers' beliefs, truth-claims requiring verification and validation. But such interpretations and evaluations are generally located within a set of specific practices and activities. They involve determining whether to continue or modify a practice, whether to imitate or import the practices or institutions of another culture. Contemporary Chinese attempts to evaluate the economic structures of the West are, for instance, focused on the issue of determining the consequences of such importation *for China*. Not unreasonably their interest in our practices takes the form "What does it mean for the Chinese? Is it good for us?" When cross-cultural interpretations and evaluations are phrased in objective terms, as if they were part of a theoretical investigation, they are not on that account judgments of goodness or rightness *überhaubt*; nor are they attempts to determine whether a particular cultural conception conforms to a Platonic idea. Even assessments of justice are placed within the context of a specific set of practices. Like intracultural evaluators, cross-cultural evaluators want to determine whether another culture's various conceptions of persons (for instance) is bound to a system of practices that could or should be avoided or imitated. Such investigations are submerged and highly particular, contextual, practical investigations, guided by specific own concerns.

II

There is a philosophical dream, a dream that moral and political ideals are not only grounded in and explained by human nature, but that fundamental moral and political principles can be derived from the narrower conditions that define persons. Though sometimes bold and wild dreamers do go so far, this dream does not ususaly express a metaphysical wish that could be satisfied by analyzing the conditions for reflective subjectivity or the psycholinguistic conditions for the reflexivity of first person attributions. More commonly, the dream is that the normative political principles concerning rights and moral principles regarding respect can be derived from what is essential to the concept of a person.

The strongest version of this dream attempts to use the (initially value-neutral) concept of a person to derive specific rights, principles, and obligations; a somewhat more modest version of the dream attempts to use the concept of a person to set constraints on such rights, principles, and obligations; a yet weaker version makes the two notions—the concept of a person and the delineation of moral and political rights—mutually explicative. But all versions of this dream press for *one* concept of a person, whose various components form a harmonious structure that could provide adjudication among competing normative claims about what does or does not fall within the domain of the rights and obligations of persons. The press for one well-structured concept that allocates priorities among its various conditions is a press for a decision procedure to settle disagreements about, and conflicts among, competing values and obligations.

But there is no such thing as *the* concept of a person, not only for the obvious historical reason that there have been dramatically discontinuous changes in the characterization of *persons*—though that is true—but for the equally obvious anthropological-cultural reason that the moral and legal practices heuristically treated as analogous across cultures in fact differ so dramatically that they capture "the concept" of person only at a vacuously vague level—though that is also true.

Social and political conceptions of persons—conceptions of their powers, rights, and limits, the criteria for their individuation and continued identity—derive from conceptions of primary, privileged activities, the activities which are thought to express human excellences and tasks. Attributes believed to be required for performing such primary activities are designated as the essential identificatory properties of persons. The significant powers and limitations of persons in a society focused on spiritual and meditational activity are, for instance, radically different from those attributed to persons in a society focused on political participation or on scientific advancement; both differ from the properties thought essential to persons in societies focused on military or civic glory. The philosophic problems concerning the identities of persons vary correspondingly: when Descartes treats scientific demonstration as the primary activity, the ego became mind, and the philosophical problems concerning persons shift to those involving the analysis of the relation between private and public interests in rights; when the self is defined by its economic activity, the philosophic problems focus on issues of rational choice. Moral and political principles cannot be derived from "the" concept of personhood because that concept is socially and politically constructed: the defining characteristics of persons are set by the primary practices and privileged actions. The norms and ideals embedded in these practices also set the rules and principles that govern just social and political associations. The two—the normic criteria for personhood and the principles of justice—are coordinate. A culture's concept of a person is one way in which the norms that govern its moral and political principles are expressed; its moral and political principles are the articulation of some of the strands in the normative concept of a person.

The various functions performed by our contemporary concept of persons do not hang together: there is some overlap, but also some tension. Indeed the various functions that "the" notion plays are so related that various attempts to structure them in a taxonomic order express quite different norms and ideals. Disagreements about primary values and goods reappear as disagreements about the priorities and relations among the various functions the concept plays, disagreements about what is essential to persons. Not only does each of the functions bear a different relation to the class of persons and human beings, but each also has a different contrast class.

These are some of the functions we—inheritors of the Judeo-Christian-Renaissance-Enlightenment-Romantic traditions—want the concept to play:

1. The attribution should give us objective grounds for being taken seriously, with respect . . . and on grounds that we cannot lose with illness, poverty, villainy, inanity, or senility. On this view the idea of person is an insurance policy. Some think of the insurance as assuring us rights; others think of it as assuring us a certain kind of regard, to be

treated as ends rather than merely as means, our activities centrally rational (or at least reasonable) and good willed (or at least well-intentioned), interpreted by an extension of the principle of charity. For some the special status of persons is justified by some set of properties: persons should be respected because they are capable of critical rationality, or because they are free inventors of their lives, or because they have divinely donated souls, or because they can be harmed, frustrated in living out their life-plans. (Cf. sections 3-5 below.) For others the special status of persons cannot be grounded by any essential properties either (a) because respect or rights are not *grounded* in the concept of a person (they are not *derived* from that concept but are necessarily part of it) or (b) because the grounds for such respect or rights consist of a range of social or political goods rather than the nature of persons.

(Among the Hellenes the contrast class for this notion was the class of slaves and barbarians. Among Christians the contrast class is that of unsouled beings. For Kantians the contrast class is that of nonrational beings, incapable of understanding the laws of nature and unable to act freely from the idea of the laws of morality. This conception of the class of persons intersects but is not identical with, nor subsumed within, the class of human beings: Martians and dolphins might be persons, as might intrapsychic homunculi.)

2. Sometimes the respect and rights of persons are assured by law: the concept of a person is treated as primarily a legal concept. The legal concept of a person is meant to assure:

(a) Liability. This is a retrospective function, defined by the conditions for presumptive agency: bodily continuity, memory, *mens rea*. (The contrast class: those with defective conditions for agency: e.g., the insane, the senile.)

(b) Legally Defined Responsibility. This is a prospective and regionalized function that defines specific duties and obligations. Such responsibilities are often institutionally defined: sometimes the legal person's duties and responsibilities are contractually fixed, with explicitly articulated sanctions for default or violation; sometimes the obligations are defined informally by commonly accepted practices and sanctions. In such cases liability is carried by the legal entity rather than by the individuals—for example, trustees, corporations, guardians, boards of directors, banks—who act as its officers. (The contrast class: minors; [once, and still in some places] women.)

(c) Specifically Defined Citizen Rights and Duties. This is a function that empowers a specifically designated class of individuals to act and speak on behalf of the State. They are, as Hobbes put it, its "artificial persons." Polities accord specific rights and duties of participation in decision-making, representation, governance. Indeed, this is one way political systems differ: by the different ways they distribute the power and the right to act or speak in the person of the State, as an agent of one of its constitutive institutions. As the frontespiece of Hobbes' *Leviathan* graphically demonstrates, the king of an absolute monarchy is the embodied Person of the State. If the State is composed of families or clans, rather than of individuals, those families or clans are the person-citizens of the State, and their heads or elders speak and act for them. Similarly, the representatives of state-defined political institutions (the judiciary, the legislative body, city officials) act in the person of the State: their decisions personify the official acts of the State. When the pope speaks *ex cathedra*, he speaks as the Personification of the Church; the voice of Parliament is the voice of the people; citizens—"We the People"—casting votes on public issues or selecting their representatives, are expressing the views of the Person(s) of the State. Even though their rights and welfare are under the legal protection of the State, the disenfranchised—etymologically, the unfree—are the subjects or wards of the State rather than citizen-persons entitled to act or speak as the Person of the State. Whether the class of citizen-persons coincides with or is a subset of the class of those who are legally liable is, of course, a political and even an ideological issue. (The contrast class is usually under contention: aliens, slaves, exiles, fetuses.)

Neither the Kantian regulative principle of respect nor the Christian idea of the immortal soul have any necessary connection with the legal function of the idea of person. Respect for the person does not entail any particular legal rights; nor does the assurance of legal personhood assure social or moral respect. Furthermore, each of the distinctive legal *personae* might well select different grounds for the attribution of personhood. For instance, an individual can claim some citizen rights (the right of *habeas corpus*, for instance) without satisfying the conditions for liability. Nor need a legal person be accorded all the rights of citizenship: universities do not, as such, vote or receive social security. The conditions for prospective responsibility are regional and relativised: whether an individual or a group is designated a legal person is characteristically a political, and sometimes an ideological, issue.

Some legal theorists have argued that no single concept of a person can—or should—be used to derive the wide variety of legislative and judicial policies required to give appropriately differentiated treatment to the varieties of legal *personae*.[1] They maintain that moral and legal practices contextualize and regionalize the status of a person: a fetus is, for example, accorded the status of a legal person in some contexts and for some issues but not for others; a corporation has the legal status of a person for some purposes, for others not. We should, they hold, draw our inclusionary and exclusionary classes contextually, following our sense of what is morally and judicially appropriate rather than attempting to derive our legal practices from a sharply—and, they suggest, arbitrarily—defined class of persons. ("First come the practices of right and wrong, and then come definitions and classifications.") The question of whether there are several distinctive legal concepts of a person, each with its own pragmatically defined domain, or whether there is one concept, with distinctive pragmatic applications, is an idle question, since neither legal theory nor legal practice are affected by the answer.

There are, of course, dramatic cultural variations in the criteria for agency, variations in the legal conditions that define persons. The class of liable and responsible persons can, for instance, exclude individuals in favor of groups of individuals (clans or families); or the heads of such groups (the chief patriarch); intrapsychic homunculi, daemonic possessors. It can be treated as an all-or-none classification or as a matter of degrees. It is often difficult to determine how to diagnose such cultural variation: Do these differences represent disagreements about the proper analysis of the concept of a person? Do some cultures lack the concept or do they have an analogue? Do some cultures lack what we consider a legal system or do they rather locate their legal system in a different network of institutions? There may be no fact of the matter: exigencies of theory construction rather than ontology may determine whether we can legitimately project our concept of a legal person to analogous bearers of liability and responsibility, or whether we should decline the attribution to individuals whose agency is defined within radically different schemes of liability and responsibility.

3. The idea of a person is also the idea of an autonomous agent, capable of self-defined and self-defining choices. There are at least two versions of this idea.

(a) The first is primarily negative and defensive, concentrating on the desire to fend off external interference: "*Noli me tangere*," or in Amerispeak: "Don't tread on me, buddy."

(b) The second is primarily positive and constructive, concentrating on capacities for self-determination.

Both the negative and the positive version come in two varieties:

(a) One emphasizes critical rationality and independent evaluation: a person is essentially capable of stepping back from her beliefs and desires to evaluate their rationality and appropriateness; she is also capable (at the very least) of attempting to form and modify her beliefs and desires, her actions, on the basis of her rational evaluations. (The contrast class: the mindless, the nonrational, the dissociated.)

(b) The other emphasizes imaginative creativity. Because their decisions and actions are intentionally identified, and because they have latitude in transforming, improvising, and inventing their intentions, persons can, in a number of significant ways, form the worlds in which they live. There are two dimensions on which such formations take place: the political and the visionary-poetic.

(i) Since the social and political domain is constructed, it can be reconstructed, if only a piece at a time. To be a person is to participate actively in public life, forming or at least modifying the social and political policies and institutions that significantly and effectively shape life. (The contrast class: the masses, whose opinions and actions can be manipulated.)

(ii) By choosing or constructing systems of values persons create the categories that structure and interpret their world, that form their ambitions, hopes, and fears. Since they determine what is important and significant, their interpretations structure both what they see and what they do. (The contrast class: the dependent, the fearful, the timid, the unimaginative.)

These differences mark differences in two faces or moments in Enlightenment political theory. The first stance is defensive: it is designed to protect the person from what is perceived as tyrannical or unjust political or epistemic authority. This concept of a person stresses negative liberty and minimal government. There is some correlation, but no necessary connection, between the defensive boundary conception of the free person and the conception of the person whose critical, rational capacities are primarily exercised in scientific discovery or poetic creativity and only secondarily in defense against error.

Although the Enlightenment concept of a person began with the Christian conception of a person as defined by his free will, his capacity to affirm or deny God's law, autonomy shifted from the freedom of the will to the rational power of independent critical judgments of truth and falsity. When the old order loses its authority, the emphasis on persons as autonomous judges preserving and protecting individual boundaries is replaced by an emphasis on autonomous legislators generating new social structures and practices. Negative liberty gives way to positive liberty; minimal government gives way to a government charged with the formation of citizen values. Protection against error gives way to the power of constructing a systematic science, and eventually to the power of the imagination in constructing a world through poetic language. There is some correlation, but no necessary connection, between the concept of a person as a constructive, self-determining legislator and the conception of a person as primarily an inventive creator. The movement from the earlier defensive to the later constructive conceptions of persons correlates in a very rough way with the movement from early Cartesian Enlightenment conceptions of the independent inquiring rational self, free of the claims of dogmatic doctrine, to late Enlightenment Romanticism, with its emphasis on positive liberty, political reform, and poetic creativity.

The conception of persons as deserving respect is sometimes grounded on the conception of a person as capable of self-definition. But of course both the rationality and the creativity version of the self-defining person (in their negative and positive forms) make individual claims to personhood empirically contingent. If claims to respect are based on the capacities for autonomy, we are in deep trouble. Constitutional and sociopolitical contingencies affect the likelihood of an individual actually (rather than notionally or potentially), developing her capacities for critical rationality; similiar contingencies determine whether she is actually (rather than notionally) capable of creative self-determination. Has the individual been well nourished and nutured, well educated and well formed? Or has she suffered irreparable traumas that make autonomy practically impossible? *Logical* or *notional* possibility is not helpful here: aardvarks, baboons, and caterpillars might notionally be capable of autonomy. It might seem as if this concept of a person provides grounds for normative political claims. Precisely because certain kinds of political structures are required to actualize otherwise only notional claims to personhood, there is a prima facie obligation to structure political systems in such a way as to allow the best development of the capacities for critical self-determination. Unfortunately many extra premises are required to substantiate this claim, premises about the primary and the proper functions of the obligations of political systems. The obligation cannot follow solely from the requirements for personhood.

(This conception of the class of persons intersects but is not identical with, or subsumed within, the class of biologically defined human beings. The contrast class is composed of all those incapable of self-correcting and self-legislating critical reflexivity.)

Christianity is, for once, surprisingly open and generous. If part of the point of the concept of a person is to assure respect, it is wiser not to rest one's hopes on such fragile and vulnerable capacities as those for autonomy or creativity. Maybe a divinely assured immortal soul—or even just a divinely assured soul, immortal or not—would provide more secure grounds for respect. To be sure, standardly conditions for rationality and autonomy are regulative rather than empirical: we might take comfort in the principle that every rational being *ought* to be treated with respect. But it takes unusually good luck to get that regulative principle realized under hard and harsh circumstances, just when it is most needed. Respect may be well-grounded without being well-assured. (What is the recourse of the unrespected when they most require it? Moral indignation? Righteousness in the eyes of history—itself a politically variable matter—is not reliably effective in assuring entitlements.)

More recently the Christian conception of persons as endowed with a free will capable of affirming or denying God's law has been redefined: the rights of persons are accorded to all those capable of suffering, those whose naturally formed life history can be harmed, shortened, frustrated. Whether the sentient are self-consciously aware of the natural shapes of their lives, whether they form plans and expectations (the transformation of the idea of the will as legislator) matters less than the fact that their lives can be painful or unfulfilled. It is the sheer fact of sentience that qualifies an individual to the rights of persons.[2]

4. Social persons are identified by their mutual interactions, by the roles they enact in the dynamic dramas of their shared lives. There are several varieties of this conception.

(a) The idea of a *dramatis persona* as the bearer of roles in a dramatic unfolding of action has its source in the theater. A *persona* is the mask of an actor, cast to play a part in developing a narrative or a plot. Essentially meshed with others, a person's scope and directions are defined by her role in a complex course of events involving the interactions of agents whose varied intentions modify the outcomes—and indeed sometimes the directions—of one another's projects. While the dramatic conception of a person has no necessary connection with the concept of a person as entitled to respect, or with that of a self-defining individual, it bears some kinship to the idea of a person as an agent, as the source of liable and responsible action. When *dramatis personae* are, in principle, able to predict their effects on one another's lives, their intentions can carry moral or legal weight. (The contrast class: whatever is inert, without the power of intentional action. Since inanimate objects and events—volcanoes, wars, famines—can forward or redirect dramatic action, they are sometimes personified, but they are accounted persons only if intentional action is attributed to them.)

(b) Some psychologists introduce a normative notion of a person as capable of taking Others seriously, capable of entering into mutually affective and effective relations. To be a person is to acknowledge the reality of Others, living in a commonly constructed world, actively and cooperatively sharing practices. Some psychologists attempt to connect the sociability with the respect-based conditions for persons, attempting to treat these as mutually supportive conditions.[3] But there is no necessary connection between the two conditions. On the one hand, respect might be grounded in the idea of (a divinely donated) soul, whose sociability is contingent on the identity and roles assigned to it; on the other, some conceptions of sociability might valorize a type of intimacy that minimizes respect-across-individual-boundaries. Such a manifestly culture-bound concept of an ideal person can readily conflict with the (equally culture-bound) concept of an ideal person as capable of radical autonomy. (The contrast class: dissociated personalities, psychopaths.)

(c) There is a presumptively ontological, prepsychological version of the concept of a person as essentially formed by its relations to others. It is the conception of a person as constituted, formed, by "The Look of The Other." According to this theory consciousness is initially unreflective, without a sense of self; it acquires an image of itself—an image that comes to form the person's somatic sense of herself—by seeing itself mirrored in the eyes of Others. We form one another's identities by the act of mutual mirroring, mutual regard. A person's life is constructed from, and constituted by, such interactive formative relations. Though there may be normative claims about how we *ought* to regard one another, the conception of a person as interactively emergent neither entails nor is entailed by the conception of a person as entitled to respect or to specific legal rights. (The contrast class: nonconscious beings, beings incapable of self-conscious reflection.)

(d) Associated but not identical with the psychological condition is the honorific attribution of personhood. Some individuals are accounted *real* persons: "She's a real *mensch!*" But although the capacities for autonomy (rationality or creativity) might be ingredient in the qualifications for being a *real* person, in contrast to the usual humanoid lump, they are not sufficient. Indeed a zealot of the concept of a person as an autonomous creator might well straightaway be disqualified as a real mensch-person. On this view—to be sure a view not widely shared as definitory of the concept of a person—a *real* person is generally distinguished by fortitude and reliability, by a sense of presence, of style and individuality, often combined with compassion and a humorous sense of proportion, an ironic recognition of human frailty and finitude. (The contrast class: the psychopath, the creep, the jerk, the whine, the brute, the neanderthal.)

5. The concept of a person is also used to sketch the norms for the appropriate shape and structure of a life. Those who identify persons by a characteristic life history or life plan require an account of a standard—or maybe not so standard!—shaping of a life, one that goes beyond biologically determined patterns of maturation and aging. This

concept of a person originally derives from the Christian conception of a soul whose life and choices move her toward salvation or damnation; it is a descendant of the picture of a person as the constructor of a fate. The emphasis shifts: the person is first identified as the *author* of the story, then by the sheer *activity* of story construction, and then simply by the emergent content of the narrative.[4]

There are two versions of this focus.

(a) The Realist "Fact of the matter" Version. On this view a culture could be mistaken: it can malform and misdirect lives, and it can misunderstand the processes by which it shapes characteristic life stories. Real alienation and malformation are possible, probably common, and often denied in good faith.

(b) The "It's all up to us" Version.

(i) It is all up to those who are individual free spirits.

(ii) It is all up to us as members of a community, forming a system of practices that define lives.

While this conception of a person is compatible with the conception that defines persons as autonomous, it neither entails nor is entailed by that conception. A person's life story need not be autonomously constructed; nor need it provide grounds for respect. Even more dramatically, the conditions for autonomy need have no bearing on the shape and events of life histories, which are, after all, contingent and heteronomous. In a Kantian framework, for example, the conditions for autonomy are purely intellectual: they neither affect nor can be affected by the contingent narrative of a life. Nor need the possibility of reflective subjectivity be essential to the construction of a life story: a life can have the shape of a well-formed narrative, without its subject experiencing anything like first-person inner subjectivity. It is the convenience of theory construction rather than of brute ontology that determines whether the life story condition for personhood requires further qualification.

As it stands, the life-story concept of a person seems to allow any subject of a narrative life story to qualify even if that subject is not conscious of itself as a subjective center of experience. An individual might have a life story without being subjectively aware of it, and certainly without being self-consciously reflective about herself shaping it. Yet if the unadorned life-story condition of personhood allows mice and mountains to qualify as persons, the additional requirement of active subjective reflection seems too strong: it appears to disqualify individuals who might, on moral or political grounds, qualify as persons. The capacities for active subjective reflection—for constructing life plans—might turn out to be consequences of, rather than presuppositions for, an individual qualifying as a social and political person. (The contrast class of the weak version of persons, as characterized by life stories, is difficult to define. Everything temporal can be construed as having a life story, even a life story with a normative form. This criterion allows squirrels, a particular patch of pachysandra, and the Mediterranean basin to qualify as persons because they have life stories with a beginning, middle, and end. The contrast class of the stronger version, with the additional condition that persons must be capable of reflecting on, if not actively forming, a life story or a life plan, is equally difficult to define. Who has the capacity for the automonous construction of a life plan? Should the class include individuals who in principle might acquire the capacities for reflective agency, for constructing and following a life plan, if they could be accorded the status of persons? How are such counterfactual claims evaluated in holistic systems?)

6. The biological conception of an individual is sometimes taken to provide the foundation or basic structure of the concept of a person. Biologists want a concept that will provide

(a) the unit of genetic individuation and

(b) *conatus*: the determination of growth and immunology, the energy and direction of action, reaction and defense.

Persons are, among other things, self-sustainers and self-starters. The biological account of organic independence provides the practical origin of the more far-reaching notion of autonomy. But the concept of an organic individual does not necessarily provide a sharp distinction between human beings and other species, let alone between persons and other sorts of organic entities. Whether there is a subclass, a variety of human beings that can be designated as persons by virtue of a special set of standardly inheritable properties is a matter for empirical determination. If rationality marks the class of persons, are the various properties and capacities that constitute rationality biologically fixed, genetically coded? How do the conditions for reflective critical rationality described by Kant and Frankfurt function in the organism's system of action and reaction, expansion and defense? If self-determination marks the class of persons, are the various properties and traits that constitute an individual's capacity for self-determination biologically fixed, genetically coded? How do the various capacities for creature self-definition affect a person's constitution? We are a long way from having a reasonable speculative theory, let alone a sound research program, connecting the moral, political, and legal notions of persons with the biological notion of a reproductive, self-sustaining, defensively structured organism. (The contrast class: inanimate entities.)

It has been argued that just as women and blacks were once

excluded from the class of persons on presumptively biological grounds, so too we are now misled by superficial speciesism to exclude dolphins and mammals. But we are a long way from an account of the criteria for appropriate classification: What formally identical or analogous constitutional structures qualify nonhumans as person? Why should baboons but not robots qualify? Or Martians but not Crustaceans? While empirical considerations are relevant (Do dolphins have central nervous systems?), they cannot settle the questions of whether corporations and robots only qualify as persons by metaphorical courtesy, while dolphins and chimpanzees qualify as full members by an appropriate, corrective extension of the class. (When is a batch of wires a central nervous system and when is it only an analogue? When is an analogue good enough? When is it all too good? When does behavioral similarity qualify for literal attribution? What are the criteria for identifying biologically based behavioral similarity?) Both the arguments for excluding corporations and the left hemisphere of the brain and the arguments for including robots and Martians depend on normatively charged conceptual analyses. Since similarities and differences can be found wholesale, some other sets of considerations are required to select the features that demarcate the class of persons. What considerations select the capacity to feel pain rather than those for rational thought as the criteria for the class? Indeed because the classification has significant political and social consequences, we should not be surprised to discover that conceptual analyses of biological functions—particularly those presumed to affect intentional agency—are strongly, though often only implicitly and unself-consciously guided by moral intuitions, ideology, and taste. Controversies among sociobiologists about drawing relevant analogies between humans and other animals—their hierarchy or altruistic behavior, their protection of property—should make us suspicious about attempts to support policies concerning the rights of persons on what are allegedly purely empirical, biological considerations. (The contrast class: inanimate objects.)

7. Psychometaphysicians have a notion of the elusive, ultimate subject of experience, the *I* that cannot be reduced to an object, even though it can treat itself objectively, as the focus of introspection and investigation.[5] But this *I* can be diachronically discontinuous: the subject of sequential experiences need not be strictly identical. And even synchronic subjects of experiences need not be united: every aspect of a complex act of awareness could, in principle, have its own subject. The subject who is aware of the acute pain of loss need not be identical with the subject who is at the same time aware of the shifting pattern of light on the leaves of a tree. Or, at any rate, the transcendental unity of

apperception (if there is such a thing) does not necessarily provide specific closure to what is, and what is not, included within the bounds of such a presumptive unity. The limits of the domain of experience cannot be set by the subject of a transcendental unity of apperception without circularity.

In any case, there are a number of distinctive construals of subjectivity as the condition for personhood, and while each has quite different consequences for the concept, none has any necessary consequences for morality or for political or legal theory. The *I* which is the subject of experience serves as the contrastive notion, but the various contrasts are not isomorphic. The person as the *I*, the subject of experience, has been identified with the interior or internal perspective in contrast to the external; the subjective in contrast to the objective; the subject-of-experiences in contrast with its experiences; with rationality and the will in contrast to causality and desire; with spontaneity and creativity in contrast to the conditioned; with the decision-maker and agent in contrast to the predictor and observer; with the knower or interpreter in contrast to the known or interpreted; with reflective consciousness in contrast to the content of reflection; with mind in contrast to body.

Although each of these marks quite a different contrast, each is guided by the intuition that persons are capable of bearing a unique reflexive, reflective relation to themselves, a relation that somehow shapes them. Persons are sometimes characterized as capable of having a distinctive set of experiences—ego-oriented attitudes of anxiety, remorse, pride, guilt—which originally give rise to the idea of the self. But the reflective *I* can reject or identify with *these* ego-oriented attitudes as easily as it can with its body or its habits. It is no more identical with any set of "existential attitudes" than it is with any of its more externally defined attributes. The *act* of reflecting on an attribute or attitude, asking "Is that *me*?" ("putting the self in question"), is always different from the attitude or attribute itself, even if the attitude reveals—as anxiety is said to do—the precarious position of the *I* as the act of self-constituting reflection. Being anxious is one thing; being the act that identifies with anxiety is another; both are different from something-perhaps-a-nothing-I-know-not-what, or a simple soul beyond experience, or a pure act of reflection that constitutes itself. All these—different as they are from one another—are far from the original starting point of the *I* as a being whose experience, and especially its experience of itself, is *sui generis*. None of these reflexive attitudes carries specific political, legal, or moral consequences. In *Notes from the Underground* Dostoyevsky's dramatic explorations of the subterranean destructiveness of the endlessly ironic self-mirroring self-consciousness

demonstrate that even rational, self-critical reflexivity can assure neither sociability nor morality, and it can destroy self-respect. (The contrast class: objects; those incapable of self-conscious reflection.)

III

The variety of functions that the concept of a person plays—the
variety of conceptions of persons we have sketched—cannot plausibly
be combined in a single concept. At most one might settle for a heterogeneous class, defined by a disjunction of heterogeneous conditions.
Even if some rough construction of a denominator common to all these
notions and functions were proposed, that conception would be so
general that it could not fulfill—nor could it generate—the various
functions performed by the various regional and substantively rich conceptions.

But this stark conclusion seems premature. Perhaps we can characterize persons by attempting some sort of synthesis of our various
conditions: *a person is a unit of agency, a unit which is (a) capable of
being directed by its conception of its own identity and by what is
important to that identity and (b) capable of acting with others in a
common world. A person is an interactive member of a community,
reflexively sensitive to the contexts of her activity, a critically reflective
inventor of the story line of her life.* Surely this is a parody of a characterization. The conditions only cohere if one does not look too closely.
Crucially, it is not clear whether these conditions are conjunctive or
whether they are nestled. After all, the conditions for strong autonomy
might well on occasion conflict with those for strong sociability. The
conditions of critical rationality might well on occasion conflict with
those of poetic creativity. The conditions for personhood—and indeed
the class of those qualifying as persons—are quite different if critical
rationality dominates over sociability rather than sociability over the
capacities for critical rationality. Societies which weight them differently
differ dramatically, and sometimes ideological or political issues determine the weighting and priority of the various conditions.

Might the metaphysical notion of a person be primary, in a way
that would settle these questions of priority? Primary to what? A univer-
salistic metaphysical notion can constrain, but it cannot select or determine the priorities among competing politically and ideologically defined persons. If the metaphysical idea of a person is rich and robust
enough to generate political consequences, it is already charged and
directed toward those consequences. If it stands neutrally above those

consequences, it is unlikely to be rich enough to do the work done by the various (strands in the) concepts of *persons*. The concept of the referent of first-person attributions, or the concept of the subject of experience, *might* be a precondition for the political or moral uses of the concept of a person. But even that is questionable: it is not conceptually necessary that the bearer of rights be capable of reflexive first-person attributions.

The notion of a human being is a notion of a biologically defined entity; the notion of a person is, however, normatively and sometimes ideologically charged. It expresses a view about what is important, valuable about being creatures like us, in having this or that set of significant traits and properties. Such creatures need not belong to our biological species. Martians or Superrobots could be persons; organically organized families and clans might qualify, as could intrapsychic daemons, homunculi, or consciences. For some, this designates a natural kind: there is a fact of the matter about what ought to be important and significant to us. For others, we are that natural kind whose primary attributes are plastic: within limits we are self-legislatively self-defining, even self-constructing creatures.

But even those who think of persons as self-defining creators of their identities do not agree about the extension of this class. For some, self-determination is a matter of individual volition; for others, only historical communities with self-perpetuating practices can be considered self-determining. For some, *every* individual, no matter how pathetically malformed, however constitutionally or socially deprived or deformed, is equally the creator of the story that is her life. No matter what story she tells about her life, that story *is* her life as a person. For others, only Nietzschean free, self-creating individual spirits, the solitary ones who transcend the herd and the conventions of the herd, are capable of self-definition. For others, only cultural and political communities can define or create themselves: individual persons are self-legislating only as members of a community defined by shared interactive practices, which define the boundaries and the essential traits of persons. On this view the definition of persons is implicit in the practices that express and reproduce the community's cultural forms, especially the practices of parenting and education, the distribution of legal and political power.

These reflections on "the" concept of a person seem unsatisfactory: all we have is a whining complaint (mis)inspired by vulgar forms of Wittgensteinianism, mock innocently shifting the burden of analysis. Instead of dispatching yet another vexed philosophic issue, counseling Quixotic philosophers to stop looking for a nonexistent essential definition of persons, we should perhaps more modestly end with an account of the many different reasons we have wanted, and perhaps needed, the notion of a person. These are, after all, honorable desires, as philosophic desires go. We have, in a sketchy way, explored some of the reasons that philosophers and legal-political theorists want the concept: those reasons are given by the heterogeneous list of functions—some of them rhetorical—that the concept has played. The Procrustean tactic of cutting limbs to fit an arbitrarily, if elegantly, designed form neither illuminates nor gains anything: it limits rather than enhances an understanding of the various functions of "the" concept.

It is, of course, possible to legislate one central notion of a person and fend off strong contending candidates for definition. Such legislation might express a moral or an ideological victory; if it is widely accepted, it might even succeed in being a culturally self-fulfilling prophecy. But it would not on that account alone constitute an insightful illumination into the nature of persons. Such legislation about the essential character of persons expresses rather than grounds or legitimates our moral and legal principles. But, significantly, the deep fissures and conflicts that are central to moral experience, and that make their way into the complexities of legal practice, are reintroduced among, and even sometimes within, the various functions of the concepts of persons. We do not even have the luxury of assuring ourselves that at least "the" concept of the person is coordinate with "the" concepts of moral and legal practices. At best we can say that the tensions and conflicts that are at the heart of moral and legal practices are reflected in, and sometimes clarified by, tensions and conflicts in conceptions of persons.

Why then is there such a metaphysical longing for *one* concept? (Or is it a longing for *one* metaphysical concept?) Perhaps the explanation is that the various functions the concept plays are each *unifying* functions: *the* locus of liability; *the* subject of experience; *the* autonomous critical reflector or creator. Since these various functions are unifying functions, there might be a strong temptation to look for the unified source of these various unifying functions. But this is an elementary error, on a par with illicitly extracting and then detaching an existential quantifier from its proper nested location. A desire for unity cannot by itself perform the conjuring trick of pulling one rabbit out of several hats: a transcendental unity of the concept of person, unifying the *variety* of distinct, independently (unifying) functions that each regional concept plays.

Our reflections leave our conclusions open: we might conclude either that there is no such thing as the concept of personhood, that there are only highly regionalized functions that seemed, erroneously, to be subsumable in a structured concept? Or we might conclude that the various functions of the concept are sometimes at odds, that the concept of a person cannot function to provide decision procedures for resolving conflicts among competing claims for rights and obligations because it embeds and expresses just those conflicts. Nothing hangs on the choice between these conclusions because neither political practice nor philosophic theory is affected by the outcome. For all practices and theoretical purposes it does not matter whether the concept of a person has multiple and sometimes conflicting functions, or whether there is no single concept which can be characterized as *the* concept of a person. Since *the* concept(s) of a person is not foundational, it does not matter whether we deny that there is a concept of a person or conclude there is a concept with multiple and sometimes conflicting functions.

Another metaphysical longing remains unsatisfied. But of course that does not mean that we shall be freed of metaphysical longing, or even of this particular metaphysical longing.[6]

IV

The desire to discover a culturally or contextually neutral concept of persons —one that is independent of the range of practices in which "persons" function— rests on the desire to provide a nontendentious way of evaluating those practices. Critics and reformers must, of course, attend to whatever facts of the matter —empirical or conceptual— might affect practices. Sometimes, when those facts undetermine the specification or justification of a practice, the holism of a culture helps to close the gap. A reform may be justified —or shown untenable— by reference to other, deeply embedded practices. But sometimes even holism fails to close the gap. When that happens, critics and defenders alike attempt to turn to what they present as neutral, extracultural principles to arbitrate their differences. It is remarkable how quickly and surely all sides of disputes manage to find extracultural principles to justify their positions, as against those of their opponents. The "justifications" of practices are often further articulations, specifications, and determinations of the general features of the practice. These further articulations are by no means merely emotive expressions or blind existential choices. They are cognitive, conceptual, and, above all, systematic formulations of practices. Specifying and justifying practices are themselves practices: the primary models, principles, and criteria for justification are themselves derived from the primary activities that are central to a culture. The criteria and procedures for justification in a culture whose central activities center around common-law juridical practices differ from those focused on the primacy of mathematical demonstrations; both differ from the primary models of justification that derive from Talmudic or Koranic commentary.

Is this a capitulation to relativism, a retreat from the high ground that judges the entire controversy to be ill-conceived? Not at all. Contextualism is perfectly compatible with realism; a sober modesty about justification and proof is compatible with a denial of skepticism. Once a context of interpretation or justification is specified, context independent facts of the matter set constraints on truth conditions. Uncertainty remains, as it does in all practical and empirical contexts where there is no final, uncontestable demonstration of the adequacy or inadequacy of an interpretation. Cross-cultural influence or interaction can, of course, involve mistaken interpretations, interpretations that are sometimes profoundly and systematically mistaken. In such cases the actions and interactions based on mistaken interpretations tend to fail, usually visibly. But such interpretations are also corrigible. When communication fails, interested interlocutors usually persist in trying to understand and to make themselves understood. It is persistent interaction rather than the assurance of independent context-neutral principles of demonstration that supports successful communication.

Notes

1. Cf. Charles Baron, "The Concept of Person in the Law," in *Defining Human Life: Medical, Legal and Ethical Implications,* ed. M. W. Shaw and A. E. Doudera (AUPHA Press, 1983); Richard Tur, "The 'Person' in Law," in *Persons and Personality*, ed. Arthur Peacocke and Grant Gillett (Oxford: Blackwell, 1987).

2. Cf. Karl Capek, *War with the Newts* (London: Unwin, 1985); Peter Singer, *Animal Liberation* (New York: Avon Books, 1977).

3. Cf. H. Kohut, *The Restoration of the Self* (New York: International Universities Press, 1977).

4. Cf. Jerome Bruner, *Actual Minds, Possible Worlds* (Cambridge: Harvard, 1986).

5. Cf. Thomas Nagel, *The View From Nowhere* (New York: Oxford, 1986).

6. I am grateful to Christopher Gill, Adam Morton, and other participants in a conference held at Aberystwyth in June 1985. An earlier and shorter version of this essay appeared in *Social Research* (54, 1 [Spring 1987]) under the title "Persons as Rhetorical Categories." Another shorter version appeared under the title "Persons and Personae" in *Persons and Human Beings*, ed. Christopher Gill (New York: Oxford University Press, 1988) and in Amélie Rorty, *Mind in Action* (Boston: Beacon Press, 1988). I am also grateful to Michael Krausz for his encouragement, patience, and suggestions.

Relativism and the Self

Mark Johnston

Is there any object, property, relation, state, event, process, or fact in this world, or in any other, which demands and therefore justifies particular responses on our part? Here is an example, bland enough, I hope, to be uncontroversial: if p is *conclusive evidence* for q (for example, if p is [r and if r then q]), then the fact that p is conclusive evidence for q demands and justifies the response of believing q given that one continues to believe p. Someone who continued to believe p and did not as a result come to believe q would be open to censure. He would have failed to make a response that was required or demanded by his believing p.

These bland remarks are seemingly compatible with the following surprising view about conclusive evidence. For any p and q, if p is conclusive evidence for q, then the fact of p's being conclusive evidence for q merely is its being the case that we are standardly disposed to believe q in consequence of believing p, and perhaps also that we are standardly disposed to censure someone who continues to believe p and fails to believe q. Of course, the counterpart of the usual objection to simple subjectivism will have to be avoided: it cannot be that the relations of conclusive evidence would change if our standard dispositions were to change. So the advocate of the surprising view should say that p's being conclusive evidence for q is merely its being the case that we, as we *actually*[1] are, would typically come to believe q in consequence of believing and continuing to believe p and typically censure someone who believed p and did not believe q. "We" is meant to embrace those of us who are standard in matters of belief fixation and epistemic censure, and "typically" is meant to leave room for our tolerating certain excuses. So, for example, someone in the position of Saul Kripke's Pierre[2] has an excuse, someone whose belief that p does not consist in a state that is relevantly related to the state that is his thought that q would not be censurable for believing p and not believing q.

On the surprising view the concept of conclusive evidence is dependent upon concepts of our patterns of belief fixation and epistemic censure and of the dispositions underlying them. Given the surprising view, no sense is to be made of a kind of skepticism to the effect that our patterns of belief fixation and epistemic censure, even under internally ideal conditions, might not pick up the real relations of conclusive evidence. Indeed, the incoherence of such skepticism might well be the place to begin to argue for the surprising view.

Can an advocate of the surprising view maintain that the fact that p is conclusive evidence for q justifies and demands the response of believing q given that one believes p? It seems so. After all, the advocate can observe that in giving p and the fact that p is conclusive evidence for q as one's justification for believing q, one would be thereby addressing others whose responses would be similar and who would endorse such responses even under conditions of ideal deliberation. What is this if it is not justifying one's response? And when, in a sphere in which justification is called for, only one response is able to be justified, that response will be required or demanded. So it seems that there can be justifiers which are *dependent*, that is, justifying facts whose obtaining constitutively involves our practices and in particular our dispositions to take certain things as justifications.

Is there any *independent* object, property, relation, state, event, process, or fact in this world, or in any other, which justifies and demands particular responses on our part? Given the foregoing, a justifier will be independent only if it is coherent to suppose that the responses we take to be appropriate to the things we take to be the justifiers might be globally misfiring; we might not be tracking the justifiers at all. Calling the surprising view "surprising" is meant to suggest that we regard facts like p's being conclusive evidence for q as independent justifiers.[3] But now, having introduced a basis for contrast, we can set aside the case of cognitive or epistemic responses like belief and ask the corresponding question about conative or orectic responses like desire or concern. Is there any independent object, property, relation, state, event, process, or fact in this world, or in any other, which justifies and demands particular orectic responses on our part?

Initially it is very plausible to suppose that the facts of personal identity—facts such as the fact that while one process will be such that I will survive, another involves my death—are independent justifiers of orectic responses like preferring processes of the first sort to processes of the second sort. Certainly, we naturally and habitually take these facts to justify such responses. And it would be a surprise to be told that what makes some process count as my surviving is that we would regard the person emerging from the process as me—as if who is who could be a matter of what we are inclined to believe. Consider, for example, how the abortion debate would be transformed if *this* surprising view were to gain general acceptance.

This paper attempts to find a coherent way of developing such a surprising view and so of representing the facts of personal identity as at most dependent justifiers. And this issue will turn out to be closely related to the issue of the coherence of relativism about the self.

As a final preliminary, notice that the question of whether the facts of personal identity are dependent or independent justifiers should be distinguished from a related question much in vogue. Several philosophers have aimed for the conclusion that the facts of personal identity are, as we might put it, derivative justifiers, that is, facts which justify preferences only because of the typical concomitants of those facts.[4] According to these philosophers the nonderivative justifiers in the case of personal identity are the impressive psychological continuities which normally accompany survival. On this view our tendency to regard the facts of personal identity as nonderivative justifiers is an illusion of importance produced by the normal correlation between personal identity and such continuities. These several philosophers suggest that this illusion of importance can be isolated and perhaps dispelled by the contemplation of bizarre cases in which personal identity and its normal concomitants come apart.

The issue emerges clearly in the following sort of case. You are persuaded that a certain process will result in your replacement by a complete duplicate who will live a life qualitatively just like the life you would have lived. (Your friends and familiars will be spared the knowledge that you have been replaced.) Does the fact that you believe that the process involves your death justify your resisting it, even though you accept that in qualitative and perhaps even causal terms nothing will be importantly different? If you answer "Yes!" then you are taking the fact or possible fact of your continued existence to be of nonderivative significance, to be a nonderivative justifer. You take its failing to hold to justify a certain response even when the typical concomitant which reinforces that response—the termination of impressive physical and psychological continuities—is not in effect.

How have the several philosophers aimed to show that taking personal identity to be of nonderivative significance—in my terms, to be a nonderivative justifier—is a deep mistake? First, they claim that the facts of personal identity just consist in facts about how the relevant sorts of cross-temporal qualitative similarity are causally secured.[5] Then their strategy is to find pairs of cases C1 and C2 such that one survives in C1 and not in C2, while the difference between C1 and C2 at the level of causal and qualitative matters is not in itself worth caring about. So the several philosophers urge: How can it be reasonable or justified to strongly prefer C1 to C2 just on the basis of the difference in respect of personal identity once one sees that this merely consists in small differences at the level of causal and qualitative matters, differences which are not in themselves worth caring about?[6] Of course, the crucial terms in this argument are "consists in" and "not in themselves worth caring about." There are uses of "consists in" according to which a thing is not strictly identical with what it consists in, so that one could admit that the facts of personal identity, though they consist in facts about qualitative and causal matters, are distinct enough from such underlying facts for us to argue in this way: the differences between C1 and C2 at the level of causal and qualitative matters are not *in themselves* important differences, but they are nonetheless differences of great derivative importance merely because upon these differences turns a difference in respect of personal identity, a difference of great nonderivative importance. The availability of a plausible form of such an "argument from above" will produce a standoff which would itself defeat the several philosophers. For their aspirations were revisionary. They were urging us to correct an alleged mistake we made about personal identity, the alleged mistake of taking it to be a nonderivative justifier. The argument from above can provide a way of defending this attitude in the very sort of case where the mistake is supposed to show up. There are delicate questions about just when the argument from above is available and plausible. But as I have argued elsewhere,[7] any way of constraining the idiom "consists in" which gives a plausible story about personal identity will make available the argument from above in some plausible form.

Let us put aside the several philosophers' argument from insignificant differences and consider another argument against taking personal identity to be a nonderivative justifier, an argument to the effect that the facts of personal identity cannot be nonderivative justifiers because, contrary to what we thought, they are only dependent justifiers. The argument will go by way of defending the coherence of a certain relativism about personal identity and will, I hope, illuminate, and suggest a solution for, the general problem which arises when we take a relativistic view of what we formerly regarded as an independent justifier. (So indeed the considerations urged here, if probative, will have their counterparts for value, free will, the passage of time, the hardness of the logical must, and so on.)

1. Can There Be an Alternative Concept of Personal Identity?

The motivation for relativism, the claim of surprising relativity in the conditions of application of some concept, often begins with the description of alternatives. In the case of personal identity, as elsewhere, something is to be learned from the initial difficulties which face any such description of alternatives. To take a concrete example, Eli Hirsch has attempted to elaborate an alternative concept of personal identity by means of his example of the Contacti.[8] The language of the Contacti is syntactically just like English, and like English speakers they have as rules of their language such things as "a person is to use the word 'I' to refer to that person." However, the Contacti mean something different by their word 'person'. The application conditions of their word 'person' involve conditions of exclusive contact in a strange way. For example, during the period when a woman is touching a man the Contacti will regard the sentence "the person who was a man is now a woman and the person who was a woman is now a man" as true. When contact is broken, the Contacti say, "The person who was first a man and who became a woman during exclusive contact has become a man again" and "The person who was first a woman and who became a man during exclusive contact has become a woman again." They say these things without believing that any changes in the anatomies of the relevant bodies occurred before, during, or after the exclusive contact. Nor do they believe that people are nonbodily substances or souls which habitually swap bodies during exclusive contact. Nor do they believe in a mysterious swapping of psychologies as a result of exclusive contact. It is just that they use the term 'person' in such a way that it has in its extension individuals with life histories made up of stages which from our point of view are strangely gerrymandered in this respect: in general, if A is a person who throughout his life history touches in an exclusive fashion first B, then C, then D, and so on then the Contacti term 'person' will have in its extension an individual whose life history consists of all the stages of the life history of A during periods when A is not exclusively touching another person, together with all the stages of the life history of B during periods when A is exclusively touching B and so on for C, D, and such.[9]

Hirsch wants us to concentrate on the case where, although the Contacti talk this way, their practical attitudes to touching and its consequences are as similar to ours as can be. For example, to put it in our terms, they are not afraid to touch a person who is in pain, nor do they expect to remember directly the experiences had by a person they touched during the period of touching. And, continuing to put things in our terms, if one of the Contacti, escaping from the scene of a crime, grabs another of the Contacti around the neck and points a gun at the hostage's head, the Contacti end up charging the same person as we would for threatening the life of an innocent bystander. On the Contacti law books we find the following law: "If during a period of exclusive touching a previously identified person is touching another person who is threatening the life of an innocent bystander the first person and not the second is guilty of the crime." As Hirsch suggests, if things were otherwise and the Contacti had the responses we would expect if we took their use of 'person' at face value, then the example of the Contacti either would be one of a tribe with our concept of personal identity and strange collateral beliefs about the effects of touching or would be difficult to develop coherently.[10]

Although Hirsch regards the Contacti as so bizarre that their ways do not represent a real psychological possibility for us, he takes the example of the Contacti to illustrate how it is possible for some community to have a concept of personal identity that is different from the concept we use. Now certainly the Contacti use the term 'person' to pick out individuals which are from our point of view bizarrely gerrymandered. Certainly they use a concept which we do not, namely, the concept of *being the same Cp as*, a concept which we could introduce into our language as follows:

A, an individual considered at t, *is the same Cp as* B, an individual at t', if either

> (i) A is not exclusively in contact with anyone at t, and B is not exclusively in contact with anyone at t', and A is the same person as B.
> (ii) $\exists X \exists Y$ (A is at t exclusively in contact with X, and B is at t' exclusively in contact with Y, and X is the same person as Y).
> (iii) A is not exclusively in contact with anyone at t but $\exists Y$ (B is at t' exclusively in contact with Y, and Y is the same person as A).
> (iv) B is not exclusively in contact with anyone at t' but $\exists X$ (A is at t exclusively in contact with X, and X is the same person as B).

However, as far as I can see, Hirsch gives us no grounds for believing that this concept, as used by the Contacti, is *their* concept of personal identity. Indeed, there are good reasons to believe just the opposite. First, the concept Cp as used by the Contacti does not direct and organize either their future-directed or retrospective concerns. Knowing what we would know when we know that we are about to hold the hand of someone who will then have his molars pulled out, any member of the Contacti has just the pattern of future-oriented concern which someone with our concept of personal identity would have. In our terms, he is concerned for the person who will suffer the pain and relieved that it is not him. Second, the concept Cp as used by the Contacti does not pick out individuals that are such that the Contacti typically hold such individuals responsible for every voluntary act in their life history. Knowing what we would know when we know that we are about to be grabbed by a hostage-taker, each of the Contacti expects just what someone with our concept of personal identity would expect when it comes to the question of who will be punished. He expects that he will not be punished just because, as we would put it, he was grabbed by a hostage-taker. Each one of the Contacti has the same pattern of anticipation of praise and blame conditional upon action as someone with our concept of personal identity would have.

Finally, the concept Cp as used by the Contacti is not such that the Contacti expect individuals satisfying the concept to typically have the capacity for remembering any recent experience they had. Knowing what we would know when we know that while masked one is to be touched by someone having visual experiences, the Contacti do not expect that after contact is broken and one's mask is taken off, one will remember the visual experiences in question. Each of the Contacti has the same pattern of anticipation of experiences and memories of those experiences as someone with our concept of personal identity would have.

In general, the concept of *being the same Cp* as used by the Contacti does not seem to be their concept of personal identity merely *because* they use that concept neither to guide their future-oriented and retrospective concerns, nor to shape their expectations about the relationship between earlier action and later desert of praise and blame, nor to focus their patterns of anticipation of experiences and memories of those experiences. The concept which the Contacti actually employ in this way is one about which they, as Hirsch presents them, are respectfully silent. It is the concept they could introduce a term to express by saying:

Let "is the same Pc as" denote the relation which holds between any A, considered at t, and B, considered at t', is either

(i) A is not at t in exclusive contact with anyone, nor is B at t', and A is the same Cp as B.

(ii) $\exists X \exists Y$ (A is at t exclusively in contact with X, and B is at t' exclusively in contact with Y, and X is the same Cp as Y).

(iii) A is not at t in exclusive contact with anyone but ∃Y (B is at
t in exclusive contact with Y, and A is the same Cp as Y).
(iv) B is not at t in exclusive contact with anyone but ∃X (A is at
t in exclusive contact with X, and X is the same Cp as B).

As a few elementary manipulations using Cp show, the Contacti
term "is the same Pc as" expresses *our* concept of personal identity. As
Hirsch describes the Contacti, they may have an alternative concept,
but they do not have an alternative concept of personal identity.

Contrast this criticism of Hirsch's claims about the Contacti with
an absolutist and ethnocentric critcism which I do not endorse. Someone might have said that when members of the human species are in
question, there is a distinguished kind—human persons—with which to
restrict the relation of absolute identity so as to get the distinguished
relation of (human) personal identity. The resultant relation is supposed
to be distinguished in the sense that in virtue of its *independent* features
it alone justifies the response on the part of members of our biological
species of organizing in terms of it what I will call the *person-directed
attitudes*, that is, (i) one's future-oriented and retrospective concerns for
oneself and others; (ii) one's expectations about experiences and memories of those experiences; (iii) one's expectations about the relations
between action and desert. That is the absolutist part. (The absolutist is
allowed enough relativism to make his view plausible—he does not
require that Martians must also apply the concept of human personal
identity to themselves.) The ethnocentric part is that *we* have got onto
the distinguished relation for members of our species. The distinguished
relation happens to be the relation we use in organizing our person-
directed concerns and expectations. So Hirsch's Contacti either employ
our concept of personal identity, that is, the concept that determines the
distinguished relation, or do not have a concept of personal identity.
Our concept of personal identity is *the* concept of personal identity (for
members of our biological species). There just cannot be truly alternative concepts of personal identity for members of our species.

The absolutist and ethnocentric response runs foul of a consequence of the fact that personal identity can sometimes be an indeterminate matter. Any plausible candidate relation for personal identity
will have certain sorts of physical and/or psychological continuities as
necessary conditions of its holding. Such continuities admit of very fine-
grained degrees, and it is implausible to suppose that questions about
whether people survive are so sensitive as to have determinate Yes or
No answers at every point throughout the full range of cases in which
physical and psychological continuities are varied from case to case by

minute amounts.[11] Here, as elsewhere, a useful model for such indeterminacies is to treat them as semantic indeterminacies.[12] So if a statement like "Sam survived vicissitude V" is neither determinately true nor determinately false, even though vicissitude V is fully specified, the explanation will be in terms of semantic features of the name 'Sam'.

The name 'Sam', we may suppose, was introduced to denote something which was essentially a person. And perhaps the term 'person' itself admits of indeterminate cases. Abstracting from the problems introduced by higher-order indeterminacy,[13] certain individuals are in the extension of 'person', certain individuals are in its antiextension (= the extension of 'nonperson'), and certain individuals are in neither. So we suppose that there are a number of roughly but not exactly coincident individuals which were there at Sam's dubbing and which exist throughout and after V. Some of these individuals are in neither the extension nor the antiextension of 'person', that is, it is not a determinate matter whether or not these individuals are persons. Some of these individuals along with some of those in the extension of 'person' were salient at the time and place where the name 'Sam' was introduced to denote a particular person. Since the name 'Sam' was introduced to denote a particular person salient on that occasion, it will not be a determinate matter as to which one of these individuals is Sam. On some of the allowable ways of making 'Sam' precise, that is, ways of taking 'Sam' to denote some then salient individual which is not definitely not a person, the sentence "Sam is identical with someone which exists throughout and after V" will come out true. On other allowable ways of making 'Sam' precise it will come out false.

Suppose that something like this is the correct or a correct account, so that we end up explaining the indeterminacy associated with a statement like 'Sam survived vicissitude V' in terms of the vagueness of our terms 'Sam' and 'person'. Then, as against the absolutist, it looks as though we had better allow for the possiblity that other communities or our own community at a later stage would still have a concept of a person even if they moved away from our concept of a person by incorporating some acceptable precisifications into either the extension or the antiextension of their term 'person'. For how could something be an acceptable precisification of the term 'person' and be such that adopting it would make it the case that the concept that then came to be associated with the term 'person' was no longer a person concept?

I can think of only two answers to this, answers which depend on problems we can set aside. First, someone might maintain that if something is to be a person-concept (for members of our species), it has to be standardly observationally grounded in the sense that in standard cases we make correct judgments of personal identity simply by looking and so in an easy and offhand way which does not pretend to detect or respect minute differences in degrees of physical or psychological continuity.[14] But then we can generate a familiar sorites structure by exploiting the fact that such a concept of personal identity is not sensitive to such minute differences. It will be plausible to describe the structure as leading by steps of such minute differences from determinate cases of personal identity through indeterminate cases to cases where personal identity determinately fails to hold. So we have a principled reason to suppose that any concept of personal identity, the use of which can be observationally grounded in this way, will admit of some indeterminate cases. And it may be plausible to suppose that any concept of personal identity suitable for the members of our species will be observationally grounded, so that we have a principled reason to suppose that any such concept of personal identity will admit of indeterminacies. If this is so, the worry can be met by considering candidates for alternative concepts of personal identity—only those that can be observationally grounded—which therefore have an associated range of indeterminate cases.

Second, someone might maintain that a precisification of 'person' with respect to a formerly indeterminate case might be adopted by the members of a community without being internalized by them, that is, without them coming to organize their person-directed concerns and expectations in terms of the (relation determined by the) concept which incorporates the stipulation. A decent worry indeed; precisifications can remain mere stipulations if there are no associated changes in attitude. So consider as candidates for alternative person-concepts only those which could organize the person-directed concerns and expectations of the members of the communities which use them.

With these caveats, given indeterminacy, there will be a range of related concepts which deserve to be called concepts of a person usable by the members of our species, and there will be a range of related concepts of personal identity (= identity restricted to persons). The relation between some of these concepts of personal identity may be given thus: if P is our concept of personal identity, then person concepts P1, P2, P3. . . are all such that whatever pairs are in the antiextension of P are in the antiextensions of each of the Pi, and whatever pairs are in the extension of P are in the extensions of each of the Pi, and the Pis differ over just which are the indeterminate cases.

If this is accepted, it seems that we can make good sense of a certain sort of relativism about personal identity. Suppose that the sentence "Sam survives vicissitude V" is indeterminate in English. Then there will be interpreted languages Lj and Lm with concepts of personal identity Pj and Pm respectively such that 'Sam survives V' is determinately true in Lj and determinately false in Lm. Supposing that they use Pj and Pm respectively to organize their concerns and expectations, neither the speaker of Lj nor the speakers of Lm will be employing a defective concept of personal identity.

Now suppose that you are Sam and you face a choice between being exposed to the particular vicissitude V and a slightly less harrowing experience V'. V and V' are not significantly different in the degree of mental continuity which they secure. Choosing V results in great benefits for you if you survive. But, unfortunately, you are a speaker of Lm and not of Lj. More, the Lm concept of personal identity, Pm, is the one you have internalized: it is the one which organizes your concerns and expectations. Since the sentence 'Sam will survive V' is false in Lm, and Pm is your concept of personal identity, you conclude that you will not survive V and that therefore you are unable to secure the great benefits that result from surviving V.

However, imagine your counterpart, Skam, in the community of Lj speakers. He considers the sentence 'Skam will survive V'. He rightly takes it to be true in Lj. Moreover, since Pj is the concept which organizes his concerns and expectations, he concludes that he will survive V and is, therefore, able to secure the great benefits that result.

Now we can state the *prima facie* argument from relativism to the conclusion that personal identity is at most a derivative justifier. Simply by giving up an absolutist view of personal identity in a way that seemed forced on us by the recognition that personal identity could sometimes be an indeterminate matter, we can make it seem implausible that personal identity is a nonderivative justifier. For if personal identity is a nonderivative justifier, Sam has a strong *prima facie* reason to shun V, whereas someone exactly like Sam in all respects compatible with his internalizing an ever so slightly different concept of personal identity has no reason to shun V. But this looks very strange. Surely all that is really going on is that Sam and Skam have simply internalized different stipulations about what previously counted as indeterminate cases. If Sam is apprised of all this, he will see Skam as both blamelessly different from him and without any reason to shun V. But then, so the argument goes, Sam would be right to doubt that *he* has reason to shun V. The fact that he has simply internalized a different stipulation about a case that was previously an indeterminate matter ought to seem to Sam too flimsy to provide a reason to shun V. He should forget what he thinks about V and go ahead.

If that is so, we have admitted that the facts of personal identity and in particular a fact like *V will involve death* is not a justifier in such cases. And if such facts are not justifiers or sources or reasons to prefer certain things and act in certain ways in such cases but are justifiers in most other cases, then it is going to be plausible to suggest that the differences that make the facts of personal identity justifiers in most cases have to do with the holding of the strong psychological and physical connections that are the normal concomitants over the short term of personal identity. In most cases a difference in respect of personal identity carries with it an important difference at the level of physical and psychological connections. So when personal identity is a justifier, a source of reasons to prefer and act, it is a derivative justifier. It justifies in virtue of its usual concomitants.

It is important that the advocate of this argument from relativism can allow that personal identity is not *in general* a matter of conventional fiat and can also allow that the constraints on the identity of human persons—for example, that human persons are in their natural condition constituted by living human bodies—make the facts of personal identity more stable and less a projection of context-dependent interests than the facts about the identity of artifacts.

That these differences should be recognized is the upshot of a fuller study of our use of the concepts of personal identity and of artifact identity than I can give here. But critical reflection on certain cases suggests the differences in question. For example, whether the original gun of Little Caesar is counted, and properly counted, the *same gun* as the gun assembled much later from parts scattered around his hideaway or is rather the same gun as the gun in his pocket which has been produced by continuous replacement of those parts may depend upon such extrinsic matters as the laws of evidence in the state in which Little Caesar is tried. We can anticipate the gun which was later assembled from the scattered parts being presented as exhibit A—according to the ballistics reports the very gun which Little Caesar used to plug his rivals. (Maybe the murder weapon has to be produced to secure a conviction for a capital offense.)

The example of Little Caesar's gun is just a variant on the case of the Ship of Theseus. The ship leaves port, it sails across the sea, the planks which make it up are gradually replaced, so that it arrives at its destination made up of planks none of which made it up when it left port. Of course, this way of describing the situation embodies the natural intuition that despite the slow replacement of planks the ship that left port arrived at its destination. This intuition can be thrown into doubt by filling out the example by supposing that as the original planks were discarded, they were collected one by one and used to assemble a ship exactly like the Ship of Theseus as it was when it left port. Is the ship consisting of the original planks the original ship? Some claim so, but the dominant intuition here is that still the ship spatiotemporally continuous with the Ship of Theseus is the Ship of Theseus, despite the fact that it is the one with none of the original planks. After all, loss and replacement of planks is the usual thing in the normal life of such a ship.

Here the important thing to notice is that "the normal life of such a ship" can plausibly be glossed as something like "the normal purposes to which we put such ships," and we can envisage a context in which our reasons for being interested in ships are different, and as a result our intuitions about identity are different. Imagine that the Ship of Theseus had become a prized exhibit. A curator in the museum in which it is stored covets the ship. He forms a plan to steal it. Every evening, when he is the last to leave, he replaces one plank in the ship with a replica he has made at home. In this way he gradually acquires all the original planks which he then puts together into a ship of the same form as the Ship of Theseus. Surely he could be prosecuted for *stealing* the Ship of Theseus and so wrongfully having it in *his* possession. This implies that the Ship of Theseus is the ship the curator put together in his backyard. Yet this consequence is at odds with the original intuition that the ship spatiotemporally continuous with the Ship of Theseus is the Ship of Theseus. As in the case of Little Caesar's gun, practical and temporary interests, and not just the intrinsic features of the processes involving the artifact, determine which judgment of cross-time identity is reasonable.

The situation with living things and humans in particular is somewhat different. There is a sense of "the life of a human being" relevant to our tracing each other which is not sensitive to the temporary and external purposes to which we put ourselves and others. A dog can be used as a weapon, a drunk as a doorstop, a ravenous rat as an instrument of torture. Yet, we would still trace these individuals in terms of continuous animal life, so that such extrinsic purposes do not to the same extent impact upon our tracing the individuals in question. Moreover, if there is any truth in the relativism to be advanced here, a human being's self-conception is sometimes relevant to the question of what kind of thing we have for the purposes of identification and reidentification. So something more than how *we* collectively think of the individual in question dominates in the case of people.

It is an advantage, then, that in order to persuade ourselves of the argument from relativism, we need not assume that personal identity and artifact identity are on all fours. We need only assume that personal identity is, in some cases, an indeterminate matter; that our concept of personal identity is, so to speak, subject to conventional determination at the edges.

Finally, we need not assume that the mere conventional fiat which involves legislating about an indeterminate case of personal identity *itself* makes it true that the case is one in which personal identity determinately holds. Instead, there is our old concept p which determines a relation Rp which neither determinately holds nor determinately fails to hold in the case in question. And there is the almost exactly similar concept P′ which determines a relation Rp′ which determinately holds in the case in question. The mere stipulation that this case and its ilk should be taken as cases of survival just amounts to suggesting that we adopt P′ as our concept of personal identity. It does not in itself make P′ our concept of personal identity. For that to come about, we must come to care about the relation Rp′ *as* personal identity, that is, we must come to employ it in organizing our person-directed concerns and expectations.

What does that actually involve? Suppose we think of a subject's person-directed concerns and expectations as those attitudes directed at what the subject takes to be the reflective subjects of mental life ("persons" in the broadest sense) with which he is familiar. Maintaining many of these attitudes will depend upon accepting substantive judgments of personal identity and difference, judgments employing a quite specific concept of personal identity. The relation determined by that concept is then said to organize the subject's person-directed concerns and expectations. As theorists employing *this* notion of a relation's organizing a subject's person-directed concerns and expectations, we need not assume that the subject himself uses or can give criteria or purely descriptive necessary and sufficient conditions for the holding of the relation which organizes his person-directed concerns and expectations. Some of the conditions of correctness for the use of a phrase like 'is the same human person as' may be causal-historical or social and may turn up yet undiscovered features of the nature of things. That is to say that we need not oppose whatever is true in the doctrine that 'human person' is or is "akin to" a natural kind term. The import of relativism is that there may be several more or less natural kinds available to associate with a term like 'human person'. Then our patterns of person-directed concern and expectation will be crucial.

2. A Concrete Alternative?

In order properly to elaborate and evaluate the argument from relativism to the claim that personal identity is at most a derivative justifier, we had better focus on a concrete example of the kind of clash of alternative conceptions of personal identity which we have so far discussed only in schematic terms.

Consider Teletransportation, a process by which a machine at one point scans one's brain and body and sends the information gathered to a receiving point, where a cell by cell duplicate is immediately produced while one's original brain and body is immediately destroyed.[15] Some philosophers believe that relative to our present concept of personal identity, it is indeterminate whether one would survive Teletransportation and walk out of the receiving station with a new but exactly similar brain and body. Some do not believe this.[16] However, surely it could have turned out that we found that our concept of personal identity was one which did count Teletransportation an indeterminate case. If it is epistemically possible that our concept be a concept of personal identity and have Teletransportation as an indeterminate case, then it seems that there is nothing incoherent in the idea of there being *some* concept of personal identity which counts Teletransportation as an indeterminate case. So we can imagine a community employing such a concept of personal identity.[17]

Given that, we can imagine such a community and two resultant communitites, the Human Beings and the Teletransporters, who come to adopt and internalize different stipulations about Teletransportation. According to the Human Beings one determinately does not survive Teletransportation. It is a means of suicide and replacement by a dupli- cate. The Teletransporters, on the other hand, regard Teletransportation as a means of very fast travel and have discovered how to adjust the mechanism at the receiving end, so that the near-duplicate body pro- duced is free of the illnesses of the body originally scanned. Thus, Teletransporters have what looks to them like superfast travel and prac- tical freedom from disease. Moreover, they have no false views about the workings of the Teletransporter. They do not suppose that it trans- fers souls from one place to another. The Teletransporters simply take themselves to survive Teletransportation.

Confronted with the Teletransporters, the Human Beings initially regard them as making a deep mistake. At first it seems to the Human Beings that the Teletransporters blame and punish people distinct from those who perpetrate crimes, are systematically deluded about just *who* had the experiences they seem to remember, and are prepared to com- mit suicide and even kill their own children by putting them into the machine. Though fully realizing that the Teletranaporters do not see things in this way, the Human Beings initially take this to be testimony to the depth of the Teletransporter's delusions.

Gradually dissent breaks out among the Human Beings as to whether the Teletransporters are making a deep mistake. Certain absolutists maintain that there is a distinguished relation—being the same human being—which in virtue of its independent features demands and justifies the response, on the part of each enculturated human animal, of organizing his or her person-directed concerns and expectations in terms of that relation. The absolutists do not make many converts, in part because the relation of being the same human being seems already gerrymandered in a way that is responsive to the core concerns and expectations of Human Beings. Human Beings, unlike the human animals which typically constitute them, can be reduced to the condition of mere brains and can survive as brains kept alive in a vat or as a result of the operations of the cardiovascular system of a beheaded tiger. While the lives of human animals may be natural joints, the lives of Human Beings need not be so natural. So if anything distinguishes the relation of being the same human being, it is not the solitary work of nature.

What most badly damages the absolutist cause is the historical discovery that the Teletransporters and the Human Beings had simply internalized different stipulations about Teletransportation, stipulations which from the point of view of the ur-community and its concept of personal identity were equally good ways of going—equally acceptable precisifications. The Human Beings then find it hard to believe that the accidents of conceptual history happened decisively to favor only them. And when they try, on the assumption that they are the victims of conceptual history and have an erroneous concept of personal identity, they are at a loss as to how to discover what that error is. But then they see that the Teletransporters are in a parallel situation—plausibly taken as neither correct by absolutist standards nor incorrect by weaker standards. So certain relativists urge that the Teletransporters are just blamelessly different. Instead of organizing their person-directed concerns and expectations in terms of the relation of being the same human being, the Teletransporters do it in terms of the more inclusive relation of being the same series-human being,[18] where a *series-human being* is an individual which has as its history the history of a series which begins with a human being and which is such that any successive member is generated from its predecessor by Teletransportation. According to the relativist the Teletransporters are no less justified in organizing the core of their concerns and expectations in terms of the relation of being the same series-human being. For since there is no distingushed relation served up by nature which demands and justifies the relevant responses on the part of any enculturated human animal, there is no obstacle to laying down conditions on a community's being correct about personal identity which are mostly internal. Tentatively accepting the standpoint of the relativists, we could take those conditions to be the following:

(1) The members of a given community C would be correct to take identity restricted to Ks to be the relation of personal identity for them *iff*

    (i) K is a more or less natural person-kind, that is, a more or less natural kind whose nondefective members never exist without the capacity for reflective mental life

and

    (ii) It is standard among the members of C to organize their person-directed concerns and expectations in terms of identity restricted to Ks.

This characterization of when a community is correct in taking some relation to be personal identity for them makes no mention of a distinguished relation which, independently of their concerns and expectations, deserves to be taken as a personal identity. Clause (i) simply ensures that the members of a given community could not be correct in taking personal identity for them to be absolute identity restricted to a kind whose instances have periods when they are ants, stars, trees, gases, rivers, or any other type of thing without the capacity for reflective mental life. Such a community might have false beliefs to the effect that such things were persons, that is, loci of reflective mental life. Or they might not. If not, and if they could manage to organize their person-directed concerns and expectations in terms of such an identity relation, then we can either say that they employ, not a concept of personal identity, but something more inclusive, or that any minimal restriction of their concept to some more or less natural person-kind would be a correct concept of personal identity for them to have.

Such relativism as is embodied in (1) has an important consequence. If it is a fact that identity restricted to Ks is the relation of personal identity for the members of C, then personal identity is at most a dependent justifier of the responses of the members of C. Putting clause (i) to one side, what makes it the case that this relation is personal identity for the members of C, and hence a relation which justifies a myriad of concerns and expectations, is just that the members of C standardly take it to be such. Here, as elsewhere, shared and standardized responses, in Hume's terms, "raise in a manner a new creation,"[19] that is, provide for the use of a concept which, though ethnocentric and relational, is, nevertheless, descriptive of the way things are. Compare the suggestion that we might understand "X is red for humans" as having as its truth condition that X would produce a particular type of experience in visually standard human beings under standard viewing conditions (where we as we actually are set the standards[20].) Since we are humans, and we mostly only talk to humans, we can drop the relativization and say that having the particular type of experience in the presence of red things and judging them red as a result is making the correct or justified response to their redness. Moreover, although the concept of being red for humans is anthropocentric and relational, the concept may well be descriptive of an intrinsic feature of red things—a feature which is constituted by their surface texture. Here we have a concept apt for describing the "new creation," an ethnocentric and relational concept, which nonetheless can be descriptive of intrinsic features of things and which can be used in the justification of the basic responses constitutive of the concept. Similarly, the concept of being the relation of personal identity for the members of C allows us to understand Cs as having a way of justifying their responses in terms of the holding of a relation which may be constituted by certain continuities, a relation which is for them personal identity. Of course, here, as with any relativistic account of justification, justifying one's basic responses can amount to no more than showing to those whom one can expect to (come to) share one's basic responses that those responses are attuned to the corresponding features of the "new creation," that is, the features of things characterizable in terms of such responses understood as standard among the member's of one's community. Here we have no special feature of relativism about *personal identity*. Any relativism which uses the notion of the "new creation" can do no more than count features of that new creation as *dependent* justifiers.

Having developed the relativistic account of personal identity vis-à-vis the Teletransporters, we can return to our fundamental question: If personal identity is at most a dependent justifier, how can it be a nonderivative justifier? So long as the worry behind the question is left unelaborated, it seems to me sufficient to answer it as follows. We can say that a dependent justifier J serves to nonderivatively justify responses S1, S2 . . . among the members of C just in case standard members of C, even under conditions of ideal deliberation,[21] would appeal to J to justify these responses and would not do this only because there were other justifiers of S1, S2 . . . which had J as their manifestation, cause, or necessary condition. Now we need simply point out that standard Human Beings, even under conditions of ideal deliberation, would take the relation of being the same human being to justify their responses of organizing their concerns and expectations in terms of that relation, and that they would not do this only because they believed that this relation was associated with other justifiers of this response. *Mutatis mutandis* for the Teletransporters—that is how dependent justifiers can be nonetheless nonderivative justifiers.

However, this reply, though formally correct, can seem not to address the real worry behind our fundamental question, a worry which can take a general or a particular form. In its general form the worry is related to what Stanley Cavell calls, "vertigo," the feeling that if we only have recourse to dependent justifiers, the firm ground which we took to support our responses will seem to have melted into thin air. The therapy for this general worry lies outside the scope of the present paper. If there is a treatment available, it may lie in showing that nothing could be an *in*dependent justifier of our orectic responses, so that we have no right to see our actual situation as one which falls short of providing justifiers that could in principle have been provided. Someone who believes that the idea of God is incoherent ought to find it difficult to see the world under the aspect of Deus Absconditus.

The particular worry remains and may be put this way. Suppose that among the Human Beings the relation of being the same human being satisfies the above condition on nonderivative justifiers and so is a nonderivative as well as a dependent justifier. Would it remain a nonderivative justifier among the Human Beings when they were fully converted to relativism and so fully apprised of the fact that it was only a dependent justifier? Would it, for example, provide any Human Being apprised of this fact with a consideration which would lead him reasonably to shun Teletransportation whether it took place before or after being recultured as a Teletransporter?

In order to approach this question, consider a representative Human Being persuaded of relativism about personal identity and confronted with a cultural waif yet to have its person-directed concerns and expectations organized in terms of any very determinate relation. Our representative and relativistic Human Being can reasonably conclude that the waif ought to be relevantly encultured in the style of the Teletransporters and so acquire their concept of personal identity. After all, given relativism, the Teletransporters have a concept of personal identity which allows them access to things everyone can see as great goods, that is, superfast travel and practical freedom from disease. But having had that thought about the waif, our Human Being ought to be susceptible to a regret that he himself was not originally encultured as a Teletransporter, thereby taking the attitude toward his earlier unformed self that is the counterpart of the attitude which he takes toward the waif. Having had the regret and being offered the means to produce something like the situation he regretted did not obtain, namely, the means for reculturation as a Teletransporter, it seems that only inertia and not reason would lead him to hesitate. For he admits that there is reason to get access to superfast travel and practical freedom from disease. And by his own relativistic lights he sees a means—reculturation—by which *he* and not some surrogate or descendant can have such access. After all, he has ordinary views about the survivability of radical conversions and so believes *he* will survive reculturation. Moreover, on account of his relativism about personal identity he believes that *having* survived reculturation and so having become properly construable as a Teletransporter, he will then survive Teletransportation. So our Human Being's concern for the holding of personal identity at no stage gives him any reason to turn down reculturation and then Teletransportation. (For those who balk at the claims of this paragraph, especially at the transition from consideration of the waif, to regret, and then to reculturation and Teletransportation, the last section of this paper is the place to look for reassurance.)

However, as a last step, suppose that the Teletransporters believe in baptisms under fire. They only offer reculturation by means of an initial Teletransportation which produces as near a duplicate human body as is compatible with its having the Teletransporters' concept of personal identity. Here the only difference is that reculturation and Teletransportation are more or less simultaneous. But how can that mere difference in timing be significant enough to provide a reason or justification, even a *prima facie* reason or justification, to turn down the Teletransporters' offer? And as indicated in section 1, if no such reason or justification is present in this purified case, then personal identity is likely not to be a nonderivative justifier.

Having thus elaborated the argument from relativism against taking personal identity to be a nonderivative justifier, I think that one can see that this last and crucial step fails in the same way in which the argument from insignificant differences fails. What is an insignificant difference at the level of timing makes for a crucial difference at the level of personal identity. Only if Teletransportation follows reculturation can our Human Being correctly see the whole process as one which provides *him* with access to superfast travel and practical freedom from disease. For only then can he properly conclude that having survived reculturation, he will then survive Teletransportation.

A parallel point applies to the more schematic claim of section 1, namely, that a mere difference in respect of which stipulation Sam has internalized cannot provide Sam with a reason for turning down Teletransportation. Given relativism, such a difference at the level of internalized stipulations makes a crucial difference in what the relevant facts of personal identity for Sam are.

3. Is Refiguring One's Self-Conception Rational?

These considerations suggest that there is no good argument from relativism against taking personal identity to be a nonderivative justifier. (That is not to say that the reasons that the facts of personal identity provide are not overrideable, only that they provide reasons which are nonderivative.) However, some will think that I have missed a prior objection to the argument from relativism that went by way of leading our representative Human Being through consideration of the waif and regret about himself to conversion to the way of the Teletransporters. The prior objection is that it is simply not correct for our representative Human Being to think that having survived reculturation, he will *then* survive Teletransportation. The objection is that since at the time at which he is deliberating his concept of personal identity is the concept of being the same human being, he ought to employ *that* concept in thinking about and evaluating all possible future situations, even possible future situations which involve his adopting a different concept of personal identity. According to the objector this is a general point about concept use with respect to possible situations. We must always clearly distinguish the concepts we presently use to describe, think about, and evaluate the situation from the concepts used *in* the situation. Thus it is not correct to say that if we come to mean by "green" what we now mean by "blue," then the concept green would apply to the sky, so that then the sky would be green. The sentence "The concept green applies to the sky" would *then* be taken by us as true, but nevertheless from our present perspective we must say that the concept green does not apply to the sky. Similarly, our representative Human Being at the time of considering the upcoming reculturation and Teletransportation should consistently employ his present concept of personal identity. From his present perspective he would not survive Teletransportation even if he were recultured first. Reculturation would simply give him false views about what he could survive. So he has no reason to refigure his pattern of concerns and expectations, and hence his concept of personal identity. Teletransportation can never provide benefits for *him*.

It is important for my purposes that this objection can be got around since the moral I wish to draw from relativism is that we are all in a situation in some ways parallel to our representative Human Being.

We may all have reason to refigure our concerns and expectations.

I think there is a way of respecting the point about concepts which is consonant with relativism and these revisionary aspirations. We must first see what form of relativism about the self is consistent with plausible principles.

A plausible principle drawn from the theory of sortals is that each individual is classifiably under one and only one substance sortal.[22] A substance sortal is a term for a sort or kind of thing, a term which is *the substance sortal for a given individual*, just in case it is the most specific kind of term such that necessarily there is no time at which the individual exists without satisfying it at that time. Thus 'person or dog' is not a substance sortal for persons, since there is at least the more specific sortal 'person'. And 'child' is not a substance sortal for individual Human Beings; it is a mere phase sortal which applies to a Human Being during what need be only a phase of his total existence. (Those who have a generous view of what individuals there are may recognize essential children, tragically short-lived individuals for which 'child' is a substance sortal. Here is a strange but compelling skepticism to which I am recurrently prone: How do I know I am not an essential child or an essential young man or an essential inhabitant of the year 1989? If my self- and other-directed concerns and expectations do not largely settle this, what does?)

The plausiblity of the plausible principle—that each individual is classifiable under a single substance sortal—lies in the fact that if we have a definite individual in mind, then there had better be specific constraints on what states it can be in and so on what changes it can survive. The full characterization of an individual's substance sortal just incorporates these specific constraints. Now persons, by reflecting on what they are, can form a conception of their substance sort or kind and hence of what changes they can survive. Applying the plausible principle to the case of persons, a minimal condition on the correctness of such self-conceptions is provided by

> *Constancy*: Necessarily, at any time X has at that time a correct conception of what he could survive iff at that time X takes himself to be able to survive all and only what a K could survive, and K is the substance kind for X.

Constancy, though a minimal condition, makes trouble for what we might call Simple (or Simpleminded) Relativism.

> *Simple Relativism*: Necessarily, at any time X is at that time correct to think of himself as able to survive all and only

what a K would survive iff K is a person kind and at that
time identity restricted to Ks is the relation which organizes
X's person-directed concerns and expectations.

Simple Relativism is inadequate in that it says nothing about the
degenerate or undeveloped, who lack person-directed concerns and expectations. However, the main problem with it survives even when such
cases are taken care of. For surely,

> *Refiguration*: It is possible for some person to refigure the relation
> which organizes his concerns and expectations, so that at two
> or more distinct times during his life distinct person-kind
> restrictions on identity play the organizing role.

A contradiction is now derivable. From Constancy and Simple
Relativism we get

> Necessarily, at any time K is a person kind and at that time
> identity restricted to Ks is the relation which organizes X's
> person-directed concerns and expectations iff at that time X
> takes himself to be able to survive all and only what
> a K could survive, and K is the substance kind for X.

But then, given that an individual cannot be properly classified under
more than one substance kind, we get

> It is not possible for any person X to be such that at two or more
> distinct times during his life distinct person kind restrictions
> on identity play the organizing role,

which contradicts Refiguration. (For those who want no truck with
modality, a contradication is derivable from the unmodalized variants of
Constancy and Simple Relativism plus the assumption that a particular
individual does refigure the relations of personal identity which organizes his concerns and expectations.) The blame for the contradiction is
properly put on Simple Relativism, which is clearly mistaken in not
taking account of what happens when an individual refigures the particular relation of personal identity which organizes his concerns and
expectations. What we need instead is

> *Modified Relativism*: Necessarily and at any time X is at that time
> correct to think that *he can survive all and only what a K can
> survive so long as he does not go on to refigure his concerns
> and expectations in terms of identity restricted to a distinct
> person-kind K'* iff K is a person kind and at that time identity
> restricted to Ks organizes his concerns and expectations.

Modified Relativism captures but appropriately limits the basic relativistic idea that the conditions for one's survival depend upon one's (person-directed) concerns and expectations. What one is at some time correct to think one can survive is not only determined by what relation *then* organizes one's concerns and expectations but is also determined by the relations that *will* come to organize them. Modified Relativism does not contradict plausible principles, but it also does not tell us what unique substance kind human persons, being capable of refiguration, fall under. Given the possibility of reculturation either way, we can not respect anything in the basic relativistic idea if we count either Human Being or Series Human Being as substance kinds for human persons. For if the basic relativistic idea is that what a person considered at a time can survive depends upon his concerns and expectations at that time, then when considering someone who has refigured his core concerns and expectations, it will seem arbitrary for the relativist to privilege this person's earlier concerns and expectations and say that they alone determine what he can survive, so that, for example, a Human Being even after reculturation as a Teletransporter remains able to survive all and only what a Human Being can survive. There should be a certain symmetry here. But then how *is* the relativist to describe such a change and give an account of the status of the kinds Human Being and Series Human Being?

The relativist should say that kinds like Human Being and Series Human Being are, in fact, *cryptophase kinds*, associated with phases which persons can live through the given, but only given, special circumstances that is refiguration. The concepts of the relations of identity restricted to these kinds are superior to the concept of *being the same Cp*, as used by the Contacti. For these concepts turned out to satisfy the initial conditions for being correct concepts of personal identity for the Human Beings and the Teletransporters respectively. Nonetheless—and this is the crucial point—although these concepts were correct concepts of personal identity modulo the restriction that no refiguration takes place, they were strictly defective. For they were concepts of identity restricted to (unobvious) phase kinds. The situation is parallel to one in which certain Human Beings mistake their substance kind as the kind Human Child, because, due to a universal disease, they never survive childhood.

So what according to Modified Relativism is the *substance* sortal under which the Teletransporters and the Human Beings fall? We could say simple 'person' where something is a person just in case in its developed and undegenerated condition it has the capability for reflective mental life. But given Modified Relativism, a more specific characterization is in the offering. This characterization incorporates the consistent form of the basic relativistic idea, that what *cryptophase* kind we fall under at a time is a matter of our person-directed concerns and expectations at that time. The characterization is 'Protean Person' where this is explained in two steps.

First, we say that a person X is at t a member of a cryptophase kind K if and only if

> (A) K is a more or less natural person kind, that is, only individuals which in their normal developed condition would be subjects of reflective mental life are its instances.
> and
> (B) either
>> (i) (normal developed persons) At t identity restricted to Ks is the relation which organizes X's person-directed concerns and expectations.
>
> or
>
>> (ii) (degenerated persons) At t no relation organizes X's person-directed concerns and expectations, but at the nearest time before t when some relation did, it was identity restricted to Ks.
>
> or
>
>> (iii) (undeveloped persons) At t X is yet to develop person-directed concerns and expectations, but he or she is naturally related to Ks in such a way that if things were to go normally, identity restricted to Ks would organize X's person-directed concerns and expectations.

Then we say

> X is a Protean Person just in case necessarily for any event e X is capable of surviving e if and only if
> (C) e is not a change at odds with X's cryptophase kind at the time of e; that is, if at the outset of e X is of cryptophase kind K, then e is an event which Ks can survive.

A refinement is necessary. To avoid intransitivities we need to understand (C) as only applying to events during which there is no refiguration, that is, no process of a type which can produce a change in an individual's crytophase kind. For suppose a complex event e_0 involves both the event, e_1, of reculturating a Human Being as a Teletransporter and the event, e_2, of Teletransporting the result. Applying (C) to e_0, we get the result the original Protean person could not and so does not survive e_0. However, applying (C) to e_1 and e_2 separately, we get the result that the original Protean person could survive e_1 and then survive e_2—intuitively the correct result for Protean persons. Here is the required refinement. Taking (c) to apply to events during which there is no refiguration, we then need to deal with two other types of events, namely, single refiguration, which replace identity restricted to one kind K with identity restricted to another kind K* as the organizing relation, and events occurring during or coincident with single refigurations. (Any complex event can be partitioned into subevents of the three types, and the condtions applied to subevents.) In general, a Protean person X will survive a particular refiguration if X survives the other events coincident with or occurring during it. And we should say that a Protean person X can survive an event e coincident with or occurring during a refiguration r just in case, if r is a refiguration of the type which replaces indentity restricted to Ks by identity restricted to K*s as the organizing relation, then e is an event which both Ks and K*s can survive. This last condition has the result that if a Teletransportation-like process were to produce an individual whose person-directed concerns and expectations were organized in terms of the relation of being the same human being, then that individual would be right to think of himself as not existing before the process.[23]

Relativism thus makes itself consistent with Constancy by recognizing that while it is up to us which cryptophase sortal we fall under at a particular time, there is, nevertheless, something invariant about our natures. We are inevitably and always Protean Persons, that is, we are inevitably and always such that the cryptophase kinds under which we fall at particular times are determined by our concerns and expectations at the respective times. Since Protean Person is a highly general kind whose associated conditions for survival are merely schematic, we need at any particular time to organize our concerns and expectations in terms of a nonschematic crytophase kind. And for practical purposes, that is, purposes for which there is no question of a refiguring in the offing, we can think of ourselves as capable of surviving all and only what would leave us instances of our present crytophase kind. The Human Beings and the Teletransporters were, therefore, right about themselves for all practical purposes. The corrections which Modified Relativism would urge them to make are relevant and useful only when the special circumstances of refiguration, for example, by reculturation, is in the offing.

With all this in place we can make short work of the original objection to the idea that there is no reason for our representative Human Being convinced of relativism to undergo reculturation and then Teletransportation. Once our representative Human Being is converted to

Modified Relativism about personal identity, he should think that his previous conviction that he could not survive any process, however complex, which brought it about that nothing around after the process is the same human being as him was a mistake, the mistake of taking a phase kind to be a substance kind. He should conclude that his substance kind is the kind Protean Person. Then he will be able to trace himself through the reculturation and even through the Teletransportation by thinking, "I will survive reculturation and then I will survive Teletransportation." Both occurrences of "I" in this thought pick out an individual of the substance kind Protean Person, and so an individual which will survive reculturation and then Teletransportation. Our representative Human Being converted to Modified Relativism can think of himself as a Protean Person who at the moment is a member of the crytophase kind Human Being and who would as a result of reculturation become a member of the crytophase kind Series Human Being. The fact that the Teletransporters' way of organizing their person-directed concerns and expectations provides for superfast travel and practical freedom from disease gives our representative Human Being a reason to realize what was always a possibility for him. So it would be with any cryptophase conception which offered the means to a better life overall.

If Modified Relativism is true, then the obvious upshot is that we should all think of ourselves as Protean persons and should seek a crytophase conception of ourselves which fits a life which is best or maximally good. This is an important result both in itself and in the context of the long debate as to whether common sense has made a deep ontological mistake about the nature of personal identity and whether such an insight could in principle justify a change in our pratical attitudes.

On the one hand, Derek Parfit and John Perry have claimed that our deep mistake was to take personal identity to be a nonderivative justifier of our orectic responses, the real justifiers being the underlying physical and psychological continuities.[24] As against this, if we have made a deep mistake about personal identity, it is instead an instance of the general absolutist mistake that something close to common sense is often prone to make. We took personal identity to be an independent justifier of our orectic responses. But perhaps nothing in this world or in any other could be such a thing.

On the other hand, as against John Rawls who suggested that no ontological discovery about personal identity could justify a revision in our practical attitudes,[25] relativism—a consequence of the ontological observation that personal identity is sometimes an indeterminate matter—does have revisionary upshot.

The revisionary upshot is *not* that we should cease to organize our person-directed concerns and expectations in terms of some specific concept of personal identity but instead in terms of the underlying physical and psychological continuities. No, the actual revisionary upshot is in a way radical and much more in need of investigation to get clearer on its requirements. It is that we all now have reason to aim to internalize a socially enactable concept of personal identity which makes available and contributes to a better life. Our representative Human Being was facing the realization of only one of the myriad possibilities for Protean Persons.

4. Epilogue

None of this as yet constitutes a complete argument for the view that our substance kind is the kind Protean Person. All we have so far is an illustration of how this view emerges from the attempt to render consistent in a nonarbitrary way the consequences of the claim that personal identity is at most a dependent justifier. Let me then conclude with a sketch of how the foregoing in conjunction with views about personal identity which I have developed elsewhere might be turned into the required argument.

The paper "Human Beings" addresses the question of how we could settle on an account of the kind of thing we are.[26] Not, it argues, by giving a primary role to "the method of cases"—the method of taking very seriously our reactions to imaginary cases which decompose in various ways the physical and psychological continuities and connections which go together in the ordinary run of cases of persnal identity. For there are many reasons to think that our reactions to such imaginary cases are the products of several potentially distorting influences. In order to sort out which of these influences are *really* distorting, we need recourse to different methodology. So it is proposed that the investigation into the kind of thing we are should be guided by a certain reconstructive aim. There is the humble and ubiquitous practice of reidentifying ourselves and each other over time. Philosophical skepticism aside, this practice is a reliable and mostly unproblematic source of knowledge about particular claims of personal identity. So the first question for a philosophical theory of personal identity to attempt to answer is this: What kind of thing is such that things of that kind can be reliably and unproblematically reidentified over time in *just the way* in which we reliably and unproblematically reidentify ourselves and each other? This constraint not only rules out Cartesian views of the facts of personal identity but can be wielded to support a conception of our-selves as of the kind Human Being, where a human being is typicallly constituted by a human animal but can be reduced to the condition of a mere functioning brain.

However, the limits of this alternative methodology must be frankly recognized. There is nothing about the reconstructive method which will settle the answer to this question: Even if we are of the kind Human Being, is this kind a substance kind or a crytophase kind? After all, it could have been the case that due to a universal disease human beings always died in adolescence. Applying the alternative reconstructive method from within such a situation we would get the (correct) result that the victims of the universal disease are of the kind Pre-Adult Human Being. Although they certainly are of this kind, what is left open by the reconstructive method is whether this kind is a substance kind or a crytophase kind. So also the corresponding question is left open in the case of ourselves, the Human Beings.

Given a reasonable skepticism about the probative force of appeals to imaginary cases in order to answer this question, where can we look for an answer? We can look only, I think, to the deliverance of philosophical reflection on the nature of the facts of personal identity, and in particu-lar on the conceptual dependence or independence of personal identity on our person-directed expectations and concerns. But once we take the view that the facts of personal identity are at most dependent justifi-ers—constituted out of our person-directed expectations and con-cerns—and then attempt to find a consistent and nonarbitrary form of this view, we get a very surprising result. Indeed, the kind Human Being is for us only a phase kind. Our substance kind is a higher-order kind nonarbitrarily defined across such phase kinds as Human Being and Series Human Being. The kind Protean Person is such a higher-order kind. Surprising as this upshot is, it is I think indicative of a general strategy which will allow the relativist consistently to see his own prac-tice merely as one among many, each perhaps equally valid on its own terms. Such relativism makes sense against the background of a higher-order constancy.[27]

Notes

1. For the use of "actually" in getting around such objections to simple subjectivism see Martin Davies and Lloyd Humberstone, "Two Notions of Necessity," *Philosophical Studies* 38 (1980): 1-30.

2. See Saul Kripke, "A Puzzle about Belief," in *Meaning and Use*, ed. A. Margalit (Reidel, 1979).

3. So I here mean neither to deny nor to endorse the surprising view of evidence.

4. See Derek Parfit, "Personal Identity," *Philosophical Review* 80 (1971); "Lewis, Perry and What Matters" in *The Identities of Persons*, ed. A. O. Rorty (University of California Press, 1976); *Reasons and Persons* (Oxford University Press, 1984), part 3, especially sections 90, 95, 102-103. See also John Perry, "The Importance of Being Identical," in *Identities of Persons*, and Sydney Shoemaker, in Sydney Shoemaker and Richard Swineburne, *Personal Identity (Great Debates in Philosophy)* (Basil Blackwell, 1984).

5. Cf. Parfit, *Reasons and Persons*, sections 78 and 79; Perry, "The Importance of Being Identical"; and Shoemaker, *Personal Identity*.

6. Or not worth caring about in the way in which we care about personal identity.

7. Mark Johnston, "Reasons and Reductionism," forthcoming.

8. Eli Hirsch, *The Concept of Identity* (Oxford University Press, 1982), chapter 10.

9. I talk about life histories and not individuals having stages because I believe that taking individuals to be sums of temporal parts has quite strong empirical consequences to which no relatively a priori account of the nature of persistence through change has a right. If there are temporal parts of concrete individuals, then they ought to be either instantaneous or arbitrarily short-lived, and it ought to be that no particular part of a temporal part outlives that part. But then, when things remain the same, for example, when X continues to be P, Q, R, and S over time, it must be that arbitrarily short-lived property instances are replaced by exactly similar and equally short-lived property instances as time passes. The world may be that way or it may not, but no philosophical answer to the question "How is it that a thing survives change?" should give such hostages to empirical fortune. For more on this worry see "Is There a Problem About Persistence?" *Proceedings of the Aristotelian Society, Supplementary Volume*, 1987.

On the other hand, one can talk in general about individuals corresponding to gerrymandered histories only if one has low standards for what counts as an individual. That our standards should be low is, I take it, the upshot of certain paradoxes which Peter Unger and Peter Van Inwagen have attempted to use to show that there are no individuals or (in Van Inwagen's case) no individuals but organisms and simples. See Peter Unger, "I Do Not Exist," in *Perception and Identity*, ed. G. MacDonald (Cornell University Press, 1979) and "Why There Are No People," *Midwest Studies in Philosophy*, vol. 4 (University of Minnesota, 1979), and Peter Van Inwagen, *Material Beings* (Cornell University Press, forthcoming).

10. Hirsch, *The Concept of Identity*, p. 292, pp. 297-299.

11. This point is made most forcefully by Derek Parfit in *Reasons and Persons*, sections 84-86.

12. For this suggestion about indeterminacy see Hartry Field, "Quine and The Correspondence Theory," *Philosophical Review* 83 (1974). As Field notes, this way of thinking about indeterminacy is suggested by David Lewis in "General Semantics," *Synthese* 22 (1970).

13. That is, indeterminacy about what counts as a determinate case of a person or, equivalently, what is in the extension of the term 'person'.

14. For more on this feature of our use of the concept of personal identity and the constraints it places on an adequate account of the concept, see Mark Johnston, "Human Beings," *The Journal of Philosophy* (1987).

15. See Parfit, *Reasons and Persons*, section 75.

16. See Johnston, "Human Beings," *The Journal of Philosophy* 89 (1987): 59-83.

17. Of course, such a community would have to use other concepts which had corresponding indeterminacies. For example, their concept of mind might have to be such that it was indeterminate whether the same mind that was the mind of the person who got into the machine is the mind of the person who gets out at the receiving end. For I am inclined to think that one of the general constraints on a community's concepts Pi and Mi being concepts of persons and minds respectively is that evaluated with respect to them, the sentence "Necessarily a person cannot be outlived by his own mind" comes out true.

In any case, someone who denies that there is a concept of personal identity that counts Teletransportation a vague matter can still take the structural points made by means of this example.

18. Parfit uses the equivalent concept of a series-person in *Reasons and Persons*, section 98. So far as I know, the idea is originally Thomas Nagel's.

19. David Hume, appendix 1 of *The Enquiry Concerning the Principles of Morals*.

20. More generally 'X is red in w for humans' has as its truth-condition that X as it is in w would produce a particular type of experience in visually standard human beings under standard viewing conditions. Of course, this is just an example, and nothing turns upon accepting the details of this account of colors.

21. That is, deliberation which brings to bear some maximally consistent subset of one's relevant beliefs about the matter.

22. On the theory of sortals see Hirsch, *The Concept of Identity*; David Wiggins, *Identity and Spatio-Temporal Continuity* (Basil Blackwell, 1967); and idem, *Sameness and Substance* (Oxford University Press, 1980). See also Neil Tennant, "Continuity and Identity," *Journal of Philosophical Logic* 6 (1977), and Anil Gupta, *The Logic of Common Nouns* (Yale University Press, 1980).

23. Since organizing the core concerns and expectations of an individual is a complex matter involving expectations about experiences and memories, future-directed and retrospective concern, and expectations about the relation between action and susceptibility to subsequent praise and blame, there is the possibility of some but not all of these expectations and concerns being organized in terms of a single relation and the possibility of this happening to different degrees. Though personal identity—identity restricted to some person kind—is not a relation which admits of degrees, whether an individual is properly construed as a member of a particular cryptophase kind K and hence whether he would, without refiguration, survive something which would not leave him a K may be a matter of degree.

Another complication arises in the case of the relation between memory experiences and the experiences remembered. If something is to be a memory of a previous experience, then there must be a causal connection between the experience remembered and the memory. We can imagine a community of people who, perhaps because they take themselves to be reincarnatable souls, take themselves to have, in dreams, memories of experiences of human beings long dead, human beings whose lives they think of as part of their own lives. Though their expectations about memory of previous experiences are organized in terms of the inclusive relation which binds together lives of different human beings from different historical eras, these expectations are mostly false since there is no pattern of causal dependence, at least of anything like the right kind, between experiences of people in earlier eras and contemporary dream experiences.

I am inclined to say that because of their false beliefs the members of this community have not *felicitously* organized their expectations about experiences and subsequent memory around the relevant relation and that strictly such felicitous organization is required for some relation to be the relevant relation of personal identity. I also feel some pull toward the view that the doctrine of reincarnatable souls might for them be a kind of "noble lie" which got them to organize their future-directed concern and their expectation about the relation between action and susceptibility to subsequent praise and blame in terms of the relevant relation. If so, we can regard the relevant relation, inclusive as it is of what we would think of as past lives, as *partially* satisfying the conditions on being the relation of personal identity for them.

24. Parfit, *Reasons and Persons*, and Perry, "The Importance of Being Identical."

25. John Rawls, "On the Independence of Moral Theory," *Proceedings of the American Philosophical Association*, 1975. See also Normal Daniels, "Moral Theory and the Plasticity of Persons," *Monist* 62 (1979), and Susan Wolf, "Self-Interest and Interest in Selves," forthcoming in *Ethics*.

26. Johnston, "Human Beings."

27. In writing this essay I have been helped by conversations with Ronald Dworkin, Gilbert Hartman, David Lewis, Thomas Nagel, Derek Parfit, Gideon Rosen, Michael Smith, Jamie Tappenden, Peter Unger, Steven White, and Crispin Wright.

Contributors

GORDON C. F. BEARN is Assistant Professor of Philosophy at Lehigh University. He has also taught at Williams College. He has published articles concerning relativism, Wittgenstein, and Nietzsche in such journals as *Metaphilosophy* and *Mind*.

DONALD DAVIDSON is currently the Willis S. and Marion Slusser Professor of Philosophy at the University of California at Berkeley. He has taught at numerous institutions, including Harvard University, Stanford University, Princeton University, and Rockefeller University. His lectureships have included the John Locke Lectures (Oxford University), the Hagerstrom Lectures (Uppsala), and the Carus Lectures. Donald Davidson is a Past President of the American Philosophical Association, a member of the American Academy of Arts and Sciences, and a Corresponding Fellow of the British Academy. His books include (with Patrick Suppes and Sidney Siegel) *Decision Making: An Experimental Approach* (1955), *Essays on Action and Events* (1980), and *Inquiries into Truth and Interpretation* (1984). He has edited (with Jaakko Hintikka) *Words and Objections* (1969) and (with Gilbert Harman) *The Semantics of Natural Language* (1972), as well as *The Logic of Grammar* (1975).

CATHERINE Z. ELGIN is Visiting Associate Professor of Philosophy at Wellesley College. She is the author of *With Reference to Reference* (1983) and (with Nelson Goodman) *Reconceptions* (1988). Her next book, a work in epistemology, is tentatively entitled *Philosophy without Foundations*.

CLIFFORD GEERTZ is Harold F. Linder Professor of Social Science at the Institute for Advanced Study in Princeton. He has taught at the University of Chicago, where he was Professor of Anthropology and Chairman of the Committee for the Comparative Study of New Nations. Clifford Geertz is a Fellow of the American Academy of Arts and Sciences, and the American Philosophical Society, and the National Academy of Sciences. His publications include *The Religion of Java* (1960), *Agricultural Involution* (1963), *Islam Observed* (1968), *Negara: The Theatre State in Nineteenth Century Bali* (1980), two volumes of essays: *The Interpretation of Cultures* (1973) and *Local Knowledge* (1983), and *Works and Lives: The Anthropologist as Author* (1988).

NELSON GOODMAN is Professor Emeritus of Philosophy at Harvard University. He is a Past President of the Eastern Division of the American Philosophical Association and is the author of *The Structure of Appearance* (1951), *Fact, Fiction, and Forecast* (1955), *Languages of Art* (1968), *Problems and Projects* (1972), *Ways of Worldmaking* (1978), *Of Mind and Other Matters* (1984), and (with Catherine Z. Elgin) *Reconceptions* (1988). Goodman masterminded the multimedia work *Hockey Seen*, directed the Harvard Summer Dance Center, and founded Project Zero, a research program in arts education.

GILBERT HARMAN is Professor of Philosophy at Princeton University, where, with George Miller, he directs the Cognitive Science Laboratory. He is the author of many articles and three books: *Change in View: Principles of Reasoning* (1981), *The Nature of Morality: An Introduction to Ethics* (1977), and *Thought* (1975). He edited *On Noam Chomsky: Critical Essays* (1982) and (with Donald Davidson) *The Semantics of Natural Language* (1972) as well as *The Logic of Grammar* (1975). His current research is aimed at understanding how people reason.

ROM HARRÉ is University Lecturer in Philosophy of Science at Oxford University and Fellow and Vice Principal of Linacre College. He has also taught at Kings College, Auckland, University of the Punjab, University of Birmingham, and the University of Leicester. Among his books are *An Introduction to the Logic of the*

Sciences (1960), *Matter and Method* (1964), *The Anticipation of Nature* (1965), *The Principles of Scientific Thinking* (1970), *The Philosophies of Science* (1972), *Social Being* (1979), *Great Experiments* (1981), and *Personal Being* (1983).

Mark Johnston is Associate Professor of Philosophy and Richard Stockton Bicentennial Preceptor at Princeton University, where he received his Ph.D. in 1984. His interests range from social theory and ethics to philosophy of mind, metaphysics, and philosophy of language. He is currently writing a book on objectivity and legitimacy.

Russell Keat is a Senior Lecturer in Philosophy at the University of Lancaster, England, and is Director of the Centre for the Study of Cultural Values. He is a member of the *Radical Philosophy* editorial collective and has been a Visiting Fellow at the Humanities Research Centre, Australian National University. Among Keat's publications are *The Politics of Social Theory* (1982) and (with John Urry) *Social Theory as Science* (1975). He is currently completing a book on conceptions of the human body in the work of Reich, Foucault, and Merleau-Ponty.

Michael Krausz is Professor of Philosophy at Bryn Mawr College and is Chairman of the Greater Philadelphia Philosophy Consortium. He has been visiting professor at several institutions in the United States, England, Israel, Egypt, and Kenya. Krausz is editor or coeditor of *Critical Essays on the Philosophy of R. G. Collingwood* (1972), *The Concept of Creativity in Science and Art* (1981), *Relativism: Cognitive and Moral* (1982), and *Rationality, Relativism, and the Human Sciences* (1986). He is General Editor of E. J. Brill's Series in Philosophy of History and Culture and is currently writing a book on rightness and reasons in cultural practices. Krausz has had numerous one-person shows of his art works in the U.S. and abroad, and is the Founder and Associate Artistic Director of the Philadelphia Chamber Orchestra.

Thomas McCarthy, Professor of Philosophy at Northwestern University, has taught previously at Boston University and the University of Munich. The author of many articles in social philosophy and philosophy of the social sciences, he has been awarded fellowships by the Alexander von Humboldt Foundation, the National Endowment for the Humanities, and the Guggenheim Foundation. McCarthy is the author of *The Critical Theory of Jurgen Habermas* (1978) and the coeditor of *Understanding and Social Inquiry* (1977), as well as *After Philosophy* (1987). In addition to having translated several of Habermas' works, he is General Editor of the series of translations and monographs *Studies in Contemporary German Social Thought*, MIT Press.

ALASDAIR MACINTYRE is W. Alton Jones Professor at Vanderbilt University. He has previously taught at the universities of Manchester, Leeds, Oxford, Essex, and Brandeis University and Wellesley College. MacIntyre is a Past President of the Eastern Division of the American Philosophical Association and is a Fellow of the American Academy of Arts and Sciences. His books include *Marxism and Christianity* (1953), *The Unconscious* (1958), *A Short History of Ethics* (1966), *Against the Self-Images of the Age* (1971), *After Virtue* (1981), and *Whose Justice? Which Rationality?* (1988).

JOSEPH MARGOLIS, Professor of Philosophy at Temple University, has previously taught at New York University, City College of the City University of New York, University of Toronto, University of Western Ontario, University of California at Berkeley, University of Minnesota, and Columbia University. Margolis is President of the American Society of Aesthetics. His books include *Persons and Minds* (1978), *Culture and Cultural Entities* (1984), and *Philosophy of Psychology* (1984). He has recently completed a trilogy, titled *The Persistence of Reality*. It includes *Pragmatism without Foundations: Reconciling Realism and Relativism* (1986), *Science without Unity: Reconciling the Human and Natural Sciences* (1987), and *Texts without Referents: Reconciling Science and Narrative* (1988).

BIMAL KRISHNA MATILAL is Spalding Professor of Eastern Religions and Ethics and Fellow of All Souls College, Oxford University. He was educated in Calcutta and Harvard, where he obtained his Ph.D. in 1965. Bimal Matilal has taught at the University of Toronto, University of Chicago, University of California at Berkeley, University of Pennsylvania, Victoria University in Wellington, New Zealand, and has been Visiting Scholar at Harvard Divinity School. His nine books include *The Navya-Nyàya Doctrine of Negation* (1965), *Logic, Language, and Reality* (1985), and *Perception: An Essay on Classical Indian Theories of Knowledge* (1986), which relates classical Indian philosophies to modern analytical philosophies. Bimal Matilal has also coedited *Analytical Philosophy in Comparative Perspective* (1985) and *Buddhist Logic and Epistemology* (1986).

JITENDRA N. MOHANTY is Professor and Chairman of the Department of Philosophy at Temple University. He was educated in the universities of Calcutta and Gottingen, where he received his Ph.D. He has taught at the University of Calcutta, University of Oklahoma, and the New School for Social Research. Mohanty has been a Visiting Fellow at All Souls College, Oxford, and was President of the Indian Philosophical Congress. He is Editor of *Husserl Studies*. In addition to studies on Husserl and Frege, Mohanty's most recent book is *The Possibility of Transcendental Philosophy* (1985). He is also finishing a book on *Reason in Indian Thought*.

MARTHA C. NUSSBAUM is the David Benedict Professor and Professor of Philosophy and Classics at Brown University. She is the author of *Aristotle's De Motu Animalium* (1978), *The Fragility of Goodness: Luck and Ethics in Greek Tragedy and Philosophy* (1986), *Love and Knowledge: Essays on Philosophy and Literature* (forthcoming), and numerous articles. She has edited *Language and Logos: Studies in Ancient Greek Philosophy Presented to G. E. L. Owen* (1982) and *Logic, Science and Dialectic: Collected Papers in Greek Philosophy* by G. E. L. Owen (1986). She is a consultant to the World Institute for Development Economics Research (WIDER), Helsinki, with whose support the paper in this volume was written.

HILARY W. PUTNAM is Walter Beverly Pearson Professor of Modern Mathematics and Mathematical Logic in the Department of Philosophy at Harvard University. He has also taught at M.I.T., Northwestern University, Princeton University, Oxford University (where he gave the John Locke Lectures), Johann Wolfgang Goethe University (Frankfurt), and Ludwig Maximilians University (Munich). He is a Past President of the Eastern Division of the American Philosophical Association, the Philosophy of Science Association, and the Association for Symbolic Logic. Putnam is a Fellow of the American Academy of Arts and Sciences and a Corresponding Fellow of the British Academy. His books include *Meaning and the Moral Sciences* (1978), three volumes of *Philosophical Papers* (1975), *Reason, Truth and History* (1981), *The Many Faces of Realism* (The Carus Lectures) (1987), and *Representation and Reality* (1988).

AMÉLIE OKSENBERG RORTY is the Matina Horner Visiting Professor at Radcliffe College and the Hannah Obermann Visiting Professor at Brandeis University and Tufts University. She is the author of *Mind in Action* (1988). With Brian MacLaughlin she has coedited *Perspectives on Self-Deception* (1988), and with Martha Nussbaum she is coediting *Essays on Aristotle's De Anima* (forthcoming). She has also edited *The Identities of Persons* (1976), *Explaining Emotions* (1980), *Essays on Aristotle's Ethics* (1980), and *Essays on Descartes' Meditations* (1986).

RICHARD RORTY, Kenan Professor of Humanities at the University of Virginia, is a Past President of the American Philosophical Association and, among other awards, has been a MacArthur Prize Fellow. Rorty has written on philosophy of mind, philosophy of language, and social philosophy, as well as on contemporary philosophers such as Sellars, Heidegger, Davidson, and Derrida. His books include *Philosophy and the Mirror of Nature* (1979), *Consequences of Pragmatism* (1982), and *Contingency, Irony and Solidarity* (1988).

AMARTYA SEN is Lamont University Professor at Harvard University, where he lectures in economics and philosophy. Sen was Drummond Professor of Political Economy at Oxford University and a Fellow of All Souls College. He was born in India and educated at Calcutta and at Cambridge. Sen is a Fellow of the British Academy, a Foreign Honorary Member of the American Academy of Arts and Sciences, a Past President of the Econometric Society, and is presently the President of the International Economic Association. His books include *Choice of Techniques* (1960), *Collective Choice and Social Welfare* (1970), *On Economic Inequality* (1973), *Poverty and Famines* (1981), *Choice, Welfare and Measurement* (1982), *Resources, Values and Development* (1984), and *On Ethics and Economics* (1987).

Richard A. Shweder, an anthropologist, is Professor of Human Development at The University of Chicago. A recipient of the American Association for the Advancement of Science's Socio-Psychological Prize, Shweder has been a Guggenheim Foundation Fellow and a Fellow at the Center for Advanced Study in the Behavioral Sciences. He is coeditor of *Culture Theory: Essays on Mind, Self and Emotion* (1984) and *Metatheory in the Social Sciences: Pluralisms and Subjectivities* (1986).

David B. Wong is Associate Professor and Chair of the Department of Philosophy at Brandeis University. He has written articles in ethical theory, the Continental rationalists, and Chinese philosophy, and is the author of *Moral Relativity* (1984). His work in progress includes a book on the possibilities of moral commitment in a pluralistic society.

Eddy M. Zemach is Professor of Philosophy at the Hebrew University of Jerusalem. He has taught in many American institutions, including Yale University, State University of New York at Stony Brook, University of Miami, University of New Mexico, Williams College, and Harvard University. He has published more than a hundred articles, mostly in the philosophy of language, ontology, philosophy of psychology, and aesthetics. And he has published, in Hebrew, two books in aesthetics and five books in literary criticism.

Index

480